The Catholic BAbY Name Book

The Catholic BABY Name Book

Patrice Fagnant-MacArthur

Foreword by Lisa M. Hendey

A CatholicMom.com Book

ave maria press AMP notre dame, indiana

© 2013 by Patrice Fagnant-MacArthur

Founded in 1865, Ave Maria Press is a ministry of the United States Province of Holy Cross.

www.avemariapress.com

Paperback: ISBN-10 1-59471-303-0, ISBN-13 978-1-59471-303-3

E-book: ISBN-10 1-59471-382-0, ISBN-13 978-1-59471-382-8

Cover image © Thinkstock.

Cover and text design by Katherine Robinson.

Printed and bound in the United States of America.

Library of Congress Cataloging-in-Publication Data

Fagnant-MacArthur, Patrice.

  The Catholic Baby Name Book / Patrice Fagnant-MacArthur.

     pages cm

  ISBN-13: 978-1-59471-303-3 (pbk.)

  ISBN-10: 1-59471-303-0 (pbk.)

  1. Names, Personal. 2. Christian saints--Names. I. Title.

  CS2377.F34 2013

  929.4--dc23

                              2012046435

Contents

Foreword

I t was completely on a whim that I registered the domain name "CatholicMom.com" so many years ago. As the mom of two young sons and married to the love of my life (then a non-Catholic), I recall feeling completely overwhelmed, not only by my motherly duties, but especially by the responsibility of raising our children in the faith. My motivations for buying a "dummies" computer book and starting a small website were largely selfish: I was desperate for support, encouragement, and information about my vocation to motherhood, and specifically to Catholic motherhood. Our desire to connect—to be in communion with one another—never ceases to amaze me. I now count many of the women I connected with back·in those early days as dear friends. Many of them have gone on to become contributors to a resource that now welcomes hundreds of thousands of women from close to two hundred countries around the world into a daily dialogue about the things that matter most in our lives. Together we have watched our babies be born and our children grow, we have prayed with and for one another, and we've done our very best to mentor the new moms who have come into our ever-blossoming fold.

These many years later, I still wake up each day and head anxiously to my desk with a joy for the mission that has become my life's work. While the ways in which our Church reaches out to us have developed and diversified over the past several years, her message remains as timeless as always. And while Catholic parents may now have new trials and possibilities to face that are born of an ever-advancing technological culture, many of the fears, questions, delights, and joys we hold in our hearts are the same ones our parents and grandparents before us grappled with and celebrated as we grew up.

As women, as wives and single women, as stay-at-home moms and nine-to-fivers, as mothers and grandmothers, and especially as Catholics and women of faith, we are on a mission: to know, love, and serve God, to share his loving care with our family and friends, and to enjoy life with him forever in heaven. Lofty goals, and ones that require a daily recommitment! This mission demands of us our very best . . . and to be at our best, we need all the help, support, and encouragement we can find.

That is why I am thrilled beyond measure to have partnered with my friends and colleagues at

Ave Maria Press to create a series of resources that will support you in your life's mission. With this series of books as a compliment to our resources at *CatholicMom.com*, we aim to educate, to inspire, and to uplift you with resources that are engaging and authentically Catholic. It's our great hope that these books will nurture your heart, mind, body, and soul—that they will go beyond the mainstream books you find about parenting and touch upon the cares that make our mothering, not simply a status, but rather a vocation.

How I dearly wish I had owned my friend Patrice Fagnant-MacArthur's amazing new resource *The Catholic Baby Name Book* when it came to the naming of our sons. As we all know, the naming of a child is a tremendous responsibility. My parents tell me that my own naming process was delayed, since my father had only imagined that his firstborn would be a son, named Patrick after both himself and his beloved mother, Patty. When I arrived on the scene—definitely a girl—I went nameless for a few days until my parents settled on "Lisa Marie." To this day, I sign my name with my middle initial "M" as a tribute to both my mother and maternal grandmother who share my "Marie" middle name, and as a token of my love for our Blessed Mother.

While it's difficult to imagine myself being a "Patrick," I followed family tradition by naming our second son Adam Patrick, not only as a hat tip to family tradition, but also as a sign of devotion to one of my favorite patrons, the Apostle of Ireland. My husband, Greg, and I gave his older brother, Eric Michael, a middle name that at once invokes the protection of our favorite archangel and pays homage to the family priest who presided over our sacrament of Matrimony.

Names have the power to create tradition, to bring honor, and to form a sense of identity that will remain with your children throughout their lives. Equally as important, by considering a patron to walk with your child, you claim for him or her a saintly companion—a trusted friend, a role model for a life of faith, and a powerful intercessor for life's challenges. I believe it a happy surprise that this book is penned by a dear friend and talented writer who shares my sister Erin's middle name, "Patrice." *The Catholic Baby Name Book* will open your heart and mind as you explore naming options for your precious baby. Patrice's book invites your family to consider heroes and heroines of the past who will become a part of your family's legacy. I hope you enjoy imagining all of the possibilities, adventures, and blessings that await you and your precious baby.

Lisa M. Hendey

Introduction

I HAVE CALLED YOU BY NAME; YOU ARE MINE. ISAIAH 43:1

When I was a little girl, I always had fun telling people I was named after a street sign! My mother had loved the name "Patrice" for years and hoped to give that name to a daughter, but she wasn't sure if it was a saint's name. Five years before I was born she took a trip to Canada where she encountered *Rue St. Patrice*, and my fate was sealed. It wasn't until I was an adult that I learned that Patrice is simply French for Patrick. That street in Canada is actually St. Patrick Street. While there is a St. Patricia, there is no official St. Patrice (at least not yet!). With Marie as a middle name and Anne as a confirmation name, I definitely have my personal patron saints.

Like my parents, my husband and I had the name of our first child chosen long before he was born. He was to be David, which was my husband's confirmation name. Meaning "beloved," it was a perfect choice for an eldest son. His patron saints are the King David of scripture as well as St. David of Wales. When we found out we were expecting a second son, I wanted to choose another biblical name. I had always liked the name Isaac, which means "one who laughs." It suits this joyful child perfectly! His patron saints are Isaac, the long-awaited son of Abraham and Sarah, and St. Isaac Jogues.

I've always had an interest in names and their meanings. As a teen, I would peruse shops that had mugs or framed art featuring names and their meanings, and I would look up all my friend's names. I've also had a longtime love of the saints. My parents supplied me with a steady stream of books about the lives of the saints, and in Catholic elementary school, I would take all the saints' biographies out of the library and read them over and over. The librarian actually felt compelled to suggest that I expand my reading to include other topics! Today, I think of the saints as my friends up in heaven and ask for their assistance daily.

Therefore, I was extremely excited when I was offered the opportunity to compile *The Catholic Baby Name Book*. I had the chance to research thousands of names and to read and write the biographies of more than 3,500 saints! I said yes to the project with no idea how I would ever accomplish the huge task in front of me. I am a busy homeschooling mom, blogger, and editor of a Catholic website. How was this ever going to get done? I went to Mass and told God that if he wanted this book to get written, he needed to provide me with the time to do it, and I asked St. Anne every day for help. I definitely believe God wanted this project to happen because the fact that it got done by the deadline verged on being miraculous.

The first task was to compile a list of the saints and well-known biblical figures who were to be included in this book. While not technically given the title "saints," biblical figures who played a role in salvation history have always been held in high esteem by the Church and are a frequent source of Christian names. There are also many cases where a canonized saint and a biblical figure share the same name. What you see on the pages before you is by no means a completely comprehensive list, but it is quite extensive. A valiant effort has been made to include as many official saints as possible. Of course, all the people who share God's glory in heaven are also saints, and no doubt some have names that are not to be found on this list.

Once the list was compiled, I researched the names to determine

their language of origin, meanings, and variations. Some of the names are so unusual that there is no information on them at all. I highly doubt that names such as Barbasymas or Dyfnog will be on the list of top 100 names any time soon, but for someone searching for a one-of-a-kind Christian name, they may be just what one is looking for. There are many such names in this list. There are also many spelling variations of what one may think of as common names, which can be a great way to put a unique twist on a traditional name. Of course, if you are searching for a classic name that has stood the test of time, there are many to choose from as well.

In addition, the meaning of names is a tricky business. Language changes over time, and the meaning of a word may evolve. In addition, especially in German names, there was a tendency to combine two name elements, usually one from both sides of the family, leading to names whose meanings don't necessarily make much literal sense. For example, the common German ending *bert* means bright and is combined with a variety of prefixes, which lead to combinations such as Gundebert, which means "bright war." By the same token, the endings *olph* or *ulf* mean "wolf." The prefix *Lud* means people. Therefore the name Ludolph means "people plus wolf." Nevertheless, once again, a concerted effort has been made to provide the most accurate information possible.

The next step was to write a short biography of a patron saint or biblical figure for each major name. Obviously, many saints share the same name (think of all the St. Johns or St. Marys). Due to space considerations, only one for each name could be profiled—the exception being where there is a biblical figure and a saint by the same name, in which case two short biographies are given. Where appropriate, a list of other saints sharing the same name is given.

As I wrote the biographies of these saints, I was incredibly impressed with their lives. A great majority I had never heard of. Some we know so little about—only that they made the ultimate sacrifice of giving up their lives for the faith. Others are so well-known that they seem like old friends. A special effort was made to include modern saints and blesseds, those beatified and canonized by Pope John Paul II and Pope Benedict XVI. If a saint falls into that category, that fact is noted in the biography included. Saints such as St. Padre Pio, St. Maximilian Kolbe, St. Gianna Molla, and St. Kateri Tekakwitha are included, as are many lesser-known saints who were martyred during World War II.

Each of the saints featured on these pages was a unique individual with a corresponding unique path to God and holiness. Some were priests or religious. Others were married or widowed. Some were kings and queens. Others were humble hermits. Some lived long lives. Others died in childhood. Some served God from the day they were born. Others led lives of ill repute before turning their lives over to God and spending the rest of their days serving Him. Each of these saints has something to teach us. Each shares in the glory of God in heaven, ready to watch over us and our children and to offer us help. We only need to ask. We live in a world in which people often name a child after a television or movie star. How much better to name a child after a star of heaven! Not only does the saint set an example for your child to imitate, your child will also have a special patron in heaven to pray for him or her.

Space considerations limited the amount of biographical data that could be included about each saint, but there are many places to search for additional information. Two books that may be helpful are *Our Sunday Visitor's Encyclopedia of Saints* (Our Sunday Visitor, 2003) and *John Paul II's Book of Saints* (Our Sunday Visitor, 2007), which includes biographies of all those canonized or beatified during his long pontificate. Both of these books are by Matthew E. Bunson, D. Min., and Margaret Bunson. There is much information to be found on the Internet as well. Two sites that I found especially helpful were *Catholic Online* (www .catholic.org/saints/) and *SPQN* (http://saints.sqpn.com/). I also want to acknowledge *Butler's Lives of the Saints: Complete Edition* edited by Herbert Hurston and Donald Attwater (Christian Classics, 1956). It is the source of many of the brief biographical sketches found in this book as well as those on various websites.

A name is one of the most important gifts you will ever give to your child. The *Catechism of the Catholic Church* offers the following guidelines for choosing a name for this magnificent new life God has entrusted to your care:

> In Baptism, the Lord's name sanctifies man, and the Christian receives his name in the Church. This can be the name of a saint, that is, of a disciple who has lived a life of exemplary fidelity to the Lord. The patron saint provides a model of charity; we are assured of his intercession. The "baptismal name" can also express a Christian mystery or Christian virtue. . . .
>
> God calls each one by name. Everyone's name is sacred. The name is the icon of the person. It demands respect as a sign of the dignity of the one who bears it. The name one receives is a name for eternity. (2156, 2158–59)

Thank you for picking up *The Catholic Baby Name Book*. I hope that you will enjoy perusing these pages, dreaming of what name would be the perfect one for your child. Whether you choose a name years before a child is conceived or after you see that beautiful face in the delivery room, I wish you a blessed and joyful search for your child's eternal name.

Prayer for Choosing a Name for Your Child

Dear God,

Thank you for the gift of our child. You know and love this child even more than we do. You have already called him by name. Help us to choose the eternal name you wish for our child. Help our child to grow in faith and wisdom in order to serve and love you all of his days and be happy with you in heaven. We ask this through Christ, our Lord.

Amen.

How to Use This Book

H ere the name Elizabeth is used to explain each element in the listing of a name. See also the chart on the following page.

→ *Elizabeth*: The name of the saint appears in bold type. The book is in two parts, boys' names and girls' names. They are in alphabetical order. When a name applies to both genders, there are instructions to refer to the name where a fuller treatment is provided, e.g., **Erica**, see Eric (boy's name). When the name is a variation of another name, you are directed to the original name, e.g., **Eliza**, see Elizabeth.

→ *Saint*: Next there is the designation of the name as that of a saint or virtue, or coming from the Old Testament or the New Testament.

→ *Top 100 Name*: Identifies the name as one of the most popular names. Please note that not all of the most popular names have a Christian or Catholic meaning. Names such as Aliya or Tyler, though popular, have been omitted since they have no Christian or Catholic meaning.

→ *Hebrew; consecrated to God:* The language of origin and the meaning of the name are given.

→ *Alizabeth, Eliabeth, Eliza, Elizabea, Elizabee, Ellizabeth, Elschen, Elysabeth, Elzbieta, Elzsébet, Helsa, Ilizzabet, Lizette, Lusa:* Variations of the name are provided in italic type. Each of these variations is also listed as a name with direction to see the name of origin, e.g., **Alizabeth**, see Elizabeth.

→ *St. Elizabeth, St. Elizabeth Ann Seton, St. Elizabeth of Hungary, St. Elizabeth of Portugal, St. Elizabeth of Schonau, St. Elizabeth Rose:* When there are numerous saints with the same name, they are listed.

→ Finally, there is some commentary about the life of the most prominent saint with this name. Other saints bearing the same name can be researched online or in the references provided in the Introduction.

Elizabeth: The name of the saint appears in bold type.

Saint: The name may be that of a saint or virtue, or come from the Old or New Testament.

Top 100 Name: Identifies the name as one of the most popular names.

Elizabeth Saint, New Testament; Top 100 Name; Hebrew; consecrated to God;

Hebrew; Consecrated to God: The language of origin of the name and the meaning are given.

Alizabeth, Eliabeth, Eliza, Elizabea, Elizabee, Ellizabeth, Elschen, Elysabeth, Elzbieta, Elzsébet, Helsa, Ilizzabet, Lizette, Lusa

St. Elizabeth, St. Elizabeth Ann Seton, St. Elizabeth Rose, St. Elizabeth of Hungary, St. Elizabeth of Portugal, St. Elizabeth of Schonau

Alizabeth, Eliabeth, Eliza, etc.: Variations of the name are provided in italic type.

St. Elizabeth Ann Seton, St. Elizabeth of Hungary, etc.: When there are numerous saints with the same name, they are listed.

St. Elizabeth (first century) was a cousin of Mary, the Mother of God. Her husband, Zachary, was a priest in Jerusalem. He was told by an angel that his wife, who was beyond childbearing age, would have a son. When he doubted this, he lost the ability to speak until after their child, John the Baptist, was born. While Mary was pregnant with Jesus, she went to visit the pregnant Elizabeth. Elizabeth's story is told in the first chapter of the Gospel of Luke.

St. Elizabeth (first century) was a cousin of Mary. . . .: Commentary about the life of the most prominent saint with this name.

BOYS'
Names

A

Aaren *see Aaron*

Aarin *see Aaron*

Aaron Old Testament; Top 100 Name; Hebrew, Aramaic; a teacher, lofty, mountain of strength, messenger

Aaren, Aarin, Aaronn, Aeron, Aran, Arren, Arrin, Arryn

Aaron in the Bible was the older brother of Moses. He spoke for Moses in dealing with the Egyptian royal court. He also performed signs which helped convince the people that they were on a mission from God. St. Aaron of Aleth (sixth century) was a hermit, monk, and abbot at a monastery on Cézembre. He attracted numerous visitors while there, including St. Malo.

Aaronn *see Aaron*

Abadios Saint; Arabic; eternal, lasting

St. Abadios (fourth century) was martyred during Emperor Diocletian's persecutions. After confessing Christ at K'balakhis, he was thrown from a rocky cliff.

Abakerazum Saint

Kirdjun

Also known as St. Kirdjun, St. Abakerazum was a reformed robber and bandit who converted to Christianity. He died as a martyr in Alexandria.

Abanoub Saint; Egyptian; king of gold

St. Abanoub (fourth century) embraced Christianity at a young age and gave away all he had to the poor. While walking to the city of Samanoud, he saw a vision of the archangel Michael. He was martyred at the age of twelve.

Abarran *see Abraham*

Abba *see Abban*

Abban Saint; Latin; white

Abba, Abben, Abbin, Abbine, Abbon

St. Abban, St. Abban of Murnevin

St. Abban (sixth century) was born in Ireland but spent his life in Abingdon, England. According to tradition, St. Gobnait was his sister. It is believed that he founded Ballyvourney, a nunnery, and entrusted it to her. He also established the churches of Cell Ailbe and Camross.

Abben *see Abban*

Abbin *see Abban*

Abbine *see Abban*

Abbo Saint; German; a man

St. Abbo (945–1004) was a monastic leader and papal representative. He was born in France. After studying at Orléans, Paris, and Remis, he was brought to Huntingdonshire, England, in 986. He became abbot of Fleury in 988. As abbot, he attended the Synod of Basel and assisted Pope Gregory V. He also helped calm the fears of many who felt the world was going to end at the year 1000. He was known as a philosopher and scholar and wrote a life of St. Edmond. He died of a stab wound on November 13, 1004.

Abbon *see Abban*

Abdas Saint; Hebrew; a servant of God

A Persian bishop, St. Abdas (d. 420) was born in Chaldor. After being ordained a priest, he built up his hometown monastery and school. He brought many people to the Christian faith, for which he was arrested, and suffered many hardships until he was miraculously released. Abdas later joined a monastery and became bishop of Kaskhar (Susa). When relations between the Christian Church and the Persian government became hostile, Abdas was one of the first martyred by being clubbed to death.

Abdiesus Saint; Latin; one who serves Jesus

St. Abdiesus (d. 342) was a deacon in the Christian community of Persia. He was martyred during the persecutions of King Shapur II.

Abdón Saint; Hebrew; servant of God, the very helpful man

St. Abdón (d. 250) was martyred along with his companion St. Sennen during the time of Emperor Diocletian. They were placed in an arena with wild animals, but when the animals refused to harm them,

gladiators were sent in to finish the job. He is the patron saint of burying the dead and coopers.

Abe *see Abel*

Abedah *see Abdón*

Abel Saint, Old Testament; Hebrew, Assyrian; breath, meadow

Abe, Abell, Abelson, Able, Adal, Avel

Abel in the Bible was the second son born to Adam and Eve. When he and his brother Cain offered sacrifice to the Lord, his gift found favor while his brother's did not. In a fit of jealousy, Cain murdered Abel, thus making him the first martyr in scripture.

St. Abel (d. 751) was an archbishop and Benedictine abbot. Born in Ireland, he accompanied St. Boniface on missions to Europe. Pope St. Zachary chose him as archbishop of Remis; however Milo, who occupied the seat, refused to relinquish it. Abel chose to live in a monastery at Lobbes where he was named abbot.

Abell *see Abel*

Abelson *see Abel*

Abercius Saint

St. Abercius Marcellus (d. 167) was a bishop of Hieropolis in Phyrgia during the reign of Marcus Aurelius. Late in life, he visited Rome and was commanded by the emperor to rid his daughter, Lucilla, of a demon. He then went on to visit and preach in Syria and the area surrounding the Euphrates River. He was later imprisoned for the faith and died in 167.

Aberham *see Abraham*

Abey *see Abraham*

Abhiram *see Abraham*

Abibas Saint; Hebrew

St. Abibas (first century) is thought to be the second son of Gamaliel, the famous Jewish teacher of St. Paul. Both Gamaliel and Abibas were early converts to the Christian faith.

Abibus Saint

A deacon, St. Abibus (d. 322 or 323) was burned at the stake in Edessa, Mesopotamia, under Emperor Licinius.

Abidianus Saint; African

St. Abidianus was an African martyr.

Abie *see Abraham*

Abiel *see Abel*

Abilius Saint; Latin

Avilius

St. Abilius (d. 98) (also known as Avilius) was the third bishop of Alexandria, Egypt after Sts. Mark and Anianus. Well respected for his chastity and knowledge of Christ, he served in that position for nineteen years and eight months. He was buried next to St. Mark the Evangelist in the Church of Bucalis in Alexandria.

Able *see Abel*

Abrahaim *see Abraham*

Abraham Saint, Old Testament; Hebrew; father of a great multitude

Abarran, Aberham, Abey, Abhiram, Abie, Abrahaim, Abrahame, Abrahamo, Abrahan, Abraheem, Abrahem, Abrahim, Abrahm, Abramo, Abrao, Arram, Avram, Bram

St. Abraham, St. Abraham Kidunaja, St. Abraham of Carrhae, St. Abraham of Kratia, St. Abraham of Rostov, St. Abraham of Smolensk, St. Abraham the Poor

Abraham in the Bible (Genesis 11:26–25:10), whose birth name was Abram, is known as the Father of Many Nations. Through his sons Ishmael and Isaac, Judaism, Christianity, and Islam all trace their traditions back to him. He and his wife Sarai, who was barren, lived in Haran, but God appeared to him and told him to depart for a land that he would show him. God promised him land and descendants as numerous as the stars. Sarai, who at a very advanced age still had no children, offered Abram her maidservant Hagar. From this union, Ishmael was born. In Genesis 17, Abram's name is changed to Abraham and Sarai becomes Sarah. Sarah would soon give birth to Isaac, proving that nothing is impossible with God. God would later test Abraham's faith by asking him to offer this much-loved son as a sacrifice. Abraham obeyed, but an angel saved Isaac at the last moment. After the death of Sarah, Abraham took another wife who bore him six more sons. He died at the age of 175.

St. Abraham (d. 480) was a hermit and confessor born in the area which is now modern Iraq. While traveling to Egypt, he was captured and held as a slave for five years. He escaped and made his way to Gaul, where he was ordained a priest and became the abbot of St. Cyriacus Abbey.

Abrahame *see Abraham*

Abrahamo *see Abraham*

Abrahan *see Abraham*

Abraheem *see Abraham*

Abrahem *see Abraham*

Abrahim *see Abraham*

Abrahm *see Abraham*

Abram Saint; short form of Abraham

Abrama, Abramo, Abrams

Abrama *see Abram*

Abramo *see Abraham*

Abrams *see Abram*

Abran Saint; Hebrew; father of a mighty nation

Gibrian

Born in Ireland, St. Abran (d. 515), also known as Gibrian, sailed to Brittany with his nine siblings, all of whom dedicated themselves to God. He lived in a hermitage on the Marne River. All of the siblings are considered saints because of their Christian influence on the Breton people.

Abrao *see Abraham*

Abudimus Saint

St. Abudimus (d. 305) was a Greek martyr born on the island of Tenedos in the Aegean. He was tortured and martyred during the persecution of Emperor Diocletian.

Abuna Saint; Arabic; our father

Frumentius

Also known as Frumentius, St. Abuna (d. 380) was born in Tyre (modern day Lebanon) and is considered one of the Apostles to Ethiopia. He was shipwrecked during a cruise on the Red Sea and was taken to the King of Axum, where he became a secretary. After the king died, he became part of the succeeding queen's court, who allowed him to preach about Christ. He was later consecrated as a bishop of Ethiopia.

Abundius Saint; Latin; abundance

St. Abundius (d. 469) was born in Thessalonica and became the fourth bishop of Como, Italy. After attending the Council of Constantinople in 450, he was sent by Pope St. Leo I the Great to the Emperor Theodosius II as a papal representative. He served in this role at the Council of Chalcedon in 451 and the Council of Milan in 452, both of which were convened to refute the Eutychian heresy. The Te

Deum is occasionally attributed to him.

Acacius Saint; Greek; a vessel, pitcher, spark

St. Acacius (d. 425) was a bishop of Amida, Mesopotamia. He resolved to help the seven thousand Persian prisoners who had been captured by the Romans and were being held in his city. He sold all the gold and silver vessels of his church to ransom and feed them. When these captives returned home to their native Persia, they told their ruler about Bishop Acacius. Emperor Bahram V was so impressed that he was reported to have ended Christian persecution in his dominion.

Acca Saint; English; oak

A bishop and scholar, St. Acca (ca. 660–740 or 742) was born in Northumbria, England. St. Wilfrid appointed him abbot of St. Andrew's Monastery in Hexham, England. Acca also accompanied Wilfrid to Rome in 692. After Wilfrid's death, Acca succeeded him as bishop of Hexham, where he spent his time erecting many churches and promoting learning. For unknown reasons, he either left or was exiled in 732 and became a hermit in Galloway. Just before his death, he returned to Hexham and received a warm welcome. He was revered as a saint immediately after his death.

Aceolus Saint; Latin; one who disagrees

St. Aceolus (d. 303) was a sub-deacon, most likely studying for the priesthood. He was taken prisoner and martyred with St. Acius, a deacon, during Emperor Diocletian's persecution near Amiens, France.

Acepsimas Saint

St. Acepsimas (fifth century) was a hermit who longed to be a priest. After praying and doing penance for almost sixty years, he was allowed to study for the priesthood. He died happy, shortly after being ordained.

Acestes Saint, New Testament; Greek; pleasing goat

St. Acestes (first century) was a soldier assigned to escort St. Paul to his death. During this assignment, St. Paul converted Acestes and two other soldiers. Immediately after Paul's execution, they proclaimed their faith and were beheaded.

Acharius Latin; ungrateful

St. Acharius (d. 640) served St. Eustace in a monastery in Luxeuil, France, and was known for his holiness and administrative capabilities. He was appointed bishop of Noyon-Tournai in 621. He is remembered for encouraging many other holy men in his era.

Achatius Saint; Hebrew; holding

St. Achatius was well-known in the Christian community

of Antioch. Some records list him as bishop of Antioch or Militene, but this is uncertain. When summoned before the local Roman official Martian, he refused to sacrifice to pagan gods or to give up the names of his fellow Christians and was sent to prison. According to legend, when Emperor Decius received Martian's report of the trial, he pardoned Achatius.

Achillas Saint; Greek; grief to the enemy

St. Achillas (d. 330) was archbishop of Larissa in Thessaly, Greece. He is known for his defense of orthodoxy during the Council of Nicaea and a miracle he performed to disprove Arianism. He told the Arians that if Christ was merely a creature of God, they should tell oil to flow from a stone. They kept quiet. Then he said, "If the Son of God is equal to the Father, as we believe, then let oil flow from this stone." When it did so, all were amazed.

Achilleus Saint; Greek; grief to the enemy

St. Achilleus Kewanuka (1869–1886) was a convert to the faith who served King Mwanga of Uganda. One of the Martyrs of Uganda, he was burned alive for his faith and canonized in 1964 by Pope Paul VI.

Acisclus Saint

Arrested in Córdoba, Spain, with his sister Victoria, St. Acisclus (fourth century) was condemned to death after considerable torture. One legend has the siblings being thrown into a fiery furnace. However, they were unharmed and instead were singing songs of joy. They were then bound with stones and cast into a river, but they floated. Next, they were suspended over a fire, but the fire instead killed hundreds of pagans. In the end, they were beheaded. After their death, their home was turned into a church.

Acius Saint; Latin; thread, yarn

Aragawi

St. Acius (d. 303) was a deacon, most likely studying for the priesthood. He was taken prisoner and martyred with St. Aceolus, a subdeacon, during Emperor Diocletian's persecution near Amiens, France.

Acllinus Saint

One of the Scillitan Martyrs, St. Acllinus (d. 180) was beheaded under Vigellius, the first persecutor of Christians in northwestern Africa.

Acquilla *see Aquila*

Acyndinus Saint

St. Acyndinus (d. 345) was a Persian priest arrested and martyred for the faith during the reign of King Shapur II.

Ad *see Adam, Adlai, Adolf*

Adal *see Abel*

Adalar Saint; German; noble eagle

St. Adalar (d. 755) was a priest and monk who served as a

missionary with St. Boniface. He was martyred with St. Boniface at Dokkum in Frisia.

Adalard Saint; German, French; noble and hardy, brave

St. Adalard (ca. 751–827) was raised in the court of his cousin Charlemagne. He entered the Monastery of Corbie in Picardy at the age of twenty, and then went to Monte Cassino, but Charlemagne ordered him to return to Corbie. He was elected abbot and then prime minister to Pepin, Charlemagne's son, the king of Italy. He was exiled in 814 after becoming entrenched in the politics of the royal family, but was cleared of all charges seven years later and was able to return. He then served the court of Louis the Pious. In 822, he and his brother Wala founded Corvey Abbey in Westphalia.

Adalbald Saint; German

St. Adalbald of Ostrevant (d. 652) was born in Flanders and was a nobleman at the court of Dagobert I of France. When he was sent to Gascony to help put down a rebellion, he met his future wife, Rictrudis. Her family objected to the match, but they wed anyway. They dedicated themselves to prayer and good works, but his in-laws eventually killed him. Many miracles were recorded at his tomb, and he was considered a martyr.

Adalbero Saint; German

St. Adalbero (d. 1005) was a monk in Gorze who became bishop of Verdun, France, in 984. He was then transferred to Metz where he founded Cluniac monasteries.

Adalbert Saint; German; nobly bright

St. Adalbert, St. Adalbert of Magdeburg, St. Adalbert of Prague

St. Adalbert (d. 740) was an Irish missionary. Born and educated in England, he accompanied St. Willibrord to Friesland, where he converted many people. He then accompanied St. Egbert to Ireland. He eventually became abbot of Epternach.

Adalgis Saint; German

St. Adalgis (d. 686) was born in Ireland. A disciple of St. Fursey, he became a missionary to France, where he worked in Arras and Laon and founded a monastery in Picardy.

Adalgott Saint; German

St. Adalgott (d. 1165) was a monk in the Benedictine monastery of Clairvaux. He became abbot in Disentis and was eventually named bishop of Chur. He was known for his care of the sick and poor and founded a hospital during his time as bishop.

Adam Saint, Old Testament; Top 100 Name; Phoenician, Hebrew; earthy, red

Ad, Adama, Adamec, Adamek, Adamik, Adamo, Adas, Addam, Adem, Adham, Adhamh, Adim, Adné, Adnon, Adok, Adom, Adomas, Adym, Adão, Edam, Edem, Edim, Edym

In Scripture, Adam (Genesis 1–5) was the first man created by God. He lived with the first woman, Eve, in the Garden of Eden where they had dominion over all the plants and animals. They were told only to avoid the fruit of the tree of the knowledge of good and evil. Eve succumbed to temptation and ate of the fruit. When she offered it to Adam, he ate as well. They were then removed from the garden and both were cursed.

St. Adam (d. 1210) was a native of Fermo, Italy. His holy life as a hermit in a cave on Mount Vissiano attracted many followers. He was invited to join the San Sabine Monastery as a Benedictine. His life of prayer and self-discipline led to his being elected abbot.

Adama *see Adam*

Adamec *see Adam*

Adamek *see Adam*

Adamik *see Adam*

Adamnan Saint; Hebrew; red earth, man

St. Adamnan, St. Adamnan of Coldingham

St. Adamnan (ca. 628–704) became a monk in Drumhome, Donegal, Ireland. In 679, he became abbot of a monastery in Iona. He worked tirelessly to convince Irish monks and monasteries to replace their Celtic practices with those of the Roman church. He also argued that women and children should be exempt from wars. When this practice was adopted, it became known as Adamnan's law. He also wrote a life of St. Columba.

Adamo *see Adam*

Adarian *see Adrian*

Adas *see Adam*

Adauctus Saint; Latin; increase

St. Adauctus (d. 312) was arrested and persecuted along with his daughter Callisthene during the reign of Coemperor Maximinus Daia, right before Constantine's Edict of Milan. While his daughter was spared, he was martyred in Ephesus.

Adaucus Saint; Latin; increase

St. Adaucus (d. 304) was an Italian noble who became a quaestor in the government of Phrygia. When Emperor Diocletian ordered Adaucus's town to be burned to the ground, he and all the other Christians in the area were martyred.

Addal Saint; Hebrew; God is my refuge

St. Addal (d. 180) was sent by St. Thomas to the court of King Abgar the Black, a second-century Osroene ruler. Legend holds that King Angar asked Christ to cure him of his mortal illness. Addal cured him in Jesus' name, and the King and his people were converted to the faith. He is recorded as having been a martyr.

Addam see Adam

Addlai see Adlai

Addlay see Adlai

Addof see Adolf

Addoff see Adolf

Ade see Adrian

Adelbert see Albert

Adelelmus Saint; German; helmet

Aleaunie

Born in Laudun, Poitou, St. Adelelmus (d. 1100) served in the military before making a pilgrimage to Rome. While on pilgrimage, he met St. Robert of Molesme and was inspired to abandon the military for life as a monk. King Alfonso and Queen Constance of Burgandy of Castile founded a monastery in Burgos, Spain, and asked him to be the abbot. Adelelmus founded a hospital and church there as well.

Adelin see Hadelin

Adelphius Saint; Greek

St. Adelphius, St. Adelphius the Confessor

St. Adelphius was one of the Nitria Mountain desert fathers and monks.

Adelphus Saint; Greek; brother

St. Adelphus (d. 670) was the grandson of St. Romaricus and served as abbot of Remiremont.

Adem see Adam

Adeodatus Saint; Latin; given by God

Pope St. Adeodatus, St. Adeodatus II

Pope St. Adeodatus (d. 618) had been a priest for forty years when he became pope in 615. During his papacy, the Lombards and Byzantines were at war and earthquakes and plagues affected the land. He was generous to the victims of these disasters as well as to the poor in general. He was the first pope to use leaden bullae to seal papal documents, which have been called bulls ever since.

Aderald Saint

St. Aderald (d. 1004) was an archdeacon at Troyes. He built the Benedictine abbey of St. Sepulchre at Samblières in part to house the large number of holy relics he had brought back from a pilgrimage to the Holy Land.

Adham see Adam

Adhamh see Adam

Adheritus Saint; Latin; to stick to

St. Adheritus (second century) was bishop of Ravenna, succeeding St. Apollinaris.

Adim see Adam

Adjutor Saint; Latin; one who helps

St. Adjutor (d. 1131) was born near Normandy, France, and became a knight in the First Crusade. He was captured by the Muslims, but legend holds that he escaped by swimming.

As a result, he is considered a patron of swimmers, boaters, and drowning victims. He spent the rest of his life as a recluse at the Abbey of Trion.

Adlai Hebrew; my ornament

Addla, Addlay

Adné *see Adam*

Adnon *see Adam*

Ado Saint; Hebrew; beauty

Born into a noble family, St. Ado (d. 875) was educated at the Benedictine abbey of Ferrieres. He gave up his inheritance and became a Benedictine at the Monastery of Prum in Germany. He spent two years in Rome on pilgrimage and then went on to Ravenna where he found an old copy of the Roman Martyrology. He wrote a new version, which was published in 858. He was appointed archbishop of Vienne by Pope Nicholas I.

Adof *see Adolf*

Adok *see Adam*

Adolf Saint; German; noble wolf

Ad, Addof, Addoff, Adof

St. Adolf (d. 1224) came from a family of counts in Westphalia. He entered a Cistercian monastery, where he was known for his piety. He became bishop of Osnabrück in 1216.

Adolph Saint; German; noble wolf

Adolphe

Bl. Adolph Koping (1813–1865) was a German priest who became president of the Catholic Association of Journeymen, which provided religious and social support to young journeymen. He worked to promote journeymen associations. He was beatified by Pope John Paul II in 1991 and is a patron of World Youth Day.

Adolphe *see Adolph*

Adolphus Saint; German; noble wolf

St. Adolphus, St. Adolphus Ludigo-Mkasa

St. Adolphus (d. 850) was one of the martyrs of Córdoba, Spain. At the time, that region was under Muslim control. He was the son of an Islamic father and a Christian mother. He was martyred during the persecutions led by the Caliph of Córdoba, Abdal-Rahman II.

Adom *see Adam*

Adomas *see Adam*

Adorjan *see Adrian*

Adrain *see Adrian*

Adreian *see Adrian*

Adreyan *see Adrian*

Adriaan *see Adrian*

Adrian Saint; Top 100 Name; Greek, Latin; rich, dark

Adarian, Ade, Adorjan, Adrain, Adreian, Adreyan, Adriaan, Adriane, Adriann, Adrianne, Adriean, Adrin, Adrion, Adrionn, Adrionne, Adron, Adryan, Adryn, Adryon, Arje

St. Adrian, St. Adrian II, III, IV, V, St. Adrian Van Hilvarenbeek, St. Adrian the Abbot

St. Adrian (d. 710) was born in Africa. He became abbot of

the monastery at Nerida, near Naples. St. Theodore, who was archbishop of Canterbury, later appointed him abbot of Sts. Peter and Paul Monastery, which would come to be known as St. Augustine's Monastery. He served in that capacity for thirty-nine years, during which time the monastery became known as a great center of learning.

Adriane *see Adrian*

Adriann *see Adrian*

Adrianne *see Adrian*

Adrianus Saint; Greek, Latin; rich, dark

St. Adrianus was martyred in Africa with Secundilla and Victorius.

Adriean *see Adrian*

Adrin *see Adrian*

Adrio Saint; Latin

St. Adrio was martyred in Alexandria, Egypt, with Basilla and Victor.

Adrion *see Adrian*

Adrionn *see Adrian*

Adrionne *see Adrian*

Adron *see Adrian*

Adryan *see Adrian*

Adryn *see Adrian*

Adryon *see Adrian*

Adulf Saint; German; of noble heritage

St. Adulf (d. 680) was a noble of Saxon or Irish heritage who became a monk. Legend names him a bishop, but that may be due to confusion of names. He did serve, along with his brother St. Butulf, as a missionary to Germany.

Adulph Saint; German; noble wolf

St. Adulph (d. 824) was born in Seville, Spain, to an Arab Muslim father and a Spanish Catholic mother named Artemia. She ultimately took her three children to Córdoba, where she could raise them more freely in the Catholic faith. St. Adulph and his brother John were martyred around 824 under the persecutions of the Muslim caliph, Abderraman II.

Aduri *see Ansurius*

Adventor Saint; Latin; guest

St. Adventor (d. 284) was martyred along with Solutor and Octavius. The three were members of the Theban Legion. When their leader was killed, they managed to escape. Adventor and Octavius were caught and killed at the Dora Riparia. Solutor suffered the same fate at Dora Baltea. According to legend, a vision of the Virgin Mary appeared in a dream to St. John Bosco and revealed the site where Adventor and Octavius were martyred. The Basilica dell' Ausiliatrice was built on that location.

Adym *see Adam*

Adão *see Adam*

Aedesius Saint; Latin; hairy, unpleasant

St. Aedesius (d. 306) of Caesarea lived during the time of

Emperor Diocletian's persecution of the Christians. He spoke up against the local Roman officials who were taking Christian virgins and placing them in brothels as part of their torture. For this, he was tortured and drowned.

Aedh Saint; Gaelic; fire

Emilian

St. Aedh MacBricc (d. 589) was the son of Bricc, or Breece, of the Hy Heill. After his brother robbed him of his inheritance, he entered the monastic life. He founded a religious community in Westmeath, and some records list him as being a bishop.

Aedyn *see Aidan*

Aeigil *see Eigil*

Aelred Saint; English; noble counsel

Ethelred

St. Aelred (ca. 1110–1167) was the son of Eilaf, a Saxon priest. He was known for his intelligence, even at a young age. When he finished his education, he became the steward to King David of Scotland. He left this position to become a monk at the Cistercian community at Rievaulx, where he eventually became abbot. He wrote his most famous work, "The Mirror of Charity," at the request of St. Bernard of Clairvaux. He is the patron of those who suffer from bladder stones.

Aemilianus Saint; Latin; industrious

Emilian

St. Aemilianus, also known as Emilian, (d. 259) was martyred with several others in Citra, Africa.

Aengus Saint; Celtic; one choice

Óengus

St. Aengus, also known as Óengus, (d. 824) was an Irish bishop, reformer, and writer. He is believed to be the author of the Festology of the Saints of Ireland, the Félire. He became a hermit on the banks of the river Nore and later moved to Maryborough in search of even more solitude. Still, people were drawn to his holiness and sought him out. This led him to enter the monastery of Tallaght, near Dublin, and it is believed that he became a bishop. Two monasteries, in counties Limerick and Laois, were named after him.

Aeodh *see Beoadh*

Aeron *see Aaron*

Aetherius Saint; Latin; ethereal

St. Aetherius (d. 602) was a priest of Lyons, France, and was a favorite pupil of St. Nicetius, who was the city's archbishop. He built St. Nicetius a bed. After the archbishop's death, the bed became associated with several miracles. Those who were ill were cured after being laid upon it. In due time, Aetherius himself became archbishop.

Pope St. Gregory I wrote to him and asked him to provide lodging and assistance to a missionary he was sending his way. This man would become St. Augustine of Canterbury.

Afan Saint; Celtic

St. Afan (sixth century) was a bishop of Brecknock, Wales. He was a cousin of St. David, patron saint of Wales.

Affonso *see Alfonso*

Africanus Saint; Latin; from Africa

St. Africanus was martyred in Africa, along with St. Theodore.

Africus Saint; Latin, Greek; sunny, not cold

St. Africus (seventh century) was a bishop and confessor in Comminges, located in southern France.

Agabius Saint; Hebrew; a locust, the father's joy or feast

St. Agabius (d. 250) was bishop of Verona, Italy.

Agabus Saint, New Testament; Hebrew; a locust, the father's joy or feast

St. Agabus (first century) was one of the seventy-two disciples mentioned by St. Luke. He is mentioned as a prophet in the Acts of the Apostles and was said to have predicted both a famine in the Roman Empire and St. Paul's imprisonment in Jerusalem. Yet, he was unable to convince St. Paul to cancel his journey there. He died as a martyr in Antioch.

Aganus Saint; Latin; act as

St. Aganus (d. 1100) was a Benedictine abbot of St. Gabriel's in Campania, Italy.

Agape *see Agape (girl's name)*

Agapitus Saint; Hebrew; the beloved one

Pope St. Agapitus I (d. 536) was the son of a priest named Gordianus, who was martyred during the reign of Pope Symmachus. Elected Pope in 535, he set to work healing the rifts in the Church at that time. Belisarius was on the verge of invading Italy, and Agapitus went to Constantinople to appeal to Emperor Justinian to halt the advance. While he knew he would not succeed in that mission, he was able to put down a religious revolt that was led by Empress Theodora and Bishop Anthemius. Agapitus died while in Constantinople, but his remains were brought back to St. Peter's in Rome.

Agapius Saint; Greek

St. Agapius (d. 306) was from Caesarea, Palestine. He was arrested four times during the persecutions of Emperor Diocletian. Three times he was tortured then released. The fourth time, he was offered pardon if he disavowed the faith. He refused and was penned up with a wild boar, but the boar did not kill him. The next day, stones were affixed to his feet and he was drowned in the Mediterranean.

Agathangelo Saint

Bl. Agathangelo Noury (d. 1638) was born with the name Francis at Vendome, France. He later entered the Capuchin monastery in Le Mans and was ordained a priest in 1625. He worked in Aleppo, Syria, where he published Catholic works in Arabic. He was then sent to Cairo where he worked to help bring Coptic Christians back into communion with Rome. He also went to Ethiopia where he was arrested in 1638. He was tried by King Gondar and found guilty of interfering with Ethiopian religious matters. He was hanged using the cord of his habit.

Agathangelus Saint; Latin; good angel

St. Agathangelus (d. 309) was a Roman deacon who was martyred during the reign of Emperor Diocletian. He had accompanied St. Clement from Rome to Ancyra where they were both beheaded.

Agatho Saint; Greek; good

Pope St. Agatho (d. 681) was a Greek born in Sicily to wealthy parents. He became a monk and was very knowledgeable in Latin and Greek. He was elected pope in 678. The sixth Ecumenical Council met during his papacy. This council proclaimed the existence of two wills in Christ and condemned Monothelitism. He died during a plague in 681.

Agathopodes Saint

St. Agathopodes (d. 150) was a deacon who along with St. Philo assisted St. Ignatius of Antioch. After St. Ignatius was martyred, the two men retrieved his relics from the Roman authorities. They also wrote the story of his life.

Agathopus Saint; Greek; brave person

St. Agathopus (d. 303) was a deacon in Thessalonica (modern Greece) who was arrested for possessing Christian scriptures. He was martyred by being thrown into the sea with heavy rocks tied around his neck.

Ageranus Saint; Latin; lord of the horses

Aja, Aye

St. Ageranus (d. 303) was a Benedictine monk in a monastery in France. When a Norman army attacked, the majority of the monks fled, but he and four other monks and one novice stayed behind and defended the altars. They were murdered by the Normans.

Agericus Saint; Latin; powerful sword

St. Agericus (d. 588) succeeded St. Desiderius as bishop of Verdun, France. He was an advisor to King Childebert II and was very generous with the poor in his area.

Agilbert Saint; German; famous sword from combat

St. Agilbert (d. 673) studied at Jouarre Monastery in Ireland. King Coenwalh of the West Saxons asked him to become bishop of Wessex. He was active in missionary activities and ordained St. Wilfrid. When the king divided his diocese, he resigned his see. He later became bishop of Paris.

Agileus Saint; Latin; spade of a fighter

St. Agileus (d. 300) was memorialized in a sermon by St. Augustine. A Christian who lived in North Africa, he was martyred in Carthage.

Agilulfus Saint; Latin; spear of the warrior

St. Agilulfus (d. 751) was an abbot of Stavelot. He later became archbishop of Cologne, Germany. He tried to convince King Pepin not to name his illegitimate son, Charles Martel, to the throne and was killed as a result.

Agilus Saint; German

Ayeul

St. Agilus (d. 650) was also known as Ayeul. Born into a noble French family, he served as a missionary in Bavaria, Germany. He later became abbot of Rebais near Paris.

Agnan *see Anianas*

Agnello Saint; Latin; reference to the Lamb of God

Bl. Agnello of Pisa (1195–1236) was born into a noble Italian family. He became a Franciscan and was appointed by St. Francis to bring the Franciscan order to England. He established houses in Canterbury and London and a school in Oxford. He was very devoted to the Franciscan ideal of poverty.

Agnellus Saint; Latin; reference to the Lamb of God

St. Agnellus (d. 596) was a hermit who later became abbot of San Gaudioso near Naples. He was known as a miracle worker and is a patron of the city of Naples.

Agnolo *see Angelo*

Agobard Saint; German

St. Agobard (ca. 775–840) fled from Spain when the Muslims entered his homeland. He went to France where he was ordained a priest. He was known for his holiness and charity and was named archbishop of Lyons. He wrote several treatises on theology and liturgical matters.

Agofredus Saint; German, Latin; spear that brings peace

St. Agofredus (d. 738) was the brother of St. Leutfridus. A Holy Cross Benedictine monk, he was known throughout Normandy, France, for his holiness.

Agostino Saint; form of Augustine; Italian; majestic

St. Agostino Roscelli (1818–1902) was born into a poor family in Bargone of Casarza Ligure. He became a priest. During his life, he served as a parish priest, worked with prison inmates, and became chaplain of a hospital. With Pope Pius IX's blessing, he founded the Sisters of the Immaculate Conception. He was canonized by Pope John Paul II in 2001.

Agrecius Saint

St. Agrecius (d. 335) was patriarch of Antioch when Pope Sylvester I named him bishop of Treves, Germany, at the request of the empress, St. Helena. She also entrusted him with what are known as the Relics of Trier, relics from the Holy Land that she collected on her pilgrimage there. He served as bishop for twenty years and attended the Council of Aries in 314.

Agricola Saint; Latin; farmer

St. Agricola (ca. 497–580) was bishop of Chalon-sur-Saone, France. He led an ascetic life, fasting all day until evening, when he ate a small meal while standing. He enlarged and beautified many of the churches in his diocese. After he died, he was buried in Saint Marcellus Church. In 879, a blind man experienced a recurring dream in which he was told to go to the tomb of St. Agricola. On his way to the tomb, his eyesight began to be restored. He could see clearly by the time he reached the tomb.

Agricolus Saint; Latin; farmer

St. Agricolus (d. 700) was the son of St. Magnus, a senator who, after his wife died, became a monk and then bishop of Lérins. Agricolus was ordained a priest. In 660, he became coadjutor to his father. He took over the see in 670. He was known for his preaching and care for the poor and sick. He was named patron of Avignon in 1647.

Agrippinus Saint; Latin; born feet first

St. Agrippinus (d. 300) was bishop of Naples. His remains are in the Naples cathedral, beside Sts. Eutychius and Aucutis.

Aguistin *see Agustin*

Agustein *see Augustine, Agustin*

Agusteyne *see Augustine, Agustin*

Agustin Saint; Latin; majestic

Aguistin, Agustein, Agusteyne, Agustis, Agusto, Agustus, Agustyn

St. Agustin Caloca Cortes (1898–1927) was born at Teul, Zacatecas, Mexico. He became a priest and was a prefect at the covert Auxiliary Seminary of Our Lady of Guadalajara. He was arrested and shot. He is one of the Martyrs of the Cristero War. He was canonized by Pope John Paul II in 2000.

Agustis *see Augustine, Agustin*

Agusto *see Augustine, Agustin*

Agustus *see Augustine, Agustin*

Agustyn *see Augustine, Agustin*

Ahriel *see Ariel (girl's name)*

Aibert Saint; German; noble and bright

St. Aibert (d. 1140) was a Benedictine ascetic and recluse from Tournai, Belgium. He was a monk for twenty-three years at the Benedictine Monastery of St. Crespin, before leaving to become a hermit. He is known for his devotion to the Rosary and saying two Masses each day—one for the living and one for the dead.

Aicardo *see Aidric*

Aichardus Saint; Latin, French; condiment

St. Aichardus (d. 687) was supposed to follow in his father's footsteps and have a military career. His mother intervened, however, and allowed him to make his own decision about what to do with his life. He decided to become a monk and entered the Benedictine Order at St. John's Abbey in Ansion, Poitou. He became prior of a new monastery founded by St. Philibert in Quincay, later becoming abbot when Philibert died.

Aidan Saint; Top 100 Name; Gaelic; fiery

Aedyn, Aiden, Aidon, Aidun, Aidwin, Aidwyn, Aidyn, Aiyden, Aydan, Aydin

St. Aidan, St. Aidan of Ferns, St. Aidan of Lindisfarne

St. Aidan (d. 651) was born in Connaught, Ireland. Even as a child, he was very pious. He spent time at St. David Monastery in Wales. He miraculously saved the monastery from being destroyed when Saxon war parties attacked. Later, he returned to Ireland where he founded a monastery in Ferns, in Wexford. He also became a bishop. In religious art, he is often portrayed with a stag because, according to legend, he made a beautiful stag invisible to save it from being hunted by hounds.

Aiden *see Aidan*

Aidon *see Aidan*

Aidred *see Aidric*

Aidric Saint; English; blessed ruler

Aicardo, Aidred, Aidrich, Aidris

St. Aidric (d. 856) grew up in the royal household of Charlemagne, where he served him and his son Louis. As an adult, he studied for the priesthood at Metz, France. Louis called him back to court once he was ordained. Later, he would be named bishop of Le Mans. He later served as a legate in the court of King Pepin in Aquitaine, France.

Aidrich *see Aidric*

Aidris *see Aidric*

Aidun *see Aidan*

Aidwin *see Aidan*

Aidwyn *see Aidan*

Aidyn *see Aidan*

Aignan *see Anianas*

Aigulf Saint

St. Aigulf (d. 676) grew up in Blois, France, and became a Benedictine monk in Fleury. Named abbot of the monastery at Lerins, he set to work to reform the monastery, which gained him some enemies. Two of the monks turned the abbot and four of his followers over to local soldiers. The prisoners were taken to Capri, Italy, where they were murdered.

Ailan *see Alan*

Ailbhe Saint; Gaelic; white

Albeus

A disciple of St. Patrick, St. Ailbhe's (d. 528) life is known mostly through legend. One such legend is that he was left in the woods as an infant and suckled by a wolf. What can be verified is that he was a missionary in Ireland and the first bishop of Emily in Munster, Ireland. He is sometimes referred to as St. Albeus and is known as the patron saint of wolves.

Aileran Saint; Celtic; wise one

St. Aileran (d. 664), known as "the wise," was a very distinguished professor at the school of Clonard in Ireland. A master of Latin and Greek, he wrote several manuscripts, including a life of St. Patrick and one on St. Brigid. His writings were studied and read in many of the scholarly institutions of Europe. He died from the yellow plague.

Ailfrid *see Alfred*

Ailfryd *see Alfred*

Ailin *see Alan*

Aimil *see Emil*

Aimo Saint; French; loved

St. Aimo (d. 1173) was born near Rennes, France, and entered the Benedictine Monastery of Savigny in the modern area of Normandy. He was full of charitable kindness, caring for two monks who had leprosy. The other monks presumed that he was a leper as well. It was only once they realized that he did not have the dreaded disease that he was allowed to be ordained to the priesthood. He is also known to have had mystical experiences.

Aindrea *see Andrea*

Airick Saint; Celtic; agreeable

St. Airick (twelfth century) was a hermit in England and a friend of St. Godric.

Aitan *see Ethan*

Aiyden *see Aidan*

Aizik *see Isaac*

Aja *see Ageranus*

Ajuture Saint; Latin; help

St. Ajuture (d. 1131) was a Norman gentleman who was taken prisoner and tortured by the Saracens but never renounced his faith. When he was freed, he returned home to spend the rest of his life in penance and prayer.

Al *see Alexander*

Alaan *see Alan*

Alan Saint; Gaelic; handsome, peaceful

Ailan, Ailin, Alaan, Aland, Alando, Alani, Alann, Alanson, Alao, Alon, Alun, Alune, Alyn, Alyne

Bl. Alan de la Roche (1428–1475) was born in Brittany. He entered the Dominican Order and studied in Paris. He became a teacher and was known as a great preacher. He was dedicated to the Rosary and founded several Confraternities of the Rosary.

Aland *see Alan*

Alando *see Alan*

Alani *see Alan*

Alann *see Alan*

Alano *see Alonso*

Alanson *see Alan*

Alanus Saint; English; attractive

Bl. Alanus de Solminihac (1593–1659) was born in a castle in Belet, Dordogne, France. He became an Augustinian Regular at Chancelade Abbey. He became superior of the abbey and was later named bishop of Cahors, a position he held for twenty-three years. He was a very active bishop who visited all of his parishes several times, founded a seminary, and supported adoration of the Eucharist. He also attended the Council of Trent.

Alanzo *see Alonso*

Alao *see Alan*

Alasdair *see Alexander*

Albain *see Alban*

Alban Saint; Latin; from Alba, Italy

Albain, Albany, Albean, Albein, Albone, Alby, Auban, Auben, Aubyn, Elbin, Ellban

St. Alban, St. Alban Bartholomew Roe, St. Alban of Mainz

St. Alban (third century) was the first martyr in England. Although he was a pagan, he hid a priest (St. Amphibalus) in his home to protect him from persecution. The priest greatly impressed him and convinced him to become a Christian. When the soldiers came to his house to arrest the priest, Alban changed clothes with him and went in his place. When the judge found out about this deception, he was furious and demanded that Alban worship the false gods, but Alban steadfastly refused. As a result, he was whipped and then beheaded.

Albany *see Alban*

Albean *see Alban*

Albein *see Alban*

Alberic Saint; German; smart, wise ruler

Alberich, Alberick, Alberyc, Alberyck, Alberyk

St. Alberic of Utrecht, St. Alberic Crescitelli

St. Alberic of Utrecht (d. 784) entered the Benedictine order at Utrecht, Netherlands. Known for his piety and preaching, he became bishop of Utrecht, succeeding St. Gregory of Utrecht, in 775.

Alberich *see Alberic*

Alberick *see Alberic*

Albert Saint; German, French; noble and bright

Adelbert, Albertik, Albrecht, Albret, Albyrt, Albyrte, Alvertos, Aubert, Dalbert, Delbert

St. Albert of Cashel, St. Albert of Como, St. Albert of Gambron, St. Albert of Genoa, St. Albert of Jerusalem, St. Albert of Louvain, St. Albert of Magdeburg, St. Albert of Montecorvino, St. Albert of Trapani, St. Albert the Great, St. Albert Chmielowski

St. Albert of Louvain (ca. 1166–1192) was the son of Duke Godrey III of Brabant and brother of Henry I, duke of Lorraine and Brabant. After serving as a knight in service to Count Baldwin V, he became a canon and then bishop of Liege. His appointment as bishop was opposed by Count Baldwin who appealed to Emperor Henry VI, who removed him from the post. St. Albert appealed to Rome, and Pope Celestine declared his appointment valid. He was then made a cardinal by Archbishop William of Reims. A group of knights working for Emperor Henry VI stabbed him to death. The emperor was forced to make public penance for this act.

Albertik *see Albert*

Albertinus Saint; Latin; noble and bright

St. Albertinus (d. 1294) was known as a peacemaker. Serving as prior general of the Benedictine order, he helped oversee the merger of that order with the Camaldolese. He also mediated a dispute between the people of Gubbio, Italy, and their bishop.

Alberto Saint; Italian; noble and bright

St. Alberto Hurtado Cruchaga (1901–1952) was a Chilean Jesuit priest, lawyer, social worker, and writer. He cared for the poor and taught future teachers. He also gave Ignatian retreats to help people discover their vocations. He became director of his diocese's Catholic Action movement and then the national director. He died of pancreatic cancer and was canonized by Pope Benedict XVI in 2005.

Albertus Saint; a form of Albert; Latin; noble and bright

Known also as St. Albert the Great, St. Albertus Magnus (d. 1280) was a German Dominican who has been honored as a Doctor of the Church. A brilliant scholar of the natural sciences, his most famous student was St. Thomas Aquinas. He advocated studying science by observing nature, a radical idea at the time. He was also very knowledgeable about the Bible and theology. He believed science and religion could inform each other and coexist peacefully. He is a patron saint of the sciences.

Alberyc see *Alberic*

Alberyck see *Alberic*

Alberyk see *Alberic*

Albeus see *Ailbhe*

Albinus see *Aubin*

Albone see *Alban*

Albrecht see *Albert*

Albret see *Albert*

Alby see *Alban*

Albyrt see *Albert*

Albyrte see *Albert*

Alcmund Saint; German; clear

St. Alcmund (d. 781) was bishop of Hexham in Northumberland, England. He was known as a miracle worker.

Alcuin Saint; Teutonic; noble friend

Bl. Alcuin (730–804) was born in York, England. A student of St. Colgan, he became a deacon and the head of the York cathedral school. Charlemagne made him Minister of Education, and he founded several schools. He established scriptoria devoted to copying ancient manuscripts. He also invented cursive writing and advocated the doctrine that the Holy Spirit proceeds from the Father and the Son.

Aldate Saint; English; old gate

St. Aldate (d. 577) was a bishop of Gloucester, England. He encouraged the people of his area to resist pagans who were trying to invade.

Aldebrandus Saint; Latin; governs with the sword

St. Aldebrandus (d. 1219) was born in Sorrivoli, Italy. As provost of Rimini, he preached against the sinful lives of those in authority. He was subject to death threats as a result and had to flee the area. In 1170, he was named bishop of Fosombrone, Italy, where he is regarded as patron.

Aldemar Saint; German; famous for nobility

St. Aldemar (d. 1080) was born in Capua, Italy, and became a monk in Monte Cassino. Princess Aloara of that area appointed him as director of the religious at a new convent she had established in Capua. When his abbot reassigned him back to Monte Cassino, the princess was very upset. Aldemar went to Bologna, but a companion involved in the dispute tried to kill him. He then fled to Bocchignano, Abruzzi, where he founded several more religious houses.

Aldericus Saint; German; old power

St. Aldericus (d. 841) was born in Gatinais, France. He became a Benedictine monk and then a priest. He served as chancellor of the diocese of Sens. He was known as an ecclesiastical scholar.

saint; English; old helmet
lhelm (d. 709) was a rela-
of King Ine of Wessex. He
was educated in Wiltshire, England. He was named abbot of
Malmesbury. He also founded
St. Lawrence Monastery in
Bradfordon-on-Avon. He later
became bishop of Sherborne.
He is known, not only for his
holiness, but as the first Englishman to promote classical
learning on the British isles.

Aldo _see Aldo (girl's name)_

Aleaunie _see Adelelmus_

Alec _see Alexander_

Alecander _see Alexander_

Alecsandar _see Alexander_

Alecsander _see Alexander_

Alecxander _see Alexander_

Aled _see Allucio_

Alejándro _see Alexander_

Alek _see Alexander_

Alekos _see Alexander_

Aleksandar _see Alexander_

Aleksander _see Alexander_

Aleksei _see Alexander_

Aleksy Saint; a form of Alexander;
Russian; defender of mankind
Bl. Aleksy Sobaszek; Bl. Aleksy
Sobaszek (1895–1942) was born
in Przygodzice, Wielkopolskie,
Poland. He became a priest and
was killed in the concentration
camp at Dachau, Oberbayern,
Germany. He is one of the 108
Polish Martyrs of World War II
beatified by Pope John Paul II
in 1999.

Alekzander _see Alexander_

Alermius _see Etherius_

Alessander _see Alexander_

Alessandro _see Alexander_

Alex _see Alexander_

Alexandar _see Alexander_

Alexander Saint; Top 100 Name;
Greek; defender of mankind
_Al, Alasdair, Alec, Alecander, Alec-
sandar, Alecsander, Alecxander,
Alejándro, Alek, Alekos, Aleksan-
dar, Aleksander, Aleksei, Alekzan-
der, Alessander, Alessandro, Alex,
Alexandar, Alexandor, Alexandr,
Alexandro, Alexandros, Alexx-
ander, Alexzander, Alic, Alick,
Alisander, Alixander, Xander_

St. Alexander, St. Alexander
Akimetes, St. Alexander I, St.
Alexander Nevski, St. Alexander of Alexandria, St. Alexander of Comana, St. Alexander
of Constantinople, St. Alexander of Gaza, St. Alexander of
Kemet, St. Alexander Sauli, St.
Alexander the Bish

St. Alexander (d. 251) studied with Origen in the Christian school of Alexandria. He
became bishop of Cappado-
cia, during which time he was
imprisoned for several years.
When he was released, he went
to Jerusalem where he became
coadjutor bishop in 212. During
the persecution of Decius, he
was once again imprisoned. He
was thrown to the wild beasts,
but they refused to attack him.
He was then taken to Caesarea
where he died in prison.

Alexandor _see Alexander_

Alexandr *see Alexander*

Alexandro *see Alexander*

Alexandros *see Alexander*

Alexes *see Alexis*

Alexey *see Alexis*

Alexios *see Alexis*

Alexis Saint; a short form of Alexander; Greek; defender of mankind

Alexes, Alexey, Alexios, Alexius, Alexiz, Alexsis, Alexsus, Alexus, Alexys

St. Alexis, St. Alexis Falconieri

St. Alexis (fifth century) was the son of a rich Roman senator. He wanted to give up his riches and serve the poor, but they had already arranged a marriage for him. He consented and married her, but on their wedding day he obtained his new wife's permission to leave her and dedicate himself to God. He went to Syria where he lived as a beggar for many years. When a picture of the Blessed Virgin spoke and declared him a "man of God," he became famous, which he did not want. He fled back to Rome and begged at his parents' home. They did not recognize him but opened their home to him, where he lived under the stairs. When he died, his family found a note on him telling them who he was.

Alexius *see Alexis*

Alexiz *see Alexis*

Alexsis *see Alexis*

Alexsus *see Alexis*

Alexus *see Alexis*

Alexxander *see Alexander*

Alexys *see Alexis*

Alexzander *see Alexander*

Aleydis *see Alice (girl's name)*

Alf *see Alfred*

Alfanus Saint

St. Alfanus (d. 1085) was a Benedictine monk at Monte Cassino who later became archbishop of Salerno, Italy. He assisted Pope St. Gregory VII on his deathbed.

Alfeo *see Alfred*

Alfons Saint; form of Alphonse; Italian, Spanish; noble and eager

Bl. Alfons Mazurek (1891–1944) was born at Baranówka, Lubelskie, Poland. He became a Discalced Carmelite and was ordained a priest. He taught at the Carmelite minor seminary and became prior of the monastery at Czerna, Poland. He was murdered by Nazis and is considered one of the 108 Polish Martyrs of World War II. He was beatified by Pope John Paul II in 1999.

Alfonse *see Alfonso*

Alfonso Saint; form of Alphonse; Italian, Spanish; noble and eager

Affonso, Alfonse, Alfonsus, Alfonza, Alfonzus

Bl. Alfonso Maria Fusco (1839–1910) was born in Angri, Salerno, Italy, to a peasant family. He was ordained a priest. Together with Maddalena

Caputo of Angri, he founded the Congregation of the Baptistine Sisters of the Nazarene, which was devoted to the care of poor youth and abandoned children. He was beatified by Pope John Paul II in 2001.

Alfonsus *see Alfonso*

Alfonza *see Alfonso*

Alfonzus *see Alfonso*

Alfred Saint; English; elf counselor, wise counselor

Ailfrid, Ailfryd, Alf, Alfeo, Alfredus, Alfreth, Alfrid, Alfried, Alfryd, Alured, Elfrid, Fred

St. Alfred the Great (848–899) was the fifth son of the King of Wessex and the godson of Pope Leo IV. He was a great scholar who translated many classics for the English people. He became king and was known for his patronage of the arts, literature, and the Christian Church.

Alfredo Saint; a form of Alfred; English, Spanish; elf counselor, wise counselor

Bl. Alfredo Ildefonso Schuster (1880–1954) was born in Rome, Italy. He became a Benedictine and was ordained a priest. He served as abbot of St. Paul-Outside-the-Walls. Pope Pius XI appointed him archbishop of Milan in 1929 and consecrated him a cardinal. He encouraged laity to take part in parish life and in Catholic Action. He opposed Fascism and worked for the poor during World War

II. He was beatified by Pope John Paul II in 1996.

Alfredus *see Alfred*

Alfreth *see Alfred*

Alfrick Saint; English; old counselor, wise judge

St. Alfrick (d. 1105) was a monk in the Benedictine Abbey of Abingdon, England. He became bishop of Wilton and then archbishop of Canterbury.

Alfrid *see Alfred*

Alfried *see Alfred*

Alfryd *see Alfred*

Alfwold Saint; English

St. Alfwold (d. 1058) was a monk in Winchester, England, who later became bishop of Sherborne. He was known for his ascetic lifestyle which served as an example for the local royalty.

Alic *see Alexander*

Alick *see Alexander*

Alifonso *see Alonso*

Alipius Saint; Latin; he whom suffering does not affect

St. Alipius (d. 430) was born in Tagaste, North Africa, and was a childhood friend of St. Augustine. He went to Rome to study law and became a magistrate. When Augustine came to Rome, Alipius resigned his post and went with him to Milan where they were both baptized by St. Ambrose and then ordained in Hippo. Alipius became bishop of Tagaste.

Alisander *see Alexander*

Alixander *see Alexander*

Allen *see Elwin*

Allerius Saint; Latin; beautiful and handsome

St. Allerius (d. 1050) was a member of the powerful Pappacarboni family in Salerno, Italy. When stricken with a serious illness, he vowed to become a monk if he was cured. When the cure came, he kept his promise and joined the monastery in Cluny, France. He later returned to Salerno and became a hermit. Twelve men joined him, and they formed the Benedictine Abbey of La Cava.

Allonzo *see Alonso*

Allowin *see Bavo*

Allucio Saint; Latin, Spanish; bright, shining

Aled, Filuned

St. Allucio (d. 1134) was a shepherd in Tuscany before he dedicated his life to acts of charity. He built two churches, a bridge over the Arno, and three hospices for pilgrims. He also helped mediate conflicts between the Tuscan city-states. He was known as a miracle worker. The group that worked with him became known as the Brothers of St. Allucio.

Allyre *see Illidius*

Almachius Saint; Latin; beautiful

Telemachus

St. Almachius (ca. 400 AD), also known as Telemachus, was an ascetic who had traveled from the East to Rome. Upon seeing the gladiatorial games going on in the arena, he went down into the stadium and attempted to separate the combatants. Almachius was killed as a result, although it is uncertain whether he was killed by the gladiators or stoned by the spectators.

Almirus Saint; Latin

St. Almirus (d. 560) was a companion of Sts. Avitus and Carifelis. He went to Maine, France, with them, where he lived as a hermit the rest of his days.

Almus Saint; Latin; nourishing

St. Almus (d. 1270) was a monk in the Cistercian monastery at Melrose, England. He was then elected abbot of Scotland's Balmerino Monastery, which had been founded by the widow of William I of Scotland.

Alnoth Saint; German

St. Alnoth (d. 700) tended cows on the lands of St. Werburga's Monastery at Weedon, Northampton, England. The bailiff who was in charge of him treated him very badly, but he bore his suffering with patience. He later became a hermit. Two robbers attacked him and killed him.

Aloisius *see Aloysius*

Alojzy Saint; form of Aloysius; Polish, German; famous warrior

Bl. Alojzy Liguda (1898–1942) was born in Winó, Opolskie, Poland. He became a member of the Society of the Divine Word. He was martyred in the concentration camp at Dachau, Oberbayem, Germany. He was one of the 108 Polish Martyrs of World War II. He was beatified by Pope John Paul II in 1999.

Alon *see Alan*

Alonso Saint; form of Alphonse; Spanish; noble and eager

Alano, Alanzo, Alifonso, Allonzo, Alonz, Alonze

St. Alonso Rodriguez (1532–1617), also known as Alphonsus, was born in Spain, the son of a wealthy merchant. He was studying with the Jesuits when his father died, and he was called home to take over the family business. He married and had children. After three of his children and his wife died, he sold his business and joined the Jesuits. He was considered unsuitable for the priesthood but was welcomed as a lay brother. He worked as a hall porter for twenty-four years. He lived a life of obedience and penance and was devoted to the Immaculate Conception.

Alonz *see Alonso*

Alonze *see Alonso*

Aloysius Saint; form of Louis; German; famous warrior

Aloisius

St. Aloysius Gonzaga (1568–1591) was born in Castiglione, Italy. His father wanted him to pursue a military career, but he was called to religious life. He joined the Jesuits at age eighteen after receiving his father's blessing. He served in a hospital during the plague of 1587 and died at the age of twenty-three of that disease.

Alphaeus Saint; Hebrew; changing

St. Alphaeus (d. 303) was a lector in the parish church in Caesarea. He was arrested and tortured during the persecutions of Emperor Diocletian. He was beheaded when he refused to renounce the faith.

Alphege Saint; English; high elf

Known as "the First Martyr of Canterbury," St. Alphege (954–1012) was a monk in the Deerhurst Monastery in Gloucester, England. He remained a few years before becoming a hermit. He later became abbot of the Abbey of Bath and bishop of Winchester where he served for twenty years, during which time he helped convert a Danish chieftain to Christianity. Pope John XVIII named him archbishop of Canterbury. He was taken captive by Danes pillaging the southern regions. He was hit with an ax and then beaten to death.

Alphius Saint; Hebrew; learned chief

St. Alphius (d. 251) was arrested during the persecutions of Emperor Trajanus Decius. He was tortured in Rome and then brought to Pozzuoli, near modern Naples. His tongue was torn from his mouth before he was martyred.

Alphonsus Saint; form of Alphonse; Latin; noble and eager

St. Alphonsus, St. Alphonsus Marie Liguori, St. Alphonsus Rodriguez

St. Alphonsus (1696–1787) was born near Naples, Italy. At age sixteen, he graduated with a law degree and was admitted to the Neopolitan bar. After losing a case in 1723, he decided to leave the law behind and become a priest. In 1732, he founded the Congregation of the Most Holy Redeemer. In 1756, he became bishop of St. Agatha, where he served until 1775 when he retired due to illness. He wrote 111 works on spirituality and theology.

Altfrid Saint

St. Altfrid (d. 874) was a Benedictine monk who helped found several female religious communities. He was the headmaster of the school at Corvey Abbey in Saxony and later became bishop of Ilildesheim, Germany. He was known for his holiness and devotion to Mary.

Altinus Saint; Latin

It is unclear when St. Altinus lived. One record has him as a first-century disciple of Christ who founded churches in France. Another has him as a martyr in the fourth century.

Altman Saint; German; old man

Altmann, Altmen, Atman

St. Altman (d. 1091) was born in Germany and educated in Paris. After being ordained, he became the ranking priest at the Paderborn cathedral school. He then became the royal chaplain of Emperor Henry II. He was named bishop of Passati, where he dedicated himself to reforming religious institutions. He aided Pope Gregory VII's efforts to end simony and clergy marriages. He was ultimately driven out of his diocese as a result of this controversy. He spent the end of his life in the abbey at Gottweig, Austria.

Altmann *see Altman*

Altmen *see Altman*

Alto Saint; Latin; high, tall

St. Alto (d. 760) was either Anglo-Saxon or Irish. He traveled to Augsburg, Germany, where he lived in a simple hut. His reputation for holiness grew and reached the ears of King Pepin, who gave him land for an abbey. The abbey was blessed by St. Boniface in 750.

Alun *see Alan*

Alune *see Alan*

Alured *see Alfred*

Alvarez Saint; German, Spanish; noble guardian

St. Alvarez, St. Alvarez of Corova

St. Alvarez (fourteenth century) was a member of the Dominican Monastery at Córdoba, Spain. He became known for his preaching ability and became the confessor of Queen Catherine and a tutor of the future King John II. He later founded a monastery in Córdoba. He led the opposition to the antipope Benedict XII (Peter de Luna).

Alverius Saint; Latin; noble guardian

St. Alverius was a soldier of the Theban legion who was martyred near Fosano.

Alvertos *see Albert*

Alvitus Saint; Latin

St. Alvitus (d. 1063) entered the Benedictine order at Sahagun, Spain, and became bishop of León. He is known for transferring the relics of St. Isidore from Seville, Spain, to León.

Alyn *see Alan*

Alyne *see Alan*

Alypius Saint; Greek

St. Alypius (fourth century) was an ascetic who sat on top of a pillar, in prayer and contemplation. He is a patron of infertile women.

Amabilis *see Amabilis (girl's name)*

Amadour Saint; Latin; one who loves

According to tradition, St. Amadour (first century) was a servant in the house of the holy family. He married St. Veronica and went with her to Gaul to spread the Christian faith. He is also reputed to have witnessed the martyrdom of Sts. Peter and Paul. After the death of St. Veronica, he became a hermit at Quircy, France, where he built a shrine to the Blessed Virgin Mary.

Amaethlu Saint; Hebrew, Arabic

St. Amaethlu (sixth century) was from Wales. He founded a church in Anglesey.

Amand Saint; Latin; worthy of love

St. Amand (584–675) joined a small monastery on the island of Yeu when he was twenty years old. He later went to Tours, where he was ordained, and then lived in Bourges for fifteen years. He became a bishop with a general commission to spread the faith. In addition to being a missionary, he is known as the founder of monasticism in ancient Belgium, where he established many monasteries. In his elder years, he retired to the monastery at Elnone, where he served as abbot for four years prior to his death. He is a patron of wine makers, beer brewers, merchants, innkeepers, bartenders, and Boy Scouts.

Amandus Saint; Latin; worthy of love

St. Amandus (d. 481) was ordained by Bishop Delphinus of Bordeaux, France, whom he later succeeded as bishop. He was an instructor of St. Paulinus of Nola and was known as an outstanding and holy bishop.

Amantius Saint; Latin; loving

St. Amantius (d. 600) is a patron saint of Città di Castello, Italy. He was a parish priest in that city, and Pope St. Gregory the Great venerated him because of his holiness.

Amarand Saint; Arabic; moon

St. Amarand (d. 700) was abbot of the Moissac Monastery before being named bishop of Albi, France.

Amaranthus Saint; Greek; immortal, unfailing

St. Amaranthus (third century) was a martyr venerated in southern France. No record remains of his life, but he was mentioned by St. Gregory of Tours.

Amarinus Saint; Greek; unfading

St. Amarinus (d. 676) was a companion of St. Praejectus. A bishop of Clermont, France, the valley of St. Amarian in Alsace, France, was named after him.

Amasius Saint; Latin; lover

St. Amasius (d. 356) fled his Greek homeland because of the Arian heresy. He escaped to Italy where he was named bishop of Teano.

Amaswinthus Saint

St. Amaswinthus (d. 982) was a monk and abbot at the Andulusian Monastery of Silva de Malaga. He lived there for forty-four years.

Amator Saint; Latin; one who loves

St. Amator (d. 418) grew up in an upper-class French family. He did not want to be married, and with the help of Bishop Valerian, who was to perform the ceremony, convinced his intended bride to enter a convent. He then became a priest and later bishop of Auxerre. He left the area for a time when threatened by Germanus, a local pagan governor, but he later returned and was able to convert him. Germanus later became bishop of the area himself. Some believe St. Amator ordained St. Patrick.

Amatus Saint; Latin; beloved

St. Amatus (d. 627) was born into a noble French family and educated at St. Maurice Abbey. He became a Benedictine monk and then lived as a hermit. St. Eustice advised him to go to Luxueil Monastery. While he was there, he converted a Merovingian noble named Romaric. Romaric founded a double monastery, and Amatus served as its first abbot.

Ambie *see Ambrose*

Ambrogio *see Ambrose*

Ambroise *see Ambrose*

Ambroisius *see Ambrose*

Ambros *see Ambrose*

Ambrose Saint; Greek; immortal

Ambie, Ambrogio, Ambroise, Ambroisius, Ambros, Ambrosi, Ambrosius, Ambross, Ambrossye, Ambrosye, Ambrotos, Ambroz, Ambrus, Amby

St. Ambrose, St. Ambrose Autpert, St. Ambrose Edward Barlow, St. Ambrose Kibuka, St. Ambrose of Alexandria

St. Ambrose (d. 397) was a successful lawyer and the governor of Milan when the bishop of Milan died, causing a riot in the cathedral. The bishop had supported the Arian heresy, and the people were fighting over whether an Arian or a Catholic would take his place. Ambrose tried to make peace between the two groups, who then decided that he should be bishop. He had no interest in the job, and was not even baptized, and asked the emperor to overturn the decision, but he refused. Ambrose reluctantly accepted and embraced the life. He gave up his property and began studying theology. He fought the Arian heresy wholeheartedly. He was also very generous with the poor.

Ambrosi *see Ambrose*

Ambrosio Saint; form of Ambrose; Greek; immortal

St. Ambrosio Kibuuka (d. 1886) was a page to King Mwanga of Uganda. A convert to the faith, he was martyred by being burned alive. He is one of the Martyrs of Uganda.

Ambrosius *see Ambrose*

Ambross *see Ambrose*

Ambrossye *see Ambrose*

Ambrosye *see Ambrose*

Ambrotos *see Ambrose*

Ambroz *see Ambrose*

Ambrus *see Ambrose*

Amby *see Ambrose*

Amedeus Saint; Latin; God's love

St. Amedeus (1420–1482) was born to a noble family

in Portugal. He became a lay Franciscan brother. After living as a hermit for a while, he was ordained as a priest and founded Franciscan monasteries.

Amic *see Amicus*

Amick *see Amicus*

Amico *see Amicus*

Amicus Saint; Latin, English; beloved friend

Amic, Amick, Amico, Amik, Amiko, Amyc, Amyck, Amycko, Amyk, Amyko

St. Amicus (d. 773) was a French knight who served Charlemagne. He fought against the Lombards in northern Italy. He is considered a martyr.

Amik *see Amicus*

Amiko *see Amicus*

Amman *see Ammon*

Ammon Saint; Egyptian; hidden

Amman

St. Ammon (d. 332) was a deacon in Thrace. He and forty of his converts died during the persecutions of Emperor Licinius. He was martyred by having a red-hot poker placed on his head.

Ammonius Saint

St. Ammonius (d. 250) was a soldier. He and his companion, Moseus, were arrested for having hired Christians. After being condemned to labor in the mines of Bithynia, they were burned to death.

Amo Saint; Latin; I love

St. Amo (fourth century) succeeded St. Mansuetus as bishop of Toul, France.

Amor Saint; Spanish, Latin; love

St. Amor, St. Amor of Amorbach, St. Amor of Aquitaine

St. Amor of Amorbach (eighth century) was a Benedictine abbot who helped St. Permin as a missionary to the Germans. He founded Amorbach Monastery in France.

Ampelius Saint; Greek, Latin; vine

St. Ampelius (d. 672) was a missionary to the Lombard people. He served as bishop of Milan, Italy.

Ampelus Saint; Greek, Latin; vine

St. Ampelus (d. 302) was a Sicilian who was martyred during the persecutions of Emperor Diocletian.

Amphianus Saint

Apian, Appian

St. Amphianus (d. 305), also known as Appian or Apian, was a young Christian in Lycia, Turkey. He accused the Roman governor of pagan sacrifice. As a result, he was arrested and tortured to death.

Amphibalus Saint; Latin; chasuble

St. Amphibalus (third century) was the priest saved by St. Alban. Alban, who was not Christian at the time, sheltered Amphibalus in his home so that he might avoid arrest. The priest converted Alban during

his time there, and when soldiers did arrive, Alban switched places with him, becoming a martyr.

Amphilocus Saint

St. Amphilocus (d. 400) was a cousin and friend of St. Gregory Nazianzus. He studied in Constantinople and was named bishop of Iconium. He fought against both the Arian and Messalian heresies. He attended the Council of Constantinople in 381.

Amphion Saint; Greek; son of Zeus (from Greek mythology)

St. Amphion (fourth century) was bishop of Epiphania, Cicilia, and then bishop of Nicomedia. He attended the Council of Nicaea in 325.

Amplias *see Ampliatus*

Ampliatus Saint, New Testament; Latin; illustrious

Amplias

St. Ampliatus (first century), also known as Amplias, was mentioned by St. Paul in Romans 16:8. He is considered one of the seventy disciples and joined St. Andrew in missionary work in the Balkans, where he was martyred with Sts. Narcissus and Urban. He may have been the first bishop of Varna, Bulgaria.

Amulwinus Saint

St. Amulwinus (d. 750) was a Benedictine abbot at the Monastery of Lobbes, Belgium.

Amyc *see Amicus*

Amyck *see Amicus*

Amycko *see Amicus*

Amyk *see Amicus*

Amyko *see Amicus*

Anacario Saint; Greek; not without grace

Bl. Anacario Benito Nozal (d. 1936) was a religious from the Passionist house of studies outside the city of Daimiel. He was martyred during the Spanish Civil War and was beatified in 1989 by Pope John Paul II.

Anacharius Saint

St. Anacharius (d. 604) was born near Orleans, France. Educated at the court of King Guntram of Burgandy, he later became bishop of Auxerre. He is known for his promotion of litanies.

Anacletus *see Cletus*

Ananias Saint, New Testament; Hebrew; he who has the grace of God

St. Ananias (first century) was a Christian in the city of Damascus. He had a vision of Christ in which he was told to seek out Saul, who would become St. Paul. Saul had made his way into the city struck blind after seeing the Lord on his way there. Ananias cured him of his blindness and baptized him. Ananias was later martyred in Eleutheropolis.

Anastacio *see Anastasius*

Anastacios *see Anastasius*

Anastagio *see Anastasius*

Anastas *see Anastasius*

Anastase *see Anastasius*

Anastasi *see Anastasius*

Anastasius Saint; Greek; resurrection

Anastacio, Anastacios, Anastagio, Anastas, Anastase, Anastasi, Anastatius, Anstcio, Anastice, Anastisis, Anaztáz, Stasio

Pope St. Anastasius I, and nineteen other popes bearing the same name, St. Anastasius the Fuller, St. Anastasius the Sinaite

A Roman by birth, Pope St. Anastasius I (d. 401) was elected pope in 399. He arranged for a council to consider the writings of Origen. This council condemned Origen's work as heterodox. He also urged the church in North Africa to continue to fight against Donatism.

Anastatius *see Anastasius*

Anastazy Saint; Polish; resurrection

Bl. Anastazy Jakub Pankiewicz (1882–1942) was a priest who was martyred at the Dachau concentration camp. He is one of the 108 Polish Martyrs of World War II. He was beatified by Pope John Paul II in 1999.

Anastcio *see Anastasius*

Anastice *see Anastasius*

Anastisis *see Anastasius*

Anathalon Saint; Greek; to renew, refresh

St. Anathalon (first century) was a companion of St. Barnabas. Barnabas sent him to Milan, Italy, where he served as bishop.

Anathony *see Anthony*

Anatole Saint; Greek; east, dawn

St. Anatole Kiriggwajjo (d. 1886) was a page of King Mwanga in Uganda. He was martyred with St. Charles Lwanga.

Anatolius Saint; Greek; from the east

St. Anatolius (ninth century) was a Scottish bishop. He left Scotland to make a pilgrimage to Rome and then became a hermit in Salins, France.

Anaztáz *see Anastasius*

Andee *see Andrea*

Andeol *see Antiochus*

Andeolus Saint

St. Andeolus (d. 208) was a subdeacon sent by Polycarp to evangelize southern Gaul. Septimus Severus, who was passing through Viviers, had him put to death.

Ander *see Leander*

Andera *see Andrea*

Anderea *see Andrea*

Anders *see Andrew*

Andery *see Andrew*

Andochius Saint

St. Andochius (second century) was a priest sent to Gaul by St. Polycarp. He was accompanied by Thyrsus, a deacon. The two converted a merchant named Felix who was staying with them. The three were arrested and martyred.

Andonis *see Andrew*

Andra *see Andrea*

Andraia *see Andrea*

Andraya *see Andrea*

Andre Saint; form of Andrew; French; strong, manly, courageous

Andrecito, Andree, Andrie, Aundré

St. Andre Bessette (1845–1937) was born as Alfred Bessette in Quebec, Canada. He was a sickly child who was orphaned at the age of twelve. Largely uneducated and unable to acquire a trade due to his poor health, he worked at various jobs. For a short time, he went to America to find work, but ultimately he returned home. His pastor noticed the young man's spiritual nature and recommended him to the Congregation of Holy Cross in Montreal. He was initially rejected, but after Archbishop Ignace Bourget got involved, they accepted him as a lay brother. He was given the job of porter at Notre Dame College in Quebec, a job he held for forty years. He was very devoted to St. Joseph and was known as a miracle worker through that saint's intercession. St. Andre began a campaign to build a chapel in honor of St. Joseph. His reputation for holiness grew, and when he died a million people filed past his coffin. He was canonized by Pope Benedict XVI on October 17, 2010.

Andrea Saint; Top 100 Name; form of Andrew; Greek; strong, courageous

Aindrea, Andee, Andera, Anderea, Andra, Andraia, Andraya, Andre, Andreah, Andreaka, Andreea, Andreja, Andreka, Andrel, Andrell, Andrelle, Andreo, Andressa, Andrette, Andriea, Andrieka, Andrietta, Andris, Andrya, Andryah, Aundrea, Ondria

Bl. Andrea Giacinto Longhin (1863–1936) was a member of the Capuchin Order. He was ordained a priest and taught other young religious. Pope Pius X appointed him bishop of Treviso, Italy. He was beatified by Pope John Paul II in 2002.

Andreah *see Andrea*

Andreaka *see Andrea*

Andreas Saint; a form of Andrew; Greek; strong, manly, courageous

Andries

Bl. Andreas Carlo Ferrari (1850–1921) was born in Lalatta, Parma. He was ordained a priest. He became a professor at the seminary in Parma, teaching many subjects including physics, mathematics, and theology. He became archbishop of Milan. He was beatified by Pope John Paul II in 1987.

Andrecito *see Andre*

Andree *see Andre*

Andreea *see Andrea*

Andreja *see Andrea*

Andreka *see Andrea*

Andre *see Andrea*

Andrelle *see Andrea*

Andreo *see Andrea*

Andressa *see Andrea*

Andrette *see Andrea*

Andrew Saint, New Testament; Top 100 Name; Greek; strong, manly, courageous

Anders, Andery, Andonis, Andrews, Andy, Anker, Antal, Audrew, Drew

St. Andrew, St. Andrew Avellino, St. Andrew Bobola, St. Andrew Chong Hwa-Gyong, St. Andrew Corsini, St. Andrew Dotti, St. Andrew Dung Lac, St. Andrew Kagwa, St. Andrew Nam-Thuong, St. Andrew of Crete, St. Andrew of Trier, St. Andrew the Scot

St. Andrew (first century) was the brother of St. Peter. The two were followers of John the Baptist before following Christ. He was Jesus' first disciple, and he in turn brought his brother to the Lord. The two were fishermen and Jesus asked them to give up their trade to become "fishers of men." After Christ's death and resurrection, Andrew went to Greece where he ultimately was crucified by being tied to a cross. He is the patron saint of Scotland and Russia, as well as of fishermen.

Andrews *see Andrew*

Andrie *see Andre*

Andriea *see Andrea*

Andrieka *see Andrea*

Andries *see Andreas*

Andrietta *see Andrea*

Andris *see Andrea*

Andriy Saint; Greek; man, warrior

Bl. Andriy Ishchak (1887–1941) was a Ukrainian Greek Catholic priest. He taught at the Lviv Theological Academy. He was killed by soldiers of the Soviet Army and was beatified by Pope John Paul II in 2001.

Andronicus Saint; Latin; a man excelling others

St. Andronicus (fifth century) was married to Athanasia. After their two children died, they became hermits in the desert, living in separate hermitages. Twelve years later, a monk named Athanasius came to visit Andronicus. The two went to Jerusalem together and later joined a monastery in Alexandria. When Athanasius died, Andronicus discovered a note on the body identifying her as Athanasia, his wife. He died soon after and they were buried together.

Andrya *see Andrea*

Andryah *see Andrea*

Andy *see Andrew*

Anectus Saint; Latin; tolerable

St. Anectus (d. 303) was martyred in Caesarea during the persecutions of Emperor Diocletian.

Angel Top 100 Name; Greek; angel, messenger

Angelelmus Saint; Greek, Latin; angel, messenger

St. Angelelmus (d. 828) was a Benedictine abbot of Sts. Gervase and Protase Monastery in Auxerre, France. He served as bishop of Auxerre from 813–828.

Angeleo *see Angelo*

Angelico Saint; Greek, Latin; angel, messenger

Bl. Fra Angelico (1395–1455) was born in Vicchio, Tuscany. He entered the Dominican order and took the name Giovanni da Fiesole. He was called "Angelico" because of his extraordinary personal piety. He began his career as an artist illuminating manuscripts. He later painted altarpieces and other works. He also painted many frescoes for the Convent of San Marco in Florence. He was hired to paint frescoes for chapels at the Vatican. He was beatified by Pope John Paul II in 1982 and was named the patron of Catholic artists.

Angelino *see Angelo*

Angelito *see Angelo*

Angello *see Angelo*

Angelo Saint; a form of Angel; Greek; angel, messenger

Agnolo, Angeleo, Angelino, Angelito, Angello, Angelos, Angelous, Angiolo, Anglo, Anjello, Anjelo

St. Angelo (1185–1220) was born to Jewish converts to the Catholic faith in Jerusalem. He and his twin brother had great spiritual and intellectual gifts and entered the Carmelite order at the age of eighteen. Five years later, the Lord called Angelo to go to Sicily. There, he converted many. He then went on to Leocata where he also brought many to the Lord. While doing so, he condemned the wickedness of a local man named Berengarius. While he was preaching, a group of this man's followers stabbed him. He died praying for his murderer.

Angelos *see Angelo*

Angelous *see Angelo*

Angelus Saint; a form of Angel; Greek, Latin; angel, messenger

Bl. Angelus of Acri, Blessed Angelus Orsucci

Bl. Angelus Orsucci (d. 1622) was born in Lucca, Italy. He became a Dominican and was sent to the Philippines and Japan as a missionary. He was arrested by the Japanese government and spent four years in prison before being burned to death in Nagasaki. He is one of the Martyrs of Japan.

Angilbert Saint; a combination of Angel and Albert; Teutonic

St. Angilbert (d. 814) grew up in the court of Charlemagne and was educated by Alcuin. After accompanying King Pepin to Italy and serving as an envoy of the court to the pope, he was named abbot of Saint-Riquier in Picardy, France, where he endowed the library with two hundred books. He also had an intimate relationship with Charlemagne's daughter Bertha, which produced two children. He repented of this relationship and lived a life of penance and austerity. Bertha entered a convent. Several years after his death, his body was found to be incorrupt.

Angiolo *see Angelo*

Anglinus Saint

St. Anglinus (d. 768) was the tenth abbot of the Benedictine monastery of Stovelot-Malmedy near Leige, Belgium.

Anglo *see Angelo*

Angus Saint; Scottish; exceptional, outstanding

Aonghas

According to legend, St. Angus MacNisse (fifth century) was both baptized and consecrated as bishop by St. Patrick. After making a pilgrimage to Rome, he returned to found a church and monastery at Kells. He is known as a miracle worker.

Anianas Saint; Latin; distress

Agnan, Aignan

St. Anianas (d. 453), also known as Aignan or Agnan, lived as a hermit in Vienne, France, for many years before he was ordained as bishop of that area. When Attila the Hun and his followers attacked Orleans, France, he sent word to General Flavius Aetius and helped him defend the area.

Anibal *see Hannibal*

Anicet Saint; Greek; invincible man of great strength

St. Anicet Adolfo (1912–1934) was a member of the Congregation of the Brothers of the Christian Schools and is one of the Martyrs of Turón. He was canonized by Pope John Paul II in 1999.

Aniceto Saint; Greek; invincible man of great strength

St. Aniceto (1912–1934) was born as Manual Seco Gutiérrez in Santander, Spain. He became a member of the Brothers of the Christian Schools in 1928. He was martyred during the persecutions of the Spanish Civil War and is considered one of the Martyrs of Turón. He was canonized by Pope John Paul II on November 21, 1999.

Anicetus Saint; Greek, Latin; invincible man of great strength

Pope St. Anicetus (d. 168) was pope from about 150 to 168. He was a Syrian from Emesa. The elderly Polycarp of Smyrna visited Rome to discuss the celebration of Passover with him. There was a dispute over whether to keep the Jewish date or celebrate it on Sunday. While the two did not agree, Anicetus did allow the Church in Smyrna to continue using the Jewish date. He was the first Roman pope to condemn a heresy. He forbid Montanism and opposed the Gnostics and Marcionism.

Aninus Saint

St. Aninus (date unknown) was a hermit from Syria, known for his austere life and as a miracle worker.

Anjello see Angelo

Anjelo see Angelo

Anker see Andrew

Annemund Saint

St. Annemund (d. 658) was the son of a prefect in Lyons, Gaul, and was raised in the court of King Dagobert I. He served as councilor to Clovis II when he took over the throne. He later was named bishop of Lyons and was friends with St. Wilfrid of York. He was slain during the political upheaval that followed Clovis's death.

Anno Saint; a form of Johann; German; God is gracious

Ano, Hanno

St. Anno (1010–1075), also known as Hanno, was highly educated and became archbishop of Cologne. He was invited to serve at court by Emperor Henry III, and after his death, Empress Agnes asked him to serve as regent for Henry IV. He worked with St. Peter Darnien to help reform the Church in the area, founded monasteries, and was known for his dedication to prayer. He retired to Sieburg Monastery, where he died.

Annobert Saint

St. Annobert (d. 869) was a Benedictine monk in

Almeneches who later became the bishop of Séez, France.

Ano *see Anno*

Anothony *see Anthony*

Ansano *see Auxanus*

Ansanus Saint; Latin; ear

St. Ansanus (285–304) was denounced by his father when he became a Christian at the age of twelve. He was a missionary to Siena and Bagnorea, Italy, where he gained the title of "the baptizer." During the reign of Emperor Diocletian, he was arrested and beheaded. He is a patron saint of Siena, Italy.

Ansbald Saint; German; peaceful God

St. Ansbald (d. 886) was born into a noble family in Luxembourg. He became a Benedictine monk, later serving as abbot of St. Huburt and then abbot of Prum. When the Normans attacked the abbey, he asked Holy Roman Emperor Charles the Fat for assistance to rebuild and was granted the funds he needed.

Ansbert Saint; German; brilliant God

St. Ansbert (d. 695) was born at Chaussy-sur-Epte, France. He served as a chancellor at the court of King Clotaire III. He became a Benedictine monk at Fontenelle Abbey in Normandy, where he later served as abbot. He became bishop of Rouen, France, and was exiled to Hainaut by Pepin of Heristal.

Anse *see Anselm*

Ansegisus Saint

St. Ansegisus (770–833) was a Benedictine monk at Fontenelle, France, where he later served as abbot. Under his leadership, the monastery became a famous center of learning. He was a great supporter of monasteries.

Anselm Saint; German; divine protector

Anse, Anselme, Anselmi, Elmo

St. Anselm, St. Anselm of Lucca, St. Anselm of Nonantola

St. Anselm (1033–1109) was born into a noble family in Piedmont. He wanted to become a monk at the age of fifteen, but the abbot refused, fearing his father's displeasure. Instead, he left the country and became a great scholar. After his father's death, at the age of twenty-seven, he entered the monastery at Bec, where he became prior. He devoted himself to the study of theology and wrote several books, including the Monologium, which explains the metaphysical proofs of the existence and nature of God. His reputation grew, and he was named as archbishop of Canterbury. After considerable protest, he reluctantly accepted the post. The pope ordered him to attend the Council at Bari, which was an attempt to reconcile the Greeks with the Catholic Church. He is considered the father of scholasticism and was proclaimed a Doctor of the Church in 1720 by Pope Clement XI.

Anselme *see Anselm*

Anselmi *see Anselm*

Ansfrid Saint; German; peaceful God

St. Ansfrid (d. 1010) was a friend of Holy Roman Emperor Otto III. He was named bishop of Utrecht. He founded a monastery at Heiligensberg, Germany, and a convent at Thorn. He became blind later in life, and he retired to the abbey.

Ansgar Saint; German; spear of the gods

Anskar

St. Ansgar (801–865), also known as St. Anskar, was born into a noble family near Amiens. He entered a monastery in Picardy, and later lived in New Corbie Monastery in Westphalia. He served as a missionary in Denmark and Sweden where he built the first Christian church in that country. He was made archbishop of Hamburg and then archbishop of Bremen when the two sees were united. Ansgar returned to Denmark and converted Erik, king of Jutland. Unfortunately, the whole area went back to being pagan after his death.

Ansillo Saint; German; protected by God

Little is known about his life, but St. Ansillo (seventh century) was a monk whose relics rest in the Benedictine Abbey of Lagny, near Meaux, France.

Anskar *see Ansgar*

Ansovinus Saint

St. Ansovinus (d. 840) was born in Camerino and was educated at the cathedral school of Pavia. He lived as a hermit for many years before serving as a counselor to the Holy Roman Emperor Louis II. He was chosen to be bishop of Camerino and attended the Council of Rome called by Pope Nicholas I in 861. He was known for his generosity to the poor.

Ansueris Saint

St. Ansueris (d. 1066) was the Benedictine abbot of St. Georgenberg Abbey near Ratzburg, Denmark. He and twenty-eight other monks were stoned to death after the death of Emperor Henry III.

Ansuinus Saint

St. Ansuinus (d. 888) was a companion of St. Ageranus. When the Normans invaded the monastery in Bleze, France, he was martyred while defending the altars.

Ansurius Saint

Aduri, Asurius, Isauri

St. Ansurius (d. 925), also known as Isauri, was elected bishop of Orense, Spanish Galicia, Spain. He founded the Abbey of Ribas de Sil and after serving as bishop for seven years gave up his post to become a monk there.

Antal *see Andrew*

Anterus Saint; Latin, Finnish; priceless

Pope St. Anterus (d. 236) served as pope for only one month and ten days. He succeeded Pope Pontian, who had been deported from Rome along with the antipope Hippolytus to Sardinia. He was a Greek who wanted to collect the acts of the martyrs into a central source. There is some dispute as to whether or not he was martyred.

Anthawn *see Anthony*

Anthelm Saint

St. Anthelm (1107–1178) was born in Savoy, France. He became a priest and then entered the Carthusian order when he was thirty. He was appointed abbot of Le Grande Chartreuse, which was in need of great repair. Under his care, it became a worthy motherhouse. He served as minister-general of the order and helped standardize rules and opened the order to women. He defended Pope Alexander against the antipope Victor IV. He was then appointed bishop of Belley, France. He is known for his care of the poor and local lepers.

Anthey *see Anthony*

Anthian *see Anthony*

Anthimus Saint

Antimo

St. Anthimus (d. 303) was born in Bithynia and was a priest of Rome. He was responsible for bringing many people into the Christian faith. He was arrested and thrown into the Tiber with a stone around his neck. When he miraculously escaped, he was recaptured and beheaded.

Anthino *see Anthony*

Antholian Saint

St. Antholian (d. 265) was martyred in Auvergne, France, during the reign of Emperor Valerian.

Anthonee *see Anthony*

Anthonio *see Anthony, Antonio*

Anthonu *see Anthony*

Anthony Saint; Top 100 Name; Latin, German; praiseworthy, flourishing

Anathony, Anothony, Anthawn, Anthey, Anthian, Anthino, Anthonee, Anthonio, Anthonu, Anthonysha, Anthoy, Anthyoine, Anthyonny

St. Anthony, St. Anthony Dainan, St. Anthony Daniel, St. Anthony Ishida, St. Anthony Kauleas, St. Anthony Mary Claret, St. Anthony Mary Gianelli, St. Anthony Mary Pucci, St. Anthony Mary Zaccaria, St. Anthony Nam-Quynh, St. Anthony of Padua

St. Anthony of Padua (1195–1231) is a Doctor of the Church. Born in Portugal, he joined the Augustinian order, but left to become a Franciscan. He was known for his ability to speak the truths of the Catholic faith in so simple and resounding a manner that everyone could understand them. He was commissioned by Brother Gratian, the local minister provincial, to be a missionary to the Lombard region. Here, he came to the attention of St. Francis, who recruited him to teach the faith to young members of the order. He also served as an envoy to Pope Gregory IX. He is a patron saint of Padua and known as a finder of lost items.

Anthonysha *see Anthony*

Anthoy *see Anthony*

Anthyoine *see Anthony*

Anthyonny *see Anthony*

Antidius Saint

St. Antidius (d. 265) was a disciple of St. Fironinus. He succeeded him as bishop of Besancon, France, before being martyred by marauders.

Antilnus Saint

St. Antilnus (eighth century) was a Benedictine abbot at Brantome, France.

Antimo *see Anthimus*

Antini *see Antoni*

Antinio *see Antonio*

Antiochus Saint; Greek; stubborn, resistent

Andeol

St. Antiochus (fifth century), also known as Andeol, was a priest in Lyons, France. When St. Justus resigned as bishop in order to become a hermit, Antiochus was sent to Egypt to convince him to return. He

failed in his mission and was named as bishop of Lyons to replace St. Justus when he returned.

Antipas Saint, New Testament; Greek; in opposition to everyone

St. Antipas (d. 90) is mentioned in the book of Revelation (Rv 2:13) as a "faithful martyr" of Pergamum. He was a disciple of St. John the Apostle, who ordained Antipas bishop of Pergamon. He is believed to have been burned to death. He is a patron against toothaches.

Antoine Saint; a form of Anthony; French; praiseworthy, flourishing

Bl. Antoine Fournier (1736–1794) was a married layman from Angers, France, who was martyred during the French Revolution. He is one of the Martyrs of Anjou who was beatified by Pope John Paul II in 1984.

Antoinio *see Antonio*

Antoino *see Antonio*

Anton Saint; a form of Anthony; Spanish; praiseworthy, flourishing

Bl. Anton Maria Schwartz, Bl. Anton Martin Slomsek

Bl. Anton Maria Schwartz (1852–1929) was born in Vienna, Austria. He became a priest and founded the Congregation of Christian Workers of Saint Joseph Calasanz. He was beatified by Pope John Paul II in 1998.

Antonello *see Antonio*

Antoneo *see Antonio*

Antoni Saint; a form of Anthony; Latin

Antini

Bl. Antoni Beszta-Borowski, Bl. Antoni Julian Nowowiejski, Bl. Antoni Leszczewicz, Bl. Antoni Rewera, Bl. Antoni Siadek, Bl. Antoni Zawistowski

Bl. Antoni Beszta-Borowski (1880–1943) was martyred at the Auschwitz concentration camp in Poland. He is one of the 108 Polish Martyrs of World War II and was beatified by Pope John Paul II in 1999.

Antonin *see Antonio*

Antoninus Saint; a form of Anthony; Italian; praiseworthy, flourishing

St. Antoninus, St. Antoninus of Sorrento

St. Antoninus (fourth century) was a stonemason in Aribazus, Syria. He spoke out against the pagan practices of his neighbors and decided to become a hermit. After living as a recluse for two years, he returned to the village and destroyed the idols. He left the town and built a church in Apamea, Syria, where he was murdered.

Antoninus *see Antonio*

Antonio Saint; a form of Anthony; Italian; praiseworthy, flourishing

Anthonio, Antinio, Antoinio, Antoino, Antonello, Antoneo, Antonin, Antoninus, Antonnio, Antonyia, Antonyio

St. Antonio Vieira, St. Antonio de Sant'Anna Galvao

St. Antonio Vieira (1608–1697) was born in Lisbon, Portugal, but traveled to Brazil as a child. He entered the Jesuit order when he was fifteen, and by the time he was eighteen, he was teaching at the college of Olinda. After being ordained as a priest, he became known for his skill as an orator. He returned to Portugal as a companion of the viceroy's son. King John IV of Portugal was so impressed by him that he named him as the royal preacher. He became a diplomat, traveling to England, France, Netherlands, and Italy. He eventually returned to Brazil, where he served as a missionary. Pope Clement X invited him to preach before the College of Cardinals, and he became a confessor to Queen Christina of Sweden.

Antonnio *see Antonio*

Antonyia *see Antonio*

Antonyio *see Antonio*

Anysius Saint; Greek; satisfaction

St. Anysius (d. 407) was a friend of St. Ambrose. He was named bishop of Salonika, Greece, as well as vicar apostolic of Illyricum. He was one of sixteen Macedonian bishops who appealed to Pope Innocent on behalf of St. John Chrysostom.

Aonghas *see Angus*

Apelles Saint, New Testament; Latin; called

St. Apelles (first century) was the first bishop of Smyrna, Turkey, and was mentioned by St. Paul in his Letter to the Romans (Romans 16:10). He was martyred for the faith.

Aphraates Saint

St. Aphraates (d. 345) was born on the Persian border near Syria. After converting to Christianity he became a hermit and attracted many people because of his holiness. He spoke out against the Arians, and Emperor Valens sent a servant to murder him. When the servant died suddenly, the emperor took it as a sign to protect Aphraates. He went on to write a large defense of the faith called *The Demonstrations*. He is referred to as "the Persian Sage."

Aphrodisius Saint; Greek; pertaining to Aphrodite

According to legend, St. Aphrodisius (first century) sheltered the Holy Family when they fled into Egypt. He was martyred along with Sts. Caralippus, Agapius, and Eusebius.

Apian *see Amphianus*

Apollinaris Saint; form of Apollo; Greek; manly

St. Apollinaris, St. Appollinaris Franco, St. Appollinaris Sidonius, St. Appollinaris Syncletica

St. Apollinaris (second century) was bishop of Hierapolis in Phrygia in the second century, held in high esteem by Eusebius, St. Jerome, and Theodoret. He defended the Christian religion to the Emperor Marcus Aurelius, reminding him of favors he had received from God because of the prayers of Christians.

Apollo Saint; Greek; manly

Apollon, Apolo, Apolonio, Appollo, Appolo, Appolonio

St. Apollo (d. 395) spent forty years as a hermit in the desert around Thebes before founding a community of monks in Hermopol, Egypt. He became their abbot and was known as a miracle worker.

Apollon *see Apollo*

Apollonius Saint; a form of Apollo; Greek; manly

St. Apollonius (d. 305) was a deacon who converted a musician named Philemon. The two were sewn into sacks and thrown into the sea during the persecution of Emperor Diocletian.

Apollos Saint, New Testament; Greek; manly

St. Apollos (first century) was instructed by Priscilla and Aquila and became an important early Christian. He was part of the church in Corinth and was with Paul in Ephesus.

He is mentioned in the First Letter of Paul to the Corinthians.

Apolo *see Apollo*

Apolonio *see Apollo*

Aponius Saint; Greek

St. Aponius (first century) was martyred with St. Andrew during the persecution of King Herod Antipas.

Appian Saint; Latin; relating to bees

St. Appian (d. 800) was born in Liguria, Italy. After entering the Benedictine Monastery of St. Peter of Ciel d'Oro in Pavia, he became a hermit. He lived alone near the Adriatic seas, but his example of holiness converted many.

Appollo *see Apollo*

Appolo *see Apollo*

Appolonio *see Apollo*

Apronian Saint; Latin

St. Apronian (d. 304) was an executioner in Rome working for Emperor Diocletian. He converted to Christianity after witnessing the faith of St. Sisinnius before the tribunal. Apronian was beheaded for his faith.

Aprus Saint; Latin

St. Aprus (sixth century) was born in Trier, Germany, and became the bishop of Toul, France. He was the sister of St. Apronia.

Apuleius Saint

St. Apuleius (first century) was originally a follower of Simon Magus, a Roman magician who confronted St. Peter and wanted to overthrow Christianity. St. Peter converted Apuleius and his friends Marcellus, Sergius, and Bacchus. They suffered martyrdom for their faith.

Aquil *see Aquila*

Aquila Saint; Latin, Spanish; an eagle

Acquilla, Aquil, Aquilas, Aquileo, Aquiles, Aquilina, Aquilino, Aquill, Aquilla, Aquille, Aquillino, Aquyl, Aquyla, Aquyll, Aquylla

St. Acquila (d. 311) was torn to pieces with iron combs for his faith in Christ. Because of his example, the prefect Arianus became a Christian and died for the faith as well.

Aquilas *see Aquila*

Aquileo *see Aquila*

Aquiles *see Aquila*

Aquilino *see Aquila*

Aquilinus Saint; a form of Acquilla; Latin; eagle

St. Aquilinus (d. 650) was born in Bavaria. He left his homeland because he didn't want to be named bishop. He went to Milan, Italy, where he preached against Arianism. Those who supported the Arians murdered him.

Aquill *see Aquila*

Aquilla *see Aquila*

Aquille *see Aquila*

Aquillino *see Aquila*

Aquyl *see Aquila*

Aquyla *see Aquila*

Aquyll *see Aquila*

Aquylla *see Aquila*

Aragawi *see Acius*

Araldo *see Harold*

Aralt *see Harold*

Aran *see Aaron*

Aranyu *see Aurelius*

Arator Saint; Latin; cultivator, plowman

St. Arator of Verdun (d. 460) was bishop of Verdun, France.

Arbogast Saint; French; inheriting guest

St. Arbogast (d. 678) was born in Aquitaine, France, and lived as a hermit in the German forest. He moved to Alsace, where he became a friend of King Dagobert II. He appointed Arbogast the archbishop of Strasbourg. After the king's son died falling off a horse, Arbogast brought him back to life.

Arcadius Saint; Spanish; bold

St. Arcadius (d. 538) was bishop of Bourges, France, and took part in the Council of Orléans, France, in 538.

Arcangelo Saint; Greek; prince of the angels

St. Arcangelo Tadini (1846–1912) was an Italian priest. He was a curate in Lodrino for two years before serving the parish of Botticino Sera for the rest of his life. He founded the Workers' Mutual Aid Association and built a spinning factory to help employ local women. He also founded the Congregation of Worker Sisters of the Holy House of Nazareth who worked in factories and helped teach women. He had a great devotion to the Blessed Sacrament. He was canonized by Pope Benedict XVI on April 19, 2009.

Archelaus Saint; Greek; the prince of the people

St. Archelaus (d. 278) was a bishop in Kashkar, Mesopotamia. He fought against Manichaeism and is thought to have debated the movement's founder, Manes.

Archippus Saint, New Testament; Greek; a master of horses

St. Archippus (first century) was a companion of St. Paul mentioned in Philemon 1:2. He is believed to have been the first bishop of Colossne.

Arcontius Saint

St. Arcontius (eighth or ninth century) was a bishop of Viviers, France. A mob of people killed him for defending the Church in a matter of local politics.

Ardagne *see Ardanus*

Ardaing *see Ardanus*

Ardal *see Arnold*

Ardalion Saint; Greek

St. Ardalion (d. 300) was performing on stage, making fun of a Christian who was condemned to die, when he suddenly was filled with grace and made a public conversion. He was arrested, condemned, and burned alive.

Ardan *see Ardanus*

Ardanus Saint

Ardagne, Ardaing, Ardan

St. Ardanus (d. 1058), also known as Ardaing, Ardan, or Ardagne, was the abbot of the Benedictine Monastery of Tournus. He was known for caring for the people surrounding the area, especially during a three-year famine.

Ardo Saint

St. Ardo (d. 843) was born in Languedoc, France, with the name Smaragdus. When he joined the Benedictine abbey at Aniane, he took the name Ardo. He directed the monastery school and accompanied St. Benedict of Aniane on his journeys. When St. Benedict became superior of the Aachen Monastery in Germany, Ardo took over the monastery at Aniane.

Arduinus Saint; Latin; brave friend

St. Arduinus (d. 1009) was a priest in Rimini, Italy. He lived as a hermit until he entered the Monastery of San Gudenzio.

Aredius Saint; Hebrew

Yrieix

St. Aredius (510–591), also known as St. Yrieix, was the son of Jocundus, a wealthy Roman. He studied at the monastery at Vigeois. At the age of fourteen, he went to Metz, where he became the chancellor to King Theudebert II of Austrasia. He decided to leave the court and join Bishop Nicetius of Trier. He then converted to Christianity. He founded the Monastery of Attanum.

Arelian *see Aurelius*

Areliano *see Aurelius*

Aresty *see Orestes*

Aretas Saint; Arabic; metal forger

St. Aretas (date unknown) was one of 505 early martyrs who died in Rome.

Arethas Saint; Greek; excellence

St. Arethas (d. 523) was the governor of the Christian city of Nadjran. When the king of Yemen, Dzu Nowass, undertook a violent persecution against Christians, he massacred the people of that area who would not renounce their faith. Arethas was beheaded.

Argeus Saint; Greek

St. Argeus (d. 320) and his brothers Narcissus and Marcellus were soldiers in the army of Coemperor Licinius Licinianus. They were martyred for the faith. Argeus and Narcissus were beheaded. Marcellus was drowned.

Argymirus Saint

St. Argymirus (d. 858) was a native of Cobra, Spain. He held a high political position but was fired because of his Christian faith. He became a monk and was ultimately beheaded for his faith.

Arialdus Saint

St. Arialdus (d. 1066) was a noble from Milan. He studied at Laon and Paris, France, before becoming a canon. He was excommunicated by Bishop Guido for preaching against abuses in the city, but he was reinstated by Pope Stephen IX. Bishop Guido was guilty of simony and immorality. His supporters killed Arialdus. He was declared a martyr by Pope Alexander II in 1067.

Arian Saint; Greek, Hebrew; enchanted, melodius

Ariana, Ariane, Ariann, Arianne, Arrian

St. Arian (d. 311) was the governor of Thebes. He was converted after witnessing the martyrdom of Sts. Apollonius and Philemon in Alexandria. Arian was drowned for his faith.

Arigius Saint

St. Arigius (d. 604) was bishop of Gap, France, for twenty years.

Aris *see Aristides*

Aristarchus Saint, New Testament; Greek; the best source

St. Aristarchus (first century) was mentioned by St. Paul in Colossians 4:10. Originally from Thessalonika in Macedonia, he became a disciple of St. Paul and traveled with him. They were imprisoned in Ephesus. He was the first bishop of Thessalonika and was beheaded with St. Paul in Rome.

Aristede *see Aristides*

Aristedes *see Aristides*

Aristeed *see Aristides*

Aristide *see Aristides*

Aristides Saint; Greek; son of the best

Aris, Aristede, Aristedes, Aristeed, Aristide, Aristidis, Arystides, Arystydes

St. Aristedes (second century) was an Athenian philosopher known for writing the *Apology of Aristides*, which was presented to Emperor Hadrian in 125.

Aristidis *see Aristides*

Aristion Saint, New Testament; Greek; selective person

St. Aristion (first century) was one of the original seventy-two disciples. He preached in Cyprus and was martyred in either Salamis or Alexandria.

Ariston Saint; Greek; the best

St. Ariston (d. 284) was martyred with several others in Campania, Italy, during the persecution initiated by Emperor Diocletian.

Aristus *see Evaristus*

Arje *see Adrian*

Arlo *see Charles*

Armagillus Saint; Latin; armor bearer

St. Armagillus (d. 570) was a Welsh missionary and a cousin of St. Samson. He joined Abbot

Carentmael as a missionary to Brittany, France.

Armand *see Ormond*

Armentarius Saint; Greek; herder of livestock

St. Armentarius (d. 451) was a bishop of Pavia, Italy.

Armogastes Saint; German; guest of the eagle

St. Armogastes (d. 455) was a member of the household of Prince Theodoric, son of the Vandal king Geiseric. Geiseric was an Arian heretic who punished Christians who refused to accept Arianism. Amogastes was banished to the mines and then forced to herd cattle in Carthage where he died.

Arn *see Arnold*

Arnald *see Arnold*

Arndt *see Arnold*

Arne *see Arnold*

Arnhold *see Arnold*

Arnol *see Arnold*

Arnold Saint; German; eagle ruler

Ardal, Arn, Arnald, Arndt, Arne, Arnhold, Arnol, Arnoldas, Arnolde, Arnoldo, Arnoll, Arnolt, Arnot, Arnott, Arnoud, Arny, Arnyld, Arynyld

St. Arnold, St. Arnold Jansen

St. Arnold was a Greek by birth. He was a confessor in the court of Charlemagne. He was noted for his charity to the poor. The village of Amold-Villiers, near Jülich, Germany, was named after him.

Arnoldas *see Arnold*

Arnolde *see Arnold*

Arnoldo *see Arnold*

Arnoll *see Arnold*

Arnolt *see Arnold*

Arnot *see Arnold*

Arnott *see Arnold*

Arnoud *see Arnold*

Arnulf Saint; a form of Arnold; German; eagle ruler

St. Arnulf, St. Arnulf of Soissons, St. Arnulf of Eynesbury

St. Arnulf (d. 640) was a member of the court of the Frankish king Theodebert II of Austrasia. He was married to Doda. Their son Ansegisel married Beggia, daughter of Pepin of Landen, beginning the Carolingian dynasty of France. Doda became a nun, and Arnulf planned to become a monk, but he was instead named bishop of Metz. In 626, he retired to a hermitage at Remiremont, France.

Arny *see Arnold*

Arnyld *see Arnold*

Aroldo *see Harold*

Arram *see Abraham*

Arren *see Aaron*

Arrian *see Arian*

Arrieal *see Ariel (girl's name)*

Arrin *see Aaron*

Arryn *see Aaron*

Arsacius Saint

St. Arsacius (d. 358) was a member of the Roman army and was imprisoned for being a Christian. After his release, he became a hermit near

Nicomedia. He warned the people of an impending earthquake on August 24, 358. He died while praying.

Arsen see *Arsenius*

Arsène see *Arsenius*

Arseneo see *Arsenius*

Arsenio see *Arsenius*

Arsenius Saint; Greek; masculine, virile

Arsen, Arsène, Arseneo, Arsenio, Arseny, Arsenyo, Arsinio, Arsinyo, Arsynio, Arsynyo

St. Arsenius, St. Arsenius the Great

St. Arsenius (d. 959) was born a Jew in Constantinople. He converted to the faith and became the first bishop of Corfu, Greece.

Arseny see *Arsenius*

Arsenyo see *Arsenius*

Arsinio see *Arsenius*

Arsinyo see *Arsenius*

Arsynio see *Arsenius*

Arsynyo see *Arsenius*

Artaldus Saint

Arthaud

St. Artaldus (1101–1206), also known as Arthaud, was born in Sothonod, Savoy. He became a Carthusian at Portes. After many years as a priest, he was sent by his prior to found a charterhouse in a valley in the Valmorey called "the cemetery." Soon after getting it established, it burned down, and he started over at a new location on the Arvieres River. When he was over eighty years old, he was named bishop of Belly. He served for two years before returning to his charterhouse to live out his days.

Artaxus Saint

St. Artaxus (third or fourth century) was martyred with several companions at Syrmium, Pannonia.

Artemas Saint, New Testament; Greek; whole

Artemis, Artimas, Artimis, Artimus

St. Artemas (first century) was mentioned by St. Paul is his Epistle to Titus (Titus 3:12). He is believed to have been the bishop of Lystra.

Artemide Saint; Greek

Artemides

Bl. Artemide Zatti (1880–1951) was born to a farming family in Boretto. In 1897, the family moved to Argentina. He joined the Salesians at Bernal when he was twenty. He contracted tuberculosis and promised Mary that he would devote his life to helping the sick if he was healed. He did recover and kept his promise. He was given the task of the pharmacy at a hospital, and later took over the direction of the whole hospital. He attended daily Mass and would visit the sick at their homes, as well as at the hospital. He died of cancer. He was beatified by Pope John Paul II in 2002.

Artemides *see Artemide*

Artemis *see Artemas*

Artemius Saint; Greek

St. Artemius (d. 396) was traveling to Spain but fell ill and ended up settling in Clermont, France, where he was named bishop.

Arthaud *see Artaldus*

Artimas *see Artemas*

Artimis *see Artemas*

Artimus *see Artemas*

Arwald Saint

St. Arwald (d. 686) is the name given to two sons of Arwald, the prince of the Isle of Wight, since their given names are unknown. The Isle was invaded and the two sons converted to Christianity shortly before being killed.

Arynyld *see Arnold*

Arystides *see Aristides*

Arystydes *see Aristides*

Asclas Saint

St. Asclas (d. 287) was brought before Arrian, the governor of Egypt, during the persecutions of Emperor Diocletian. Arrian attempted to cross the Nile but was unable to do so. Asclas told him he would not be able to cross the Nile unless he acknowledged Christ in writing. He obeyed and was able to successfully cross. However, once he made it to the other side, he had Asclas thrown into the Nile.

Asclepiades Saint

St. Asclepiades (d. 217) was a bishop of Antioch.

Ashley Saint; English; ash-tree meadow

Asheley, Ashelie, Ashely, Ashlan, Ashlea, Ashlee, Ashleigh, Ashlen, Ashli, Ashlie, Ashlin, Ashling, Ashlinn, Ashlone, Ashly, Ashlyn, Ashlynn, Aslan

Bl. Ralph Ashley (d. 1606) was from England and served as a cook at Douai College before going to Valladolid, Spain, and becoming a Jesuit brother. He later returned to England, where he was captured and tortured for being Catholic. He served two years in the tower of London before being executed. He was beatified in 1929.

Asicus Saint

Tassac, Tassach

St. Asicus (d. 490) was converted to Christianity by St. Patrick. He became the first abbot-bishop of Elphim Monastery in Roscommon, Ireland, but he resigned the office to become a hermit. After seven years, monks from the monastery found him and convinced him to return, but he died on the journey.

Aslan *see Ashley*

Aspasius Saint

St. Aspasius (d. 560) was the bishop of Eauze, near Auch, France. He took part in the Councils of Orléans in 533, 541, and 549.

Aspren Saint

St. Aspren (first century) was a native of Naples, in Campania, Italy. St. Peter cured him when he became ill and later baptized him. Aspren was made bishop of Naples.

Astericus Saint; Greek

St. Astericus (d. 1035) was born in Bohemia. He became a Benedictine and an ambassador to King Stephen of Hungary. He was named abbot of Brevnov, as well as abbot of Pannonhalma in Hungary. He went to Rome on behalf of King Stephen to negotiate the recognition of Hungary by Pope Sylvester II.

Asterius Saint; Greek; of the sun

St. Asterius (date unknown) was a senator who was martyred for the faith in Caesarea, Israel. He was slain for having buried the remains of Marinus, another Christian martyr.

Astius Saint; Latin; one who belongs

St. Astius (d. 117) was bishop of Dynhachium in Macedonia. He was crucified during the persecutions of Emperor Trajan.

Asurius *see Ansurius*

Athan *see Tathal*

Athanasius Saint; Greek; immortal

St. Athanasius, St. Athanasius Badzekuketta, St. Anthanasius the Athonite

St. Athanasius (296–373) was born in Alexandria to Christian parents. As a young man, he made a retreat with St. Anthony in the desert. He became a deacon and spoke out against the Arian heresy. This was to become his life's work. At the recommendation of Bishop Alexander of Alexandria, Athanasius was selected to succeed him. Because of his opposition to Arianism, he spent seventeen years in exile. He is a Doctor of the Church.

Athelm Saint

St. Athelm (d. 926) was an uncle of St. Dunstan. He was a Benedictine monk at Glastonbury, England, where he was named abbot. He later became bishop of Wells and archbishop of Canterbury.

Athenodorus Saint; Greek

St. Athenodorus (d. 304) was martyred in Mesopotamia. He was severely tortured but refused to give up the faith. When he was condemned to die, he started to pray and the executioner collapsed. No one dared to touch him, and he died while praying.

Athenogenes Saint; Greek

St. Athenogenes (d. 305) was the author of the hymn *Phos Hilaron*, known in Latin as *Lumen Hilarem*, which is used in the Byzantine vespers liturgy. He was a theologian who was burned to death along with ten followers at Sebaste. He entered the flames singing the *Phos Hilaron* in joy.

Atilano Saint; Latin; he who walks with difficulty

St. Atilano Cruz Alvarado (1901–1928) tended cattle as a boy in Mexico. He began studying for the priesthood at the age of seventeen and was ordained in July of 1927, a time in which the Mexican government was violently persecuting Christians. When the young priest and his pastor, St. Justino Orona Madrigal, were discussing matters at a local ranch, soldiers raided the area and shot them both. He was canonized by Pope John Paul II on May 21, 2000.

Atman *see Altman*

Attala Saint; Greek; young

St. Attala (d. 800) was the abbot of a Benedictine monastery at Taormina, in Sicily.

Attalas Saint; Greek; young

St. Attalas (d. 627) was born in Burgandy, France. He became a monk at Lérins but later moved to Luxeuil where he learned from St. Columban. He served as Columban's companion when they went to Bobbio, Italy, to found a monastery there. Attalas succeeded Columban as abbot when he died. Attalas spoke out strongly against Arianism.

Atticus Saint; Latin; from Attica (outside of Athens)

St. Atticus (d. 425 or 426) was archbishop of Constantinople. He had been an opponent of St. John Chrysostom, but after Chrysostom's death he became one of his supporters. He rebuilt a small church located where the Hagia Sophia would later be built and was an opponent of the Pelagians.

Attilanus Saint

St. Attilanus (937–1007) was born in Tarazona, near Saragossa, Spain. He became a Benedictine monk at Mareruela and later became bishop of Zamora.

Atto Saint; English; steep ridge

St. Atto (1070–1153) was born in Badajoz, Spain, and became a Benedictine monk at Vallambrosa, Italy. He became abbot-general and then bishop of Pistoia. He wrote the lives of St. Gualbert and St. Bernard of Parma and the history of the shrine of Compostela in Spain.

Auban *see Alban*

Aubary *see Aubrey*

Auben *see Alban*

Aubert *see Albert, Autbert*

Aubeu *see Austremonius*

Aubery *see Aubrey*

Aubin Saint; Latin, French; white

Albinus

St. Aubin (d. 550), also known as Albinus, entered the monastery at Tincilloc in Brittany at a young age. When he was thirty-five, he became abbot and later was named bishop of Angers. He was known for being generous to the sick and poor, especially ransoming slaves and caring for them. He was also known as a miracle worker.

Aubray *see Aubrey*

Aubrea *see Aubrey*

Aubreah *see Aubrey*

Aubrette *see Aubrey*

Aubrey Top 100 Name; German, French; noble, bearlike, blond ruler

Aubary, Aubery, Aubray, Aubrea, Aubreah, Aubrette, Aubry, Aubrya, Aubryah, Aubury, Avery

St. Aubrey Crescitelli (1863–1900), or Alberic, was born in 1863 in Altavilla, Beneventa, Italy. He was ordained a priest and joined the Milan Foreign Missionary Society. He served as a missionary in China. He was arrested, tortured, and murdered. He is one of the Martyrs of China.

Aubry *see Aubrey*

Aubrya *see Aubrey*

Aubryah *see Aubrey*

Aubury *see Aubrey*

Aubyn *see Alban*

Auctus Saint; Latin; growth, enlargement, increase

St. Auctus (date unknown) was martyred with Taurion at Amphipolis in Macedonia.

Audard *see Theodard*

Audrew *see Andrew*

Augebert Saint; English

St. Augebert (seventh century) was an Englishman who was sold into slavery in France. After Pope St. Gregory I the Great ransomed him, he became a deacon. He was martyred by pagans in Champagne, France, while he was preparing to return to England as a missionary.

Augie *see August*

Augulus Saint

St. Augulus (d. 303) was a bishop who was martyred in either London, England, or Normandy, France.

August Saint; form of Augustine; Latin; majestic

Augie, Auguste, Gus

Bl. August Czartoryski (1858–1893) was a prince of the Polish Czartoryski family. He was born in Paris and was a rather sickly child. He joined the Salesians in Turin after meeting with Don Bosco and receiving his blessing. He was ordained a priest but died one year later of tuberculosis. He was beatified by Pope John Paul II in 2004.

Augustalus Saint; form of Augustine; Latin; majestic

St. Augustalus (d. 450) was a bishop of Gaul.

Auguste *see August*

Augusteen *see Augustine*

Augustein *see Augustine*

Augusteyn *see Augustine*

Augusteyne *see Augustine*

Augustinas *see Augustine*

Augustine Saint; Latin; majestic

Agustein, Agusteyne, Agusteyne, Agustis, Agusto, Agustus,

Agustyna, Augusteen, Augustein, Augusteyn, Augusteyne, Augustinas, Augustino, Augustyn, Augustyne

St. Augustine Moi, St. Augustine of Canterbury, St. Augustine of Hippo, St. Augustine of Huy, St. Augustine Webster

St. Augustine of Hippo (354–430) was the son of St. Monica, who prayed for her wayward son to convert and reform his life for many years. Her prayers worked. Through the influence of St. Ambrose, he was baptized, and then he became a priest and a bishop. He wrote more than a hundred works and is best known for his *Confessions*, which tell the story of his life and conversion. He is a Doctor of the Church.

Augustino *see Augustine*

Augusto Saint; form of Augustine; Latin; majestic

St. Augusto Andres (1910–1934) was a member of the Brothers of the Christian Schools. One of the Martyrs of Turón killed during the Spanish Civil War, he was canonized by Pope John Paul II in 1999.

Augustus Saint; form of Augustine; Latin; majestic

St. Augustus, St. Augustus Chapdelaine, St. Augustus Schoffler

St. Augustus Schoffler (1822–1851) was born in Mittelbronn, Lorraine. He joined the Society of Foreign Missions in Paris and was sent to Indochina in 1848. When a persecution of Christians broke out, he was arrested and beheaded. He was canonized by Pope John Paul II in 1988 as one of the Martyrs of Indochina.

Augustyn *see Augustine*

Augustyne *see Augustine*

Aundré *see Andre*

Aurek *see Aurelius*

Aurèle *see Aurelius*

Aurelian Saint; form of Aurelius; Latin; golden

St. Aurelian (d. 551) was a bishop of Aries located in Gaul. Pope Vigilius named him a papal vicar of Gaul.

Aurelius Saint; Latin; golden

Aranyu, Arelian, Areliano, Aurek, Aurèle, Aurelyus, Aurey, Auriel, Aury

St. Aurelius (d. 429) was a friend of St. Augustine of Hippo. He was a deacon at Carthage and later became bishop of that area. He led a number of ecclesiastical councils on Christian doctrine.

Aurelyus *see Aurelius*

Aureus Saint; Latin; golden

St. Aureus (date unknown) was the bishop of Mainz, Germany. He went into exile when the Huns attacked the city, but he later returned to celebrate Mass at the cathedral. During the service, he was martyred.

Aurey *see Aurelius*

Auriel *see Aurelius*

Aury *see Aurelius*

Ausonius Saint; Latin

St. Ausonius (third century) was a disciple of St. Martial of Limoges. He served as the first bishop of Angouleme, France, and was martyred for the faith.

Auspicius Saint; Latin; protector

St. Auspicius (second century) was a bishop of Trier, Germany.

Austell *See Austell (girl's name)*

Austindus Saint; Latin; great, magnificent

St. Austindus (d. 1068) was born in Bordeaux, France. He became a Benedictine monk at St. Oren's Abbey in Auch. He later served as abbot where he instituted Cluniac reforms. He was named archbishop of Auch in 1041.

Austregisilus Saint

St. Austregisilus (d. 624) was the son of a Bourges nobleman. He became a priest and joined Nazaire Abbey in Lyon where he became abbot. He was later named bishop of Bourges, France.

Austremonius Saint

Aubeu

St. Austremonius (third century) was the first bishop of Clermont. Pope Fabian sent him and six other missionaries from Rome to Gaul. He is believed to have been martyred.

Autbert Saint

Aubert

St. Autbert (d. 725), also known as Aubert, was a bishop of Avranches, France, who founded the now-famous monastery of Mont St. Michel on the Normandy coast.

Autbod Saint

Autbodus

St. Autbod (d. 690) was a native of Ireland who served as a missionary to France. He spread the faith in Artois, Picardy, and the Belgian region of Hainaut. He became a hermit in Laon, France.

Autbodus *see Autbod*

Authaire Saint

St. Authaire (seventh century) was a courtier of King Dagobert I, king of the Franks. He was the father of St. Oys of Rouen.

Autonomous Saint; Greek; self-governing

St. Autonomous (d. 300) was an Italian bishop. He fled to Bithynia to escape Emperor Diocletian's persecution. There he spread the faith until he was arrested and martyred by the Roman authorities.

Autor Saint; Latin; increase, enlargement

St. Autor (fifth century) was a bishop of Metz, France.

Auxanus Saint; Greek; one who grows

Ansano

St. Auxanus (d. 568), also known as Ansano, was bishop of Milan, Italy.

Auxentius Saint; Latin; to exalt, praise

St. Auxentius (d. 321) was a soldier in the army of Coemperor Licinius Licinianus. Because he refused to take part in pagan sacrifices, he was persecuted. He left the military and became a priest. He was later named bishop of Mopsuestia, in Cilicia.

Auxibius Saint; Greek; powerful, alive

St. Auxibius (first century) was baptized by St. Mark and appointed bishop of Soil on Cyprus by St. Paul.

Avel *see Abel*

Aventanus Saint; Latin

St. Aventanus (d. 1380) was born in Limoges, France. He became a lay Carmelite. He was a mystic, known for his ecstasies, miracles, and visions. He died of the plague while attempting to make a pilgrimage to the Holy Land.

Aventine Saint; Latin; one of the seven hills of Rome

St. Aventine of Troyes (d. 538) served as steward and almoner, in charge of the cathedral's treasury, to St. Loup, the bishop of Troyes. He later became a hermit. He was known for his love of animals. He rescued fish that were caught in pitchers of water that were drawn from a brook, returning them to the water. He also saved a deer that was being pursued by hunters.

Aventinus Saint; Latin; one of the seven hills of Rome

St. Aventinus, St. Aventinus of Chartres

St. Aventinus (d. 1180) was a companion of St. Thomas Becket. He lived as a hermit in Tours, France, until he was ordained as a deacon by Becket. He then traveled with Becket to the Synod of Tours. After Becket was martyred, Aventinus lived out his days in Touraine, France.

Avilius *see Abilius*

Avitus Saint; Latin; from grandfather St. Avitus, St. Avitus of Clermont, St. Avitus of Vienne

St. Avitus (470–519) was the son of Bishop Isychius, a former Roman senator. He took over as bishop of Vienne in 490. He was known for his wisdom and charity, and he converted members of the Frankish tribes who lived in the area. He presided over the Council of Epaon in 517 and was noted for his writings.

Avram *see Abraham*

Aydan *see Aidan*

Aydin *see Aidan*

Aye *see Ageranus*

Ayeul *see Agilus*

Aymard Saint; French

Bl. Aymard (d. 965) was abbot in Citany, France, where he continued the reform of St. Odo. He served as abbot until blindness forced him to retire.

Aymil *see Emil*

Azas Saint; Hebrew; strong

St. Azas (d. 304) and approximately 150 companions were martyred in Isauria during the persecutions of Emperor Diocletian.

B

Babylas Saint; Hebrew

St. Babylas (d. 253) was a bishop of Antioch, Turkey. He and several of his students were arrested during the persecutions of Emperor Trajanus Decius. He died while awaiting execution.

Badilo Saint; Spanish, Italian; ford

St. Badilo (d. 870) was a monk at Vezelay in France and became abbot of Leuze in Hainault, Belgium.

Badulfus Saint

St. Badulfus (d. 850) was a Benedictine abbot of Ainay, Lyons, France.

Baglan Saint

St. Baglan (sixth century) was a hermit who lived at Baglan in South Wales. He may have been a Breton prince, the son of Ithel Hael.

Bagne Saint

Bagnus, Bain

St. Bagne (d. 710) was a Benedictine monk at Fontenelle Abbey in France. He was named a bishop and served as a missionary in the area of modern Calais, in France. He was later named abbot of Fontenelle.

Bagnus *see Bagne*

Bain *see Bagne*

Bairre *see Finbar*

Bairtrand *see Bertrand*

Baithin Saint

St. Baithin (d. 598) was a cousin of St. Columba. He was abbot of Tiree Abbey in Ireland and then served as abbot of Iona in Scotland.

Baldemer *see Baldomerus*

Balderic Saint; German; brave ruler

St. Balderic (seventh century) was the brother of St. Bova. He and his sister were the children of King Sigebert of Austrasia. They may also have been related to King Dagobert. Balderic became a priest and founded the Monastery of Montfaucon in the province of Lorraine. He also established a convent in Reims for his sister, where she served as abbess.

Baldmar *see Baldomerus*

Baldmare *see Baldomerus*

Baldomerus Saint; German; bold, famous

Baldemer, Baldmar, Baldmare, Baumar, Baumer

St. Baldomerus (d. 650) was a locksmith prior to entering the Monastery of St. Justus in Lyons, France. He is a patron saint of locksmiths.

Baldred Saint; English; bold counselor

Balther

St. Baldred (d. 757), also known as Balther, was a bishop of Scotland who founded a monastery at Tyninghame. He later lived as a hermit in the Firth of Forth.

Baldus *see Bond*

Baldwin Saint; German; brave friend

St. Baldwin (d. 680) was the son of St. Salaberga and the brother of St. Anstrude. He was an archdeacon of León, Spain. He was martyred for the faith.

Bali *see Balin*

Balin Saint; Hindu; mighty soldier

Bali, Baline, Balyn, Balyne, Baylen, Baylin, Baylon

St. Balin (seventh century) was a brother of St. Gerald. He was a disciple of St. Colman, whom he accompanied to Iona in Scotland. He then took up residence in Connaught, Ireland.

Baline *see Balin*

Ballas *see Blaise*

Balta *see Bartholomew*

Balther *see Baldred*

Balyn *see Balin*

Balyne *see Balin*

Balyse *see Blaise*

Bandaridus Saint; Latin; flag

Bandarinus, Banderik, Bandery

St. Bandaridus (d. 556) was a bishop of Soissons, France. He founded Crépin Abbey. When King Clotaire I banished him because of a disagreement, he went to England, where he lived as an anonymous gardener. After seven years, he was recalled by the king.

Bandarinus *see Bandaridus*

Banderik *see Bandaridus*

Bandery *see Bandaridus*

Bane *see Barnabas*

Banjamin *see Benjamin*

Banjaminn *see Benjamin*

Banjamyn *see Benjamin*

Bannerjee *see Benjamin*

Baradates Saint

St. Baradates (d. 460) was a hermit who lived in Syria. Emperor Leo I wrote to him, asking for advice about the Council of Chalcedon.

Barbasymas Saint

St. Barbasymas (d. 346) was bishop of Seleucia and Ctesiphon. He was arrested along with sixteen priests during the persecution of King Shapur II. He and his companions refused to worship the Persian god and were martyred. Barbasymas was beheaded.

Barbatian Saint; Latin; bearded

St. Barbatian (fifth century) was a priest in Antioch, Turkey. He traveled to Rome where the Empress Galla Placidia sought his advice. She built a monastery for him at Ravenna.

Barbatus Saint; Latin; bearded

St. Barbatus (610–682) was born in Italy and became a priest in Marcona. He was sent to

Benevento where he converted many. He became bishop of Benevento and attended the Council of Constantinople in 680.

Bardo Saint; German; bright wolf

St. Bardo (d. 1053) was born in Oppershafen, Wetterau, Germany. He was educated at Fulda Abbey and became a Benedictine. He was later made abbot of two monasteries. He became archbishop of Mainz and served as chancellor and chief almoner for the empire.

Barhadbesciabas Saint

St. Barhadbesciabas (d. 355) was a deacon in Arbele. During the persecution conducted by Sassanid King Shapur II, he was arrested and tortured. He was beheaded.

Barlaam Saint; Greek; son of Laam

St. Barlaam (d. 1193) was born with the name "Alexis" into a wealthy family from Novgorod. After his parents' death, he became a hermit on the Volga. He attracted several followers and had to start a monastery. At that time, he changed his name to Barlaam.

Barn *see Barnard*

Barna *see Barnabas*

Barnaba *see Barnabas*

Barnabas Saint, New Testament; Greek, Hebrew, Latin; son of the missionary

Bane, Barna, Barnaba, Barnabe, Barnabus, Barnaby, Barnebas, Barnebus, Barney, Barnibas, Barnibus, *Barnybas, Barnybus, Bernaby, Berneby, Burnabas*

St. Barnabas (d. 61) was a Jewish man, born in Cyprus with the name of Joseph. He was one of the earliest converts to Christianity in Jerusalem. The apostles gave him the name Barnabas. He accompanied St. Paul from Tarsus to Antioch. He served as a missionary with both Paul and John Mark, who was his cousin. Tradition holds that he was stoned to death.

Barnabe *see Barnabas*

Barnabus *see Barnabas*

Barnaby *see Barnabas*

Barnard Saint; a form of Bernard; French; brave as a bear

Barn, Barnhard, Barnhardo, Barnhart

St. Barnard (d. 841) was a member of the court of Charlemagne, where he was educated. He became a Benedictine monk and was named abbot of Ambronay Abbey. He later became archbishop of Vienne, France, and founded Romans Abbey, where he died.

Barnardo *see Bernardo*

Barnebas *see Barnabas*

Barnebus *see Barnabas*

Barney *see Barnabas*

Barnhard *see Barnard*

Barnhardo *see Barnard, Bernardo*

Barnhart *see Barnard*

Barnibas *see Barnabas*

Barnibus *see Barnabas*

Barnoc *see Barrog, Brannock*

Barnybas *see Barnabas*

Barnybus *see Barnabas*

Barr *see Finbar*

Barrfoin Saint

St. Barrfoin (sixth century) was an Irish saint who was a friend of Saints Columba and Brendan. He was in charge of a church founded by St. Columba in Drum Cullen, Offaly. He also served as a missionary.

Barrog Saint; Gaelic; embrace

Barnoc, Barroq

St. Barrog (seventh century), also known as Barroq and Barnoc, was a hermit who lived on Barry Island, off the coast of Glamorgen.

Barroq *see Barrog*

Barry *see Finbar*

Barsabas Saint; Hebrew; son of return, son of rest

St. Barsabas (d. 342) was a Persian abbot who was martyred along with twelve of his monks during a persecution led by Sassanid King Shapur II. He was known as a wonder-worker.

Barsanuphius Saint

St. Barsanuphius (d. 550) was a hermit in Gaza, Israel, for fifty years. He refused to speak but communicated through writing. Eight hundred of his letters are still in existence. He was known for being able to live without eating or drinking.

Barsimaeus Saint

St. Barsimaeus (d. 250) was a bishop of Edessa in Syria

known for converting many in the area.

Bart *see Bartholomew*

Bartek *see Bartholomew*

Bartel *see Bartholomew*

Bartelmes *see Bartholomew*

Barteo *see Bartholomew*

Barth *see Bartholomew*

Barthelemy *see Bartholomew*

Bartho *see Bartholomew*

Bartholde *see Berthold*

Bartholo *see Bartholomew*

Bartholomaus *see Bartholomew*

Bartholomeo *see Bartholomew*

Bartholomeus *see Bartholomew*

Bartholomew Saint, New Testament; Hebrew; son of Talmai

Balta, Bart, Bartek, Bartel, Bartelmes, Barteo, Barth, Barthelemy, Bartho, Bartholo, Bartholomaus, Bartholomeo, Bartholomeus, Bartholomieu, Bartholomu, Bartimous, Bartlett, Bartolomeo, Bartolommeo, Bartome, Bartz

St. Bartholomew, St. Bartholomew Alvarez, St. Bartholomew Buonpedoni, St. Bartholomew of Fame, St. Bartholomew of Rossano

St. Bartholomew (first century) was one of the original twelve apostles. Called Bartholomew in the synoptic gospels, it is believed he is the same person as the Nathaniel mentioned in the Gospel of John. According to tradition, he preached in India and Greater Armenia. He was martyred by being flayed and then beheaded.

Bartholomieu *see Bartholomew*

Bartholomu *see Bartholomew*

Bartimous *see Bartholomew*

Bartlett *see Bartholomew*

Bartlomiej Saint

Blessed Bartlomiej Osypiuk (1843–1874) was a married father of two from Bohukaly, Poland. He was shot by Russian soldiers in Podlasie, Poland. He is one of the Martyrs of Podlasie and was beatified in 1996 by Pope John Paul II.

Bartold *see Berthold*

Bartolomeo *see Bartholomew*

Bartolomeu Saint; form of Bartholomew; Aramaic; son of Talmai

Bl. Bartolomeu Fernandes dos Martires (1514–1590) was born in Lisboa, Portugal. He joined the Dominicans and took part in the Council of Trent. He became archbishop of Braga, Portugal, and built hospitals and hospices. He wrote a Portuguese catechism and Biblical commentaries. He retired and spent the last eight years of his life as a monk and teacher. He was beatified by Pope John Paul II in 2001.

Bartolommeu *see Bartholomew*

Bartome *see Bartholomew*

Bartz *see Bartholomew*

Baruch Hebrew; one who is blessed

Boruch

Barula Saint

According to tradition, St. Barula (d. 304) was a seven-year-old boy who was martyred with St. Romanus in Syria.

Barypsabas Saint

St. Barypsabas (first century) was from the East. He lived as a hermit and was martyred in Dalmatia, Yugoslavia. Tradition holds that he took a vial of Christ's blood to Rome.

Bas *see Basil*

Basal *see Basil*

Base *see Basil*

Baseal *see Basil*

Basel *see Basil*

Basil Saint; Greek, Latin; royal, kingly

Bas, Basal, Base, Baseal, Basel, Basile, Basilius, Basino, Basle, Bassel, Baxley, Bazek, Bazel, Bazil, Bazyli, Bekel

St. Basil, St. Basil of Ancyra, St. Basil the Great, St. Basil the Younger, Blessed Basil Moreau

St. Basil the Great (320–379) was born in Caesarea of Cappadocia, one of the ten children of St. Basil the Elder and St. Emmelia. Before becoming a monk, he opened a school of oratory and practiced law. He then founded several monasteries and became bishop of Caesarea. He fought Arianism and simony and insisted on rigid clerical discipline. He was known for his intelligence and holiness. He was referred to as "The Great" even during his life. After his death, he was named a Doctor of the Church.

Basile *see Basil*

Basileus Saint; Greek; royal, kingly

St. Basileus (d. 319) was a bishop of Amasea. He was drowned because of his faith. One of his disciples, Elidiphorus, was led by an angel to find his body and give the martyr a Christian burial.

Basilides Saint; Greek; son of the king

St. Basilides (d. 205) was a soldier of the guard of the prefect of Egypt. When he was leading St. Potamiana to her execution, he protected her against the insults of the mob. She promised to remember him when she reached heaven. Three days after her death, she appeared to him and placed a crown on his head as a pledge that he, too, would soon die as a martyr. He was baptized and beheaded the next day.

Basiliscus Saint; Greek; little king

St. Basiliscus (d. 312) was bishop of Comana. He was beheaded and his remains were thrown into a river. He appeared to St. John Chrysostom shortly before that saint's death.

Basilius *see Basil*

Basino *see Basil*

Basinus Saint

St. Basinus (d. 705) was abbot of St. Maximin Abbey in Trier, Germany. He then became bishop of Trier. He was a patron of the English missionaries of the time, including St. Willibrord.

Basle *see Basil, Basolus*

Basolus Saint

Basle

St. Basolus (555–620), also known as Basle, was born in Limoges, France. He became a monk in Reims and then lived as a hermit for forty years. He was known as a miracle worker.

Bassel *see Basil*

Bassian Saint

St. Bassian (320–409) was a Sicilian who was sent to Rome for his education. He became bishop of Lodi in Lombardy, Italy. He attended the Council of Aquilcia in 381. A friend of St. Ambrose of Milan, he was with him when he died.

Bassus Saint; Latin; thick, fat, stumpy

St. Bassus (d. 250) was the bishop of Nice, France. He was martyred during the persecutions of Emperor Trajanus Decius by being nailed with two large brads to a board.

Bastian *see Sebastian*

Bastien *see Sebastian*

Basura Saint; Spanish; trash

St. Basura (third century) was a bishop of Masil who was martyred during Emperor Diocletian's persecutions.

Bathus Saint

St. Bathus (d. 370) was burned to death, along with several

others, in a church by order of the local king.

Baudacarius Saint

St. Baudacarius (d. 630) was a monk in the Abbey of Bobbio, Italy. He was in charge of the vineyard where thirty other monks were assigned to assist him in chasing away birds and animals that were prone to eating the vineyard's crop. He wanted to be able to give the monks a meal, but he had nothing. When the prior rebuked him for not planning for this need, he trusted in God and was miraculously able to feed all of the monks with one cooked duck.

Baudelius Saint; Latin; victory

St. Baudelius (d. 297) was born in Orleans, France. A married man, he preached the faith throughout Nimes, France. When he interrupted a festival in honor of the Roman deity Jupiter, he was beheaded.

Baudolino Saint; Latin; victory

St. Baudolino (700–740) was born into a noble family, but he gave all his wealth away prior to becoming a hermit in Forum Fulvii, near the river Tanaro. He is known for his holiness and having the gift of prophecy. He is the patron of Alessandria.

Baumar *see Baldomerus*

Baumer *see Baldomerus*

Bavo Saint

Allowin

St. Bavo (622–659), also called Allowin, was a widower who was converted to the faith by St. Amand. He went to a monastery in Ghent and dedicated his life to penance and living virtuously. He became a companion of St. Amand on his missionary journeys to France and Flanders. He later became a hermit, building himself a cell at Mendonck. After some time, he returned to the monastery in Ghent, where he once again lived as a recluse. He is the patron saint of Ghent.

Baxley *see Basil*

Baylen *see Balin*

Baylin *see Balin*

Baylon *see Balin*

Bazek *see Basil*

Bazel *see Basil*

Bazil *see Basil*

Bazyli *see Basil*

Bean Saint; Gaelic; life

St. Bean (eleventh century) was the founder of the bishopric of Mortlach in Banff, which was the forerunner of the diocese of Aberdeen.

Beandan *see Brandan*

Beandon *see Brandan*

Bear *see Bernard*

Bearnard *see Bernard*

Beatus Saint; Latin; happy, blessed

St. Beatus, St. Beatus of Vendome

St. Beatus (d. 798) was a member of St. Martin's Monastery near Santander, Spain. He opposed the Adoptionist heresy put forth by Archbishop Elipandus of Toledo. Together with Etherius, the bishop of Osma, he wrote the Liber Adversus Elipandum. After the heresy was put down, he retired to the Monastery of Valcavado.

Becan Saint; Celtic; small

St. Becan (sixth century) was an Irishman related to St. Columba. He founded a monastery at Kill-Beggan, Westmeath, which eventually became a Cistercian abbey.

Behnjamin *see Benjamin*

Bejamin *see Benjamin*

Bekel *see Basil*

Bellinus Saint; English; name of a king

St. Bellinus (d. 1151) was bishop of Padua, Italy. He was martyred for the faith.

Ben *see Benjamin*

Benardo *see Bernardo*

Benat *see Bernard*

Benci *see Benedict*

Bendek *see Benedict*

Bendic *see Benedict*

Bendick *see Benedict*

Bendict *see Benedict*

Bendictus *see Benedict*

Bendik *see Benedict*

Bendix *see Benedict*

Bendrick *see Benedict*

Benedek *see Benedict*

Benedetto Saint; Latin; blessed

St. Benedetto Menni (1841–1914) was born in Milan, Italy, the fifth of fifteen children. He was a brother in the Order of Saint John of God Hospitaler. He studied at the Gregorian Pontifical University in Rome and was ordained in 1866. In 1881, he founded the Congregation of Hospitaller Sisters of the Sacred Heart of Jesus. He was known for his care of the sick, elderly, mentally ill, and abandoned children. He was canonized by Pope John Paul II in 1999.

Benedic *see Benedict*

Benedick *see Benedict*

Benedict Saint; Latin; blessed

Benci, Bendek, Bendic, Bendick, Bendict, Bendictus, Bendik, Bendix, Bendrick, Benedek, Benedic, Benedick, Benedictas, Benedictus, Benedik, Benediktas, Benedit, Benedix, Benedyc, Benedyck, Benedyct, Benedyk, Benen, Venedict

St. Benedict of Nursia, Pope St. Benedict II, Bl. Pope Benedict XI

St. Benedict of Nursia (480–547) was the son of a Roman noble in Nursia. His twin sister was St. Scholastica. He founded twelve communities of monks at Subiaco before moving to Monte Cassino in the mountains of southern Italy. He is most known for his "Rule," which provided a framework of life for the monks. It was known for its balance of prayer and work, and many of the monasteries of the Middle Ages adopted it. He is often called the founder of western Christian monasticism.

He is a patron saint of Europe and of students.

Benedictas *see Benedict*

Benedik *see Benedict*

Benediktas *see Benedict*

Benedit *see Benedict*

Benedix *see Benedict*

Benedyc *see Benedict*

Benedyck *see Benedict*

Benedyct *see Benedict*

Benedyk *see Benedict*

Benejaminas *see Benjamin*

Benek *see Bernard*

Benen *see Benedict*

Bengamin *see Benjamin*

Bengamon *see Benjamin*

Bengamyn *see Benjamin*

Beniam *see Benjamin*

Beniamino *see Benjamin*

Benito Saint; Italian; blessed; form of Benedict

St. Benito de Jesus (1910–1934) was a member of the Brothers of the Christians Schools. He is one of the Martyrs of Turón killed during the Spanish Civil War. He was canonized in 1999 by Pope John Paul II.

Benja *see Benjamin*

Benjahmin *see Benjamin*

Benjaim *see Benjamin*

Benjam *see Benjamin*

Benjamain *see Benjamin*

Benjamin Saint, Old Testament; Top 100 Name; Hebrew; son of my right hand

Banjamin, Banjaminn, Banjamyn, Bannerjee, Behnjamin, Bejamin, Ben, Benejaminas, Bengamin, Bengamon, Bengamyn, Beniam, Beniamino, Benja, Benjahmin, Benjaim, Benjam, Benjamain, Benjamine, Benjaminn, Benjamino, Benjamon, Benjamyn, Benjamynn, Benjemin, Benjermain, Benjermin, Benkamin, Bennjamin, Bennjamon, Bennjamyn, Binyamin

St. Benjamin Julian (Vicente Alonso) Andres (Spain), St. Benjamin, St. Benjamin the Great of Nitra

Benjamin in the Old Testament was the last born of Jacob's twelve sons, the second son of Rachel.

St. Benjamin (d. 424) was a Persian deacon who was imprisoned a year for his faith. He was released on the condition that he would no longer speak about God. However, he declared that he could not be silent and preached about Christ wherever he went. He was arrested and tortured and finally killed by having a knotted snake inserted into his bowels to rend and tear him.

Benjamine *see Benjamin*

Benjaminn *see Benjamin*

Benjamino *see Benjamin*

Benjamon *see Benjamin*

Benjamyn *see Benjamin*

Benjamynn *see Benjamin*

Benjemin *see Benjamin*

Benjermain *see Benjamin*

Benjermin *see Benjamin*

Benkamin *see Benjamin*

Bennjamin *see Benjamin*

Bennjamon *see Benjamin*

Bennjamyn *see Benjamin*

Benno Saint; Hebrew; son

St. Benno (d. 1106) was born in Hildesheim, Germany. He became a chaplain to Emperor Henry III and then bishop of Meissen. He was deeply embroiled in political matters of the day. He is a patron saint of anglers and weavers.

Benonee *see Benoni*

Benoney *see Benoni*

Benoni Old Testament; Hebrew; son of my sorrow

Benonee, Benoney, Benonie, Benony

Benoni in the Bible was the name that Rachel (wife of Jacob) originally gave to her son as she was dying. Jacob renamed him Benjamin (Gn 35:18).

Benonie *see Benoni*

Benony *see Benoni*

Benvenutus Saint; Latin, Italian; welcome

St. Benvenutus Scotivoli (d. 1282) studied law in Bologna. He was named archdeacon of Ancona, became a Franciscan, and then was made bishop of Osimo, Italy.

Benyamin *see Benjamin*

Benyamino *see Benjamin*

Beoadh Saint; Celtic

Aeodh

St. Beoadh (d. 518) was called Aeodh. He was a bishop of

Ardcarne who received the prefix "Beo" due to his holiness.

Beoc Saint; Celtic

St. Beoc (fifth or sixth century) was an Irish monk who founded a monastery in Lough Derg, in Donegal.

Beocca Saint; English

St. Beocca (d. 870) was martyred in England when the Danes raided Anglo-Saxon abbeys. He and ninety other monks were killed in Surrey.

Ber *see Bernard*

Berach Saint; Gaelic; sharp

St. Berach (d. 595) was raised by his uncle, St. Freoch, and became a disciple of St. Kevin. He founded an abbey at Clusin-Coirpte in Connaught, Ireland. He is the patron saint of Kilbarry, County Dublin.

Berarius Saint

St. Berarius (d. 680) was a bishop of Le Mans, France, who is known for moving the relics of St. Scholastica from Monte Cassino to Le Mans.

Berchan *see Berthane*

Bercharius Saint

St. Bercharius (636–696) was a native of Aquitaine. He received his instruction from St. Nivard, archbishop of Reims. He became a monk at Lexeuil and was ordained into the priesthood. He then became an abbot at Hautvilliers and founded a monastery at Moutier-en-Der and a convent at Puellemontier. He was stabbed by a deranged monk and died two days later. He is considered a martyr.

Bercthun Saint

St. Bercthun (d. 733) was a Benedictine and the first abbot of Beverley Monastery in France. He was a disciple of St. John of Beverley.

Beregisius Saint

St. Beregisius (d. 725) was the founder of the Abbey of Saint-Hubert in the Ardennes region of France.

Berencardus Saint

St. Berencardus (d. 1293) was a Benedictine monk at the St. Papoul Abbey in Languedoc, France. He was known for his charity.

Berend *see Bernard*

Bern *see Bernard*

Bernaby *see Barnabas*

Bernad *see Bernard*

Bernados *see Bernard*

Bernal *see Bernard*

Bernaldo *see Bernardo*

Bernard Saint; German; brave as a bear

Bear, Bearnard, Benat, Benek, Ber, Berend, Bern, Bernad, Bernados, Bernal, Bernardel, Bernardin, Bernardus, Bernardyn, Bernarr, Bernat, Bernek, Bernel, Bernerd, Berngards, Bernhard, Bernhards, Bernhardt, Bernhart, Bernon, Burnard

St. Bernard, St. Bernard degli Uberti, St. Bernard Due, St. Bernard of Arce, St. Bernard of Bagnorea, St. Bernard of Calvo, St. Bernard of Carinola, St. Bernard of Clairvaux, St. Bernard of Montjoux, St. Bernard of Valdeiglesias, St. Bernard Valeara

St. Bernard of Clairvaux (1090–1153) was born into a noble family in Burgandy, France. From a young age, he was known for his intelligence and piety. He became a Cistercian and was sent to begin a new monastery, which would become the famous Abbey of Clairvaux. He was named as abbot. During his life, he founded many other monasteries and wrote many books. He was the secretary of the Council of Troyes in 1128. He was also known as a miracle worker. Pope Pius VIII named him a Doctor of the Church.

Bernardel *see Bernard*

Bernardi *see Bernardo*

Bernardin *see Bernard*

Bernardine Saint; a form of Bernard; English, German; brave as a bear

Bernadeen, Bernadeena, Bernadeenah, Bernadeene, Bernaden, Bernadena, Bernadenah, Bernadene, Bernadin, Bernadina, Bernadinah, Bernadyn, Bernadyna, Bernadynah, Bernadyne, Bernardina, Berni

St. Bernardine of Siena (1380–1444) was a native of Tuscany. Orphaned at six, he was raised by his aunt. Once he completed his education, he served the sick in hospitals. He caught the bubonic plague and nearly died. He joined the Observant branch of the Order of Friars Minor and was ordained a priest in 1405. He spent thirty years preaching all over Italy. He was put on trial for heresy and was found innocent. Pope Martin V asked him to preach in Rome. In time, he became vicar-general of the Franciscan Order in Italy.

Bernardino Saint; a form of Bernard; Spanish; brave as a bear

St. Bernardino Realino (1530–1616) was born into a noble Christian family of Capri, Italy. He studied medicine for a while but then devoted himself to the law and received his doctorate in 1563. He went to Naples, where he was appointed auditor and lieutenant general. The Blessed Mother appeared to him, and he decided to join the Society of Jesus. He was sent to Lecce where he spent the rest of his life. He was known for his intellect, teaching ability, and service to the poor. He died with the names of Jesus and Mary on his lips.

Bernardo Saint; a form of Bernard; Spanish; brave as a bear

Barnardo, Barnhardo, Benardo, Bernaldo, Bernardi, Bernhard, Bernhardo, Burnardo, Nardo

St. Bernardo of Corleone, St. Bernardo Tolomei

St. Bernardo of Corleone (1605–1667) was a shoemaker and was known for his ability in dueling.

After wounding a man in a duel, he sought refuge in the Church of the Capuchin Friars Minor in Palermo. After undergoing a true conversion, he became a Capuchin lay brother in 1632. He spent the rest of his life in self-imposed penances to atone for his earlier life.

Bernardus *see Bernard*

Bernardyn *see Bernard*

Bernarr *see Bernard*

Bernat *see Bernard*

Berneby *see Barnabas*

Bernek *see Bernard*

Bernel *see Bernard*

Bernerd *see Bernard*

Berngards *see Bernard*

Bernhard *see Bernard, Bernardo*

Bernhardo *see Bernardo*

Bernhards *see Bernard*

Bernhardt *see Bernard*

Bernhart *see Bernard*

Berno Saint; German; bear

St. Berno (850–927) was the son of the French nobleman Odon who helped provide refuge for a group of Benedictine monks that had been driven from their monastery by Normans. Berno assisted his father in this effort. When his father died, he gave away his inheritance and joined the Benedictine Monastery of St. Martin in Autun. He was named abbot of Baume, and, having proved himself in that position, was later named abbot of Cluny, one of Europe's most important monasteries.

Bernon *see Bernard*

Bernward Saint; German; protected by the bear

St. Bernward (960–1022) was raised by his uncle, Bishop Volkmar of Utrecht. After being ordained, he became chaplain and tutor to the child Emperor Otto III. He was elected bishop of Hildesheim and built St. Michael's Church and Monastery there. Late in life, he became a Benedictine.

Beronicus Saint

St. Beronicus (date unknown) was martyred in Antioch, Syria, with Pelagia and forty-nine companions.

Bert *see Engelbert, Herbert, Hubert, Lambert, Norbert*

Bertain *see Bertin*

Bertaud *see Berthaldus*

Berthaldus Saint

Bertaud

St. Berthaldus (d. 540), also known as Bertaud, was a hermit who lived in the Ardennes region of France. He was ordained by St. Remigius.

Berthane Saint

Berchan

St. Berthane (d. 840), also known as Berchan, was a monk of Iona and a bishop of Kirkwall in Scotland. He died in Ireland and is known as "the Man of Two Countries."

Bertharius Saint

St. Bertharius (810–883) was a poet and a writer. Born a member of the royal house of France, he joined the monastery of Monte Cassino, in Italy. He became abbot of that house and helped to protect it against Muslim invasion. However, in 883, invading Saracens martyred him and several other monks while they were in the chapel.

Berthelot *see Berthold*

Berthoald Saint; German; bright strength

St. Berthoald (seventh century) was the fifth bishop of Cambrai Arras, France. He worked hard to protect his flock during a time of severe upheaval in France.

Berthold Saint; German; bright, illustrious

Bartholde, Bartold, Berthelot, Berthoud, Bertoide, Bertold, Bertoldi, Bertolt, Burthold, Burtholde

St. Berthold (d. 1195), also known as Bertold and Bartold, is considered by some to be the founder of the Carmelite order. He was born in Limoges, France, and studied at the University of Paris. After being ordained a priest, he went on a crusade. He joined a group of hermits at Mount Carmel and created a rule for them. Aymeric, the Latin patriarch of Antioch, appointed him the first Carmelite superior general.

Berthoud *see Berthold*

Bertin Saint; Spanish; distinguished friend

Bertain, Bertinus, Bertyn, Burtin, Burtyn

St. Bertin (seventh century) was born in Constance, France, and was educated at the Abbey of Luxeuil. He and two other monks joined St. Omer in founding a monastery in Pas-de-Calais, which was called St. Mommolin. Eight years later, they established another monastery at Sithui dedicated to St. Peter. St. Bertin served as abbot there for sixty years, and after his death it was named for him.

Bertinus *see Bertin*

Bertoide *see Berthold*

Bertold *see Berthold*

Bertoldi *see Berthold*

Bertolt *see Berthold*

Bertram *see Bettelin*

Bertran *see Bertrand*

Bertrand Saint; German; bright shield

Bairtrand, Bertran, Bertrando, Bertranno, Bertrant, Burtrand

St. Bertrand, St. Bertrand of Comminges

St. Bertrand (d. 623) was ordained by St. Germanicus and became bishop of Le Mans, France. He was very interested in growing grapes. Because he supported the Neustrian kings, he was exiled, but he was reinstated by King Clotaire II. He founded a church, a monastery, and a hospice.

Bertrando *see Bertrand*

Bertranno *see Bertrand*

Bertrant *see Bertrand*

Bertuin Saint; German; brilliant

St. Bertuin (d. 698) was an Anglo-Saxon monk who spent two years in Rome. He became a bishop and was sent to Malonne, in the area of Namur, Belgium. He became abbot of a monastery he founded there.

Bertulf Saint; Teutonic; the warrior who shines

St. Bertulf (d. 640) was a German who converted to Christianity due to the influence of his relative Arnulf of Metz. He entered the Monastery of Luxeuil in France. When Abbot Attala from Bobbio came to visit Luxeuil, Bertulf gained permission to leave and join that community. He later became the abbot of Bobbio, where he preached against Arianism.

Bertyn *see Bertin*

Bessarian *see Bessarion*

Bessarion Saint; Greek; the walker

Bessarian

St. Bessarion the Great (third or fourth century), also known as Bessarian, was a native of Egypt, where he became a disciple of St. Antony and then of St. Macarius. He remained silent and observed a strict fast. He was known as a miracle worker. Some of his miracles include making salt water fresh and bringing rain during a drought.

Bessis Saint; Hebrew; God's promise

St. Bessis (unknown) was a hermit martyred at Sanctuary, Val Soana, Irrea diocese.

Besuss Saint

St. Besuss (date unknown) was a Theban legionnaire and martyr.

Betharius Saint

St. Betharius (d. 623) was a bishop of Chartres, France, for over twenty-five years. He attended the Council of Sens.

Bettelin Saint

Bertram

St. Bettelin (eighth century), also known as Bertram, was a disciple of St. Guthlac. According to legend, he was a noble who married an Irish princess. She died giving birth in a forest while he went for help, and she was eaten by a wolf. He then became a hermit, living under the auspices of Croyland Monastery.

Betto Saint; Latin, Italian;

blessed;

St. Betto (d. 918) was a monk at Saint-Columbe Abbey in Sens, France, and was later named bishop of Auxerre.

Beuno Saint

St. Beuno (d. 640) was a monk in Wales who evangelized much of North Wales and founded a monastery at Clynnog Fawr. According to legend, he restored the head of St. Winifred after she was beheaded. He is a patron of sick children and against diseased cattle.

Beuvon *see Bobo*

Beuzec *see Budoc*

Bicor Saint

St. Bicor (date unknown) was a Persian bishop who was martyred in the persecution conducted by Sassanid King Shapur II.

Bieuzy Saint; French

St. Bieuzy (seventh century) followed St. Gildas to Brittany, France, where he was martyred.

Bilfrid Saint

St. Bilfrid (eighth century) was a Benedictine hermit who lived off the coast of Northumbria. He used his silversmith skills to aid Bishop Eaddfrid in binding the Lindisfarne Gospels.

Bill *see William*

Billy *see William*

Binyamin *see Benjamin*

Birillus Saint

St. Birillus (d. 90) was the first bishop of Catania, Sicily. He was ordained by St. Peter.

Birinus Saint; Latin; reddish

St. Birinus (600–649) was a priest in Rome and became bishop of Genoa, Italy. He was then sent on a missionary apostolate to Britain by Pope Honorius I. He converted King Cynegils, who gave him the area of Dorchester as his see.

Birnstan *see Birrstan*

Birrstan Saint

Birnstan, Brynstan

St. Birrstan (d. 934) was a disciple of St. Grimbold. He was a

Benedictine and became bishop of Winchester, England.

Blaan *see Blane*

Bladulph *see Blidulf*

Bladus Saint; Latin; knife, sword

St. Bladus (date unknown) was one of the early bishops of the Isle of Man off the Scottish coast.

Blain *see Blane*

Blaine *see Blane*

Blais *see Blaise*

Blaise Saint; Latin; stammerer

Ballas, Balyse, Blais, Blaisot, Blaize, Blasi, Blasien, Blasius, Blay

St. Blaise (fourth century) was a bishop of Sebastea in Armenia. According to legend, he went to the hills to escape persecution, where sick animals sought him out to be healed. Legend also holds that a boy who had a fishbone stuck in his throat was brought to him. He saved the boy from death. He was ultimately captured and sentenced to be starved to death. He is a patron saint of animals and throat illnesses.

Blaisot *see Blaise*

Blaithmaic Saint

St. Blaithmaic (d. 823) was an Irish abbot. He went to England to preach to the Danes, who murdered him on the altar steps of the abbey church at Iona.

Blaize *see Blaise*

Blane Saint; Gaelic; thin, lean

Blaan, Blain, Blaine, Blayne

St. Blane (d. 590), also known as Blaan, was born on the island of Bute, Scotland. After studying in Ireland for seven years, he became a priest and returned to Scotland as a missionary. He was consecrated as a bishop and known as a miracle worker.

Blasi *see Blaise*

Blasien *see Blaise*

Blasius *see Blaise*

Blay *see Blaise*

Blayne *see Blane*

Blidulf Saint

Bladulph

St. Blidulf (d. 630), also known as Bladulph, was a monk at Bobbio, Italy. He denounced King Arioald of the Lombards for his heretical views.

Blier *see Blitharius*

Blinlivet Saint

St. Blinlivet (ninth century) was the twenty-fifth bishop of Vannes in Brittany, France. After he retired, he became a monk and was known for his asceticism and prayerfulness.

Blitharius Saint

Blier

St. Blitharius (seventh century), also known as Blier, was a native of Scotland. He traveled as a missionary to France with St. Fursey.

Blitmund Saint

St. Blitmund (d. 660) was a monk in Bobbio, Italy. He went with St. Valery to France, where they founded an abbey at Leucone, where he served as abbot.

Boadin Saint

St. Boadin (date unknown) was originally from Ireland but joined the Benedictine order in France. He was known for his kindness and adherence to the monastic rule.

Boaz Old Testament; Hebrew; swift

Boz

Boaz was the husband of Ruth (Ru 2:1).

Bob *see Robert*

Bobby *see Robert*

Bobinus Saint

St. Bobinus (d. 766) was born in Aquitaine and became a Benedictine monk at Moulier-la-Celle. He later became bishop of Troyes.

Bobo Saint; Ghanaian; born on a Tuesday

Beuvon

St. Bobo (d. 985), also known as Beuvon, fought against Saracens as a French knight before becoming a hermit. He died at Pavia, in Lombardy, Italy, while on a pilgrimage to Rome.

Bodagisil Saint

St. Bodagisil (d. 588) founded an abbey on the banks of the Meuse River in Belgium, where he became abbot.

Bodfan Saint

St. Bodfan (seventh century) was a monk at Beaumaris, Wales. He is a patron saint of Ahern, in Gwynredd, Wales.

Bodo Saint; German; leader

St. Bodo (d. 678) was born in Toul, France, and was a brother of St. Salaberga. After he was married, his wife became a nun and he became a Benedictine monk at Laon. He later became bishop of Toul and founded several abbeys.

Boetharius Saint

St. Boetharius (seventh century) was bishop of Chartres and chaplain to King Clotaire II of France.

Boethian Saint; Celtic; victorious

St. Boethian (seventh century) was born in Ireland. He was a Benedictine monk who built the Pierrepoint Abbey near Laon, France. Rebellious monks murdered him.

Bogumilus Saint

St. Bogumilus (1135–1182) was born into a noble family near Dobrow, Poland. He studied in Paris and was ordained a priest. He was named chancellor and then archbishop of Gnesen. He founded a Cistercian abbey at Coronowa. After he resigned his position as bishop, he joined the Camaldolese at Uniedow, Poland.

Boisil *see Boswell*

Bolcan Saint

Olcan

St. Bolcan (d. 840), also known as Olcan, was baptized by St. Patrick. He was then sent to France, where he studied for the priesthood. After he was ordained, St. Patrick named him bishop of Derban.

Boleslas *see Boleslaw*

Boleslaw Saint; Slavic; the most glorious of the glorious

Boleslas

Bl. Boleslaw Strzelecki (1896–1941) was born in Poniemon, Podlaskie, Poland. He served the diocese of Radom, Poland, as a parish priest. He was arrested during the Nazi persecution of the Church and was sent to Auschwitz, where he died. He was beatified by Pope John Paul II in 1999.

Bonaventure Saint; Italian; good luck

St. Bonaventure, St. Bonaventure of Miako

St. Bonaventure (1221–1274) was born in Bagnorea in Tuscany. He entered the Franciscan order when he was twenty-two. After his ordination, he traveled to Paris, where he studied under Alexander of Hales and John of Rochelle. He became friends with St. Thomas Aquinas and King St. Louis. He was named general of the Franciscan order and wrote the life of St. Francis. Pope Gregory X named him cardinal and bishop of Albano. He died while attending the Second Council of Lyons. He is a Doctor of the Church.

Bond Saint; English; tiller of the soil

Baldus, Bonde, Bondie, Bondon, Bonds, Bondy

St. Bond (seventh century), also known as Baldus, was from Spain. He became a hermit and public penitent, trained by St. Artemius.

Bonde *see Bond*

Bondie *see Bond*

Bondon *see Bond*

Bonds *see Bond*

Bondy *see Bond*

Bonet *see Bonitus*

Bonfilius Saint; Latin; good son

St. Bonfilius (1040–1125) was born in Piceno, Italy. He became a Benedictine monk and was later named bishop of Storace. In 1078, he became bishop of Foligno. After making a pilgrimage to the Holy Land, he retired to a Benedictine abbey.

Boniface Saint; Latin; do-gooder

Bonifacio, Bonifacius, Bonifacy

St. Boniface, St. Boniface Curitan, Pope St. Boniface I, St. Boniface IV, St. Boniface of Lausanne, St. Boniface of Mainz

St. Boniface of Mainz (675–754) was originally known as Winfrith in England, where he was a respected scholar, teacher, and priest. In his midforties, he set off on a missionary trip to Friesland (modern-day Holland) but was forced to return home in defeat when he wasn't allowed to preach. He then set off to Rome, where Pope Gregory II sent him on a test mission to Thuringia in Germany and gave him the new name of Boniface. He later was consecrated as a bishop. He spread the Word of God in both Hesse and Thuringia. In his later years, he returned to Friesland, where he was martyred. He is known as the Apostle of Germany and is a patron saint of brewers and World Youth Day.

Bonifacio *see Boniface*

Bonifacius *see Boniface*

Bonifacy *see Boniface*

Bonitus Saint; Latin; worthy

Bonet

St. Bonitus (623–706) was born in Auvergne, France. Thiery III named him governor of Marseilles, and he was later made bishop of Clermont. When doubts were raised about his election, he resigned his see and became a hermit at the Benedictine Abbey of Manglieu at Clermont.

Bononio *see Bononius*

Bononius Saint

Bononio

St. Bononius (d. 1026), also known as Bononio, was a disciple of St. Romuald. That saint sent him to preach in Egypt and Syria, where he helped build some Christian churches. After spending some time as a hermit in Sinai, he became abbot of the Benedictine Abbey of Lucedo in Italy.

Boruch *see Baruch*

Bosa Saint; English

St. Bosa (d. 705) was a Benedictine monk at Whitby, England, which was ruled by St. Hilda. After St. Wilfrid was forced into exile because he refused to accept the division of his see of York, Bosa became bishop of York. St. Bede referred to him as "a man beloved of God."

Bosvile *see Boswell*

Boswall *see Boswell*

Boswel *see Boswell*

Boswell Saint; English; boar enclosure by the stream

Boisil, Bosvile, Boswall, Boswel, Bozwel, Bozwell

St. Boswell (d. 661), also known as Boisil, became abbot of Melrose, England. He was a biblical scholar who had the gift of prophecy and was known for his preaching. He died of the plague.

Botuid Saint

Botwid

St. Botuid (d. 1100), also known as Botwid, was from Sweden. While on a journey to England he converted to Christianity. He returned to Sweden as a missionary and was martyred by a Finnish slave.

Botulph Saint; English; messenger wolf

St. Botulph (d. 680) was from England. He and his brother St. Adulph traveled to Belgic Gaul, where they established churches and schools. Adulph was named bishop of Maestricht. Botulph returned to

England where he established a monastery at Ikanho. He was known for his holiness and patience in the face of sickness. He is a patron saint of travelers and farming.

Botwid *see Botuid*

Boz *see Boaz*

Bozwel *see Boswell*

Bozwell *see Boswell*

Braiano *see Brian*

Bram *see Abraham*

Brandan Saint; English; beacon hill

Beandan, Beandon, Brandon, Brandyn, Branton, Breandan, Breendan

St. Brandan (fifth century) was an Irish monk who traveled to England. He fled to Gaul beause of the cruel treatment he had received there. He was later named as an abbot.

Brandon *see Brandan*

Brandyn *see Brandan*

Brannoc *see Brannock*

Brannock Saint Welsh

Barnoc, Brannoc

St. Brannock (sixth century), also known as Barnoc or Brannoc, was a Welsh monk who traveled to Devon, England. He founded a monastery at Braunton in Devonshire, where he served as abbot.

Branton *see Brandan*

Branwallader Saint

Breward

St. Branwallader (sixth century), also known as Breward,

was a bishop of Jersey, England. He served with St. Samson in Cornwall and the Channel Islands and may have also traveled to Brittany.

Brauli *see Braulio*

Braulio Saint; Italian; meadow on the hillside

Brauli, Brauliuo

St. Braulio (590–651) was educated by St. Isidore in Seville. He became bishop of Saragossa and fought against the Arian heresy. He took part in the fourth, fifth, and sixth Councils of Toledo. He was known for his preaching, care for the poor, and devotion to prayer. Toward the end of his life, his eyesight failed, which was a great trial for the scholar. Realizing his end was near, he spent the last day of his life reciting the psalms. He is a patron of Aragon.

Brauliuo *see Braulio*

Breandan *see Brendan*

Breendan *see Brandan, Brendan*

Bregowine *see Bregwin*

Bregwin Saint

Bregowine, Bregwine

St. Bregwin (d. 764), also known as Bregowine or Bregwine, was the twelfth archbishop of Canterbury.

Bregwine *see Bregwin*

Bren *see Brendan*

Brendan Saint; Gaelic, English; little raven, sword

Breandan, Breendan, Bren, Brendano, Brenden, Brendin, Brendis, Brendon, Brenn, Brenndan, Bryn

St. Brendan, St. Brendan of Birr St. Brendan (d. 577) is an Irish saint known as "the Navigator," "the Voyager," or "the Bold." He was taught by St. Ita. He founded a monastery at Clonfert. According to legend, he traveled to the "Isle of the Blessed," also called St. Brendan's Island. Some believed he discovered America.

Brendano *see Brendan*

Brenden *see Brendan*

Brendin *see Brendan*

Brendis *see Brendan*

Brendon *see Brendan*

Brenn *see Brendan*

Brenndan *see Brendan*

Bretannio *see Bretannion*

Bretannion Saint

Bretannio, Vetranio, Vetranion

St. Bretannion (d. 380), also known as Bretannio, Vetranio, or Vetranion, was a bishop of Tomi, Romania. When the Emperor Valens visited the area and tried to convince the people to convert to Arianism, Bretannion spoke out against him and was exiled. He was allowed to return due to public outcry.

Breward *see Branwallader*

Brian Top 100 Name; Gaelic; strong, virtuous, honorable

Braiano, Briand, Briann, Briano, Briant, Briaun, Brien, Brin, Briny, Bryan, Bryon

Bl. Brian Lacey (d. 1591) was born in Norfolk, England. He was arrested in 1586 for helping and hiding priests. He was released but was arrested a second time in 1591. He was tortured and condemned to death. He was hung at Tyburn, London, England.

Briand *see Brian*

Briann *see Brian*

Briano *see Brian*

Briant *see Brian*

Briarch Saint

St. Briarch (d. 627) became a monk in Wales. He traveled with St. Tudwal to Britanny, France, where he built a monastery and served as abbot.

Briaun *see Brian*

Briavel Saint; Celtic

St. Briavel (sixth century) was a hermit in Gloucestershire, England.

Brice Saint; Welsh, English; alert, ambitious

Bricen, Briceton, Bricio, Brise, Brisen, Britius, Brizio, Bryce

St. Brice (370–444), also known as Britius, was raised by St. Martin of Tours. He suffered from vanity and ambition and treated Martin poorly. He asked for Martin's forgiveness and succeeded him as bishop of Tours, but he soon went back to his previous way of life. He was exiled due to his behavior. After seven years in Rome, he completely changed his life. When he returned to his see, he was known for his humility and holiness.

Bricen *see Brice*

Briceton *see Brice*

Bricio *see Brice*

Brictus Saint; Latin; speckled

St. Brictus (d. 312) was bishop of Martola near Spoleto, Italy. He was imprisoned during the reign of Emperor Diocletian, but was not martyred.

Brien *see Brian*

Brieuc Saint; Celtic; power, nobility, respect

Brioc, Briocus, Briomaglus

St. Brieuc (420–510), also known as Briocus, Briomaglus, or Brioc, was born in Wales. After being ordained in France, he returned to England as a missionary, where he converted his parents and the ruler of Brittany. He founded a monastery in Brittany and was known as a miracle worker.

Brin *see Brian*

Briny *see Brian*

Brioc *see Brieuc*

Briocus *see Brieuc*

Briomaglus *see Brieuc*

Brise *see Brice*

Brisen *see Brice*

Brithwald Saint

St. Brithwald (d. 731) was educated at Canterbury, England. He became a Benedictine and served as abbot of Kent until 692, at which time he became archbishop of Canterbury.

Britius *see Brice*

Brito Saint; Latin; from Brittany, France

Britonius

St. Brito (d. 386), also known as Britonius, was bishop of Trier, Germany. He worked to convert the Priscillian heretics in his region.

Britonius *see Brito*

Britwin Saint; English

St. Britwin (d. 733) was a Benedictine abbot of Beverley, England, who worked to promote monasticism and culture in England.

Brizio *see Brice*

Brocard Saint; English; armed warrior

St. Brocard (d. 1231) was born in France. He went to Mount Carmel, where he became prior for thirty-five years. Under his direction, the Carmelite Rule was formally approved.

Broderick *see Roderic*

Brogan Saint; Gaelic; a heavy work shoe

Brogen, Broghan, Broghen, Brogin, Brogon

St. Brogan (seventh century) was abbot of Ross Tuire, Ossory, Ireland, and known for writing a hymn to St. Brigid.

Brogen *see Brogan*

Broghan *see Brogan*

Broghen *see Brogan*

Brogin *see Brogan*

Brogon *see Brogan*

Bron Saint; African; source

Brone

St. Bron (d. 511) was a follower of St. Patrick. He was bishop of Cassellrra, near Sligo, Ireland. He brought literary and artistic standards to Irish monasticism.

Brone *see Bron*

Bronislav *see Bronislaw*

Bronislaw Saint; Polish; weapon of glory

Bronislav, Bronyslav, Bronyslaw

Bl. Bronislaw Kostkowski (1915–1942) was a Polish seminarian who was arrested during the Nazi persecution and died at the Dachau concentration camp. He is one of the 108 Polish Martyrs of World War II. He was beatified in 1999 by Pope John Paul II.

Bronyslav *see Bronislaw*

Bronyslaw *see Bronislaw*

Bruno Saint; German, Italian; brown haired, brown skinned

St. Bruno, St. Bruno of Segni, St. Bruno Seronkuma

St. Bruno (1030–1101) was born in Cologne and studied at the cathedral school at Rheims. After being ordained, he served that school as a professor of theology and then headmaster. He later became chancellor of Rheims. When he spoke out against the archbishop, he was forced into exile. He returned several years later and became a hermit. Bishop St. Hugh of Grenoble gave him and his followers some land at La Grande Chartreuse. This was the start of the Carthusian order.

Brunon Saint; German, Italian; brown haired, brown skinned

Bruno

Bl. Brunon Zembol (1905–1942), also known as Bruno, was born in Letownia, Malopolskie, Poland. He was a Franciscan friar who was arrested by the Nazis and sent to Dachau concentration camp. He is one of the 108 Polish Martyrs of World War II and was beatified in 1999 by Pope John Paul II.

Bryan *see Brian*

Bryce *see Brice*

Brychan Saint; Welsh; speckled

St. Brychan (fifth century) was born in Ireland to Prince Anlach and his wife, Marchel. He married three times and had twenty-four children, all known for their holiness.

Bryn *see Brendan*

Brynach Saint; Welsh

St. Brynach (sixth century) is a Welsh saint who traveled to Rome and Brittany and then to Milford Haven. He established several oratories. Land was given to him in Nevern by the local lord, Clether, to begin a monastery.

Brynoth Saint

St. Brynoth (d. 1317) was bishop of Scara in West Gottland, Sweden.

Brynstan *see Birrstan*

Bryon *see Brian*

Buchard *see Burkard*

Budoc Saint

Beuzec, Budeux

St. Budoc (sixth century), also known as Budeux and Beuzec, was the son of a king of Brittany and of Azenor, a French princess. He was born at sea while his mother was exiled and was raised in a monastery near Waterford, Ireland. He became abbot and was later named Bishop of Dol, Brittany.

Budeux *see Budoc*

Buonfiglio Saint; good son; Italian

St. Buonfiglio Monaldo (thirteenth century) was one of seven Florentines who joined the Confraternity of the Blessed Virgin. They later became the Servants of Mary, or Servites. Buonfiglio served as the first prior general.

Burchard Saint; English; castle strong

St. Burchard (d. 754) was a priest of Wessex, England. He went to Germany, where St. Boniface consecrated him the first bishop of Würzburg. He founded the Abbey of St. Andrew's.

Burkard Saint; English; castle strong

Buchard

St. Burkard (d. 754), also known as Buchard, was an English priest and Benedictine monk. He became the first bishop of Würzburg and founded three abbeys. After retiring his see,

he spent the rest of his life in a monastery.

Burnabas *see Barnabas*

Burnard *see Bernard*

Burnardo *see Bernardo*

Burthold *see Berthold*

Burtholde *see Berthold*

Burtin *see Bertin*

Burtrand *see Bertrand*

Burtyn *see Bertin*

Byblig Saint

St. Byblig (fifth century) is a holy man associated with Caenarvon, Wales.

C

Cachi *see Casimir*

Cadfan Saint; Welsh; battle summit

St. Cadfan (sixth century) was born in Brittany, France. He served as a missionary to Wales, where he founded several churches.

Cadfarch Saint; Welsh; battle horse

St. Cadfarch (sixth century) was a disciple of St. Illtyd. He began churches at Penegoes and Abererch in Wales, England.

Cadoc Saint; Welsh; eager for war

Cadvael, Cathmael, Docus

St. Cadoc (497–580), also known as Docus, Cathmael, or Cadvael, founded Llancarfan Monastery near Cardiff, Wales, which was known as a center of learning. He later served as a missionary to Brittany, France. After he returned to the British areas, he was martyred by Saxons near Weedon, England.

Cadog Saint; Welsh; battle

St. Cadog (fifth century) is associated with Llangardock, in Dyfed, Wales.

Cadroe Saint; Scottish; soldier for the Lord

Cathroe, Kadroe

St. Cadroe (d. 971), also known as Cathroe or Kadroe, was a Scottish prince. He studied in Ireland and then went to England. He became a Benedictine monk in Fleury, France, and was named abbot of Waulsort Monastery in Belgium. He was later named abbot of St. Clement's Monastery in Metz, France. He was known as a miracle worker.

Cadvael *see Cadoc*

Cadwalla *see Cadwallader*

Cadwallader Saint; Welsh; battle leader

Cadwalla, Caedwalla

St. Cadwallader (659–689), also known as Cadwalla or Ceadwalla, was king of the West Saxons. He also gained control of Surrey and Kent. He was wounded during the conquest of the Isle of Wight and abdicated his throne soon after. He traveled to Rome where he was baptized and died ten days later.

Caecilius Saint; Latin; blind

St. Caecilius (third century) was a priest of Carthage responsible for converting St. Cyprian.

Caedmon Saint; Gaelic; wise warrior

St. Caedmon (d. 680) was a Celt who, as an old man, joined Whitby Monastery, where he was responsible for tending the animals. In a dream one night, he had a vision where he learned a new song, "The Hymn of Creation." After waking, he could recite it perfectly. He became known as the first poet working in vernacular English. Although he was illiterate, he helped translate the Latin scriptures into English for the people.

Caedwalla *see Cadwallader*

Caelab *see Caleb*

Caeleb *see Caleb*

Caerealis Saint; Latin

St. Caerealis (d. 251) was a Roman soldier. He and his wife Sallustia were converted by Pope St. Cornelius. They were martyred during the persecutions of Emperor Trajanus Decius.

Caesarius Saint; Latin; long haired

St. Caesarius, St. Caesarius of Arles, St. Caesarius of Nazianzus

St. Caesarius (d. 309) was the father of Eudoxius, known for being an Arian heretic. Although his own life was less than ideal, Caesarius would not deny the faith and died as a martyr in Armenia during the reign of Emperor Galerius.

Caesidius Saint; Latin; pale

St. Caesidius (third century) may have been the son of St. Rufinus. He was one of a group of Christians martyred on the shore of Lake Fucino in Italy.

Cagnoald Saint; German; illustrious

Cagnou, Chagnoald

St. Cagnoald (d. 635), also known as Chagnoald or Cagnou, was the brother of St. Faro and St. Burgundofara. He became a monk at Luxeuil and was later ordained bishop of Laon. He criticized Emperor Theodoric I for his immoral conduct and was exiled. He worked as a missionary for many years before returning to Laon. He attended the Council of Reims in 630.

Cagnou *see Cagnoald*

Caian Saint; Welsh

St. Caian (fifth century) was a son or grandson of the local king of Brecknock. He was from Wales, England.

Caidoc Saint; Gaelic

St. Caidoc (seventh century) was an Irish missionary who worked with St. Fricor in northern France.

Cailab *see Caleb*

Caillin Saint; Gaelic; pup

St. Caillin (seventh century) founded a famous monastery at Fenagh, Ireland. According to legend, he turned druids into stone when they refused to convert to Christianity.

Caimin Saint; Gaelic; stooped, bent

St. Caimin (d. 635) was an Irish hermit of Inniskeltra. Together with St. Senan, he founded a monastery and chapel on the Island of the Seven Churches.

Cairlon Saint; Gaelic

Caorlan

St. Cairlon (sixth century), also known as Caorlan, died while he was serving as an abbot, but St. Dageus brought him back to life. He later became archbishop of Cashel, Ireland.

Cairnech *see Carantac*

Caius *see Gaius*

Cajetan Saint; Latin; person from Caieta

St. Cajetan (1480–1547) was from Vicenza. He became a priest and helped reestablish a confraternity dedicated to promoting God's glory. He also founded an oratory in Verona dedicated to caring for the poor and sick. Together with other clergy who hoped to reform the Church, which was suffering from a great deal of corruption at the time, he formed a religious order focused on solid foundations of religious life. They became known as the Theatines Clerks Regular. While they didn't succeed in changing the lives of many religious, they did convert many souls. He died a very discouraged man. He is the patron saint of the unemployed, gamblers, and good fortune.

Cal *see Caleb*

Calab *see Caleb*

Calabe *see Caleb*

Caleb Old Testament; Top 100 Name; Hebrew, Arabic; dog, faithful

Caelab, Caeleb, Cailab, Cal, Calab, Calabe, Callob, Calob, Calub, Calyb, Caylab, Cayleb, Caylebb

Caleb was from the house of Judah in the Bible. He and Joshua were the only two Israelite spies to return from Canaan and report that God could bring it into the Israelites' hands. Because the Hebrews didn't listen to them, they were forced to spend forty years in the desert. Joshua and Caleb were the only two adults allowed to live to enter into the Promised Land. Caleb is called "my servant" by God in Numbers 14:24, a position of the highest honor heretofore used only for Moses.

Calepodius Saint; Latin

St. Calepodius (d. 232) was a Roman priest who was martyred with several companions during the reign of Emperor Severus Alexander.

Caletricus Saint; Latin

St. Caletricus (d. 580) was bishop of Chartres, France.

Calimerius Saint; Latin; he who ushers in a beautiful day

St. Calimerius (d. 280) was a Greek educated in Rome. He was made bishop of Milan and was known as "the Apostle of the Valley of the Po River." He was martyred by being thrown head first into a well during the reign of Emperor Commodus. He is a patron invoked against drought.

Calixtus Saint; Greek; the best and most beautiful

Pope St. Callixtus I (d. 222) was a slave in his youth. After losing some of his master's money, he was sentenced to work in the mines of Sardinia. In time, he was released, and he became a deacon. Pope Zephyrinus put him in charge of the burial chambers along the Appian Way. He succeeded Zephyrinus as bishop of Rome. He died as a martyr.

Callinicus Saint; Latin; he who secures a beautiful victory

St. Callinicus (third century) was martyred by being burned to death in Gangra, Paphlagonia, in Asia Minor.

Calliopus Saint; Latin

St. Calliopus (d. 303) was martyred at Pompeiopolis by being crucified upside down.

Callisto Saint; Greek; most beautiful

St. Callisto Caravario (1903–1930) was born in Turin, Italy. He became a priest and served as a missionary in China. He was attacked by communist pirates and was shot while trying to protect young people who were with him. He was canonized in 2000 by Pope John Paul II.

Callistratus Saint; Latin; beautiful warrior

St. Callistratus (d. 300) was martyred along with forty-nine other soldiers in Constantinople. They were sewn into sacks and drowned in the sea.

Callistus Saint; Latin; most beautiful

St. Callistus, St. Callistus Caravario

St. Callistus (d. 1003) was born in Aragon, Spain. He went to France with St. Mercurialis, where he died fighting the Saracens.

Callob *see Caleb*

Calmin *see Calminius*

Calminius Saint; Latin; calm

Calmin

St. Calminius (d. 690), also known as Calmin, founded three French abbeys.

Calob *see Caleb*

Calocerus Saint; Latin

St. Calocerus (d. 130) was an officer in the Roman army and was stationed in Brescia in Lombardy, Italy. He preached the faith in Albenga and was martyred there.

Calogerus Saint; Latin; beautiful at old age

St. Calogerus (d. 486) lived as a hermit for over thirty years near Girgenti in Sicily. Known as "the Anchoret," he also served as a missionary on the isles of Lepari.

Calub *see Caleb*

Calupan Saint

St. Calupan (d. 575) was a monk of Meallot, in Auvergne, France. He later became a hermit, living in a cave.

Calyb *see Caleb*

Camelian Saint; English; camelia flower

St. Camelian (d. 525) was bishop of Troyes, France, from 478 until his death.

Cameran *see Cameron*

Camerin *see Cameron*

Cameron Top 100 Name; Scottish; crooked nose

Cameran, Camerin, Camerron, Camerun, Cameryn, Camiren, Camiron, Cammeron

St. Cameron (date unknown) was martyred for the faith in Cagliari, Italy.

Camerron *see Cameron*

Camerun *see Cameron*

Cameryn *see Cameron*

Camillus Saint; Latin; child born to freedom

St. Camillus de Lellis (d. 1607) was born in Bocchianico, Italy. He lost all his money because of gambling and entered the Capuchin order. He cared for the sick and became director of St. Giacomo Hospital in Rome. He then established a new order, the Ministers of the Sick, dedicated to caring for the ill. They served Holy Ghost Hospital in Rome, plague-stricken ships in Rome, and wounded troops in Hungary and Croatia. He is a patron of the sick, nurses, and doctors.

Camiren *see Cameron*

Camiron *see Cameron*

Cammeron *see Cameron*

Candidus Saint; Latin; pure, sincere

St. Candidus (d. 259) was martyred in Alexandria or Carthage with twenty other Africans.

Candres Saint

St. Candres (fifth century) was a missionary to Maastricht.

Canice Saint; Gaelic; handsome

Kenneth

St. Canice (515–600), also known as Kenneth, was a native of Glengiven, Ireland. He was a friend of St. Columba of Iona and witnessed many of that saint's miracles. He is known as one of the Twelve Apostles of Ireland and preached extensively throughout Ireland and Scotland. He was known as a man of virtue and learning.

Cannatus Saint

St. Cannatus (fifth century) was a bishop of Marseilles, France.

Cannen *see Kanten*

Canog Saint; Welsh

St. Canog (d. 492) was the eldest son of the king of Brecknock in Wales. He was martyred by barbarians at Merthyr-Cynog.

Cantianus Saint; Latin

St. Cantianus (d. 304), with his siblings St. Cantius and St. Cantianella, was a member of the Roman Anicii family, orphaned

as a child and raised by a Christian named Protus. After freeing their slaves and giving their money to the poor, he and his siblings fled to Aquileia, Italy, to escape Emperor Diocletian's persecution. They were captured at Aquae Gradatae and were beheaded.

Cantius Saint; Latin

St. Cantius (d. 304), with his siblings St. Cantianus and St. Cantianella, was a member of the Roman Anicii family, orphaned as a child and raised by a Christian named Protus. After freeing their slaves and giving their money to the poor, he and his siblings fled to Aquileia, Italy, to escape Emperor Diocletian's persecution. They were captured at Aquae Gradatae and were beheaded.

Canute Saint; Latin, Scandinavian; white haired, knot

King St. Canute IV, St. Canute Lavard

St. Canute Lavard (1096–1131) was the son of King Eric the Good of Denmark. He became the duke of Jutland and defended the area against the Vikings. He later became king of the Western Wends. His uncle, King Nils of Denmark, opposed this and had him killed by his cousin's bear Ringsted.

Caorlan *see Cairlon*

Capito Saint; Latin; big head

St. Capito (date unknown) was martyred with Meneus.

Caprais *see Caprasius*

Caprasius Saint; Latin; regarding the goat

Caprais

St. Caprasius (d. 430), also known as Caprais, was a hermit in Provence, France. Along with Sts. Honoratus and Venantius, he traveled to Greece to start a hermitage there. He also founded a monastery at Lerins.

Caradoc Saint; Welsh; love

St. Caradoc (d. 1124) was a Welsh hermit at St. Cendydd Church in Gower. He later moved to Barry Island at St. Issels. When King Henry I invaded the area, he went to Haroldston.

Carantac Saint; Welsh; victorious

Carrannog, Cairnech, Karanteg

St. Carantac (sixth century), also known as Carannog, Cairnech, and Karanteg, founded a church at Llangrannog, Wales, and a monastery at Cernach.

Caranus Saint

St. Caranus (seventh century) was a bishop who served in Eastern Scotland.

Caraunus Saint; Latin

Ceraunnus, Cheron

St. Caraunus (fifth century), also known as Cheron or Ceraunnus, was a Roman preacher in Gaul. He was killed by robbers near Chartres.

Carilefus Saint

St. Carilefus (d. 536) was born in Auvergne, France, and was raised at Menat Monastery near Riom. He was ordained at Micy Abbey. He lived as a hermit in Maine but attracted so many disciples that he needed to begin a monastery where he served as abbot.

Carl *see Karl*

Carlito *see Carlos*

Carlitos *see Carlos*

Carlos Saint; Top 100 Name; a form of Carlton; Spanish; Carl's town

Carlito, Carlitos, Carlus, Carolus, Charlos, Karlos

Bl. Carlos Manuel Rodriguez Santiago (1918–1963) was born in Caguas, Puerto Rico. He was a layman who served the Church as a catechist and choir manager and who helped promote the liturgical movement in Puerto Rico. He died of intestinal cancer. He was beatified in 2001 by Pope John Paul II.

Carlus *see Carlos*

Carman *see Carmel (girl's name)*

Carmel *see Carmel (girl's name)*

Carmen *see Carmel (girl's name)*

Carmon *see Carmel (girl's name)*

Carmyn *see Carmel (girl's name)*

Carnealous *see Cornelius*

Carnelius *see Cornelius*

Carolus *see Carlos*

Carponius Saint; Greek, Latin; valuable fruit

St. Carponius (d. 303) was martyred in Caesarea in Palestine during the reign of Emperor Diocletian. He died with his sister, Fortunata, and his brothers, Evaristus and Priscian.

Carpophorus Saint; Greek, Latin; he who carries nuts and dried fruit

St. Carpophorus (d. 300) was a priest martyred in either Spoleto, Italy, or Seville, Spain, during the reign of Emperor Diocletian.

Carpus Saint; Greek, Latin; fruit, fruitful

St. Carpus (d. 150) was bishop of Gurdos, Lydia. He was martyred in Pergamos with several companions.

Carrannog *see Carantac*

Carterius Saint; Greek; solid, sensible

St. Carterius (d. 304) was a priest martyred in Caesarea in Capadocia during the reign of Emperor Diocletian.

Carthach Saint; Gaelic; loving

Carthage

St. Carthach, St. Carthach the Younger

St. Carthach (d. 540), also known as Carthage, was an Irish bishop. He founded the monastery of Druim Fertain and another at Lough Sheelin, County Meath.

Carthage *see Carthach*

Cas *see Casimir*

Caseus *see Cassius*

Cashemere *see Casimir*

Cashi *see Casimir*

Cashmeire *see Casimir*

Cashmere *see Casimir*

Casimere *see Casimir*

Casimir Saint; Polish; peacemaker

Cachi, Cas, Cashemere, Cashi, Cashmeire, Cashmere, Casimere, Casimire, Casimiro, Castimer, Cazimier, Cazimir, Kasimir, Kazio, Kazmer

St. Casimir (1461–1484) was a Polish prince, the second son of King Casimir IV and Elizabeth of Austria. From his youth, he rejected the trappings of castle life. He wore plain clothes, slept little, and dedicated his life to prayer. He obeyed the wishes of his father and led a campaign to take over the Hungarian throne. He felt it was wrong, however, and was happy to go home when the mission failed. His father exiled him, sending him to Dobski. Casimir also rejected a marriage alliance his father had formed for him. He died at the age of twenty-three from lung disease. He is the patron saint of Poland and Lithuania.

Casimire *see Casimir*

Casimiro *see Casimir*

Casius *see Cassius*

Caspar Saint; Persian; treasurer

Kaspar

St. Caspar del Bufalo (1786–1837) was born in Rome and became a priest. When Napoleon invaded Rome, Caspar was exiled for refusing to give up his allegiance to the pope. He returned to Rome after the fall of Napoleon. He founded the Congregation of the Most Precious Blood. The pope asked him to establish six houses in Naples, a crime-filled area. He was known for his dramatic preaching style and as a miracle worker.

Casshus *see Cassius*

Cassia *see Cassius*

Cassian Saint; Latin; empty, poor, robbed

St. Cassian of Autun, St. Cassian of Benevento, St. Cassian of Imola, St. Cassian of Tangier St. Cassian of Tangier (d. 298) was a court recorder at the trial of St. Marcellus the Centurion. When St. Marcellus was given the death penalty, Cassian declared that he was a Christian as well. He was beheaded and is the patron of modern stenographers.

Cassio *see Cassius*

Cassius Saint; Latin, French; box, protective cover

Caseus, Casius, Casshus, Cassia, Cassio, Cazzie, Cazzius, Kasius, Kassio, Kassius, Kazzius

St. Cassius (d. 303) was martyred with Florentius and other companions at Bonn, Germany, during the persecution of Coemperor Maximian.

Castar *see Castor*

Caster *see Castor*

Castimer *see Casimir*

Castir *see Castor*

Caston *see Castor*

Castor Saint; Greek; beaver

Castar, Caster, Castir, Caston, Costard, Coster, Kastar, Kaster, Kastor, Kastyr

St. Castor (d. 420) was born in Nimes, France. He became a lawyer and married a wealthy widow. With her permission, he entered religious life, and she joined a nunnery. He started Monanque Monastery in Provence, where he served as abbot.

Castorius Saint; Greek, Latin; beaver

St. Castorius (third century) was one of four carvers at Sirmium (Mitrovica, Yugoslavia) who came to the attention to Emperor Diocletian. He commissioned them to complete several carvings, which they did, but they refused to carve a statue of Aesculapius because of their Christian beliefs. When they refused to sacrifice to the gods, they were imprisoned. They were later executed. St. Castorius is the patron saint of sculptors, stonemasons, and stonecutters.

Castritian Saint; Italian

St. Castritian (third century) was a bishop of Milan, Italy, for forty-two years.

Castulus Saint; Latin; chaste

St. Castulus (d. 286) was a chamberlain of Emperor Diocletian. He sheltered Christians in his home and provided for religious services inside the palace. When this activity was discovered, he was brought before the prefect of the city. He was tortured and then buried alive.

Castus Saint; Latin; chaste

St. Castus (d. 250) was taken prisoner twice as a Christian. The first time, he denied Christ while he was being tortured, and he was released. The second time, he did not waiver in his faith and was burned to death. He was praised by St. Augustine of Hippo.

Catald Saint; Greek; outstanding in war

St. Catald (400–480) was an Irish monk who taught at Lismore. He resigned that position and made a pilgrimage to Jerusalem. On his return trip, he stopped at the Italian city of Taranto, where he was named bishop. He is known as a miracle worker.

Catan *see Cathan*

Catellus Saint; Latin; puppy

St. Catellus (ninth century) was a friend of St. Antoninus of Sorrento. Catellus became a bishop of Castellamore, Italy, but he really wanted to be a hermit. He lived at Monte Aureo and cared for his diocese on a sporadic basis. With St. Antoninus, he established the stone oratory known as Monte San Angelo.

Cathan Saint; Celtic; little battle

Catan, Cattan

St. Cathan (sixth or seventh century), also known as Catan

or Cattan, was one of the first Irish missionaries to come to the Isle of Bute, where he served as bishop. He was the uncle of St. Blane.

Cathmael *see Cadoc*

Cathroe *see Cadroe*

Cattan *see Cathan*

Catulinus Saint; Latin; little dog

St. Catulinus (date unknown) was a deacon martyred in Carthage with several companions.

Cawrdaf Saint; Welsh

St. Cawrdaf (sixth century) was a Welsh chief who later entered a monastery.

Caylab *see Caleb*

Cayleb *see Caleb*

Caylebb *see Caleb*

Cazimier *see Casimir*

Cazimir *see Casimir*

Cazzie *see Cassius*

Cazzius *see Cassius*

Ceadd *see Chad*

Ceallach Saint; Gaelic; bright headed

Celsus, Kellach

St. Ceallach (sixth century), also known as Kellach or Celsus, was a bishop of Killala, Ireland. He lived as a hermit later in life and may have died a martyr.

Cearan Saint; Gaelic; bright, famous

Ciaran

St. Cearan (d. 870), also known as Ciaran, was an abbot of Belluch-Duin in Ireland.

Cecil *see Cecilia (girl's name)*

Cedd Saint; English

St. Cedd (620–664) preached among the Middle Angles. After being ordained, he served as a missionary to Essex. He became bishop and founded several monasteries. He also became abbot of the monastery of Lastingham. He died of the plague.

Ceferino Saint; Greek; he who caresses the wind

Bl. Ceferino Jimenez Malla (1861–1936) was born in Catalonia, Spain. He was uneducated and joined the Church as an adult. He became a mule-trader and settled in Barbastro. He became a city councilman, catechist, Eucharistic minister, choir director, and Rosary leader. He became a Dominican tertiary in 1926. He was arrested during the Spanish Civil War for hiding priests and was shot by a firing squad. He was beatified in 1997 by Pope John Paul II.

Céin *see Cian*

Ceitho Saint; Welsh

St. Ceitho (sixth century) is a Welsh saint who founded a church in Liangeith in Dyfed. He lived as a hermit.

Cele Saint; Latin; celestial, heavenly

St. Cele-Christ (d. 728) was the bishop of Leinster, England.

Celerinus Saint; Latin; fast

St. Celerinus (d. 250) suffered during the persecutions of Emperor Trajunus Decius in Rome. After he was freed, he went to Carthage where he was ordained a deacon by St. Cyprian.

Celestine Saint; Latin; celestial, heavenly

Celestino, Celestyn, Selestin, Selestine, Selestyn

Pope St. Celestine I (d. 432) was born in Campania. He lived with St. Ambrose in Milan for a time. He served as a deacon. He was elected pope in 422. He fought against Pelagianism in Gaul and England. He sent Palladius to evangelize Ireland.

Celestino *see Celestine*

Celestyn *see Celestine*

Cellach Saint; Celtic; war

St. Cellach (1080–1129) was a Benedictine monk who taught at Oxford, England, until 1106, when he was made archbishop of Armagh. He became a priest, ending the policy that had been in place since 966 that the head of the Irish church had to be a layman.

Celsus *see Ceallach*

Censurius Saint; Latin; critic

St. Censurius (d. 486) succeeded St. Germanus as the bishop of Auxerre, France.

Ceolfrid Saint; Teutonic; God's peace

St. Ceolfrid (642–716) was born in Northumbria. He joined

the monastery at Ripon. He went with St. Benedict Biscop to Rome in 675 and was later named abbot of St. Paul's in Wearmouth. He developed the monastery into a cultural center. The oldest known copy of the Vulgate Bible in one volume was produced under his direction. He was the warden of St. Bede from the age of seven. When he retired, he set off for Rome, but died en route.

Ceollach Saint; Celtic

St. Ceollach (seventh century) was an Irish bishop of the Mercians in England. He died in Ireland.

Ceolwulf Saint; English

St. Ceolwulf (d. 764) was King of Northumbria, England. He gave up the throne and became a monk, entering the monastery at Lindisfarne. St. Bede dedicated his eccelesiastical history to him.

Ceratius Saint

St. Ceratius (fifth century) was bishop of Grenoble and was present at the Council of Orange in 441.

Ceraunus Saint; Greek, Latin; thunder

St. Ceraunus (d. 614) was bishop of Paris, France.

Ceraunnus *see Caraunus*

Cerbonius Saint; Latin

St. Cerbonius (493–575) succeeded St. Regulas as bishop of Populonia. When King Totila of the Ostragoths invaded

Tuscany, he had Cerbonius arrested and sentenced to death for hiding Roman soldiers. The bear that was supposed to kill him instead licked his feet. The king exiled Cerbonius instead, sending him to Elba, where he lived out his days.

Cerek *see Cyril*

Cerel *see Cyril*

Ceril *see Cyril*

Cerneuf *see Serenus*

Ceslas *see Czeslaw*

Cettin Saint

St. Cettin (fifth century) was a bishop who worked with St. Patrick.

Cewydd Saint; Welsh; giant

St. Cewydd (sixth century) is associated with Anglesey, Wales.

Chaad *see Chad*

Chad Saint; English; warrior

Ceadd, Chaad, Chaddi, Chaddie, Chaddy, Chade, Chadleigh, Chadler, Chadley, Chadlin, Chadlyn, Chadmen, Chado, Chadrick, Chadron, Chadryk, Chady

St. Chad (634–672) was a younger brother of St. Cedd. He was taught by St. Aidan in Lindisfarne and England. In time, he was made archbishop of York. Theodore, the archbishop of Canterbury, accused him of impropriety. But Theodore was so won over by his behavior that he named Chad bishop of Mercia.

Chaddi *see Chad*

Chad *see Chad*

...y *see Chad*

Chade *see Chad*

Chadleigh *see Chad*

Chadler *see Chad*

Chadley *see Chad*

Chadlin *see Chad*

Chadlyn *see Chad*

Chadmen *see Chad*

Chado *see Chad*

Chadrick *see Chad*

Chadron *see Chad*

Chadryk *see Chad*

Chady *see Chad*

Chaeromon Saint

St. Chaeromon (d. 250) was bishop of Nilopolis, Egypt. An elderly man, he fled to the Arabian Desert to escape the persecutions of Emperor Trajanus Decius. He is considered a martyr.

Chaffre *see Theofrid*

Chagnoald *see Cagnoald*

Chainaldus Saint

St. Chainaldus (d. 633) became a monk at Luxeuil. He accompanied St. Columban on his missionary efforts. He later became bishop of Laon and attended the Council of Reims, France, in 630.

Chanton Saint; French; we sing

St. Chanton (d. 303) was martyred during the reign of Emperor Diocletian.

Charalampias Saint

St. Charalampias (d. 203) was a priest martyred in Asia Minor during the persecution of Emperor Septimus Severus.

Charbel Saint; Syrian; the story of God

St. Charbel (1828–1898) was born Youssef Antoun Makhlouf in North Lebanon. He joined Our Lady of Maifouk Monastery and then St. Maron Monastery in Annaya, where he took the name Charbel. He was ordained a priest and lived for sixteen years in the monastery before becoming a hermit. He died twenty-three years later on Christmas Eve. A few months later, dazzling lights were seen around his grave, and pilgrims began flocking to the site. Many miracles were attributed to him.

Chareles *see Charles*

Charels *see Charles*

Charisius Saint

St. Charisius (third century) was martyred by drowning at Corinth, Greece.

Charl *see Charles*

Charle *see Charles*

Charlen *see Charles*

Charles Saint; Top 100 Name; German, English; farmer, strong and manly

Arlo, Chareles, Charels, Charl, Charle, Charlen, Charlese, Charlot, Charlz, Charlzell, Xarles

St. Charles Borromeo, St. Charles Garnier, St. Charles Hoyn Song-mun, St. Charles Joseph Eugene de Mazenod, St. Charles Lwanga and

Companions, St. Charles of Sezze, St. Charles of Mount Argus

St. Charles Borromeo (1538–1584) was the son of Count Gilbert Borromeo and Margaret Medici, sister of Pope Pius IV. He entered the Benedictine Abbey of Sts. Gratian and Felinus at Arona when he was twelve. He served Pope Pius IV as a cardinal and administrator of Milan. He also helped the pope reconvene the Council of Trent and was influential in that session. He oversaw the creation of the catechism, missal, and breviary that came out of that council. He is a patron of learning and the arts.

Charlese see Charles

Charlos see Carlos

Charlot see Charles

Charlz see Charles

Charlzell see Charles

Cheledonius Saint; Phoenician; new town

St. Cheledonius (fourth century) was from Spain and was martyred at Calahorra, Old Castile.

Chencho see Lorenzo

Cheron see Caraunus

Chi Saint; Chinese, Nigerian; younger generation, personal guardian angel

St. Chi Zhuze (d. 1900) is one of the Martyrs of China canonized by Pope John Paul II in 2000. He was eighteen years old at the time of his death.

Chillien Saint

St. Chillien (seventh century) was a relative of St. Fiacre. He was from Ireland but served as a missionary in Artois, France.

Chirstian Saint; form of Christian; Greek; follower of Christ

St. Chirstian (d. 1138) was the brother of St. Malachy of Armagh. He was named bishop of Clogher, Ireland.

Chretien see Christian

Chris see Christopher

Chrisopherson see Christopher

Christé see Christian

Christepher see Christopher

Christerpher see Christopher

Christhoper see Christopher

Christiaan see Christian

Christian Saint; Top 100 Name; Greek; follower of Christ

Chretien, Christia, Christé, Christiaan, Christinana, Christiane, Christiann, Christianna, Christianno, Christiano, Christianos, Christino, Christion, Christon, Christyan, Christyon, Chritian, Chrystain, Chrystian, Crystek

Bl. Christian O'Conarchy (d. 1186) was the abbot of the first Cistercian monastery established in Ireland. Little is known of his life, but he may have been bishop of Lismore and papal legate for Ireland.

Christianno see Christian

Christiano see Christian

Christianos see Christian

Christino see Christian

on *see Christian*

ipher *see Christopher*

Christo *see Christopher*

Christobal *see Christopher*

Christof *see Christopher*

Christoher *see Christopher*

Christon *see Christian*

Christopher Saint; Top 100 Name; Greek; Christ-bearer

> *Chris, Chrisopherson, Christepher, Christerpher, Christhoper, Christipher, Christo, Christobal, Christof, Christoher, Christopherr, Christophor, Christophr, Christophre, Christophyer, Christophyr, Christorpher, Christovao, Christpher, Christphere, Christphor, Christpor, Christrpher, Chrystopher, Kristopher, Topher*

St. Christopher (third century) is a martyr whose life is mostly legendary. He wanted to serve the greatest king there was. He served the king of Canaan, but when he saw him make the Sign of the Cross at the mention of the devil, he learned there was a higher king. Christopher went to search for the devil, but then he learned that the devil feared Christ, so he went out to find him. A hermit instructed Christopher in the faith and suggested that the large man could serve Christ by carrying people across a dangerous river. One day, a little child asked to be carried across. The child seemed unusually heavy. The child told Christopher, "You had on your shoulders not only the whole world but him who made it." Christopher was beheaded at Lycia.

Christopherr *see Christopher*

Christophor *see Christopher*

Christophr *see Christopher*

Christophre *see Christopher*

Christophyer *see Christopher*

Christophyr *see Christopher*

Christorpher *see Christopher*

Christovao *see Christopher*

Christpher *see Christopher*

Christphere *see Christopher*

Christphor *see Christopher*

Christpor *see Christopher*

Christrpher *see Christopher*

Christyan *see Christian*

Christyon *see Christian*

Chritian *see Christian*

Chromatius Saint; Greek

> St. Chromatius (d. 406) was from Aquileia, Italy. As a priest, he took part in the Synod of Aquileia that condemned Arianism. Later, he was named bishop of that area. He was a friend of St. Jerome, who described Chromatius as "a most learned and holy man." He was also a defender of St. John Chrysostom.

Chrysanthus Saint; Greek

> St. Chrysanthus, St. Chrysanthus Eunuchus

> St. Chrysanthus (d. 283) was the son of an Egyptian noble named Polemius. His father brought him to Rome where, despite his father's objections,

he was baptized. He married Daria, whom he brought to the faith. The two maintained vows of chastity and worked to bring many to the Christian faith. Both were arrested, tortured, and ultimately buried alive.

Chrysogonus Saint; Greek

St. Chrysogonus (fifth century) was a priest beheaded at Aquileia.

Chrysolius Saint; Greek

St. Chrysolius (fourth century) was a native of Armenia who fled to Rome during the persecution of Emperor Diocletian. Pope Marcellus I sent him to northeast Gaul as a missionary. He was then named a bishop. He was arrested and beheaded. He is the patron saint of Komen, Belgium.

Chrysoteins Saint; Greek

St. Chrysoteins

St. Chrysoteins (d. 250) was a priest who was beheaded for the faith. He was martyred in Babylon during the reign of Emperor Trajanus Decius.

Chrystian *see Christian*

Chrystopher *see Christopher*

Chuniald Saint; Celtic

St. Chuniald (seventh century) was a missionary working in southern Germany and Austria. He worked with St. Gislar and was a disciple of St. Rupert of Salzburg.

Cian Saint; Celtic; ancient

Céin, Cianán, Cyan, Kian

St. Cian (sixth century) lived as a hermit in Caernarvonshire, Wales.

Cianan Saint; form of Cian; Celtic; ancient

St. Cianan (d. 489) was descended from the kings of Munster and was a pupil of Nathan. He was one of fifty hostages the princes of Ireland gave to King Leogair. After being freed, he traveled to France and then returned home, where he converted many. He established a church in Leinster and another in Owen.

Cianán *see Cian*

Ciaran *see Cearan*

Cillene Saint; Celtic; a church

St. Cillene (d. 752) was from Ireland. He served as an abbot in Iona, Scotland.

Cillian *see Kilian*

Cindeus Saint; Greek; one who escapes danger

St. Cindeus (d. 300) was a priest who was burned at the stake in Asia Minor.

Ciprian *see Cyprian*

Cipriano *see Cyprian*

Ciprien *see Cyprian*

Ciril *see Cyril*

Cirilio *see Ciril*

Cirilio *see Ciril*

Cirill *see Cyril*

Cirillo *see Cirilo*

Cirilo Saint; form of Cyril; Greek, Italian; lordly

Cirilio, Cirillo, Cyrilo, Cyryllo, Cyrylo, Kiril, Kiryl, Kyrillos

St. Cirilo Bertrán (1888–1934) was a member of the Brothers of the Christian Schools and was director of his house in Turón, Asturias, Spain. He is one of the Martyrs of Turón who were killed during the Spanish Civil War. He was canonized by Pope John Paul II in 1999.

Cirrillo *see Cyril*

Cissa Saint; Swedish; blind, sixth

St. Cissa (seventh century) was a Benedictine hermit who lived near Lindisfarne, England.

Citanus *see Clether*

Cittinus Saint

St. Cittinus (d. 180) was beheaded in northwestern Africa under Vigellius, the first Christian persecutor.

Clarus Saint; Latin; clean, transparent

St. Clarus (d. 875) was born in Rochester, England. He went to Normandy, where he became a Benedictine monk. He then lived as a hermit at Naqueville, near Rouen. He was beheaded for refusing the advances of a noblewoman.

Clateus Saint; Greek, Latin; honored

St. Clateus (d. 64) was one of the first bishops of Brescia, Italy. He was martyred during the persecution of Emperor Nero.

Claud Saint; form of Claude; Latin; lame

St. Claud (d. 699) was born to a senatorial family in Franche-Comté. He served as a priest in Besancon for twelve years before joining the Monastery of Condate in the Jura mountains. He later served as abbot, during which time he enforced the Rule of St. Benedict. In 685, he was named bishop of Besancon, a position he held for seven years before retiring back to the monastery.

Claudan *see Claude*

Claudanus *see Claude*

Claude Saint; Latin; lame

Claudan, Claudanus, Claudel, Claudell, Claudi, Claudian, Claudianus, Claudien, Claudin, Claudis, Claudy

St. Claude La Columbriere (1641–1682) was born to French nobles. He joined the Jesuits, where he served with distinction. He became the spiritual director of St. Margaret Mary Alacoque and helped promote devotion to the Sacred Heart of Jesus. In 1676, he was sent to England, where he served Mary of Modena, Duchess of York, who later became queen. He was an active missionary during his time there. He was arrested for being a conspirator to the English throne and was exiled. He spent the last two years of his life in Lyon. He was canonized by Pope John Paul II in 1992.

Claudel *see Claude*

Claudell *see Claude*

Claudey *see Claude*

Claudi *see Claude*

Claudian *see Claude*

Claudianus *see Claude*

Claudien *see Claude*

Claudin *see Claude*

Claudio Saint; form of Claude; Latin; lame

Bl. Claudio Granzotto (1900–1947) was born into a peasant farming family in Treviso, Italy. He was the youngest of nine children, and his father died when he was nine. He was drafted into the Italian army at age fifteen and served in it for three years. He then attended the Academy of Fine Arts in Venice, Italy. He joined the Order of Friars Minor and was known for his prayer, his artistic ability, and his service to poor. He died of a brain tumor. He was beatified in 1994 by Pope John Paul II.

Claudis *see Claude*

Claudy *see Claude*

Cleatus *see Cletus*

Cledis *see Cletus*

Cleer *see Clether*

Clement Saint, New Testament; Latin; mild, good, merciful

Clementius, Clemmons

St. Clement Maria Hofbauer, St. Clement of Alexandria, St. Clement of Okhrida, Pope St. Clement I of Rome

Pope St. Clement I (d. 100?) was one of the first popes. Some lists have him as second, while others list him as fourth. Relatively little is known of him, but he was a disciple of St. Peter and possibly St. Paul. During his pontificate, there was a schism at Corinth, which inspired him to write to that community. He asserted the authority of the presbyters as rulers of the church.

Clemente Saint; form of Clement; Latin, Italian, Spanish; mild, good, merciful

Clemento, Clemenza, Klemens

Bl. Clemente Marchisio (1833–1903) was born in Cuneo, Italy. He became a priest in Turin and founded the Institute of the Daughters of St. Joseph. He was beatified in 1984 by Pope John Paul II.

Clementinus Saint; form of Clement; Latin; mild, good, merciful

St. Clementinus (date unknown) was martyred with Theodotus and Philornenus in Heraclea, Thrace.

Clementius *see Clement*

Clemento *see Clemente*

Clementa *see Clemente*

Clemenza *see Clemente*

Clemmons *see Clement*

Cleodus *see Clether*

Cleonicus Saint; Greek; famous

St. Cleonicus (d. 308) was martyred with several companions by Emperor Galerius in the province of Pontus on the Black Sea.

Cleophas Saint, New Testament; Greek; glory of his father

St. Cleophas (first century) was one of the two disciples who met Christ on the road to Emmaus. He was the father of one of the Marys who stood at the foot of the Cross and may also have been the father of St. James the Less and a brother of St. Joseph.

Cleotis *see Cletus*

Clerus Saint; Latin; lot, share

St. Clerus (d. 300) was a Syrian deacon martyred in Antioch.

Clete *see Cletus*

Clether Saint; Welsh; famous

Citanus, Cleer, Cleodus, Clydog

St. Clether (d. 520), also known as Cleer, Clydog, Citanus, or Cleodus, was a descendent of a Welsh king. He went to England, where he was martyred.

Cletis *see Cletus*

Cletus Saint; Greek; illustrious

Anacletus, Cleatus, Cledis, Cleotis, Clete, Cletis, Cleytus, Kletos

Pope St. Cletus (d. 92), also known as St. Anacletus, was the third pope, after St. Peter and St. Linus. Tradition holds that during his papacy he divided Rome into twenty-five parishes.

Cleytis *see Cletus*

Clicerius Saint; Greek; sweet

St. Clicerius (d. 438) was a bishop of Milan, Italy.

Clinius Saint; Latin

St. Clinius (date unknown) was born in Greece and served as an abbot at the Benedictine Abbey of Monte Cassino, Italy. He also served as superior of St. Peter's near Pontecorvo.

Clodoald Saint; Teutonic; illustrious captain

Cloud

St. Clodoald (522–560), also known as Cloud, was a grandson of King Clovis of the Franks and a son of King Clodomir of Orleans. St. Clotilda, his grandmother, raised him. His uncle, Clotaire, had two of his brothers killed while they were still children. Clodoald escaped by being sent to Provence, France. He became a hermit. He is a patron saint of nail makers and of St. Cloud, Minnesota.

Clodulf Saint; German; glory

St. Clodulf (605–697) was the son of St. Arnulf. He married Goda, with whom he had a son, Aunulf. Goda became a nun when Clodulf was ordained. He was named bishop of Metz and held that office for forty years.

Cloud *see Clodoald*

Clydog *see Clether*

Codratus Saint; Latin; fourth

Quadratus

St. Codratus, St. Codratus of Corinth

St. Codratus of Corinth (d. 258), also known as Quadratus, grew up in the wild after his mother died during Emperor Trajanus Decius's persecution of Christians. He was arrested during the reign of Valerian. He was given to wild animals, but they would not touch him, so he was beheaded.

Coelchu *see Colga*

Coenraad *see Conrad*

Cofen *see Govan*

Cogitosus Saint; Celtic

St. Cogitosus (eighth century) was a monk of Kildare, Ireland, who wrote a biography of St. Brigid.

Colemann *see Colman*

Colga Saint; Celtic; thorn, sword

Coelchu

St. Colga (d. 789), also known as Coelchu, was the abbot of the monastic school of Clonmacnoise, Ireland. He was dedicated to the teachings of St. Paul and studied them intently. He may have had visions from that saint as well. He wrote a prayer in which the apostles, evangelists, saints, angels, prophets, and patriarchs beg for mercy and forgiveness from God.

Colgan Saint; Celtic; thorn, sword

St. Colgan (d. 796) was a friend of Bl. Alcuin and served as an abbot of Clanmacroise in Offaly, Ireland. He was known as "the Wise" and "the Chief Scribe of the Scots."

Colin *see Culen*

Colman Saint; Latin, English; cabbage farmer, coal miner

Colemann, Koleman

St. Colman McRhoi, St. Colman of Armagh, St. Colman of Cloyne, St. Colman of Dromore,

St. Colman of Elo, St. Colman of Glendalough, St. Colman of Kilmacduagh, St. Colman of Kilroot, St. Colman of Lindisfarne, St. Colman of Lismore, St. Colman of Stockerau

St. Colman of Cloyne (522–600) was born in Munster, Ireland. He was a poet and served as the royal bard at Cashel. When he was fifty years old, he was baptized by St. Brendan and became a priest. He, in turn, taught St. Columba. He was named the first bishop of Cloyne in eastern Cork.

Colombe *see Columba*

Columb *see Columba*

Columba Saint; Latin; dove

Colombe, Columb, Columbe, Columbia, Columbina, Columbinah, Columbine, Columbyna, Columbynah, Columbyne, Colym

St. Columba, St. Columba Kim Hyo-im, St. Columba of Sens

St. Columba (521–597) was born into a noble family in Donegal, Ireland. He was ordained and spent fifteen years preaching and setting up foundations. Because of a family feud, he left Ireland and traveled to Iona, Scotland. He started what became a very well-known monastery there and established a monastic rule that was followed by many, prior to the establishment of St. Benedict's Rule. He is one of the Twelve Apostles of Ireland and is a patron saint of Derry, floods, bookbinders, poets, Ireland, and Scotland.

Columban Saint; Latin; dove

Columbanus

St. Columban (559–615) was born in Leinster, Ireland. He was educated by Sinell, abbot of Cluaininis in Lough Erne, and Abbott Congall in Bangor, County Down, Northern Ireland, but he wanted to leave Ireland. At the age of thirty, he set out for Gaul with twelve other monks. There, he preached the faith. King Gontram of Burgandy offered him a Roman castle at Annegray for him and his monks. The number of monks grew and they were forced to seek additional space. They found it at Luxeuil. Many years later, due to political difficulties, he sought refuge in Milan, where he spoke out against the Arian heresy. He also founded a monastery at Bobbio, where he died.

Columbanus *see Columban*

Columbe *see Columba*

Columbine *see Columba*

Columbinus Saint; Latin; dove

St. Columbinus (d. 680) was a Benedictine abbot at Lure, in the Vosges, France.

Columbyna *see Columba*

Columbynah *see Columba*

Columbyne *see Columba*

Colym *see Columba*

Comgall Saint; Celtic

St. Comgall (516–601) was born in Ylster, Ireland. He served as a soldier, then studied at Clonard with St. Finian and at Clonmacnoise with St. Ciaran. He followed a very austere form of monastic life for a few years. He then established a monastery at Bangor, where he served as abbot of eight thousand monks. He accompanied St. Columba as a missionary to Scotland, where he founded a monastery at Heth. He died at Bangor.

Comgan Saint; Gaelic; twin

St. Comgan (eighth century) was the son of a prince of Leinster, Ireland. His brother was St. Kentigern. After being wounded in battle, he fled to Scotland. He settled in Lochaise, where he built a monastery.

Cominus Saint; Latin; common, universal

St. Cominus (date unknown) was an Irish abbot who is the patron saint of Ardcavan, Ireland.

Conall Saint; Gaelic, Scottish; strong wolf

St. Conall (seventh century) was abbot of Inniscoel Monastery in County Donegal, Ireland.

Conan Saint; Gaelic, Scottish; praised, exalted, wise

Conant, Conary, Connen, Connon, Konan

St. Conan (d. 648) was from Scotland. He taught St. Fiacre and then traveled as a missionary to the Isle of Man, where he was made bishop.

Conant *see Conan*

Conar *see Conor*

Conary *see Conan*

Concordius Saint; Latin; harmony, union

St. Concordius (ca. 178) was a subdeacon who, during the reign of Marcus Aurelius, was arrested in the desert and brought before Torquatus, governor of Umbria. Even while being beaten with clubs and stretched on the rack, he cheerfully sang, "Glory be to thee, Lord Jesus!" Three days later, soldiers were sent to behead him in the dungeon unless he worshipped an idol. In response, Concordius spit on the idol and was rewarded with martyrdom.

Conde *see Condedus*

Condede *see Condedus*

Condedus Saint; Latin; count, companion

Conde, Condede

St. Condedus (d. 685), also known as Conde or Condede, was from Briton. He became a hermit at Fontaine Saint Valery, France, and later entered the Benedictine Monastery at Fontanelle. He later resumed his life as a hermit, this time settling on the island of Belcinae in the Seine near Caudebec. King Therry III gave him an island on which he built two chapels.

Coner *see Conor*

Conlaid *see Conleth*

Conlaith *see Conleth*

Conleth Saint; Celtic; chaste fire

Conlaid, Conlaith

St. Conleth (d. 519), also known as Conlaith or Conlad, lived as a hermit at Old Connell on the Liffey. St. Brigid asked him to serve as spiritual director for her community. He became the first bishop of Kildare in 490. He was known as a skilled illuminator of manuscripts. He was killed by wolves on a pilgrimage to Rome.

Conn Saint; Gaelic; chief

Bl. Conn O'Rourke (1549–1579) was born in Breifne, Ireland. He became a Franciscan priest and was martyred. He was beatified in 1992 by Pope John Paul II.

Connen *see Conan*

Conner *see Conor*

Connon *see Conan*

Connor *see Conor*

Conny *see Cornelius*

Conogon Saint

St. Conogon (d. 460) was a bishop in Brittany, France.

Conon Saint; Greek; dust

St. Conon, St. Conon of Naso

St. Conan (d. 275) was the name of both a father and twelve-year-old son martyred at Iconium in Asia Minor. They were roasted over a fire and killed on the rack.

Conor Saint; Gaelic; lover of hounds

Conar, Coner, Conner, Connor,
Conour, Konner

Bl. Conor O'Devany (1532–
1612) was an Irish Franciscan
priest who became the bishop
of Down and Connor. He was
martyred by English authorities
in Dublin in 1612 on a trumped-
up charge of treason. He was
offered a pardon if he denied
his Catholic faith, which he
steadfastly refused to do. He is
one of the Irish Catholic Martyrs who were beatified in 1992
by Pope John Paul II.

Conour *see Conor*

Conrad Saint; German; brave
counselor

Coenraad, Conrade, Konrad

St. Conrad, St. Conrad of Par-
zham, St. Conrad of Trier

St. Conrad (d. 975) was the
son of Count Henry of Alt-
dorf. After being ordained,
he was made provost of Constance Cathedral and then was
named bishop of Constance.
He was very generous, giving
his inheritance to the Church
and the poor. He was friends
with Emperor Otto I, whom he
accompanied to Italy in 962. He
founded a number of churches
and a hospital at Kreuzlingen.

Conrade *see Conrad*

Conran Saint; Gaelic, Scottish

St. Conran (date unknown) was
a bishop of the Orkney Islands
in Scotland.

Considine *see Constantine*

Constabilis Saint; Latin;
established

St. Constabilis (1070–1124) was
born in Lucania to a noble family. From the age of seven, he
studied under St. Leo at Cava
Monastery near Salerno. He
later became abbot of that monastery. He founded the town
of Castelabte and is its patron
saint.

Constadine *see Constantine*

Constandine *see Constantine*

Constandios *see Constantine*

Constans *see Constantine*

Constanstine *see Constantine*

Constant *see Constantine*

Constantian Saint; Latin; firm,
constant

Constantianus

St. Constantian (d. 570), also
known as Constantianus, was
a monk at Micy, France. He then
lived as a hermit in the forest
of Nuz. St. Innocent, bishop
of Le Mans, asked him to be
ordained so that he could minister to the people of the area.
He was known for his holiness
and as a miracle worker. He
attracted many followers, and
he founded Javron Abbey.

Constantianus *see Constantian*

Constantin *see Constantine*

Constantine Saint; Latin; firm,
constant

Considine, Constadine, Constan-
dine, Constandios, Constans, Con-
stanstine, Constant, Constantin,
Constantinos, Constantinus,

Constantios, Costa, Costandinos, Costantinos

St. Constantine, St. Constantine the Great

St. Constantine the Great (272–337) was the son of Constantius I Chlorus and St. Helena. When his father died, he was named junior emperor of York, England. After defeating his main rivals, he became a ruler of the Roman Empire. He fought with the insignia of Christ on his banners. He and Coemperor Licinius issued the Edict of Milan in 313, which allowed Christianity to be practiced freely. Constantine presided over the Council of Nicaea and founded the city of Constantinople. He was baptized on his deathbed.

Constantinos *see Constantine*

Constantinus *see Constantine*

Constantios *see Constantine*

Constantius Saint; Latin; constant, steadfast

St. Constantius (d. 520) was a bishop of Aquino, Italy.

Contardo Saint; Teutonic; he who is daring and valiant

St. Contardo (d. 1294) was a member of the Este family of Ferrara, Italy. He is known as "the Pilgrim." He died in Broni, while on pilgrimage to Compostela, Spain. Miracles were reported at his grave.

Contentius Saint; Latin; happy, content

St. Contentius (d. 510) was a bishop of Bayeux, France.

Conus Saint; Latin

St. Conus (d. 1200) was born in Diano, Italy. He joined the Benedictine monastery at St. Maria di Cadossa. He was known for his holiness and died at a young age. He is a patron saint of Teggiano, Italy.

Conval *see Conwall*

Convoyon Saint

St. Convoyon (d. 868) was born into a family that was descended from Roman senators. He was an archdeacon of Vannes and then took up life as a hermit. He later became a Benedictine monk and established St. Savior Monastery near Redon. He was driven out of the abbey by Norsemen.

Conwall Saint; Scottish

Conval

St. Conwall (d. 630), also known as Conval, was a priest and a disciple of St. Kentigern. He preached and worked in Scotland.

Corbican Saint; Gaelic

St. Corbican (eighth century) was an Irish hermit from the area now known as the Netherlands, Belgium, and Luxembourg. He spent his life educating the local peasants.

Corbinian Saint; Latin; raven, crow

St. Corbinian (670–730) was born at Châtres. As an adult, he lived in that area as a hermit for fourteen years. He soon attracted a following. He decided to travel to Rome with some of his disciples. Pope Gregory II sent him to Friesling, in Bavaria, Germany, as a bishop. He founded a monastery and a school. He incurred the wrath of the local duke, Grimoald, by criticizing his marriage. Grimoald's wife tried to have him killed, and he fled the area. He returned to Friesling after Grimoald died. He is a patron saint of Munich, Germany.

Corbmac Saint; Gaelic; charioteer

St. Corbmac (sixth century) was a disciple of St. Columba, who made him abbot of Durrow Monastery.

Corebus Saint; Latin; fool

St. Corebus (d. 138) was a prefect of Messina, on Sicily. He was martyred during the persecution of Emperor Hadrian.

Corentin Saint; Latin; he who helps

Corentinus, Corentius, Cury

St. Corentin (d. 460) was a hermit at Plomodiern. He was later named the first bishop of Cornouaille, now known as Quimper, Brittany. He is regarded as one of the seven founder saints of Brittany. He is a patron saint of Cornouaille, Brittany, and of seafood.

Corentinus *see Corentin*

Corentius *see Corentin*

Cormac Saint; Gaelic; raven's son

Cormack, Cormick

St. Cormac (sixth century) was a friend of St. Columba. He served as an abbot.

Cormack *see Cormac*

Cormick *see Cormac*

Cornall *see Cornelius*

Cornealous *see Cornelius*

Corneili *see Cornelius*

Corneilius *see Cornelius*

Corneille *see Cornelius*

Corneilus *see Cornelius*

Cornelias *see Cornelius*

Corneliaus *see Cornelius*

Cornelie *see Cornelius*

Cornelious *see Cornelius*

Cornelis *see Cornelius*

Corneliu *see Cornelius*

Cornelius Saint; Latin, Greek; cornel tree, horn colored

Carnealous, Carnelius, Conny, Cornall, Cornealous, Corneili, Corneilius, Corneille, Corneilus, Cornelias, Corneliaus, Cornelie, Cornelious, Cornelis, Corneliu, Cornellious, Cornellis, Corneliu, Cornellius, Cornellus, Cornelous, Corneluis, Cornelus, Corney, Cornie, Cornielius, Corniellus, Corny, Cournelius, Cournelyous, Kornell, Nelius, Nellie

Pope St. Cornelius, St. Cornelius of Armagh

Pope St. Cornelius (d. 253) succeeded Fabian as Pope after the election was delayed fourteen months because of Decius's persecution of the Christians. A main issue of his pontificate was how to deal with those who had renounced the Christian faith during the persecutions. Some felt that they would need to be rebaptized. Others, including Cornelius, maintained that they needed only to repent their sin and perform penance. During his pontificate, Novatian, a Roman priest, declared himself pope—the first antipope. A synod of bishops in 251 declared Cornelius the true pope. When Emperor Gallus began persecuting Christians, Cornelius was exiled and died a martyr.

Cornellious *see Cornelius*

Cornellis *see Cornelius*

Cornellius *see Cornelius*

Cornellus *see Cornelius*

Cornelous *see Cornelius*

Corneluis *see Cornelius*

Cornelus *see Cornelius*

Corney *see Cornelius*

Cornie *see Cornelius*

Cornielius *see Cornelius*

Corniellus *see Cornelius*

Corny *see Cornelius*

Cos *see Cosmas*

Cosimo *see Cosmas*

Cosmas Saint; Greek; orderly, harmonious, universe

Cos, Cosimo, Cosmo, Cosmos, Cozmo, Kosmas, Kosmo

St. Cosmas, St. Cosmas of Aphrodisia, St. Cosmas of Maiuma

St. Cosmas (d. 283) and his brother Damian were born in Arabia. They were skilled doctors but never took money for their services. They were persecuted during the reign of Emperor Diocletian. They were hung on a cross, shot with arrows, and finally died by beheading. They are the patron saints of pharmacists.

Cosmo *see Cosmas*

Cosmos *see Cosmas*

Costa *see Constantine*

Costandinos *see Constantine*

Costantinos *see Constantine*

Costard *see Castor*

Coster *see Castor*

Cottidus Saint

St. Cottidus (date unknown) was a deacon who was martyred in Cappadocia.

Cournelius *see Cornelius*

Cournelyous *see Cornelius*

Cozmo *see Cosmas*

Craton Saint; Greek; he who rules

St. Craton (d. 273) was a philosopher who was converted by St. Valentine of Terni. He was martyred with his wife and family.

Credan Saint; English; belief

St. Credan (d. 780) served as abbot of the Benedictine monastery in Evesham, England, during the reign of King Offa of Mercia.

Crepin *see Crispin*

Crescens Saint, New Testament; Latin; growing, increasing

St. Crescens (first century) was mentioned by St. Paul in his Second Letter to Timothy (2 Tm 4:8–10). He was a missionary who was appointed bishop of

Galatia. He was martyred during the persecutions of Emperor Trajan.

Crescentian Saint; Latin; growth

St. Crescentian (d. 287) was a soldier who was beheaded at Saldo, near Citta di Castello, in Italy.

Crescentio Saint; Latin; he who constantly increases his virtue

St. Crescentio (date unknown) was a Roman martyr who died with St. Narcissus. A cemetery on the Via Saleria is named for him.

Crescentius Saint; Latin; he who constantly increases his virtue

St. Crescentius (first century) was only eleven years old when he was martyred. He was brought from Perugia, Italy, to Rome, where he stood trial. He was tortured and beheaded.

Crewanna Saint; Gaelic

St. Crewanna (fifth century) accompanied St. Breaca from Ireland to Cornwall, England.

Cripin *see Crispin*

Cris *see Crispin*

Crispe *see Crispin*

Crispian *see Crispin*

Crispin Saint; Latin; curly haired

Crepin, Cripin, Cris, Crispe, Crispian, Crispino, Crispo, Crispyn, Cryspyn, Krispin

St. Crispin, St. Crispin of Viterbo

St. Crispin (fourth century) was bishop of Ecija in Andalusia, Spain. He was beheaded

during the reign of Coemperor Maximilian.

Crispino *see Crispin*

Crispo *see Crispin*

Crispulus Saint; Latin; curly haired

St. Crispulus (first century) was martyred with St. Restitutus in Rome during the reign of Emperor Nero.

Crispus Saint, New Testament; Latin; curled

St. Crispus (first century) was baptized by St. Paul at Corinth, Greece. He is mentioned in 1 Corinthians 1:14. He later served as bishop of Chalcedon and was martyred.

Crispyn *see Crispin*

Cristiolus Saint; Welsh; anointed

St. Christiolus (seventh century) was from Wales. The brother of St. Suilain, he founded several Christian churches.

Cristobal Saint; form of Christopher; Greek; Christ-bearer

Cristoval, Cristovao

St. Cristobal Magallanes Jara (1869–1927) was born in Totatiche, Mexico, the son of farmers. After working as a shepherd, he studied for the priesthood and was ordained at the age of thirty. He became a parish priest in his hometown, where he helped found schools, carpentry shops, and the planning of water works. He worked to evangelize the Huichol people. He was accused of promoting the Cristero rebellion in the area. He was arrested while en route to celebrate Mass and was martyred four days later. He was canonized by Pope John Paul II in 2000.

Cristoval *see Cristobal*

Cristovao *see Cristobal*

Croidan Saint; Celtic

St. Croidan (sixth century) was a disciple of St. Petroc with Sts. Medan and Degan.

Cronan Saint; Celtic; little dark one

St. Cronan, St. Cronan Beg, St. Cronan of Roscrea, St. Cronan the Wise

St. Cronan of Roscrea (d. 640) was born in the Ely O'Carroll, Ireland. He lived as a hermit before founding fifty monasteries, the first of which was Puay and the most famous of which was Roscrea, where he also established a school. He may have been a bishop of Nendrum.

Crummine Saint; Celtic

St. Crummine (fifth century) was a disciple of St. Patrick, who appointed him the head of the church in Lachan County, Westmeath.

Cryspyn *see Crispin*

Crystek *see Christian*

Cuan Saint; Celtic; little hound

Mochua, Moncan

St. Cuan (sixth century), also known as Moncan or Mochua, was an Irish abbot who founded many churches and monasteries.

Cuaran Saint; Celtic; stooped, bent

St. Cuaran (d. 700) was an Irish bishop who retired his post and became a hermit in Iona, Scotland.

Cuby *see Cybi*

Cucufa *see Cucuphas*

Cucuphas Saint; Phoenician; he who likes to joke

Cucufa, Cugat

St. Cucuphas (269–304), also known as Cugat or Cucufa, was born into a noble family in Scillis, Africa. He was traveling to Spain when he was martyred near Barcelona.

Cugat *see Cucuphas*

Culen Saint; Gaelic; handsome

Colin

St. Culen (d. 971), also known as Colin, became King of Scotland when he defeated Dubh. Culen was defeated and killed by the Britons.

Cumgar Saint; Welsh

St. Cumgar (470–520) was a native of Devon who founded monasteries at Budgworth, Somerset, England, and at West Glamorgan, Wales.

Cumine Saint; Scottish; bent, crooked

St. Cumine (d. 669) was born in Ireland and served as abbot of Iona, Scotland. He was known as "the White" and wrote a biography of St. Columba.

Cummian Saint; Celtic

St. Cummian, St. Cummian Fada

St. Cummian Fada (d. 662) was a monk in Clonfert, Ireland. He founded a monastery at the area that came to be called Kilcummin.

Cunegundes *see Cunegunda* (girl's name)

Curcodomus Saint

St. Curcodomus (d. 680) was a Benedictine abbot at Maroilles, in the dioceses of Cambrai, France.

Curig Saint; Welsh

St. Curig (sixth century) was a bishop of Llanbadarn, Wales.

Curomotus Saint

St. Curomotus (d. 258) was bishop of Lycaonia in Asia Minor. He was martyred.

Cury *see Corentin*

Cuthbert Saint; English; brilliant

Cuthberte, Cuthburt

St. Cuthbert, St. Cuthbert Mayne

St. Cuthbert (634–687) was from one of the British Isles. He was orphaned as a young child, worked as a shepherd, and then became a monk at Melrose Abbey, where he later served as prior. He served as a missionary and was named prior of Lindisfarn. He eventually retired from missionary life to become a hermit. He was called away from hermitage to become bishop of Lindisfarn. He was known as a miracle worker and for having the gift of prophecy. He is a patron saint of Northumbria.

Cuthberte *see Cuthbert*

Cuthburt *see Cuthbert*

Cuthman Saint; English

St. Cuthman (eighth century) was a shepherd in southern England. He cared for his mother and built a church in Steyning. He was known as a miracle worker.

Cyan *see Cian*

Cybard *See Epaphroditus*

Cybi Saint; Welsh

Cuby, Kabius

St. Cybi (sixth century), also known as Cuby or Kabius, was born in Cornwall, England, and was a cousin of St. David of Wales. He studied under St. Anda and then founded a monastery called Caer Cybi on an island near Holyhead, Wales.

Cybor *see Eparchius*

Cydney *see Sidney*

Cynfran Saint; Welsh; chief crow

St. Cynfran (fifth century) was the son of a Welsh king. He founded a church in Gwynedd.

Cynibild Saint; Welsh

St. Cynibild (seventh century) was the brother of Sts. Chad and Cedd. He preached to the Anglo-Saxons.

Cynllo Saint; Welsh

St. Cynllo (fifth century) was a Welsh saint. He may have been the brother of St. Teilo. Several churches are named for him, but little is known of his life.

Cynwl Saint; Welsh

St. Cynwl (sixth century) was a Welsh hermit known for his austere life. He was the brother of St. Deinoil.

Cyprian Saint; Latin; from the island of Cyprus

Ciprian, Cipriano, Ciprien, Cyprianus, Cyprien, Cyprryan, Thasius

St. Cyprian, St. Cyprian of Toulon, St. Cyprian, Bishop of Carthage

St. Cyprian, Bishop of Carthage (d. 258), also known as Thasius, was born to a wealthy family in North Africa. He became an orator, lawyer, and teacher of rhetoric. After his baptism, he gave away some of his wealth to the poor of Carthage. He was elected bishop of Carthage. He fled the area during the persecutions of Emperor Decian, but he continued to rule his see from afar. He was an important writer of the early Church and was a staunch defender of the primacy of the pope. In time, he was brought before the Roman proconsul and was imprisoned. He was beheaded.

Cyprianus *see Cyprian*

Cyprien *see Cyprian*

Cyprryan *see Cyprian*

Cyrel *see Cyril*

Cyrell *see Cyril*

Cyrelle *see Cyril*

Cyriac *see Cyriacus*

Cyriacus Saint; Greek; of the Lord

Cyriac, Quiriacus

St. Cyriacus (d. 133), also known as Quiriacus, was bishop of either Ancona, Italy, or Jerusalem. He was martyred while making a pilgrimage to the Holy Land.

Cyril Saint; Greek; lordly

Cerek, Cerel, Ceril, Ciril, Cirill, Cirille, Cirrillo, Cyrel, Cyrell, Cyrelle, Cyrill, Cyrille, Cyrillus, Cyryl, Kirill, Kyrill, Syrell, Syril

St. Cyril of Alexandria, St. Cyril of Jerusalem

St. Cyril of Alexandria (376–444) was born at Alexandria, Egypt. He received a classical education and was ordained by his uncle, Theophilus, who was patriarch of the city. He became patriarch of Alexandria after his uncle's death. He battled Nestorius, patriarch of Constantinople, who maintained that Mary should not be called the Mother of God. He convinced Pope Celestine I to convoke a synod at Rome which condemned Nestorius. He spent much of his life writing treatises on the Trinity and the Incarnation. He is a Doctor of the Church.

Cyrill *see Cyril*

Cyrille *see Cyril*

Cyrillus *see Cyril*

Cyrilo *see Cirilo*

Cyrinus Saint

St. Cyrinus (third century) was a Roman martyr mentioned in the *Acts of St. Marcellinus.*

Cyrus Saint; Persian; sun

St. Cyrus, St. Cyrus of Carthage

St. Cyrus (third century) was a doctor from Alexandria. He helped bring many of his patients to the Christian faith. He and an Arabian colleague, John, offered emotional support to Athanasia and her young daughters who were being tortured for the faith in Canopus, Egypt. For this action, the two doctors were tortured and beheaded.

Cyryl *see Cyril*

Cyryllo *see Cirilo*

Cyrylo *see Cirilo*

Czeslaw Saint; Slavic; adoring glory

Ceslas

Bl. Czeslaw Odrowaz (1180–1242) was born in Krakow, Poland. He became a Dominican priest and a doctor of canon law and theology. He served as the director of vocations at the Dominican convent at Prague. He later became the spiritual director of St. Hedwig of Poland and a traveling preacher through Moravia, Saxony, Prussia, and Pomerania. His prayers were known to work many miracles.

D

Dabi *see David*

Dabid *see David*

Dabius Saint

Davius

St. Dabius (date unknown), also known as Davius, was an Irish missionary to Scotland.

Dacius *see Datius*

Daclan *see Declan*

Dadas Saint; Greek; torch

St. Dadas (d. 368) was a Persian noble related to King Shapur II. He and his wife, Casdoe, were martyred.

Daemien *see Damien*

Daevid *see David*

Daevyd *see David*

Dafydd *see David*

Dagan *see Decuman*

Dagobert Saint; German; shining like the sun

St. Dagobert II of Austrasia (650–679) was the son of King Sigebert II. Dagobert took the throne as a child and was sent into exile. He went to Ireland with Bishop Dido of Poitiers, France. Dagobert reclaimed his throne as King of Austrasia in 675. He was martyred while on a hunting trip.

Dai *see David*

Daig Saint; Celtic; flame, fire

St. Daig Maccairaill (d. 586) was the son of Cayrill. He founded a monastery at Iniskeen, Ireland. He is known as one of the "Three Master Craftsman of Ireland."

Dainel *see Daniel*

Dairus *see Darius*

Daived *see David*

Daivid *see David*

Daivyd *see David*

Dalbert *see Albert*

Dallan Saint; Celtic; blind

St. Dallan Forgaill (d. 598) was born in Connaught. He was a Christian poet known for writing a poem in honor of St. Columba. He lost his sight, but legend holds that when the poem was published after St. Columba's death, his sight was restored. He was murdered by pirates at Triscoel.

Dalmatius Saint; Latin; from Dalmatia

St. Dalmatius of Rodez, St. Dalmatius of Pavia, St. Dalmatius of Constantinople

St. Dalmatius of Pavia (d. 304) preached in Italy and France. He was named bishop of Pavia, Italy, in 303, and was martyred the following year during the persecution of Coemperor Maximian.

Damaiaon *see Damian*

Damaien *see Damian*

Damasus Saint; Latin; tamer

Pope St. Damasus I (306–384) was born in either Rome or Spain. He became a deacon and later an archdeacon. He was named bishop of Rome when he was sixty years old. He was the pope who commissioned St. Jerome to translate the scriptures into Latin.

Damaun *see Damian*

Damayon *see Damian*

Damean *see Damian*

Damen *see Damian*

Dameon *see Damien*

Damian Saint; Greek; tamer, soother

Damaiaon, Damaien, Damaun, Damayon, Damean, Damen, Damiane, Damiann, Damiano, Damianos, Damiyan, Damján, Damyan, Damyen, Damyin, Damyyn, Daymian, Demyan

St. Damian (d. 710) was bishop of Pavia, in Lombardy, Italy. He served as a mediator between the Lombards and the emperors of the Byzantine Empire.

Damiane *see Damian*

Damiann *see Damian*

Damiano *see Damian*

Damianos *see Damian*

Damianus Saint; Greek; tamer, soother

St. Damianus Nam Myong-Hyog (nineteenth century) was one of the Martyrs of Korea canonized by Pope John Paul II in 1984.

Damie *see Damien*

Damien Saint; Greek; to tame

Daemien, Dameon, Damie, Damieon, Damiion, Damine, Damiyon, Dammion, Damyen, Damyon

St. Damien de Veuster (1840–1889), also known as St. Damien of Molokai, was born in Belgium and joined the Sacred Heart Fathers. He was sent to Honolulu, Hawaii, where he was ordained in 1864. In 1873, he volunteered to go to the leper colony on Molokai. He worked tirelessly to improve conditions for the lepers and contracted the disease himself twelve years later. He was canonized by Pope Benedict XVI in 2009.

Damieon *see Damien*

Damiion *see Damien*

Damine *see Damien*

Damiyan *see Damian*

Damiyon *see Damien*

Damján *see Damian*

Dammion *see Damien*

Damyan *see Damian*

Damyen *see Damian, Damien*

Damyin *see Damian*

Damyon *see Damien*

Damyyn *see Damian*

Dan *see Daniel*

Daneel *see Daniel*

Daneil *see Daniel*

Danel *see Daniel*

Daniel Saint, Old Testament; Top 100 Name; Hebrew; God is my judge

Dainel, Dan, Daneel, Daneil, Danel, Danielius, Daniell, Daniels, Danielson, Danny, Danukas, Dasco, Deiniol, Deniel, Doneal, Doniel, Donois, Nelo

St. Daniel Comboni, St. Daniel, St. Daniel the Stylite

Daniel has a book of the Old Testament named after him. He was a prophet who could interpret dreams and visions. Perhaps the most famous story associated with him is of his time in the lion's den. King Darius had made a decree that no one was to offer prayer to any god but him for thirty days. Daniel continued to pray. He was arrested and thrown into a lion's den, but the lions would not harm him.

St. Daniel (d. 1221) was a Franciscan provincial in Calabria, Italy. He and several other friars served as missionaries in Morocco. They were arrested in Ceuta, North Africa. They refused to convert to Islam and were beheaded.

Danielius *see Daniel*

Daniell *see Daniel*

Daniels *see Daniel*

Danielson *see Daniel*

Danny *see Daniel*

Danukas *see Daniel*

Dariess *see Darius*

Darieus *see Darius*

Dario *see Darius*

Darioush *see Darius*

Darius Saint; Greek; wealthy

Dairus, Dariess, Darieus, Dario, Darioush, Dariuse, Dariush, Dariuss, Dariusz, Darrias, Darrios, Darrus, Darus, Daryos, Daryus

St. Darius (fourth century) was martyred at Nicaea, Turkey, with Zosimus, Paul, and Secundus.

Dariuse *see Darius*

Dariush *see Darius*

Dariuss *see Darius*

Dariusz *see Darius*

Darrias *see Darius*

Darrios *see Darius*

Darrus *see Darius*

Darus *see Darius*

Daryos *see Darius*

Daryus *see Darius*

Dasco *see Daniel*

Dasius Saint; Latin; baron

St. Dasius (d. 300) was a Roman soldier chosen to lead a local festival in Durosturum, Bulgaria. When he refused to worship the god Kronos, he was beheaded.

Dathus Saint

St. Dathus (d. 190) was bishop of Ravenna.

Datius Saint; Latin; to give

Dacius

St. Datius (d. 552), also known as Dacius, was a monk who was elected bishop of Milan in 530. When the city was attacked by Goths, he was taken prisoner for a time. After he was freed, he went to Constantinople to support Pope Vigilius against Emperor Justinian during the Three Chapter Controversy. He died at Chalcedon.

Dativus Saint; Latin; term from Roman law, applied to educators

St. Dativus (d. 304) was martyred with Saturninus and many others in Africa during the reign of Emperor Diocletian.

Daudi Saint; Hebrew; beloved

Bl. Daudi Okelo (1902–1918) was born in Uganda. He was a convert to the Catholic faith and served as a catechist. He was martyred for teaching the Gospel. He was beatified in 2002 by Pope John Paul II.

Dauid *see David*

Dav *see David*

Dave *see David*

Daved *see David*

Daveed *see David*

Daven *see David*

David Saint, Old Testament; Top 100 Name; Hebrew; beloved

Dabi, Dabid, Daevid, Daevyd, Dafydd, Dai, Daived, Daivid, Daivyd, Dauid, Dav, Dave, Daved, Daveed, Daven, Davidd, Davidde, Davide, Davidek, Davido, Davis, Davood, Davoud, Davyd, Davydas, Davydd, Davyde, Dayvid, Deved, Devid, Devidd, Devidde, Devod, Devodd, Devyd , Devydd, Devydde, Dodya

St. David, St. David I of Scotland, St. David of Sweden

David in the Bible was the second king of Israel, succeeding Saul. He was the ancestor of Jesus through Joseph and Mary. He was known as a shepherd boy, warrior, musician, and poet. Many of the psalms were attributed to him. His story is told in the books of Samuel, 1 Kings, and 1 Chronicles.

St. David (d. 589) was the son of King Sant of South Wales and St. Non. He was ordained a priest and founded several monasteries, including Menevia in southwestern Wales,

...ch was known for its ascetic lifestyle. He was named an archbishop. He died at the monastery at Menevia and is a patron of Wales.

Davidd *see David*

Davidde *see David*

Davide *see David*

Davidek *see David*

Davido *see David*

Davinus Saint; form of David; Hebrew; beloved
St. Davinus (d. 1051) was a pilgrim. He died while traveling to Rome and Constantinople. He died in Lucca, Italy, where he is venerated.

Davis *see David*

Davius *see Dabius*

Davood *see David*

Davoud *see David*

Davyd *see David*

Davydas *see David*

Davydd *see David*

Davyde *see David*

Day Saint; form of Daniel; Hebrew; God is my judge
St. Day (date unknown) is a patron saint of a Cornish church near Redruth, England.

Daymian *see Damian*

Dayvid *see David*

Declan Saint; Gaelic; man of prayer
Daclan, Deklan, Diclan, Dyclan
St. Declan (fifth century) was baptized by St. Colman and preached in Ireland shortly before St. Patrick's arrival. St.

Patrick established the episcopal see of Ardmore, and Declan became the bishop there. He was known as a miracle worker.

Deco *see Dominic*

Decorosus Saint; Latin; he is practical
St. Decorosus (d. 695) was bishop of Capua, Italy, and attended the Council of Rome in 680.

Decuman Saint; Latin; very large
Dagan
St. Decuman (d. 706) was born to a noble family in Wales. He crossed the Bristol Channel and settled at Watchet. He lived as a hermit with a cow for his companion. He was beheaded by a pagan.

Deicolus Saint; Latin; he who cultivates a relationship with God
St. Deicolus (530–625) was born in Leinster and studied at Bangor. He was one of the twelve disciples to accompany St. Columbanus as a missionary. He traveled to Gaul, Austrasia, and Burgundy. When St. Columbanus was exiled by Theuderic II, Deicolus was too old to follow him and instead settled at Lure, where he started the Abbey of Lure.

Deifer Saint
St. Deifer (sixth century) was the founder of Bodfare Monastery in Clwyd, Wales.

Deiniol Saint; Welsh; God is my judge
Denoual

St. Deiniol (d. 584), also known as Denoual, founded a monastery at the site where Bangor Cathedral now stands. He was the bishop of Bangor and attended the Synod of Llandddewi Brefi with St. David in 545.

Deklan *see Declan*

Delbert *see Albert*

Delphinus Saint; Greek; from Delphi, Greece

St. Delphinus (d. 404) was a bishop of Bordeaux, France. He corresponded with St. Ambrose and attended the Synod of Saragossa, Spain.

Demeitrius *see Demetrius*

Demenico *see Domenico*

Demeterious *see Demetrius*

Demetreus *see Demetrius*

Demetri *see Demetrius*

Demetrian *see Demetrius*

Demetrias *see Demetrius*

Demetrio *see Demetrius*

Demetriu *see Demetrius*

Demetrium *see Demetrius*

Demetrius Saint; Greek; lover of the earth

Demeitrius, Demeterious, Demetreus, Demetri, Demetrian, Demetrias, Demetrio, Demetriu, Demetrium, Demetrois, Demetrus, Demetryus, Demtrius, Demtrus, Dmetrius, Dymek, Dymetrias, Dymetrius, Dymetriys, Dymetryas, Dymetryus

St. Demetrius (d. 912), also known as Demetrian, was born in Sika, Cyprus. After his wife

died, he entered St. Anthony's Monastery and became a priest. He later became abbot and then bishop of Khytri.

Demetrois *see Demetrius*

Demetrus *see Demetrius*

Demetryus *see Demetrius*

Demingo *see Dominic*

Democritus Saint; Greek; arbiter of the village

St. Democritus (date unknown) was martyred with Secundus and Dionysius in Africa or Phrygia.

Demtrius *see Demetrius*

Demtrus *see Demetrius*

Demyan *see Damian*

Denick *see Devinicus*

Deniel *see Daniel*

Denoual *see Deiniol*

Dentlin Saint

St. Dentlin (seventh century) was the son of St. Vincent Madelgarys and St. Waldestrudis. He died when he was only seven years old, and a church in Cleves, Germany, was named for him.

Deochar Saint

St. Deochar (d. 847) was a hermit in Franconia before becoming abbot of Herriedon Abbey, established by Emperor Charlemagne.

Deodatus Saint; Latin; gift to God

St. Deodatus (d. 679) was a hermit. He later became bishop of Nevers, France. He founded the Abbey of Ebersheimmunster and Jointures Abbey.

Deogratius Saint; Latin; thanks be to God

St. Deogratius (d. 457) was bishop of Carthage. He was responsible for ransoming many Italian captives and was slain by Arian heretics.

Derek *see Theodore*

Dermot Saint; Gaelic; free from envy

Diarmaid, Diarmis

St. Dermot (sixth century), also known as Diarmis or Diarmaid, was the founder of a monastery on Innis-Closran Island, where he served as abbot. He trained St. Kiernan of Clonrnacnois.

Derrick *see Theodore*

Desideratus Saint; Spanish; desired

St. Desideratus (d. 790) was the son of St. Waningus, who founded the abbey at Fecamp. He became a Benedictine monk and most likely resided at the abbey his father had started.

Desiderius Saint; Spanish; desired

Dizier

St. Desiderius (d. 407), also known as Dizier, was from Genoa, Italy. He became bishop of Langres, France. He was slain when the Vandals invaded the region.

Deusdedit Saint; Latin; given to God

Pope St. Deusdedit (d. 618) was pope for three years. During his tenure, there was a skin epidemic in Rome that resembled leprosy. He personally helped the victims and directed other clergy to do so as well.

Deved *see David*

Devereux *see Dubricus*

Devid *see David*

Devidd *see David*

Devidde *see David*

Devinicus Saint; Scottish; poet

Denick

St. Devinicus (sixth century) was a Scottish missionary and bishop who helped evangelize Caithness.

Devod *see David*

Devodd *see David*

Devyd *see David*

Devydd *see David*

Devydde *see David*

Diaconus Saint; Greek, Latin; friend, servant

St. Diaconus (sixth century) was a deacon martyred in Marsi, Italy, at the hands of the Lombards.

Diarmaid Saint; Celtic; without envy

St. Diarmaid (d. 851) was an Irish bishop of Armagh. Forau, a usurper, took over the see, and Diarmaid went into exile in Connacht.

Diarmis *see Dermot*

Dichu Saint; Gaelic; great hound

St. Dichu (fifth century) was the first convert of St. Patrick in Ulster, Ireland. He gave St. Patrick a church in Saul.

Diclan *see Declan*

Dictinus Saint

St. Dictinus (d. 420) was part of the Priscillianism heresy but recanted at the Council of Toledo in 400. He was bishop of Astorga, Spain.

Didacus Saint; Latin, Spanish; teacher

St. Didacus (1400–1463) was born to a poor family in San Nicolas of del Puerto in the diocese of Seville. He joined a local hermit for some time before joining the Observant Friar Minors at Arrizafa. He served as a missionary in the Canary Islands. After he was recalled to Spain, he traveled to Rome in 1450. His devotion to a sick friend led to his being named director of the infirmary at Ara Caeli. He lived the rest of his life in Spain. He is a patron saint of the Franciscan laity.

Didymus Saint; Greek; a twin brother

St. Didymus (d. 304) was a pagan who rescued Theodora, a Christian, when she was sentenced to a brothel as punishment. He was converted by her example, and they both were martyred.

Diego Saint; Top 100 Name; form of Jacob, James; Spanish; supplanter, substitute

Bl. Diego Oddi (1839–1919) was born into a farm family in Vallinfreda, Italy. He wanted to enter religious life, but his family objected. He decided to become a Franciscan lay brother and lived a life of simple service and prayer. He was beatified in 1999 by Pope John Paul II.

Digain Saint

St. Digain (fifth century) was the son of Constantine, chieftain of Cornwall. He founded a church in Llangernyw and was known for his virtue, writing, and preaching.

Diman Saint; Latin; to lose

St. Diman (d. 658) was a monk under the direction of St. Columba. He served as a bishop of Connor, Ireland.

Dingad Saint; Welsh

St. Dingad (fifth century) was a son of King Brychan of the Welsh kingdom of Brycheiniog. He lived as a hermit in Llangingad, Llangovery.

Diodorus Saint; Greek; gift of God

St. Diodorus (third century) was martyred in Laodicia, Syria, with Diomedes and Didymus, during the reign of Emperor Diocletian.

Diomedes Saint; Greek; he who trusts in God's protection

St. Diomedes (fourth century) was born in Tarsus. A physician, he preached the faith with enthusiasm. He was arrested and was beheaded during the persecution of Emperor Diocletian.

Diomma Saint; Celtic

St. Diomma (fifth century) taught St. Declan of Ardmore and other Irish evangelists. He is the patron saint of Kildimo County, Limerick.

Dionysius Saint; Greek; celebration

Pope St. Dionysius, St. Dionysius, St. Dionysius of Alexandria, St. Dionysius of Augsburg, St. Dionysius of Corinth, St. Dionysius of Milan, St. Dionysius Sebuggwao, St. Dionysius the Deacon, St. Dionysius the Great

Pope St. Dionysius (d. 268) served as pope from 259–268. He helped rebuild the Church after the persecution conducted by Emperor Valerian. He fought against the Sebellianism heresy and condemned Paul of Samosata for heretical teaching.

Dioscorides Saint; Greek; relative of he who is of the Lord

St. Dioscorides (date unknown) was martyred in Smyrna.

Dioscorus Saint; Greek, Latin; he who is of the Lord

St. Dioscorus (d. 305) was martyred by being burned with hot irons in Egypt.

Disen *see Disibod*

Disibod Saint; German; bold, wise one

Disen, Disibode

St. Disibod (619–700), also known as Disen or Disibode, was an Irish monk and bishop. He went to Germany as a missionary and founded a monastery at Bingen, where St. Hildegard would later live.

Disibode *see Disibod*

Dismas Saint, New Testament; Greek; sunset

St. Dismas (first century) was the good thief crucified with Christ, whom Jesus told "would be with him that day in Paradise"(Lk 23:43).

Diuma Saint; Celtic

St. Diuma (seventh century) was an Irish priest who was brought to Mercia by Peada of Mercia. He became bishop of Mercia.

Dizier *see Desiderius*

Dmetrius *see Demetrius*

Dochow Saint

St. Dochow (d. 473) founded a monastery in Cornwall, England. He may have been a bishop.

Docus *see Cadoc*

Dodo Saint; Hebrew; lovable

St. Dodo (d. 750) was a Benedictine monk at Lobbes, Belgium. He later became abbot of Wallers-en-Faigne, France.

Dodolinus Saint

St. Dodolinus (seventh century) was the bishop of Vienne in Dauphine, France.

Dodya *see David*

Dogfan Saint; Welsh

St. Dogfan (fifth century) was descended from Chieftain Brychan of Brecknock. He was martyred by pagan invaders at Dyfed, Wales.

Dogmael Saint; Welsh

St. Dogmael (sixth century) was a monk at Cunedda and

preached in Pembrokeshire, Wales, and Brittany, France.

Dom *see Dominic*

Domangard Saint

Donard

St. Domangard (d. 500), also known as Donard, was a contemporary of St. Patrick. He lived as a hermit and is the patron of Maghera, County Down, Ireland.

Domeka *see Dominic*

Domenico Saint; form of Dominic; Italian; belonging to the Lord

Demenico, Domicio, Dominico, Dominiko, Menico

Bl. Domenico Lentini (1770–1828) was born into a poor family in Lauria, Potenza, Italy. He became a priest and served his hometown parish for the rest of his life. He was known for his devotion to poverty, the Eucharist, and Our Lady of Sorrows. He was also a teacher, opening his home to students. He was beatified by Pope John Paul II in 1997.

Domicio *see Domenico*

Dominator Saint; Latin; one who rules

St. Dominator (d. 495) was a bishop of Brescia, Italy, during the time when Germanic tribes were in control of Italy.

Domingo Saint; Spanish; born on Sunday

St. Domingo Hanh Van Nguyen, St. Domingo Nicolas Dat Dinh

St. Domingo Hanh Van Nguyen (1772–1838) was a Dominican priest in Vietnam. He was arrested during the persecutions of Vietnemese Emperor Minh Mang. When he refused to trample on a cross, he was tortured and then martyred. He was canonized by Pope John Paul II in 1988.

Domini *see Dominic*

Dominic Saint; Top 100 Name; Latin; belonging to the Lord

Deco, Demingo, Dom, Domeka, Domini, Dominick, Dominie, Dominik, Dominitric, Dominy, Domminic, Domnenique, Domokos, Nick

St. Dominic, St. Dominic de la Calzada, St. Dominic del Val, St. Dominic Doan Xuyen, St. Dominic Doan Xuyen, St. Dominic Henares, St. Dominc Loricatus, St. Dominic Mao Trong Ha, St. Dominic Nicholas Dat, St. Dominic of Brescia, St. Dominic of Silos

St. Dominic (1170–1221) was born at Calaruega, Spain, and studied at the University of Palencia. He was ordained a priest and became canon at Osma. In 1203, he accompanied Bishop Diego de Avezedo of Osma to Languedoc, where he spoke against the Albigensians. In 1214, he and six followers founded an order devoted to the conversion of the Albigensians. Pope Honorius III gave approval to the Order of Preachers. Dominic spent the rest of his life preaching, traveling all over Italy, Spain, and France, and establishing new houses of the order. He is the patron saint of astronomers.

Dominick *see Dominic*

Dominico *see Domenico*

Dominicus Saint; Latin; belonging to the Lord

St. Dominicus (d. 180) was martyred in Africa with several companions under the author of Vigellius. He was beheaded.

Dominie *see Dominic*

Dominik *see Dominic*

Dominiko *see Domenico*

Dominitric *see Dominic*

Dominy *see Dominic*

Domitian Saint; Latin; tamed

St. Domitian, St. Domitian of Chalons

St. Domitian (d. 440) was born in Rome, became a monk at Lerins, France, and founded a monastery at Bebron, now called St. Lambert de Joux.

Domitius Saint; Latin; tamed

St. Domitius (d. 361) was a Phyrgian who entered the circus in Caesarea and encouraged the people to deny the pagan gods. He was martyred by the sword.

Domminic *see Dominic*

Domnenique *see Dominic*

Domninus Saint; Latin; lord, master

St. Domninus of Fidenza (d. 304) was born in Parma, Italy. He was chamberlain to Emperor Maximian, where he was keeper of the royal crown. When he converted to Christianity, the emperor went after him. He rode through the streets of Piacenza, holding a cross, while being chased by the imperial forces. He was caught and beheaded outside of Fidenza, where the Cathedral of San Donnino would later stand.

Domnio Saint; Latin; lord, master

St. Domnio (fourth century) was a Roman priest and confessor, praised by Sts. Jerome and Augustine for his holiness.

Domnoc *see Modomnoc*

Domnolus Saint

St. Domnolus (d. 581) was an abbot of a monastery in Paris. He refused to become bishop of Avignon, but later agreed to be bishop of Le Mans, France, a position he held for twenty-one years. He attended the Council of Tours in 566 and built churches, monasteries, and a hospice.

Domnus Saint; Latin; lord, master

St. Domnus of Vienne (d. 657) was bishop of Vienne, France. He was known for ransoming captives taken in local wars.

Domokos *see Dominic*

Donald Saint; Scottish; world leader, proud ruler

Donalt, Donát, Donaugh, Doneld, Donild, Donnell, Donyld

St. Donald of Ogilvy (eighth century) is a Scottish saint. He and his wife raised nine daughters. After his wife's death, he and their daughters founded a religious group known as the Nine Maidens, or Nine Virgins. After Donald's death, they entered a monastery at Abernathy.

Donalt *see Donald*

Donan Saint; Celtic; mighty

Donnan

St. Donan (d. 617), also known as Donnan, was from Ireland and went to Galloway. He served as a missionary before forming a monastery on the island of Eigg. He and fifty-two monks were martyred by intruders.

Donard *see Domangard*

Donat Saint; Latin; gift

Dunwyd

St. Donat (sixth century), also known as Dunwyd, is the patron saint of Llandunwyd, Glamorgan, Wales. He may have been a bishop.

Donát *see Donald*

Donatian Saint; Latin; gift

St. Donatian (d. 390) was born in Rome and served as bishop of Reims, France, from 360 until his death. He is the patron saint of Bruges, Belgium.

Donatus Saint; Latin; gift

St. Donatus, St. Donatus of Besancon, St. Donatus of Corfu, St. Donatus of Fiesole

St. Donatus (d. 874) was born to a noble Irish family. He made a pilgrimage to Rome,

where he visited the tombs of the apostles. On his return trip, he stopped at the Cathedral of Fiesole. The people gathered there were praying for a new bishop to lead them. When he entered, candles miraculously lit and bells rang. The people elected Donatus as bishop. He was known for his piety and as a scholar. He served as an advisor to Lothair I and his son, Louis II.

Donaugh *see Donald*

Doneal *see Daniel*

Doneld *see Donald*

Doniel *see Daniel*

Donild *see Donald*

Donnan *see Donan*

Donnell *see Donald*

Donois *see Daniel*

Donyld *see Donald*

Dore *see Isidore*

Dorotheus Saint; Greek; gift of God

St. Dorotheus of Gaza (sixth century) joined the monastery near Gaza. He later founded his own monastery and served as abbot. He wrote instructions for monks that were compiled into *Directions on Spiritual Training*.

Dositheus Saint; Greek; God's possession

St. Dositheus (d. 530) visited Jerusalem, where he was baptized. He became a monk and cared for the sick at Gaza, Israel.

Dotto Saint; Italian; scholar

St. Dotto (sixth century) was abbot of a monastery of the Orkney Islands in Scotland.

Doucis *see Dulcidius*

Drausinus Saint

Drausius

St. Drausinus (d. 576), also known as Drausius, was educated by St. Anseric. He became bishop of Soissons, France, where he built a monastery, two churches, and a convent.

Drausius *see Drausinus*

Drew *see Andrew*

Drithelm Saint; English

St. Drithelm (d. 700) was a wealthy man from Northumbria, England. He died and experienced a powerful vision of heaven, hell, and purgatory, before coming back to life. He distributed his possessions among his wife, children, and the poor and became a monk at Melrose Abbey, where he lived as a hermit.

Droctonius *see Droctoveus*

Droctoveus Saint

Droctonius, Drotte

St. Droctoveus (d. 580), also known as Droctonius or Drotte, was born in Auxerre, France. He became a monk at St. Symphian Abbey at Autun, France. He was later named abbot. When St. Germanus founded a new abbey under the patronage of King Childebert I, Droctoveus was called there to become abbot.

Drogo Saint; German; to bear, to carry

Droun

St. Drogo (1105–1186), also known as Droun, was born in Flanders. He was a pilgrim and then served as a shepherd. After acquiring an illness in his twenties that made him physically repulsive, he became a hermit, living in a hut at Sebourg for forty years. He had no human contact except a small window through which he received the Eucharist and food.

Drostan Saint; Celtic; the noisy one

Drustan, Dustan, Throstan

St. Drostan (d. 610), also known as Drustan, Dustan, or Throstan, was a member of the royal Cosgrach family of Ireland. He was trained by St. Columba, under whose direction he became a monk. He was the founder and first abbot of the monastery of Old Deer in Aberdeenshire, Scotland, and is considered an apostle to Scotland.

Drotte *see Droctoveus*

Droun *see Drogo*

Drustan *see Drostan*

Drusus Saint; Latin; the strong one

St. Drusus (date unknown) was martyred with Zosimus and Theodore in Syria.

Druthmar Saint; German

St. Druthmar (d. 1046) was a Benedictine named abbot of Corvey, in Saxony, Germany, by Emperor St. Henry II.

Dubricus Saint; English; dark ruler
Devereux, Dyfrig

St. Dubricus (465–550), also known as Dyfrig or Devereux, was born in Madley, Wales, the illegitimate grandson of King Peibio Clafrog of Ergyng. He founded monasteries at Henllan and Moccas. He later became bishop of Ergyng. According to legend, he was named archbishop of Wales and crowned King Arthur.

Dubtach Saint; Celtic; dark one

St. Dubtach (d. 513) was archbishop of Armagh, Ireland, from 497 until his death.

Dulas Saint; Greek; slave

St. Dulas (d. 310) was from Zephyrium, Cilicia. He was arrested for refusing to worship Apollo and the other Roman gods. He was tortured and died while traveling to Tarsus.

Dulcardus Saint; Latin; sweet

St. Dulcardus (d. 584) was a monk at Micy in Orleans. He later became a hermit at Saint-Doulchard, France.

Dulcet *see Dulcidius*

Dulcidius Saint; Latin; sweet
Doucis, Dulcet

St. Dulcidius (d. 450), also known as Dulcet or Doucis, was bishop of Agen, France.

Dun *see Dunstan*

Dunchadh Saint; Celtic; fortress

St. Dunchadh (d. 717) was abbot of Iona, in Scotland.

Dunchaid Saint; Celtic

St. Dunchaid O'Braoin (d. 988) was a hermit. Later, he became abbot at Clanmocnoise, near Westmeath, Ireland.

Dunstan Saint; English; brownstone fortress
Dun, Dunsten, Dunstin, Dunston, Dunstyn

St. Dunstan (909–988) was born into a noble family near Glastonbury, England. He was educated by Irish monks. His uncle, St. Alphege, ordained him. King Edmund appointed him abbot of Glastonbury Abbey, which he made into a great center of learning. He served as a minister of state for several English kings. At the end of his life, he taught at the cathedral school at Canterbury. He was a musician and was skilled at working with metal and illuminating manuscripts. According to legend, the devil tempted him, and he pulled the devil by the nose with redhot tongs. He is the patron of armorers, goldsmiths, locksmiths, and jewelers.

Dunsten *see Dunstan*

Dunstin *see Dunstan*

Dunston *see Dunstan*

Dunstyn *see Dunstan*

Dunwyd *see Donat*

Dustan *see Drostan*

Duthac Saint; Scottish; black
Duthus

St. Duthac (1000–1065), also known as Duthus, was

educated in Ireland and became bishop of Ross, Scotland. He was known for his miracles and prophecies and was said to have predicted the Danish invasion.

Duthus *see Duthac*

Dyclan *see Declan*

Dyfan Saint; Celtic; day, constant

St. Dyfan (second century) was sent by Pope St. Eleutherius to be a missionary to the Britons.

Dyfnan Saint; Welsh; deep brook

St. Dyfnan (fifth century) was the son of the Welsh chieftain Brychan of Brecknock. He was the founder of Angelsey, Wales.

Dyfnog Saint; Welsh

St. Dyfnog (sixth century) was a Welsh confessor of the Caradog family.

Dyfrig *see Dubricus*

Dymek *see Demetrius*

Dymetrias *see Demetrius*

Dymetrius *see Demetrius*

Dymetriys *see Demetrius*

Dymetryas *see Demetrius*

Dymetryus *see Demetrius*

E

Eadbert Saint; Teutonic; wealthy

St. Eadbert (d. 698) was abbot and bishop of Lindisfarne, Ireland. He was known for his knowledge of scriptures.

Eaden *see Eden*

Eadfrid Saint; English

St. Eadfrid (d. 675) was a priest who served in Northumbria and Mercia, England. He founded Leominster Priory.

Eadin *see Eden*

Eadmund *see Edmund*

Eadnot Saint; English

St. Eadnot (d. 1016) was a bishop of Dorchester, England, who was martyred by the invading Danes.

Eadsimus *see Eadsin*

Eadsin Saint; English

Eadsimus, Edsige

St. Eadsin (d. 1050), also known as Edsige or Eadsimus, became a monk at Christ Church, Canterbury. He later became archbishop of Canterbury. He crowned King St. Edward the Confessor.

Eadward *see Edward*

Eadwin *see Edwin*

Eadwinn *see Edwin*

Eadyn *see Eden*

Eamon *see Edmund*

Earnest *see Ernest*

Eata Saint; English

St. Eata (d. 686) was educated by St. Aidan at Lindisfarne. He became a monk and a priest and at the request of St. Colman became abbot of Lindisfarne. He later became abbot of Melrose and founded a monastery at Ripon in Yorkshire. He was named bishop of Bernicia. When that see was split in two, he became bishop of Hexham.

Eathan *see Ethan*

Eathen *see Ethan*

Eathin *see Ethan*

Eathon *see Ethan*

Eathyn *see Ethan*

Eavan *see Evan*

Ebbo Saint; German; wild boar

St. Ebbo (d. 740) was born in Tonnerre. He became a Benedictine at St. Pierre-leVef in Sens, France. He later became bishop of Sens and saved the city from a Saracen attack.

Eberard *see Evrard*

Eberbard Saint; German

St. Eberbard (d. 1164) was born to a noble family of Nuremberg, Germany. He became a priest and a Benedictine monk. He served as abbot of Biburg and was later named archbishop of Salzburg. He served as a peace-maker during the "Investiture Contraversy," mediating the dispute between Pope Alexander III and Emperor Frederick I Barbarossa.

Eberhard *see Evrard*

Ebon *see Ebontius*

Ebontius Saint; Hebrew; rock

Ebon, Ponce, Pontius

St. Ebontius (d. 1104), also known as Ebon, Pontius, or Ponce, was born in Comminges, Haute Garonne, France. He became a Benedictine and abbot and was later named bishop of Babastro, Spain.

Ebrulf Saint; Teutonic; wolf

Evroult

St. Ebrulf (626–706), also known as Evroult, was born in Bayeux, Normandy, France, and was a courtier to King Childebert III. Through mutual agreement, he and his wife separated in order to enter religious life. He entered Deux Jumeaux Abbey and then became a hermit in Ouche Forest. He attracted many followers and had to start a monastery.

Ecclesius Saint; Latin; church

St. Ecclesius (d. 532) was bishop of Ravenna, Italy. He built the Church of San Vitale and was known for his great compassion.

Echa Saint; English; noble

Etha

St. Echa (d. 767), also known as Etha, was a Benedictine who lived as a hermit at Crayk, near York, England.

Edam *see Adam*

Edbert Saint; English; wealthy, bright

Ediberto

St. Edbert (d. 960) was king of Northumbria, England, for twenty years before becoming a Benedictine monk at York.

Edburga Saint; English; strong boar

St. Edburga, St. Edburga of Bicester, St. Edburga of Winchester

St. Edburga (d. 751) was born into the royal family of Kent, England. She became a Benedictine abbess of

Minster-in-Thanet, where she built a church. She was also a noted calligrapher. She corresponded with St. Boniface, whose missions she supported.

Edek *see Edgar*

Edem *see Adam*

Eden Old Testament; Hebrew; pleasure; delight

Eaden, Eadin, Eadyn, Edenson, Edyn, Eiden

Eden was the Garden of God described in Genesis 2–3.

Edenson *see Eden*

Edeyrn Saint; English

St. Edeyrn (sixth century) was a companion of King Arthur before becoming a hermit in Armonica, an area in Brittany.

Edgar Saint; English; successful spearman

Edek, Edgars, Edger, Edgir

St. Edgar the Peaceful (943–975) was the younger son of King Edmund I. He later became king himself and was a patron of St. Dunstan, who served as his counselor. During his reign, the monastic-reform movement took place, restoring Benedictine Rule to England's monastic communities. His daughter was St. Edith of Wilton.

Edgars *see Edgar*

Edger *see Edgar*

Edgir *see Edgar*

Ediberto *see Edbert*

Edik *see Edward*

Edim *see Adam*

Edison *see Edward*

Edistius Saint

St. Edistius (d. 303) was martyred in Ravenna, Italy.

Edko *see Edward*

Edlin *see Edwin*

Edman *see Edmund*

Edmand *see Edmund*

Edmaund *see Edmund*

Edmond *see Edmund*

Edmun *see Edmund*

Edmund Saint; English; prosperous protector

Eadmund, Eamon, Edman, Edmand, Edmaund, Edmond, Edmun, Edmundo, Edmunds

St. Edmund Arrowsmith, St. Edmund Campion, St. Edmund Genings, St. Edmund Rich, St. Edmund the Martyr

St. Edmund Campion (1540–1581) was born in London and was raised Catholic. He attended St. John's College, where he was known for his brilliance. He took the Oath of Supremacy declaring Queen Elizabeth the head of the English Church and became an Anglican deacon in 1564. He had great doubts about this, however, and after studying in Ireland he returned to the Catholic faith. He went to France in order to escape the persecution of Catholics. He joined the Jesuits and was ordained. He returned to England as a missionary and was ultimately captured, tortured, hung, drawn, and quartered at Tyburn. He was canonized in 1970.

Edmundo *see Edmund*

Edmunds *see Edmund*

Edoardo Saint; form of Edward; Italian; prosperous guardian

Bl. Edoardo Giuseppe Rosaz (1830–1903) was born in Susa, Piedmont, Italy, and was ordained in France. He founded the Sisters of the Third Order of Saint Francis of Susa. He also founded a home for abused and abandoned children. He later served as bishop of Susa. He was beatified by Pope John Paul II in 1991.

Edorta *see Edward*

Edsige *see Eadsin*

Eduino *see Edwin*

Edus *see Edward*

Edvard *see Edward*

Edvardo *see Edward*

Edwald *see Edward*

Edwan *see Edwin*

Edward Saint; English; prosperous guardian

Eadward, Edik, Edison, Edko, Edorta, Edus, Edvard, Edvardo, Edwald, Edwardo, Edwards, Edwy, Edzio, Etzio, Ewart

St. Edward the Confessor, St. Edward the Martyr

St. Edward the Confessor (d. 1066) was born at Islip, England, the son of King Ethelred III. When the Danes invaded England, he and his mother traveled to Normandy, where he was brought up. In 1042, he

became king of England. He married Edith, the daughter of Earl Godwin. The early years of his reign were marked by political activity, but he later withdrew, and royal power decreased. He was known for his piety. Shortly after he died, the Normans conquered England.

Edwardo *see Edward*

Edwards *see Edward*

Edwige *see Hedwig (girl's name)*

Edwin Saint; English; prosperous friend

Eadwin, Eadwinn, Edlin, Eduino, Edwan, Edwinn, Edwyn, Edwynn

St. Edwin (586–633) was the king of Northumbria. He married Ethelburga, the daughter of St. Ethelbert, king of Kent, and promised to allow her to practice her Christian faith. King Edwin converted to the faith and was baptized on Easter in 627. He died during battle against the Welsh Cadwalon who fought with Penda of Mercia, a pagan. He is considered a martyr.

Edwinn *see Edwin*

Edwold Saint; English

St. Edwold (ninth century) was the brother of St. Edmund the Martyr, king of East Anglia, England. He lived as a hermit in Cerne, Dorsetshire.

Edwy *see Edward*

Edwyn *see Edwin*

Edwynn *see Edwin*

Edym see Adam

Edyn see Eden

Edzio see Edward

Eeathen see Ethan

Efan see Ethan

Efen see Ethan

Effan see Ethan

Effen see Ethan

Effin see Ethan

Efflam Saint; Celtic; flame

St. Efflam (d. 700) was the son of a British prince who founded a monastery in Brittany, France.

Effon see Ethan

Effyn see Ethan

Efin see Ethan

Efon see Ethan

Efyn see Ethan

Egbert Saint; English; bright sword

Egbirt, Egburt, Egbyrt

St. Egbert (639–729) was a monk at Northumbria. He wanted to travel to Germany as a missionary but because of a vision did not continue with that plan. Instead, he went to Iona, where he lived as a monk. He convinced the other monks there to adhere to the Roman form of computing Easter, which had been established at the Synod of Whitby in 664. He died on the first Easter that this date was observed by the monks.

Egbirt see Egbert

Egburt see Egbert

Egbyrt see Egbert

Egdunus Saint

St. Egdunus (d. 303) was martyred with seven companions in Nicomedia.

Egelred Saint; English

St. Egelred (d. 870) was a Benedictine monk at Crayland Abbey, Great Britain. He was martyred when the Danes invaded the monastery.

Egelwine Saint; English

St. Egelwine (seventh century) was a prince of the house of Wessex. A confessor, he lived at Athelny, in Somersetshire, England.

Egidio Saint; Greek; he who carries the goatskin sword in battle

St. Egidio Maria of St. Joseph (1729–1812) was born Francis Postillo in Taranto, Apulia. Because he was uneducated, he couldn't become a priest and instead became a lay brother. He served in Naples where he helped the sick and socially excluded. He was canonized in 1996 by Pope John Paul II.

Egilhard Saint; German; edge of a sword

St. Egilhard (d. 881) was a Benedictine abbot of Cornilmunster, Germany, who was martyred by Normans at Bercheim.

Egilo Saint; German

Eigil

St. Egilo (d. 875), also known as Eigil, was abbot of Prum, near Trier, Germany. Emperor Charles the Bald directed him to restore Flavigny Abbey in

Dijob, France. He also founded Corbigny Abbey in Yonne.

Egino Saint; German

St. Egino (d. 1122) was born in Augsburg, Bavaria, Germany, and grew up in the abbey of Sts. Ulric and Afra. He became abbot of that monastery, but he was exiled for a time when he supported Pope Callistus II against Emperor Henry V. He returned but experienced a second exile when he opposed Bishop Hermann, who was practicing simony.

Egwin Saint; English; friend

St. Egwin (d. 717) was an English noble. He became bishop of Worcester, England, but his clergy found him to be overly strict, and he went to Rome. When he returned to England, he founded Eversham Monastery.

Ehric see Eric

Eiden see Eden

Eigil Saint; Scandinavian; edge of a sword

Aeigil

St. Eigil (750–822), also known as Aeigil, was the nephew of St. Sturm. He was born into a noble family of Norica who sent him to Fulda Abbey for his education. He later became abbot of Fulda. He was known for his gentleness and the many building projects that took place under his leadership.

Eigrad Saint; English

St. Eigrad (sixth century) was the brother of St. Samson of York. Trained by St. Illtyd, he founded a church in Anglesey, Wales.

Eingan Saint; German; doorway

Anianas, Einon, Eneon

St. Eingan (sixth century), also known as Anianus, Einon, or Eneon, was the son of a chieftain in Cumberland, Wales. He lived as a hermit at Llanengan, near Bangor.

Einon see Eingan

Eitan see Ethan

Eithan see Ethan

Eithen see Ethan

Eithin see Ethan

Eithon see Ethan

Eithyn see Ethan

El see Elijah

Elaeth Saint; Welsh

Eleth

St. Elaeth (sixth century), also known as Eleth, was a British king who was driven out of his territory. He traveled to a monastery in Anglesey in northern Wales. He was known for his religious poetry.

Elaphius Saint; Greek; deer

St. Elaphius (d. 580) was a bishop of Chalons-sur-Marne, France. He died on the way to Spain, where he was to serve as an ambassador.

Elbin see Alban

Eldrad see Heldrad

Elerius Saint; Welsh

St. Elerius (sixth century) was an abbot in a monastery in northern Wales. He was a companion of St. Winefred.

Elesbaan Saint; African

St. Elesbaan (d. 540) was a Christian king of Ethiopia. He fought against the Jewish Dunaan, who had tortured Christians. He resigned his throne and became a hermit.

Eleth *see Elaeth*

Eleuchadius Saint

St. Eleuchadius (d. 112) was from Greece. St. Apollinaris converted him to the Christian faith. He became bishop of Ravenna.

Eleutherius Saint

St. Eleutherius, St. Eleutherius of Tournai

St. Eleutherius (d. 585) was abbot of St. Mark's near Spoleto. He was a miracle worker, said to have raised a dead man to life. He spent his life in fasting, penance, and prayer. After he resigned his abbacy, he lived at St. Andrew's Monastery in Rome, where he died.

Elfrid *see Alfred*

Elgar Saint; German; noble spearman

St. Elgar (d. 1100) was born in Devonshire, England. After being held captive in Ireland for several years, he became a hermit on the isle of Bardsey, off the coast of Cearnarvon, Wales.

Eli Old Testament; Top 100 Name; Hebrew; the offering or lifting up

Eli was a Jewish High Priest of Shiloh. He was responsible for the training of Samuel.

Elian Saint; Greek; sunshine

St. Elian (sixth century) was a missionary in Cornwall, England.

Elias Saint; Greek; the Lord is my God

St. Elias Facchini, St. Elias

St. Elias (d. 660) was the Benedictine bishop of Syracuse, Italy, who sponsored monastic expansion in the region.

Eligius Saint

Eloi

St. Eligius (590–660), also known as Eloi, was born near Limoges, France. A metalsmith, he was appointed master of the mint under Clotaire II of Paris. He shared his fortune with the poor and built several churches and a monastery. He also established a major convent in Paris. He was later ordained a priest and became bishop of Noyon and Tournai. He is the patron saint of metalworkers.

Elija *see Elijah*

Elijah Old Testament; Top 100 Name; Hebrew; the Lord is my God

El, Elija, Elijiah, Elijio, Elijuah, Elijuo, Eliya, Eliyah, Eliyahu, Ellija, Ellijah, Elliot, Ellis, Ellyjah

Elijah was a prophet in the Northern Kingdom of Israel during the reign of Ahab. His story is told in the book of Kings.

Elijiah *see Elijah*

Elijio *see Elijah*

Elijuah *see Elijah*

Elijuo *see Elijah*

Eliphius Saint; Latin, Arabic; first
Eloff

St. Eliphius (d. 362), also known as Eloff, was originally from Ireland or Scotland. He was martyred in Toul, France.

Elisha Old Testament; Hebrew; salvation of God

Elisha was a prophet of the Northern Kingdom of Israel. He was a disciple of Elijah and took over his role of prophet after Elijah was brought up into the heavens by chariot. His story is told in 1 and 2 Kings.

Eliya *see Elijah*

Eliyah *see Elijah*

Eliyahu *see Elijah*

Ellban *see Alban*

Ellidius Saint

St. Ellidius (seventh century) is the patron saint of Himant, Powys, Wales.

Ellija *see Elijah*

Ellijah *see Elijah*

Elliot *see Elijah*

Ellis *see Elijah*

Ellyjah *see Elijah*

Elmo *see Anselm, Erasmus*

Eloff *see Eliphius*

Eloi *see Eligius*

Eloque Saint; Gaelic

St. Eloque (d. 666) was a Benedictine abbot at Lagny.

Elpidius Saint; Greek; he who has hopes

St. Elpidius (d. 422) was a bishop of Lyon, France.

Elsiar Saint

St. Elsiar (d. 1015) was a Benedictine monk at Saint-Savin Monastery in Lavedan.

Elstan Saint; English; Eli's town

St. Elstan (d. 981) was a Benedictine who became bishop of Winchester, England.

Elvan Saint; form of Alvin; English; white, light skinned

St. Elvan (second century) and his companion, St. Mydwyn, were Britons sent by King St. Lucius to Pope St. Eleutherius to ask for missionaries.

Elvis *see Elwin*

Elwin Saint; form of Alvin; English; white, light skinned
Allen, Elvis

St. Elvin (sixth century), also known as Elvis or Allen, accompanied St. Breaca from Ireland to Cornwall, England.

Elzear Saint; Hebrew; God has helped

St. Elzear (1285–1323) was born to noble parents at a castle in Ansouis, Province, France. After being educated at St. Victor's Monastery in Marseilles, he married Delphina of Glandieves. She had taken a vow of celibacy, and he respected that. He became lord of Ansouis and count of Ariano. He also served as a tutor to the son of King Robert of Naples. He was a tertiary of the Franciscan order. Both he and his wife were known for their holiness and piety.

Eman *see Emmanuel*

Emebert Saint; German; mighty bright

St. Emebert (d. 710) was the son of Duke Witger of Lotharingia and St. Amalberga of Maubeuge. He was the brother of four other saints. He served as bishop of Cambrai, in Flanders, Belgium.

Emek *see Emmanuel*

Emeric Saint; German; industrious leader

St. Emeric (d. 1031) was the son of St. Stephen, Hungary's first Christian king. He was educated by St. Gerhard, who was bishop of Csanád. He did not live to take over the throne, however, and was killed in a hunting accident while in his twenties. His grave was the site of many miracles and healings.

Emeritus Saint; Latin; veteran, licensed

St. Emeritus (d. 304) was martyred with Saturninus and many others in Algiers.

Emerius Saint

Emerus

St. Emerius (eighth century) was the son of St. Candida. He became a Benedictine monk in France and founded St. Stephen of Banoles Abbey in Catalonia, Spain.

Emerus *see Emerius*

Emidius *see Emygdius*

Emiel *see Emil*

Emil Saint; Latin, German; flatterer, industrious

Aimil, Aymil, Emiel, Emile, Emilek, Emilio, Emill, Emils, Emilyan, Emyl, Emyll

Bl. Emil Szramek (1887–1942) was born in Tworkov, Poland. He was ordained a priest and served in the Archdiocese of Katowice. He was arrested by the Nazis and sent to the Dachau concentration camp. He is one of the 108 Polish Martyrs of World War II and was beatified in 1999 by Pope John Paul II.

Emilas Saint; Latin; friendly, industrious

St. Emilas (d. 852) was a deacon martyred in Córdoba, Spain, by Caliph Abd-al-Rahman II.

Emile *see Emil*

Emilek *see Emil*

Emilian Saint; Latin; friendly, industrious

St. Emilian, St. Emilian Cucullatus

St. Emilian (d. 520) was a hermit for forty years before becoming bishop of Vercelli in Piedmont, Italy.

Emilio *see Emil*

Emilius Saint; Latin; friendly, industrious

St. Emilius (d. 250) was taken prisoner with Castus in Africa. The first time, they renounced the faith and were released. The second time, they were faithful and were burned to death.

Emill *see Emil*

Emils *see Emil*

Emilyan *see Emil*

Emiterio *see Hemiterius*

Emmahnuel *see Emmanuel*

Emmanel *see Emmanuel*

Emmaneuol *see Emmanuel*

Emmanle *see Emmanuel*

Emmanual *see Emmanuel*

Emmanueal *see Emmanuel*

Emmanuel Saint; Hebrew; God with us

Eman, Emek, Emmahnuel, Emmanel, Emmaneuol, Emmanle, Emmanual, Emmanueal, Emmanuele, Emmanuell, Emmanuelle, Emmanuil, Imanol, Imanual, Imanuel, Imanuele, Immanual, Immanuel, Immanuele, Immuneal, Manny

St. Emmanuel Trieu Van Nguyen, St. Emmanuel Phung St. Emmanuel Trieu Van Nguyen (1756–1798) was a seminarian with the Paris Foreign Mission Society and was ordained at Pong-King. He served as a parish priest in Cochinchina. He was arrested while visiting his mother and was martyred. He is one of the Martyrs of Vietnam canonized by Pope John Paul II in 1988.

Emmanuele *see Emmanuel*

Emmanuell *see Emmanuel*

Emmanuelle *see Emmanuel*

Emmanuil *see Emmanuel*

Emmeramus Saint

St. Emmeramus (d. 690) was from Poitiers, France. Duke Theodo asked him to go to Bavaria, Germany. He became the abbot of Regensburg Monastery and later served as bishop of that city. He was assassinated in Munich while on a pilgrimage to Rome.

Emygdius Saint

Emidius

St. Emygdius (279–309), also known as Emidius, was from Trier, Germany. After he converted to Christianity, he visited Rome and destroyed a pagan temple. He was made a bishop by Pope Marcellus I and was sent to Ascoli Piceno, where he was later martyred.

Emyl *see Emil*

Emyll *see Emil*

Enda Saint; Gaelic; birdlike

St. Enda (d. 530) was an Irish soldier. His sister, St. Fanchea, convinced him to lay down his arms and settle down. When his fiancé died, he became a monk and traveled to Rome, where he was ordained. He returned to Ireland, where he built churches and the Monastery of Killeaney.

He is one of the founders of Irish monasticism.

Eneco Saint; Latin; fiery

Inigo

St. Eneco (d. 1057) was a Benedictine monk in San Jaun de la Pena in Aragon, Spain. He became abbot of Ona in Old Castile.

Eneon *see Eingan*

Engelbert Saint; German; bright as an angel

Bert, Engelburt, Englebert, Englebirt, Engleburt, Englebyrt

St. Engelbert (d. 1225) was the son of the count of Berg. He became archbishop of Cologne, as well as tutor to the son of Emperor Frederick II. He crowned Henry, king of the Romans. When his cousin attempted to steal from the nuns of Essen, Engelbert stopped him. The cousin hired assassins to kill him. He was murdered at Gevelsberg.

Engelburt *see Engelbert*

Engelmer Saint

St. Engelmer (d. 1096) was the son of a poor laborer. He lived as a hermit near Passau, Germany, and was killed by a treasure hunter.

Engelmund Saint; English

St. Engelmund (d. 739) was born in England. He became the abbot of a monastery. He later traveled to Frisia, in the Netherlands, with St. Willibrord and helped evangelize the area.

Enghenedl Saint; Welsh

St. Enghenedl (seventh century) was from Anglesey, Wales.

Englatius Saint; Scottish

St. Englatius (d. 966) was a bishop who lived at Tarves, in Aberdeenshire, Scotland.

Englebert *see Engelbert*

Englebirt *see Engelbert*

Engleburt *see Engelbert*

Englebyrt *see Engelbert*

Ennodius Saint

St. Ennodius (474–521) was born Magnus Felix Ennodius in Arles, France, and he was educated in Milan, Italy. He was married, but they separated. She entered a convent, and he was ordained. He became bishop of Pavia. He served as a papal ambassador to Emperor Anastasius I. He was well-known as a poet.

Enoder Saint

St. Enoder (sixth century) was a grandson of King Brychan of Brecknock and became an abbot.

Enodoch Saint

St. Enodoch (d. 520) is a Welsh saint of the line of King Brychan of Brecknock.

Enogatus Saint

St. Enogatus (d. 631) was bishop of Aleth, in Brittany, France.

Enrico Saint; form of Henry; Italian; ruler of the household

Enzio, Rico

Bl. Enrico Rebuschini (1860–1938) was born in Lake Como,

Italy. He served in the military and worked in a silk factory before entering the seminary. He fell ill and had to return home. He lived as an ascetic in his home. He later joined the Camillians, Servants of the Sick, in Verona and was ordained a priest. He dedicated his life to serving the sick. He was beatified by Pope John Paul II in 1997.

Enrigué *see Enrique*

Enriq *see Enrique*

Enrique Saint; form of Henry; Spanish; ruler of the household

Enrigué, Enriq, Enriqué, Enriquez

St. Enrique de Osso y Cervello (1840–1896) wanted to become a priest from an early age, but his father objected, instead sending him to learn the textile business. His father finally relented, and he studied at Barcelona, where he served as a subdeacon, and at Tortosa. He was ordained in 1867. He founded the Association of Young Catholic Daughters of Mary and Saint Teresa of Jesus, the Institute of Josephine Brothers, and the Congregation of Saint Teresa. He also wrote a great deal. He was canonized in 1993 by Pope John Paul II.

Enriqué *see Enrique*

Enriquez *see Enrique*

Enzio *see Enrico*

Eoban Saint; Gaelic

St. Eoban (d. 754) was an Irish Benedictine monk and a companion of Sts. Willibrord and Boniface. He was martyred with Boniface at Dokkum, Holland.

Eochod Saint

St. Eochad (d. 697) is considered the Apostle of the Picts of Galloway, Scotland. He was sent by St. Columba to spread the faith to northern Britain.

Eoghan *see Eugene*

Eoin *see Owen*

Epagaphras Saint

St. Epagaphras (first century) served as bishop in Colossae, where he was martyred.

Epaphroditus Saint, New Testament; Greek; agreeable, handsome

Cybard

St. Epaphrodius (first century) is mentioned in Phillipians 2:25–30. He was sent by St. Paul to the Phillipians. He is believed to have been the first bishop of Philippi, Macedonia.

Eparchius Saint

Cybor

St. Eparchius (d. 581), also known as Cybor, was the duke of Perigord. He lived in a walled-up cell at Angouleme, France. He attracted many followers, and a community grew around him. He was ordained by a local bishop, left his cell, and became abbot.

Ephrem Saint; Hebrew; fruitful

St. Ephrem (d. 373) was born into a Christian family in Syria. He served as a teacher under four bishops of Nisbis. He began to write hymns in order to counteract several heresies. He was influential in helping the Church realize the power of music to help spread the faith. When Christians were forced to leave Nisbis, Ephrem fled the city and went to Edessa, where he became a hermit.

Ephysius Saint; Greek

St. Ephysius (d. 303) was martyred in Sardinia, Italy.

Epicharis Saint; Greek

St. Epicharis (d. 300) was the wife of a Roman senator who was martyred in Byzantium.

Epifanio Saint; Greek; he who gives off brilliance

Bl. Epifanio Sierra Conde (1916–1936) was one of the Passionist Martyrs of Daimiel who was martyred during the Spanish Civil War. They were beatified by Pope John Paul II in 1989.

Epimachus Saint; Greek; easy to attack

St. Epimachus (d. 250) was martyred in Alexandria, Egypt.

Epiphanius Saint; Greek

St. Epiphanius, St. Epiphanius of Salamis

St. Epiphanius (310–403) was born in Besanduk, Palestine, and became an expert in scriptural languages. He served as abbot of a monastery at Eleutheropolis. He later became bishop of Cyprus and opposed the Arians.

Equitius Saint; Greek, French; equal, just, impartial

St. Equitius (490–570) was from Abruzzi, Italy. He lived as a hermit and later founded a monastery at Terni. He also founded a number of monasteries in Valeria.

Erasme *see Erasmus*

Erasmo *see Erasmus*

Erasmus Saint; Greek; lovable

Elmo, Erasme, Erasmo

St. Erasmus (d. 303), also known as Elmo, was bishop of Formiae, Campagna, Italy. He fled to Mt. Lebanon to escape Emperor Diocletian's persecutions. He lived as a hermit and, according to legend, was fed by a raven. When the emperor discovered where he was, he was tortured and imprisoned. An angel released him, and he went to Illyricum, where he was eventually martyred. According to legend, if blue light appears at the mastheads before and after a storm, it is a sign of St. Erasmus's protection, also called "St. Elmo's Fire."

Eraste *see Erastus*

Erastious *see Erastus*

Erastus Saint, New Testament; Greek; beloved

Eraste, Erastious, Ras, Rastus

St. Erastus (first century) was treasurer for the city of Corinth. After being converted by St. Paul, he was sent with St. Timothy to Macedonia. He later became a bishop and was martyred.

Erbert *see Herbert*

Erbin Saint; Welsh

Erbyn, Ervan

St. Erbin (fifth century), also known as Ervan or Erbyn, was king of Dumnonia. Churches in Cornwall, England, are dedicated to him.

Erbyn *see Erbin*

Ercongotha Saint

St. Ercongotha (d. 660) was the daughter of a king of Kent and St. Sexburga. She became a Benedictine nun at Faremoutiers-en-Brie.

Erek *see Eric*

Erembert Saint; German; Mighty, bright

St. Erembert (d. 672) was appointed bishop of Toulouse, France, by King Clotaire III. He held the office for twelve years before resigning because of poor health. He then lived at Fontenelle Monastery.

Erhard Saint; German; strong, resolute

Erhardt, Erhart

St. Erhard (d. 686) was born in Ireland. He served as a missionary bishop to Bavaria, Germany, and founded several monasteries.

Erhardt *see Erhard*

Erhart *see Erhard*

Eriberto *see Herbert*

Eric Saint; Top 100 Name; Scandinavian, English, German; ruler of all, brave ruler

Ehric, Erek, Erica, Ericc, Erico, Erik, Erric, Eryk, Rick

St. Eric IX of Sweden (d. 1160) became king of Sweden in 1150. He codified the laws of his kingdom and helped the spread of Christianity. He convinced the English Bishop Henry of Uppsala to evangelize the Finns. He was killed by Swedish nobles serving under Magnus, the son of the king of Denmark, who had invaded his territory. He is considered the patron saint of Sweden.

Ericc *see Eric*

Erico *see Eric*

Erik *see Eric*

Erkemboden Saint; German; recognized envoy

St. Erkemboden (d. 714) was a monk of St. Sithin, at St. Omer, France. He later became bishop of Therouanne, France.

Erlafrid Saint

St. Erlafrid (d. 830) was the count of Caiw in Swabia, Germany. He founded Hirschau Abbey, where he served as abbot.

Erluph Saint

St. Erluph (d. 830) was from Scotland and served as a missionary in Germany. He became bishop of Werden, Germany. He was martyred by pagans.

Ermano *see Herman*

Ermenfridus Saint; German; soldier of peace

St. Ermenfridus (d. 670) was a Benedictine monk at Luxeuil who was trained by St.

Waldeburt. He founded Causance Monastery in France.

Ermin see Herman

Erminold Saint; German; government of strength

St. Erminold (d. 1121) was sent to Hirschau Monastery, in Wurzburg, Germany, as a small child. He became abbot of Lorsch, but he resigned and returned to Hirschau when his election was disputed. He later became abbot of Pruffening, where he was martyred by a lay brother at the monastery.

Erminus Saint; English; noble

St. Erminus (d. 737) was the abbot of Lobbes Monastery in Belgium. He later became bishop of that area.

Ernest Saint; English; earnest, sincere

Earnest, Ernestino, Ernestus, Ernist, Ernyst

St. Ernest (d. 1148) was born in Steisslingen, Germany. He became abbot of the Benedictine Zwiefalten Abbey. He went on the Second Crusade organized by Conrad III and stayed in the Holy Land after it ended. He preached in Arabia and Mecca. He was captured and taken to Mecca, where he was martyred.

Ernestino see Ernest

Ernestus see Ernest

Ernist see Ernest

Ernyst see Ernest

Erotis Saint; Greek; love

St. Erotis (fourth century) was a Greek martyr who died at the stake.

Erric see Eric

Erth Saint; English; earth

St. Erth (sixth century) was an Irish missionary who evangelized Cornwall, England.

Ervan see Erbin

Eryk see Eric

Esequiel see Ezekiel

Esidore see Isidore

Eskill Saint; Norwegian; God vessel

St. Eskill (d. 1080) was from England. He traveled with St. Sigfrid as a missionary to Sweden. He was named bishop of Strangnas. When he denounced a pagan festival, King Sweyn the Bloody had him stoned to death.

Esra see Ezra

Esrah see Ezra

Essaiah see Isaiah

Estefan see Stephen

Esternus Saint

St. Esternus (d. 660) was the ninth bishop of Evreux, France.

Esterwine Saint; English

St. Esterwine (d. 668) was born into a noble family in Northumbria, England. He served as abbot of Wearmouth Abbey.

Estevon see Stephen

Etan see Ethan

Etha see Echa

Ethaen see Ethan

Ethan Old Testament; Top 100 Name; Hebrew; strong, the gift of the island

Aitan, Eathan, Eathen, Eathin, Eathon, Eathyn, Eeathen, Efan, Efen, Effan, Effen, Effin, Effon, Effyn, Efin, Efon, Efyn, Eitan, Eithan, Eithen, Eithin, Eithon, Eithyn, Etan, Ethaen, Ethe, Ethian, Ethin, Ethon, Ethyn, Eythan, Eythen, Eythin, Eython, Eythyn

Ethan in the Bible was a cymbal player in King David's court. He is the author of Psalm 89.

Ethbin Saint; English

St. Ethbin (d. 600) was a monk at Taurac, Brittany. After the monastery was attacked by the Franks in 556, he traveled to Ireland where he lived as a hermit at Kildare.

Ethe *see Ethan*

Etheihard Saint; English

St. Etheihard (ninth century) served as archbishop of Canterbury.

Etheired Saint; English; noble counsel

St. Etheired (d. 670) was a great grandson of King Ethelbert of Kent, England. He was martyred.

Ethelbert Saint; English; noble, bright, famous

St. Ethelbert, St. Ethelbert of Kent

St. Ethelbert of Kent (d. 616) was the king of Kent, England. He married Bertha, a Christian daughter of King Charibert of Paris. After he was baptized, he was responsible for bringing a great many souls into the faith, including the king of the East Saxons and the king of the East Angles. He founded the Abbeys of Christ Church, Saints Peter and Paul in Canterbury, and St. Andrew's in Rochester.

Ethelnoth Saint; English; noble

St. Ethelnoth (d. 1038) was called "the Good." He was a monk at Glastonbury before becoming the archbishop of Canterbury. King Canute II helped him in his work. He was known for his wisdom.

Ethelred *see Aelred*

Ethelwald Saint; English; noble

St. Ethelwald (d. 699) was a disciple of St. Cuthbert. He was a monk at Ripon before living as a Benedictine hermit on Fame Island, England.

Ethelwin Saint; English; noble friend

St. Ethelwin (d. 700) served as the second bishop of Lindsey, England. He went with St. Egbert to Ireland, where he died.

Ethelwold Saint; English; noble

St. Ethelwold (d. 984) was born in Winchester, England. He was ordained by St. Alphege the Bald and later joined the Benedictines at Glastonbury, where he was under the direction of St. Dunstan. He became abbot of Abingdon and later was named bishop of Winchester.

Known as "the Father of Monks," he helped bring about a monastic revival in England after the Danish invasions. He helped start or restore several monasteries.

Etherius Saint; Greek; pure air

Alermius

St. Etherius (d. 602), also known as Alermius, was a bishop of Lyons, France.

Ethernan Saint; Gaelic

St. Ethernan (ninth century) was from Scotland, but he became an Irish monk and bishop. He built a series of monasteries and hermitages on the Isle of May and along the coast of Fife. He was martyred by invading Vikings.

Ethian *see Ethan*

Ethin *see Ethan*

Ethon *see Ethan*

Ethyn *see Ethan*

Etian *see Etienne*

Etien *see Etienne*

Etienne Saint; form of Stephen; French; crowned

Etian, Etien, Ettien

St. Etienne-Theodore Cuenot (1802–1861) was born into a poor family in Beaulieu, France. After being ordained a priest, he entered the Paris Society for Foreign Missions and set out for Vietnam. He became an auxiliary bishop of the Vietnamese missions. He ordained fifty-six native priests and oversaw Vietnamese translations of *The*

Imitation of Christ and part of the Bible. He was imprisoned in 1861 but died before he could be executed. He was canonized by Pope John Paul II in 1998.

Ettien *see Etienne*

Etto Saint; Greek, Gaelic; pearl

St. Etto (d. 670) was an Irish missionary bishop in Belgium.

Etzio *see Edward*

Eubert *see Hubert*

Eucharius Saint; Greek; generous, gracious

St. Eucharius (d. 250) was the first bishop of Trier, Germany.

Eucherius Saint; Greek; generous, gracious

St. Eucherius (380–449) was married and had two sons, Salonius and Veranus. After his wife died, he withdrew from the world and joined Lerins Monastery, where his children were educated. He then became a hermit, but word of his holiness spread and he was chosen as the bishop of Lyon. His two sons became bishops as well.

Eudes *see Eudo*

Eudo Saint; Teutonic; youngster

Eudes, Eudon, Odo

St. Eudo (d. 760), also known as Eudon, Eudes, or Odo, was a Benedictine abbot who founded Carmery-en-Valay Abbey in France.

Eudon *see Eudo*

Eudoxius Saint; Greek; he who is famous

St. Eudoxius (d. 311) was part of a large group of soldiers martyred at Melitene, Armenia.

Eufridus Saint; German; peace

St. Eufridus (seventh century) was a Benedictine monk.

Eugeen *see Eugene*

Eugeene *see Eugene*

Eugen *see Eugene*

Eugendus Saint; Greek; born to nobility

St. Eugendus (d. 510), was an abbot of the Abbey of Condat. He led a very austere life, prayed almost continuously, and was very well educated, but he was never willing to be ordained a priest. After the wooden abbey burned down, he rebuilt it out of stone. He also built a church in honor of Sts. Peter, Paul, and Andrew.

Eugene Saint; Greek; born to nobility

Eoghan, Eugeen, Eugeene, Eugen, Eugenio, Eugenius, Eujean, Eujeane, Eujeen, Eujein, Eujeyn, Jaugen, Ugine

Pope St. Eugene I, St. Eugene de Mazenod

Pope St. Eugene I (d. 657) was born in Rome. He became a priest and was known for his holiness, gentleness, and charity. A year and two months after pope Martin I was banished by Byzantine Emperor Constans II, Eugene was named pope. Eugene probably would have met with the same fate as Pope Martin, except for the fact

that the Muslims invaded and defeated Constans. During his two-year reign as pope, Eugene consecrated twenty-one bishops for different parts of the world.

Eugenian Saint; Greek; born to nobility

St. Eugenian (fourth century) was a bishop of Autun, France. He was an enemy of Arianism and was martyred as a result.

Eugenio *see Eugene*

Eugenius *see Eugene*

Eugraphos Saint; Greek

St. Eugraphus (d. 235) was a Christian secretary to an army officer, Menas, who encouraged Christians who were being persecuted. They were both martyred in Africa.

Eugyppius Saint; Greek

St. Eugyppius (d. 511) was an African priest of Rome. He was a companion of St. Severinus of Noricum, whose biography he later wrote.

Eujean *see Eugene*

Eujeane *see Eugene*

Eujeen *see Eugene*

Eujein *see Eugene*

Eujeyn *see Eugene*

Eulampius Saint; Greek; brilliant

St. Eulampius (d. 310) was arrested in Nicomedia while seeking bread for many Christians hiding outside the city in caves. After he was scourged, his sister, St. Eulampia, ran out and embraced him. She was arrested as well, and both were martyred.

Eulogius Saint; Greek; well spoken

St. Eulogius and Companions, St. Eulogius of Alexandria, St. Eulogius of Córdoba, St. Eulogius of Edessa

St. Eulogius of Córdoba (d. 859) was a noted scripture scholar. He was named archbishop of Córdoba or Toledo, but before he could be consecrated, he was arrested and beheaded.

Eumenes Saint; Greek; opportune, favorable

St. Eumenes (third century) was the bishop of Gortyna. He was known as a miracle worker. He died in exile.

Euphrasius Saint; Greek; mirth

St. Euphrasius of Corfu (second century) was a criminal who was converted while he was in prison. He was then martyred for the faith by being boiled in oil on the Greek island of Corfu.

Euphronius Saint; Greek; good cheer

St. Euphronius (d. 573) was bishop of Tours, France, when the city was destroyed by fire. He devoted his life to help rebuild the city.

Euplius Saint; Greek

St. Euplius (d. 304) was a deacon at Catania, Sicily. He was found guilty of possessing a copy of scripture. After he refused to sacrifice to the gods, he was beheaded.

Euprepius Saint; Greek

St. Euprepius (first century) was the first bishop of Verona.

Eupsychius Saint; Greek; good soul

St. Eupsychius (d. 362) led a group of Christians who destroyed the temple of the goddess Fortuna in Caesarea. They were all martyred.

Eurgain Saint; Welsh; gold, beautiful

St. Eurgain (sixth century) was the daughter of chieftain Caradog of Glamorgan, Wales. She founded Cor-Eurgain, later called Llanwit.

Eusebius Saint; Greek; with good feelings

St. Eusebius, St. Eusebius of Bologna, St. Eusebius of Cremona, St. Eusebius of Milan, St. Eusebius of Rome, St. Eusebius of Samosata, St. Eusebius of Vercelli

St. Eusebius of Rome (d. 192) was martyred with Antony, Julius, Peregrinus, Pontian, and Vincent.

Euseus Saint; Celtic; hospitable

St. Euseus (fourteenth century) was from the Piedmont region of Italy. He was a hermit who supported himself by working as a cobbler.

Eusignius Saint; Greek; good sign

St. Eusignius (252–362) was a veteran of the Roman Imperial Army. He refused to sacrifice to the Roman gods and was beheaded at Antioch when he was 110 years old.

Eustace Saint; Latin, Greek; productive, stable, calm

Eustacee, Eustache, Eustachio, Eustachius, Eustachy, Eustashe, Eustasius, Eustatius, Eustazio, Eustes, Eustice, Eustis, Eustiss

St. Eustace, St. Eustace White

St. Eustace (d. 118) was a Roman military officer, originally named Placidus, who converted after experiencing a vision. He and his family were baptized, and he changed his name to Eustace. His faith was tested by a series of calamities, but like Job, he never lost his trust in God. When he refused to offer sacrifice to a pagan god, Emperor Hadrian had him and his family roasted to death.

Eustacee *see Eustace*

Eustache *see Eustace*

Eustachio *see Eustace*

Eustachius *see Eustace*

Eustachy *see Eustace*

Eustashe *see Eustace*

Eustasius *see Eustace*

Eustatius *see Eustace*

Eustazio *see Eustace*

Eusterius Saint; Greek; very free

St. Eusterius (fifth century) was the fourth bishop of Salerno, Italy.

Eustes *see Eustace*

Eustice *see Eustace*

Eustis *see Eustace*

Eustiss *see Eustace*

Eustochins Saint; Greek; produces many ears of corn

St. Eustochins (d. 461) was a bishop of Tours, France.

Eustochium *see Eustochium (girl's name)*

Eustorgius Saint; Greek; well loved

St. Eustorgius II (d. 518) was a Greek who lived in Rome. He was made bishop of Milan and ransomed many Christians who had been captured by Barbarians. He was known for his holiness.

Eustratius Saint; Greek; good soldier

St. Eustratius (fourth century) of Armenia and his servant were imprisoned during the persecution of Emperor Diocletian. His grace under torture convinced a soldier named Orestes to convert to Christianity. Eustratius, his servant, and Orestes were all martyred for the faith.

Euthymius Saint; Greek; in good spirits

St. Euthymius, St. Euthymius of Sardis, St. Euthymius the Younger

St. Euthymius (d. 377–473) was born into a wealthy family at Militene, Armenia. After being ordained, he was appointed supervisor of the monasteries in the diocese. When he was twenty-nine, he became a monk in Jerusalem, and then he became a hermit. He attracted so many followers, however, that Patriarch Juvenal of Jerusalem consecrated him a bishop so that he could minister to them. He spent sixty-six years in the desert.

Eutropius Saint; Greek; good character

St. Eutropius (third century) was a companion of St. Denis of Paris, France. He was a Roman who lived as a hermit near Saintes. After he converted the daughter of the local Roman governor, the governor had him killed by having his head split open with an ax.

Eutychian Saint; Greek; fortunate

Pope St. Eutychian (d. 283) served as pope from 275–283. The records of his papacy were destroyed during the reign of Emperor Diocletian, so little is known of him, other than that he was a Tuscan who buried many martyrs. He was the last pope buried in the papal crypt in the cemetery of Callixtus.

Eutychius Saint; Greek; happy, fortunate

Eutychus

St. Eutychius and Domitian, St. Eutychius of Alexandria, St. Eutychius

St. Eutychius (first century) was a disciple of St. John the Evangelist. He was born in Phyrgia and was with St. John in Patmos, Greece. He was imprisoned and tortured for the faith.

Eutychus *see Eutychius*

Ev *see Evan*

Evagrius Saint; Latin; from the fields

St. Evagrius (d. 380) was bishop of Constantinople, but after only a few months he was banished by Emperor Valens who was an Arian. He remained in exile until his death.

Evaine *see Evan*

Eval Saint; Greek; defends justice

Uval, Urfol

St. Eval (sixth century), also known as Uval or Urfol, was bishop of Cornwall, England.

Evan Saint; Top 100 Name; Hebrew; God is gracious

Eavan, Ev, Evaine, Evann, Evason, Even, Evonson, Evun, Ewen

St. Evan (ninth century) was a hermit in Ayrshire, Scotland.

Evann *see Evan*

Evaristus Saint; Greek; the excellent one

Aristus

Pope St. Evaristus (d. 107), also known as Aristus, was the fifth pope. He was the son of a Hellenic Jew from Bethlehem and was elected during the reign of Roman Emperor Domitian, a time of great persecution.

Evasius Saint; Latin; flee, escape

St. Evasius (d. 362) was the first bishop of Asti, Italy. Driven out by Arians, he was martyred at Casale Monferrato.

Evason *see Evan*

Evellius Saint; Hebrew; he who gives life

St. Evellius (d. 66) was a counselor to Emperor Nero. He was so impressed by the faith of the Christians of Rome that he converted. He was martyred at Pisa.

Even *see Evan*

Everard *see Evrard*

Evergislus Saint; English; friend of the boar

St. Evergislus (fifth century) was bishop of Cologne. He was possibly martyred by pagan robbers.

Evermarus Saint

St. Evermarus (d. 700) was on a pilgrimage when he was martyred by robbers at Rousson in Belgium.

Evermod Saint

Evermode

St. Evermod (d. 1178) was an abbot at Gottesgnaden and later at Magdeburg, Germany. In 1154, he became the first bishop of Ratzeburg. He is known as "the Apostle to the Wends."

Evermode *see Evermod*

Evermund Saint; English

St. Evermund (d. 720) was born in Bayeux, France. He was married, but he and his wife separated to enter religious life. He founded the Abbey of Fountenay-Louet in the diocese of Seez, France.

Evilasius Saint

Evodius Saint; Greek; he who follows a good road

St. Evodius (d. 69) was the first person to identify the followers of Christ as "Christians." He converted to Christianity through the efforts of St. Peter. He succeeded that saint as bishop of Antioch.

Evonson *see Evan*

Evortius Saint; Latin

St. Evortius (d. 340) was a Roman who became bishop of Orleans, France.

Evrard Saint; German; brave, strong boar

Eberard, Eberhard, Everard

St. Evrard (815–866), also known as Eberard, Eberhard, or Everard, was from France. He served as a soldier and married Gisela, the daughter of Emperor Louis the Pious. The couple was very devoted to their faith and used their wealth to help the poor, build churches, and start the French Abbey of Cysoing. Two of their sons became abbots. He also had a great love of learning and kept a large library.

Evroult *see Ebrulf*

Evun *see Evan*

Ewald Saint; German, English; always powerful, powerful layman

Sts. Ewald the Dark and Ewald the Fair (d. 692) were two brothers and priests from Northumbria, England, who shared the same name. They were differentiated by the color of their hair. They traveled to Germany, where they planned to serve as missionaries. Pagans martyred them.

Ewart *see Edward*

Ewen *see Evan*

Exuperantius Saint; Latin; abundant

St. Exuperantius (d. 418) was the bishop of Ravenna, Italy. He is credited with building the town of Argenta and with convincing Magister Militum not to pillage the cathedral when he occupied Ravenna.

Exuperius Saint; Latin; he who exceeds expectations

Soupire

St. Exuperius (d. 411), also known as Soupire, was a friend of St. Jerome and a bishop of Toulouse, France. He donated large sums of money to the Christian monks in Palestine, Lybia, and Egypt. He also provided for the poor of his own community. He is best known as the recipient of a list of the canonical scriptures as they are known today. He had written Pope Innocent I, requesting such a list.

Eythan *see Ethan*

Eythen *see Ethan*

Eythin *see Ethan*

Eython *see Ethan*

Eythyn *see Ethan*

Eyvan *see Ivan*

Ezakeil *see Ezekiel*

Ezéchiel *see Ezekiel*

Ezeck *see Ezekiel*

Ezeckiel *see Ezekiel*

Ezeeckel *see Ezekiel*

Ezekeial *see Ezekiel*

Ezekeil *see Ezekiel*

Ezekeyial *see Ezekiel*

Ezekial *see Ezekiel*

Ezekiel Old Testament; Hebrew; the strength of God

Esequiel, Ezakeil, Ezéchiel, Ezeck, Ezeckiel, Ezeeckel, Ezekeial, Ezekeil, Ezekeyial, Ezekial, Ezekielle, Ezell, Eziakah, Eziechiele, Haskel, Zeke

Ezekiel was a Jewish prophet. He wrote the Book of Ezekiel and prophesied about the destruction of the temple.

Ezekielle *see Ezekiel*

Ezell *see Ezekiel*

Ezequiel Saint; Hebrew; the strength of God

Ezekiel

St. Ezequiel Moreno y Diaz (1848–1906), also known as Ezekiel, was born in Alfaro, La Rioja, Spain. He joined the Order of Augustinian Recollects and was sent as a missionary to the Phillipines. He served as the military chaplain of a penal colony in Puerto Princesa City. He was named superior to the seminary in Monteagudo in 1885 and became the head of the Recollect Mission in Columbia in 1888. He was named bishop of Pasto, Columbia, in 1893. He was canonized by Pope John Paul II in 1992 and is a patron saint of cancer patients.

Eziakah *see Ezekiel*

Eziechiele *see Ezekiel*

Ezra Old Testament; Hebrew; helper, strong

Esra, Esrah, Ezrah, Ezri, Ezry

Ezra (480–440 BC) was a scribe. He may also have been a high priest. He returned from the Babylonian exile and reintroduced the Torah in Jerusalem. His story is told in the books of Ezra and Nehemiah.

Ezrah *see Ezra*

Ezri *see Ezra*

Ezry *see Ezra*

F

Fabain *see Fabian*

Fabayan *see Fabian*

Fabe *see Fabian*

Fabean *see Fabian*

Fabein *see Fabian*

Fabek *see Fabian*

Fabert *see Fabian*

Fabi *see Fabian*

Fabian Saint; Latin; bean grower

Fabain, Fabayan, Fabe, Fabean, Fabein, Fabek, Fabert, Fabi, Fabijan, Fabin, Fabion, Fabiyan, Fabyan, Fabyen, Fabyous, Faybian, Faybien

Pope St. Fabian (d. 250) came to Rome after Pope Anteros died in 236. He was a layperson and not well-known. He had most likely come just out of curiosity, but when they were trying to decide who would become the next pope, a dove descended upon him, and he was elected. Emperor Philip was friendly to Christians, and while he reigned, Pope Fabian was able to help build up the church of Rome, but when he died and Decius took over, persecutions began in earnest. Pope Fabian died as a martyr.

Fabijan *see Fabian*

Fabin *see Fabian*

Fabion *see Fabian*

Fabius Saint; Latin; bean grower

St. Fabius (d. 300) was a soldier in Caesarea, Mauretania, who was martyred for refusing to carry a Roman standard that bore pagan emblems.

Fabiyan *see Fabian*

Fabrician Saint; Latin; craftsman

St. Fabrician (date unknown) was martyred with St. Philibert in Toledo, Spain.

Fabyan *see Fabian*

Fabyen *see Fabian*

Fabyous *see Fabian*

Fachanan Saint; Gaelic

St. Fachanan (d. 600) is an Irish saint who was born at Tulachteann and was a pupil of St. Ita. He founded the monastery of Molana and the monastic school of Ross, which flourished for three hundred years. He was known for his generosity and his gift of preaching.

Facio Saint; Latin; to make, accomplish

St. Facio (d. 512) was the bishop of Masstricht, Netherlands. He faced pagan opposition and barbarian invasions.

Faciolus Saint; Latin

St. Faciolus (d. 950) was a Benedictine monk at St. Cyprian Abbey in Poitiers, France. He was known for his holiness.

Facius *see Fazzio*

Facundius Saint; Latin; he who makes convincing arguments

Fides, Foy

St. Facundius (date unknown) was a bishop of Taino in Umbria, Italy.

Facundus Saint; Latin; he who makes convincing arguments

St. Facundus (d. 300) and his friend St. Primitivus were natives of León who were beheaded on the site of Sahugan, Spain. A Benedictine monastery was founded at that location, dedicated to these two martyrs.

Falito *see Raphael*

Famianw Saint; Latin; he who has acquired fame

Quardus

St. Famianw (d. 1150), also known as Quardus, was a native of Cologne, Germany. He traveled to Rome, the Holy Land, and Spain on a pilgrimage. He decided to stay at Compostela and live as a hermit. He later joined a Cistercian abbey. He died in Umbria, Italy.

Fandila Saint; Greek; priest

St. Fandila (d. 852) was from Cadiz, Spain. He became a Benedictine monk in Córdoba. He was asked to become a priest for the religious community at San Salvador Monastery at Pinna Mellaria. After he was ordained, he preached the faith with great zeal. He was beheaded for appearing before a Moorish magistrate and refuting Islam.

Farannan Saint; Gaelic

St. Farannan (d. 590) was a follower of St. Columba on Iona, Scotland. He went to Ireland, where he lived as a hermit at Allernan, Sligo.

Faro Saint; Portuguese; beacon

St. Faro (d. 675) was raised in the court of King Thibert of Austrasia. He married Blidechild, but they separated so that the two could enter religious life. He became a monk, was named bishop of Meaux, France, and served as chancellor to King Dagobert I of the Franks.

Fatius *see Fazzio*

Fauss *see Faustus*

Faust *see Faustus*

Faustin *see Faustino*

Faustine *see Faustino*

Faustinian Saint; Latin; lucky, fortunate

St. Faustinian (fourth century) was the second bishop of Bologna, Italy. He was an ardent foe of the Arian heresy and was tortured during the persecutions of Emperor Diocletian, but he survived.

Faustino Saint; Latin; lucky, fortunate

Faustin, Faustine, Faustyn

Bl. Faustino Miguez (1831–1925) was born in a village of River Acevedo, Celanova, in the province of Orense. He joined the Pious Schools of San Fernando in Madrid and was ordained a priest. He devoted his life to working with the young, the poor, and those who were sick. He was beatified by Pope John Paul II in 1998.

Faustinus Saint; Latin; lucky, fortunate

St. Faustinus (d. 120) was martyred in Brescia with his sibling Jovita. The two are honored as patron saints of Brescia.

Faustis *see Faustus*

Faustise *see Faustus*

Faustos *see Faustus*

Faustus Saint; Latin; lucky, fortunate

Fauss, Faust, Faustis, Faustise, Faustos, Faustyce, Faustys

St. Faustus of Riez (d. 490) was born in Brittany, France, and may have been trained as a lawyer before becoming abbot of Lerins. He was later named bishop of Riez, France. He was known as a Christian writer and for speaking out against the Arian and Pelagian heresies.

Faustyce *see Faustus*

Faustyn *see Faustino*

Faustys *see Faustus*

Faybian *see Fabian*

Faybien *see Fabian*

Fazius *see Fazzio*

Fazzio Saint; Italian; good worker

Facius, Fatius, Fazius

St. Fazzio (1190–1272), also known as Facius, Fatius, or Fazius, was born in Verona, Italy. He founded the charitable society known as the Order of the Holy Spirit at Cremona, which cared for the pilgrims and sick.

Fearghas *see Fergus*

Fearghus *see Fergus*

Feargus *see Fergus*

Fechin Saint; Gaelic; little raven

Feichin

St. Fechin (d. 665), also known as Feichin, was born at Leyney, Ireland. He founded Fobhare, or Fore, Monastery where he served as abbot. He died of the plague.

Fee *see Felix*

Feeleep *see Felipe*

Feichin *see Fechin*

Felep *see Felipe*

Felic *see Felix*

Felice Saint; Latin; fortunate, happy

St. Felice da Nicosia (1715–1787) was born Giacomo Amoroso, the son of a shoemaker in

Nocosia, Italy. When he was nineteen, he tried to enter the Capuchin order but was refused several times. After eight years, they admitted him. He served as beggar for the house. He had a great devotion to the Blessed Sacrament and the gifts of healing and bilocation. He was canonized by Pope Benedict XVI in 2005.

Felician Saint; form of Felix; Latin; fortunate, happy

St. Felician of Foligno (160–251) was the bishop of Foligno, Italy, an office he held for more than fifty years. He was arrested at age ninety-four for refusing to sacrifice to the Roman gods. He was tortured and died en route to Rome, where he was to be martyred.

Feliciano *see Felix*

Felicissimus Saint; Latin; most fortunate, most happy

St. Felicissimus (d. 303) was martyred in Perugia, Italy.

Felike *see Felix*

Feliks *see Felix*

Felinus Saint; Latin; kitty

St. Felinus (d. 250) was martyred with a fellow soldier, Gratian, in Perugia, Italy.

Felip *see Felipe*

Felipe Saint; form of Philip; Spanish; lover of horses

Feeleep, Felep, Felip, Felo, Filip, Filippo

Bl. Felipe Ripoll Morata (1878–1939) was a priest, professor,

and spiritual director who was martyred during the Spanish Civil War. He was beatified in 1995 by Pope John Paul II.

Felix Saint; Latin; happy, fortunate

Fee, Felic, Feliciano, Felike, Feliks, Felizio, Felo, Filix, Filyk, Fylix, Fylyx

St. Felix, Pope St. Felix I, III, IV, St. Felix of Bologna, St. Felix of Bourges, St. Felix of Brescia, St. Felix of Cantalice, St. Felix of Como, St. Felix of Fondi, St. Felix of Fritzlar, St. Felix of Metz, St. Felic of Nantes, St. Felix of Pavia, St. Felix

St. Felix of Valois (1127–1212) lived as a hermit in a forest in the diocese of Meaux. St. John of Martha joined him and suggested that they start a religious order dedicated to ransoming captives from the Moors. They went to Rome to appeal to Pope Innocent III and, after much deliberation, he gave his blessing to the new order, known as the Order of the Most Holy Trinity for the Redemption of Captives. They began the monastery of Cerfroid in France and within forty years had established six hundred monasteries.

Felizio *see Felix*

Felo *see Felipe, Felix*

Ferdinan *see Ferdinand*

Ferdinand Saint; German; daring, adventurous

Ferdinan, Ferdinandus, Ferdynand, Fernando, Ferynand

St. Ferdinand III of Castile, St. Ferdinand of Aragon

St. Ferdinand III of Castile (1199–1252) was the son of Alfonso IX, king of Leon, and Berengaria, daughter of Alfonso III, king of Castile (Spain). Ferdinand became king of Castile when he was eighteen. He also was king of Palencia, Valladolid, and Burgos. He married Princess Beatrice of Germany, and they had ten children. He fought against the Moors and founded the Cathedral of Burgos and the University of Salamanca. He also started hospitals, monasteries, and churches. He was a secular member of the Franciscan order.

Ferdinandus *see Ferdinand*

Ferdynand *see Ferdinand*

Feredarius Saint

St. Feredarius (d. 863) was an Irish abbot of Iona, Scotland, who moved the relics of St. Columba to Ireland during the Danish raids.

Ferghas *see Fergus*

Ferghus *see Fergus*

Fergie *see Fergus*

Fergna Saint; Gaelic; having strength

St. Fergna (d. 637) was a relative of St. Columba. Known as "the White," he served as abbot of Iona, Scotland.

Fergus Saint; Gaelic; strong, manly

Fearghas, Fearghus, Feargus, Ferghas, Ferghus, Fergie, Ferguson,
Fergusson, Fergustian, Firgus, Firgusen, Firguson, Furgus, Furgusen, Furguson

St. Fergus (d. 721), also known as Fergustian, was an Irish bishop who went to Scotland as a missionary. He founded churches in Strogeth and Caithness and attended the Roman Council in 721.

Ferguson *see Fergus*

Fergusson *see Fergus*

Fergustian *see Fergus*

Fernando *see Ferdinand*

Ferreolus Saint; Latin; referring to iron

St. Ferreolus (d. 591) was a bishop of Limoges, France.

Ferrutio Saint; Latin, Italian; iron

St. Ferrutio (d. 212) was a deacon, originally from Asia Minor, who served in Besancon, France, as a missionary. He served for thirty years before being arrested, tortured, and beheaded during the persecution of Alexander Severus.

Ferrutius Saint; Latin; iron, sword

St. Ferrutius (date unknown) was a Roman soldier serving in Mainz, Germany, who was arrested for refusing to take part in a pagan ceremony. He died from being tortured while in prison.

Ferynand *see Ferdinand*

Fiace Saint

Fiech

St. Fiace (d. fifth century), also known as Fiech, was a disciple of St. Patrick. He served as an Irish bishop and wrote a hymn in honor of St. Patrick.

Fiachan Saint; Celtic; crow

St. Fiachan (seventh century) was from Munster, Ireland. He lived as a monk in Lismore Abbey.

Fiacre Saint; Latin; soldier

St. Fiacre (d. 670) was born in Ireland, where he lived at a hermitage in County Kilkenny. He was known for being holy, as well as for his skill with herbs and the ability to heal. He attracted many followers and for this reason went to France to seek greater solitude. St. Faro, the bishop of Meaux, gave him a spot in Breuil, where he built an oratory in honor of Mary, a hospice for receiving visitors, and a cell where he lived. He never allowed any woman to enter his monastery. He is a patron saint of gardeners and cab drivers.

Fiari *see Phaebadius*

Fibitius Saint

St. Fibitius (d. 500) was an abbot who later served as bishop of Trier, Germany.

Fidel *see Fidelis*

Fidele *see Fidelis*

Fidelio *see Fidelis*

Fidelis Saint; Latin; faithful

Fidel, Fidele, Fidelio, Fidell, Fido, Fydal, Fydel

St. Fidelis, St. Fidelis of Como, St. Fidelis of Sigmaringen

St. Fidelis of Como (d. 304) was a Roman soldier stationed in Milan, Italy. He was martyred for helping Christian prisoners escape.

Fidell *see Fidelis*

Fidentius Saint; Latin; trusting, fearless

St. Fidentius (second century) was a bishop of Padua, Italy.

Fides *see Facundius*

Fidharleus Saint; Celtic

St. Fidharleus (d. 762) was an Irish abbot responsible for restoring Rathin Abbey.

Fido *see Fidelis*

Fidouls Saint

St. Fidouls (d. 540) was the son of a Roman official who was taken prisoner and sold into slavery. After he was ransomed by Aventinus, the abbot of Aumont Abbey near Troyes, France, he joined the monastery. He later served as abbot.

Fidweten Saint

St. Fidweten (d. 888) was a Benedictine monk at Redon Abbey, Brittany, France.

Fiech *see Fiace*

Filaster *see Philaster*

Filbert *see Philibert*

Filip Saint; form of Philip; Greek; lover of horses

Bl. Felip Geryluk (1830–1874) was a married father from Zaczopki, Poland. He was shot by Russian soldiers in Podlasie, Poland. He is one of the Martyrs of Podlasie and was beatified by Pope John Paul II in 1996.

Filippo *see Felipe*

Filippo Saint; form of Philip; Greek; lover of horses

St. Filippo Smaldone (1848–1923) was born in Naples, Italy. He became a priest and worked with plague victims. He contracted the disease but was miraculously cured through Our Lady of Pompei. He founded a school for deaf-mutes in Lecce, Italy, which later became the motherhouse of the Congregation of the Salesian Sisters of the Sacred Hearts. Filippo expanded the school's mission to include working with blind, orphaned, and abandoned children. He also founded the Eucharistic League of Priest Adorers. He was canonized by Pope Benedict XVI in 2006.

Filix *see Felix*

Fillan Saint; Celtic; little wolf

Foelan

St. Fillan (eighth century), also known as Foelan, was son of Feriarch and St. Kentigerna. He became a monk and lived near St. Andrew's Monastery in Scotland. He served as abbot for a time before resigning that position to resume his life as a hermit. This time he settled at Glendochart, Pertchire, where he built a church. He was known as a miracle worker.

Filo *see Philo*

Filomeno *see Philemon*

Filuned *see Allucio, Almedha (girl's name)*

Filyk *see Felix*

Finan Saint; Gaelic; light skinned, white

St. Finan, St. Finan of Lindisfarne

St. Finan of Lindisfarne (d. 661) was born in Ireland. He became a monk at Iona in Scotland and was later elected bishop of Lindisfarne.

Finbar Saint; Celtic; fair haired

Bairre, Barr, Barry, Finnbarr

St. Finbar (550–620) was born in Connaught, Ireland. He was educated by the monks at Kilmacahil, Kilkenney. He made two pilgrimages to Rome and preached in Ireland and Scotland. He lived as a hermit at Lough Eiroe and then began a monastery that started the city of Cork. He served as the first bishop of Cork. He was known as a miracle worker.

Findan Saint; Celtic; fair

Fintan

St. Findan (d. 879), also known as Fintan, was born in Leinster, Ireland. Norse raiders captured him and made him a slave. After he escaped, he traveled to Rome and became a Benedictine at Sabina. He lived as a hermit at the Rheinan Abbey in Switzerland for more than twenty years.

Fineen *see Finian*

Fingar Saint; Celtic; fair garden or enclosure

St. Fingar (fifth century) was born in Ireland. He and his

sister Phiala and other companions were martyred at Hoyle, near Penzance, by pagans.

Finian Saint; Gaelic; light skinned, white

Fineen, Finien, Finn, Finnen, Finnian, Finyan, Fionan, Fionna, Fynyan

St. Finian, St. Finian Lobhar, St. Finian Munnu, St. Finian of Clonard

St. Finian (d. 579) was born into a royal family in Strangford, Lough, Ulster, in Ireland. He became a monk in Strathclyde and was ordained in Rome. He founded several monasteries in Ulster and became abbot of Moville in County Down, Ireland. He was known as a miracle worker.

Finien *see Finian*

Finlugh Saint; Celtic

St. Finlugh (sixth century) was born in Ireland, trained in Scotland, and then returned to Ireland to become the abbot of a monastery in County Deify.

Finn *see Finian*

Finnbarr *see Finbar*

Finnen *see Finian*

Finnian *see Finian*

Fintan Saint; Gaelic; from Finn's town

Finten, Fintin, Finton, Fintyn, Fyntan, Fynten, Fyntin, Fynton, Fyntyn

St. Fintan (d. 603) was a hermit in Clonenagh, Leix, Ireland. He attracted many followers and

became their abbot. He was known for the gifts of clairvoyance and prophecy, as well as for being a miracle worker.

Finten *see Fintan*

Fintin *see Fintan*

Finton *see Fintan*

Fintyn *see Fintan*

Finyan *see Finian*

Fionan *see Finian*

Fionna *see Finian*

Fionnchu Saint; Celtic; fair hound, fair warrior

St. Fionnchu (sixth century) was an abbot of Bangor Abbey in Ireland.

Firgus *see Fergus*

Firgusen *see Fergus*

Firguson *see Fergus*

Firmatus Saint; Latin; firm

St. Firmatus (date unknown) was a deacon who was martyred in Auxerre, France.

Firmian Saint; Latin; firm, sure

St. Firmian (d. 1020) was a Benedictine abbot of San Piceno in Italy.

Firminus Saint; Latin; firm, sure

St. Firminus, St. Firminus of Amiens, St. Firminus of Metz, St. Firminus of Uzes

St. Firminus (sixth century) was a bishop of Viviers, France. He was known for his charity and his support of monasticism.

Firmus Saint; Latin; firm, sure

St. Firmus, St. Firmus of Tagaste

St. Firmus (d. 290) was a martyr persecuted under Maximian.

Fitzhugh *see Hugh*

Flabio *see Flavius*

Flainn *see Flannan*

Flan *see Flannan*

Flanan *see Flannan*

Flanin *see Flannan*

Flann *see Flannan*

Flannan Saint; Gaelic; redhead

Flainn, Flan, Flanan, Flanin, Flann, Flannen, Flannery, Flannin, Flannon, Flanon, Flanyn

St. Flannan (seventh century) was the son of an Irish chieftain. On a pilgrimage to Rome, he was consecrated a bishop by Pope John IV. He served as the first bishop of Killaloe.

Flannen *see Flannan*

Flannery *see Flannan*

Flannin *see Flannan*

Flannon *see Flannan*

Flanon *see Flannan*

Flanyn *see Flannan*

Flavel *see Flavian*

Flavelle *see Flavian*

Flavian Saint; Latin; blond, golden haired

Flavel, Flavelle, Flavien, Flavyan, Flawian, Flawiusz, Flawyan

St. Flavian, St. Flavian of Autun, St. Flavian of Constantinople

St. Flavian (d. 512) was patriarch of Antioch. He was exiled by Emperor Anastasius I, who was a Monophysite. He died in the city of Petra, Jordan.

Flavias *see Flavius*

Flavien *see Flavian*

Flavio *see Flavius*

Flavious *see Flavius*

Flavius Saint; Latin; blond, golden haired

Flabio, Flavias, Flavio, Flavious, Flavyo

St. Flavius, St. Flavius Clemens

St. Flavius (d. 300) was bishop of Nicomedia. He was martyred along with his brothers Augustine and Augustus.

Flavyan *see Flavian*

Flavyo *see Flavius*

Flawian *see Flavian*

Flawiusz *see Flavian*

Flawyan *see Flavian*

Flocellus Saint; Celtic; small flower

St. Flocellus (second century) was martyred in Autun, France, by being thrown to wild beasts.

Floraz *see Florian*

Florbert *see Floribert*

Florentino Saint; Latin; blooming

Florentyno

Bl. Florentino Asensio Barroso (1877–1936) was a Spanish priest who served as pastor of Villaverde de Medina before being transferred to Valladolid. He became bishop of Valladolid. He was arrested during the Spanish Civil War. He was tortured for two weeks before being shot. He was beatified by Pope John Paul II in 1997.

Florentinus Saint; Latin; blooming

St. Florentinus of Trier (fourth century) was a bishop of Trier, Germany.

Florentius Saint; Latin; blooming

St. Florentius, St. Florentius of Carracedo, St. Florentius of Strasbourg, St. Florentius of Vienne

St. Florentius (fifth century) was a Bavarian who was ordained by St. Martin of Tours and sent to France as a missionary. He lived as a hermit on Mount Glonne in Anjou. Due to the large number of followers he attracted, he founded a monastery, now called St. Florent le Vieux.

Florentyno *see Florentino*

Flores *see Florian*

Florian Saint; Latin; flowering, blooming

Floraz, Flores, Florien, Florion, Floriz, Florrian, Flory, Floryan, Floryant, Floryante

St. Florian (d. 304) was an officer in the Roman army. He declared himself to be Christian when the soldiers of Aquilinus were rounding the Christians up. He was scouraged, flayed, set on fire, and then thrown into the river Enns with a stone around his neck. He is a protector of those in danger of fire or water.

Floribert Saint; German; brilliant master

Florbert

St. Floribert, St. Floribert of Leige

St. Floribert (d. 660), also known as Florbert, served as abbot of Mont-Bladin and Saint-Bavon in Ghent, Belgium.

Florien *see Florian*

Florion *see Florian*

Floriz *see Florian*

Florrian *see Florian*

Florus Saint; French; flowers

St. Florus (d. 389) was the bishop of Lodeve in Languedoc, France.

Flory *see Florian*

Floryan *see Florian*

Floryant *see Florian*

Floryante *see Florian*

Flosculus Saint; Latin; wildflower

Flou

St. Flosculus (d. 480), also known as Flou, was a bishop of Orleans, France.

Flou *see Flosculus*

Foelan *see Fillan*

Foellan Saint; Celtic

St. Foellan (eighth century) was from Ireland, the son of St. Kentigem. He traveled with his holy mother to Scotland, where he became a monk and served as a missionary.

Forannan Saint; Celtic

St. Forannan (d. 932) was a bishop in Ireland. After having a vision directing him to travel to Meuse, he went to Belgium with twelve companions. There, he founded an abbey at Waulsort, where he served as abbot.

Forseus *see Fursey*

Fortchern Saint; Celtic; overlord

St. Fortchern (sixth century) was bishop of Trim, Ireland, a position he resigned in order to live as a hermit in Meath.

Fortun *see Fortunatus*

Fortunatus Saint; Latin; fortune, fortunate

Fortun, Fortune, Fortunio

St. Fortunatus, St. Fortunatus of Spoleto

St. Fortunatus of Spoleto (d. 400) was a native of Montefalco, a hill town near Spoleto in Umbria, Italy. He was a parish priest known for his charity and care for the poor.

Fortune *see Fortunatus*

Fortunio *see Fortunatus*

Foster *see Vedast*

Foy *see Facundius*

Fragan Saint

St. Fragan (fifth century) and his wife, Gwen, were the parents of Sts. Jacut, Guithem, and Winwaloe. They traveled to Brittany, France, in order to escape the pagan barbarians of England.

Fran *see Francis*

France *see Francis*

Francesco Saint; form of Francis; Italian; free, from France

St. Francesco Antonio Fasani, St. Francesco Fogolla, St. Francesco Lantrua

St. Francesco Antonio Fasani (1681–1742) was born in Lucera, Foggia, Italy, as Antony Fasani. He entered the Conventional Franciscan Order in 1695, where he took the name Francesco. He was a teacher, provincial of the

order, master o pastor. He was k tic and for his care o₁ ᵤ He was canonized in 1986 by Pope John Paul II.

Francis Saint; Latin; from France

Fran, France, Franciskus, Franco, Francys, Frank, Frannie, Franny, Franscis, Fransis, Franus, Frencis

St. Francis of Assisi, St. Francis Borgia, St. Francis Caracciolo, St. Francis Ch'oe Kyong-Hwan, St. Francis de Morales, St. Francis de Sales, St. Francis Fasani, St. Francis Galvez, St. Francis Isidore Gagelin, St. Francis Jaccard, St. Francis Jerome

St. Francis of Assisi (1181–1226) was born at Assisi in Umbria, Italy. His father, Pietro Bernardone, was a wealthy cloth merchant who wanted his son to follow in his footsteps. Francis was charismatic and attracted a group of friends who were leading a wild youth, but he most of all wanted to be a knight. He left for the Fourth Crusade but returned after having a vision that God wanted him to return home. At the church at San Damiano, he heard Christ ask him to "repair my church." He dedicated himself to this project, and his father disowned him. The bishop supported his efforts, however. Francis soon began to preach and to attract followers. He wanted them all to live by the Gospel and live a life of poverty. He was the founder of the Franciscan order and is known for his love of all creation. He is the patron saint of animals, merchants, and ecology.

Francisco Saint; form of Francis; Portuguese, Spanish; free, from France

Fransysco, Frasco

St. Francisco Fernandez de Capillas (1607–1648) was a Spanish missionary in China. He was beheaded and became the first Catholic martyr in China. He was canonized in 2000 by Pope John Paul II.

Franciskus *see Francis*

Franciszek Saint; form of Francis; Latin; free, from France

Bl. Franciszek Dachtera, Bl. Franciszek Drzewiecki, Bl. Franciszek Kesy, Bl. Franciszek Rogaczewski, Bl. Franciszek Roslaniec, Bl. Franciszek Stryjas

Bl. Franciszek Dachtera (1910–1942) was a Polish priest who was imprisoned and martyred at the Dachau concentration camp. He is one of the 108 Polish Martyrs of World War II who were beatified by Pope John Paul II in 1999.

Franco *see Francis*

Francois Saint; form of Francis; French; free, from France

Francoise

St. Francois Gagelin (1799–1833) grew up in a family that helped protect loyal priests during the French Revolution. He later joined the Paris-based Society for Foreign Missions.

He headed for Asia and was ordained a priest in Vietnam. He gave himself up to the pagan authorities in 1833 when they were persecuting Christians. He had always longed to be a martyr and was granted his wish when he was beheaded. He was canonized in 1988 by Pope John Paul II.

Francoise *see Francois*

Francys *see Francis*

Frank *see Francis*

Frannie *see Francis*

Franny *see Francis*

Franscis *see Francis*

Fransis *see Francis*

Fransysco *see Francisco*

Franus *see Francis*

Frasco *see Francisco*

Fraternus Saint; Latin; brotherly

St. Fraternus (d. 450) was a bishop and martyr of Auxerre, France.

Fred *see Alfred*

Fredderick *see Frederick*

Fredegand Saint; Celtic

St. Fredegand (d. 740) was born in Ireland and was a student of St. Foillan of Fosses. He lived as a monk at Kerkelodor Abbey near Antwerp, Belgium. He later served as abbot.

Fredek *see Frederick*

Frederick Saint; German; peaceful ruler

Fredderick, Fredek, Frederrick, Fredwick, Fredwyck

St. Frederick (780–838) was bishop of Utrecht, Germany. He sent many missionaries into the northern part of Germany to fight the paganism there. He was assassinated while celebrating Mass.

Frederico Saint; form of Frederick; Spanish; peaceful ruler

Frederigo, Fredrico

Bl. Frederico Albert (1820–1876) was born in Torino, Italy. He became a priest and founded the Congregation of the Vincentian Sisters of Mary Immaculate (the Albertines). He was beatified by Pope John Paul II in 1984.

Frederigo *see Frederico*

Frederrick *see Frederick*

Frediano Saint; Latin, Italian; cold

Frigidanus, Frigidian

St. Frediano (d. 588), also known as Frigidanus or Frigidian, was a prince of Ireland who went on a pilgrimage to Rome. The pope named him bishop of Lucca. He also founded a group of eremitical canons.

Fredo *see Sigfrid*

Fredrico *see Frederico*

Fredwick *see Frederick*

Fredwyck *see Frederick*

Frencis *see Francis*

Friard Saint; Latin; brother

St. Friard (d. 577) was a companion of St. Secundel. He lived as a hermit on the island of Vindomitte, near Nantes, France.

Fricor Saint

Adrian

St. Fricor (seventh century), sometimes called Adrian, was an Irish missionary in northern France.

Fridolin Saint; Teutonic; he who loves peace

St. Fridolin (d. 540) was from Ireland. He settled in Poitiers, France, and rebuilt the monastery of St. Hilary. He then lived as a hermit on the Rhine, where he started the Abbey of Sackingen.

Frigidanus *see Frediano*

Frigidian *see Frediano*

Frithestan Saint; English

St. Frithestan (d. 933) served as bishop of Winchester, England, from 909 until 931.

Frodobert Saint; German; bright, wise

St. Frodobert (d. 673) was a Benedictine monk at Luxeuil, France, and later founded Moutier la Celle Abbey near Troyes.

Frodulphus Saint

St. Frodulphus (d. 750) was a monk at Autun, France. Because of the Saracen invasion, he fled to Barjon, on the Cote d'Or.

Fromundus Saint

St. Fromundus (d. 690) was a Benedictine bishop of Coutances, France.

Fronto Saint; Latin; he who thinks

St. Fronto (first century) was a follower of Christ and was

baptized by St. Peter. He accompanied St. Peter to Rome and was then sent as a missionary to Gaul. He was the first bishop of Perigueux.

Fructuosus Saint; Latin; he who bears much fruit

St. Fructuosus of Braga, St. Fructuosus of Tarragona

St. Fructuosus of Tarragona (d. 259) was a bishop of Tarragona, Spain. He and two deacons, Augurius and Eulogius, were arrested by the Roman governor Emilian and were burned at the stake.

Fructus Saint; Latin; he who bears much fruit

St. Fructus (642–715) was born to a noble family of Segovia, Spain. After his parents' death, he and his brother and sister gave all their wealth to the poor and lived as hermits. Moors martyred his siblings, but Fructus died of natural causes.

Frugentius Saint; Latin

St. Frugentius (d. 675) was a Benedictine monk who was martyred with St. Aigulphus on the island of Capria, near Corsica.

Frumentius Saint; Latin; he who provides wheat

Abuna

St. Frumentius (d. 380) was born in Tyre, Lebanon. He was shipwrecked while on a voyage on the Red Sea and was taken to the Ethiopian royal court, where he became a secretary.

He and his brother, St. Aedesius, introduced Christianity to Ethiopia. Frumentius was consecrated the first bishop of Axum.

Fugatius Saint; Latin

St. Fugatius (second century) was a missionary sent by Pope St. Eleutherius to Britain.

Fulbert Saint; German; he who shines

St. Fulbert (d. 1028) was born in France and studied at Rheims, under future Pope Sylvester II. He became bishop of Chartres, where he rebuilt the cathedral after it burnt down. He was known for his defense of monasticism and orthodoxy. He was also a poet.

Fulco Saint; Spanish; village

St. Fulco (d. 1229) was bishop of Piacenza, Italy. He was later transferred to the see of Pavia. He was extremely generous, even sharing his meals with the poor.

Fulcran Saint; French

St. Fulcran (d. 1006) was bishop of Lodeve, in Languedoc, France. He upheld high moral values among the clergy and religious orders and rebuilt many churches and monasteries. He also cared for the sick and started several hospitals.

Fulgencio Saint; Latin; he who shines and stands out

Bl. Fulgencio Calvo Sanchez (1916–1936) was one of the Passionist Martyrs of Daimiel who was martyred during the Spanish Civil War. He was beatified by Pope John Paul II in 1989.

Fulgentius Saint; Latin; he who shines and stands out

St. Fulgentius (d. 633) was the brother of Sts. Isidore, Leander, and Florentina. He was bishop of Ecija in Andalusia, Spain.

Fulk Saint; English; folk, people

St. Fulk (1164–1229) was born in Piacenza, Italy, to Scottish parents. He studied in Paris and then was named bishop of Piacenza. Pope Honorius III later sent him to Pavia.

Fulrad Saint; French

St. Fulrad (710–784) was born in Alsace, France. He served as abbot of St. Denis Abbey near Paris. He served Pepin, Carloman, and Charlemagne. He and St. Burchard helped win the approval of Pope St. Zachary to have Pepin be named king of the Franks. He later aided Pepin in giving Ravenna, Italy, to the Holy See. He also founded monasteries.

Furgus see *Fergus*

Furgusen see *Fergus*

Furguson see *Fergus*

Fursa see *Fursey*

Furseus see *Fursey*

Fursey Saint; Gaelic

Forseus, Fursa, Furseus, Fursy

St. Fursey (d. 650) was born to a noble family on the island of Inisguia en Lough Carri, Ireland. He founded Rathmat

Abbey. Later, he went to East Anglia, England, and founded a monastery near Ugremouth. He also built a monastery at Lagny, near Paris, France.

Fursy see *Fursey*

Fuscian Saint; Latin; dark

St. Fuscian (d. 287) was a Christian missionary to the Morini people of Gaul. He was tortured in Amiens and beheaded at Saint Aux-Bois.

Fydal see *Fidelis*

Fydel see *Fidelis*

Fylix see *Felix*

Fylo see *Philo*

Fylyx see *Felix*

Fymbert Saint; German

St. Fymbert (seventh century) was a bishop of western Scotland ordained by Pope St. Gregory the Great.

Fyntan see *Fintan*

Fynten see *Fintan*

Fyntin see *Fintan*

Fynton see *Fintan*

Fyntyn see *Fintan*

Fynyan see *Finian*

G

Gabe see *Gabriel*

Gabinus Saint; form of Gabriel; Hebrew; devoted to God

St. Gabinus (d. 295) was the brother of Pope St. Gaius and the father of St. Susanna. Even though he was related to Emperor Diocletian, he was beheaded for refusing to sacrifice to pagan gods.

Gabis *see Gabriel*

Gabrael *see Gabriel*

Gabraiel *see Gabriel*

Gabrell *see Gabriel*

Gabrian *see Gabriel*

Gabriel Saint, Angel; Top 100 Name; Hebrew; God is my strength

Gabe, Gabbyn, Gabis, Gabrael, Gabraiel, Gabreil, Gabrell, Gabrian, Gabriël, Gabrielus, Gabrile, Gabris, Gabryel, Gebereal, Gebreil, Gebrell, Genereal, Gereil, Ghabriel, Riel

St. Gabriel, St. Gabriel Francis of Our Lady of Sorrows, St. Gabriel Jusuke, St. Gabriel Lalement, St. Gabriel Taurin Dufresse, St. Gabriel the Archangel

St. Gabriel the Archangel appears in scripture as a messenger from God. In the book of Daniel, he explains Daniel's visions. In the Gospel of Luke, he foretells the births of both John the Baptist and of Jesus. He is the patron saint of communication workers.

Gabrielus *see Gabriel*

Gabrile *see Gabriel*

Gabris *see Gabriel*

Gaetan *see Gaetano*

Gaetano Saint; Italian; from Gaeta, a city in southern Italy

Gaetan, Gaetono

St. Gaetano Catanoso, St. Gaetano Errico

St. Gaetano Catanoso (1879–1963) was born to wealthy landowners in Chorio di San Lorenzo, Reggio Calabria, Italy. After being ordained a priest, he served the rural parish of Pentidattilo. He started the Confraternity of the Holy Face in 1920. He was later moved to the larger parish of Santa Maria de la Candelaria, where he served for almost twenty years. He also served as a hospital chaplain and spiritual director. In 1934, he started the Congregation of the Daughters of St. Veronica, Missionaries of the Holy Face. He was canonized by Pope Benedict XVI in 2005.

Gaetono *see Gaetano*

Gagericus Saint

Gery, Gau

St. Gagericus (d. 625), also known as Gery or Gau, became bishop of Cambrai and Arras, France. He founded St. Medard Monastery in Brussels, Belgium.

Gaimo *see Giacomo*

Gaius Saint; Latin; rejoicer

Caius

Pope St. Gaius, St. Gaius Francis, St. Gaius of Korea

Pope St. Gaius (d. 296), also known as Caius, was from Solana, a member of a noble family related to Emperor Diocletian. He became pope in 283 and spent the last eight years of his papacy in the catacombs of Rome. He died a martyr.

Galagnus Saint

St. Galagnus (d. 1181) lived as a hermit on Mount Siepe in Tuscany, Italy.

Galation Saint; Latin; to freeze

St. Galation (d. 251) was the son of Sts. Clitaphon and Leucippe. He converted his wife, Episteme, to Christianity. He then became a hermit, and she lived with a community of virgins. They did not see each other again until he was being martyred. Episteme went to his side and was martyred with him.

Galdinus Saint; Latin; pale green

St. Galdinus (1100–1176) was a member of the Della Scala family of Milan, Italy. He served in various clerical offices before being forced into exile when Emperor Frederick I Barbarossa took revenge on Milan. He later returned and was named archbishop and, later, cardinal of Milan. He helped rebuild the city.

Galfrido *see Walfrid*

Gall Saint; Gaelic; from Gaul

St. Gall (550–646) was a companion of St. Columban. He was one of the twelve Irishmen who accompanied Columban to France, where Gall helped found Luxeuil Monastery. He later followed Columban to Switzerland, where he became a hermit on the Steinach River.

Gallgo Saint; Celtic; foreign, stranger

St. Gallgo (sixth century) was the founder of Llanalgo Anney in Anglesey, Wales.

Gallicanus Saint; Latin; from Gaul, France

St. Gallicanus (d. 541) was the fifth bishop of Embrun, France.

Gamaliel Saint; Hebrew; recompense of God, camel of God

St. Gamaliel (first century) was a rabbi who taught St. Paul. He advised the Jewish Sanhedrin in Jerusalem to release St. Peter and other apostles. He later became a Christian himself.

Gamelbert Saint; German; distinguished because of his age

Bl. Gamelbert of Michaelsbuch (720–802) was born to a wealthy family in Bavaria. He served as a parish priest in Michaelsbuch, Germany, for more than fifty years and founded the Benedictine Metten Abbey.

Gamo Saint

St. Gamo (eighth century) was a Benedictine abbot of Bretigny, near Noyon, France. He was a patron of the arts who helped monastic expansion during that era.

Gangulphus Saint

St. Gangulphus (d. 760) was a landowner in Burgundy, France. He went away to war and to preach the Gospel in Frisia. When he returned, he discovered that his wife was having an affair with a priest. He withdrew to his castle at

Avallon, where he lived as a hermit, performing works of charity and penance. Unfortunately, his wife's lover decided to kill him. He intended to behead him but missed and hit his thigh instead. The wound would prove to be fatal. He is a patron saint of unhappily married husbands, tanners, shoemakers, children, and horses, and is invoked against knee pains, marital difficulties, and adultery.

Gaon *see Godo*

Garald *see Gerald, Harold*

Garbhan Saint; Gaelic; little rough one

St. Garbhan (seventh century) was an Irish abbot who worked to preserve knowledge and culture in Ireland.

Garcey *see Garcia*

Garcia Saint; Spanish; mighty with a spear

Garcey, Garcios, Garcya, Garcyah, Garsias, Garsya, Garsyas

St. Garcia (d. 1073) was from Quintanilla, Spain. He was named abbot of Artanza Abbey in 1039. He was a counselor to King Ferdinand I of Castile, Spain, and advised him on his military campaigns.

Garcios *see Garcia*

Garcya *see Garcia*

Garcyah *see Garcia*

Garibaldus Saint; German; he who is bold with a lance

St. Garibaldus (d. 762) was a noted scholar who became bishop of Regensburg, Germany.

Garold *see Gerald, Harold*

Garolds *see Gerald*

Garrat *see Gerard*

Garratt *see Gerard*

Garsias *see Garcia*

Garsya *see Garcia*

Garsyas *see Garcia*

Garvais *see Gervase*

Garvaise *see Gervase*

Garvas *see Gervase*

Garvase *see Gervase*

Gaspar Saint; form of Casper; French; treasurer, imperial

Gaspard, Gaspare, Gaspari, Gasparos, Gasper, Gazpar, Gazsi

St. Gaspar, St. Gaspar Bertoni

St. Gaspar (1786–1837) was born in Rome. Soon after being ordained a priest, he was exiled by Napoleon's army. He returned after the fall of Napoleon. In 1815, he founded the Congregation of the Most Precious Blood. Pope Pius VII asked him to start six houses in Naples, which at the time was a center for crime. The order soon spread throughout Italy.

Gaspard *see Gaspar*

Gaspare *see Gaspar*

Gaspari *see Gaspar*

Gasparos *see Gaspar*

Gasper see Gaspar

Gaston see Vedast

Gatian Saint; Hebrew; family

St. Gatian (d. 337) was the first bishop of Tours, France.

Gau see Gagericus

Gaubert see Waldebert

Gaucher see Gaucherius

Gaucherius Saint; French; left

Gaucher

St. Gaucherius (1060–1140) was born in Meulan sur Seine, France. He and a friend, Germond, lived as hermits in the forest of Limoges. They soon attracted followers, and Gaucherius started St. John's Monastery as well as a convent for women.

Gaudencio see Gaudentius

Gaudentius Saint; Latin; happy, content

Gaudencio, Gaudioso

St. Gaudentius (d. 1004) was a friend of St. Adalbert and traveled to Prussia with him. He was appointed the first bishop of Gnesen by Emperor Otto III.

Gaudioso see Gaudentius

Gaudiosus Saint; Latin; happy, content

St. Gaudiosus of Naples (d. 455), also known as St. Gaudiosus the African, was bishop of Abitina in North Africa. He fled from the area during the persecutions of Genseric, a Vandal king. He settled in Naples, Italy, where he started a monastery.

Gazpar see Gaspar

Gazsi see Gaspar

Gearald see Gerard

Gearalt see Gerald

Gebereal see Gabriel

Gebhard Saint; German; brave gift

St. Gebhard (949–995) was the founder of the Benedictine Abbey of Petershausen.

Gebizo Saint

Gerizo

St. Gebizo (d. 1087), also known as Gerizo, was from Cologne, Germany. He lived as a monk at Monte Cassino, Italy. Pope St. Gregory VII sent him to Croatia to crown their new king.

Gebreil see Gabriel

Gebrell see Gabriel

Gebuinus Saint

St. Gebuinus (d. 1080) was archbishop of Lyons, France.

Gedeon Saint; form of Gideon; Hebrew; tree cutter

St. Gedeon (d. 796) was bishop of Besancon, France, for six years.

Gelasius Saint; Greek; cheerful and happy

Pope St. Gelasius I (d. 496) was born in Rome, the son of an African. Known for his learning, holiness, and charity, he was elected pope on March 1, 492. He and the patriarch of Constantinople clashed over the Acacian heresy. He also ordered reception of the Eucharist under both bread and wine in order to oppose the Manichaeans.

Gellert *see Gerald*

Gemellus Saint; Latin; little twin

St. Gemellus (d. 362) was a native of Paphlagonia who was martyred at Ancyra, Turkey. He had traveled there to criticize Emperor Julian for apostasy. He was arrested and tortured. He was said to be the last Christian killed by crucifixion.

Geminian Saint; Latin; identical twin

Geminus

St. Geminian (d. 348) was a bishop of Modena, Italy, who was known for opposing heresy.

Geminus *see Geminian*

Gemus Saint; Latin; jewel, precious stone

St. Gemus (date unknown) was a Benedictine monk at Moyenmoutier in Alsace, France.

Genereal *see Gabriel*

Generosus Saint; Latin, Spanish; generous

St. Generosus (date unknown) was martyred in Tivoli, Italy.

Genesius Saint; Latin; genes

St. Genesius, St. Genesius of Arles

St. Genesius (third century) was an actor. He was performing before Emperor Diocletian, playing a catechumen about to be baptized in a disrespectful play, when he suddenly converted to Christianity. He was tortured and then beheaded. He is the patron saint of actors.

Genistus *see Gennadius*

Genitus Saint; Latin; begotten

St. Genitus (third century) served with his father, St. Genulfus, as a missionary to France. They lived as hermits at Cellessur Nahon, France, and attracted many followers.

Gennadius Saint; Greek; noble, generous

Genistus

St. Gennadius (d. 936), also known as Genistus, was a Benedictine monk at Argeo, Spain. He became abbot of San Pedro de Montes at Vierzo. Later, he served as bishop of Astorga, Spain, for more than thirty years before living as a recluse for the last five years of his life.

Gennard Saint

St. Gennard (d. 720) was an abbot of Flay Monastery but retired to Fontenelle Abbey.

Gennaro Saint; Italian; of Janus

Bl. Gennaro Maria Sarnelli (1702–1744) was born in Naples, Italy. He became a lawyer when he was twenty, but a stint caring for the sick in the Hospital for the Incurables led him to enter the priesthood. As a priest, he cared for at-risk boys and girls. He then entered the Redemptorists and continued his ministry to the youth, poor, and those in prison. Over the course of his life, he wrote more than thirty books on a variety of subjects. He was beatified by Pope John Paul II in 1996.

Gentian Saint; Latin

St. Gentian (d. 287) died as a martyr with Sts. Victorius and Fuscian in Gaul. He was an elderly man who was trying to protect the other two.

Genulfus Saint

St. Genulfus (third century) and his son, St. Genitus, were sent from Rome to France as missionaries. They lived as hermits at Caellessur Nahon, France, where they attracted many followers. St. Genulfus was the first bishop of Canors.

Geoff *see Jeffrey*

Geoffrey *see Jeffrey*

Georgas *see George*

George Saint; Greek; farmer

Georgas, Georget, Gheorghe, Giorgos, Goerge, Goerget, Gordios, Gorje, Gorya, Grzegorz

St. George, St. George Gervase, St. George Liminotes, St. George Napper, St. George Precca, St. George of Amastris, St. George of Antioch, St. George Swallowell, St. George of Lodeve, St. George of Vienne

St. George (d. 303) was a Roman soldier in the Guard of Diocletian. He refused to offer sacrifice to the Roman gods and loudly renounced Diocletian's edict. The emperor attempted to bribe him, but George steadfastly refused. He had George tortured before he was martyred by beheading. Legend tells of St. George slaying a dragon who was terrorizing the people

of Silene. A princess was going to be sacrificed to the dragon, but St. George protected himself with the Sign of the Cross, slayed the dragon, and rescued the princess. The people were so thankful, they converted to Christianity. St. George is a patron saint of England.

Georget *see George*

Geovanni *see Giovanni*

Gerad *see Gerard*

Gerald Saint; German; mighty spearman

Garald, Garold, Garolds, Gearalt, Gellert, Geraldo, Gerale, Gerrald, Gerrell, Gerrild, Gerrin, Gerritt, Gerrold, Geryld, Giraldo, Giraud, Girauld, Jerold, Jerry

St. Gerald, St. Gerald of Sauve-Majeure

St. Gerald (d. 1109) was born in Cahors, Gascony, and became the abbot of Moissac, France. The archbishop of Toledo had been directed by the pope to bring about ecclesiastical reform in Spain. He appointed Gerald as the director of the Cathedral of Toledo. He was recognized for his holiness and was elected to be bishop of Brega. He spent his time eradicating ecclesiastical abuses, especially the administering of ecclesiastical investiture by laymen.

Geraldo *see Gerald*

Gerale *see Gerald*

Gerard Saint; English; brave spearman

*Garrat, Garratt, Gearald, Gerad,
Geraro, Gerd, Gere, Gerrard, Gerrick, Girard*

St. Gerard de Lunel, St. Gerard
Majella, St. Gerard Miles, St.
Gerard Sagredo, St. Gerard of
Saint-Wandrille

St. Gerard Majella (1726–1755)
was born in Muro, Italy. He
joined the Redemptorists and
became a professed lay brother.
Because of his great piety, he
was able to serve as a spiritual
director to religious women. He
was a mystic who had the gifts
of levitation and bilocation. He
was devoted to obedience, charity, and mortification for Christ.
He died of tuberculoisis at the
age of twenty-nine. Because
his prayers for a woman in
labor helped lead to a miracle,
he is a patron saint of expectant
mothers.

Geraro *see Gerard*

Gerasimus Saint; Greek; award,
recompense

St. Gerasimus (d. 475) was a
merchant born in Lycia, Asia
Minor. After meeting some
hermits in Egypt, he returned
to Palestine to start an eremitical community in Jericho, Israel.
He was known as a miracle
worker.

Gerbold Saint; German; brave
spear-fighter

St. Gerbold (d. 690) founded the
abbey of Livray. He was later
made bishop of Bayeux, France.

Gercon Saint

St. Gercon (third century) was
a martyr associated with either
Xanten or Bonn.

Gerd *see Gerard*

Gere *see Gerard*

Gerebald Saint; German

St. Gerebald (d. 885) was a
bishop of Chalons sur Seine,
France.

Gerebern *see Gerebrand*

Gerebrand Saint; German; sword
Gerebern

St. Gerebrand (seventh century), also known as Gerebern,
accompanied St. Dymphna to
Belgium when she was attempting to escape her father. He was
martyred.

Gereil *see Gabriel*

Geremiah *see Jeremiah*

Gereon Saint; Greek; old man

St. Gereon (d. 304) was an officer in the Theban Legion who
was martyred with over three
hundred companions on the
Lower Rhine River at Xanten.
He is invoked against headaches and migraine and is a
patron saint of Cologne.

Gergely *see Gregory*

Gergo *see Gregory*

Gerintius Saint; Latin

St. Gerintius of Italica (first century) was a missionary in Spain,
where he served as bishop of
Talco. He was martyred.

Gerinus Saint; German; lance

St. Gerinus (d. 676) and his brother, St. Leger, were martyred by Ebroin. Gerinus was stoned to death near Arras, France.

Gerivas *see Gervase*

Gerizo *see Gebizo*

Gerlac Saint; German; spear thrower

St. Gerlac (1100–1170) was a Dutch soldier and sailor. After his wife died, he spent seven years serving the sick and poor in Rome. He then became a hermit in Holland. He was a correspondent of St. Hildegard.

Gerland Saint; German

Germana

St. Gerland (d. 1100) was ordained bishop of Girgenti by Pope Urban II. He worked to Christianize Sicily after the Saracens had been expelled from that area.

Germain *see Germaine (girl's name)*

Germana *see Gerland*

Germane *see Germaine (girl's name)*

Germanicus Saint; Latin; from Germany

St. Germanicus (d. 155) was martyred in Smyrna. He was thrown to wild beasts, but they would not attack. He had to provoke them into killing him.

Germano Saint; Latin; he who sprouts

Bl. Germano Perez Giminez (1906–1936) was one of the Passionist Martyrs of Daimiel who was martyred during the Spanish Civil War. They were beatified by Pope John Paul II in 1989.

Germanus Saint; Latin; he who sprouts

St. Germanus (d. 250) was martyred in Caesarea, Cappadocia, with Theophilus, Caesarius, and Vitalis.

Germayn *see Germaine (girl's name)*

Germayne *see Germaine (girl's name)*

Germerius Saint

St. Germerius (480–560) was born in Angouleme and became bishop of Toulouse, France. He would serve in that capacity for fifty years. He founded two churches and a monastery and cared for the poor.

Germin *see Germaine*

Germoc Saint

St. Germoc (sixth century) was an Irish chieftain and the brother of St. Breaca. He lived in Cornwall, England.

Germon *see Germaine (girl's name)*

Germyn *see Germaine (girl's name)*

Gerold Saint; form of Gerald; German; mighty spearman

St. Gerold (d. 978) was born into the Rhaetian family of Saxony counts. He gave his land to Einsiedeln Monastery, where his sons lived as monks. He then became a recluse, living as a hermit in a forest near Mitternach in the Waalgu.

Gerome *see Jerome*

Geronimo *see Jerome*

Gerontius Saint; Latin; old man

St. Gerontius of Cervia (d. 501) was bishop of Cervia, Italy. He was martyred on the Flaminian Way while returning home from a synod in Rome.

Gerrald *see Gerald*

Gerrard *see Gerard*

Gerrell *see Gerald*

Gerrick *see Gerard*

Gerrild *see Gerald*

Gerrin *see Gerald*

Gerritt *see Gerald*

Gerrold *see Gerald*

Gerulph Saint; German; spear, wolf

St. Gerulph (d. 746) was Flemish and the heir to a vast estate. A greedy relative killed him shortly after Gerulph made his confirmation. He forgave his attacker with his dying breath.

Gervais *see Gervase*

Gervas *see Gervase*

Gervase Saint; French; honorable

Garvais, Garvaise, Garvas, Garvase, Gerivas, Gervais, Gervas, Gervasio, Gervaso, Gervasy, Gervays, Gervayse, Gervis, Gerwazy, Jarvis

St. Gervase (date unknown), his parents, and his twin brother were all martyred for the faith. Gervase was beaten to death with a lead-tipped whip. He is a patron saint of haymakers and is invoked for the discovery of thieves.

Gervasio *see Gervase*

Gervaso *see Gervase*

Gervasy *see Gervase*

Gervays *see Gervase*

Gervayse *see Gervase*

Gervis *see Gervase*

Gerwazy *see Gervase*

Gery *see Gagericus*

Geryld *see Gerald*

Getulius Saint; Latin; of the Gaetuli, a tribe in North Africa

St. Getulius (d. 120) was the husband of St. Symphorosa. He resigned his post as officer in the Roman army after he became a Christian. He settled in Tivoli, Italy, where he converted Caerealis, who had been sent to arrest him. Getulius, Caerealis, Amantius, and Primitivus were martyred at Tivoli.

Ghabriel *see Gabriel*

Gheorghe *see George*

Ghislain Saint; French; pledge

Gislenus

St. Ghislain (d. 680), also known as Gislenus, was a hermit who lived in a forest in Hainault, Belgium. He attracted many followers and built an abbey near Mons, Belgium. He was a teacher of Sts. Waltrude, Lambert, and Valerius.

Giacamo *see Giacomo*

Giaco *see Giacomo*

Giacobbe *see Giacomo*

Giacobo *see Giacomo*

Giacomo Saint; form of Jacob; Italian; supplanter, substitute

Gaimo, Giacamo, Giaco, Giacobbe, Giacobo, Giacopo, Gyacomo, Jacopo

Bl. Giacomo Alberione (1884–1971) was born in San Lorenzo di Fossano, Cuneo, Italy. He became a priest and served the parish in Narzole. He was also a spiritual director at the Alba seminary. He founded the Society of St. Paul and the Daughters of St. Paul, as well as the Sister Disciples of the Divine Master and the Sisters of the Good Shepherd. All of these congregations are devoted to publishing materials to aid in spreading the Word of God. He was beatified by Pope John Paul II in 2003.

Giacopo *see Giacomo*

Gian *see Giovanni*

Giannino *see Giovanni*

Gib *see Gilbert*

Gibardus Saint; German; strong gift

St. Gibardus (d. 888) was a Benedictine abbot of Luxeuil, France. Gibardus and his monks were captured and martyred.

Gibb *see Gilbert*

Gibrian Saint

Abran

St. Gibrian (d. 515) was born into an Irish family of ten children. He and several of his siblings moved to France. Gibrian lived as a hermit near the Coole and Marne Rivers. His siblings settled nearby, and Gibrian served as their spiritual leader.

Gide *see Giles*

Gideon Old Testament; Hebrew; tree cutter

Gedeon, Gideone, Gydeon, Hedeon

Gideon was a judge of the Hebrews. His story is told in Judges 6–8. There was peace in Israel for forty years during his life, but after his death the Israelites once again returned to pagan worship.

Gideone *see Gideon*

Gilbert Saint; English; brilliant pledge, trustworthy

Gib, Gibb, Gilberto, Gilburt, Gilibeirt, Gillbert, Gillburt, Gilleabert, Giselbert, Giselbertus, Gisselberto, Guilbert, Gylbert, Gylbirt, Gylburt, Gylbyrt

St. Gilbert of Sempringham (1083–1190) was born the son of a wealthy Norman knight in England. He was ordained a priest and served as an advisor to a group of religious women who were living together. They started a new religious order and opened several new foundations. Pope Eugene III approved the community, which became known as the Gilbertine order. It grew to have twenty-six monasteries before being suppressed by Henry VIII.

Gilberto *see Gilbert*

Gilburt *see Gilbert*

Gildard Saint; German; good

St. Gildard (d. 514) was the brother of St. Medard. He

served as bishop of Rouen, France.

Gilduin Saint; French

St. Gilduin (1052–1077) was a young priest from Brittany. He was elected bishop of Dol but felt unworthy of the post, so he traveled to Rome, where Pope Gregory VII released him from the charge. He died on the return journey.

Giles Saint; French; goatskin shield

Gide, Gyles, Gylles

St. Giles, St. Giles of Assisi, St. Giles, Abbot

St. Giles of Assisi (d. 1263) was a native of Assisi, Italy. He was one of the earliest followers of St. Francis and accompanied that saint on many of his missions. When he traveled to Tunis to attempt to evangelize the Saracens, the Christians there put him back on the boat in order to avoid repercussions from his religious fervor. He spent the rest of his life living as a hermit near Perugia. He was known for his mystical experiences, his austerity, and silence.

Gilibeirt *see Gilbert*

Gillbert *see Gilbert*

Gillburt *see Gilbert*

Gilleabert *see Gilbert*

Gilstlian Saint

St. Gilstlian (fifth or sixth century) was the uncle of St. David of Wales and a monk at Menevia Abbey.

Giona *see Jonah*

Giorgio Saint; form of George; Italian; farmer

St. Giorgio Preca of Malta (1880–1962) was born in Malta. He joined the Carmelites and was ordained a priest. He founded the Society of Christian Doctrine, which was dedicated to the education of youth. He was canonized by Pope Benedict XVI in 2007.

Giorgos *see George*

Giotto *see Godfrey*

Giovann *see Giovanni*

Giovanni Saint; form of John; Italian; God is gracious

Geovanni, Gian, Giannino, Giovann, Giovannie, Giovanno, Giovon, Giovonathon, Giovonni, Giovonnia, Giovonnie, Givonni, Vannie, Vonny

St. Giovanni Calabria (1873–1954) was born to a poor family in Verona, Italy. After serving in the military, he enrolled at the Faculty of Theology Seminary. One night he found an abandoned baby and brought him into the house. From that moment on, he was dedicated to working on behalf of the orphans and the abandoned. In 1907, he founded the Congregation of the Poor Servants of Divine Providence. He was canonized by Pope John Paul II in 1999.

Giovannie *see Giovanni*

Giovanno *see Giovanni*

Giovon *see Giovanni*

Giovonathon *see Giovanni*

Giovonni *see Giovanni*

Giovonnia *see Giovanni*

Giovonnie *see Giovanni*

Giraldo *see Gerald*

Girard *see Gerard*

Giraud *see Gerald*

Girauld *see Gerald*

Giselbert *see Gilbert*

Giselbertus *see Gilbert*

Gislar Saint

St. Gislar (seventh century) was a missionary to southern Germany and Austria.

Gislenus *see Ghislain*

Gisselberto *see Gilbert*

Giuseppe Saint; form of Joseph; Italian; God will add, God will increase

Giuseppi, Giuseppino, Guiseppe, Guiseppi, Guiseppie, Guisseppe

Bl. Giuseppe Alllamano, Bl. Giuseppe Baldo, Bl. Giuseppe Benedetto Dusmet, Bl. Giuseppe Nascimbeni, Bl. Giuseppe Tovini

Bl. Giuseppe Benedetto Dusmet (1818-1894) was born into a noble family in Palermo, Sicily. He became a Benedictine monk at Monte Cassino and taught philosophy and theology. He served as the head of several monasteries, including San Servino, San Flavio, and Dan Nicolo l'Arena. He was beatified by Pope John Paul II in 1988.

Giuseppi *see Giuseppe*

Giuseppino *see Giuseppe*

Givonni *see Giovanni*

Glastian Saint; Scottish

St. Glastian (d. 830) was the bishop and patron of Kinglassie, Fife, and Scotland.

Glaves *see Gluvias*

Glavis *see Gluvias*

Glodesind *see Glodesind (girl's name)*

Glushallaich Saint

St. Glushallaich (seventh century) was an Irish hermit who was a follower of St. Kevin.

Gluvias Saint; French, English; lance, spear

Glaves, Glavis

St. Gluvias (sixth century) was the brother of St. Cadoc of Llancarfan, Wales. He was a monk who may have started an abbey.

Glycerius Saint; Latin; sweetness

St. Glycerius (d. 303) was a priest who was tortured and burned at the stake at Nicomedia during the persecutions of Emperor Diocletian.

Goar Saint; Scottish

St. Goar (d. 575) was a parish priest in Aquitaine, France. He decided to become a hermit and lived near the Rhine River at Oberwesel, Germany. He was accused of sorcery by the local bishop, but he was cleared of the charge. Emperor Charlegmagne later built a church where Goar's hermitage had been.

Goban Saint; Celtic; little smith

St. Goban (sixth century) was an abbot who served in Tascaffin, County Limerick, Ireland.

Gobrain Saint; Celtic

St. Gobrain (d. 725) was a monk who became bishop of Vannes in Brittany, France. When he was eighty-seven, he retired his see and lived out his days as a hermit.

Goddfree *see Godfrey*

Goddfrey *see Godfrey*

Godefroi *see Godfrey*

Godewin *see Godwin*

Godfree *see Godfrey*

Godfrey Saint; Gaelic, German; God's peace

Giotto, Goddfree, Goddfrey, Godefroi, Godfree, Godfry, Godofredo, Godoired, Godrey, Goffredo, Gofraidh, Gofredo, Gorry

St. Godfrey (d. 1572) is actually the name of two martyrs, Godfrey of Duynen and Godfrey of Merville. They were both hanged at Briel by Calvinists. They are honored among the Martyrs of Gorkum.

Godfry *see Godfrey*

Godo Saint; German

Gaon

St. Godo (d. 690), also known as Gaon, was born in Verdun, France. He was a Benedictine monk who founded Oye Abbey, near Sezanne en Brie, where he served as abbot.

Godofredo *see Godfrey*

Godoired *see Godfrey*

Godrey *see Godfrey*

Godwen *see Godwin*

Godwin Saint; English; friend of God

Godewin, Godwen, Godwinn, Godwyn, Godwynn, Goodin, Gooding, Goodwin, Goodwyn, Goodwynn, Goodwynne

St. Godwin (d. 690) was a noted scholar who served as the Benedictine abbot of Stravelot Malmedy Monastery in Belgium.

Godwinn *see Godwin*

Godwyn *see Godwin*

Godwynn *see Godwin*

Goerge *see George*

Goerget *see George*

Goeric Saint; German

St. Goeric of Metz (d. 643) was a married man with two daughters who served as a courtier at the court of King Dagobert. After being struck blind and recovering miraculously, he joined the clergy. He founded a monastery at Epinal for his daughters and built the church of St. Peter's. He also became bishop of Metz.

Goeznoveus Saint; Celtic, Latin; having knowledge of vision

St. Goeznoveus (d. 675) was the brother of St. Maughan. He became bishop of Quimper, France.

Goffredo *see Godfrey*

Gofraidh *see Godfrey*

Gofredo *see Godfrey*

Gohardus Saint

St. Gohardus (d. 843) was a bishop of Nantes, France. He was celebrating Mass at Sts. Peter and Paul Church when the church was attacked by Normans. He, as well as many others, was killed in the attack.

Gollen Saint; Welsh

St. Gollen (seventh century) was a Welsh saint, associated with Llangollen, in Clwyd, Wales.

Golvinus Saint

St. Golvinus (seventh century) was born in Brittany, France. He served as the bishop of St. Pol de Leon.

Goncalve *see Gonsalo*

Gonclaco Saint

St. Gonclaco Garcia (d. 1597) was a Spanish Fransiscan who served as a missionary to Japan. He was crucified at Nagasaki, Japan, with St. Paul Miki and other companions.

Gondebert *see Gumbert*

Gonen *see Govan*

Goneri Saint; French

St. Goneri (sixth century) was a hermit who lived near Treguier in Brittany, France.

Gonsalo Saint; Spanish; wolf

Goncalve, Gonsalve, Gonsalvo, Gonzales, Gonzalo, Gonzalos, Gonzalous, Gonzelee, Gonzolo, Gundisalvus

St. Gonsalo Garcia (1556–1597), also known as Gundisalvus, was born in Vasai, India. He was taught by the Jesuits for eight years. Fr. Sabastian Goncalves, a Jesuit priest, took him to Japan when he was fifteen years old. He quickly learned the language and became a merchant. He then went to Manila in the Philippines as a lay missionary and joined the Seraphic order as a lay brother, before being formally ordained as a Franciscan. In 1592, he was sent on a diplomatic mission to Japan. Four years later, he and several other missionaries were placed under house arrest. Their left ears were cut off, and they were later crucified. Upon approaching his cross, he knelt down and embraced it. The other missionaries followed his example and did the same.

Gonsalve *see Gonsalo*

Gonsalvo *see Gonsalo*

Gonzaga Saint; Spanish; battle elf

St. Gonzaga Gonza (d. 1886) was one of the Martyrs of Uganda, murdered by King Mwanga II of Buganda.

Gonzales *see Gonsalo*

Gonzalo *see Gonsalo*

Gonzalos *see Gonsalo*

Gonzalous *see Gonsalo*

Gonzelee *see Gonsalo*

Gonzolo *see Gonsalo*

Goodin *see Godwin*

Gooding *see Godwin*

Goodwin *see Godwin*

Goodwyn *see Godwin*

Goodwynn *see Godwin*

Goodwynne *see Godwin*

Goran Saint; form of George; Greek; farmer

St. Goran (sixth century) was a missionary of the district of Cornwall, England.

Gordian Saint; Latin; from Gordium

St. Gordian (d. 362) was martyred by being beheaded in Rome.

Gordios *see George*

Gorfor Saint

St. Gorfor (date unknown) is a patron saint of Llanover, in Gwent, Wales.

Gorje *see George*

Gorman Saint; Gaelic; small, blue eyed

St. Gorman (d. 965) was a Benedictine bishop of Schleswig, in Denmark, where he served as a missionary.

Gormcal Saint; Gaelic

St. Gormcal (d. 1016) was an abbot of Ardoilen Abbey in Galway, Ireland.

Gorry *see Godfrey*

Gorya *see George*

Gosbert Saint; German; God bright

St. Gosbert (d. 859) was a Benedictine bishop of Osnabruck, Germany. He was a friend of St. Angsar.

Goswin Saint; Teutonic; friend of God

St. Goswin (1086–1165) was born in Douai, France, and studied in Paris. He taught theology in Douai before entering Anchin Abbey. He later served as abbot of that monastery.

Gotteschalk Saint; German; servant of God

Gottschalk

St. Gotteschalk (d. 1066) served in the army of King Canute of Denmark and married the king's daughter. He established a Slavic kingdom on the Elbe, brought in Saxon monks, and built churches. He was murdered by agents of his brother-in-law. He is a patron of languages, linguists, lost vocations, princes, and translators.

Gottschalk *see Gotteschalk*

Govan Saint; Celtic, Welsh; smith, ditch

Cofen, Gonen

St. Govan (500–586), also known as Cofan or Gonen, was a hermit who lived on a cliff near Bosherston, in Wales. That area is now known as St. Govan's Head.

Graig *see Gregory*

Gratia Saint; Latin; grace

Bl. Gratia (d. 1508) was a native of Cattaro in Dalmatia. He was a sailor until he was thirty, when he heard a sermon by an Augustinian friar that deeply moved him. He joined that order as a lay brother at Monte Ortono, where he worked in the gardens. When he was transferred to the Friary of St. Christopher at Venice, miracles began to take place. He had a deep devotion to the Eucharist.

Gratian Saint; Latin; grace

St. Gratian (d. 250) was a soldier in the army of Emperor Trajanus Decius and was martyred with St. Felinus at Perugia, Italy.

Gratus Saint; Latin; one recognized by God

St. Gratus (d. 470) attended the Synod of Milan in 451 as a priest. He later became bishop of Aosta, Italy, where he promoted evangelization and charity. He is a patron saint of Aosta and vineyards. He is invoked against insects, dangerous animals, fire, hail, and storms.

Greagoir *see Gregory*

Greagory *see Gregory*

Gredifael Saint; Welsh

St. Gredifael (seventh century) was an abbot of Whitland, in Dyfed, Wales, who accompanied St. Paternus from Brittany to Wales.

Greer *see Gregory*

Gregary *see Gregory*

Greger *see Gregory*

Gregery *see Gregory*

Gregg *see Gregory*

Grégoire *see Gregory*

Gregorey *see Gregory*

Gregori *see Gregory*

Grégorie *see Gregory*

Gregorio *see Gregory*

Gregorious *see Gregory*

Gregors *see Gregory*

Gregory Saint; Latin; vigilant watchman

Gergely, Gergo, Graig, Greagoir, Greagory, Greer, Gregary, Greger, Gregery, Gregg, Grégoire, Gregorey, Gregori, Grégorie, Gregorio, Gregorious, Gregors, Gregos, Gregrey, Gregroy, Gregry, Greigoor, Greigor, Greigore, Greogry, Gries, Grisha, Grzegorz

St. Gregory II, St. Gregory VII, St. Gregory Barbarigo, St. Gregory Nazianzus, St. Gregory of Nyssa, St. Gregory of Ostia, St. Gregory Palamas, St. Gregory Thaumaturgus, St. Gregory the Enlightener, St. Gregory the Sinaite, St. Gregory the Great

St. Gregory the Great (540–604) was the son of a Roman senator. He gave up the world and turned to God, becoming one of the seven deacons of Rome. He was appointed Chief Magistrate of Rome by Emperor Justin the Elder. He built six monasteries in Sicily and one in Rome. He became a Benedictine monk when he was thirty-five. He was elected pope in 590. He was a prolific writer and made great contributions to the liturgy of the Mass and the Divine Office. He is a Doctor of the Church and a patron saint of teachers.

Gregos *see Gregory*

Gregrey *see Gregory*

Gregroy *see Gregory*

Gregry *see Gregory*

Greigoor *see Gregory*

Greigor *see Gregory*

Greigore *see Gregory*

Greogry *see Gregory*

Gries *see Gregory*

Grimbald Saint; German; helmet bold

Grimwald

St. Grimbald (827–901), also known as Grimwald, was a Benedictine monk at the French Abbey of Saint-Bertin. He was invited to England by King Alfred, who wanted him to serve as bishop of Canterbury. He declined the office, instead becoming the abbot of New Minster Abbey at Winchester. He is credited with restoring learning to England.

Grimoaldo Saint; Spanish; confessor

Bl. Grimoaldo Santamaria (1883–1902) was born in Pontecorvo, Frosinone, Italy. As a child, he was an altar server, member of the church choir, and part of the Solidality of the Immaculate Conception. He entered the Passionists at the age of sixteen and devoted himself to the ascetic lifestyle. He died of acute meningitis. He was beatified by Pope John Paul II in 1995.

Grimoaldus Saint; Spanish; confessor

St. Grimoaldus (d. 1137) was of English descent and became an archpriest of Pontecorvo, Italy.

Grimwald *see Grimbald*

Grisha *see Gregory*

Grwst Saint; strong warrior

St. Grwst (seventh century) was the son of a prince of Rheged. He became a missionary and traveled to Wales, where he became a hermit.

Grzegorz Saint; Greek, Polish; watchful, vigilant

Bl. Grzegorz Boleslaw Frackowiak (1911–1943) was a Polish friar who was guillotined in Dresden. He is one of the 108 Polish Martyrs of World War II who were beatified by Pope John Paul II in 1999.

Guasacht Saint; Gaelic; danger, pearl

St. Guasacht (fourth century) was the son of Maelchu, who had been St. Patrick's master when he was a slave in Ireland. Guasacht later became an Irish bishop.

Gudwal Saint; Welsh

St. Gudwal (sixth century) was a native of Wales. He became a priest and then a bishop. He set off for Cornwall with 188 monks. When they arrived, he founded a monastery at Devon.

Guenhael Saint; French; white angel

St. Guenhael (d. 550) was trained by St. Winelae at Landevnee Abbey in Brittany, France. Guenhael later became abbot of that monastery.

Guenninus Saint

St. Guenninus (seventh century) was a bishop of Vannes in Brittany, France.

Guerembaldus Saint

St. Guerembaldus (d. 695) was a Benedictine bishop of Hirschau, Germany.

Guesnoveus Saint

St. Guesnoveus (d. 675) was a bishop of Quimper, in Brittany, France. He founded a monastery near Brest.

Guethenoc Saint; English

St. Guethenoc (fifth century) was a son of Sts. Fagan and Gwen. He was forced to leave Britain and travel to France when the Saxons invaded.

Guevrock Saint

St. Guevrock (sixth century) was from Britain. He became abbot of Loc Kiroc, in Brittany, France.

Guido Saint; form of Guy; Italian; valley, warrior

St. Guido Maria Conforti (1865–1931) was born in Ravadese, Parma, Italy. As a child, he would converse with the crucified Christ in his parish church. He became a priest and served as a professor at the seminary in Parma. He became vice-rector of the seminary and then Vicar of Clergy for the diocese. He founded the Xaverian Missionaries. He was named archbishop of Ravenna and then archbishop of Parma. He was canonized by Pope Benedict XVI in 2011.

Guie *see Guy*

Guier Saint; French, English; guide

St. Guier (date unknown) was a priest who lived as a hermit in Cornwall, England.

Guilbert *see Gilbert*

Guilen *see Guillaume*

Guiliano *see Julian*

Guillaume Saint; form of William; French; determined guardian

Guilen, Guillaums, Guilleaume, Guyllaume

Bl. Guillaume Joseph Chaminade (1761–1850) was born in Perigeux, France. He went to the College of Mussidan, where he spent twenty years. He was ordained a priest and ministered to people in secret during the French Revolution. He was exiled to Spain during the French Directorate. When he returned to France, he founded the Sodalities of Our Lady, devoted to sharing Our Lady's mission of bringing Christ to the world. He also founded the Daughters of Mary Immaculate and the Society of Mary. He was beatified by Pope John Paul II in 2000.

Guillaums *see Guillaume*

Guilleaume *see Guillaume*

Guinizo Saint

St. Guinizo (d. 1050) was a Benedictine from Spain who lived as a hermit at Monte Cassino, in Italy.

Guiseppe Saint; form of Joseph; Hebrew, Italian; he will enlarge

St. Guiseppe Marello, St. Guiseppe Moscati, St. Guiseppe Maria Cardinal Tomasi

St. Guiseppe Moscati (1880–1927) was born to a noble family in Benevento, Italy. He moved to Naples when he was eight and spent most of his life there. He received his doctorate in Medicine from the University of Naples in 1903. He joined the staff of the Ospedali Riuniti degli Incurabili, where he became an administrator. He was a skilled doctor; many considered him a miracle worker. He was deeply committed to his faith—taking a vow of chastity, attending daily Mass, and sometimes including the sacraments as part of his treatment for patients. He was canonized by Pope John Paul II in 1987.

Guiseppi *see Giuseppe*

Guiseppie *see Giuseppe*

Guisseppe *see Giuseppe*

Guitmarus Saint

St. Guitmarus (d. 765) served as abbot of Saint Riquier Abbey of France.

Gulstan Saint

St. Gulstan (d. 1010) was a Benedictine monk at St. Gildas of Rhuys Abbey in Brittany, France.

Gumbert Saint; German

Gondebert

St. Gumbert (seventh century) was married to St. Bertha.

Unable to have children, they decided to separate so that they could both enter religious life. Gumbert donated all his property to the Church in order to start two monasteries. He then went to Ireland where he became a monk. He was martyred by a band of pirates who came to loot the monastery.

Gumesindus Saint; German

St. Gumesindus (d. 852) was a priest and one of the Martyrs of Córdoba.

Gummarus Saint

St. Gummarus (717–774) was a son of the lord of Emblem who grew up at the court of Pepin. Pepin suggested he marry Guinimaria, which Gummarus agreed to do. This marriage was most unhappy since his wife was mean to him and abusive to their servants. He did all he could to make restitution to those she had harmed when he was away at war and tried to convert her to gentler ways, but to no avail. In time, they separated, and he founded the abbey at Lierre, where he lived as a hermit. He is a patron saint of childless people, courtiers, cowherds, difficult marriages, hernia sufferers, separated spouses, and woodcutters.

Gundebert Saint; German; bright war

St. Gundebert (d. 676) was a Benedictine bishop of Sens, France. He founded the Abbey of Senores.

Gundenis Saint; German

St. Gundenis (d. 203) was a virgin who was martyred during the persecution of Septimius Severnus.

Gundisalvus *see Gonsalo*

Gundulphus Saint; German; battle wolf

St. Gundulphus (sixth century) was a bishop in Gaul.

Gunifort Saint; Gaelic

St. Gunifort (date unknown) was martyred in Pavia, Italy.

Gunioc Saint; Scottish

St. Gunioc (d. 838) was a Scottish bishop.

Gunthiern Saint; Welsh

St. Gunthiern (d. 500) was a Welsh prince who lived as a hermit in Brittany, France.

Gurloes Saint; French

St. Gurloes (d. 1057) was a Benedictine abbot of Sainte Croix of Quimperle in Brittany, France.

Gus *see August*

Guthagon Saint

St. Guthagon (eighth century) was from Ireland. He lived as a hermit in Belgium.

Guthlac Saint; English; war offering

St. Guthlac (673–714) was related to the royal house of Mercia and served in the army of Ethelred of Mercia for nine years. He then became a monk at Repton. He later became an anchorite on an island in the marshes of Lincolnshire. Attacked by Britons, he was rescued by St. Bartholomew. The site of his hermitage ultimately became a monastery called Crowland.

Guy Saint; Hebrew, German; valley, warrior

Guie, Guyon

St. Guy, St. Guy of Anderlecht, St. Guy of Pomposa

St. Guy of Anderlecht (950–1012) was born near Brussels. He lived an austere life and died after returning home from a seven-year pilgrimage he had taken on foot to Jerusalem and Rome. He is a patron saint of bachelors, epileptics, horned animals, laborers, outbuildings, sacristans, and workhorses, and against mad dogs.

Guyllaume *see Guillaume*

Guyon *see Guy*

Gwenno *see Winwaloc*

Gwerir Saint; Welsh

St. Gwerir (ninth century) was a monk and hermit in Liskeard, Cornwall. King Alfred was said to have been cured of a serious illness when he visited his grave.

Gwrnerth Saint; Welsh; man strength

St. Gwrnerth (sixth century) was a Welsh monk.

Gwynllyw Saint; Welsh; fair leader

St. Gwynllyw (450–500) was the husband of St. Gladys and father of St. Cadoc. He was king of Gwynllwg in South Wales and is the legendary founder of Newport. St. Cadoc's example convinced St. Gwynllyw to give up his life of violence and seek forgiveness for his sins. He and his wife then became hermits.

Gyacomo *see Giacomo*

Gyavire Saint

St. Gyavire (d. 1886) was martyred in Uganda. He was known as "the good runner of messages" before being killed by King Mwanga.

Gydeon *see Gideon*

Gylbert *see Gilbert*

Gylbirt *see Gilbert*

Gylburt *see Gilbert*

Gylbyrt *see Gilbert*

Gyles *see Giles*

Gylles *see Giles*

H

Habet Deus Saint; Latin; having God

St. Habet Deus (d. 500) was a bishop of Luna, in Tuscany, Italy, who was martyred by Arabian heretics.

Hadelin Saint

Adelin

St. Hadelin (d. 690), also known as Adelin, was born in Gascony, France. He founded Chelles Abbey in Liege, where he served as abbot. He later became a hermit, living near the Meuse River.

Haduin Saint; German, French; battle friend

Harduin

St. Haduin (d. 662), also known as Harduin, was bishop of Le Mans, France. He founded several monasteries, including Notre Dame d'Evron.

Hadulph Saint; German; the combat wolf

St. Hadulph (d. 662) was known as a scholar and patron of the arts. He was a benedictine bishop of Arras Cambrai, France.

Hagar *see Hagar (girl's name)*

Hager *see Hagar (girl's name)*

Hagir *see Hagar (girl's name)*

Hagor *see Hagar (girl's name)*

Hagyr *see Hagar (girl's name)*

Hakob *see Jacob (girl's name)*

Hallvard Saint; Norse; guardian of the rock

Hallverd, Halverd

St. Hallvard (1020–1042) was a Norwegian who became a trader in the Baltic Islands. A pregnant woman sought sanctuary on his ship after being falsely accused of theft by three men. He offered to make restitution to the three men, but instead they killed both Hallvard and the woman with arrows. He is a patron saint of Oslo.

Hallverd *see Hallvard*

Halverd *see Hallvard*

Hanibal *see Hannibal*

Hank *see Henry*

Hannibal Saint; Phoenician; grace of God

Anibal, Hanibal, Hannybal, Hanybal

St. Hannibal Maria di Francia (1851–1927) was born at Messina, Italy. His father, who died when Hannibal was very young, was a papal vice-consul, a knight, and honorary captain of the Navy. He was called to religious life when he was seventeen years old. After being ordained, he devoted himself to working with the poor. He founded the Daughters of Divine Zeal in 1887 and the Rogationists in 1897. He was considered a saint even during his life and was formally canonized in 2004 by Pope John Paul II.

Hanno *see Anno*

Hannybal *see Hannibal*

Hans *see Jan*

Hanybal *see Hannibal*

Harald *see Harold*

Harbert *see Herbert*

Hardoin Saint; French

St. Hardoin (seventh century) was bishop of St. Pol de-Leon in Brittany, France.

Harduin *see Haduin*

Hardulph Saint; German, English; brave wolf

St. Hardulph (date unknown) was a hermit of Leicester, England.

Hareld *see Harold*

Harild *see Harold*

Hariolfus *see Herulph*

Harold Saint; Scandinavian; army ruler

Araldo, Aralt, Aroldo, Garald, Garold, Harald, Hareld, Harild, Harrell, Haryld, Herald, Hereld, Herold, Heronim, Heryld

St. Harold (d. 1168) was a child who was martyred at Gloucester, England. His martyrdom was blamed on Jews, which was most likely due to the anti-Semitism of the era.

Harrell *see Harold*

Harro *see Henry*

Harv *see Harvey*

Harvee *see Harvey*

Harvey Saint; German; army warrior

Harv, Harvee, Harvi, Harvie, Harvy

St. Harvey (521–556), also known as Hervé, from Breton, was blind, but he still became abbot of Plouvien Monastery. He later moved to Lanhourneau. He was known as a miracle worker. He is a patron saint of the blind, bards, and musicians and is invoked against eye disease.

Harvi *see Harvey*

Harvie *see Harvey*

Harvy *see Harvey*

Haryld *see Harold*

Haskel *see Ezekiel*

Hatebrand Saint

St. Hatebrand (d. 1198) was a native of the Netherlands. He was the Benedictine abbot of

Olden Koaster in Frisia and is credited with reviving monasticism in that area.

Hazikiah *see Hezekiah*

Hebert *see Herbert*

Hébert *see Herbert*

Heberto *see Herbert*

Heda *see Hedda*

Hedah *see Hedda*

Hedaya *see Hedda*

Hedda Saint; German; battler

Heda, Hedah, Hedaya, Heddah, Hedia, Hedu

St. Hedda (d. 870) was the Benedictine abbot of Peterborough, England. When the Danes invaded, he and eighty-four other monks were killed.

Heddah *see Hedda*

Hedeon *see Gideon*

Hedia *see Hedda*

Hedu *see Hedda*

Hedwig *see Hedwig (girl's name)*

Hegesippus Saint

St. Hegesippus (d. 180) was a Jewish convert to Christianity. He is known as the Father of Church History and was the first to record the succession of popes from St. Peter to St. Eleutherius.

Heike *see Henry*

Heimrad Saint; German; advisor of the homeland

St. Heimrad (d. 1019) was born in Germany, the son of poor parents. He became a priest and then lived as a perpetual pilgrim, traveling to both Rome

and Jerusalem. He eventually became a hermit on Mount Hasung near Kassel, Germany. He was known for his asceticism and deliberately took on eccentric mannerisms so that others would think him a fool.

Helanus Saint; Greek; light

St. Helanus (sixth century) traveled from Ireland to France with several of his siblings. He later became a priest.

Heldrad Saint; German; counselor of warriors

Eldrad

St. Heldrad (d. 842), also known as Eldrad, was from Provence, France. On his way to Rome, he stopped at the Abbey of Novalese in the Italian Alps. He became abbot and served in that capacity for thirty years. He built a hospice and devised ways of rescuing travelers in the Alps. He also added to the abbey's library.

Helier Saint; English; cover, roof

St. Helier (sixth century) was born in Tongres, Belgium, to pagan parents. His infertile parents had turned to St. Cunibert to ask for help in having a child. He advised them to pray and to have their child raised as a Christian. Their prayers were answered, and St. Cunibert raised Helier, but Helier's father grew jealous of the relationship and had Cunibert killed. Helier fled and joined the monks at Saint Marculf at

Nanteuil. He traveled to Jersey, Britain, as a missionary. He was martyred there.

Helimenas Saint; Greek

St. Helimenas (d. 250) was a priest who was beheaded near Babylon during the persecutions of Emperor Trajanus Decius.

Heliodorus Saint; Greek; gift of the sun

St. Heliodorus (third century) was martyred in Africa during the persecutions of Emperor Diocletian.

Helladius Saint; Greek; of Greece

St. Helladius, St. Helladius of Auxerre

St. Helladius (d. 632) was a counselor to Visigoth King Sisibut. He later became abbot of Agali Monastery. In 615, he was made archbishop of Toledo, Spain.

Hemiterius Saint; Greek

Emiterio

St. Hemiterius (fourth century) was a martyr who died in Calahorra, Old Castile, Spain.

Henery *see Henry*

Henraoi *see Henry*

Henrim *see Henry*

Henrry *see Henry*

Henry Saint; Top 100 Name; German; ruler of the household

Hank, Harro, Heike, Henery, Henraoi, Henrim, Henrry, Heromin

St. Henry, St. Henry II, St. Henry of Cocket, St. Henry of Sweden, St. Henry Walpole

St. Henry (972–1024) was the son of Henry, duke of Bavaria, and Gisells, daughter of Conrad, king of Burgundy. He was educated by St. Wolfgang and became duke of Bavaria when his father died. In 1002, he was elected emperor. He was committed to helping the Church and built the Cathedral of Bamberg. He was also victorious in war against the Saracens. He and his wife, St. Cunegundes, had both made vows of chastity. He is a patron saint of the childless, the handicapped, and those rejected by religious orders.

Henryk Saint; form of Henry; Dutch; ruler of the household

Bl. Henryk Hlebowicz, Bl. Henryk Kaczorowski, Bl. Henryk Krzysztofik

Bl. Henryk Kaczorowski (1888–1942) was born in Bierzwiennej, Wielkopolskie, Poland. He was ordained a priest and served as rector of the major seminary of Wloclawek in Poland. He was arrested by the Nazis and died at the Dachau concentration camp. He is one of the 108 Polish Martyrs of World War II and was beatified by Pope John Paul II in 1999.

Heraclas Saint; Greek; glorious gift

St. Heraclas (d. 247) was one of Origen's first pupils in Alexandria. He succeeded Origen as head of the school. He ultimately became patriarch of Alexandria, excommunicated Origen, and sent him out of Egypt.

Heraclius Saint; Greek; he who is drawn to the sacred

St. Heraclius, St. Heraclius of Sens

St. Heraclius of Sens (d. 515) was bishop of Sens, present when Clovis was baptized. He built the Abbey of St. John the Evangelist in Sens.

Heradius Saint; Greek

St. Heradius (d. 303) was martyred with several companions at Nyon on Lake Geneva, Switzerland.

Herald *see Harold*

Herb *see Herbert*

Herbert Saint; German; glorious soldier

Bert, Erbert, Eriberto, Harbert, Hebert, Hébert, Heberto, Herb, Herberte, Herbirt, Herburt, Herbyrt, Heriberto, Hirbert, Hirbirt, Hirburt, Hirbyrt, Hurbert, Hyrbert, Hyrbirt, Hyrburt, Hyrbyrt

St. Herbert, St. Herbert Hoscam, St. Herbert of Derwentwater

St. Herbert of Derwentwater (d. 687) was a priest who lived as a hermit on an island in Lake Derwentwater, England. He was a friend of St. Cuthbert.

Herberte *see Herbert*

Herbirt *see Herbert*

Herburt *see Herbert*

Herbyrt *see Herbert*

Herculafilis Saint; Greek

St. Herculafilis (second century) was a martyred Roman soldier.

Herculaflus Saint; Greek

St. Herculaflus (d. 549) was bishop of Perugia, Italy. He was martyred by King Totila of the Ostragoths. He died by beheading.

Herculanils Saint; Greek

St. Herculanils (d. 180) was martyred at Porto, near Rome.

Herebald Saint; English

St. Herebald (eighth century) was a hermit who lived in Brittany, France.

Hereld *see Harold*

Heribert Saint; German; ruler

St. Heribert (970–1021) was born in Worms. He was ordained a priest and later became the archbishop of Cologne, Germany. He accompanied Emperor Otto III to Italy. After Otto's death, he served Emperor St. Henry. He built the monastery of Deutz on the Rhine. He miraculously ended a drought and is therefore considered the patron saint of rain.

Heriberto *see Herbert*

Hermaan *see Herman*

Herman Saint; Latin; noble, soldier

Ermano, Ermin, Hermaan, Hermann, Hermano, Hermie, Herminio, Hermino, Hermon, Hermy, Hermyn, Heromin

St. Herman Joseph (1150–1241) was born in Cologne. He was known as a mystic and was deeply respected throughout Germany. He entered the Prae-monstratensians, where he was ordained. He had long been considered a saint but was officially canonized in 1958.

Hermann *see Herman*

Hermano *see Herman*

Hermas Saint; Greek; messenger

St. Hermas (first century) was mentioned by St. Paul in his Epistle to the Romans (Rom 16:14). He was bishop of Philippi, Greece, and a martyr.

Hermengaudis Saint; Greek; messenger of joy

St. Hermengaudis (d. 1035) was bishop of Urgell, in the Spanish Pyrenees, where he built a cathedral.

Hermengild Saint; German; he who offers sacrifice to God

St. Hermengild (d. 586) was the son of Leovigild the Visogoth, king of Spain. He was raised as an Arian. When his wife converted him from that heresey, he was disinherited by his father and was subsequently martyred by being axed to death.

Hermenland Saint; Greek

St. Hermenland (d. 720) was born near Noyon, France. He became a monk at Fontenelle Abbey. He and twelve other monks went as missionaries to Nantes, where he started an abbey on an island in the Loire. He was known as a miracle worker and had the gift of prophecy.

Hermes Saint; Greek; messenger

St. Hermes (d. 120) was martyred with several companions in Rome.

Hermias Saint; Greek; messenger

St. Hermias (d. 160) was a Roman soldier who was martyred at Comana, in Cappadocia.

Hermie *see Herman*

Herminio *see Herman*

Hermino *see Herman*

Hermogenes Saint; Greek; sent from Hermes

St. Hermogenes, St. Hermogenes of Alexandria

St. Hermogenes (fourth century) was martyred by being driven into a marshland to die of exposure.

Hermogius Saint

St. Hermogius (d. 942) was born at Tuy, Spain. He founded Labrugia Monastery in Spanish Galicia, Spain. He was taken prisoner by the Moors in Córdoba, but St. Pelagius took his place, and he was released.

Hermolaus Saint; Greek; messenger of God

St. Hermolaus (d. 305) was an elderly priest who converted St. Pantaleon. He was martyred with Hermippus and Hermocrates.

Hermon *see Herman*

Hermy *see Herman*

Hermylus Saint; Greek

St. Hermylus (d. 315) was a deacon who was martyred by

being drowned in the Danube, at Belgrade, Serbia.

Hermyn *see Herman*

Hernan Saint; German; peacemaker

St. Hernan (sixth century) fled from his home in Briton when the Anglo-Saxons conquered the area. He became a hermit in Loc Horn, in Brittany, France.

Herodion Saint; Greek; song of the hero

St. Herodion (d. 136) was a bishop of Antioch, Turkey, who was martyred.

Herold *see Harold*

Heromin *see Henry, Herman*

Heron Saint; Latin; hero

St. Heron (d. 250) was scourged for the faith in Egypt and then set free.

Heronim *see Harold*

Herulph Saint; German

Hariolfus

St. Herulph (d. 785), also known as Hariolfus, was the son of a count of Ellwengen, Germany. He started an abbey at Ellwangen in 764. He later became bishop of Langres, France.

Herv *see Herve*

Herve Saint; form of Harvey; French; army warrior

Herv, Hervee, Hervey, Hervi, Hervie, Hervy

St. Herve (d. 1021) was from Touraine, France. He became a hermit and monk at St. Martin of Tours Abbey.

Hervee *see Herve*

Hervey *see Herve*

Hervi *see Herve*

Hervie *see Herve*

Hervy *see Herve*

Heryld *see Harold*

Hesychius Saint; Greek, Latin; quiet, serene

St. Hesychius, St. Hesychius of Antioch

St. Hesychius (d. 302) was a Roman soldier who consoled St. Julius before he was martyred. He was then martyred himself.

Hew *see Hugh*

Hezekia *see Hezekiah*

Hezekiah Old Testament; Hebrew; God gives strength

Hazikiah, Hezekia, Hezekyah, Hezikyah

Hezekiah was the fourteenth king of Judah. He saw the destruction of the northern kingdom of Israel by the Assyrians. He removed the worship of pagan deities from the Temple in Jerusalem. Isaiah and Micah were prophets during his reign. His story is told in 2 Kings and 2 Chronicles.

Hezekyah *see Hezekiah*

Hezikyah *see Hezekiah*

Hidulphus Saint; Latin, German; battle wolf

St. Hidulphus (d. 707) was a courtier in the royal court of Austrasia and the husband of St. Agia. The couple separated in order to enter religious life.

He became a monk at Lobbes Abbey, which he had helped start.

Hiero Saint; Greek; holy

Iero

St. Hiero (d. 885) was from Ireland. He served as a missionary to Holland, where he was martyred.

Hieron Saint; Greek; holy place

St. Hieron (d. 300) was martyred with thirty Armenians at Melitene.

Hieronides Saint; Greek

St. Hieronides (d. 300) was an elderly deacon who was martyred in Alexandria, Egypt.

Hieu *see Hieu (girl's name)*

Higbald *see Hygbald*

Hil *see Hilary*

Hilair *see Hilary*

Hilaire *see Hilary*

Hilare *see Hilary*

Hilarie *see Hilary*

Hilarion Saint; Latin; happy, content

St. Hilarion (291–371) was born in Tabatha, Palestine, and was educated in Alexandria, Egypt, where he spent time with St. Anthony the Great. He then became a hermit at Majuma, near Gaza, Israel. He later traveled to Dalmatai, Croatia, and Cyprus with St. Hesychius. He was known as a miracle worker, and crowds flocked to see him wherever he went.

Hilarius Saint; Latin; happy, content

St. Hilarius (d. 449) was raised as a pagan. He converted to Christianity and became a monk at the Abbey of Lerins. He later served as bishop of Arles, where he sometimes was reproved by both civic and ecclesiastical authorites because of his zeal. Despite these issues, he was well respected for his faith.

Hilary Saint; Latin; cheerful

Hi, Hilair, Hilaire, Hilare, Hilarie, Hilery, Hill, Hillary, Hillery, Hilliary, Hillien, Hilly, Hylarie, Hylary

St. Hilary, St. Hilary Pope, St. Hilary of Poitiers

St. Hilary of Poitiers (315–368) was born into a noble pagan family. He married, had children, and studied the Bible. As he did so, he came to realize the truth found there and converted to the faith. He became bishop of Poitiers. The emperor wanted to run the Church, and Hilary opposed him. For this, he was exiled. He devoted himself to writing and teaching. His words converted many. He was proclaimed a Doctor of the Church in 1851. He is a patron saint against snake bites.

Hildebert Saint; German; fortress

St. Hildebert (d. 752) was abbot of the Abbey of St. Peter at Ghent, Belgium. He was martyred for his defense of holy images.

Hildegrin Saint; German

St. Hildegrin (d. 827) was the younger brother of St. Ludger. He was bishop of Chalons sur Marne, France, and later served as abbot at Werden Abbey.

Hildegund *see Hildegund (girl's name)*

Hildemar Saint; German; known in battle

St. Hildemar (d. 844) was a monk at Corbie. He later served as Benedictine bishop of Beauvais, France.

Hilduard Saint

St. Hilduard (d. 750) was a Benedictine missionary in Flanders, Belgium. He founded St. Peter's Abbey in Dickelvenne, near Ghent.

Hilery *see Hilary*

Hill *see Hilary*

Hillary *see Hilary*

Hillery *see Hilary*

Hilliary *see Hilary*

Himelin Saint

St. Himelin (d. 750) was an Irish priest. On his way home from a pilgrimage to Rome, he fell ill at the side of the road in Belgium. He begged a woman carrying a pitcher for some water. She hesitated because of the plague that many were suffering from, but she offered to take him to the nearby rectory and give him food and drink there. He insisted on drinking from the pitcher and promised that the priest for whom the water was intended would be "well satisfied." She finally allowed him to drink. When she reached the rectory, the priest was astounded to discover the water was now wine. The priest went in search of Himelin and brought him back to the rectory where he died.

Himerius Saint

St. Himerius (d. 560) was bishop of Amelia, in Umbria, Italy.

Hipparchus Saint; Greek

St. Hipparchus (d. 297) was a magistrate who was martyred for refusing to take part in a pagan celebration when Emperor Maximian defeated the Persians. He was one of the Martyrs of Samosata (in modern Turkey).

Hippolytus Saint; Greek; horseman

St. Hippolytus, St. Hippolytus of Porto

St. Hippolytus (d. 775) was a Benedictine abbot of St. Claude, in France.

Hirbert *see Herbert*

Hirbirt *see Herbert*

Hirburt *see Herbert*

Hirbyrt *see Herbert*

Homfree *see Humphrey*

Homfrey *see Humphrey*

Homobonus Saint; Latin; good man

St. Homobonus (d. 1197) was born in Cremona, Italy. He was a married merchant who was known as a model of virtue. He died while attending Mass at St. Giles Church in Cremona. He is a patron of tailors and cloth workers.

Homphree *see Humphrey*

Homphrey *see Humphrey*

Homphry *see Humphrey*

Honestus Saint; English; truthfulness

St. Honestus (d. 270) was from Nimes, France, but was sent to Spain where he was martyred in Pampeluna.

Honorat Saint; Spanish; honorable

Bl. Honorat a Biala Podlaska Kozimski (1829–1916) was born in Biala Podlaska. He lost his faith as a young man, but when he was imprisoned for political reasons, he returned to it. After being released, he entered the Capuchin order and was ordained a priest. He founded the Felician Sisters and the Capuchin Sisters of St. Clare. He also served as the Capuchin Commissary General. He died in Nowe-Miasto and was beatified by Pope John Paul II in 1988.

Honoratus Saint; Latin; honorable

Honore

St. Honoratus, St. Honoratus of Amiens, St. Honoratus of Toulouse, St. Honoratus of Vercelli

St. Honoratus of Amiens (d. 600) was bishop of Amiens, France. He is a patron of bakers, confectioners, bakers of altar bread, candle makers, florists, and flour merchants.

Honore *see Honoratus*

Honorino Saint; Latin; honorable

Bl. Honorino Carracedo Ramos (1916–1936) was one of the Passionist Martyrs of Daimiel who were martyred during the Spanish Civil War. He was beatified by Pope John Paul II in 1989.

Honorius Saint; Latin; honorable

St. Honorius, St. Honorius of Brescis, St. Honorius of Canterbury, St. Honorius II, III, IV

St. Honorius (d. 1250) was a cattle merchant whose servants stole from him while he was away. When he discovered this robbery, the servants killed him. He is venerated as a martyr.

Hormisdas Saint; Persian; the great wise one

Pope St. Hormisdas (450–523) was born in Frosinone, Campagna di Roma, Italy. He was married and widowed prior to becoming a priest. His son would become Pope St. Silverius. Hormisdas became pope in 514. He helped end the Acacian Schism, which led to the Church in Constantinople being reconciled to Rome.

Hortulanus Saint; Latin; gardener

St. Hortulanus (fifth century) was a North African bishop who was exiled by the Arian Vandal King Genseric.

Hoystill *see Austell (girl's name)*

Hryhory Saint; Ukranian; awake

Bl. Hryhory Khomyshyn (1867–1947) was born in Hadynkivsti, Ternopil District, Ukraine.

He was ordained a priest and became rector of the seminary in Lviv, Ukraine. He served as bishop of Stanislaviv. He was arrested for his faith by the NKVD and died in prison. He is one of the martyrs killed under communist regimes in Eastern Europe. He was beatified by Pope John Paul II in 2001.

Hubbert *see Hubert*

Huber *see Hubert*

Hubert Saint; German; bright mind, bright spirit

Bert, Eubert, Hubbert, Huber, Hubertek, Huberto, Hubertson, Hubirt, Huburt, Hubyrt, Hugibert, Huibert, Uberto

St. Hubert (d. 714) became a Benedictine monk when he was twelve years old. He lived at the Abbey of Bretigny, near Noyon, France.

Hubertek *see Hubert*

Huberto *see Hubert*

Hubertson *see Hubert*

Hubirt *see Hubert*

Huburt *see Hubert*

Hubyrt *see Hubert*

Huey *see Hugh*

Hugh Saint; short form of Hubert; English; bright mind, bright spirit

Fitzhugh, Hew, Huey, Hughe, Hughes, Huw, Huwe

St. Hugh, St. Hugh dei Lippi Uggucioni, St. Hugh of Ambronay, St. Hugh of Anzy le Duc, St. Hugh of Grenoble, St. Hugh of Lincoln, St. Hugh of Noara,

St. Hugh of Rouen, St. Hugh the Great, St. Hugh the Little

St. Hugh of Lincoln (twelfth century) was born at Avalon Castle in Burgundy, the son of the lord of Avalon. He was educated at a convent at Villard-Benoit and became a deacon at age nighteen. He later became a Carthusian and was ordained a priest. He became the abbot of the first Carthusian monastery in England, which had been built by King Henry II. He served as bishop of Lincoln and was known for his wisdom and justice.

Hughe *see Hugh*

Hughes *see Hugh*

Hugibert *see Hubert*

Hugo *see Ugo*

Huibert *see Hubert*

Hum *see Humbert, Humphrey*

Humbert Saint; German; brilliant strength

Hum, Humbirt, Humburt, Humbyrt

St. Humbert (d. 680) was a Benedictine monk who helped found Morailles Abbey in Flanders, Belgium, where he became abbot.

Humbirt *see Humbert*

Humburt *see Humbert*

Humbyrt *see Humbert*

Humfredo *see Humphrey*

Humfree *see Humphrey*

Humfrey *see Humphrey*

Humfri *see Humphrey*

Humfrid *see Humphrey*

Humfry *see Humphrey*

Humilis Saint; Latin; humble

St. Humilis of Bisignano (1582–1637) was born at Bisignano, Calabria, Italy, and became a Franciscan lay brother. Known for his holiness, he was summoned to Rome to be a counselor to both Pope Gregory XV and Pope Urban VIII. He was canonized in 2002.

Humph *see Humphrey*

Humphery *see Humphrey*

Humphree *see Humphrey*

Humphrey Saint; German; peaceful strength

Homfree, Homfrey, Homphree, Homphrey, Homphry, Hum, Humfredo, Humfree, Humfrey, Humfri, Humfrid, Humfry, Humph, Humphery, Humphree, Humphry, Humphrys, Hunfredo

St. Humphrey, St. Humphrey Lawrence

St. Humphrey (d. 871) was a monk at Prum and later served as bishop of Therouanne, France. He fled when the Normans invaded but then later returned to help rebuild the city. He also became abbot of St. Bertin in France.

Humphry *see Humphrey*

Humphrys *see Humphrey*

Hunegund Saint

St. Hunegund (d. 690) was forced to marry, but Pope St. Vitalian released her from her vows so that she could become a nun. She entered the abbey at Homblieres, France.

Hunfredo *see Humphrey*

Hunger Saint; English; need for food

St. Hunger (d. 866) was a bishop of Utrecht, Netherlands. Forced to flee when the Normans invaded, he settled in Prum, Germany, where he died.

Huno Saint; German; chicken

St. Huno (d. 690) was a priest of Ely, England, who helped St. Aetheldreda as she was dying. He then became a hermit in Fens.

Hurbert *see Herbert*

Huw *see Hugh*

Huwe *see Hugh*

Hyacinth Saint; Greek; botany

Hyacintha, Hyacinthia, Hyacinthie, Hycinth, Hycynth

St. Hyacinth, St. Hyacinth Castaneda, St. Hyacinth Orfanel

St. Hyacinth (1185–1257) was born in Oppeln, Poland. He was a priest and a doctor of sacred studies. After seeing St. Dominic perform a miracle in Rome, he decided to become a Dominican friar. He received the habit from St. Dominic himself. Hyacinth preached throughout Poland, Sweden, Norway, Denmark, Scotland, Russia, Turkey, and Greece. He is invoked by those in danger of drowning.

Hyacinthe Saint; Greek, French; botany

Bl. Hyacinthe Marie Cormier (1832–1916) was born in Orleans, France. He was ordained a priest and joined the Dominican order. He suffered from ill health, but a special exemption was made in order for him to make his vows. He was later named master general of the order. He was known for his preaching ability and his enthusiasm for sacred music. He was beatified in 1994 by Pope John Paul II.

Hybald *see Hygbald*

Hydroc Saint

St. Hydroc (fifth century) is the patron saint of Lanhydroc Cornwall, England.

Hygbald Saint; English

Higbald, Hybald

St. Hygbald (d. 690), also known as Higbald or Hybald, was a Benedictine abbot of Lincolnshire, England.

Hyginius Saint; Greek

St. Hyginius (d. 140) was pope from 136 to 140. He was Greek by birth and was a philosopher before converting to Christianity. During his reign, the Gnostics began to preach their heretical views.

Hylarie *see Hilary*

Hylary *see Hilary*

Hypatius Saint; Latin; highest

St. Hypatius (366–450) was born in Phrygia and became a monk. After having a vision, he traveled to Thrace, where he became a hermit. He gave shelter to St. Alexander Akimetes and others who were threatened by Nestorian heretics. He was also known for miracles and prophecies.

Hyperechios Saint

St. Hyperechios (date unknown) was an Egyptian hermit and a Desert Father.

Hyrbert *see Herbert*

Hyrbirt *see Herbert*

Hyrburt *see Herbert*

Hyrbyrt *see Herbert*

Hywyn Saint; Welsh; eminent

St. Hywyn (d. 516) founded several monasteries and churches in Wales.

I

Iacob *see Jacob*

Iacov *see Jacob*

Ibar Saint; Norse; bow army

Ivor

St. Ibar (fifth century), also known as Ivor, was a missionary to Ireland who helped evangelize Leinster and Meath. He also started Beggary Monastery on the island of Beg Eire.

Icek *see Isaac*

Idus Saint; Latin; to divide

St. Idus (fifth century) was a disciple of St. Patrick who became the bishop of Alt Fadha in Leinster, Ireland.

Iero *see Hiero*

Ignaas *see Ignatius*

Ignac *see Ignatius*

Ignace *see Ignatius*

Ignacey *see Ignatius*

Ignacio Saint; form of Ignatius; Italian; fiery or ardent

St. Ignacio Delgado y Cebrian (1761–1838) was from Villa Felice, Spain. He became a Dominican and was sent as a missionary to Vietnam, where he would spend the next fifty years. He became the bishop of East Tonkin. He was arrested during the persecutions of Minh Mang. He was tortured, which led to his death. After his death, his body was further desecrated by being beheaded and thrown into a river. He was canonized by Pope John Paul II in 1988.

Ignacius *see Ignatius*

Ignacy Saint; form of Ignatius; Latin; fiery or ardent

Bl. Ignacy Franczuk (1824–1874) was a married father from Derlo, Poland. He was one of the Martyrs of Podlasie and was beatified by Pope John Paul II in 1996.

Ignas *see Ignatius*

Ignatios *see Ignatius*

Ignatious *see Ignatius*

Ignatius Saint; Latin; fiery or ardent

Ignaas, Ignac, Ignace, Ignacey, Ignacio, Ignacius, Ignas, Ignatios, Ignatious, Ignatus, Ignatys, Ignatz, Ignaz, Ignazio

St. Ignatius, St. Ignatius Loyola, St. Ignatius of Africa, St. Ignatius of Antioch, St. Ignatius of Laconi

St. Ignatius Loyola (1491–1556) was born into a noble Spanish family and served as a page in the court of Ferdinand and Isabella. He served as a soldier and was injured in battle. As he recovered from that injury, he read a life of Christ and lives of the saints. This reading and his reflection on it led to his conversion. He became a hermit and then worked to convert Muslims. He later started the Society of Jesus, which received papal approval in 1534.

Ignatus *see Ignatius*

Ignatys *see Ignatius*

Ignatz *see Ignatius*

Ignaz *see Ignatius*

Ignazio Saint; form of Ignatius; Italian; fiery or ardent

St. Ignazio of Santhia (1686–1770) was from Vercelli, Italy, and served as a parish priest for several years before entering the Capuchins in Turin, Italy. He served as a sacristan and novice master. Later, he became the head chaplain of the armies of the king of Piedmont. After serving in that capacity, he returned to Capuchin Hill, where he served the poor and blessed the many pilgrims who came to see him. He was canonized in 2002 by Pope John Paul II.

Ike *see Isaac*

Ikey *see Isaac*

Ikie *see Isaac*

Ildephonse Saint; German; totally prepared for combat

Bl. Ildephonse (Alfredo) Schuster (1880–1954) was born in Rome, Italy. He joined the Order of St. Benedict and earned a doctorate of philosophy and then a doctorate in theology. He was ordained a priest and was later named the archbishop of Milan. Pope Pius XI consecrated him a cardinal in 1929. He served as a papal legate and took part in the conclave that elected Pope Pius XII. He was beatified by Pope John Paul II in 1996.

Ildephonsus Saint; German; totally prepared for combat

St. Ildephonsus (607–667) was born to a noble Spanish family. He entered the Benedictine Monastery of Agilia near Toledo, where he later served as abbot. In 657 he was named archbishop of Toledo. He wrote a famous work about the perpetual virginity of Mary as well as another on the history of the Spanish Church.

Illadan Saint; Celtic

St. Illadan (sixth century) was a bishop of Rathlipthen, in Offaly, Ireland.

Illidius Saint; Latin; troop

Allyre

St. Illidius (d. 385), also known as Allyre, was bishop of Clermont, France. He helped develop that area into a cultural center.

Illtyd Saint; Welsh; multitude of land

St. Illtyd (seventh century) was a Welsh saint. He and his wife, Tyrnihild, were members of Glamorgan's chief's army before becoming hermits. He later founded the abbey of Llanilltud Fawr in Glamorgan, Wales. According to legend, he was a cousin of King Arthur and one of the three Knights of the Holy Grail.

Illuminatus Saint; Latin; shining

St. Illuminatus (d. 1000) was a Benedictine monk at San Mariano Anney in Sanservino, Italy, where he later served as abbot.

Imanol *see Emmanuel*

Imanual *see Emmanuel*

Imanuel *see Emmanuel*

Imanuele *see Emmanuel*

Immanual *see Emmanuel*

Immanuel *see Emmanuel*

Immanuele *see Emmanuel*

Immuneal *see Emmanuel*

Indes Saint

St. Indes (d. 303) was martyred at Nicomedia with Domna, Agapes, and Theophila during the persecutions of Emperor Diocletian.

Indract Saint; Celtic

St. Indract (d. 710) was an Irish chieftain who was martyred either on the return trip from a pilgrimage in Rome or by Saxons near Glastonbury.

Ine Saint

St. Ine (d. 727) was king of Wessex 688–726. During his reign, he established the see of Sherborne and restored Glastonbury Abbey. In 726, he retired and he and his wife, St. Ethelburga, moved to Rome where he founded an English school.

Inigo *see Eneco*

Injuriosus Saint; Latin; injustice

St. Injuriosus (d. 550) and his wife, St. Scholastica, lived a celibate marriage, devoting themselves to God. They resided in Auvergne.

Innocent Saint; Latin; innocent

Pope St. Innocent, St. Innocent of Tortuna, Blessed

Pope St. Innocent I (d. 417) was born in Albano, Italy. According to St. Jerome, he was the son of Pope St. Anastasius, whom he succeeded as pope, born before his father's entry into the clergy. Innocent became pope in 401. As pope, he emphasized papal supremacy. He also was greatly in favor of clerical celibacy and fought the removal of St. John Chrysostom.

Innocentius Saint; Latin; innocent

Innocenty *see Inocencio*

Innocentz *see Inocencio*

Innocenz *see Inocencio*

Innocenzio *see Inocencio*

Innocenzyo *see Inocencio*

Inocenci *see Inocencio*

Inocencio Saint; Italian; innocent

Innocenty, Innocentz, Innocenz, Innocenzio, Innocenzyo, Inocenci, Inocente, Inocenzio, Inosente, Sencio

St. Inocencio de la Immaculata (1887–1934) was born Manuel Canoure Arnau in Cecilia del Valle de Oro, Lugo, Spain. He became a Passionist priest and was martyred during the Spanish Civil War. He is one of the Martyrs of Turón canonized by Pope John Paul II in 1999.

Inocente *see Inocencio*

Inocenzio *see Inocencio*

Inosente *see Inocencio*

Irenaeus Saint; Greek; lover of peace

St. Irenaeus, St. Irenaeus of Sirmium

St. Irenaeus (125–202) was born in Asia Minor. He became a priest and served under St. Pothinus. Irenaeus was sent to Rome in 177 and escaped the persecution that was going on in Lyons. When he returned there, it was to serve as bishop. He spoke out against Gnosticism and wrote a treatise in five books to expose that heresy's errors. He is known as one of the Fathers of the Church.

Irmina *see Irmina (girl's name)*

Isaac Saint, Old Testament; Top 100 Name; Hebrew; he will laugh

Aizik, Icek, Ike, Ikey, Ikie, Isaack, Isaak, Isaakios, Isacco, Isaic, Ishaq, Isiac, Isiacc, Issac, Issca, Itzak, Yeshak

St. Isaac, St. Isaac of Cordoba, St. Isaac of Spoleto, St. Isaac the Great, St. Isaac Jogues

Isaac in the Bible is the long-awaited son of Abraham and Sarah. At the direction of God, Abraham brought him to Moriah intending to offer him as a sacrifice, but an angel of the Lord stopped him and said that he had passed the test. At age forty, he married Rebekah. Their children were Jacob and Esau. Isaac lived to be 180, the longest-living patriarch.

St. Isaac Jogues (1607–1646) was born in Orleans, France. He became a Jesuit and became a missionary to Canada, where he worked among the Hurons and Petuns in the area of the Great Lakes. He was captured by the Mohawks in 1642. After thirteen months, he escaped and returned to France to recover from the ill treatment he had received. In 1644 he returned to the New World. He was martyred by being tomahawked in the head by an Iroquois chief in what is now New York State.

Isaack *see Isaac*

Isaak *see Isaac*

Isaakios *see Isaac*

Isacco *see Isaac*

Isador *see Isidore*

Isadore *see Isidore*

Isadorios *see Isidore*

Isai *see Isaiah*

Isaia *see Isaiah*

Isaiah Saint, Old Testament; Top 100 Name; Hebrew; the salvation of the Lord

Essaiah, Isai, Isaia, Isaid, Isaish, Isaya, Isayah, Isia, Isiash, Issia, Izaiah, Izaiha, Izaya, Izayah, Izayaih, Izayiah, Izeyah, Izeyha

Isaiah in the Bible was a prophet in the kingdom of Judah. Many of the New Testament teachings of Jesus refer to the book of Isaiah. Gregory of Nyssa described Isaiah as "more of an Evangelist than a Prophet, because he described all of the Mysteries of the Christ so vividly that you would assume he was not prophesying about the future, but rather composing a history of past events."

Isaiahs *see Isaias*

Isaias Saint; form of Isaiah; Hebrew; God is my salvation

Isaiahs, Isais, Izayus

St. Isaias (d. 309) was martyred with thirty-seven companions by pagan Arabs in the Red Sea area.

Isaic *see Isaac*

Isaid *see Isaiah*

Isais *see Isaias*

Isaish *see Isaiah*

Isarnus Saint; German; eagle of iron

Ysarn

St. Isarnus (d. 1048), also known as Ysarn, was a Benedictine abbot of St. Victor's in Toulouse, known for his care of criminals.

Isauri *see Ansurius*

Isaurus Saint; Greek, Latin; from Isauria

St. Isaurus (date unknown) was martyred by being beheaded at Appalonia, Macedonia.

Isaya *see Isaiah*

Isayah *see Isaiah*

Ischyrion Saint

St. Ischyrion (d. 250) was a procurator of an Egyptian city, possibly Alexandria. He was martyred for refusing to worship pagan gods.

Iser *see Israel*

Ishaq *see Isaac*

Isia *see Isaiah*

Isiac *see Isaac*

Isiacc *see Isaac*

Isiash *see Isaiah*

Isidor *see Isidore*

Isidore Saint; Greek; gift of Isis

Dore, Esidore, Isador, Isadore, Isadorios, Isidor, Isidro, Issy, Ixidor, Izador, Izadore, Izidor, Izidore, Izydor

St. Isidore the Confessor, St. Isidore the Farmer, St. Isidore of Seville

St. Isidore of Seville (560–636) was born in Cartegena, Spain. He struggled in school but turned this care over to God and became a very learned man. He became a priest and then served as archbishop of Seville. He was a prolific writer whose works included a dictionary, an encyclopedia, and a history of the world. He also introduced the works of Aristotle to Spain. He was named a Doctor of the Church in 1722. He is a patron saint of students, computer users, and the internet.

Isidro *see Isidore*

Israel Old Testament; Hebrew; wrestled with God

Iser, Israele, Israhel, Isrell, Isrrael, Isser, Izrael, Yisrael

Israel was the name given to the patriarch Jacob (Gn 32:28). The Jewish people came to be known as the "Children of Israel" or "Israelites." The land of Canaan came to be known as the land of Israel.

Israele *see Israel*

Israhel *see Israel*

Isrell *see Israel*

Isrrael *see Israel*

Issac *see Isaac*

Issca *see Isaac*

Isser *see Israel*

Issia *see Isaiah*

Issy *see Isidore*

Ithamar Saint; Hebrew; island of the palms

St. Ithamar (d. 656) was born in Kent and became bishop of Rochester, Britain, in 644. He was known for his learning.

Itzak *see Isaac*

Iustin *see Justin*

Ivan Saint; form of John; Russian; God is gracious

> *Eyvan, Ivann, Ivano, Ivas, Iven, Ivin, Ivon, Ivun, Iwan, Ovyn, Yvan, Yvann*

> St. Ivan (ninth century) was a courtier in the court of Bohemia, but he gave it up to become a hermit.

Ivann *see Ivan*

Ivano *see Ivan*

Ivas *see Ivan*

Iven *see Ivan*

Ivin *see Ivan*

Ivo Saint; German; yew wood, bow wood

> *Yvo*

> St. Ivo, St. Ivo (Yves) of Kermartin

> St. Ivo (1253–1303) studied in Paris and became bishop of Chartres. He was a counselor to King Philip, who imprisoned him for a time when he opposed the king's plan to leave his wife in order to marry another woman. He wrote widely on canon law. He is a patron saint of Brittany, lawyers, and abandoned children.

Ivon *see Ivan*

Ivor *see Ibar*

Ivun *see Ivan*

Iwan *see Ivan*

Iwi *see Ywi*

Ixidor *see Isidore*

Izador *see Isidore*

Izadore *see Isidore*

Izaiah *see Isaiah*

Izaiha *see Isaiah*

Izaya *see Isaiah*

Izayah *see Isaiah*

Izayaih *see Isaiah*

Izayiah *see Isaiah*

Izayus *see Isaias*

Izeyah *see Isaiah*

Izeyha *see Isaiah*

Izidor *see Isidore*

Izidore *see Isidore*

Izrael *see Israel*

Izydor *see Isidore*

J

Jaan *see Jan*

Jaasen *see Jason*

Jaasin *see Jason*

Jaason *see Jason*

Jaasun *see Jason*

Jaasyn *see Jason*

Jacen *see Jason*

Jachob *see Jacob*

Jacindo *see Jacinto*

Jacint *see Jacinto*

Jacinto Saint; Portuguese, Spanish; hyacinth

> *Jacindo, Jacint, Jacynto*

> Bl. Jacinto de los Angeles (1660–1700) was born in Mexico. As a child he was an altar boy. He then helped assist the local priests in protecting public morality. He was married and had two children. He was martyred by local pagans after

stopping an idolatrous ceremony. He was beatified in 2002 by Pope John Paul II.

Jackques *see Jacques*

Jackquise *see Jacques*

Jaco *see Jacob*

Jacob Saint, Old Testament; Top 100 Name; Hebrew; supplanter, substitute

Hakob, Iacob, Iacov, Jachob, Jaco, Jacobb, Jacub, Jaecob, Jaicob, Jakov, Jalu, Jecis, Jeks, Jeska, Jocek, Jock, Jocob, Jocobb, Jokubas

St. Jacob of Mahdjudh, St. Jacob of Nisibis

Jacob in the Bible is the younger son of Isaac and Rebekah. His story is told in Genesis 25–50. He bought the birthright from his older twin, Esau, and later tricked his father into bestowing his blessing upon him. He married Leah and Rachel and had twelve sons. His name was later changed to Israel, and his children became the twelve tribes of Israel.

St. Jacob of Nisbis (d. 350) was the first bishop of Nisbis and took part in the Council of Nicaea. He founded the theological school of Nisibis and was known for his learning and holiness.

Jacobb *see Jacob*

Jacopo *see Giacomo*

Jacot *see Jacques*

Jacque *see Jacques*

Jacquees *see Jacques*

Jacques Saint; form of Jacob; French; supplanter, substitute

Jackques, Jackquise, Jacot, Jacque, Jacquees, Jacquese, Jacquess, Jacquet, Jacquett, Jacquis, Jacquise, Jaq, Jarques, Jarquis

St. Jacques Fremin (1628–1691) was born in Rheims, France. He became a Jesuit and was sent to Canada as a missionary. He established the first Catholic settlement in Vermont on Isle La Motte. He converted more than 10,000 souls.

Jacquese *see Jacques*

Jacquess *see Jacques*

Jacquet *see Jacques*

Jacquett *see Jacques*

Jacquis *see Jacques*

Jacquise *see Jacques*

Jacub *see Jacob*

Jacut Saint

St. Jacut (fifth century) and his brother, St. Guethenoc, were sons of Sts. Fagan and Gwen, who were forced to leave Britain to escape invading Saxons. They traveled to Brittany.

Jacynto *see Jacinto*

Jadviga *see Hedwig (girl's name)*

Jaecob *see Jacob*

Jaemes *see James*

Jaesan *See Jason*

Jaesen *see Jason*

Jaesin *see Jason*

Jaeson *see Jason*

Jaesun *see Jason*

Jaesyn *see Jason*

Jahn *see Jan*

Jahsan *see Jason*

Jahsen *see Jason*

Jahson *see Jason*

Jaicob *see Jacob*

Jaime *see James*

Jaimes *see James*

Jaison *see Jason*

Jakim *see Joachim*

Jakob Saint; form of Jacob; Hebrew; supplanter, substitute

Bl. Jakob Gapp, Bl. Jakob Kern

Bl. Jakob Gapp (1897–1943) was born in Wattens, Austrian Tirol. He served as an Austrian soldier during World War I. He was wounded and became a prisoner of war. He was released in 1919. He entered the Marianist seminary and was ordained a priest. He worked as a teacher and chaplain in Marianist schools. He preached against Nazism. He went to France to escape Nazi persecution and worked there as a chaplain and librarian. He was ultimately arrested and brought to Berlin. He was condemned to death for speaking out against the Nazi party. He was beatified by Pope John Paul II in 1996.

Jakov *see Jacob*

Jalu *see Jacob*

Jambert Saint; English

St. Jambert (d. 792) was an abbot of St. Augustine's monastery and became archbishop of Canterbury. He was known for his care of the poor.

James Saint, New Testament; Top 100 Name; Hebrew; supplanter, substitute

Jaemes, Jaime, Jaimes, Jamesie, Jameson, Jamesy, Jamies, Jamse, Jamyes, Jemes

St. James Buzabalio, St. James Intercisus, St. James Kisai, St. James Lacop, St. James Nam, St. James of Manug, St. James of the Marches, St. James of Sasseau, St. James of Tarentaise, St. James of Toul, St. James the Deacon, St. James the Greater

St. James the Greater (d. 44) was the son of Zebedee and Salome and the brother of St. John the Apostle. He may have been the cousin of Jesus. He is called "the Greater" because he became an apostle of Jesus prior to the other James, known as "the Lesser." He was a disciple of St. John the Baptist and left everything when Jesus invited him to become a "fisher of men." After Christ's resurrection, he preached in Samaria, Judea, and Spain. He was stabbed with a sword by King Herod Agrippa I in Jerusalem.

Jamesie *see James*

Jameson *see James*

Jamesy *see James*

Jamies *see James*

Jamse *see James*

Jamyes *see James*

Jan Saint; form of John; Slavic; God is gracious

Hans, Jaan, Jahn, Jana, Janae, Jann, Janne, Jano, Janos, Jenda, Jhan, Yan

St. Jan Sarkander (1576–1620) was born in Austrian Silesia and educated at Prague. He became a priest and defended the faith against the Hussites. In 1618, Protestants took control of the government. Jan was taken prisoner two years later. He was tortured and martyred. Pope John Paul II canonized him in 1995.

Jana *see Jan*

Janae *see Jan*

Janathan *see Jonathan*

Janco *see John*

Jann *see Jan*

Jano *see Jan*

Janos *see Jan*

Januarius Saint; Latin; gate, passageway

St. Januarius (d. 305) was born in Italy and served as bishop of Benevento. When he went to visit two deacons and two other Christians in prison, he was also taken prisoner. He was sentenced to be killed by wild beasts, but the beasts would not attack. He was then beheaded. He is a patron saint of blood banks, Naples, and volcanic eruptions.

Jaq *see Jacques*

Jaramia *see Jeremiah*

Jardan *see Jordan*

Jarden *see Jordan*

Jaremay *see Jeremy*

Jaremy *see Jeremy*

Jarlath Saint; Latin; in control

St. Jarlath (d. 540) was a member of the Conmaicne family, one of the most important families of Galway during the time. He became a priest and then founded the Monastery of Cluain Fois, outside of Tuam, where he served as abbot. He later opened a school there as well, which became known as a center of learning.

Jarogniew Saint; Slavic, Polish; spring, anger

Bl. Jarogniew Wojciechowski (1922–1942) was one of the 108 Polish Martyrs of World War II. He was beatified by Pope John Paul II in 1999.

Jarques *see Jacques*

Jarquis *see Jacques*

Jarvis *see Gervase*

Jasan *see Jason*

Jasaun *see Jason*

Jasin *see Jason*

Jason Saint, New Testament; Top 100 Name; Greek; healer

Jaasen, Jaasin, Jaason, Jaasun, Jaasyn, Jacen, Jaesan, Jaesen, Jaesin, Jaeson, Jaesun, Jaesyn, Jahsan, Jahsen, Jahson, Jaison, Jasan, Jasaun, Jasin, Jasten, Jasun, Jasyn

St. Jason (first century) was one of the seventy disciples. He is mentioned in the Bible in Acts 17 and Romans 16:21. He was appointed bishop of Tarsus by St. Paul. He traveled to Corfu, where he helped bring many to the Christian faith. He was thrown into prison by the king of Corfu. That king eventually was drowned while pursuing Christians fleeing his island. The new king embraced Christianity and allowed Jason to preach freely until he died of old age.

Jasten *see Jason*

Jastin *see Justin*

Jasun *see Jason*

Jasyn *see Jason*

Jaugen *see Eugene*

Jazeps *see Joseph*

Jean Saint; form of John; French; God is gracious

Jéan, Jeane, Jeannah, Jeannie, Jeannot, Jeano, Jeanot, Jeanty, Jeen, Jene

St. Jean de Brebeuf (1593–1649) was born in France. He became a Jesuit and was sent to the New World as a missionary to the Native Americans. He worked among the Hurons for many years before being taken prisoner by the Iroquois. They tortured and martyred him. He is a patron saint of Canada.

Jeane *see Jean*

Jeannah *see Jean*

Jeannot *see Jean*

Jeano *see Jean*

Jeanot *see Jean*

Jeanty *see Jean*

Jecho *see Jesus*

Jecis *see Jacob*

Jeen *see Jean*

Jeff *see Jeffrey*

Jeffery *see Jeffrey*

Jeffrey Saint; German, French; God's peace

Geoff, Geoffrey, Godfrey, Jeff, Jeffery, Jefrey

St. Jeffrey of Amiens, St. Jeffrey of Cappenberg, St. Jeffrey of Duynen, St. Jeffrey of Kappenburg, St. Jeffrey of Loudon, St. Jeffrey of Merville

St. Jeffrey of Cappenberg (1097–1127), also known as Godfrey, was a descendent of both Charlemagne and the dukes of Swabia. After becoming Christian, this count of Westphalia turned his castle into a Premonstratensian Abbey and turned his land and money over to St. Norbert of Xanten. He then joined the order as a monk. His wife became a nun at a convent he founded. He also started several hospitals.

Jefrey *see Jeffrey*

Jeks *see Jacob*

Jem *see Jeremiah*

Jemeriah *see Jeremiah*

Jemes *see James*

Jemiah *see Jeremiah*

Jen *see John*

Jenaro Saint; Latin; born in January

Saint Jenaro Sánchez Delgadillo (1876–1927) was born in Zapopan, Jalisco. He was vicar of Tamazulita, the parish of Tecolotlán, Jalisco (diocese of Autlán) and was known for his skill in preaching. He was martyred in Mexico and was canonized by Pope John Paul II in 2000.

Jenda *see Jan*

Jene *see Jean*

Jeramiha *see Jeremiah*

Jeramy *see Jeremy*

Jere *see Jeremy, Jerome*

Jereamy *see Jeremy*

Jereias *see Jeremiah*

Jeremaya *see Jeremiah*

Jeremia *see Jeremiah*

Jeremiah Saint, Old Testament; Top 100 Name; Hebrew; God will uplift

Geremiah, Jaramia, Jem, Jemeriah, Jemiah, Jeramiha, Jereias, Jeremaya, Jeremia, Jeremial, Jeremija, Jeremya, Jeremyah, Jerimiah, Yeremia

Jeremiah in the Bible was a major Old Testament prophet who is credited with authoring the book of Jeremiah, 1 Kings, 2 Kings, and Lamentations.

St. Jeremiah (d. 852) was beheaded in Spain by Caliph Abd-al-Rahman II. He is one of the Martyrs of Córdoba.

Jeremial *see Jeremiah*

Jeremija *see Jeremiah*

Jeremry *see Jeremy*

Jeremy Saint; Hebrew; God will raise up

Jaremay, Jaremy, Jeramy, Jere, Jereamy, Jeremry, Jeremye, Jereomy, Jeriemy, Jerime, Jerimy, Jeromy, Jerremy

St. Jeremy (d. 309) ministered to Christians who were working in the mines of Cilicia as punishment under Maximus. He, too, was arrested for the faith and was beheaded by order of Governor Firmilian.

Jeremya *see Jeremiah*

Jeremyah *see Jeremiah*

Jeremye *see Jeremy*

Jereomy *see Jeremy*

Jeriemy *see Jeremy*

Jerime *see Jeremy*

Jerimiah *see Jeremiah*

Jerimy *see Jeremy*

Jermaine *see Germaine (girl's name)*

Jeroen *see Jerome*

Jerold *see Gerald*

Jerom *see Jerome*

Jerome Saint; Latin; holy

Gerome, Geronimo, Jere, Jeroen, Jerom, Jeromo, Jerrome, Jerron, Jerrone

St. Jerome, St. Jerome de Torres, St. Jerome Emiliani, St. Jerome Hermosilla, St. Jerome of Pavia, St. Jerome of Werden

St. Jerome (347–419) was born to a rich pagan family. He studied in Rome and became a lawyer. He began to study theology and converted to the faith. He became a monk and lived as a hermit in the Syrian desert. He became a priest and served as a secretary to Pope Damasus I, who commissioned him to revise the Latin text of the Bible, which became known as the Vulgate translation. He then returned to life in the desert, where he wrote prolifically, including translations of histories, biographies, and works of Origen. He is a Doctor of the Church and patron of archeologists, archivists, Bible scholars, librarians, schoolchildren, and students.

Jeromo *see Jerome*

Jeromy *see Jeremy*

Jerremy *see Jeremy*

Jerrome *see Jerome*

Jerron *see Jerome*

Jerrone *see Jerome*

Jerry *see Gerald*

Jersey *see Jerzy*

Jerzey *see Jerzy*

Jerzi *see Jerzy*

Jerzy Saint; form of George; Polish; farmer

Jersey, Jerzey, Jerzi, Jurek

Bl. Jerzy Matulevicz (1871–1927) was born into a poor farm family in Lugine, Lithuania. He was orphaned at the age of ten. He suffered from tuberculosis of the bone in his leg for most of his life. He earned his doctorate of theology at the University of Fribourg, Switzerland, and was ordained a priest as a member of the Congregation of Marian Fathers. He was a noted teacher, preacher, and spiritual director. He became superior general of the Marian Fathers. He founded the Sisters of the Immaculate Conception and the Sisters Servants of Jesus in the Eucharist. He was named bishop of Vilnius, Lithuania.

He was beatified by Pope John Paul II in 1987.

Jescee *see Jesse*

Jese *see Jesse*

Jesee *see Jesse*

Jesi *see Jesse*

Jeska *see Jacob*

Jesous *see Jesus*

Jesse Old Testament; Hebrew; wealthy

Jescee, Jese, Jesee, Jesi, Jezze, Jezzee

Jesse in the Bible was the son of Obed and the grandson of Ruth and Boaz. He was the father of King David and is therefore a forefather of Jesus.

Jessus *see Jesus*

Jesu *see Jesus*

Jesus New Testament; Top 100 Name; form of Joshua; Hebrew; savior, deliverer

Jecho, Jesous, Jessus, Jesu, Jezus, Josu

Jezus *see Jesus*

Jezze *see Jesse*

Jezzee *see Jesse*

Jhan *see Jan*

Jian *see John*

Jildo Saint

Bl. Jildo Irwa (1905–1918) was born in Uganda. He converted to the faith at age eleven and taught others about the Gospel. When he refused to stop teaching, he was martyred. He was beatified in 2002 by Pope John Paul II.

Joacheim *see Joachim*

Joachim Saint; Hebrew; God will establish

Jakim, Joacheim, Joaquin, Joaquyn, Joaquynn, Joquin, Juaquyn

St. Joachim, St. Joachim Ho, St. Joachim Royo, St. Joachim Sakachibara

St. Joachim (first century BC) is traditionally known as the father of Mary and grandfather of Jesus. After years of childlessness, an angel appeared to him and his wife, Anne, to tell them that they would have a child. They promised to dedicate the child to God.

Joahan *see Johann*

Joannicus Saint; Hebrew, Latin; God is gracious

St. Joannicus (d. 846) was born in Bithynia, in modern Turkey. He was an iconoclast before he converted at the age of forty. He became a hermit who lived on Mount Olympus in Bithynia. He went up against Emperor Theophilus and said that sacred images would be restored to churches. Empress Theodora followed Joannicus's direction and did restore the icons.

Joaquim *see Joshua*

Joaquin *see Joachim*

Joaquyn *see Joachim*

Joaquynn *see Joachim*

Jobst *see Justin*

Jocek *see Jacob*

Jock *see Jacob*

Jocob *see Jacob*

Jocobb *see Jacob*

Jodoc Saint; Latin, English; lord

St. Jodoc (d. 668) was the son of King Juthael of Amorica. Jodoc became king but abdicated after making a pilgrimage to Rome. He was ordained a priest and then lived as a hermit at Runiacum. He felt a calling to pray for soldiers. He is invoked against fire, storms, and shipwrecks, and is a patron of boatmen, sailors, and watermen.

Joel Old Testament; Hebrew; God is willing

Joell, Joelle, Joely, Jole, Yoel

Joel was one of the prophets of the Old Testament. The Book of Joel is one of the twelve prophetic books known as the Minor Prophets because of the length of the text.

Joell *see Joel*

Joelle *see Joel*

Joely *see Joel*

Joen *see John*

Johahn *see Johann*

Johan *see Johann*

Johanan *see John*

Johane *see Johann*

Johann Saint; form of John; German; God is gracious

Joahan, Johahn, Johan, Johane, Johannan, Johaun

Bl. Johann Nepomuk Tsciderer von Gleifheim (1777–1860) was from Tyrol. He was ordained a priest and served the diocese of Trent, where he taught moral and pastoral theology at the seminary. He then became a parish priest at Sarnthal and Meran. He was later named bishop of Heliopolis and then bishop of Trent. He was known for his charity to the poor and sick. He was beatified by Pope John Paul II in 1995.

Johannan *see Johann*

Johaun *see Johann*

John Saint, New Testament; Top 100 Name; Hebrew; God is gracious

Janco, Jen, Jian, Joen, Johanan, Johne, Jone, Sean, Shawn, Yohan

St. John, St. John Almond, St. John Angeloptes, St. John Baptist Chon Chang-Un, St. John Baptist Con, St. John Baptist de la Salle, St. John Baptist Machado, St. John Baptist Nam Chong-Sam, St. John Baptist Rossi, St. John Baptist Scalabrini, St. John Baptist Thank, St. John Baptist Vianney, St. John Berchmans, St. John Bosco, St. John Boste, St. John Calabytes, St. John Camillus the Good, St. John Cantius, St. John Cassian St. John de Brebeaf and Companions, St. John de Britto, St. John de Massians, St. John de Ortega, St. John de Ribera, St. John del Prado, St. John Eudes, St. John Fisher, St. John Francis Regis, St. John Gaulbert, St. John Grove, St. John Hoan, St. John Houghton, St. John Jones, St. John Joseph of the Cross, St. John Kemble, St. John Charles Cornay, St. John Chrysostom, St. John Climacus, St. John Dat, St. John de Atares, St. John de Brebeuf, St. John de Britto, St. John de Massias, St. John de Ortega, St. John Kokumbuko, St. John Leonardi. St. John Maria Muzeyi, St. John Mark, St. John Mary Mzec, St. John Nepomucene, St. John Nepomucene Neumann, St. John Neumass, St. John of Autun, St. John of Avila, St. John of Bergamo, St. John of Beverly, St. John of Bridlington, St. John of Capistrano, St. John of Chalons, St. John of Chinon, St. John of Cologne, St. John of Constantinople, St. John of Damascus, St. John of Edessa, St. John of Egypt, St. John of God, St. John of Gorze, St. John of Kanty, St. John of Lodi, St. John of Martha, St. John of Matera, St. John of Meda, St. John of Monte Marano, St. John of Nicomedia, St. John of Osterwick, St. John of Perugia, St. John of Pulsano, St. John of Ratzeburg, St. John of Ravenna, St. John of Reomay, St. John of Rila, St. John of Ruysbroeck, St. John of Sahagun, St. John of Shutp, St. John of Syracuse, St. John of the Cross, St. John of the Goths, St. John of the Grating, St. John of Tuy, St. John of Verona, St. John Ogilvie, St. John Payne, St. John Plessington, St. John Rigby, St. John Roberts, St. John Serapion, St. John Soan de Goto, St. John Southworth, St. John Stone, St. John the Almoner, St. John the Almsgiver, St. John the Apostle, St. John the Baptist, St. John the Dwarf, St. John the Evangelist,

St. John the Hermit, St. John the Iberian, St. John the Merciful, St. John the Silent, St. John the Syrian of Pinna, St. John the Wonder-Worker, St. John Theristus, St. John Vianney, St. John Vincent, St. John Wall, St. John Yano

St. John (first century) was a son of Zebedee and Salome, the brother of St. James the Greater. He was a follower of St. John the Baptist when he was called by Jesus to become a "fisher of men." He was one of the Lord's closest friends and is referred to as "the one Jesus loved." After the Resurrection, he was the first to recognize Christ when he appeared to them on the shore. According to tradition, he cared for the Virgin Mary at Ephesus. Although he was tortured for the faith, he was not martyred, and as an older man he wrote the Gospel of John and the book of Revelation.

John Paul Saint; combination of John and Paul

Bl. Pope John Paul II (1920–2005) was born Karol Wojtyla in Wadowice, Poland. He enrolled in a school for drama, but when the university was closed, he went to work in a chemical factory. In 1942, he began studying for the priesthood in the secret seminary in Krakow. After World War II, he continued his studies and was ordained in 1946. He studied in Rome and earned

his doctorate in theology. He served as professor at the University of Lublin for twenty years. He was then named an auxiliary bishop of Krakow. He attended Vatican II as bishop of Krakow and worked to implement its reforms in his homeland. He was named a cardinal in 1967 and was elected pope in 1978. He was known for his opposition to communism, his promotion of the culture of life, and his writings on the theology of the body. He served as pope for twenty-six years and was beatified by Pope Benedict XVI in 2011.

Johnatan *see Jonathan*

Johnathan *see Jonathan*

Johne *see John*

John-Joseph Saint; combination of John and Joseph

St. John-Joseph of the Cross (1654–1739) was born Carlo Gaetano Calosirto on Ischia Island. He joined the Franciscans and became a priest. He served as superior of the Italian branch of the order but was most known as a prophet and mystic.

John-Louis Saint; French; combination of John and Louis

St. John-Louis Bonnard (1824–1852) was born in France. He became a priest and joined the Paris Society of Foreign Missions. He was sent to Vietnam where he was arrested and beheaded. One of the Martyrs of Vietnam, he was canonized by Pope John Paul II in 1988.

Johsua *see Joshua*

Johusa *see Joshua*

Jokubas *see Jacob*

Jole *see Joel*

Jolyon *see Julian*

Jona *see Jonah*

Jonah Old Testament; Hebrew; dove

Giona, Jona, Yonah, Yunus

Jonah (sixth century BC) was an Old Testament prophet sent to Ninevah to warn the people to change their ways. The book of Jonah in the Bible tells how he attempted to run from God's order, so God had him swallowed by a giant fish, where he lived for three days before being spit out on Ninevah's shore.

Jonahs *see Jonas*

Jonas Saint; Hebrew; he accomplishes

Jonahs, Jonasco, Jonass, Jonaus, Jonelis, Jonukas, Jonus, Jonutis, Jonys, Joonas, Yon

St. Jonas (third century) was a companion of St. Denis of Paris. He was martyred in Paris.

Jonasco *see Jonas*

Jonass *see Jonas*

Jonatan *see Jonathan*

Jonatha *see Jonathan*

Jonathan Old Testament; Hebrew; given of God

Janathan, Johnathan, Johnatan, Jonatan, Jonatha, Jonathin, Jonathun, Jonathyn, Jonethen, Jonnathun

Jonathan in the Bible was the son of King Saul and a close friend of King David. His story is told in 1 Samuel.

Jonathin *see Jonathan*

Jonathun *see Jonathan*

Jonathyn *see Jonathan*

Jonatus Saint; form of Jonathan; Hebrew; given of God

St. Jonatus (d. 690) was a Benedictine abbot of Marchiennes and Elnone.

Jonaus *see Jonas*

Jone *see John*

Jonelis *see Jonas*

Jonethen *see Jonathan*

Jonnathun *see Jonathan*

Jonukas *see Jonas*

Jonus *see Jonas*

Jonutis *see Jonas*

Jonys *see Jonas*

Joonas *see Jonas*

Joosef *see Josef*

Jooseppi *see Joseph*

Joquin *see Joachim*

Jorandus Saint

St. Jorandus (d. 1340) lived as a Benedictine hermit at Kergist and Saint-Juhec in Pedernec.

Jordaan *see Jordan*

Jordae *see Jordan*

Jordain *see Jordan*

Jordaine *see Jordan*

Jordan Saint; Top 100 Name; Hebrew; the river of judgment, descending

Jardan, Jarden, Jordaan, Jordae, Jordain, Jordaine, Jordane, Jordani, Jordanio, Jordann, Jordanny, Jordano, Jordany, Jordayne, Jorden, Jordian, Jordun, Jorrdan

Bl. Jordan of Saxony (1190–1237) was born into a noble family in Saxony. From an early age, he was dedicated to helping the poor. He received his master's degree in theology from the University of Paris and joined the Dominicans, serving under St. Dominic. He succeeded St. Dominic as master general of the Order of Preachers. He helped spread the order throughout Germany and Denmark. He also wrote a biography of St. Dominic. He drowned off the coast of Syria while on a pilgrimage to the Holy Land.

Jordane *see Jordan*

Jordani *see Jordan*

Jordanio *see Jordan*

Jordann *see Jordan*

Jordanny *see Jordan*

Jordano *see Jordan*

Jordany *see Jordan*

Jordayne *see Jordan*

Jorden *see Jordan*

Jordian *see Jordan*

Jordun *see Jordan*

Jorrdan *see Jordan*

Josaphat Saint; Hebrew; God's judgment

St. Josaphat Kuncevyc (1580–1623) was raised in the Orthodox Ruthenian Church, which united with the Church of Rome in 1595. He became a monk in the Ukranian Order of St. Basil. He was later ordained a Byzantine Rite priest. He was a famous preacher who worked to bring unity among the faithful. He became bishop of Vitebsk, Belarus, and then archbishop of Polotsk, Lithuania. He was martyred by a mob of anti-Uniats (those against the unification of the Church with Rome).

Jose Saint; Top 100 Name; form of Joseph; Spanish; God will add

Josean, Josecito, Josee, Joseito, Joselito, Joses, Josito

St. Jose Thi Dang Le, St. Jose Uyen Dinh Nguyen

St. Jose Thi Dang Le (1825–1860) was a captain in the army of the Vietnamese emperor, Tu Duc. Because he was Catholic and knew he was in a dangerous situation, he resigned his post, but he was arrested soon after. He encouraged other Catholics who were imprisoned and was able to receive the last sacraments before his execution. He was strangled to death. He was one of the Martyrs of Vietnam canonized by Pope John Paul II in 1988.

Josean *see Jose*

Josecito *see Jose*

Josee *see Jose*

Josef Saint; form of Joseph; German, Portuguese, Czech, Scandinavian; God will add

Joosef, Josif, Jossif, Juzef, Juzuf

St. Josef Bilczewski (1860–1923) was born into a peasant family in Austria. He entered the seminary in Krakow, Poland, and was ordained in 1884. Two years later he obtained a doctorate degree in theology from the University of Vienna. He became a theology professor at the University of Lviv. He was named archbishop of Leopoli in 1900 and cared for his flock during several wars, including World War I and the start of communist oppression. He was canonized in 2005 by Pope Benedict XVI.

Joseito *see Jose*

Joselito *see Jose*

Josemaria Saint; Hebrew; combination of Joseph and Maria

St. Josemaria Escriva (1902–1975) was born in Barbastro, Spain. His father died while he was in the seminary, and he had to support his family while continuing his studies. He was ordained in 1925. In 1927, he moved to Madrid to study law. In 1928, he started Opus Dei, designed to help the faithful on their path to holiness. During the Spanish Civil War, he went into hiding and ministered in secret. After the war, he was able to return to public study and ministry. In 1943, he founded the Priestly Society of the Holy Cross. He was canonized by Pope John Paul II in 2002.

Josep *see Joseph*

Joseph Saint, New Testament; Top 100 Name; Hebrew; God will add

Jazeps, Jooseppi, Josep, Josephe, Josephie, Josephus, Josheph, Josip, Jóska, Joza, Joze, Jozeph, Jozhe, Jozio, Jozka, Jozsi, Jozzepi, Jupp, Jusepe, Juziu, Yosef, Zef

St. Joseph, St. Joseph Abibos, St. Joseph Cafasso, St. Joseph Calasanctius, St. Joseph Canh, St. Joseph Chang Song-jib, St. Joseph Cottolengo, St. Joseph Hien, St. Joseph Khang, St. Joseph Luu, St. Joseph Marchand, St. Joseph Mary Tommasi, St. Joseph Mosc

St. Joseph (first century) was the husband of Mary and the foster father of Jesus. He was a carpenter descended from the line of King David. When he found out that Mary, his betrothed, was pregnant, he planned to divorce her quietly, but he received a visit from an angel telling him to take her as his wife. A second angel would later tell him to leave Bethlehem and take his family to Egypt. Both times he obeyed without question. His last appearance in scripture is when he and Mary searched for Jesus when he was lost in the Temple. Most believe he died prior to Jesus' public ministry. He is patron of the Universal Church, fathers, workers, and a happy death.

Josephe *see Joseph*

Josephie *see Joseph*

Josephus *see Joseph*

Joses *see Jose*

Josh *see Joshua*

Joshau *see Joshua*

Joshaua *see Joshua*

Joshauh *see Joshua*

Joshawah *see Joshua*

Josheph *see Joseph*

Joshia *see Joshua*

Joshiah *see Josiah*

Joshu *see Joshua*

Joshua Old Testament; Top 100 Name; Hebrew; God is my salvation

Joaquim, Johsua, Johusa, Josh, Joshau, Joshaua, Joshauh, Joshawah, Joshia, Joshu, Joshuaa, Joshuea, Joshuia, Joshula, Joshus, Joshusa, Joshuwa, Joshwa, Jousha, Jozshua, Jozsua, Jozua, Jushua

Joshua (in the Bible) was the successor of Moses as leader of the Israelites. He led them into Canaan.

Joshuaa *see Joshua*

Joshuea *see Joshua*

Joshuia *see Joshua*

Joshula *see Joshua*

Joshus *see Joshua*

Joshusa *see Joshua*

Joshuwa *see Joshua*

Joshwa *see Joshua*

Josia *see Josiah*

Josiah Old Testament; Top 100 Name; Hebrew; the Lord burns, the fire of the Lord

Joshiah, Josia, Josiahs, Josian, Josias, Josie, Josya, Josyah

Josiah was a king of Judah. He became king at the age of eight after his father, King Amom, was assassinated. He served for thirty-one years and was responsible for much reform. He is mentioned in the geneaology of Jesus in the Gospel of Matthew.

Josiahs *see Josiah*

Josian *see Josiah*

Josias *see Josiah*

Josie *see Josiah*

Josif *see Josef*

Josip *see Joseph*

Josito *see Jose*

Jóska *see Joseph*

Jossif *see Josef*

Jost *see Justin*

Josu *see Jesus*

Josya *see Josiah*

Josyah *see Josiah*

Jousha *see Joshua*

Jovinian Saint; Latin; relating to Jove (a Roman god)

St. Jovinian (d. 300) was a bishop who was a missionary companion of St. Peregrinus of Auxerre. He was martyred.

Jovinus Saint; Latin; jovial

St. Jovinus (d. 258) was martyred in Rome with St. Basileus.

Joza *see Joseph*

Joze *see Joseph*

Jozef Saint; form of Joseph; German, Portuguese, Czech, Scandinavian; God will add

Jozeff, József

St. Jozef Sebastian Pelczar (1842–1924) was born in Korczyna in southeastern Poland. He was ordained a priest in 1864. Soon after, he was sent to Rome to earn doctoral degrees in theology and canon law. He wrote "On the Spiritual Life," which was widely read. He served as a seminary professor and as dean of the theology department and rector at Jagiellonian University in Krakow. He founded the Congregation of the Handmaids of the Sacred Heart of Jesus in Krakow in 1894. He was named bishop of Przemysl in 1899. He was canonized by Pope John Paul II in 2003.

Jozeff *see Jozef*

Jozeph *see Joseph*

Jozhe *see Joseph*

Jozio *see Joseph*

Jozka *see Joseph*

József *see Jozef*

Jozshua *see Joshua*

Jozsi *see Joseph*

Jozsua *see Joshua*

Jozua *see Joshua*

Jozzepi *see Joseph*

Juan Saint; Top 100 Name; Spanish; God is gracious

Juanch, Juanchito, Juane, Juann, Juaun, Juwan

St. Juan Capistrano, St. Juan Diego Cuauhtlatoatzin, St. Juan Grande Roman, O.H.

St. Juan Diego (1474–1548) was born in Cuauhtitian in Mexico.

He was a farm worker, field laborer, and mat maker. Married with no children, he converted to the Catholic faith when he was fifty years old. He was widowed in 1529. On his way to daily Mass in 1531, he saw a beautiful vision of a young woman dressed as an Aztec princess. She said she was the Virgin Mary and asked Juan Diego to ask the bishop to build a church at that site. The bishop asked him to bring proof of the woman's identity. Mary told him to gather flowers in his cloak. When he returned to the bishop and gave him the flowers, the inside of his cloak featured a glowing image of Mary—now known as Our Lady of Guadalupe. Juan Diego was canonized in 2002 by Pope John Paul II.

Juanch *see Juan*

Juanchito *see Juan*

Juane *see Juan*

Juann *see Juan*

Juaquyn *see Joachim*

Juaun *see Juan*

Jucundus Saint; Latin; pleasant

St. Jucundus, St. Jucundus of Bologna

St. Jucundus (d. 250) was martyred in the persecutions of Decius with several other companions.

Judah Old Testament; Hebrew; praised

Judah in the Bible was the fourth son of Jacob and Leah

and the founder of the tribe of Judah.

Judas Saint, New Testament; form of Judah; Hebrew; praised

St. Judas Cyriacus (d. 133) was a bishop of Ancona, Italy, who was martyred while on a pilgrimage to Jerusalem.

Jude Saint; short form of Judah, Judas; Hebrew; praised

St. Jude Thaddaeus (first century) was one of the twelve apostles and the brother of St. James the Lesser. He preached in Judea, Samaria, Idumaea, Syria, Mesopotamia, and Lybia, returning to Jerusalem in 62. He is an author of a letter to the churches of the East. He was martyred in Armenia. He is invoked in desperate situations.

Julean *see Julian*

Juleo *see Julio*

Juliaan *see Julian*

Julian Saint; Top 100 Name; form of Julius; Latin; youthful

Guiliano, Jolyon, Julean, Juliaan, Julianne, Julianne, Julion, Julyan, Julyin, Julyon

St. Julian, St. Julian of Anazarbus, St. Julian of Apamea, St. Julian of Auvergne, St. Julian of Bolgna, St. Julian of Caesarea, St. Julian of Cagliari, St. Julian of Cuenca, St. Julian of Egypt, St. Julian of Le Mans, St. Julian of Lyons, St. Julian of Sora, St. Julian of Toledo, St. Julian Sabas the Elder, St. Julian the Hospitaler, St. Julian Alfredo (Vilfridio Fernandez) Zapico (Spain)

St. Julian of Le Mans (third century) was the first bishop of Le Mans, France. He was known as a miracle worker. He cared deeply for the poor, the infirm, and orphans.

Julias *see Julius*

Julio Saint; form of Julius; Spanish; youthful

Juleo, Juliyo, Julyo

St. Julio Alvarez Mendoza (1866–1927) was born in Guadalajara, Jalisco, Mexico. He was ordained in 1894 and ministered to the people of Mechoacanejo, Jalisco, Mexico. During the Catholic persecution in Mexico, he conducted Mass on farms and baptized in mountain streams. He was arrested for being a priest and was martyred. He was canonized by Pope John Paul II in 2000.

Julion *see Julian*

Julious *see Julius*

Julius Saint; Greek, Latin; youthful

Julias, Julious, Juliusz, Jullius, Juluis

Pope St. Julius, St. Julius of Novara

Pope St. Julius (d. 352) was a native Roman. He was elected pope in 337. He became embroiled in the Arian controversy when Eusebius of Nicomedia opposed having Athanasius as bishop of Alexandria. Eusebius elected George, and the Arians elected Pistus. Julius declared that Athanasius was the rightful bishop and reinstated him. Julius also built several basilicas and churches in Rome.

Juliusz *see Julius*

Juliyo *see Julio*

Jullius *see Julius*

Juluis *see Julius*

Julyan *see Julian*

Julyin *see Julian*

Julyo *see Julio*

Julyon *see Julian*

Junian Saint; Latin; young

St. Junian (d. 587) was the founder of Mariacum Abbey in Poitou, where he served as abbot. He later became a hermit at Chaulnay.

Junipero Saint; Spanish; juniper tree

Bl. Junipero Serra (1713–1784) was born in Petra, Spanish Majorca. He joined the Franciscan order, was ordained a priest, and taught philosophy and theology at the Lullian University. In 1749, he traveled to the New World as a missionary. He served on the west coast, founding twenty-one missions and converting many Native Americans. He was beatified by Pope John Paul II in 1988.

Jupp *see Joseph*

Jurek *see Jerzy*

Jurmin Saint; English

St. Jurmin (seventh century) was an East Anglian prince in England. He is remembered as a confessor.

Jusa *see Justin*

Jusepe *see Joseph*

Jushua *see Joshua*

Just Saint; Latin; just

St. Just (d. 303) was from Trieste, Italy. He was known for his penance and charity. During the persecutions of Emperor Diocletian, he was weighed down and thrown into the sea.

Justain *see Justin*

Justan *see Justin*

Justek *see Justin*

Justen *see Justin*

Justian *see Justin*

Justice Virtue; form of Justin; just, righteous

Justin Saint; Latin; just, righteous

Jastin, Jobst, Jost, Jusa, Justain, Justan, Justek, Justen, Justian, Justinas, Justinian, Justinius, Justinn, Justins, Justinus, Justo, Juston, Justton, Justukas, Justun, Justyn, Iustin, Ustin

St. Justin, St. Justin de Jacobis, St. Justin Martyr, St. Justin of Chieti

St. Justin Martyr (100–165) was born in Nabius, Palestine. He was a pagan philosopher who converted to the faith after witnessing the example of martyrs and studying the scriptures. He then used what he had learned to argue with pagans. He was one of the first Christian apologists, and he opened a school of debate in Rome, Italy. He was arrested and beheaded. He is a patron saint of apologists, lecturers, orators, and philosophers.

Justinas *see Justin*

Justinian *see Justin*

Justiniano Saint; form of Justin; Spanish; just, righteous

Bl. Justiniano Cuesta Redonda (1910–1936) was a Passionist priest in Spain. He was one of the Martyrs of Daimiel who died in the Spanish Civil War. He was beatified by Pope John Paul II in 1989.

Justinius *see Justin*

Justinn *see Justin*

Justino Saint; form of Justin; Spanish; just, righteous

St. Justino Orona Madrigal (1877–1928) was born to a poor family in Atoyac, Mexico. He was ordained a priest at the age of twenty-seven and started the Claretian Brothers of the Sacred Heart. During the Catholic persecution, he went into hiding at a local ranch, along with Fr. Atilano Cruz Alvarado. On July 1, 1928, forty government troops stormed the house. Fr. Justino was gunned down. He was canonized by Pope John Paul II in 2000.

Justins *see Justin*

Justinus *see Justin*

Justo *see Justin*

Juston *see Justin*

Justton *see Justin*

Justukas *see Justin*

Justun *see Justin*

Justus Saint; form of Justin; French; just, righteous

St. Justus, St. Justus of Beauvais, St. Justus of Cantebury, St. Justus of Lyons, St. Justus of Poland, St. Justus of Trieste, St. Justus of Urgel

St. Justus of Beauvais (278–287) lived in Auxerre, France, with his father. The two traveled to Amiens to ransom a relative. While there, they were reported as Christians. Justus, only nine years old, defended his faith and was beheaded.

Justyn *see Justin*

Juvenal Saint; Latin; young

Juventin, Juventino, Juventyn, Juvon, Juvone

St. Juvenal (d. 369) was a physician who became the first bishop of Narni, Italy.

Juventin *see Juvenal*

Juventino *see Juvenal*

Juventius Saint; Latin; one that represents youth

St. Juventius (first century) was bishop of Pavia, Italy. He and St. Syrus evangelized that region.

Juventyn *see Juvenal*

Juvon *see Juvenal*

Juvone *see Juvenal*

Juwan *see Juan*

Juzef *see Josef*

Juziu *see Joseph*

Juzuf *see Josef*

K

Kaarle *see Karl*

Kaarlo *see Karl*

Kabius *see Cybi*

Kadroe *see Cadroe*

Kaiven *see Kevin*

Kale *see Karl*

Kamen Saint; Slavic, German, Jewish; stone, rock

Bl. Kamen Vitchev (1893–1952) was born in the Burgas region of Bulvaria to a pious, orthodox Eastern Rite family. He was educated in Austria and Turkey and then joined the Congregation of the Assumption. He was ordained and then received a doctorate in theology. He taught and served as dean of studies at the College of St. Augustine in Plovidiv. He was also a prolific writer. He was arrested and killed by the communists for being a priest. He was beatified by Pope John Paul II in 2002.

Kanten Saint

Cannen

St. Kanten (eighth century), also known as Cannen, founded Llangeanten Abbey in Powya, Wales.

Karal *see Karol*

Karalos *see Karol*

Karanteg *see Carantac*

Karcsi *see Karl*

Karl Saint; form of Charles; German; farmer

Carl, Kaarle, Kaarlo, Kale, Karcsi, Karlitis, Karlo, Karlton, Kjell

Bl. Karl (Carl) Leisner, Bl. Karl of Austria

Bl. Karl Leisner (1915–1945) was born in Germany. He tried to organize Catholic youth groups in Germany, but the Nazis would not allow it, so he would take the youth to Belgium and the Netherlands. He was ordained a deacon in 1939 and was arrested for criticizing Hitler. He was sent to Dachau, where he was secretly ordained a priest. He was still alive when the camp was liberated, but he was suffering from tuberculosis and died a few months later. He was beatified in 1996 by Pope John Paul II.

Karlitis *see Karl*

Karlo *see Karl*

Karlos *see Carlos*

Karlton *see Karl*

Karol Saint; form of Charles; Czech, Polish; farmer

Karal, Karalos, Karolek, Karolis, Károly, Karrel, Karrol, Karroll

Bl. Karol Herman Stepien (1910–1943) was a priest who was one of the 108 Polish Martyrs of World War II. He was beatified in 1999 by Pope John Paul II.

Karolek *see Karol*

Karolis *see Karol*

Károly *see Karol*

Karrel *see Karol*

Karrol *see Karol*

Kasimir *see Casimir*

Kasius *see Cassius*

Kaspar *see Caspar*

Kassio *see Cassius*

Kassius *see Cassius*

Kastar *see Castor*

Kaster *see Castor*

Kastor *see Castor*

Kastyr *see Castor*

Kazimierz Saint; Slavic; keeping the peace

Bl. Kazimierz Gostynski, Bl. Kazimierz Grelewski, Bl. Kazimierz Sykulski

Bl. Kazimierz Gostynski (1884–1942) was a priest who died in the Dachau concentration camp. He is one of the 108 Polish Martyrs of World War II. He was beatified in 1999 by Pope John Paul II.

Kazio *see Casimir*

Kazmer *see Casimir*

Kazzius *see Cassius*

Kea Saint; Greek, English; male, manly, brave

St. Kea (sixth century) was the son of King Lleuddun Luyddog of Lothian. He became bishop of North Britain before becoming a hermit. He went to Wales and then traveled south, founding churches as he went. He died in Brittany.

Keane *see Keyne (girl's name)*

Keaven *see Kevin*

Keene *see Keyne (girl's name)*

Keeran *see Kieran*

Keeren *see Kieran*

Keerin *see Kieran*

Keeron *see Kieran*

Keiron *see Kieran*

Keivan *see Kevin*

Kellach *see Ceallach*

Ken *see Kenneth*

Kenan Saint; Hebrew, Irish; to acquire

St. Kenan (d. 500) was an Irish bishop who built the first stone cathedral at Danberg, in Meath, Ireland.

Kenelm Saint; English; brave helmet

St. Kenelm (d. 821) was the son of King Kenulf of Mercia. He was murdered by henchmen working for one of his sisters.

Keneth *see Kenneth*

Kenneith *see Kenneth*

Kennet *see Kenneth*

Kenneth Saint; Gaelic, English; handsome, royal oath

Ken, Keneth, Kenneith, Kennet, Kennethen, Kennett, Kennieth, Kennith, Kennyth, Kenyth

St. Kenneth (sixth century) was the son of a chieftain. He became a hermit on the peninsula of Gower, Wales, which was later named Llangenydd in his honor.

Kennethen *see Kenneth*

Kennett *see Kenneth*

Kennieth *see Kenneth*

Kennith *see Kenneth*

Kennyth *see Kenneth*

Kentigern Saint; Gaelic; kind ruler
St. Kentigern Mungo (d. 603) was the son of a British princess and was raised by St. Serf. He became a hermit near Glasgow, Scotland, and was later named the first bishop of the Strath-cylde Britons. He was driven into exile in Wales, where he founded St. Asaph Monastery at Llanelwy. He later returned to Scotland to continue his work there. He is a patron saint of Glascow and against bullies.

Kenyth *see Kenneth*

Kernan *see Kieran*

Kessag Saint; Gaelic
St. Kessag (460–520) was a prince of Cashel, Ireland, who traveled to Scotland as a missionary bishop. He was known as a miracle worker and was martyred.

Kev *see Kevin*

Kevan *see Kevin*

Kevern *see Keverne*

Keverne Saint; Gaelic; handsome, gentle
Kevern, Kevirn
St. Keverne (sixth century) was from Cornwall, England, and was a friend of St. Kieran.

Keverne *see Kevin*

Kevian *see Kevin*

Kevien *see Kevin*

Kevin Saint; Top 100 Name; Gaelic; handsome
Kaiven, Keaven, Keivan, Kev, Kevan, Keverne, Kevian, Kevien,
Kevinn, Kevins, Kevis, Kevun, Kevvy, Keyvin
St. Kevin (498–618) was the son of Leinster nobility. He lived with monks from the age of twelve and studied for the priesthood at Cell na Manach. After being ordained, he lived as a hermit for seven years. He attracted many followers and founded a monastery at Glendalough, where he served as abbot. In time, it became a town and then a see, now part of the archdiocese of Dublin.

Kevinn *see Kevin*

Kevins *see Kevin*

Kevirn *see Keverne*

Kevis *see Kevin*

Kevun *see Kevin*

Kevvy *see Kevin*

Keyne *see Keyne (girl's name)*

Keyvin *see Kevin*

Kian *see Cian*

Kiaron *see Kieran*

Kiarron *see Kieran*

Kieran Saint; Gaelic; little and dark
Keeran, Keeren, Keerin, Keeron, Keiron, Kernan, Kiaron, Kiarron, Kierien, Kierin, Kiernan, Kierrian
St. Kieran, St. Kieran of Saighir
St. Kieran (516–546) was born in Connacht, Ireland. He became a monk at Clonnard, where he was well-known for his scholarly abilities. He then spent seven years at Inishmore with St. Enda. Spending some time at Isel monastery, he was asked to leave because of his "excessive

charity." He eventually established the famous Clonmacnois Abbey, where he served as abbot. He was known as a miracle worker.

Kierien *see Kieran*

Kierin *see Kieran*

Kiernan *see Kieran*

Kierrian *see Kieran*

Kilean *see Kilian*

Kilian Saint; Gaelic; little warrior
Cillian, Kilean, Kiliane, Kilien, Killian, Killie, Killiean, Killien, Killienn, Killion, Killy, Kylien, Kyllian, Kyllien
St. Kilian (640–689) was an Irish monk who was named bishop. Pope Conon gave him permission to evangelize Franconia. He was beheaded for objecting to the duke of Wurzburg's forbidden marriage.

Kiliane *see Kilian*

Kilien *see Kilian*

Killian *see Kilian*

Killie *see Kilian*

Killiean *see Kilian*

Killien *see Kilian*

Killienn *see Kilian*

Killion *see Kilian*

Killy *see Kilian*

Kingsmark Saint; English; mark of the king
St. Kingsmark (fifth century) was a Scottish chieftain who lived in Wales.

Kirdjun *see Abakerazum*

Kiril *see Cirilo*

Kirill *see Cyril*

Kiryl *see Cirilo*

Kjell *see Karl*

Klaas *see Nicholas*

Klas *see Nicholas*

Klemens *see Clemente*

Kletos *see Cletus*

Kogantianus Saint
St. Kogantianus (d. 303) was martyred during Emperor Diocletian's persecutions.

Koleman *see Colman*

Konan *see Conan*

Konner *see Conor*

Konrad *see Conrad*

Konstanty Saint; form of Constantine; Greek; firm, constant
Bl. Konstanty Bojko (1825–1874) and Bl. Konstanty Lukaszuk (1829–1874) were both married men who were shot by Russian soldiers in Podlasie, Poland. They are Martyrs of Podlasie and were beatified by Pope John Paul II in 1996.

Kornell *see Cornelius*

Kosmas *see Cosmas*

Kosmo *see Cosmas*

Krispin *see Crispin*

Kristopher *see Christopher*

Krys *see Krystyn*

Krystein *see Krystyn*

Krystek *see Krystyn*

Krystin *see Krystyn*

Krystyn Saint; form of Christian; Polish; Christian
Kristin, Krys, Krystein, Krystek, Krystin

Bl. Krystyn Gondek (1909–1942) was a Franciscan priest who died at the Dachau concentration camp. He is one of the 108 Polish Martyrs of World War II and was beatified by Pope John Paul II in 1999.

Kyle *see Kennocha (girl's name)*

Kylien *see Kilian*

Kyllian *see Kilian*

Kyllien *see Kilian*

Kyrill *see Cyril*

Kyrillos *see Cirilo*

L

Laci *see Laszlo*

Lacko *see Laszlo*

Lactali Saint

St. Lactali (d. 672) was from County Cork, Ireland. He studied in Bangor under Sts. Comgall and Molus. He founded Achadh-Ur Abbey at Freshford, Kilkenny.

Ladislas *see Laszlo*

Laetantius Saint; Latin; joyful

St. Laetantius (d. 180) was martyred in Carthage during the persecutions of Vigellius.

Laetus Saint; Latin; joyful

St. Laetus (d. 553) was a priest in Orleans, France.

Lamalisse Saint

St. Lamalisse (seventh century) was a Scottish hermit.

Lambert Saint; German; bright land

Bert, Lamberto, Lamberts, Lambirt, Lambirto, Lambrett, Lamburt,
Lamburto, Lambyrt, Lambyrto, Lampard, Landbert, Landberto, Landbirt, Landbirto, Landburt, Landburto, Landbyrt, Landbyrto, Landebirt, Landeburt, Landebyrt, Lombard

St. Lambert, St. Lambert of Lyon, St. Lambert of Maastricht, St. Lambert of Sargossa

St. Lambert (d. 688) was raised in the court of King Clotaire III. He became a monk at Fontenelles, France, where he later served as abbot. He also founded Donzere Abbey. He was later named archbishop of Lyons.

Lamberto *see Lambert*

Lamberts *see Lambert*

Lambirt *see Lambert*

Lambirto *see Lambert*

Lambrett *see Lambert*

Lamburt *see Lambert*

Lamburto *see Lambert*

Lambyrt *see Lambert*

Lambyrto *see Lambert*

Lampard *see Lambert*

Lancelot *see Laszlo*

Landbert *see Lambert*

Landberto *see Lambert*

Landbirt *see Lambert*

Landbirto *see Lambert*

Landburt *see Lambert*

Landburto *see Lambert*

Landbyrt *see Lambert*

Landbyrto *see Lambert*

Landebirt *see Lambert*

Landeburt *see Lambert*

Landebyrt *see Lambert*

Landeilnus Saint; Teutonic; he who is a friend of the earth

St. Landeilnus (d. 686) was raised by St. Autbert of Cambrai, France. He led a life of crime for a time, but repented, was ordained, and founded four abbeys including Lobbes Abbey and Crespin Abbey.

Landericus Saint; Teutonic; powerful in the region

St. Landericus (seventh century) was the son of Sts. Vincent Madlegarus and Waldetrudis. He became bishop of Meaux, in France. After resigning his see, he became abbot of Soignies, Belgium.

Landoald Saint; German, French; one who brings victory

St. Landoald (d. 668) was a Lombard who was ordained a priest in Rome. Pope St. Martin I sent him as a missionary to Belgium and northeastern France. He served with St. Amand.

Landray see Landry

Landre see Landry

Landri see Landry

Landrie see Landry

Landrue see Landry

Landry Saint; French, English; ruler

Landericus, Landray, Landre, Landri, Landrie, Landrue

St. Landry (eleventh century), also known as Landericus, was a monk at the Benedictine Monastery of Novalese, Italy.

He was a priest who cared for the people in the villages of Lanslevillard and Bonneval. A group of sinners who refused to repent grew so angry at Landry's efforts to convert them that they drowned him in the Arc River.

Landulf Saint; German; land, territory, wolf

St. Landulf (d. 1134) was a monk at San Michele, in Ciel d'Oro, Pavia. He later became bishop of Asti, Italy.

Lanny see Laurence

Lantfrid Saint; German

St. Lantfrid (d. 770) was a Benedictine abbot of Beneddiktbeuren in Bavaria, Germany. He was a brother of Sts. Elilantus and Waltram.

Lanty See Lawrence

Larance see Laurence

Laranz see Laurence

Laren see Lawrence

Larenzo see Lorenzo

Larian see Lawrence

Larien see Lawrence

Larka see Lawrence

Larrance See Laurence, Lawrence

Larrence see Lawrence

Larya see Lawrence

Laserian Saint; Gaelic; flame

St. Laserian (d. 639) was born in Ireland and was a brother of St. Goban. He became a monk in Iona, Scotland. He traveled to Rome, where he was ordained by Pope St. Gregory the Great. He was later made a bishop and papal legate to Ireland. He also served as abbot of Leighlin.

Lashi *see Louis*

Lasho *see Louis*

Laslo *see Laszlo*

Laszlo Saint; Hungarian; famous ruler

Laci, Lacko, Ladislas, Lancelot, Laslo, Lazlo

St. Laszlo (1040–1095), also known as Ladislas and Lancelot, was the son of King Bela I of Hungary. He took over the throne in 1077. During his reign, he annexed Dalmatia and Croatia and expelled the Huns, Poles, Tatars, and Russians from his territories. He also made Christianity the national religion. He was to serve in the First Crusade, but he died before it began.

Latinus Saint; Latin; the Latin man, Roman

St. Latinus (d. 115) was the third bishop of Brescia, Italy. He was imprisoned and tortured for the faith.

Laurance *see Laurence*

Laurans *see Laurence*

Laureano *see Laurence*

Laurence Saint; form of Lawrence; Latin; crowned with laurel

Lanny, Larance, Laranz, Larrance, Laurance, Laurans, Laureano, Laurencho, Laurentij, Laurentios, Laurentiu, Laurentius, Laurentz, Laurentzi, Laurenz, Laurie, Laurin, Laurits, Lauritz, Laurnet, Lurance

St. Laurence (d. 258) was an archdeacon of Rome and "keeper of the treasures of the Church." On August 6, 258, Pope St. Sixtus II and six deacons were beheaded. The pope had told Laurence that he would join them in four days, so he took advantage of that time to disperse the money the Church had at its disposal so that the Roman authorities would not get it. On August 10, he was summoned to appear for his execution and to bring the treasure the pope had trusted him with. He arrived surrounded by the poor and sick, because they were the true treasures of the Church. He was martyred by being cooked to death on a gridiron. He is a patron of the poor, ill, librarians, and cooks.

Laurencho *see Laurence*

Laurentij *see Laurence*

Laurentinus Saint; Latin; crowned with laurel

St. Laurentinus (d. 258) was put to death along with his brother and sister. They were martyred in Carthage during the reign of Decius.

Laurentios *see Laurence*

Laurentiu *see Laurence*

Laurentius *see Laurence*

Laurentz *see Laurence*

Laurentzi *see Laurence*

Laurenz *see Laurence*

Laurenzo *see Lorenzo*

Laurianus Saint; form of Lawrence; Latin; crowned with laurel

St. Laurianus (d. 544) was from Hungary. He was ordained in Milan, Italy, and became archbishop of Seville, Spain. He was martyred in Bourges, France.

Laurie *see Laurence*

Laurin *see Laurence*

Laurino Saint; form of Lawrence; Latin; crowned with laurel

Bl. Laurino Proano Cuesta (1916–1936) was one of the Passionist Martyrs of Daimiel who were killed during the Spanish Civil War. He was beatified by Pope John Paul II in 1989.

Laurinzo *see Lorenzo*

Laurits *see Laurence*

Lauritz *see Laurence*

Laurnet *see Laurence*

Laurus Saint; form of Lawrence; Latin; crowned with laurel

Lery

St. Laurus (seventh century), also known as Lery, was from Wales. He traveled to Brittany, France, where he founded an abbey on the river Doneff that was later named for him.

Laurynzo *see Lorenzo*

Lauto Saint

St. Lauto (d. 568) was a bishop of Constance in Normandy, France, a position he held for forty years.

Lavi *see Leo*

Lavon *see Levan*

Law *see Lawrence*

Lawdog Saint; Welsh

St. Lawdog (sixth century) was associated with Wales, where four churches are named for him.

Lawren *see Lawrence*

Lawrence Saint; Latin; crowned with laurel

Lanty, Laren, Larian, Larien, Larka, Larrance, Larrence, Larya, Law, Lawren, Lawron, Lawry, Loreca, Lorenis, Lourenco, Lowrance, Lowrence

St. Lawrence, Martyr, St. Lawrence Giustiniani, St. Lawrence Huong, St. Lawrence Huong Van Nguyen, St. Lawrence Imbert, St. Lawrence of Brindisi, St. Lawrence of Canterbury, St. Lawrence of Novara, St. Lawrence of Siponto, St. Lawrence of Spoleto, St. Lawrence O'Toole, St. Lawrence Ruiz

St. Lawrence Guistiniani (1381–1456) was born into a noble Venetian family, the son of a pious mother. He joined the canons of St. George in Alga. He was ordained in 1406 and was made prior of the community. He later became bishop of Castello. That see was then joined with the patriarchate of Grado, and the seat was moved to Venice. Lawrence therefore became the first patriarch of Venice. He was also known as a mystic and writer.

Lawron *see Lawrence*

Lawry *see Lawrence*

Lazarius *see Lazarus*

Lazaros *see Lazarus*

Lazarus Saint, New Testament; Greek; God has helped

> *Lazarius, Lazaros, Lazorus*
>
> St. Lazarus, St. Lazarus Zographos, St. Lazarus of Dives
>
> St. Lazarus (first century) was the brother of Sts. Martha and Mary, who lived in Bethany. After he died, Jesus raised him from the dead (Jn 11–12). Nothing is mentioned in scripture about his life after being brought back from the dead, but various traditions have him becoming a bishop.

Lazlo *see Laszlo*

Lazorus *see Lazarus*

Leahon *see Leon*

Leanard *see Leonard*

Leanardas *see Leonard*

Leanardus *see Leonard*

Leander Saint; Greek; lion-man

> *Ander*
>
> St. Leander of Seville (534–600) was born at Cartegena, Spain, the brother of Sts. Isadore, Fulgentius, and Florentina. He became a monk and then bishop of Seville. Due to his conversion of two of King Leovigild's sons, he was exiled to Constantinople, where he became friends with the future Pope St. Gregory the Great. When he returned to Spain, he spoke out against Arianism. He also created a rule for nuns and was the first to introduce the Nicene Creed at Mass.

Leaon *see Leon*

Leavi *see Levi*

Lebuin Saint

> St. Lebuin (d. 773) was an English monk who worked with St. Boniface and St. Marchelm. He was a missionary among the Frisians and earned the respect of the Westphalian Saxons.

Leeo *see Leo*

Leevi *see Levi*

Leevie *see Levi*

Leger Saint; German; people of the spear

> *Leodegarius*
>
> St. Leger (615–679), also known as Leodegarius, grew up at the court of King Clotaire II. He was ordained and became abbot of Maxentius Abbey. He helped St. Bathilda govern when Clovis II died and was named bishop of Autun in 663. Because of his involvement in some political infighting and the fact that he spoke out against Childeric's marriage, he was exiled to Luxeuil. He returned to his see when Childeric was murdered. Later, he was falsely accused of that murder and was imprisoned, tortured, and ultimately put to death.

Leio *see Leo*

Lencho *see Lorenzo*

Lennart *see Leonard*

Leo Saint; Latin; lion

> *Lavi, Leeo, Leio, Léocadie, Leos, Leosoko, Lio, Liutas, Loesko*

St. Leo, St. Leo Karasuma, St. Leo Luke, St. Leo of Catania, St. Leo of Lucca, St. Leo of Melun, St. Leo of Nonantula, St. Leo of Rouen, St. Leo Satsuma, St. Leo of Sens, St. Leo Tanaka, St. Leo of Troyes, Pope St. Leo the Great, St. Leo II, III, IV, IX

Pope St. Leo the Great (d. 461) was born in Tuscany. He became pope in 440. During his pontificate, he convinced Emperor Valentinian to recognize the primacy of the bishop of Rome. He was also responsible for forming the doctrine of the Incarnation. He is also remembered for encountering Attila the Hun, meeting him at the gates of Rome and persuading him to turn back.

Leobald Saint; Latin; brave lion

St. Leobald (d. 650) was a Benedictine abbot of Fleury Abbey in France.

Leobard Saint; form of Leonard; Italian; brave as a lion

St. Leobard (d. 593) was a hermit who lived near Marmoutier, France.

Leobinus Saint; German, French; dear friend

St. Leobinus (d. 556) was a hermit priest and abbot. He later became bishop of Chartres, France. He lived in a monastery near Lyons, which was attacked by raiders. He was tortured and left to die.

Léocadie *see Leo*

Leodegarius *see Leger*

Leon Saint; form of Leonard, Napoleon; German; brave as a lion

Leahon, Leaon, Leonas, Léonce, Leoncio, Leondris, Leone, Leonek, Leonetti, Leoni, Leonirez, Leonizio, Leonon, Leons, Leontes, Leontios, Leontrae, Leyon, Lion, Lionni, Lyon

Bl. Leon Nowakowski, Bl. Leon Wetmanski

Bl. Leon Nowakowski (1913–1939) was a Polish diocesan priest who was shot in the town of Piotrków Kujawski as he defended the faith. He is one of the 108 Polish Martyrs of World War II and was beatified by Pope John Paul II in 1999.

Leonard Saint; German; brave as a lion

Leanard, Leanardas, Leanardus, Lennart, Leonardis, Leonardo, Leonart, Leonerd, Leonhard, Leonhardt, Leonidas, Leonnard, Leontes, Lernard, Lienard, Linek, Lionard, Lnard, Londard, Lonnard, Lonya, Lynnard, Lyonard

St. Leonard, St. Leonard Kimura, St. Leonard Muraildo, St. Leonard of Noblac, St. Leonard of Port Maurice, St. Leonard of Reresby, St. Leonard Vandoeuvre, St. Leonard Wegel

St. Leonard (d. 559) was a Frank courtier who converted and became a monk at Micy. He lived as a hermit at Limoges. The king asked him to pray for the queen who was having a difficult delivery. When she delivered successfully, the king offered him all the land he could ride around on a donkey for a day. On that land, he founded Noblac Monastery. He is invoked to help women in labor and for prisoners of war.

Leonardis *see Leonard*

Leonardo *see Leonard*

Leonart *see Leonard*

Leonas *see Leon*

Léonce *see Leon*

Leoncio *see Leon*

Leondris *see Leon*

Leone *see Leon*

Leonek *see Leon*

Leonerd *see Leonard*

Leonetti *see Leon*

Leonhard *see Leonard*

Leonhardt *see Leonard*

Leoni *see Leon*

Leonianus Saint; form of Leonard; Greek; brave as a lion

St. Leonianus (d. 570) was from Pannonia, where he was taken by raiders and brought to France. After he was freed, he became a hermit near Autun.

Leonid Saint; form of Leonard; Russian; brave as a lion

Bl. Leonid Feodorov (1879–1935) was born in St. Petersburg, Russia. He was raised Russian Orthodox but converted to Catholicism in his twenties. He earned a doctorate in philosophy and a degree in theology. He was ordained a Greek Catholic priest in 1911

and entered the Studite monastery in Bosnia. Over the course of his life, he was arrested and exiled several times. He is one of the Martyrs under Communism in Eastern Europe. He was beatified by Pope John Paul II in 2001.

Leonidas *see Leonard*

Leonides Saint; form of Leonard; Russian; brave as a lion

St. Leonides (d. 202) was the father of Origin. A scholar, he was imprisoned in Alexandria and was beheaded. He is a patron saint of large families.

Leonirez *see Leon*

Leonizio *see Leon*

Leonnard *see Leonard*

Leonon *see Leon*

Leons *see Leon*

Leontes *see Leon, Leonard*

Leontios *see Leon*

Leontius Saint; form of Leonard; Greek; brave as a lion

St. Leontius, St. Leontius of Cuesaren, St. Leontius the Elder, St. Leontius the Younger St. Leontius the Younger (d. 565) was a married soldier. When he was chosen by public acclaim to be bishop of Bordeaux, France, his wife entered a convent, and he accepted the office.

Leontrae *see Leon*

Leopardinus Saint; Latin; leopard

St. Leopardinus (seventh century) was abbot of St. Symphorian Monastery in Vivaris, France. He was martyred.

Leopardus Saint; Latin; leopard

St. Leopardus (d. 362) was a martyred slave or servant of Julian the Apostate. He was martyred in Rome.

Leopold Saint; German; brave people

Leopoldo, Leorad, Lipót, Luepold, Luitpold, Poldi

St. Leopold, St. Leopold Mandic

St. Leopold (1050–1136) was born at Melk, Austria. At age twenty-three, he became military governor of Austria. He was married to the daughter of Emperor Henry IV. Together, they had eighteen children (eleven of whom lived to adulthood). He was known for his piety and charity. He also established three monasteries.

Leopoldo *see Leopold*

Leorad *see Leopold*

Leos *see Leo*

Leosoko *see Leo*

Leothade Saint

St. Leothade (d. 718) was a Frankish noble who served as abbot of Moissac and later became bishop of Auch, France.

Leovigild Saint

St. Leovigild (d. 852) was a priest who was martyred in Córdoba, Spain, during the persecution of Abd al-Rahman II.

Lernard *see Leonard*

Lery *see Laurus*

Letard *see Liudhard*

Leucius Saint; Latin; light

St. Leucius of Brindisi (d. 180) was a missionary from Alexandria, Egypt, who served as bishop of Brindisis, Italy.

Leudomer Saint; German, French

St. Leudomer (d. 585) was a bishop of Chartres, France.

Leufroy *see Leutfridus*

Leutfridus Saint

Leufroy

St. Leutfridus (d. 738), also known as Leufroy, was born near Evreux, France. He was a teacher of young boys at Evreux before becoming a hermit. Later in life, he founded La Croix-Saint-Qu'en Abbey.

Lev *see Levi*

Levan Saint; French; quick on one's feet

Lavon, Levin

St. Levan (sixth century), also known as Levin, was Irish. He traveled to Cornwall, England, as a missionary.

Levey *see Levi*

Levi Old Testament; Top 100 Name; Hebrew; joined in harmony

Leavi, Leevi, Leevie, Lev, Levey, Levie, Levitis, Levy, Lewi, Leyvi

Levi in the Bible was the third son of Jacob and Leah and the founder of the Israelite tribe of Levi (the Levites), which became the priestly caste.

Levie *see Levi*

Levin *see Levan*

Levitis *see Levi*

Levy *see Levi*

Lewi *see Levi*

Lewrenzo *see Lorenzo*

Leyon *see Leon*

Leyvi *see Levi*

Lezin Saint

St. Lezin (540–609) was born into the Frankish aristocracy, but he gave it up to enter the service of the Church. He was later named bishop of Angers.

Liafdag Saint

St. Liafdag (d. 980) was a bishop of Jutland, Denmark, where he was martyred by pagans.

Libentius Saint

St. Libentius (d. 1013) was born in Swabia, Germany. He became bishop of Hamburg.

Liberalis Saint; Latin; lover of liberty

St. Liberalis (d. 940) was born in Brive, France. He became a hermit in the Alps near Embrun. He was chosen by the people there to become their bishop. He was known for his great humility.

Liberatus Saint; Latin; the liberated one

St. Liberatus (d. 483) was abbot of an African monastery. He was martyred in Carthage by the Arian ruler of the Vandals, Hunneric.

Liberius Saint; Latin; he who spreads abundance

Pope St. Liberius, St. Liberius of Ravenna

St. Liberius of Ravenna (d. 200) was bishop of Ravenna, Italy.

He is considered the founder of the see of Ravenna.

Libert Saint; Latin; he who spreads abundance

St. Libert (d. 783) was a Benedictine monk who was martyred at Saint-Trond Abbey in France.

Liborius Saint; Hebrew, Latin; inspired

St. Liborius (d. 390) was a bishop of Le Mans, France. He is a patron saint of Paderborn, Germany, and invoked against fever, colic, and gall stones.

Licerius Saint; Greek; pertaining to light

Lizier

St. Licerius (d. 548), also known as Lizier, was born in Spain but became bishop of Couserans, France.

Licinius Saint; Latin; has flowing hair

St. Licinius (d. 616) was the count of Anjou under the Merovingian King Chilperic. He gave up the title to become a monk. He was later chosen to be bishop of Angers and was ordained by St. Gregory of Tours.

Lidanus Saint

St. Lidanus (1026–1118) founded Sezze Abbey in the Papal States, where he served as abbot.

Lienard *see Leonard*

Liephard Saint

St. Liephard (d. 640) was an English bishop who

accompanied King Caedwalla on a pilgrimage to Rome. He was martyred near Cambrai, France.

Liewellyn Saint; Welsh; lionlike

Llewellyn

St. Liewellyn (sixth century) was a Welsh monk.

Lifard *see Liphardus*

Limuneus Saint

St. Limuneus (fifth century) was a hermit who lived in a cave near Cyrrhus. He was known as a healer who built two houses for the blind.

Linas *see Linus*

Linek *see Leonard*

Linis *see Linus*

Liniss *see Linus*

Linn *see Linus*

Lino *see Linus*

Linous *see Linus*

Linus Saint, New Testament; Greek; flaxen haired

Linas, Linis, Liniss, Linn, Lino, Linous, Linux, Lynis, Lyniss, Lynus

St. Linus (d. 76) was the second pope, succeeding St. Peter in that office. He is mentioned in 2 Timothy 4:21 and was consecrated bishop by St. Paul.

Linux *see Linus*

Lio *see Leo*

Lion *see Leon*

Lionard *see Leonard*

Lionni *see Leon*

Liphard *see Liudhard*

Liphardus Saint; German; holy, intelligent

Lifard

St. Liphardus (d. 550), also known as Lifard, was a judge in Orleans, France. He gave up that life to become a hermit when he was forty years old. He attracted so many followers, he founded the monastery of Meung-sur Loire, France, where he served as abbot.

Lipót *see Leopold*

Liudhard Saint; German; holy, intelligent

Letard, Liphard

St. Liudhard (d. 600), also known as Liphard and Letard, was a Frankish bishop who served as chaplain to Queen Bertha, daughter of King Charibert of Paris, France. He helped convert King Ethelbert.

Liutas *see Leo*

Liutwin Saint; German; friend of the people

St. Liutwin (660–722) was bishop of Trier, Germany, and founded Mettlach Abbey.

Liuz *see Lucian*

Livinus Saint; Latin, Celtic; belong to the family of Livia

St. Livinus (580–657) was the son of a Scottish noble and an Irish princess. He became a bishop and traveled to Flanders, Belgium, as a missionary. He was martyred near Clost, in Brabant.

Lizier *see Licerius*

Lleudadd Saint; Welsh; to praise

St. Lleudadd (sixth century) was the abbot of Bardsey in Gwynedd, Wales. He accompanied St. Cadfan to Brittany, France.

Llewellyn *see Llewellyn*

Lnard *see Leonard*

Loaran Saint; Celtic

St. Loaran (fifth century) was a disciple of St. Patrick. He may have been bishop of Downpatrick, Ireland.

Lodovico Saint; Italian, German; famous warrior

Bl. Lodovico Pavoni (1784–1849) was born in Brescia, Italy. He was ordained a priest and founded a school for poor boys in Brescia. He became rector of St. Barnabas Church and founded an orphanage and trade school. He also started the Publishing House of the Institute of Saint Barnabas (today known as Ancora). He also took in deaf and mute students. In 1825, he founded the Brothers of Mary Immaculate. He was beatified by Pope John Paul II in 2002.

Loesko *see Leo*

Loman Saint; Gaelic, Slavic; bare, sensitive

Lomen

St. Loman (d. 450) was the nephew of St. Patrick. He accompanied his saintly uncle to Ireland and served as bishop of Trim, in Meath, Ireland.

Lomar *see Lomer*

Lombard *see Lambert*

Lomen *see Loman*

Lomer Saint; French; son of Omer

Lomar

St. Lomer (d. 593) was a hermit who founded Corbion Monastery near Chartres, France.

Londard *see Leonard*

Longinus Saint, New Testament; Latin; long

St. Longinus (first century) was the centurion who pierced Jesus' side during the crucifixion. He exclaimed, "Indeed, this was the Son of God!" (Mk 15:39). He converted and became a monk in Cappadocia. He was arrested and beheaded for the faith.

Longis Saint; Latin; long

St. Longis (d. 653) was a founder of a monastery in Maine, France. He was wrongly accused of having an improper relationship with St. Agnofleda, a recluse in his care. Their innocence was miraculously proven.

Lonnard *see Leonard*

Lonya *see Leonard*

Lorantzo *see Lorenzo*

Loreca *see Lawrence*

Lorenc *see Lorenzo*

Lorence *see Lorenzo*

Lorenco *see Lorenzo*

Lorencz *see Lorenzo*

Lorenczo *see Lorenzo*

Lorenis *see Lawrence*

Lorens *see Lorenzo*

Lorenso *see Lorenzo*

Lorentz *see Lorenzo*

Lorentzo *see Lorenzo*

Lorenz *see Lorenzo*

Lorenzo Saint; form of Lawrence; Italian, Spanish; crowned with laurel

Chencho, Larenzo, Laurenzo, Laurinzo, Laurynzo, Lencho, Lewrenzo, Lorantzo, Lorenc, Lorence, Lorenco, Lorencz, Lorenczo, Lorens, Lorenso, Lorentz, Lorentzo, Lorenz, Loretto, Lorinc, Lorinzo, Loritz, Lorrenzo, Lorrynzo, Lorynzo, Lourenza, Lourenzo, Lowrenzo, Nenzo

St. Lorenzo Ruiz (1600–1637) was born in Binondo, Manila, and was educated by Dominicans. He was a member of the Confraternity of the Rosary, married with two sons and a daughter. He worked as a calligrapher. He left the Phillipines in 1636. When he arrived in Japan, he was arrested together with fifteen companions for being Christian. He was hung from a gallows by his feet and died after two days of agony. He and his companions were canonized by Pope John Paul II in 1987.

Loretto *see Lorenzo*

Lorinc *see Lorenzo*

Lorinzo *see Lorenzo*

Loritz *see Lorenzo*

Lorrenzo *see Lorenzo*

Lorrynzo *see Lorenzo*

Lorynzo *see Lorenzo*

Lot Old Testament; Hebrew; one who is veiled, hidden

The story of Lot, who flees God's destruction of Sodom and Gomorrah is told in Genesis 19.

Lotharius Saint; German; distinguished warrior

St. Lotharius (d. 756) was the founder of Saint-Loyer-des-Champs Monastery in Argentan, France. He served as bishop of Seez.

Lott *see Lot*

Loudovicus *see Louis*

Louies *see Louis*

Louis Saint; German; famous warrior

Lashi, Lasho, Loudovicus, Louies, Lucho, Lude, Ludek, Ludirk, Ludis, Ludko, Lughaidh, Lutek

St. Louis Bertrand, St. Louis de Montfort, St. Louis Ibachi, St. Louis IX, St. Louis King of France, St. Louis Mary Grignion, St. Louis of Omora, St. Louis of Toulouse, St. Louis von Bruck

St. Louis de Montfort (1673–1716) was born in Montfort, France. He was educated at Rennes and was ordained. He founded the Sisters of Divine Wisdom. Pope Clement XI appointed him as an apostolic missionary. He was deeply devoted to the Blessed Mother and the Rosary. In 1715, he founded the Missionaries of the Company of Mary. He is known for writing *True Devotion to the Blessed Virgin*.

Lourenco *see Lawrence*

Lourenza *see Lorenzo*

Lourenzo *see Lorenzo*

Louthiem Saint

St. Louthiem (sixth century) is an Irish saint who is a patron of St. Ludgran in Cornwall, England.

Lowrance *see Lawrence*

Lowrence *see Lawrence*

Lowrenzo *see Lorenzo*

Lua Saint; Latin; moon

Lugud

St. Lua (d. 609), also known as Lugud, was born in Limerick, Ireland. He helped St. Comgall and contributed to the founding of 120 monasteries.

Lucais *see Lucian*

Lucan *see Lucian*

Lucanus *see Lucian, Lucius*

Lucas *see Luke*

Luccheus *see Lucius*

Luce *see Lucius*

Lucerius Saint; Latin, Spanish; bringer of light

Lucero

St. Lucerius (d. 740) was from Provence, France, and was raised at Farfa Abbey, where he later served as abbot.

Lucero *see Lucerius*

Luchesio Saint; Italian

St. Luchesio (d. 1260) was married to Bl. Buona dei Segni but was indifferent to religion. He spent his time chasing wealth,

working as a grocer, a money changer, and a corn merchant. When his children all died in his thirties, he converted and dedicated his life to serving the poor and sick. He and his wife became Franciscan tertiaries. He is a patron of those who have had children die and of lost vocations.

Lucho *see Louis*

Luchok *see Luke*

Lucian Saint; form of Lucius; Latin; light, bringer of light

Liuz, Lucais, Lucan, Lucanus, Luciano, Lucianus, Lucias, Lucien, Lucio, Lucjan, Lucyan, Lukianos, Lukyan, Luzian

St. Lucian, St. Lucian of Antioch

St. Lucian of Antioch (240–312) was a scripture scholar from Samosata. He was ordained at Antioch as a presbyter. He was a prolific writer, and St. Jerome used his writings as sources for his own works. Lucian also established the theological school of Antioch. He was arrested in Nicomedia and was martyred for the faith.

Luciano *see Lucian*

Lucianus *see Lucian*

Lucias *see Lucian*

Lucidius Saint; Latin; bright, shining, clear

St. Lucidius (d. 938) was a Benedictine monk at St. Peter's Monastery in southern Italy and later lived as a hermit in Santa Maria del Piano.

Lucien *see Lucian*

Lucillian Saint; Latin; light, bringer of light

St. Lucillian (d. 273) was an old man when he converted, but he was arrested and martyred by crucifixion at Byzantium. His wife, St. Paula, was martyred on the same day.

Lucio *see Lucian*

Lucious *see Lucius*

Lucis *see Lucius*

Lucius Saint; Latin; light, bringer of light

Lucanus, Luccheus, Luce, Lucious, Lucis, Lucyas, Lusio, Luzius

Pope St. Lucius, St. Lucius of Cyrene

Pope St. Lucius I (d. 254) was elected pope in 253 and served in that capacity for eighteen months. He was exiled during to the persecutions of Emperor Gallus shortly after being consecrated, but he was allowed to return. He condemned the Novationists for their refusal to readmit Christians who had denied the faith under persecution.

Lucjan *see Lucian*

Luck *see Luke*

Lucyan *see Lucian*

Lucyas *see Lucius*

Ludain *see Ludan*

Ludan Saint; Gaelic; puddle, glen

Ludain, Luden

St. Ludan (d. 1202), also known as Ludain or Luden, was the son of a Scottish prince. Returning from a pilgrimage to Jerusalem, he stopped at Scherkirchen, France, where he died. When he died, the local church bells miraculously started to ring.

Lude *see Louis*

Ludek *see Louis*

Luden *see Ludan*

Ludger Saint; Netherlands; people's spear

St. Ludger (742–809) was born in Zullen, Holland. He studied under St. Gregory at Utrecht and then under Bl. Alcuin at York, England. He became a priest and served as a missionary. Charlemagne then made him the spiritual director of five provinces. He became the first bishop of Munster in 804.

Ludirk *see Louis*

Ludis *see Louis*

Ludko *see Louis*

Ludoiph Saint; German

St. Ludoiph (d. 983) was the abbot of New Corvey in Westphalia, Germany.

Ludolf *see Ludolph*

Ludolph Saint; German; people, wolf

Ludolf

St. Ludolph (d. 1250) was bishop of Ratzeburg, Schleswig-Holstein, Germany. He was exiled and imprisoned. He was given shelter by Duke John of Mecklenburg but died because of the suffering he had experienced in prison.

Ludovico Saint; form of Louis; German; famous warrior

Ludowic

Bl. Ludovico of Casoria Palmentieri (1814–1885) was born at Casoria, Italy. He became a Franciscan friar and taught philosophy and math to young members of the order. He opened several institutions to care for the poor and needy. He founded the Grey Friars of Charity and the Franciscan Sisters of St. Elizabeth. He was beatified in 1993 by Pope John Paul II.

Ludowic *see Ludovico*

Ludvig *see Ludwik*

Ludwig *see Ludwik*

Ludwik Saint; form of Louis; German; famous warrior

Ludvig, Ludwig, Lutz

Bl. Ludwik Gietyngier, Bl. Ludwik Mzyk, Bl. Ludwik Pius Bartosik

Bl. Ludwik Gietyngier (1904–1941) was a Polish diocesan priest who died in the Dachau concentration camp. He is one of the 108 Polish Martyrs of World War II who were beatified by Pope John Paul II in 1999.

Ludwin Saint; German, Polish; famous warrior

St. Ludwin (d. 713) was born in Austrasia. After his wife died, he founded the Abbey of Mettlach. He later served as bishop of Trier, Germany.

Luepold *see Leopold*

Lughaidh *see Louis*

Lugud *see Lua*

Lui *see Luigi*

Luiggi *see Luigi*

Luigi Saint; form of Louis; Italian; famous warrior

Lui, Luiggi, Luigino, Luigy

St. Luigi Orione, St. Luigi Scrosoppi

St. Luigi Orione (1872–1940) was born in Pantecurone, Italy. He joined the Franciscans but had to return to his family because of poor health. He studied under St. John Bosco and was miraculously cured of his illness while attending that saint's funeral. He then studied for the priesthood. He opened San Luigi House at San Bernardino, a home for the poor and homeless. He would later start the Hermits of Divine Providence as well as the Ladies of Divine Providence and the Little Missionaries of Charity. He was canonized in 2004 by Pope John Paul II.

Luigino *see Luigi*

Luigy *see Luigi*

Luis Saint; Top 100 Name; form of Louis; Spanish; famous warrior

St. Luis Batiz Sainz (1870–1926) was born in San Miguel del Mazquital, Mexico. He was ordained and served as a parish priest at Chalchihuites the rest of his life. He worked with Catholic Action and started schools for poor children. He was arrested and accused of plotting antigovernment uprisings. When he refused to recognize the legitimacy of Calle's antireligious government, he was shot by a firing squad. He is one of the Martyrs of the Cristero War. He was canonized by Pope John Paul II in 2000.

Luitpold *see Leopold*

Luk *see Luke*

Lukasz Saint; form of Lucius; Latin; light, bringer of light

Bl. Lukasz Bojko (d. 1874) was one of the Martyrs of Podlasie, shot by Russian soldiers. He was beatified by Pope John Paul II in 1996.

Luke Saint, New Testament; Top 100 Name; Latin; light, bringer of light

Lucas, Luchok, Luck, Luk, Luken, Lukes, Lukian, Lukyan, Lusio

St. Luke, St. Luke Banabakiutu, St. Luke Kiemon, St. Luke Kirby, St. Luke Loan, St. Luke the Younger

St. Luke (d. 74) was born to pagan Greek parents. He was a physician who studied in Antioch and Tarsus. According to legend, he was also an artist who may have painted portraits of Jesus and Mary. He met St. Paul at Troas and helped evangelize Greece and Rome. He wrote a gospel and the Acts of the Apostles. He is a patron of artists, bachelors, bookbinders, and doctors.

Luken *see Luke*

Lukes *see Luke*

Lukian *see Luke*

Lukianos *see Lucian*

Lukyan *see Lucian, Luke*

Lull Saint; Latin; to relax

St. Lull (710–787) was from England. A relative of St. Boniface, he joined that saint in Germany. After spending some time in Rome, he succeeded St. Boniface as bishop of Mainz, Germany.

Lupercus Saint; Latin; he who frightens off wolves

St. Lupercus (d. 300) was a martyred bishop.

Lupicinus Saint; Latin; wolf charmer

St. Lupicinus (d. 480) was a brother of St. Romanus of Condant. He founded abbeys in the Jura mountains and the Lauconne districts of France.

Lupus Saint; Latin; wolf

St. Lupus, St. Lupus of Bayeux, St. Lupus of Chalons, St. Lupus of Lyons, St. Lupus of Sens, St. Lupus of Soissons, St. Lupus of Verona

St. Lupus (383–478) was born at Toul, Gaul. He married, but after six years they parted in order to enter religious life. He became a monk at Lerins Abbey and was later named bishop of Troyes. He persuaded Attila the Hun to spare Troyes when he attacked Gaul, but he was taken as a hostage. Lupus was accused of helping the Huns escape and was forced to leave Troyes. He then lived as a hermit.

Lurance *see Laurence*

Lusio *see Lucius, Luke*

Lutek *see Louis*

Lutz *see Ludwik*

Luxorius Saint; Latin

St. Luxorius (d. 303) was a soldier who was martyred in Sardinia, Sicily, Italy.

Luzian *see Lucian*

Luzius *see Lucius*

Lynis *see Linus*

Lyniss *see Linus*

Lynnard *see Leonard*

Lynus *see Linus*

Lyon *see Leon*

Lyonard *see Leonard*

Lyutis Saint

St. Lyutis (d. 1038) was a monk at Monte Cassino before becoming a hermit at La Cava, Italy.

M

Maartan *see Martin*

Maartin *see Martin*

Maarton *see Martin*

Maartyn *see Martin*

Mabel *see Mael*

Macaille Saint; Celtic

St. Macaille (d. 489) was a bishop of Croghan, Offaly, Ireland. He was present when St. Brigid took her vows.

Macanisius Saint; Celtic

St. Macanisius (d. 514) was baptized by St. Patrick, who later consecrated him as a bishop. Macanisius founded Kells Monastery in Ireland. He was known as a miracle worker.

Macarius Saint; Greek; happy, blessed

St. Macarius, St. Macarius of Alexandria, St. Macarius of Fayum, St. Marcarius of Jerusalem, St. Macarius of Ghent, St. Macarius the Great, St. Macarius the Wonder-Worker

St. Macarius the Great (d. 1012) was a bishop of Antioch in Pisidia. He was captured by the Saracens but escaped. He then traveled throughout Europe. He was known as a miracle worker. He died of the plague in Ghent, Belgium, and is a patron saint against epidemic diseases.

Macartan Saint; Celtic; son of Artan

St. Macartan (d. 505) was a friend and disciple of St. Patrick. He served as a missionary and became the first bishop of Clogher. He was known as a miracle worker.

Maccaldus *see Maughold*

Maccalin Saint; Celtic; son of Calin

St. Maccalin (d. 978) was a Benedictine monk at Gorze Abbey, where he served as abbot. He later became abbot of St. Michael's Monastery at Thierache, France.

Maccallin Saint; Celtic; son of Callin

St. Maccallin of Lusk (d. 497) was bishop of Lusk, Ireland, where he built a church and founded a monastery.

Macedonius Saint; Greek; he who triumphs and grows in stature

St. Macedonius (d. 304) was married to St. Patricia and was father of St. Modesta. All three were martyred in Nicomedia.

Machabeo Saint; Celtic

St. Machabeo (d. 1174) was abbot of Sts. Peter and Paul Monastery in Armagh, Ireland, a position he held for thirty years.

Machael *see Michael*

Machai Saint

St. Machai (fifth century) was a student of St. Patrick's. He founded a monastery on the isle of Bute, Ireland, where he served as abbot.

Machan Saint; French, Scottish; stonemason

St. Machan (date unknown) was from Scotland, educated in Ireland, and ordained as a bishop in Rome.

Machar Saint; Hebrew, Celtic; tomorrow

St. Machar (d. 540) was baptized by St. Colman and became a companion of St. Columba. He served as a missionary to the island of Mull. He became a bishop and founded Aberdeen, Scotland.

Machas *see Michael*

Machudd Saint; Welsh

St. Machudd (seventh century) founded Llanfechell Abbey in Anglesey, Wales, where he served as abbot.

Macrobius Saint; Greek; he who enjoys a long life

St. Macrobius (d. 321) was martyred near the Black Sea during the persecutions of Emperor Licinius.

Macull *see Maughold*

Madelgisilus Saint; Celtic

St. Madelgisilus (d. 655) accompanied St. Fursey from Ireland to England and then to France. When St. Fursey died, he entered the Monastery of Saint-Riquier, but he later left to become a hermit at Monstrelet.

Madern Saint; Celtic, English; lucky, fortunate

Madrun

St. Madern (d. 545) was a monk and hermit from Cornwall, England.

Madrun *see Madern*

Mael Saint; Celtic; prince

Mabel

St. Mael (sixth century), also known as Mabel, was a hermit on the isle of Bardsey. He was known for his holiness and wisdom.

Maeleachlainn *see Malachi*

Maelmuire Saint; Celtic; devotee of Mary

St. Maelmuire O'Gorman (twelfth century) was abbot of Knock, Louth, Ireland. He was an Irish poet.

Maelrhys Saint; Welsh

St. Maelrhys (sixth century) was a hermit on the isle of Bardsey.

He is venerated in northern Wales.

Magdalevus Saint

St. Magdalevus (d. 776) was a monk at Saint-Vannes in France. He was later named bishop of Verdun, France.

Magenulf Saint; German

St. Magenulf (d. 857) was archdeacon of Paderborn. He donated much of his property to found a convent of nuns.

Maghnus *see Magnus*

Maginus Saint; Latin; sage, charmer

St. Maginus (date unknown) helped evangelize Tarragona, Spain. He was arrested during the Roman persecutions and was beheaded.

Magnericus Saint; German; well mannered

St. Magnericus (d. 596) was raised by St. Nicetius of Trier, Germany, and went with him into exile. Magnericus later returned to Trier and was named bishop of that city.

Magnes *see Magnus*

Magnus Saint; Latin; great

Maghnus, Magnes, Magnuss, Manius

St. Magnus (d. 660) was born in Avignon, France, where he later served as governor. He became the father of St. Agricola. After his wife died, he became a monk at Lerins and was then named a bishop.

Magnuss *see Magnus*

Magorianus Saint; Latin

St. Magorianus (d. 415) lived in Trent, Italy, with his mother and his brothers, Sts. Claudianus and Vigilius. He became a priest and served as Vigilius's assistant when he was bishop of Trent. He devoted himself to prayer, fasting, and good works.

Maharsapor Saint

St. Maharsapor the Persian (d. 421) was a Persian noble who was raised as a Christian. He was arrested and imprisoned for three years, suffering great torture. He was offered his freedom in exchange for renouncing the faith, but he would not. He was eventually thrown into a pit to starve. He died three days later while praying.

Maikal *see Michael*

Maimbod Saint; Celtic

St. Maimbod (d. 880) was an Irish missionary who traveled throughout Gaul and northern Italy, visiting tombs of saints and martyrs, and preaching to any people he met on his way. He was martyred.

Maincin *see Munchin*

Maine Saint; French; mainland

Mavenus, Meen, Mevenus, Mewan

St. Maine (sixth century) was the founder of Saint-Meon in Brittany, France. Originally from Wales or Cornwall, he is also known as Meen, Mevanus, Mavenus, or Mewan.

Maitias *see Mathias*

Maitiú *see Matthew*

Majar *see Major*

Maje *see Major*

Majer *see Major*

Majolus Saint; Latin; greater

Mayeul

St. Majolus (906–994), also known as Mayeul, was an archdeacon of Macon, France. When he thought he might be made bishop, he instead went to Cluny Abbey to live as a monk. He later served as abbot. He also served as a counselor to Emperors Otto I and Otto II.

Major Saint; Latin; greater, military rank

Majar, Maje, Majer

St. Major (fourth century) was martyred with Saturninus and several companions in north-western Africa.

Majoricus Saint; Latin; greater, military rank

St. Majoricus (d. 484) was the son of St. Dionysia. He was martyred during the persecutions of Hunneric, the Arian Vandal.

Makael *see Michael*

Makaio *see Matthew*

Makal *see Michael*

Makel *see Michael*

Makell *see Michael*

Makis *see Michael*

Maksimilian *see Maximilian*

Maksimillian *see Maximilian*

Maksym *see Maximilian*

Maksymilian Saint; form of Maximilian; Latin; greatest

Bl. Maksymilian Binkiewicz (1908–1942) was a Polish diocesan priest who died in the Dachau concentration camp. He is one of the 108 Polish Martyrs of World War II and was beatified by Pope John Paul II in 1999.

Malachai *see Malachi*

Malachi Old Testament; Hebrew; my messenger; my angel

Maeleachlainn, Malachai, Malachia, Malachie, Malaki, Malchija, Maleki

Malachi was a minor prophet who gives his name to the last book of the Old Testament.

Malachia *see Malachi*

Malachie *see Malachi*

Malachy Saint; form of Malachi; Hebrew, Gaelic; angel of God

St. Malachy (1095–1138) was born in Armagh, Ireland. He was ordained a priest and served as abbot of Bangor. In that capacity, he replaced the Celtic liturgy with the Roman. In 1125, he became bishop of Connor. Four years later, he was named archbishop of Armagh. He resigned that post in 1138 and traveled to Rome on pilgrimage. When he returned to Rome, he founded Mellifont Abbey and served as a papal legate to Ireland. He was known as a miracle worker. In 1597, a series of papal prophecies were found which were attributed to him, but that authorship is doubtful.

Malaki *see Malachi*

Malard Saint; French; maker of hammers

St. Malard (seventh century) was a bishop of Chartres, France, who attended the Council of Chalons-sur-Saone in 650.

Malchija *see Malachi*

Malchus Saint; Hebrew; king, counselor

St. Malchus (d. 250) was one of "the Seven Sleepers" who were martyred during the persecutions of Decius. Their remains were found walled up in a cave.

Maleki *see Malachi*

Malentus Saint; Latin

St. Malentus (d. 329) was martyred by either revolting Donatists or pagans.

Malo Saint; Latin; bad

St. Malo (d. 287) was a soldier who served in Upper Egypt during the reign of Emperor Maximian Herculeus. His entire legion of over 6,000 men was martyred when they refused to participate in pagan sacrifice.

Mamas Saint; African; Saturday born

St. Mamas (259–275) was the son of Sts. Theodotus and Rufina. He was a shepherd who was martyred in Caesarea. He is a patron saint of babies who are breastfeeding and the protector of those suffering from broken bones and hernias.

Mamertinus Saint

St. Mamertinus of Auxerre (d. 462) was abbot of Sts. Damien and Cosmas Monastery at Auxerre, France.

Mamertius Saint

St. Mamertius (d. 477) was archbishop of Vienne, France, and was known for his great learning and for restoring the faith to this region. He was known as a miracle worker and was credited with stopping a fire that was destroying the city of Vienne one Easter night.

Manaen Saint, New Testament

St. Manaen (first century) is mentioned in Acts 13:1 as one of the prophets and teachers in the Gentile church in Antioch. He is described as "the foster brother" of King Herod Antipas.

Mancus Saint

St. Mancus (sixth century) was an Irish missionary who evangelized in Cornwall, England.

Manettus Saint

St. Manettus (d. 1268) was one of the seven founders of the Servants of Mary. He helped spread the order in France and served as fourth prior general of the Servites. He attended the Council of Lyons in 1246.

Manius *see Magnus*

Mannuel *see Manuel*

Manny *see Emmanuel*

Mano *see Manuel*

Manolete *see Manuel*

Manolito *see Manuel*

Manolón *see Manuel*

Mansuetus Saint; Latin; he who is peaceful, docile

St. Mansuetus (d. 483) was martyred with nine companions by the heretical Monophysites.

Manual *see Manuel*

Manuale *see Manuel*

Manue *see Manuel*

Manuel Saint; form of Emmanuel; Hebrew; God is with us

Mannuel, Mano, Manolete, Manolito, Manolón, Manual, Manuale, Manue, Manuell, Manuelli, Manuelo, Manuil, Manyuil, Minel

St. Manuel (1898–1929) was a seminarian in Durango, Mexico. He was arrested while speaking at a rally. He refused to denounce the Church. He is considered a Martyr of the Cristero War and was canonized in 2000 by Pope John Paul II.

Manuell *see Manuel*

Manuelli *see Manuel*

Manuelo *see Manuel*

Manuil *see Manuel*

Manyuil *see Manuel*

Maolruain Saint; Celtic

St. Maolruain (d. 792) was an Irish Abbot who founded Tallaght Abbey.

Marc *see Mark*

Marcantonio Saint; Italian; Mark and Anthony

Bl. Marcantanio Durando (1801–1880) was born in Mondavi, Italy. He was a priest in the Congregation of the Mission of Saint Vincent de Paul and founded the Institute of the Sisters of Jesus the Nazarene. He was beatified by Pope John Paul II in 2000.

Marcarius Saint; Latin; martial, warlike

St. Marcarius (d. 335) was bishop of Jerusalem and fought against Arianism. He attended the Council of Nicaea and played a large role in the writing of the Creed. He was with St. Helena when she discovered the true Cross, and Emperor Constantine directed him to build the Church of the Holy Sepulcher.

Marcel Saint; Latin, French; little warrior

Bl. Marcel Callo (1921–1945) was born in Rennes, France. During World War II, he was ordered by the Germans to report to the Service of Obligatory Work or else have his family be arrested. He complied. He organized a group of Christian workers and a theatrical group. He also arranged for a French Mass to be offered. He was arrested for being "too much of a Catholic." He died in prison. He was beatified by Pope John Paul II in 1987.

Marcelino *see Marcellin*

Marcellin Saint; Latin; martial, warlike

Marcelino

St. Marcellin Champagnat (1789–1840) studied under

St. John Marie Vianney and became a priest. He founded the Little Brothers of Mary (Marists) in 1817, a community devoted to Our Lady and preaching the Word of God to young men. He was canonized in 1999 by Pope John Paul II.

Marcellinus Saint; Latin; little Marcus

St. Marcellinus (d. 304) was a priest who was imprisoned along with Peter, and he was an exorcist. The two converted their jailer and his family. They were beheaded.

Marcellus Saint; Latin; little warrior

Pope St. Marcellus (d. 309) was elected pope in 307 during the end of the persecutions by Emperor Diocletian. He was very merciful to those who had repented after having denied their faith to avoid persecution. Emperor Maxentius sent St. Marcellus into exile when he refused to pardon those who would not do penance for their apostasy. He died while in exile.

Marcian Saint; Italian, Spanish; martial, warlike

St. Marcian, St. Marcian of Auxerre, St. Marcian of Ravenna, St. Marcian of Syracuse

St. Marcian (d. 304) was a convert to Christianity and was beheaded for the faith at Rome.

Marciano Saint; Italian, Spanish; martial, warlike

St. Marciano Jose (1900–1934) was a member of the Brothers of the Christian Schools and one of the Martyrs of Turón from the Spanish Civil War. He was canonized by Pope John Paul II in 1999.

Marck see Mark

Marco Saint; Latin; martial, warlike

Bl. Marco d'Aviano (1631–1699) was born in Aviano, Italy. He entered the Capuchin order at Conegliano, Italy. He was ordained a priest and served as a missionary throughout Italy. After praying over a sister who had been bedridden for thirteen years, she was miraculously healed, and his fame grew. He became a counselor to Emperor Leopold I of Austria and served as a papal legate for Pope Bl. Innocent XI. He worked as a peacemaker throughout Europe. He was beatified by Pope John Paul II in 2003.

Marculf Saint; German; border wolf

St. Marculf (d. 558) was born into a noble family at Bayeux, France. He became a priest and served as a missionary to the pagans of Gaul. He left that life to become a hermit and founded a monastery at Nanteuil, France.

Marcus Saint; form of Mark; Latin; martial, warlike

Pope St. Marcus (d. 336) was pope for less than a year. During that brief reign, he built the Basilica of San Marco in Rome, Italy, and the Juxta Pallcinis Basilica outside the city.

Mardonius Saint; Persian; the male warrior

St. Mardonius (d. 303) was an official of the Roman court who was martyred by being drowned in a well during the persecutions of Emperor Diocletian.

Mareas Saint; Hebrew; bitter

St. Mareas (d. 360) was a bishop in Persia who was martyred in the persecutions of King Sapor II.

Marek Saint; form of Mark; Slavic; martial, warlike

Marko

St. Marek Krizin (1589–1619), also known as Marko, was born into a noble Croat family. He studied in Rome and was ordained a priest. When he returned to Hungary, he became a canon at Esztergom. He served as a missionary in Slovakia, where he was taken prisoner, tortured, and martyred. He was canonized in 1995 as one of the Martyrs of Kosice by Pope John Paul II.

Marian *see Marian (girl's name)*

Mariano Saint; form of Mark; Italian; martial, warlike

Bl. Mariano de Jesus Euse Hoyos, Bl. Mariano da Roccacasale

Bl. Mariano de Jesus Euse Hoyos (1845–1926) was born in Yarumel, Columbia. He was ordained a priest and worked at the parishes of San Pedro and Yarumel before being assigned to Angostura, where he would spend the rest of his life. This area was suffering from civil war, and he ministered to his people during very difficult times. He was beatified by Pope John Paul II in 2000.

Marianus Saint; form of Mark; Hebrew, Latin; martial, warlike

St. Marianus (d. 283) was martyred during the persecutions of Numerian.

Marinus Saint; Latin; sea

St. Marinus (d. 262) was a soldier in the Roman army. He was Christian but kept his faith a secret. When he was up for a position as centurion, he was told he would have to offer sacrifice to the emperor. He refused and said he was a Christian. He was given three hours to change his mind. When he refused, he was beheaded.

Marius Saint; Latin; sailor

St. Marius (d. 555) was a monk who founded Bodon Abbey at La-Val-Benois, France, where he served as abbot. He went on a pilgrimage to the tombs of St. Martin of Tours and St. Dionysius and was cured of an illness by an apparition of St. Dionysius. He also received a prophetic vision about the destruction of his monastery.

Mark Saint, New Testament; Latin; martial, warlike

Marc, Marck, Marke, Markee, Markey, Markk, Markusha, Marq

St. Mark, St. Mark Chong Ui-bae, St. Mark of Galilee, St. Mark of Lucera, St. Mark the Faster

St. Mark (first century), sometimes referred to as John Mark, is the author of the second gospel. His mother's house in Jerusalem was a meeting place for Christians. He accompanied St. Paul and St. Barnabas on their missionary journey through Cyprus and founded the church in Alexandria. He wrote his gospel in Greek for the Gentile converts to Christianity. He is a patron saint of notaries.

Marke *see Mark*

Markee *see Mark*

Markey *see Mark*

Markk *see Mark*

Marko *see Marek*

Markusha *see Mark*

Maro Saint; Japanese; myself

St. Maro (d. 410) was a hermit in the city of Cyrrhus in Syria. Many were attracted to his spiritual wisdom and he established three monasteries.

Maroveus Saint

St. Maroveus (d. 650) was the founder of the Benedictine Monastery of Precipiano, near Tortona, Italy, where he served as abbot.

Marq *see Mark*

Mart *see Martin*

Martain *see Martin*

Martainn *see Martin*

Martan *see Martin*

Martel *see Martin*

Martial Saint; form of Mark; Latin, French; martial, warlike

St. Martial (d. 304) was one of the Martyrs of Saragossa who died during the persecutions of the Emperor Diocletian.

Martijn *see Martin*

Martin Saint; Latin, French; martial, warlike

Maartan, Maartin, Maarton, Maartyn, Mart, Martain, Martainn, Martan, Martel, Martijn, Martine, Martinien, Marto, Marton, Marts, Martyn, Mattin, Mertin, Mertyn, Morten

St. Martin, St. Martin Cid, St. Martin de Aguirre, St. Martin de Hinojosa, St. Martin de Porres, St. Martin Loynaz of the Ascension, St. Martin Manuel, St. Martin of Arades, St. Martin of Braga, St. Martin of Leon, St. Martin of Tongres, St. Martin of Ver

St. Martin de Porres (1579–1639) was born in Lima, Peru, the son of a Spanish gentleman and a Black freedwoman from Panama. He joined the Dominican Friary at Lima as a lay brother, where he worked in a variety of capacities. He devoted himself to severe penances and had a great love of all animals. He was a miracle worker who also had the gifts of aerial flights and bilocation.

Martine *see Martin*

Martinian Saint; Latin; martial, warlike

St. Martinian (d. 435) was bishop of Milan and attended the Council of Ephesus. He fought the Nestorian heresy that claimed that Mary was not the Mother of God.

Martinien *see Martin*

Martius Saint; Latin; he who gives a testament of faith

St. Martius (d. 530) was a hermit who founded Clermont Abbey.

Marto *see Martin*

Marton *see Martin*

Marts *see Martin*

Martyn *see Martin*

Martyrius Saint; Latin; testimony

St. Martyrius (d. 397) was a subdeacon who was martyred in Trent.

Maruthas Saint

St. Maruthas (d. 415) was a friend of St. John Chrysostom. He served as bishop of Maiferkat, in Syria, and wrote an account of the Martyrs of Persia. He was known as a medical specialist and is called "the Father of the Syrian Church."

Massimo *see Maximilian*

Mata *see Matthew*

Matai *see Matthew*

Matek *see Matthew*

Mateo Saint; form of Matthew; Spanish; gift of God

Matteo

St. Mateo Correa Magallanes (1866–1927) was a parish priest in Tepechitlan, Mexico. He was arrested while traveling to bring Holy Communion to an invalid. He consumed the host to avoid having it be desecrated. When he was imprisoned, he was asked to hear the confessions of several members of the insurgency. He did so. When he was asked to reveal what he was told, however, he refused, saying that a priest must die rather than reveal what is told to him in confession. He was shot to death and was canonized by Pope John Paul II in 2000.

Marian *see Marian (girl's name)*

Maternus Saint; Latin; motherly

St. Maternus (d. 307) was chosen bishop of Milan, Italy, by public acclamation. He served during the Roman persecutions but managed to escape martyrdom.

Matfei *see Matthew*

Mathe *see Matthew*

Mathi *see Mathias*

Mathian *see Matthew*

Mathias Saint; form of Matthew; German, Swedish; gift of God

Maitias, Mathi, Matios, Matthia, Matthias, Matthieus, Matus

St. Mathias Mulumba (1836–1886) was a Ugandan chief who was martyred by King Mwanga. He is one of the Martyrs of Uganda.

Mathieson *see Matthew*

Mathurin Saint; Latin; timely

St. Mathurin (d. 300) was born into a pagan family at Larchant, France. He converted at age twelve and was ordained a priest by St. Polycarp. He eventually converted his parents as well. He served as a missionary and exorcist and was known as a miracle worker.

Matios *see Mathias*

Matro *see Matthew*

Matronian Saint; Latin; mother

St. Matronian (date unknown) was a hermit in Milan, Italy.

Matt *see Matthew*

Matteas Saint; Scandinavian; gift of God

Matthaios, Mattheaus, Matthews

Bl. Matteas Cardona (1902–1936) was a priest in Calahoora, Spain, during the Spanish Civil War. He was arrested and shot. He was beatified by Pope John Paul II in 1995.

Matteo *see Mateo*

Matthaios *see Matteas*

Matthaus *see Matthew*

Mattheaus *see Matteas*

Matthew Saint, New Testament; Top 100 Name; Hebrew; gift of God

Maitiú, Makaio, Mata, Matai, Matek, Matfei, Mathe, Mathian, Mathieson, Matro, Matt, Matthaus, Mattmais, Matvi, Mayhew, Maztheson

St. Matthew, St. Matthew Alonso Leziniana, St. Matthew of Beauvais, St. Matthew Phuong

St. Matthew (first century), also known as Levi, was a son of Alphaeus. He was a Roman tax collector when he was called by our Lord to become one of the chosen twelve. He wrote his gospel to convince a Jewish audience that Jesus was the promised Messiah. He is a patron saint of bankers.

Matthews *see Matteas*

Matthia *see Mathias*

Matthias Saint; form of Matthew; German, Swedish; gift of God

St. Matthias, St. Matthias Murumba, St. Matthias of Meako

St. Matthias of Meako (d. 1597) was from Meako, Japan. He became a Franciscan tertiary and offered himself as a substitute for one of the twenty-six Christians to be killed by Toyotomi Hideyoshi. He was crucified in Nagasaki. He is one of the Martyrs of Japan.

Matthieus *see Mathias*

Mattin *see Martin*

Mattmais *see Matthew*

Matus *see Mathias*

Matvi *see Matthew*

Maudez *see Mawes*

Maughold Saint; Celtic

Maccaldus, Macull, Morgan

St. Maughold (d. 488), also known as Macull or Maccaldus, was converted by St. Patrick and entered religious life.

He evangelized the Isle of Man, where he served as bishop.

Maur *see Maurice*

Maurance *see Maurice*

Maurell *see Maurice*

Maureo *see Maurice*

Mauri *see Maurice*

Maurice Saint; Latin; dark skinned, moor, marshland

Maur, Maurance, Maurell, Maureo, Mauri, Mauricio, Maurids, Mauriece, Maurikas, Maurin, Maurino, Maurise, Mauritius, Maurius, Mauro, Maurrel, Maurtel, Mauryce, Maurycy, Maurys, Mauryse, Meurig, Meurisse, Morice, Moritz, Morrice, Morris

St. Maurice, St. Maurice of Carnoet

St. Maurice of Carnoet (1117–1191) was a monk at the Monastery of Langonnet, France, where he served as abbot. He drove out some aggressive wolves that were encroaching upon the monastery by invoking the names of Jesus and Mary.

Mauricio *see Maurice*

Maurids *see Maurice*

Mauriece *see Maurice*

Maurikas *see Maurice*

Maurilio Saint; Italian; dark skinned

Bl. Maurilio Macho Rodriguez (1915–1936) was one of the Passionist Martyrs of Daimiel who were killed during the Spanish Civil War. He was beatified by Pope John Paul II in 1989.

Maurilius Saint; Latin; dark skinned, moor, marshland

St. Maurilius (430–453) was born in Milan, Italy, but moved to France, where he became bishop of Angers.

Maurin *see Maurice*

Maurino *see Maurice*

Maurise *see Maurice*

Mauritius *see Maurice*

Maurius *see Maurice*

Mauro *see Maurice*

Maurontus Saint

St. Maurontus (d. 700) was a Benedictine monk who founded Saint-Florentle-Vieil Abbey in Anjou, France.

Maurrel *see Maurice*

Maurtel *see Maurice*

Maurus Saint; form of Maurice; Latin; dark skinned, moor, marshland

St. Maurus, St. Maurus II

St. Maurus (d. 946) was born in Rome and was a nephew of Pope John IX. He was a monk at Classe in Ravena, where he later served as abbot. He then became bishop of Cesana, Italy.

Mauryce *see Maurice*

Maurycy *see Maurice*

Maurys *see Maurice*

Mauryse *see Maurice*

Mauvier *see Meneleus*

Mavenus *see Maine*

Mavilus Saint; Latin; to not want

St. Mavilus (d. 212) was martyred in North Africa by being

hurled to wild beasts during the reign of Emperor Caracalla.

Mawes Saint

Maudez

St. Mawes (sixth century), also known as Maudez, was a hermit near Falmouth, in Cornwall, England. He founded monasteries and churches in Cornwall and Brittany.

Maxamilian *see Maximilian*

Maxamillion *see Maximilian*

Maxemilian *see Maximilian*

Maxemilion *see Maximilian*

Maxentiolus Saint; Latin

St. Maxentiolus (fifth century) founded Our Lady of Cunault Abbey in France, where he served as abbot.

Maxentius Saint; Latin; greatest

St. Maxentius (445–515) was born at Agde, France. He was taught by St. Severus and became a monk in his abbey, but he later joined the monastery at Poitou. He later served as abbot and as a counselor to King Clovis I.

Maxima *see Maxima (girl's name)*

Maximaian Saint; Latin; greatest

St. Maximaian (d. 250) was one of "the Seven Sleepers" who had been martyred after confessing their faith at Ephesus and whose relics were found in a cave.

Maximalian *see Maximilian*

Maximian Saint; Latin; greatest

St. Maximian, St. Maximian of Constantinople, St. Maximian

of Ravenna, St. Maximian of Syracuse

St. Maximian (d. 404) was bishop of Bagae, Numidia, in North Africa. He was hurled from a tower by proponents of the Donatist heresy, but he survived and went to Italy.

Maximili *see Maximilian*

Maximilian Saint; Latin; greatest

Maksimilian, Maksimillian, Maksym, Massimo, Maxamilian, Maxamillion, Maxemilian, Maxemilion, Maximalian, Maximili, Maximilianos, Maximilianus, Maximillion, Maxmilian, Maxmillion, Maxon, Maxximillion, Maxymilian

St. Maximilian, St. Maximilian Kolbe, St. Maximilian of Lorch

St. Maximilian Kolbe (1894–1941) was born in Poland. He became a Franciscan and was ordained. Even before becoming a priest, he founded the Immaculata Movement, devoted to Our Lady. He earned a doctorate in theology and started a magazine, *The Knight of the Immaculata*. He served in Japan and India. He returned home to Poland and was arrested in 1939 during the Nazi Invasion. He was released but was imprisoned again in 1941. This time, he was sent to Auschwitz. He offered to take the place of a young husband and father who was chosen to die. After suffering two weeks of starvation, he died. He was canonized by Pope John Paul II in 1982.

Maximilianos *see Maximilian*

Maximilianus *see Maximilian*

Maximillion *see Maximilian*

Maximinus Saint; Latin; greatest

St. Maximinus, St. Maximinus of Aix, St. Maximinus of Trier

St. Maximinus (d. 520) served as the first abbot of the Abbey of Micy, near Orleans, France. This abbey had been founded by King Clovis I, and he chose to have Maximinus serve as abbot.

Maximus Saint; Latin; greatest

St. Maximus, St. Maximus of Aquila, St. Maximus of Jerusalem, St. Maximus of Nola, St. Maximus of Padua, St. Maximus of Reiz, St. Maximus of Turin, St. Maximus the Confessor

St. Maximus (d. 470) founded Chinon Abbey in Tours, where he served as abbot.

Maxmilian *see Maximilian*

Maxmillion *see Maximilian*

Maxon *see Maximilian*

Maxximillion *see Maximilian*

Maxymilian *see Maximilian*

Mayeul *see Majolus*

Mayhew *see Matthew*

Maztheson *see Matthew*

Mbaga Saint

St. Mbaga Tuzinde (d. 1886) was a page to King Mwanga of Uganda. He was burned alive at Namuyango after professing

the faith. He is one of the Martyrs of Uganda.

Medard Saint; German; boldly powerful

St. Medard (d. 545) was born in Salency, Picardy. He became a priest and was known for his ability as a preacher. He served as a missionary and was later named bishop of Vermandois.

Medericus Saint; Latin

Merry

St. Medericus (d. 700), also known as Merry, was born in Autun, France. He became a monk at St. Martin's Monastery, where he later served as abbot.

Medrald Saint

Merald, Merault

St. Medrald (d. 850), also known as Merald or Merault, was a Benedictine monk who served as abbot of Vendome, France.

Medran Saint; Celtic

St. Medran (sixth century) was a follower of St. Kieran of Saghir in Ireland.

Meen *see Maine, Meinuph*

Megingaud Saint

St. Megingaud (d. 794) was a Frank who became a monk at Fritzlar Monastery in Germany, where he later served as abbot. In 754, he became bishop of Wurzburg, Germany. He spent his last days at Neustadt Abbey.

Mehran *see Myron*

Mehrayan *see Myron*

Meikil *see Michael*

Meikyl *see Michael*

Meilseoir *see Melchior*

Meinard Saint; German; strong, firm

St. Meinard (1130–1196) served as a missionary in Livonia (modern day Latvia). He settled in Iskile, where he built a church dedicated to Our Lady and a fort. In 1186 he became the first bishop of Livonia.

Meingold Saint

St. Meingold (d. 892) was born into a noble family of Liege, Belgium. He was known for his holiness and was murdered while returning from a pilgrimage. He is a patron saint of bakers.

Meinrad Saint; German; strong counsel

St. Meinrad (d. 861) was the founder of Einsiedeln in Switzerland. He later lived as a hermit. He was killed by two people to whom he had given shelter.

Meinuph Saint; German

Magenulf, Meen

St. Meinuph (d. 859), also known as Magenulf or Meen, was a noble from Westphalia. He became a priest and opened the Abbey of Bodekan for nuns. He is known as one of the apostles to Westphalia.

Mekil *see Michael*

Mekyl *see Michael*

Mel Saint; form of Melvin; Gaelic, English; armored chief, mill friend, council friend

St. Mel (d. 489) was the nephew of St. Patrick. He traveled with his uncle and helped evangelize Ireland. St. Patrick ordained him as bishop of Ardagh.

Melan Saint; Greek; having black skin

St. Melan (d. 549) was bishop of Viviers, France.

Melanie Saint; Greek; having black skin

St. Melanie (d. 535) was born in Brittany and became a close friend of King Clovis I. He served as bishop of Rennes, France. He played a leading role in the Council of Orléans in 511.

Melanius Saint; Greek; having black skin

Mellon

St. Mellanius (d. 314), also known as Mellon, was a pagan. While making a sacrifice to the god Mars in Rome, he heard Pope St. Stephen I preaching and was converted. He gave his wealth to the poor and became a priest. He traveled to Rouen where he evangelized and became the first bishop of that area. He was known as a miracle worker.

Melas Saint; Greek; black, dark

St. Melas (fourth century) was bishop of Rhinoclusa in Egypt. He was arrested and exiled because of a decree by Emperor Valens that all bishops who were opposed to Arianism should be exiled. When the soldiers came to arrest him, he was in simple garb and served them dinner before revealing who he was. When they were going to let him escape, he refused and went with them so to stand in solidarity with his fellow bishops.

Melasippus Saint

St. Melasippus (d. 360) was martyred with his wife and son at Ancyra.

Melchior Saint; Polish, Persian; king

Meilseoir, Melker, Melkior

St. Melchior, St. Melchoir Garcia Sampedro

St. Melchoir Garcia Sampedro (1821–1858) was born into a poor family in Cortes, Spain. He entered the Dominican order and served in the missions at Vietnam. After St. Jose Diaz Sanjuro was martyred, he was named the new bishop. He was soon arrested and imprisoned in a cage. He was martyred by having his body parts amputated one by one. During this torture, he prayed aloud.

Meldan *see Meldon*

Melden *see Meldon*

Meldin *see Meldon*

Meldon Saint; English; mill hill

Meldan, Melden, Meldin, Meldyn

St. Meldon (sixth century) was an Irish hermit who may have also served as a bishop in France.

Meldyn *see Meldon*

Meletius Saint; Greek; a cautious man

St. Meletius, St. Meletius of Antioch

St. Meletius (d. 295) was bishop of Pontus. He was known for his eloquence in preaching.

Melito Saint; Greek; sugary sweet, pleasant

St. Melito of Sardis (d. 180) was bishop of Sardis, near Asia Minor. He is known for forming a list of Old Testament scriptures and recommending that Marcus Aurelius make Christianity the official religion of the Roman Empire. He was a scholar and exegete who examined parallels between the Old and New Testaments.

Melker *see Melchior*

Melkior *see Melchior*

Mellitus Saint; Greek; honey

St. Mellitus (d. 624) was a monk at St. Andrew's Monastery in Rome. Pope St. Gregory the Great sent him to Kent, England, as a missionary. He became the first bishop of London and later became archbishop of Canterbury. According to tradition, his prayers saved Canterbury from a dangerous fire.

Mellon Saint; Gaelic; small pleasant one

St. Mellon (d. 314) was from Cardiff, Wales. He traveled to Rome, where he converted to Christianity. Pope St. Stephen sent him to France as a missionary. He became the first bishop of Rouen, France.

Memmius Saint; Latin

Menge

St. Memmius (d. 300), also known as Menge, was the first bishop of Chalons-sur-Maine.

Memorius Saint; Latin; memory

St. Memorius (d. 451) was a deacon of Troyes, France, who was put to death by Attila the Hun after he had been sent to ask the invading Attila to spare the town.

Menas Saint; Greek; months

St. Menas (d. 552) was a native of Alexandria, Egypt. He was a superior of the hospice of St. Samson and was consecrated as patriarch of Constantinople by Pope St. Agapitus in 536. Because of his support of Emperor Justinian's efforts to reconcile the Monophysite heretics to the Church, he was excommunicated by Pope Vigilius in 551, but he was reconciled to the Church before his death.

Meneleus Saint; Greek, Latin; strength of the people

Mauvier

St. Meneleus (d. 720), also known as Mauvier, was born in Anjou, France. He became a monk at Carmery, Auvergne. He later restored Menat Monastery, near Clermont, France, where he served as abbot.

Menge *see Memmius*

Menico *see Domenico*

Menignus Saint; Latin; powerful as fire

St. Menignus (d. 251) was a dyer in Parium who tore down an edict against Christianity that had been posted. He was arrested, had his fingers cut off, and was beheaded.

Mennas Saint; Greek; months

St. Mennas (sixth century) was from Asia Minor. He lived as a hermit in the Abruzzi region in Italy.

Menulphus Saint

St. Menulphus (seventh century) was an Irish pilgrim who became bishop of Quimper in Brittany, France.

Merald *see Medrald*

Merault *see Medrald*

Mercurialis Saint; Latin; he who pays attention to business

St. Mercurialis (d. 406) was the first bishop of Forli, Italy. He spoke out against the Arian heresy.

Mercurius Saint; Latin; he who pays attention to business

St. Mercurius (224–250) was from Cappadocia in Asia Minor. He became a military hero when Rome was invaded by Barbarians. He was beheaded for refusing to take part in pagan sacrifices.

Meriadoc Saint; Welsh

St. Meriadoc (d. 1302) was a native of Brittany. He became a hermit, but his reputation for holiness led to his being named bishop of Vannes. As bishop, he worked on behalf of the poor.

Merililaun Saint

St. Merililaun (eighth century) was from England. He was martyred in Rheims, France, while on pilgrimage to Rome.

Merinus Saint; Latin; from Merina

Merryn

St. Merinus (565–620), also known as Merryn, evangelized the area of Strathclyde, Scotland. He founded Paisley Abbey, where he served as abbot.

Merry *see Medericus*

Merryn *see Merinus*

Mertin *see Martin*

Mertyn *see Martin*

Merulus Saint; Latin; he who is fine as a blackbird

St. Merulus (d. 590) was a Benedictine monk at St. Andrew's Monastery in Rome, Italy, who was known as a miracle worker.

Mesrop Saint; Armenian

St. Mesrop (361–440) was born in Taron, Armenia. After spending time as a hermit with St. Nerses the Great, he worked as a missionary with St. Isaac the Great. He knew Greek, Syriac, and Persian, and he founded schools in Armenia and Georgia.

Methodius Saint; Greek, Latin; pursuit, method

St. Methodius I, St. Methodius of Olympus

St. Methodius (826–885) was a brother of St. Cyril. He taught philosophy at the University of Constantinople. He and Cyril were sent to convert the Jewish Khazars of Russia and were successful in their efforts. The brothers helped develop the Slavonic language now known as Cyrillic, and they translated the Bible and liturgy into that language.

Metranus Saint; Greek, Latin; he who measures

St. Metranus (d. 250) was martyred in Alexandria during the persecutions of Emperor Trajanus Decius.

Metrophanes Saint; Greek; mother appearing

St. Metrophanes (d. 325) was a nephew of Emperor Probus. He converted to the faith and became a priest. He was later named bishop of Byzantium.

Meugant Saint

St. Meugant (sixth century) was a hermit of Britain who died on the island of Bardsley. Churches in Wales and Cornwall are named for him.

Meurig *see Maurice*

Meuris Saint

St. Meuris (d. 307) was a virgin from Gaza, Palestine, who died from being tortured for the faith in Alexandria, Egypt.

Meurisse *see Maurice*

Mevenus *see Maine*

Mewan *see Maine*

Mhichael *see Michael*

Micah *see Michael*

Micahel *see Michael*

Mical *see Michael*

Michael Saint, New Testament; Hebrew; who is like God?

Chelle, Machael, Machas, Maikal, Makael, Makal, Makel, Makell, Makis, Meikil, Meikyl, Mekil, Mekyl, Mhichael, Micaela, Micah, Micahel, Mical, Michaela, Michaele, Michaell, Michalel, Michau, Michelet, Michella, Michelle, Michiel, Micho, Michoel, Miekil, Miekyl, Mihail, Mihalje, Mihkel, Misha, Miska, Myshell

St. Michael de Sanctis, St. Michael Fedres Cordero, St. Michael Garicoits, St. Michael Ho-Dinh-Hy, St. Michael Kozaki, St. Michael My, St. Michael of the Saints, St. Michael of Synnada, St. Michael the Confessor, St. Michael the Archangel

St. Michael the Archangel was "one of the chief princes" and the leader of the forces of good angels against the angels that had chosen to go against God. He is a patron saint of police, mariners, paratroopers, grocers, and those who are sick. During the Middle Ages, he was a patron saint of knights.

Michaell *see Michael*

Michak *see Michal*

Michal Saint; form of Michael; Polish

Michak, Michalek, Michall

Bl. Michal Ozieblowski, Bl. Michal Piaszczynski, Bl. Michal Wozniak

Bl. Michal Ozieblowski (1900–1942) was a priest of the archdiocese of Warsaw. He died in the Dachau concentration camp. He is one of the 108 Polish Martyrs of World War II and was beatified in 1999 by Pope John Paul II.

Michalek *see Michal*

Michalel *see Michael*

Michall *see Michal*

Michau *see Michael*

Michelet *see Michael*

Michiel *see Michael*

Micho *see Michael*

Michoel *see Michael*

Midan Saint

Nidan

St. Midan (d. 610), also known as Nidan, evangelized Anglesey, Wales.

Mieczyslaw Saint; Polish

Bl. Mieczyslaw Bohatkiewicz (1904–1942) was a Polish priest who was shot in Berezwecz. He is one of the 108 Polish Martyrs of World War II and was beatified by Pope John Paul II in 1999.

Miekil *see Michael*

Miekyl *see Michael*

Migdonius Saint; Latin

St. Migdonius (d. 303) was martyred by being burned at the stake during the reign of Emperor Diocletian.

Migeal *see Miguel*

Migeel *see Miguel*

Miguel Saint; form of Michael; Portuguese, Spanish; who is like God?

Migeal, Migeel, Miguelly, Miguil, Mikkel, Miquel, Myguel, Myguele, Myguell, Myguelle

St. Miguel De La Mora, St. Miguel Cordero

St. Miguel Cordero (1854–1910) was born in Ecuador. He became a De La Salle brother and worked as a teacher and writer. In 1907, he was sent to Europe to translate books into Spanish. He died of pneumonia. He was canonized by Pope John Paul II in 1984.

Miguelly *see Miguel*

Miguil *see Miguel*

Mihail *see Michael*

Mihalje *see Michael*

Mihkel *see Michael*

Mikkel *see Miguel*

Milas *see Milles*

Miles *see Milles*

Milles Saint; Greek, Latin, German; millstone, soldier, merciful

Milas, Miles, Milson

St. Milles (d. 380) was a Persian bishop who was martyred by King Shapur II of Persia.

Milson *see Milles*

Miltiades Saint; Greek; red earth

Pope St. Miltiades (d. 314) was a Roman of African descent who was elected pope in 311. In 313, he convened a council that condemned Donatus.

Minel *see Manuel*

Minervius Saint; Greek; power, young

St. Minervius (third century) was martyred in Lyons, France.

Minias Saint; German; great, strong

Miniato

St. Minias of Florence (d. 250), also known as Miniato, was a soldier who was martyred during the reign of Emperor Trajanus Decius.

Miniato *see Minias*

Minnborinus Saint

St. Minnborinus (d. 986) was born in Ireland. He served as abbot of St. Martin Monastery in Cologne, Germany.

Miquel *see Miguel*

Mirocles Saint; Greek, Latin; admirer

St. Mirocles (d. 318) was archbishop of Milan, Italy, and attended the Council of Rome in 313. He also helped originate Ambrosian chant and liturgy.

Miska *see Michael*

Mitrius Saint

St. Mitrius (d. 314) was a Christian slave who was beheaded by his master in Aix, Provence, France.

Mochelloc Saint; Celtic

St. Mochelloc (d. 639) is a patron saint of Kilmallock, Limerick, Ireland.

Mochoemoc Saint; Celtic

St. Mochoemoc (d. 656) was trained by St. Ita at Munster, Ireland, and was ordained by St. Comgall at Bangor. He founded Liath Mochoemoc Monastery at Tipperary, Ireland, as well as Arderin Abbey.

Mochta Saint; Celtic; great

St. Mochta (d. 535) was born in Britain but went to Ireland as a child. He became a follower of St. Patrick and was made a bishop by Pope St. Leo I. He founded Louth Monastery.

Mochua *see Cuan*

Modan Saint

St. Modan (sixth century) was the son of an Irish chieftain. He founded Dryburgh Monastery in Scotland, where he served as abbot. He later retired and became a hermit.

Modanic Saint

St. Modanic (eighth century) was a Scottish bishop known as a scholar and reformer.

Moderan Saint; Gaelic; descendent of great one

Moran

St. Moderan (d. 730), also known as Moran, was bishop of Rennes, France. In 720, he made a pilgrimage to Rome and resigned his see in order to live as a hermit at Barceto Abbey in Parma, Italy.

Modeste Saint; Latin; modest

St. Modeste Andlauer (1847–1900) was born in Rosheim. He joined the Society of Jesus at St. Acheul. After being ordained, he taught at the colleges of Amiens, Lille, and Brest. He then served as a missionary to China. He is one of the Martyr Saints of China who were canonized by Pope John Paul II in 2000.

Modestino Saint; Latin; modest

Bl. Modestino of Jesus and Mary (1802–1854) was a Franciscan priest from Italy who served the poor and sick. He cared for those suffering from a cholera epidemic and ultimately died of that same disease. He was beatified by Pope John Paul II in 1995.

Modestus Saint; Latin; modest

St. Modestus (d. 489) was bishop of Trier during the time when the Franks ruled the area.

Modoaldus Saint; Latin, German; very happy

Romoaldus

St. Modoaldus (d. 640), also known as Romoaldus, was born to a noble family in Aquitaine, France. He served as bishop of Trier and attended the Council of Rheims. He was also a counselor of King Dagobert I of the Franks and caused the king to change his immoral ways.

Modomnoc Saint; Gaelic

Domnoc

St. Modomnoc (d. 550), also known as Domnoc, was a member of the Irish royal family of O'Neil. He studied with St.

David of Wales before returning home to Ireland to live as a hermit at Tibraghny in Kilkenny. According to tradition, when he returned to Ireland, swarms of bees followed him and were thereby introduced into Ireland.

Moelray Saint

St. Moelray (d. 493) was installed as abbot of Nendrum Monastery by St. Patrick. He was a teacher of Sts. Finian and Colman.

Molagga Saint

St. Molagga (d. 650) was born in Ireland but traveled to Wales, where he became a follower of St. David of Wales and founded Fermoy Monastery.

Moling Saint

Myllin

St. Moling (d. 697), also known as Myllin, was a monk at Glendalough and then founded an abbey at Achad Cainigh. He also served as bishop of Ferns.

Moloc Saint; Hebrew; king

St. Moloc (d. 572) was born into a noble Scottish family. He was educated by St. Brendan the Elder in Ireland. He then returned to Scotland, where he served as a missionary in the Hebrides region.

Molonachus Saint

St. Molonachus (seventh century) was bishop of Lismore, in Argyl, Scotland.

Monaldus Saint

St. Monaldus (d. 1286) was a Franciscan missionary in Armenia, where he was martyred by pagans.

Monan Saint

St. Monan (d. 874) was a monk at St. Andrew's Abbey. He served as a missionary to Scotland and was murdered in the area of Firth of Forth by Danish raiders.

Monas Saint

St. Monas (second or third century) served as bishop of Milan.

Moncan *see Cuan*

Monitor Saint; Latin; he who counsels

St. Monitor (d. 490) was bishop of Orleans, France. He was a great proponent of monasticism.

Monon Saint; Greek; alone

St. Monon (d. 645) was from Scotland but moved to France to become a hermit in Ardennes. He was murdered in Luxembourg.

Montanus Saint; Spanish; mountain

St. Montanus (d. 300) was a soldier who was martyred by drowning on the island of Ponza, off the Italian coast.

Moran *see Moderan*

Morand Saint; French; to stay

St. Morand (d. 1115) was born into a noble family near Worms, Germany. After he was ordained, he entered the Benedictines at Cluny. Count Frederick Pferz asked him to become his counselor. He was known as a miracle worker. He is a patron saint of wine growers because one Lent he ate nothing but grapes.

Morgan *see Maughold*

Morice *see Maurice*

Moritz *see Maurice*

Moroc Saint

St. Moroc (ninth century) was abbot of Dunkeld in Scotland. He later became bishop of Dunblane.

Morrice *see Maurice*

Morris *see Maurice*

Morten *see Martin*

Moses Saint, Old Testament; Hebrew; drawn out of the water

St. Moses, St. Moses of Balkim, St. Moses of Psammanius, St. Moses the Black of Scete, St. Moses the Ethiopian

Moses in scripture brought the Israelite people out of Egypt. He is considered a great prophet, and the authorship of the Torah (the first five books of the Bible) is traditionally attributed to him. After being placed in a basket by his mother, he was found by Pharoah's daughter and raised as a prince. He killed an Egyptian slaveholder and fled to Midian, where God spoke to him via a burning bush. After ten plagues upon the Egyptian people, he led the Israelites out of Egypt. He received the Ten Commandments at Mount Sinai and died at age 120, within sight of the Promised Land.

St. Moses (d. 251) was of Jewish heritage. He was a priest who opposed the Novatian heresy. He was imprisoned and martyred during the persecutions of Emperor Trajanus Decius.

Moseus Saint; Hebrew; drawing out

St. Moseus (d. 250) was a soldier who was imprisoned in the mines of Bithynia, in Asia Minor. He was martyred by being burned alive.

Mucius Saint; Latin; he who endures silence

St. Mucius (d. 304) was a priest who destroyed an altar of the god Bacchys at Amphipolis, Macedonia. He was set on fire and given to wild beasts but survived both attempts on his life. He was martyred by being beheaded at Constantinople.

Mugagga Saint

St. Mugagga (d. 1886) was a Martyr of Uganda. A royal clothmaker, he was martyred by King Mwanga.

Muirchu Saint; Celtic

St. Muirchu (seventh century) was from Ireland. He wrote the lives of Sts. Brigid and Patrick.

Mukasa Saint; African; chief administrator of the lord

St. Mukasa Kiriwawanyu (d. 1886) was a servant of King Mwanga before being martyred for the faith. He is one of the Martyrs of Uganda.

Mummolinus Saint; Latin

St. Mummolinus (d. 686) was born in Constance, Switzerland. In his life, he lived at Luxeuil, St. Omer, Saint-Mommonlin, and Sithin. In 660, he became bishop of Noyon-Tournai.

Mummolus Saint; Latin

St. Mummolus (d. 678) was a Benedictine abbot of Fleury in France. He brought relics of Sts. Benedict and Scholastica from Monte Cassino to France.

Mun Saint; Scottish, Irish; mouth

St. Mun (fifth century) was a nephew of St. Patrick. He lived as a hermit in Lough Ree, Ireland.

Munchin Saint; Gaelic; little monk

Maincin

St. Munchin (seventh century), also known as Maincin, was the traditional founder of the church of Luimnech, which grew to become Limerick, Ireland. He is known as a patron of that city.

Mundus Saint; Latin; world

St. Mundus (d. 962) founded abbeys in Argyle, Scotland.

Mura Saint; Japanese; village

Muran

St. Mura (d. 645), also known as Muran, was abbot of Fahan in County Derry, Ireland. He was a follower of St. Columba.

Muran *see Mura*

Murtagh Saint; Gaelic; wealthy sailor

St. Murtagh (sixth century) was a member of the royal family of King Laoghaire. He was appointed bishop of Killala, Ireland, by St. Patrick, and later lived as a hermit on Inismurray Island.

Mutien Saint

St. Mutien-Marie Wiaux (1841–1917) was born in Mellet, Belgium, the son of a blacksmith. He took the name "Mutien" when he became a Christian Brother. He taught art and music at St. Bertuin's School in Maloone for fifty-eight years. At first, it was very difficult for him, but he persevered and became known as a model teacher. He was canonized by Pope John Paul II in 1989.

My *see Myron*

Mybrad Saint

St. Mybrad (sixth century) was a missionary in Cornwall, England.

Mydwyn Saint; Celtic

St. Mydwyn (second century) was sent by King St. Lucius to Pope St. Eleutherius to ask for missionaries in Briton. He was a companion of St. Elvan.

Myguel *see Miguel*

Myguele *see Miguel*

Myguell *see Miguel*

Myguelle *see Miguel*

Mykola Saint; Greek, Ukranian; victory of the people

Bl. Mykola Charnetsky, Bl. Mykola Conrad, Mykola Tsehelskyi

Bl. Mykola Charnetsky (1884–1959) was born in Samakivtsi, Horodensk District, Halychyna, Ukraine. He was ordained a Greek Catholic priest and earned a doctorate in dogmatic theology in Rome. He joined the Redemptorists. He was the apostolic exarch in Volyn and Pidlyashia during the Bolshevik occupation. He was arrested and sentenced to six years of labor in Siberia. He served eleven years and even after his release continued to be tortured. He is one of the martyrs killed under communist regimes in Eastern Europe and was beatified in 2001 by Pope John Paul II.

Myllin *see Moling*

Myran *see Myron*

Myron Saint; Greek; fragment ointment

Mehran, Mehrayan, My, Myran, Myrone

St. Myron (d. 250) was a bishop of Crete known as "the Wonder Worker." He lived to be one hundred years old.

Myrone *see Myron*

Myrope *see Myrope (girl's name)*

N

Nabor Saint; Hebrew; the prophet's light

St. Nabor (d. 303) was martyred in Milan, Italy.

Naethan *see Nathan*

Naethanael *see Nathanael*

Naethanial *see Nathanael*

Naethin *see Nathan*

Naethun *see Nathan*

Naethyn *see Nathan*

Nafanael *see Nathanael*

Nafanail *see Nathanael*

Nafanyl *see Nathanael*

Nafanyle *see Nathanael*

Naithan *see Nathan*

Naithanael *see Nathanael*

Naithanyael *see Nathanael*

Naithanyal *see Nathanael*

Naithin *see Nathan*

Naithon *see Nathan*

Naithun *see Nathan*

Naithyn *see Nathan*

Namphanion Saint; Greek, Latin; perfumed, aromatic

St. Namphanion (d. 180), known as "the Archmartyr," was born in Carthage and was martyred at Madaura, Numidia.

Namphasius Saint

St. Namphasius (eighth century) was a soldier and friend of Charlemagne. He then lived as a hermit at Marcillac, France.

Narcissus Saint; Greek; daffodil

Narkissos

St. Narcissus (d. 215) became bishop of Jerusalem when he was already a very old man. Falsely accused of a crime, he went to live as a hermit. After he was acquitted, he returned to his see and continued to serve for many more years. A miracle attributed to him is that he turned water into lamp oil so that Holy Saturday services could take place. St. Alexander of Cappadocia helped him rule the diocese toward the end of Narcissus's life. He died when he was 116.

Narcyz Saint; Polish

Bl. Narcyz Putz, Bl. Narcyz Turchan

Bl. Narcyz Putz (1877–1942) and Bl. Narcyz Turchan (1879–1942) were both Polish priests who were killed at the Dachau concentration camp. They are two of the 108 Polish Martyrs of World War II and were beatified by Pope John Paul II in 1999.

Nardo *see Bernardo*

Narkissos *see Narcissus*

Narnus Saint; Latin; he who was born in the Italian city of Narnia

St. Narnus (d. 345) was the first bishop of Bergamo, Italy.

Nasseus Saint

St. Nasseus (d. 329) was martyred at Renault, Algiers, by either Donatists or pagans.

Natalis Saint; Latin; born on Christmas day

St. Natalis (sixth century) was a follower of St. Columba and one of the founders of monasticism in Northern Ireland. He served as abbot of Naile, Daunhinis, and Cill.

Natan *see Nathan*

Natanael *see Nathanael*

Nataniele *see Nathanael*

Nate *see Nathan*

Nathan Old Testament; Top 100 Name; form of Nathaniel; Hebrew; gift of God

Naethan, Naethin, Naethun, Naethyn, Naithan, Naithin, Naithon, Naithun, Naithyn, Natan, Nate, Nathann, Nathean, Nathian, Nathin, Nathun, Nathyn, Natthan, Naythan, Naythun, Naythyn, Nethan

Nathan in the Bible was a prophet who lived in the time of King David. He reprimanded David for his relationship with Bathsheba. He also wrote histories of the reigns of King David and King Solomon. King David named one of his sons after him. His story is told in the books of Samuel, 1 and 2 Kings, and 2 Chronicles.

Nathanae *see Nathanael*

Nathanael Saint, New Testament; Hebrew; gift of God

Naethanael, Naethanial, Nafanael, Nafanail, Nafanyl, Nafanyle, Naithanael, Naithanyael, Naithanyal, Natanael, Nataniele, Nathanae, Nathanal, Nathaneal, Nathaneil, Nathanel, Nathaneol, Nathanual, Nathanyal, Natthanial, Natthanyal, Nayfanial, Naythaneal, Naythanial, Nithanial, Nithanyal, Nothanial, Nothanyal

St. Nathanael (first century), also known as Bartholomew, was one of the twelve apostles. After the Resurrection, he spread the faith in India and Greater Armenia. He was martyred by being flayed and beheaded.

Nathanal *see Nathanael*

Nathaneal *see Nathanael*

Nathaneil *see Nathanael*

Nathanel *see Nathanael*

Nathaneol *see Nathanael*

Nathann *see Nathan*

Nathanual *see Nathanael*

Nathanyal *see Nathanael*

Nathean *see Nathan*

Nathian *see Nathan*

Nathin *see Nathan*

Nathun *see Nathan*

Nathyn *see Nathan*

Natthan *see Nathan*

Natthanial *see Nathanael*

Natthanyal *see Nathanael*

Nayfanial *see Nathanael*

Naythan *see Nathan*

Naythaneal *see Nathanael*

Naythanial *see Nathanael*

Naythun *see Nathan*

Naythyn *see Nathan*

Nazarius Saint; Hebrew; dedicated to God

St. Nazarius (first century) was born to a pagan Roman army officer and a Christian mother. He was brought up as a Christian and evangelized in Milan with St. Celsus. He was martyred during the first persecution of Nero.

Neachtian Saint

St. Neachtian (fifth century) was a friend of St. Patrick.

Nebridius Saint; Greek; graceful like the fawn

St. Nebridius (sixth century) was bishop of Egara and then bishop of Barcelona. He was a Benedictine who was very knowledgable about the scriptures and wrote interpretations of them. He was a brother of Sts. Justus, Elpidius, and Justinian.

Nectan Saint; Scottish

St. Nectan (468–510) lived as a hermit in Devonshire, England. He founded churches in both Devonshire and Cornwall. He was beheaded by robbers. He may have been a son of King Brychan of Brecknock.

Nectarius Saint; Greek; he who sweetens life with nectar

St. Nectarius (fourth century) was born in Tarsus. The emperor chose him to become bishop of Constantinople even though he had not even been baptized. He was installed properly and, during his sixteen years as bishop, spoke out against Arianism.

Nelius *see Cornelius*

Nellie *see Cornelius*

Nelo *see Daniel*

Nemesius Saint; Latin; punishment of the gods

St. Nemesius, St. Nemesius of Alexandria

St. Nemesius (d. 260) was a Roman military tribune who was converted to the faith by Pope St. Stephen I. He served as a deacon in Rome and became the father of St. Lucilla. He was beheaded during the persecutions of Valerian.

Nennus Saint

St. Nennus (sixth century) was from Ireland. He served as abbot of monasteries on the isles of Arran and Bute.

Nenzo *see Lorenzo*

Neol Saint; Latin, French; day of birth, Christmas

St. Neol Chabanel (1613–1649) was a Jesuit who served as a professor of rhetoric at several colleges. In 1643, he went to New France as a missionary to work among the native peoples. He was assigned to the mission at Sainte-Marie and worked with Fr. Charles Garnier. He was martyred by a Huron and is considered one of the North American Martyrs.

Neopolus Saint; form of Napoleon; Spanish; lion of the woodland

St. Neopolus (third century) was martyred in Alexandria during the reign of Emperor Diocletian.

Neot Saint; Celtic; good swimmer

St. Neot (d. 870) was a relative of King Alfred the Great. He lived as a monk in Glastonbury, England, and was ordained a priest. He then went to live as a hermit in Cornwall.

Nepotian Saint

St. Nepotian (fourth century) was a bishop of Clermont.

Nereus Saint; Greek; sea traveler

St. Nereus (first century) was a soldier in the Roman army who helped persecute Christians. He converted to the faith and left the army. He was later martyred.

Nerses Saint; Greek; from Nersae, an ancient city

St. Nerses, St. Nerses Glaietsi, St. Nerses Lambronazi, St. Nerses the Great

St. Nerses the Great (d. 373) was educated in Cappadocia. He was the father of St. Isaac the Great. King Arshak III exiled him, and he was later poisoned by King Pap.

Nestor Saint; Greek; traveler, wise

St. Nestor (fourth century) was martyred in Thassolonika during the persecutions of Emperor Diocletian.

Nethan *see Nathan*

Nicanor Saint; Greek; victorious

St. Nicanor (first century) was one of the seven deacons of Jerusalem chosen by the apostles. He later traveled to Cyprus, where he was martyred.

Nicasio *see Nicasius*

Nicasius Saint; Greek; victory

Nicasio

St. Nicasius, St. Nicasius Jonson

St. Nicasius (d. 451) was a bishop of Rheims, France. He had a vision that the barbarians would invade the area. When that vision came true, he tried to slow their attack so that his parishioners could escape. He was beheaded in the doorway of his church.

Niccolas *see Nicholas*

Niceforo Saint; Greek; he who brings victory

Bl. Niceforo of Jesus and Mary (1893–1936) was the Provincial Superior of the Passionists. He was one of the Passionist Martyrs of Daimiel who were killed during the Spanish Civil War. He was beatified by Pope John Paul II in 1989.

Nicephorus Saint; Greek; he who brings victory

St. Nicephorus, St. Nicephorus, Presbyter at Tiberiopolis

St. Nicephorus (d. 829) was the son of a secretary of Emperor Constantine V. He was chosen to be an imperial commissioner. He founded a monastery near the Black Sea and then was named to the office of patriarch of Constantinople. In that capacity, he fought against the iconoclasts, which ultimately led to his being exiled to the monastery he had founded.

Nicetas Saint; Greek; victorious

St. Nicetas, St. Nicetus of Pereaslav, St. Nicetas of Remesiana, St. Nicetus of Trier

St. Nicetas of Remesiana (fourth century) was a friend of St. Paulinus of Nola. He served as a missionary bishop in Decia. He wrote many theological works and may have written the famous hymn *Te Deum*.

Nichalas *see Nicholas*

Nichelas *see Nicholas*

Nichlas *see Nicholas*

Nichlos *see Nicholas*

Nicholaes *see Nicholas*

Nicholaos *see Nicholas*

Nicholas Saint; Top 100 Name; Greek; victorious people

Klaas, Klas, Niccolas, Nichalas, Nichelas, Nichele, Nichlas, Nichlos, Nichola, Nicholaes, Nicholaos, Nicholase, Nichole, Nicholias, Nicholl, Nichollas, Nicholus, Nikolai, Nikos, Niocol, Nycholas

St. Nicholas, St. Nicholas Chrysoberges, St. Nicholas Factor, St. Nicholas I, V, St. Nicholas Owen, St. Nicholas Peregrinus, St. Nicholas Pieck, St. Nicholas Poppel, St. Nicholas Studites, St. Nicholas Tavigli, St. Nicholas vin Flue

St. Nicholas (d. 346) was a bishop of Myra, Lycia. He was known for his generosity to the poor. One of the most famous stories regarding him is that in order to stop a poor man from selling his daughters into prostitution, he threw three bags of gold through the window. This helped inspire his association with Santa Claus. He is also credited with helping to save a ship that was being threatened by a strong storm. For this reason, he is considered a patron saint of sailors.

Nicholase *see Nicholas*

Nicholias *see Nicholas*

Nichollas *see Nicholas*

Nicholus *see Nicholas*

Nick *see Dominic*

Nicodem *see Nicodemus*

Nicodemius *see Nicodemus*

Nicodemus Saint, New Testament; Greek; conquerer of the people

Nicodem, Nicodemius, Nikodem, Nikodema, Nikodemious, Nikodemo, Nikodim

St. Nicodemus (first century) was a member of the Sanhedrin during the life of Jesus. John 3:1–21 tells how he met with Jesus at night to be taught by him. He helped St. Joseph of Arimathea place Jesus' body in the tomb after the crucifixion. According to tradition, he was martyred, but no details are known.

Nicolas Saint; form of Nicholas; Italian; victorious people

Bl. Nicolas Bunkerd Kitbamrung, Bl. Nicolas da Gesturi, St. Nicholas of Tolentino

Bl. Nicolas Bunkerd Kitbamrung (1895–1944) was born in Sam Phran, Nakhon Pathom, Thailand. He was ordained a priest for the archdiocese of Bangkok. He served as a missionary in Vietnam. He was accused of spying for the French and was arrested. He ministered to the other prisoners and baptized at least sixty-eight people before dying from tuberculosis coupled with the hardships of prison life. He was beatified in 2000 by Pope John Paul II.

Nicolaus Saint; form of Nicholas; Italian; victorious people

Bl. Nicolaus (Niels) Stensen (1638–1686) was born in Denmark to a Lutheran family. He was a scientist who made important discoveries in geology and stratigraphy. He converted to Catholicism and decided to become a priest. He played an active role in the Counter-Reformation in Northern Germany. He was beatified by Pope John Paul II in 1988.

Nicomedes Saint; Greek; he who prepares the victories

St. Nicomedes (first century) was a priest from Rome who was martyred for helping persecuted Christians and providing them with a Christian burial.

Nicon Saint; Greek; the victorious one

St. Nicon (d. 250) was a Roman soldier who converted to Christianity while traveling in Palestine. He attempted to lead two hundred Christians to Sicily in order to avoid persecution, but they were all captured and martyred.

Nicostratus Saint; Greek; the general who leads the victory

St. Nicostratus (third century) was a leader of a cohort of Roman soldiers. He was martyred in Caesarea, Palestine, during the reign of Emperor Diocletian.

Nidan *see Midan*

Nikodem *see Nicodemus*

Nikodema *see Nicodemus*

Nikodemious *see Nicodemus*

Nikodemo *see Nicodemus*

Nikodim *see Nicodemus*

Nikolai *see Nicholas*

Nikolaus Saint; form of Nicholas; Greek; victorious people

Bl. Nikolaus Gross (1898–1945) was born in Niederwenigern, Germany. He was a miner and became the director of the Catholic Workers' Movement newspaper. He opposed Nazism and was declared an enemy of the state. His newspaper was shut down, but he continued to publish anyway. He was arrested for treason and killed. He was beatified by Pope John Paul II in 2001.

Nikos *see Nicholas*

Nilus Saint; Greek

St. Nilus the Elder, St. Nilus the Younger

St. Nilus the Elder (d. 430) was a member of the imperial court at Constantinople, but he left that life to become a monk on Mount Sinai along with his son, Theodulus. After his son was kidnapped by Arab raiders and Nilus was successful in finding him, both father and son became priests. Nilus later served as bishop of Ancyra.

Nimatullah Saint; Lebanese; blessing of God

St. Nimatullah al-Hardini (1808–1858) was born in Hardin, Lebanon. A priest of the Maronite Church, he was known as a miracle worker and as one who had visions of the future. He saved his students by asking them to move immediately before a wall would have fallen on them. He also saved some cows from a barn collapse and cured an altar boy of sickness. He was canonized by Pope John Paul II in 2004.

Ninian Saint; Gaelic

St. Ninian (360–432) was the son of a Christian chieftain of the Cumbrian Britons. He studied under Pope St. Damasus I in Rome for fifteen years. He became a priest and a bishop and then returned home to Briton to evangelize. He helped establish the Church in Scotland. He built the White House Monastery, now known as Whithorn Abbey. He was known as a miracle worker.

Nino *see Nina (girl's names)*

Niocol *see Nicholas*

Nissen Saint; Hebrew; sign, omen, miracle

St. Nissen (fifth century) was converted by St. Patrick and became abbot of Mountgarret Monastery in Wexford.

Nithanial *see Nathanael*

Nithanyal *see Nathanael*

Nithard Saint; German; brave, hardy, anger, envy

St. Nithard (ninth century) was a monk at Corbie, Saxony. He became a companion of St. Ansgar and served with him, preaching in Scandinavia. He was martyred.

Nivard Saint

Nivo

St. Nivard (seventh century), also known as Nivo, was bishop of Rheims. He restored Haut-villiers Abbey. He was also the brother-in-law of King Childeric II of Austrasia.

Nivo *see Nivard*

Noach *see Noah*

Noah Old Testament; Top 100 Name; Hebrew; peaceful, restful

Noach, Noak

Noah in the Bible was a faithful man in a time of evil. When God decided to destroy the world by a flood, he instructed Noah to build an ark to save his family and the animals. His story is told in the book of Genesis.

Noak *see Noah*

Noe Saint; Hebrew, Spanish; quiet, peaceful

St. Noe Mawaggali (d. 1886) was a potter in Uganda. He was arrested during the persecutions of King Mwanga and was martyred by being stabbed with a spear and torn apart by wild dogs. He is one of the Martyrs of Uganda.

Nollie *see Oliver*

Nonossus Saint

St. Nonossus (d. 560) was a Benedictine monk who lived at Mt. Soracte, near Rome.

Norbert Saint; Scandinavian; brilliant hero

Bert, Norberto, Norburt, Norbyrt, Northbert, Northburt, Northbyrt

St. Norbert (1080–1134) served as an almoner for Emperor Henry V. He felt becoming a priest was a good career move and joined the Benedictines at Siegberg. After he nearly died, he experienced a conversion. He became a wandering preacher and founded a community of Augustinian canons that became known as the Norbertines of Premonstratensians.

Norberto *see Norbert*

Norburt *see Norbert*

Norbyrt *see Norbert*

Northbert *see Norbert*

Northburt *see Norbert*

Northbyrt *see Norbert*

Nothanial *see Nathanael*

Nothanyal *see Nathanael*

Nothlem Saint; English

St. Nothlem (d. 739) was a priest in London who later became archbishop of Canterbury. He compiled research on the history of Kent, which was later used by Venerable Bede when he wrote his Ecclesiastical History.

Novatus Saint; Latin; new

St. Novatus (d. 151) was the son of the Roman senator Pudens and the brother of Sts. Praxedes and Pudentiana.

Numerian Saint; Latin; one who enumerates

St. Numerian (d. 666) was a Benedictine monk at Remiremont Monastery at Trier, Germany.

Numidicus Saint; Greek, Latin; from Numidia, Africa

St. Numidicus (third century) was burned at the stake in Carthage. According to tradition, he survived this and went on to be ordained by St. Cyprian of Carthage.

Nuno Saint; Basque; monk

St. Nuno Alvares Pereira (1360–1431) was a constable of the kingdom of Portugal. He served as a knight and prior of the Order of St. John of Jerusalem. He married and fought as a soldier for Portuguese independence. After his wife died, he became a lay brother in the Order of Friars of the Bl. Virgin Mary of Mount Carmel. He later founded a monastery in Lisbon. He was canonized in 2009 by Pope Benedict XVI.

Nycholas *see Nicholas*

O

Oalo *see Paul*

Obed Old Testament; Hebrew; a servant, workman

Obed in the Bible was the son of Boaz and Ruth, the father of Jesse, and grandfather of King David. He is an ancestor of Jesus.

Obitius Saint; Latin; departure, encounter

St. Obitius (1150–1204) was a knight in Brescia, Italy. He was married and had four children. When he nearly drowned, he experienced a vision of hell which convinced him to dedicate his life to God. Despite resistance from his family, he became a Benedictine monk and spent his life doing penance and working for nuns in his hometown.

Oceanis *see Oceanus*

Oceanos *see Oceanus*

Oceanous *see Oceanus*

Oceanus Saint; Greek; ocean

Oceanis, Oceanos, Oceanous, Oceanys

St. Oceanus (d. 310) was martyred by being burned at the stake during the persecutions of Emperor Maximian Herculeus.

Oceanys *see Oceanus*

Octavee *see Octavian*

Octavey *see Octavian*

Octavian Saint; Latin; eighth

Octavee, Octavey, Octavia, Octavio, Octavous, Octavus, Octavyos, Octavyous, Octavyus, Ottavio, Ottavios, Ottavious, Ottavius, Tavey

St. Octavian (d. 484) was an archdeacon of Carthage who was martyred by the Arian Vandals.

Octavio *see Octavian*

Octavius Saint; Latin; eighth

St. Octavius (d. 297) was martyred at Turin, Italy.

Octavous *see Octavian*

Octavus *see Octavian*

Octavyos *see Octavian*

Octavyous *see Octavian*

Octavyus *see Octavian*

Odhran Saint; Gaelic; pale

Oran, Otteran

St. Odhran (d. 563), also known as Otteran and Oran, was from Ireland and served as abbot of Meath. He traveled as a missionary to Scotland with St. Columba. He died at Lona.

Odhrán *see Odran*

Odilo Saint; German; fortunate, prosperous

St. Odilo (962–1049) was born into a noble French family. He became a monk at Cluny and a few years later was named abbot, a position he would hold until his death. He was a proponent of the Truce of God, which suspended military hostilities for religious reasons. He also instituted the feast now known as All Souls' Day. He was offered the archbishopric of Lyon, but turned it down.

Odo Saint; form of Otto; Norwegian; rich

St. Odo, St. Odo of Beauvais, St. Odo of Urgell, St. Odo the Good

St. Odo (870–959) was born to a noble pagan Danish family. He converted and became a Benedictine monk. He served as bishop of Rambury, Wessex, England, and later served as archbishop of Canterbury. He was an advisor to King Edmund and King Edgar.

Odon *see Otto*

Odran Saint; Gaelic; pale green

Odhrán, Odren, Odrin, Odryn

St. Odran (d. 452) drove St. Patrick's chariot. A pagan chieftain vowed to kill Patrick. Odran overheard the plot and changed places with Patrick in the chariot so that he was killed instead.

Odren *see Odran*

Odrian Saint; Gaelic; pale

St. Odrian (fifth century) was a bishop of Waterford, Ireland.

Odrin *see Odran*

Odryn *see Odran*

Odulf Saint; German; prosperous wolf

St. Odulf (d. 855) was born in Oorsch, North Brabant. He became an Augustinian canon and was ordained. He served as a missionary to Friesland, where he established a church and founded a monastery at Stavoren.

Oduvald Saint; German

St. Oduvald (d. 695) was the abbot of Melrose in Scotland.

Óengus *see Aengus*

Ogmund Saint; Norse; young protector

St. Ogmund (d. 1121), also known as Jon Helgi Ogmundarson, was an evangelist in Iceland. He served as the first bishop of Holar, Iceland.

Olaf Saint; Scandinavian; ancestor

Olaff, Olafur, Olaph, Olav, Ole, Olef, Olen, Olof, Oluf, Olyn

St. Olaf, St. Olaf of Norway, St. Olaf of Sweden

St. Olaf of Norway (995–1164) was the son of the king of Norway. He was a Viking pirate before converting to Christianity. He then helped Ethelred of England fight against pagan Danish invaders. He became king of Norway and invited missionaries to come and evangelize his people. The people did not want the faith thrust upon them, and Olaf was exiled to Russia. He fought to retake the throne, but was killed in battle.

Olaff *see Olaf*

Olafur *see Olaf*

Olaph *see Olaf*

Olav *see Olaf*

Olcan *see Bolcan*

Ole *see Olaf*

Olef *see Olaf*

Olegari *see Ollegarius*

Oleksiy Saint; Ukranian; defending men, warrior

Bl. Oleksiy Zarytsky (1912–1963) was born in Bilche, Lviv District, Ukraine. He was ordained a priest and became pastor of the archeparchy of Lviv for the Ukrainians. He was arrested and sent to a labor camp. He died at the labor camp of Karaganda. He was beatified by Pope John Paul II in 2001.

Olen *see Olaf*

Olivar *see Oliver*

Oliver Saint; Top 100 Name; Latin, Scandinavian; olive tree, kind, affectionate

Nollie, Olivar, Oliverio, Olivier, Olivio, Ollivar, Olliver, Ollivor, Ollyvar, Ollyver, Ollyvir, Ollyvyr, Olvan, Olven, Olvin, Olyvar

St. Oliver, St. Oliver Plunkett

St. Oliver Plunkett (1629–1681) was born in Loughcrew in County Meath, Ireland. He was ordained a priest at the Propaganda College in Rome. There was religious persecution going on in Ireland, so he remained in Rome teaching until 1669, when he was named archbishop of Armagh. In 1673, he was forced to go into hiding. He continued to encourage his people via letter until it was safe for him to return. He was arrested, falsely accused of treason, and sentenced to death. He is a patron of peace and reconciliation in Ireland.

Oliverio *see Oliver*

Olivier *see Oliver*

Olivio *see Oliver*

Ollegarius Saint; English; very diligent

Olegari

St. Ollegarius (1060–1137), also known as Olegari, was born in Barcelona, Spain, the son of Visigoth parents. He entered the Augustinian canons and became prior at St. Aidan's Monastery. He became bishop of Barcelona and then archbishop of Tarragona. He helped rebuild that area after it had been attacked by the Moors and promoted the works of the Knights Templar. He attended the First Lateran Council in 1123 and was made a papal legate by Pope Callistus II.

Ollivar *see Oliver*

Olliver *see Oliver*

Ollivor *see Oliver*

Ollyvar *see Oliver*

Ollyver *see Oliver*

Ollyvir *see Oliver*

Ollyvyr *see Oliver*

Olof *see Olaf*

Oluf *see Olaf*

Olvan *see Oliver*

Olven *see Oliver*

Olvin *see Oliver*

Olympiades Saint; Greek; heavenly

St. Olympiades (d.303) was martyred at Almira, Italy, during the persecutions of Emperor Diocletian.

Olympius Saint; Greek; heavenly

St. Olympius (d. 343) was bishop of Enos, in Rumelia, and fought Arianism. As a result, Emperor Constantius II removed him from his see.

Olyn *see Olaf*

Olyvar *see Oliver*

Omeer *see Omer*

Omeljan Saint; Ukranian

Bl. Omeljan Kove (1884–1944) was born near Kosiv, Ukraine. He was a married Greek Catholic priest and a father of six.

He organized pilgrimages and youth groups and cared for the poor and orphaned. To help save Jews during the Nazi invasion, he began baptizing them and listing them as Christians. He was arrested for this and sent to the Majdanek concentration camp, where he was gassed and burned. He was beatified by Pope John Paul II in 2001.

Omer Saint; form of Omar; Arabic, Hebrew; reverent

Omeer, Omero

St. Omer (595–670) was born near Constance, France. He entered Luxeuil Monastery. Twenty years later, he was named bishop of Therouanne. As bishop, he cared for the sick and poor. He also founded the monastery of Sithiu.

Omero *see Omer*

Oncho Saint

Onchuo

St. Oncho (d. 600) was from Ireland. He was known as a poet and pilgrim who was dedicated to preserving Celtic traditions, especially the relics of Irish saints. He died at Clonmore Monastery.

Onchuo *see Oncho*

Onek *see Otto*

Onesimus Saint; Greek; useful, worthwhile

St. Onesimus (d. 361) was bishop of Soissons, France, the successor of Sts. Crepinus and Crepinianus.

Onesiphorus Saint, New Testament; Greek; bears much fruit

St. Onesiphorus (d. 81) is mentioned in St. Paul's letters to Timothy (1 Timothy 1:16–18 and 2 Timothy 4:19). He and Porphyrius traveled to Spain and were martyred by being tied to wild horses and torn apart.

Onouphrius Saint; Greek; he who is continuingly good

St. Onouphrius (fourth century) was a monk at a monastery near Thebes, which he left in order to become a desert hermit. He lived as a hermit for over sixty years.

Onufry Saint; form of Humphrey; Polish; peaceful strength

Bl. Onufry Wasyluk (1853–1894) was one of the Martyrs of Podlasie killed by Russian soldiers. He was beatified by Pope John Paul II in 1996.

Optatian Saint; Latin; desired

St. Optatian (d. 550) was bishop of Brescia, Italy.

Optatus Saint; Latin; desired

St. Optatus of Milevis (d. 387) was a Christian convert. He became bishop of Milevis, Numidia, in Africa. He wrote six treatises against Donatism.

Oran *see Odhran*

Ordonius Saint; Latin

St. Ordonius (d.1066) was a monk at Sahagiin, Leon, Spain. He later was named bishop of Astorga.

Orentius Saint; Latin

St. Orentius (d. 439) was a hermit who lived near Tarbes, France. He later served as bishop of Auch for forty years.

Orest *see Orestes*

Oreste *see Orestes*

Orestes Saint; Greek; mountain man

Aresty, Orest, Oreste

St. Orestes (d. 304) was martyred in Cappadocia during the persecutions of Emperor Diocletian.

Oriculus Saint; Latin

St. Oriculus (d. 430) was martyred in Carthage, Africa, by Arian vandals.

Ormande *see Ormond*

Ormon *see Ormond*

Ormond Saint; English; bear mountain, spear protector

Armand, Ormande, Ormon, Ormonde, Ormondo, Ormundy

St. Ormond (sixth century), also known as Armand, was abbot of Saint Maire. He was active in monastic expansion and evangelization.

Ormonde *see Ormond*

Ormondo *see Ormond*

Ormundy *see Ormond*

Orsisius Saint; Latin

St. Orsisius (d. 380) was a hermit who served as the head of the cenobites at Tabennisi. He was a writer. St. Jerome translated his treatise on ascetical theology into Latin.

Osimund *see Osmund*

Osman *see Osmund*

Osmand *see Osmund*

Osmond *see Osmund*

Osmonde *see Osmund*

Osmondo *see Osmund*

Osmont *see Osmund*

Osmonte *see Osmund*

Osmund Saint; English; divine protector

> *Osimund, Osman, Osmand, Osmond, Osmonde, Osmondo, Osmont, Osmonte, Osmunde, Osmundo, Osmunt, Osmunte, Ozment*

St. Osmund (d. 1099) was born in Seez, Normandy, France, the son of the count of Seez. He later became count as well. He was part of the force that invaded England under the direction of William the Conqueror in 1066. He helped prepare the Domesday Book, which analyzed the resources of England. He later became bishop of Salisbury, England. He is a patron of mentally ill and paralyzed people.

Osmunde *see Osmund*

Osmundo *see Osmund*

Osmunt *see Osmund*

Osmunte *see Osmund*

Ostwald *see Oswald*

Oswal *see Oswald*

Oswald Saint; English; God's power

> *Ostwald, Oswal, Oswaldo, Oswall, Oswalt, Oswel, Osweld, Oswell, Oswold*

St. Oswald (d. 992) was born a Dane but studied in Fleury, France. He became bishop of Worcester, England. During his tenure, he built many monasteries, including the Abbey of Ramsey in Huntingdonshire. He later was named archbishop of York. Together with Sts. Dunstan and Ethwelwold, he is considered one of the three saints who brought English monasticism back to life.

Oswaldo *see Oswald*

Oswall *see Oswald*

Oswalt *see Oswald*

Oswel *see Oswald*

Osweld *see Oswald*

Oswell *see Oswald*

Oswold *see Oswald*

Otek *see Otto*

Otello *see Otto*

Otfried *see Otto*

Othmar Saint; Turkish; ruler, servant of God

St. Othmar (689–759) was a Benedictine monk who served as abbot of the Abbey of St. Gall in Switzerland. He also established a monastery school at that location, as well as an almshouse and hospital. He was exiled to the small island of Werd in Lake Constance after being falsely accused.

Otho *see Otto*

Othon *see Otto*

Otik *see Otto*

Otilio *see Otto*

Otman *see Otto*

Oto *see Otto*

Otoe *see Otto*

Otow *see Otto*

Ottavio *see Octavian*

Ottavios *see Octavian*

Ottavious *see Octavian*

Ottavius *see Octavian*

Otteran *see Odhran*

Otto Saint; German; rich

> *Odo, Odon, Onek, Otek, Otello, Otfried, Otho, Othon, Otik, Otilio, Otman, Oto, Otoe, Otow, Otton, Ottone*
>
> St. Otto of Bamberg (1060–1139) was born to a noble family in Swabia. He served Emperor Henry V in various capacities, although he disagreed with the emperor's position regarding the pope. Otto was appointed bishop of Bamberg and worked to reconcile the emperor and the pope. King Boleslav of Poland asked him to lead a missionary effort to Pomerania. He was successful and is known as the Apostle of Pomerania.

Otton *see Otto*

Ottone *see Otto*

Oudaceus Saint

> St. Oudaceus (d. 615) was raised in Wales. He became a monk and then abbot of Llandeilo Fawr, Carmarthenshire. He was later named a bishop and is one of the four saints to whom the cathedral of Llandaff, Wales, is dedicated.

Ouen Saint; French; young warrior, well born

> St. Ouen (609–686) was born at Sancy, France, the son of St. Authaire. He served King Clotaire II and was chancellor for Dogobert I and Clovis II. He was ordained and became archbishop of Rouen. He was a great supporter of education and missionary activities. He also brokered a peace treaty between Neustria and Austrasia.

Ovyn *see Ivan*

Owain *see Owen*

Owaine *see Owen*

Owan *see Owen*

Owayn *see Owen*

Owayne *see Owen*

Owen Saint; Top 100 Name; Gaelic, Welsh; born to nobility, young warrior

> *Eoin, Owain, Owaine, Owan, Owayn, Owayne, Owens, Owin, Owine, Owon, Owone, Owyn, Owyne*
>
> St. Owen (d. 680) was a steward in the household of St. Etheldreda. He later became a monk at Lastingham, England, where St. Chad was serving as abbot. Owen followed St. Chad to Litchfield.

Owens *see Owen*

Owin *see Owen*

Owine *see Owen*

Owon *see Owen*

Owone *see Owen*

Owyn *see Owen*

Owyne *see Owen*

Ozment *see Osmund*

P

Paavel *see Pavel*

Pabiali Saint

St. Pabiali (fifth or sixth century) was a descendant of a Welsh king. A chapel in Wales is named for him.

Pabo Saint; Spanish; small, humble

St. Pabo (d. 510) was a warrior who renounced that life to become the founder of a monastery in Anglesey, Scotland.

Pachomius Saint; St. Pachomius, St. Pachomius (Bidjimi), St. Pachomius the Younger

St. Pachomius (292–348) was born in Egypt and served in the emperor's army. He was so impressed by the kindness that Christians at Thebes exhibited that he converted after he left the army. He became the disciple of an anchorite, Palemon. The two lived an extremely austere life. They later built a monastery at Tabbennisi. Soon, many men joined him. During his life, he opened ten monasteries and two convents. He was the first monk to establish a rule of life for those in the monasteries.

Pacian Saint; Latin; belonging to the peace

St. Pacian (310–390) was bishop of Barcelona, Spain. He wrote on many topics, including ecclesiastical discipline, Baptism, papal supremacy, and penance.

Pacificus *see Patto*

Padarn Saint; Latin, Welsh; fatherly

Paternus

St. Padarn (490–550), also known as Paternus, was from France. He traveled to Wales, where he founded a monastery at Llanbadarn Fawr. He became that area's first bishop. He was known for his life of prayer and self-denial and for spreading the faith throughout the area.

Padraig *see Patrick*

Paduinus Saint

St. Paduinus (d. 703) became a Benedictine monk at St. Vincent's near Le Mans, France. He later served as abbot of St. Mary's Abbey.

Pafnucy *see Paphnutius*

Paganus Saint; Latin; country dweller, rustic

St. Paganus (d. 1423) was a Benedictine monk at a monastery in Sicily who later left to become a hermit.

Pakelika *see Patrick*

Palaemon Saint; Greek; sea god

Palemon

St. Palaemon (d. 325), also known as Palemon, was an Egyptian hermit. Together with his disciple St. Pachomius, he established a monastery at Tabennisi.

Paldo Saint

St. Paldo (eighth century) and his brothers, Sts. Tato and Taso, became monks at Fara in Sabina, Italy. They later established the Monastery of San Vincenzo, where each took a turn serving as abbot.

Palemon *see Palaemon*

Palladius Saint; Greek

St. Palladius (d. 661) served as abbot of St. Germanus in Auxerre, France, until he became bishop of the city. He also founded monasteries in the area.

Palmatius Saint; Latin; adorned with palm leaves

St. Palmatius (d. 287) was martyred in Trier, Germany, during the reign of Emperor Diocletian.

Pambo Saint

Panbis

St. Pambo (d. 375), also known as Panbis, was a disciple of St. Anthony. He then became a hermit in the Nitrian Desert. Many traveled to seek his counsel. St. Melania the Elder was with him when he died.

Pammachius Saint

St. Pammachius (d. 409) was a Roman senator who was married to St. Paula's daughter Paulina. After his wife died, he devoted his life to caring for the poor and sick. He opened the first hospice for pilgrims in Rome and set up a church in his home. He was also a frequent correspondent with St. Jerome—the two debated many topics.

Pamphilus Saint; Greek; friend of everyone

St. Pamphilus (d. 309) was a biblical scholar who studied at the Catechetical School of Alexandria. After he was ordained at Caesarea, he became the head of a school there which became known for its library. One of his students was the historian Eusebius. He was arrested for being a Christian and was beheaded after spending two years in prison.

Panbis *see Pambo*

Pancharius Saint

St. Pancharius (d. 303) was a Roman senator who served Coemperor Maximian. At first, he denied his faith or kept it hidden, but then, after his mother and sister encouraged him, he acknowledged he was a Christian and was beheaded at Nicomedia.

Pancras Saint; Greek; all powerful

Pancratius, Pancrazio

St. Pancras (d. 304) was an orphan who was brought up by his uncle in Rome. He was beheaded when he was fourteen years old during the persecutions of Emperor Diocletian. St. Augustine of Canterbury, England, dedicated his first church to him.

Pancratius *see Pancras*

Pancrazio *see Pancras*

Pandonio *see Pandwyna (girl's name)*

Pantaenus Saint; Greek

St. Pantaenus (d. 200) was a Stoic philosopher who taught

in Alexandria. After he converted to Christianity, he tried to reconcile the faith with Greek thought. He became head of the catechectical school in Alexandria. He may also have traveled to India or Ethiopia as a missionary.

Pantaleon Saint; Greek; lion

St. Pantaleon (275–303) was from Nicomedia, near the Black Sea in Asia. A famous doctor, he provided medical care to the emperor. He was Christian, but under pagan influence abandoned his faith. A priest named Hermolaos pointed out the error of his ways, and Pantaleon repented. He dedicated his life to caring for sick and poor without expecting any payment. He was tortured and martyred during the persecutions of Emperor Diocletian.

Paolo Saint; form of Paul; Italian; small

Bl. Paolo Manna (1872–1952) was born in Avellino, Italy. He studied at the Gregorian University in Rome and was ordained in Milan. He served as a missionary to Burma until ill health forced him to return to Italy. He founded the Missionary Union of the Clergy and Sacred Heart Seminary and helped found the Missionary Sisters of the Immaculate. He was beatified by Pope John Paul II in 1989.

Paphnutius Saint; Egyptian; man of God

Pafnucy

St. Paphnutius (fourth century) was an Egyptian who lived as a hermit for many years before becoming bishop of Upper Thebaid. During the persecutions of Emperor Maximinus, he lost an eye and was sent to work in the mines. After peace was restored, he returned to his flock. He fought against the Arian heresy and attended the Nicaean Council. Although he was celibate, he fought against clerical celibacy and felt that men should only be forbidden to marry after ordination.

Papias Saint; Greek; venerable father

St. Papias (d. 250) was a shepherd who was martyred in Pamphylia, Asia Minor, during the persecutions of Emperor Trajanus Decius.

Papinianus Saint; Latin

St. Papinianus (fifth century) was a bishop in Africa who was martyred by the Arian Vandal King Geiseric.

Papulus Saint; Latin; a nation

St. Papulus (d. 300) was a priest who evangelized in southern Gaul. He was martyred during the persecutions of Emperor Diocletian.

Paramon Saint; Latin; important

St. Paramon (d. 250) was one of the 375 martyrs who were put to death on the same day during the persecutions of Emperor Trajanus Decius.

Paras *see Paris*

Pardulphus Saint; German; brave warrior

St. Pardulphus (657–737) was from Limoges, France. He became a Benedictine monk at Gueret and later served as abbot. When the monastery was attacked by Arabs, the other monks left, but he remained behind and continued to pray. The monastery was spared.

Paree *see Paris*

Pares *see Paris*

Parese *see Paris*

Parie *see Paris*

Paris Saint; Greek; lover

Paras, Paree, Pares, Parese, Parie, Parys

St. Paris (d. 346) was a bishop of Teano, Italy.

Parisio *see Parisius*

Parisius Saint; form of Paris; Greek; lover

Parisio

St. Parisius (1160–1267), also known as Parisio, was from Italy. After he was ordained a priest, he served as chaplain and spiritual director to the Camaldolese nuns of St. Christina Convent at Treviso. He was known to have the gift of prophecy and to perform miracles.

Parmenas Saint; Greek; he that abides

St. Parmenas (d. 98) was one of seven deacons appointed by the apostles to work with the Hellenized Jews of Jerusalem. He preached in Asia Minor and was martyred in Philippi, Macedonia.

Parmenius Saint; Greek; he that abides

St. Parmenius (d. 250) was a priest who was martyred near Babylon during the persecutions of Emperor Trajanus Decius.

Parthenius Saint; Greek; virgin

St. Parthenius (third century) served as a eunuch in the court of Emperor Trajanus Decius. He was accused of embezzlement and of being a Christian. He defended the faith and was martyred by being beaten with flaming brands.

Parys *see Paris*

Pascal *see Paschal*

Pascale *see Paschal*

Pascall *see Paschal*

Pascalle *see Paschal*

Paschal Saint; Hebrew, French; having to do with Easter or Passover

Pascal, Pascale, Pascall, Pascalle, Paschalis, Pasco, Pascoe, Pascoli, Pascow, Pascual

St. Paschal, St. Paschal Baylon

St. Paschal Baylon (1540–1592) was born in Aragon, where he worked as a shepherd. Even as a child, he was known to perform miracles and live an austere life.

He became a Franciscan lay brother and worked as a door-keeper. He had a deep love of the Eucharist and defended the doctrine of the Real Presence against a Calvinist preacher. He is a patron saint of Eucharistic congresses and associations.

Paschalis *see Paschal*

Pascharius Saint; Hebrew, Latin; relating to Easter

Pasquier

St. Pascharius (d. 680), also known as Pasquier, was bishop of Nantes, France. He also founded the Abbey of Andre.

Paschasius Saint; Hebrew, Latin; relating to Easter

St. Paschasius, St. Paschasius Radbertus

St. Paschasius (d. 312) was a bishop of Vienne, France.

Pasco *see Paschal*

Pascoe *see Paschal*

Pascoli *see Paschal*

Pascow *see Paschal*

Pascual *see Paschal*

Pasko *see Paul*

Pasquier *see Pascharius*

Pastar *see Pastor*

Paster *see Pastor*

Pastir *see Pastor*

Pastor Saint; Latin; spiritual leader

Pastar, Paster, Pastir, Pastyr

St. Pastor (d. 311) was martyred at Nicomedia.

Pastyr *see Pastor*

Pat *see Patrick*

Patapius Saint; Greek

St. Patapius (fourth century) was from Egypt but traveled to Constantinople, where he lived as a hermit.

Paterius Saint; Greek; born in Pateria

St. Paterius (d. 606) was a monk from Rome. He was later named bishop of Brescia, Italy. He was also a friend of Pope Gregory the Great.

Patermuthius Saint

St. Patermuthius (d. 363) was an Egyptian hermit who was martyred with Alexander, a converted Roman soldier.

Paternian Saint; Latin; belonging to the father

Paterniano

St. Paternian (275–360) was a bishop of Fano, Italy, who escaped the persecutions of Emperor Diocletian by hiding in the mountains.

Paterniano *see Paternian*

Paternus Saint; Latin; belonging to the father

St. Paternus (482–565) was born in Poitiers, Poitou. His father left the family to become a her-mit in Ireland. Paternus lived as a monk at Marnes Abbey in France. He then traveled to Wales, where he founded Llan-patenvaur Monastery before becoming a hermit himself.

Patiens Saint; Latin; patient

St. Patiens (d. 491) was arch-bishop of Lyones, Gaul. He was known for his charity to the poor and for rebuilding churches that had been destroyed because of invasions. He also opposed Arianism.

Patric *see Patrick*

Patricain Saint; Latin; nobleman

St. Patricain (fifth century) was a Scottish bishop who was forced from his see by pagan raiders.

Patrick Saint; Latin; nobleman

Padraig, Pakelika, Pat, Patric, Patrickk, Patricus, Patrik, Patrique, Patrizius, Patryk, Patton, Pattrick

St. Patrick, St. Patrick of Prusa

St. Patrick (d. 461) was from Britain but was kidnapped as a teen and brought to Ireland as a slave. After six years of working as a shepherd, he had a vision which told him to escape. He studied in several European monasteries and became a priest and a bishop. Pope Celestine asked him to go back to Ireland as a missionary. He spent thirty-three years evangelizing there. He is known as the Apostle of Ireland.

Patrickk *see Patrick*

Patricus *see Patrick*

Patrik *see Patrick*

Patrique *see Patrick*

Patrizius *see Patrick*

Patroccus *see Patroclus*

Patroclus Saint; Greek; glory of the father

Patroccus

St. Patroclus (d. 259) was from Troyes, France. During the persecutions of Emperor Valerian,

he was arrested. He refused to worship pagan gods and was tortured for three days. When questioned again, he still refused. He was ultimately martyred by being beheaded.

Patryk *see Patrick*

Patto Saint; English; from the warrior's town

Pacificus

St. Patto (d. 788), also known as Pacificus, was from Britain. He was an abbot in Saxony and later served as bishop of Werden in Saxony, Germany.

Patton *see Patrick*

Pattrick *see Patrick*

Paul Saint, New Testament; Latin; small

Oalo, Pasko, Paulin, Paulis, Paull, Paulle, Paulot, Pauls, Paulus, Pavlos, Poul

St. Paul, St. Paul Aurelian, St. Paul Aybara, St. Paul Hanh, St. Paul I, St. Paul Loc, St. Paul Loc Van Le, St. Paul Lucius, St. Paul Miki, St. Paul My, St. Paul Ngan, St. Paul of Constantinople, St. Paul of Cyprus, St. Paul of Gaza, St. Paul of Latros

St. Paul (d. 65) was originally known as Saul. He was a tentmaker and member of the Jewish Pharisees. He persecuted Christians and took part in the stoning of St. Stephen. While traveling to Damascus, he was struck blind by a great light and experienced a vision of Christ. He converted to the faith, regained his sight, and changed his name to Paul. He spent the rest of his life preaching the faith. Many of his letters are included in the New Testament. He is known as the Apostle to the Gentiles. He was beheaded in Rome.

Paulhen Saint; form of Paul; Latin; small

Paulinus, Pewlin, Polin

St. Paulhen (sixth century), also known as Paulinus, Polin, or Pewlin, was a student of St. Illtyd. He founded the Monastery of Whitland.

Paulillus Saint; Latin; small

St. Paulillus of Salamanca (d. 437) was a courtier in the court of King Gensaric. During the Christian persecution, he was banished from court and later imprisoned, tortured, and martyred.

Paulin *see Paul*

Paulinus Saint; form of Paul; Latin; small

St. Paulinus of Antioch, St. Paulinus of Aquileia, St. Paulinus of Brescia, St. Paulinus of Capua, St. Paulinus of Nola, St. Paulinus of Sinigaglia, St. Paulinus of Trier, St. Paulinus of York

St. Paulinus of Trier (d. 358) was from Gascony and followed his teacher St. Maximinus to Trier. He became bishop of Trier and was a supporter of St. Athanasius. Because of his staunch opposition to Arianism, Emperor Constatius II exiled Paulinus to Phrygia, where he died.

Paulis *see Paul*

Paull *see Paul*

Paulle *see Paul*

Paulot *see Paul*

Pauls *see Paul*

Paulus *see Paul*

Pausis Saint; Greek; cessation

St. Pausis (d. 303) was beheaded in Caesarea, Palestine, during the persecutions of Emperor Diocletian.

Paval *see Pavel*

Pavel Saint; Russian; small

Paavel, Paval, Pavil, Pavils, Pavlik, Pavlo, Pavol

Bl. Pavel Peter Gojdic (1888–1960) was born at Ruské Peklany, the son of a Greek Catholic priest. He was ordained and served as an assistant parish priest with his father. He later joined the Order of St. Basil the Great and became apostolic administrator of Presov. He became a bishop. The communists seized power in 1948, but he remained steadfast in the face of persecution. He was imprisoned and convicted of treason. He died in a prison hospital. He was beatified by Pope John Paul II in 2001.

Pavil *see Pavel*

Pavils *see Pavel*

Pavlik *see Pavel*

Pavlo *see Pavel*

Pavlos *see Paul*

Pavol *see Pavel*

Peater *see Peter*

Pedrin *see Pedro*

Pedro Saint; form of Peter; Spanish; rock

Pedrin, Petronio

St. Pedro de Jesus Maldonado Lucero, St. Pedro Poveda Castroverde

St. Pedro Poveda Castroverde (1874–1936) was born in Linares, Spain. He became a priest and received his licentiate in theology in Seville in 1900. He served a very poor group of people in Guadix and built a school for their children and provided vocational training for the adults. He was transferred to Madrid. In 1911, he founded the Saint Teresa of Avila Academy and opened teacher-training centers. In 1914, he opened Spain's first university residence for women. In 1921, he became chaplain of the Royal Palace. He was martyred during the Spanish Revolution. He was canonized by Pope John Paul II in 2003.

Peirre *see Pierre*

Peiter *see Peter*

Pelagius Saint; Greek; excellent sailor

Pelayo

St. Pelagius, St. Pelagius of Córdoba, St. Pelagius of Laodicea

St. Pelagius of Córdoba (912–925), also known as Pelayo, was a young boy from Asturias who was a hostage of the Moors in Córdoba. After three years, no one came to ransom him, and the ruler offered to free him if he would convert to the Muslim faith. He refused and was martyred.

Pelayo *see Pelagius*

Peleus Saint; Greek

Peleusius

St. Peleus (d. 310) was an Egyptian bishop who was imprisoned and forced to work as a laborer before being burned alive.

Peleusius *see Peleus*

Pelgrim *see Peregrine*

Pelinus Saint

St. Pelinus (d. 361) was martyred in Confinium during the reign of Emperor Julian the Apostate.

Pellegrino *see Peregrine*

Peran *see Piran*

Pere Saint; form of Pedro; Catalon; rock

Bl. Pere Tarres I Claret (1905–1950) was from Manresa, Spain. While in medical school, he served as president of the Federation of Young Christians of Catalonia. After becoming a doctor, he founded a clinic in Barcelona for those who could not otherwise afford care. The Spanish Civil War convinced him to become a priest. He served as a priest for seven years before dying of lymphatic cancer. He was beatified by Pope John Paul II in 2004.

Peregrin Saint; form of Peregrine; Latin; traveler, pilgrim, falcon

St. Peregrin (d. 192) was martyred during the persecutions of Emperor Commodus. He was stretched on the rack, clubbed, burned, and beaten to death with lead-tipped whips.

Peregrin *see Peregrine*

Peregrine Saint; Latin; traveler, pilgrim, falcon

Pelgrim, Pellegrino, Peregrin, Peregryn, Peregryne, Perergrin, Perergryn, Perine

St. Peregrine Laziosi (1260–1345) was born into a wealthy family at Forli, Italy. As a youth, he was a member of an anti papal party. He struck St. Philip Benizi in the face. When Philip turned the other cheek, Peregrine was so impressed that he converted. He joined the Servites. He was known for his austerities as well as for his preaching and being a good confessor. He developed cancer of the foot and was scheduled to have it amputated, but he prayed and was healed. This led to him being a patron saint of cancer patients.

Peregrinus Saint; form of Peregrine; Latin; traveler, pilgrim, falcon

St. Peregrinus of Auxerre (third century) was a Roman sent by Pope Sixtus II to evangelize Gaul. He was the first bishop of Auxerre and was martyred during the persecutions of Emperor Diocletian. He is a patron against snake bites.

Peregryn *see Peregrine*
Peregryne *see Peregrine*
Perergrin *see Peregrine*
Perergryn *see Peregrine*
Perfectus Saint; Latin; perfect

St. Perfectus (d. 851) was a priest from Córdoba, Spain. He was martyred by the Moors on Easter Sunday.

Pergentinus Saint; St. Pergentinus

St. Pergentinus (d. 251) was martyred at Arezzo with his brother St. Laurentinus during the persecutions of Emperor Trajanus Decius.

Perine *see Peregrine*
Pero *see Piero*
Perpetuus Saint; Latin; having an unchanging goal

St. Perpetuus (d. 490) was born into a senatorial family. He became bishop of Tours in 460, a position he held for thirty years. He built monasteries and churches and rebuilt the Basilica of St. Martin. He was also known for enforcing clerical discipline and regulating feast days.

Perran *see Piran*
Peter Saint, New Testament; Greek, Latin; rock

Peater, Peiter, Peterke, Peterus, Petrus, Piaras, Pieor, Piter, Piti, Pjeter, Pyeter

St. Peter, St. Peter Arbues, St. Peter Baptist, St. Peter Canisius, St. Peter Ch'oe Hyong, St. Peter Chanel, St. Peter Chrysologis, St. Peter Claver, St. Peter

Damian, St. Peter de Betancur, St. Peter Domoulin Bori, St. Peter Duong, St. Peter Khoa

St. Peter (1–64) was named Simon and was originally a fisherman, before being called by Jesus to become a "fisher of men." He was a brother of St. Andrew. Jesus changed his name to "Peter," which means "rock," because he would be the foundation upon which he would build his Church. He became the first pope. He was martyred in Rome. At his request, he was crucified head down because he did not feel worthy to die the same way our Lord had done. He is a patron of the Universal Church, popes, fishermen, shipbuilders, and watchmakers.

Peterke *see Peter*

Peterus *see Peter*

Petra Saint; form of Peter; Greek, Latin; rock

Bl. Petra of St. Joseph Perez Florida (1845–1906) was born in Málaga, Spain. She wanted to become a nun from the time she was a child. She joined with three companions and began serving the poor. This group became the Congregation of the Mothers of the Helpless and of St. Joseph of the Mountain. She was beatified by Pope John Paul II in 1994.

Petro Saint; form of Peter; Greek, Latin; rock

Bl. Petro Verhun (1890–1957) was born in Horodok, Lviv District, Ukraine. He was a Greek Catholic. He became a doctor of philosophy, was ordained a priest, and served Ukrainian Catholics at Berlin, Germany. He was arrested and exiled to Siberia. He was beatified by Pope John Paul II in 2001.

Petroc Saint; form of Peter; Greek, Latin; rock

St. Petroc (d. 564) was born in Wales. He became a monk and studied in Ireland. He then settled in Cornwall. After thirty years, he made a pilgrimage to Rome and Jerusalem. For a time, he lived as a hermit on an island near the Indian Ocean. When he returned to Cornwall, he established a monastery at Padstow and then lived as a hermit at Bodmir Moor. He was known for his miracles.

Petronax Saint

St. Petronax (670–747) was from Brescia, Italy. He became a Benedictine monk and was asked by Pope St. Gregory II to travel to Monte Cassino to examine it after the Lombards attacked. He took over the rebuilding of that abbey and is known as "the Second Founder of Monte Cassino." He served as abbot there for thirty years.

Petronio *see Pedro*

Petronius Saint; Greek, Latin; small rock

St. Petronius (d. 463) was the son of a Roman senator.

Originally from Avignon, France, he became a monk at Lerins. He was later named bishop of Die.

Petrus *see Peter*

Pewlin *see Paulhen*

Phaebadius Saint

Fiari

St. Phaebadius (d. 392), also known as Fiari, was a bishop of Agen in southern Gaul. He worked with St. Hilary of Poitiers against the Arian heresy.

Phelim Saint; Celtic; beauty, goodness

St. Phelim (sixth century) was an Irish monk and follower of St. Columba. He is a patron saint of Kilmore.

Phil *see Philip*

Philamin *see Philemon*

Philamine *see Philemon*

Philamyn *see Philemon*

Philaster Saint

Filaster

St. Philaster (d. 387), also known as Filaster, was from Spain but became bishop of Brescia, Italy. He was a stauch opponent of Arianism. He wrote the "Catalogue of Heresies," which featured both Jewish and Christian heresies.

Philbert *see Philibert*

Phileman *see Philemon*

Philemon Saint, New Testament; Greek; kiss

Filomeno, Philamin, Philamine, Philamyn, Phileman, Philmon,

Philmyn, Philmyne, Phylmin, Phylmine, Phylmon

St. Philemon, St. Philemon of Alexandria, St. Philemon the Dancer

St. Philemon (first century) was the recipient of a letter from St. Paul, now included in the New Testament. A house church met in his home in Colosse, Phrygia. He and his wife, Apphia, were stoned to death during the reign of Emperor Nero.

Philetus Saint; Greek; beloved

St. Philetus (d. 121) was a senator who lived in Illyria. He was martyred with his family during the persecutions of Emperor Hadrian.

Philibert Saint; English; brilliant

Filbert, Philbert

St. Philibert (608–684) was born in Gascony, France. He lived at the court of King Dagobert I of the Franks before becoming a monk at Rebais Abbey. He later served as abbot but left because of disagreements with some of the other monks. He founded the Monastery of Jumieges near Fontenelle, France. He was exiled by the mayor and sent to Herio Island. He then founded Noirmoutier Abbey and rebuilt Qincay Abbey.

Philip Saint, New Testament; Greek; lover of horses

Phil, Philipine, Philippa, Philippina, Philippine, Philippo, Phillipus, Phillp, Philp, Phyleap,

Phyleep, Phylip, Phylyp, Pilib, Pippo

St. Philip, St. Philip Benizi, St. Philip Howard, St. Philip Minh, St. Philip Neri, St. Philip of Agirone, St. Philip of Gortyna, St. Philip of Heraclea, St. Philip of Jesus, St. Philip of Vienne, St. Philip of Zell, St. Philip the Deacon

St. Philip (first century) was one of the twelve apostles. He was a native of Bethsaida, the same city that Peter and Andrew lived in. He was responsible for bringing Nathaniel to Christ. After Pentecost, tradition holds that he preached in Greece and was martyred by being crucified upside down at Hierapolis.

Philippo *see Philip*

Phillipus *see Philip*

Phillp *see Philip*

Philmon *see Philemon*

Philmyn *see Philemon*

Philmyne *see Philemon*

Philo Saint; Greek; love

Filo, Fylo, Phylo

St. Philo (d. 150) was a deacon who aided St. Ignatius of Antioch. After his death, he and a fellow deacon named Agathopodes brought Ignatius's relics from Rome back to Antioch.

Philogonius Saint; Greek

St. Philogonius (d. 324) was a lawyer in Antioch, Syria. After his wife died, he joined the Church. In time, he became bishop of Antioch. He was known as one of the first opponents of Arianism.

Philologus Saint, New Testament; Greek, Latin; scholar, learned person

St. Philologus (first century) was a member of the Christian community in Rome mentioned in St. Paul's Letter to the Romans (Rom 16:15).

Philomenus Saint; Greek; to love strength

St. Philomenus (d. 275) was martyred in Ancyra, Galatia, during the reign of Emperor Aurelian.

Philosophus Saint; Greek; lover of wisdom

St. Philosophus (d. 252) was martyred in Alexandria during the persecutions of Decius.

Philoterus Saint; Greek

St. Philoterus (d. 303) was a noble from Nicomedia who was martyred during the reign of Emperor Diocletian.

Philp *see Philip*

Phocas Saint; Greek; a seal

St. Phocas, St. Phocas the Gardener

St. Phocas (d. 320) was martyred by drowning during the persecutions of Emperor Licinius.

Phyleap *see Philip*

Phyleep *see Philip*

Phylip *see Philip*

Phylmin *see Philemon*

Phylmine *see Philemon*

Phylmon *see Philemon*

Phylo *see Philo*

Phylyp *see Philip*

Piaras *see Peter*

Piat *see Piaton*

Piato *see Piaton*

Piaton Saint; Latin

Piat, Piato, Piatus

St. Piaton (d. 286), also known as Piat, Piatus, or Piato, was from Benevento, Italy. He was sent to evangelize areas of Gaul, especially Chartres and Tournai. He was martyred in Toumai by having the top part of his skull sliced off.

Piatus *see Piaton*

Pieor *see Peter*

Pieran *see Piran*

Piere *see Pierre*

Pieren *see Piran*

Pierius Saint; form of Peter; French; rock

St. Pierius (d. 310) was the director of the Catechetical School of Alexandria. He was a priest known for his writings on philosophy and theology.

Piero Saint; form of Peter; Italian; rock

Pero, Pierro

Bl. Piero Giorgio Frassati (1901–1925) was born in Turin, Italy. He was involved with Catholic youth groups, the Apostleship of Prayer, Catholic Action, and he became a Third Order Dominican. He helped establish *Momentum*, a newspaper based on the principles of the papal encyclical *Rerum Novarum*. He died of poliomyelitis. He was beatified by Pope John Paul II in 1990.

Pierre Saint; form of Peter; French; rock

Peirre, Piere, Pierrot

St. Pierre-Francois Neron (1818–1860) became a priest of the Paris Society for Foreign Missions when he was twenty-nine years old. He was sent to Vietnam, where he served as a missionary for eleven years. He was arrested and imprisoned for three months before being beheaded. One of the Martyrs of Vietnam, he was canonized in 1988 by Pope John Paul II.

Pierro *see Piero*

Pierrot *see Pierre*

Pieryn *see Piran*

Pietro Saint; form of Peter; Italian; rock

Bl. Pietro Bonilli, Bl. Pietro Casani

Bl. Pietro Bonilli (1841–1935) was born in Spoleto, Perugia, Italy. He became a priest and founded the Sisters of the Holy Family. He was beatified by Pope John Paul II in 1988.

Pigmenius Saint

St. Pigmenius (d. 362) was a priest in Rome who was martyred by being drowned in the Tiber River during the reign of Emperor Julian the Apostate.

Pilib *see Philip*

Pinytus Saint

St. Pinytus (d. 180) was born in Greece. He became a bishop of Cnossus, Crete. He was known for his ecclesiastical writings.

Pio Saint; Latin; devout, pious

Pyo

St. Pio of Pietrelcina (1887–1968), commonly known as Padre Pio, was born in Benevento, Italy, as Francesco Forgione. He joined the Capuchin Friars and became a priest at age twenty-two. In 1918, he received the stigmata. As word of this got out, many sought him out, both out of devotion and curiosity. He had the ability to read people's souls in confession, as well as to bilocate, levitate, and perform miracles. In 1956, he founded the House for the Relief of Suffering. Upon his death, the wounds of the stigmata healed and no trace of them could be found. He was canonized by Pope John Paul II in 2002.

Pionius Saint

St. Pionius (d. 250) was a priest who was arrested along with fifteen companions. He preached the faith whenever he was taken out of his cell to anyone who would listen. He was burned at the stake for refusing to sacrifice to pagan gods.

Pior Saint

St. Pior (d. 395) was a hermit and follower of St. Anthony in Egypt. He lived in a cave in the Baid desert on the Nile River.

Piotr Saint; form of Peter; Bulgarian; rock

Piotrek

Bl. Piotr Bonifacy Zjukowski, Bl. Piotr Edward Dankowski

Bl. Piotr Bonifacy Zjukowski (1913–1942) was born in Lithuania. He became a Franciscan Conventual friar. He was arrested by the Nazis and sent to Pawiak Prison in Warsaw, Poland. He died at the Dachau concentration camp. He is one of the 108 Polish Martys of World War II and was beatified by Pope John Paul II in 1999.

Piotrek *see Piotr*

Pipenon Saint

St. Pipenon (d.203) was martyred in Carthage.

Pippo *see Philip*

Piran Saint; Gaelic; prayer

Peran, Perran, Pieran, Pieren, Pieryn, Pyran

St. Piran (sixth century), also known as Peran or Perran, was a hermit near Padstow in Cornwall. He is a patron saint of tin miners.

Pirmin Saint; Latin; firm, steadfast

St. Pirmin (700–753) was born in Aragon, Spain. When the Arabs invaded that area, he fled and traveled to the Rhineland. He founded monasteries at Reichenau, Amorbach, and Murbach. He also brought Dissentia Abbey under Benedictine

Rule. In addition, he wrote a catechism and a collection of quotations from scripture and the Church Fathers.

Piter *see Peter*

Piti *see Peter*

Pius Saint; Latin; dutiful, godly, holy

Pope St. Pius I, Pope St. Pius V, Pope St. Pius X

Pope St. Pius I (d. 154) was from Aquileia, Italy, and was elected pope in 140. He fought the Valentiniand and Gnosticism. He also decreed that Easter should only be celebrated on a Sunday.

Pjeter *see Peter*

Placid Saint; Latin, Spanish; serene

Placido

St. Placid (sixth century) was the son of a nobleman and was entrusted to the care of St. Benedict at Subiaco. He followed Benedict to Monte Cassino. Little is known of his later life.

Placido *see Placid*

Platan *see Plato*

Platen *see Plato*

Platin *see Plato*

Plato Saint; Greek; broad shouldered

Platan, Platen, Platin, Platoe, Platoh, Platon, Platun, Platyn

St. Plato (d. 306) was tortured and martyred in Ancyra, Turkey. His skin was burned and ripped off. He suffered this way for eight days before being beheaded. He is a patron saint of captives.

Platoe *see Plato*

Platoh *see Plato*

Platon *see Plato*

Platonides *see Platonides (girl's name)*

Platun *see Plato*

Platyn *see Plato*

Plechelm Saint; English

St. Plechelm (d. 730) was from Northumbria, England. A priest, he helped St. Wiro found a monastery at Odilienburg. He is a patron saint of the Netherlands.

Plegmund Saint; English

St. Plegmund (d. 914) was born in Mercia, England. He lived as a hermit near Chester before being named archbishop of Canterbury by Pope Stephen V. He was a tutor of King Alfred the Great.

Plutarch Saint; Greek; rich prince

St. Plutarch (d. 202) studied at the Catechetical School of Alexandria. He was martyred during the persecutions of Emperor Septimius Severus.

Podius Saint

St. Podius (d. 1002) was the son of a Margrave of Tuscany. He joined the Augustinians and was later named bishop of Florence.

Poemen Saint; Greek; shepherd

Poemon

St. Poemen (d. 450) was a leader of a group of hermits in the Egyptian desert of Skete. He led a very ascetical life and was known for his wisdom. He was a proponent of frequent Communion for all.

Poemon *see Poemen*

Poldi *see Leopold*

Polin *see Paulhen*

Pollio Saint; Greek; to destroy

St. Pollio (third century) was from Cybalae, Pannonia. He was martyred during the persecutions of Emperor Diocletian.

Polycarp Saint; Greek; rich in fruit

St. Polycarp of Smyrna, St. Polycarp of Alexandria

St. Polycarp of Smyrna (69–155) was a disciple of St. John the Apostle. He served as bishop of Smyrna and fought Gnosticism. He was burned alive in Smyrna but was unharmed. He was then killed by a dagger.

Polydore Saint; Greek

St. Polydore Plasden (1563–1591) was a native of London who studied for the priesthood at Reims. He then returned to England, where he was arrested, hanged, drawn, and quartered. He is one of the Forty Martyrs of England and Wales.

Polyeuctus Saint; Greek; much prayed to

St. Polyeuctus (d. 259) was from Greece. He became an official in the Roman government and was martyred during the persecutions of Emperor Valerian.

Pompeius Saint; Greek; he who heads the procession

St. Pompeius Maria Pirotti, St. Pompeius

St. Pompeius (d. 290) was a bishop of Pavia. He was possibly tortured for the faith but is not listed as a martyr.

Pomponius Saint; Latin; lover of grandeur

Pomponia

St. Pomponius (d. 536) was a bishop of Naples who opposed Arianism.

Ponce *see Ebontius*

Ponsiano *see Pontian*

Pontian Saint; Greek; coming from the sea

Ponsiano

St. Pontian, St. Pontian Ngondwe, St. Pontian Pope

St. Pontian Ngondwe (d. 1886) was a member of the Royal Guard of King Mwanga of Uganda. He was martyred.

Pontianus Saint; Greek; coming from the sea

St. Pontianus (d. 169) was martyred in Spoleto, Italy, during the reign of Marcus Aurelius.

Pontius Saint; Greek; coming from the sea

St. Pontius, St. Pontius of Carthage, St. Pontius of Cimella

St. Pontius of Carthage (d. 260) was a deacon who served under St. Cyprian of Carthage. He was present at that saint's execution and subsequently wrote about the event.

Poppo Saint; German

St. Poppo (978–1048) was born in Flanders and served in the military. After making a pilgrimage to Rome and the Holy Land, he became a Benedictine monk. He was named abbot of Stavelot Malmedy by Emperor St. Henry II. Poppo worked to revive monastic discipline.

Porcarius Saint; Latin; swineherd

St. Porcarius (d. 732) was the Benedictine abbot of Lerins. He had a vision that the monastery was going to be attacked, thereby allowing most of the monks to escape. He stayed behind with a few other monks. He was martyred when the monastery was massacred.

Porphyrius Saint; Latin; purple stone

St. Porphyrius, St. Porphyrius the General

St. Porphyrius (d. 250) was a priest in Umbria, Italy. He was martyred during the persecutions of Emperor Trajanus Decius.

Porphyry Saint; Latin; purple stone

St. Porphyry (347–420) was born to a wealthy Greek family in Thessalonika, Macedonia. He lived as a hermit in Egypt for a time before becoming a priest. He was named bishop of Gaza, where he worked hard to root out paganism.

Portianus Saint; Latin; to carry

St. Portianus (d. 533) was a slave who earned his freedoms and became a monk. He served as abbot of a monastery in Gaul. He convinced King Thierry I of Austrasia into releasing prisoners.

Possessor Saint; Latin; to possess

St. Possessor (d. 485) was bishop of Verdun, France, in the dark years immediately following the fall of the Western Roman Empire.

Possidius Saint

Possidus

St. Possidius (d. 440) was a follower of St. Augustine of Hippo and was with him when he died. He became bishop of Calama, in Numidia. Arian vandals drove him into exile. He moved to Apulia, Italy, and wrote a biography of St. Augustine.

Possidus *see Possidius*

Potamon Saint; Greek, Latin

St. Potamon (d. 340) was bishop of Heraclea, Upper Egypt. He was arrested and had one eye taken out and one leg made lame. After he was freed, he took part in the Council of Nicaea. He was a strong opponent of Arianism. It is possible that he was beaten to death by Arian followers.

Pothinus Saint; Greek, Latin

St. Pothinus (87–177) was bishop of Lyons, in Roman Gaul (later known as France). He was imprisoned when he was ninety years old. He died while in prison.

Poul *see Paul*

Praejectus Saint; Greek, Latin

Prest, Prix, Projectus

St. Praejectus (d. 676), also known as Prest, Prix, or Projectus, was born in Auvergne, France. He was appointed bishop of Clermont. He helped increase monasticism and was known for his care of the poor. He was assassinated by soldiers as a result of a political misunderstanding.

Praetextatus Saint; Greek, Latin

Prix

St. Praetextatus (d. 586), also known as Prix, was bishop of Rouen. He became involved in the political dispute between the sons of King Clotaire I. He accused Fredegunde, the wife of Chilperic, of murder. As a result, she had him exiled and killed.

Pragmatius Saint; Latin; practical

St. Pragmatius (d. 520) was bishop of Autun, France.

Pratt *see Protus*

Prest *see Praejectus*

Primael Saint; Latin; chosen first

St. Primael (fifth century) was from Britain. He lived as a hermit in Quimper.

Primitivus *see Primus*

Primulus Saint; Latin; first

St. Primulus (d. 259) was martyred in Carthage.

Primus Saint; Latin; first

Primitivus

St. Primus (d. 297) was born into a noble Roman family. He and his brother Felician cared for Christian prisoners. The two were arrested, scourged, and ultimately beheaded.

Principius Saint; Latin; head, manager

St. Principius (d. 205) was bishop of Soissons.

Prior Saint; English; monastic official

St. Prior (fourth century) was an Egyptian hermit. He helped St. Anthony establish the monastic system in Egypt.

Priscus Saint; Latin; old, from another time

St. Priscus (d. 272) was an officer in the Roman Legion who was martyred along with a group of fellow soldiers in Auxerre during the persecutions of Emperor Aurelian.

Privatus Saint; Latin; private

St. Privatus (d. 223) was martyred in Rome during the reign of Emperor Alexander Severus.

Prix *see Praejectus, Praetextatus*

Probus Saint; Latin; having moral conduct

St. Probus (d. 175) was bishop of Ravenna.

Processus Saint; Latin; moving forward

St. Processus (first century) was a prison guard at Mamertine Prison in Rome. He guarded Sts. Peter and Paul when they were imprisoned there and was converted by them. He was martyred.

Prochorus Saint; Greek; he who prospers

St. Prochorus (first century) was one of the Seven Deacons of Jerusalem chosen by the apostles. He later became bishop of Nicomedia. He was martyred in Antioch.

Proclus Saint; Latin; glorious before others

St. Proclus (d. 115) was martyred in Ancyra during the reign of Trajan.

Procopius Saint; Greek; he who progresses

St. Procopius of Scythopolis (d. 303) was born in Jerusalem. He became a reader and interpreter in the Syriac language when he moved to Scythopolis. He was arrested and martyred during the persecutions of Emperor Diocletian.

Proculus Saint; Latin; born far from home

St. Proculus (d. 304) was a Roman officer who was martyred in Bologna, Italy, during the persecutions of Emperor Diocletian.

Projectus see Praejectus

Prosper Saint; Latin; fortunate

Prospero

St. Prosper of Aquitaine (390–455) was a disciple of St. Augustine who defended that saint's positions on grace and predestination. Prosper and his friend Hilary traveled to Rome to ask Pope Celestine I to affirm the truth of Augustine's statements.

He later served as a secretary to Pope Leo the Great. He also wrote a world history.

Prospero see Prosper

Protase Saint; Greek; preferred one

Protasio

St. Protase (d. 165) was the son of Sts. Vitalis and Valeria of Milan. He and his brother St. Gervase were martyred.

Protasio see Protase

Prote see Protus

Proteus see Protus

Prothadius Saint; German

St. Prothadius (d. 624) was a bishop of Besancon and served as a counselor to the Frankish King Clotaire II.

Proto see Protus

Protogenes Saint; Greek

St. Protogenes (fourth century) was bishop of Carrhae, Syria. He was exiled by Arian Emperor Valens but recalled by Emperor Theodosius I.

Protus Saint; Greek; precedes all the rest

Pratt, Prote, Proteus, Proto

St. Protus (d. 257), also known as Proteus, Prote, Proto, or Pratt, was martyred in Rome during the reign of Emperor Valerian I.

Provinus Saint; Latin; location

St. Provinus (d. 420) was born in Gaul and was a disciple of St. Ambrose in Milan. He served as coadjutor with St. Felix, bishop of Como, and later served as bishop of Como himself.

Prudentius Saint; Latin; works with sensitivity and modesty

St. Prudentius, St. Prudentius Galindo

St. Prudentius (d. 700) was a hermit who became bishop of Tarazona in Aragon.

Psalmet *see Psalmodius*

Psalmodius Saint; Latin; song

Psalmet, Sauman

St. Psalmodius (seventh century), also known as Psalmet and Sauman, was born to a noble family in Scotia and became a disciple of St. Brendan. He traveled to Gaul with that saint and lived as a hermit in Limoges, France.

Ptolemaeus *see Ptolemy*

Ptolemy Saint; Greek; aggressive, warlike

Ptolemaeus

St. Ptolemy (d. 165), also known as Ptolemaeus, was a Christian in Rome. He was imprisoned and sentenced to death. Lucius and an unnamed man protested his sentence and joined him in martyrdom.

Publius Saint; Latin; from the village, common

St. Publius, St. Publius of Carthage

St. Publius (33–125) was the prefect of Malta when St. Paul was shipwrecked there. St. Paul cured Publius's father. Publius went on to become the first bishop of Malta. He was martyred during the persecutions of Emperor Hadrian.

Pudens Saint; Hebrew; shamefaced

St. Pudens (first century) was a Roman senator, converted by the apostles, who was martyred.

Pyeter *see Peter*

Pyo *see Pio*

Pyran *see Piran*

Q

Qeuntin *see Quentin*

Quadragesimus Saint; Latin

St. Quadragesimus (d. 590) was a shepherd and subdeacon from Policastro, Italy. He was known as a miracle worker and was said to have raised a man from the dead.

Quadratus Saint; Latin; fourth

St. Quadratus (third century) was bishop of Utica, France. He and much of his flock were martyred by the Romans.

Quantin *see Quentin*

Quaratus Saint, New Testament; Latin; fourth

Quartus

St. Quaratus (first century) was one of the seventy-two disciples mentioned in Luke 10. He may also have been mentioned in Romans 16:23.

Quardus *see Famianw*

Quartus *see Quaratus*

Queintin *see Quentin*

Quent *see Quentin*

Quentan *see Quentin*

Quentilien *see Quentin*

Quentin Saint; Latin; fifth

> *Qeuntin, Quantin, Queintin, Quent, Quentan, Quentilien, Quentine, Quentyn, Quentynn, Quientin, Quintan, Quintina, Quito, Quyntan, Quyntyn, Qwentan, Qwentin, Qwentyn, Qwyntan, Qwyntyn*

St. Quentin (d. 287) was the son of a Roman senator. He converted to Christianity and served as a missionary to Gaul. He was arrested and beheaded.

Quentine *see Quentin*

Quentyn *see Quentin*

Quentynn *see Quentin*

Quientin *see Quentin*

Quinidius Saint; Latin; fifth

St. Quinidius (d. 579) was born to a noble Christian family in Vaison-la-Romaine, France. He became a hermit near Toulon and then at Lerins Abbey. He became bishop of Vaison. He was known for his charity and fairness. He also attended the Councils of Paris of 558 and 573.

Quintan *see Quentin*

Quintian Saint; Latin; fifth

St. Quintian (d. 430) was the leader of a group of Christians martyred in Africa by Arian ruler King Hunneric of the Vandals.

Quintius Saint; Latin; fifth

St. Quintius (d. 570) was a Christian courtier in the palace of a Frankish king. When he refused the queen's attentions, she had him assassinated.

Quintus Saint; Latin; fifth

St. Quintus (d. 255) was martyred in Africa during the persecutions of Emperor Trajanus Decius.

Quiriacus Saint; Greek; lord

St. Quiriacus (sixth century) was a Greek hermit who lived in Palestine and was known for his holiness.

Quirinus Saint; Latin; he who carries a lance

St. Quirinus of Siscia (d. 309) was the bishop of Siscia, Croatia. He was arrested and ordered to make sacrifices to the gods by the Roman magistrate. He refused and was drowned in the Raab River.

Quito *see Quentin*

Quodvultdeus Saint; Latin; what God wants

St. Quodvultdeus (d. 450) was a friend and correspondent of St. Augustine of Hippo. He served as bishop of Carthage. He was exiled by Arian Vandals who invaded the area. He traveled to Naples and fought the Pelagian heresy in Campagna.

Quyntan *see Quentin*

Quyntyn *see Quentin*

Qwentan *see Quentin*

Qwentin *see Quentin*

Qwentyn *see Quentin*

Qwyntan *see Quentin*

Qwyntyn *see Quentin*

R

Racho Saint

Ragnobert

St. Racho (d. 660), also known as Ragnobert, was the first bishop of Autun, France.

Radbod Saint

St. Radbod (850–917) was educated by his Uncle Gunther, who was bishop of Cologne, Germany. He became bishop of Utrecht, Holland. He also joined the Benedictines. He was known for his care for the poor and as a poet. After his see was invaded by the Danes, he moved to Deventer, France, where he died.

Radmond *see Raymond*

Radolphus *see Ralph*

Radulf *see Ralph*

Raemond *see Raymond*

Rafael Saint; form of Raphael; Spanish; God has healed

Rafaell, Rafaelo, Rafal, Rafeal, Rafeé, Rafel, Rafello, Raffaelo, Raffanell, Raffanello, Raffeal, Raffel, Raffiel, Rafiel, Ravel

St. Rafael Arnaiz Baron, St. Rafael Guizar Valencia

St. Rafael Guizar Valencia (1878–1938) was bishop of Veracruz, Mexico, and a member of the Knights of Columbus. He cared for the sick and dying during the Mexican Revolution. Forced from his diocese, he lived out the remainder of his life in Mexico City. He was canonized by Pope Benedict XVI in 2006.

Rafaell *see Rafael*

Rafaelo *see Rafael*

Rafal *see Rafael*

Rafe *see Ralph*

Rafeal *see Rafael*

Rafeé *see Rafael*

Rafel *see Rafael*

Rafello *see Rafael*

Raffaelo *see Rafael*

Raffanell *see Rafael*

Raffanello *see Rafael*

Raffeal *see Rafael*

Raffel *see Rafael*

Raffelo *see Raphael*

Raffiel *see Rafael*

Rafiel *see Rafael*

Ragnebert *see Rambert*

Ragnobert *see Racho, Rainbert*

Ragnulf *see Ranulphus*

Raimond *see Raymond*

Rainbold Saint; German

Rainnold

St. Rainbold (d. 1001), also known as Rainnold, was a monk at St. Maximinus at Trier, Germany. He was later made the abbot of St. Emmeram.

Rainnold *see Rainbold*

Rainold *see Reinold*

Ralf *see Ralph*

Ralph Saint; English; wolf counselor

Radolphus, Radulf, Rafe, Ralf, Ralpheal, Ralphel, Raul, Rolf, Rolph

St. Ralph (d. 866) was educated under Abbot Bertrand at Solignac, France. He later served as abbot at St. Medard, Soissons. He was named bishop of Bourges. In that position, he founded several monasteries and convents.

Ralpheal *see Ralph*

Ralphel *see Ralph*

Rambert Saint; German; strong, brilliant

Ragnebert, Ragnobert, Rambirt, Ramburt, Rambyrt

St. Rambert (d. 680), also known as Ragnebert or Ragnobert, was a member of the court of King Thierry III of Neustria. When he opposed the corruption of Ebroin, the mayor of the palace, he was exiled and then murdered in the Jura Mountains.

Rambirt *see Rambert*

Ramburt *see Rambert*

Rambyrt *see Rambert*

Ramey *see Remy*

Ramirus Saint; Latin, Spanish; supreme judge

St. Ramirus (sixth century) was prior of St. Claudus Monastery in Leon, Spain. The entire community was martyred by Arian Visigoths.

Ramon Saint; form of Raymond; Spanish; mighty, wise protector

St. Ramon of Barbastro (d. 1126) was born in France and became the bishop of Barbastro in Aragon, Spain.

Ramonde *see Raymond*

Ramone *see Raymond*

Ranald *see Ronald*

Ranulphus Saint; German

Ragnulf

St. Ranulphus (d. 700), also known as Ragnulf, was the father of St. Haduiph and served as bishop of Arras Cambrai in France.

Raphael Angel, Old Testament; Hebrew; God has healed

Falito, Raffelo, Raphaello, Raphale, Raphel, Raphello, Raphiel, Rephael

St. Raphael is an archangel who was sent by God to help Tobit, Tobiah, and Sarah in the book of Tobit. He appears as the companion of Tobiah and goes by the name of Azarias. After Tobit's blindness is healed, he reveals himself as the "angel Raphael, one of the seven, who stand before the Lord" (Tb 12:15). He is a patron of medical workers, matchmakers, and travelers.

Raphaello *see Raphael*

Raphale *see Raphael*

Raphel *see Raphael*

Raphello *see Raphael*

Raphiel *see Raphael*

Ras *see Erastus*

Rastus *see Erastus*

Rasyphus Saint

St. Rasyphus (fifth century) was from Britain. He and St. Ravennus fled that area to escape the Anglo-Saxon invasion. They lived as hermits in Gaul, where they were martyred.

Raul *see Ralph*

Ravel *see Rafael*

Raven *see Ravennus*

Ravenne *see Ravennus*

Ravennus Saint; English; raven

Raven, Ravenne

St. Ravennus (fifth century) was from Britain. He and St. Rasyphus fled that area to escape the Anglo-Saxon invasion. They lived as hermits in Gaul, where they were martyred.

Rayfus *see Rufus*

Rayment *see Raymond*

Raymond Saint; English; mighty, wise protector

Radmond, Raemond, Raimond, Ramon, Ramonde, Ramone, Rayment, Raymont, Raymund, Raymunde, Raymundo, Redmond, Reimond, Reimund

St. Raymond Nonnatus, St. Raymond of Barbastro, St. Raymond of Fitero, St. Raymond of Pennafort, St. Raymond of Toulouse

St. Raymond of Pennafort (1175–1275) was born to a noble family in Aragon. He became a philosophy teacher and lawyer. He was ordained a priest and joined the Dominicans. Pope Gregory IX called him to Rome, and he was assigned to collect all the official letters of the popes since 1150. He compiled five volumes and helped write Church law. In 1238, he was named master general of the Dominicans, but he stepped down after two years to focus on parish work. He is a patron saint of lawyers.

Raymont *see Raymond*

Raymund *see Raymond*

Raymunde *see Raymond*

Raymundo *see Raymond*

Raynald Saint; Spanish; king's advisor

St. Raynald of Nocera (1150–1225) was born to German parents in Umbria, Italy. He became a Benedictine monk and was later named bishop of Nocera. He is a patron saint of that city.

Raynerius Saint; German; counselor

St. Raynerius, St. Raynerius of Spalatro

St. Raynerius (d. 1160) was born in Pisa, Italy. He lived a life of ill repute until he converted after making a pilgrimage to Jerusalem. He lived as a conventual oblate at the Benedictine Abbey of St. Andrew at Pisa. He became known as a miracle worker and often used holy water as a means of healing.

Redemptus Saint; Latin; redeemed

St. Redemptus (d. 586) was the bishop of Ferentini in Italy. Pope St. Gregory the Great wrote of his holiness.

Redmond *see Raymond*

Regimbald Saint; German

Reginbald

St. Regimbald (d. 1039) lived as a monk in Augsburg, Germany, and then at Edersberg.

He became abbot of Lorsch and was later named bishop of Speyer.

Reginbald *see Regimbald*

Regulus Saint; Latin; king

Reol

St. Regulus (d. 698), also known as Reol, was a Benedictine monk who served as archbishop of Reims, France. He founded the Abbey of Orbais.

Reimond *see Raymond*

Reimund *see Raymond*

Reinaldo *see Ronald*

Reinold Saint; Latin; ruler's advisor

Rainold, Reynold

St. Reinold (d. 960), also known as Rainold or Reynold, was a Benedictine monk at Pantaleon Monastery in Cologne, Germany. He was the head of the building program there but was murdered by stonemasons who were upset that he worked harder than they did. He is a patron saint of stonemasons.

Remaclus Saint

St. Remaclus (d. 663) was born in Acquitaine, France. He was ordained a priest and served as abbot of Solignac and was later named abbot of the Abbey of Cougnon, Luxembourg. King Sigebert II of Austrasia invited him to join his court and named him abbot of the monastery of Stavelot, Belgium. He later served as bishop of Maastricht in the Netherlands. During his tenure, he spread monasticism

in that region. He died at Stavelot Monastery.

Rembert Saint; German; bright counsel

St. Rembert (d. 888) was born in Flanders, Belgium. He entered Turholt Monastery and served as a missionary in Scandinavia. He was named bishop of Hamburg Bremen in Germany with his see including Denmark, Sweden, and parts of Germany. He also wrote a biography of St. Ansgar, whom he had worked with.

Remedius Saint; Latin; medicine

St. Remedius (sixth century) was a bishop in the French Alps.

Remee *see Remy*

Remey *see Remy*

Remi *see Remigius*

Remigius Saint; Latin; he who mans the oars

Remi

St. Remigius (438–533) was the son of Emilius, count of Laon, and St. Celina. When he was twenty-two, he was named bishop of Rheims, a position he held for seventy-four years. He helped spread the faith throughout Gaul. He converted Clovis, king of the Franks, which helped established the Church in France. He is a patron saint of Rheims and is invoked against epidemics, fever, and religious indifference.

Remis *see Remy*

Remmee *see Remy*

Remmey *see Remy*

Remmy *see Remy*

Remy Saint; French; from Rheims, France

Ramey, Remee, Remey, Remis, Remmee, Remmey, Remmy

St. Rémy Isoré (1852–1900) was born in France, where he entered the Jesuits. He became a missionary to China and was stationed in Weixian during the Boxer Rebellion. He was martyred by being beheaded, and his head was placed on the village gates as a warning to other missionaries. He is one of the Martyrs of China and was canonized by Pope John Paul II in 2000.

Renan *see Ronan*

Renat *see Renatus*

Renatis *see Renatus*

Renato *see Renatus*

Renatus Saint; Italian; reborn

Renat, Renatis, Renato, Renatys, Rend

St. Renatus (d. 422) was bishop of Angers, France, and Sorrento, Italy. It is possible that there were two bishops by the same name, whom tradition has merged into one.

Renatys *see Renatus*

Renay *see Rene*

Rend *see Renatus*

Rene Saint; French; reborn

Renay, Renne, Renee, Rennie

St. Rene Goupil (1606–1642) was born in Anjou, France. He was deaf but studied medicine and worked as a medic for Jesuit missionaries in America. He served as a missionary to the Hurons and assisted St. Isaac Jocques. He was captured by the Iroquois after he made the Sign of the Cross over a child's head. The Iroquois had mistaken the gesture as a curse. St. Isaac received Rene into the Jesuits while they were imprisoned. Rene was martyred by being tomahawked in the head. He is a patron saint of anesthesiologists.

Renee *see Rene*

Renne *see Rene*

Rennie *see Rene*

Renovatus Saint; Latin; to make new

St. Renovatus (d. 633) converted to the faith from Arianism. He became abbot of Cauliana in Lusitania and then served as bishop of Merida more than twenty years.

Reol *see Regulus*

Rephael *see Raphael*

Restitutus Saint; Latin; he who returns to God

St. Restitutus (d. 299) was martyred during the persecution of Emperor Diocletian.

Reverianus Saint; Latin; to fear again

St. Reverianus (d. 272) was from Italy. He and a priest named Paul served as missionaries in Gaul and were martyred during the persecution of Emperor Aurelian.

Revocatus Saint; Latin; to speak again

St. Revocatus (d. 203) was a slave who was arrested with St. Perpetua. He was martyred.

Reynold *see Reinold*

Rheticus Saint; Greek

Rhett

St. Rheticus (d. 334) was a bishop of Autun, France, who condemned Donatism.

Rhett *see Rheticus*

Rhian Saint; form of Ryan; Gaelic; little king

Rhyan, Rian, Ryan

St. Rhian (date unknown) was a Welsh Abbot. Llanrhian, Dyfed, Wales, is named for him.

Rhoderick *see Roderic*

Rhoderik *see Roderic*

Rhoderyc *see Roderic*

Rhoderyck *see Roderic*

Rhoderyk *see Roderic*

Rhodri *see Roderic*

Rhodric *see Roderic*

Rhuddlad Saint; Welsh

St. Rhuddlad (seventh century) was a Welsh virgin who is the patroness of Llanrhyddlad in Anglesey, Wales.

Rhyan *see Rhian*

Ribert Saint; German; brilliant because of his power

St. Ribert (seventh century) was a monk of Valery-sur-Some in France, where he later served as abbot. He also was the bishop of Normandy and Picardy.

Ricardo *see Richard*

Rich *see Richard*

Richar *see Richard*

Richard Saint; German, English; rich and powerful ruler

Ricardo, Rich, Richar, Richards, Richaud, Richerd, Richird, Richshard, Rickard, Rickert, Rihardos, Riocard, Rychard, Ryszard

St. Richard, St. Richard Gwyn, St. Richard Martin, St. Richard Pampuri, St. Richard Reynolds, St. Richard of Andria, St. Richard of Chichester, St. Richard of Vaucelles, St. Richard of Wyche

St. Richard (d. 722) was from Wessex, England, and was the father of Sts. Willibald, Winnebald, and Walburga. He died in Lucca, Italy, while on pilgrimage to Rome. Many miracles were reported at his tomb.

Richards *see Richard*

Richaud *see Richard*

Richerd *see Richard*

Richird *see Richard*

Richshard *see Richard*

Rick *see Eric*

Rickard *see Richard*

Rickert *see Richard*

Rico *see Enrico*

Riel *see Gabriel*

Rigobert Saint; German; splendid, wealthy

Rigoberto

St. Rigobert (d. 743) was abbot of Orbais before being named archbishop of Rheims, France. He was exiled by Charles Martel. When he was allowed to return, he did not return to his former position. Instead, he became a hermit. He was known for his patience and as a miracle worker.

Rigoberto *see Rigobert*

Rihardos *see Richard*

Riobard *see Robert*

Riobart *see Robert*

Riocard *see Richard*

Rioch Saint; Celtic; grey

St. Rioch (d. 480) was a nephew of St. Patrick. He was a missionary bishop and abbot of Inisboffin, Ireland.

Riquier Saint; French

St. Riquier (d. 645) was born near Amiens, France. He rescued two Irish missionaries from the hands of local pagans. He traveled to England, where he studied for the priesthood. Returning to Ireland, he founded an abbey at Celles. He served as abbot there for a while before leaving to become a hermit.

Ritbert Saint

St. Ritbert (d. 690) was abbot of a monastery at Varennes.

Robars *see Robert*

Robart *see Robert*

Rober *see Robert*

Roberd *see Robert*

Robers *see Robert*

Robert Saint; Top 100 Name; English; famous brilliance

Bob, Bobby, Riobard, Riobart, Robars, Robart, Rober, Roberd, Robers, Roberte, Roberto, Robirt, Robson, Robyrt, Rosertas, Rudbert

St. Robert Bellarmine, St. Robert Lawrence, St. Robert Southwell, St. Robert of Bury St. Edmonds, St. Robert of Chaise Dieu, St. Robert of Frassinoro, St. Robert of Molesmes, St. Robert of Newminster, St. Robert of Syracuse

St. Robert Bellarmine (1542–1621) was born in Montepulciano, Italy. He joined the Society of Jesus and was ordained. He taught at Louvain and became rector at Roman College and then provincial of Naples and a cardinal. He spoke out against King James I of England and worked against the heretics of his time. He was a very important figure of the Counter-Reformation and is a Doctor of the Church.

Roberte *see Robert*

Roberto *see Robert*

Robirt *see Robert*

Robson *see Robert*

Robustian Saint; Latin; strong as the wood of an oak tree

St. Robustian (first century) was martyred in Milan, Italy.

Robyrt *see Robert*

Rocco *see Roch*

Roch Saint; English; rocky spring

Rocco, Rock

St. Roch (1295–1327) was born in Montpelier, France. Of noble birth, he gave away his inheritance and became a traveling pilgrim. He ministered to those suffering from the plague and miraculously cured many. He contracted the disease himself and went to the forest to die, but a dog befriended him and made sure he had food, and Roch recovered. He returned to France, where he was arrested for being a spy. He spent five years in jail before he died of natural causes.

Rock *see Roch*

Rodaric *see Roderic*

Rodarick *see Roderic*

Rodarik *see Roderic*

Rodderick *see Roderic*

Roderic Saint; German; famous ruler

Broderick, Rhoderick, Rhoderik, Rhoderyc, Rhoderyck, Rhoderyk, Rhodri, Rhodric, Rodaric, Rodarick, Rodarik, Rodderick, Roderich, Roderik, Roderikus, Roderrick, Roderyc, Roderyck, Roderyk, Rodgrick, Rodrique, Rorick, Ruderic

St. Roderic (d. 837), also known as Ruderic, was a priest in Spain. He had two brothers, one a Muslim and the other a lapsed Catholic. The two beat him until he was unconscious when he tried to break up an argument between them. The Muslim brought him to the authorities, and he was imprisoned and ultimately beheaded at Córdoba.

Roderich *see Roderic*

Roderik *see Roderic*

Roderikus *see Roderic*

Roderrick *see Roderic*

Roderyc *see Roderic*

Roderyck *see Roderic*

Roderyk *see Roderic*

Rodge *see Roger*

Rodgrick *see Roderic*

Rodingus Saint; Celtic

St. Rodingus (seventh century) was from Ireland. He traveled to Germany, where he evangelized the local pagans. He then went to France, where he lived as a hermit in the Argonne forest. In order to accommodate his many followers, he began a community there later known as Beaulieu.

Rodolph *see Rudolph*

Rodrigo Saint; form of Roderic; Italian, Spanish; famous ruler

St. Rodrigo Aguilar Alemán (1875–1927) was a Mexican priest and a member of the Knights of Columbus. During the Mexican persecution, he took refuge in a ranch, where he continued to minister to his people, but he was found and arrested. The following day, he was hung in the main plaza of Ejutla. He is one of the Saints of the Mexican Cristero War that were canonized by Pope John Paul II in 2000.

Rodrique *see Roderic*

Rog *see Roger*

Rogatian Saint

St. Rogatian (d. 256) was a priest in Carthage who was martyred.

Rogellus Saint; Latin; prayed for, wished for

St. Rogellus (d. 852) was a monk in Spain who was martyred

in Córdoba by the Moors for speaking out against the Muslim faith.

Roger Saint; German; famous spearman

Rodge, Rog, Rogerick, Rogerio, Rogers, Rogier, Rogir, Rogyer, Rüdiger, Ruggiero

Bl. Roger Cadwallador, Bl. Roger da Todi

Bl. Roger da Todi (d. 1237) was a follower of St. Francis, receiving the habit from him. He became the spiritual director of Bl. Philippa Mareria's community of Poor Clares.

Rogerick *see Roger*

Rogerio *see Roger*

Rogers *see Roger*

Rogier *see Roger*

Rogir *see Roger*

Rogyer *see Roger*

Rolf *see Ralph*

Rolph *see Ralph*

Roman Saint; Latin; from Rome, Italy

Romann, Romman

St. Roman Adame Rosales (1859–1927) was born in Jalisco, Mexico. He became a parish priest, serving at Nochistlan, Zacatecas. He was known for his care of the sick and his devotion to Our Lady. He founded the Daughters of Mary of Nocturnal Adoration. He was arrested after conducting a Lenten service at Rancho Veladones. He was tortured and denied food and drink. When some of his parishioners offered to buy the priest's freedom, the commander took the $6,000 and had Roman executed anyway. He was canonized by Pope John Paul II in 2000.

Romann *see Roman*

Romanus Saint; Latin; from Rome

St. Romanus Aybara, St. Romanus of Condat, St. Romanus of Le Mans, St. Romanus of Nepi, St. Romanus Ostiarus, St. Romanus of Rouen, St. Romanus of Subiaco, St. Romanus the Melodist

St. Romanus of Rouen (d. 639) grew up in the court of King Clotaire II, who later appointed him bishop of Rouen. He was known for his opposition to paganism to the extent of personally taking down a temple to Venus. He was also known for his care of prisoners and as a miracle worker.

Romaric Saint; Latin; from Rome, Italy

St. Romaric (d. 653) was a lord of Austrasia who was part of the court of King Clotaire. After his conversion by St. Amatus, he became a monk at Luxeuil Abbey in Burgandy. He helped found the monastery of Habendum at Remiremont, where he later served as abbot.

Romman *see Roman*

Romoaldus *see Modoaldus*

Romolo *see Romulus*

Romono *see Romulus*

Romuald Saint; German; the glorious king

St. Romuald (950–1027) was born in Ravenna, Italy, into an aristocratic family. After watching his father kill an opponent in a duel, he was moved to do penance for forty days. He moved to St. Apollinare Monastery, where he later served as abbot. He founded several monasteries and started the Order of Camaldoli in Tuscany. He was known for his austere way of life.

Romulo *see Romulus*

Romulus Saint; Latin; citizen of Rome

Romolo, Romono, Romulo

St. Romulus (d. 112) was a member of the imperial court in Rome. When he defended the Christians to Emperor Trajan, Trajan had him martyred.

Ronal *see Ronald*

Ronald Saint; Scottish; king's advisor

Ranald, Reinaldo, Ronal, Ronnald, Ronnold, Rynald

St. Ronald (d. 1158) was a warrior chieftain from Scotland. He built the Cathedral of St. Magnus at Kirkwall and was later murdered by rebelling warriors.

Ronan Saint; Gaelic; seal

Renan, Ronat, Rumon

St. Ronan (eighth century) was a bishop of Lismore, Ireland.

Ronat *see Ronan*

Ronnald *see Ronald*

Ronnold *see Ronald*

Roque Saint; Italian; rock

St. Roque Gonzalez de Santa Cruz (1576–1628) was born in Asuncion, Paraguay, the son of Spanish nobles. He became a priest and entered the Society of Jesus. He served as a missionary to Brazil. He worked hard to cultivate the trust of the local people and helped establish what are now the cities of Posadas and Encarnacion. He was martyred by Chief Nhecu. Pope John Paul II canonized him in 1988.

Rorick *see Roderic*

Rosendo *see Rudesind*

Rosertas *see Robert*

Ruadan Saint; Celtic; red haired

St. Ruadan (d. 584) was born in Leinster, Ireland. He founded the Monastery of Lothra in Tipperary and is considered one of the Twelve Apostles of Ireland.

Rudbert *see Robert*

Ruderic *see Roderic*

Rudesind Saint; Teutonic; excellent gentleman

Rosendo

St. Rudesind (907–977), also known as Rosendo, was born to a noble family in Galicia, Spain. He became bishop of Mondonedo when he was only eighteen. Because of a battle with a dissolute bishop of Compostela, he was exiled. Rudesind went to the Monastery of St. John Caveiro. He founded the Abbey of Celanova at Villar, where he served as abbot, as well as many other monasteries. His spiritual counsel was sought by many, and he was also known as a miracle worker.

Rüdiger *see Roger*

Rudolph Saint; German; famous wolf

Rodolph

St. Rudolph of Gubbio (d. 1066) was a student of St. Peter Damian. He became a Benedictine and was named bishop of Gubbio, Italy. He was known for his charity.

Ruefus *see Rufus*

Ruellinus Saint

St. Ruellinus (sixth century) was bishop of Treguier in Brittany, France.

Ruepert *see Rupert*

Rueperth *see Rupert*

Rufe *see Rufus*

Ruffinus Saint; form of Rufus; Latin; red head

St. Ruffinus (seventh century) was a Prince of Mercia who, along with his brother St. Wulfhade, was baptized by St. Chad. Their pagan father martyred the two brothers at Staffordshire, England.

Ruffis *see Rufus*

Ruffus *see Rufus*

Rufillus Saint; Latin; red-haired

St. Rufillus (fourth century) was the first bishop of Forum Pompilii, Emilia, Italy.

Rufino *see Rufus*

Rufinus Saint; form of Rufus; Latin; red head

St. Rufinus (d. 287) was a missionary in Gaul. He was martyred at Soissons during the reign of Emperor Diocletian.

Rufo *see Rufus*

Rufous *see Rufus*

Rufus Saint; Latin; red head

Rayfus, Ruefus, Rufe, Ruffis, Ruffus, Rufino, Rufo, Rufous

St. Rufus, St. Rufus of Metz, St. Rufus of Rome

St. Rufus (d. 295) was a deacon who was martyred at Capua, Italy, during the reign of Emperor Diocletian.

Ruggiero *see Roger*

Rumold Saint; German; fame, to rule

St. Rumold (d. 775) was an Irish monk who was consecrated as a bishop in Rome. He served with St. Willibrord in Belgium and was martyred by two men he had angered by pointing out their evil ways.

Rumon *see Ronan*

Rupert Saint; form of Robert; German, English; famous brilliance

Ruepert, Rueperth, Ruperth, Ruperto, Rupirt, Rupyrt

St. Rupert (660–710) was born into a noble Frankish family. He became bishop of Worms, Germany, and evangelized the German people. With the help of Duke Thedo of Bavaria, he helped establish Salzburg, Austria, and became its first archbishop. He is considered the Apostle of Bavaria and Austria.

Ruperth *see Rupert*

Ruperto *see Rupert*

Rupirt *see Rupert*

Rupyrt *see Rupert*

Rusticus Saint; Latin; country dweller

St. Rusticus (d. 462) was born in Gaul, the son of Bishop Bonosus. He became a monk at Lerins, France, and was later named bishop of Narbonne and fought against the Arians. He attended the Council of Ephesus, which condemned Nestorianism. He also built the Cathedral at Narbonne.

Rutilius Saint; German; shining brightly

St. Rutilius (d. 250) was from Roman Africa. He attempted to flee the persecutions of Emperor Trajanus Decius, but he was captured and martyred for the faith.

Ryan Top 100 Name; Gaelic; little king

Rhian, Rian

St. Ryan of Llanrhian (sixth century) of Pembrokshire, Wales, was an abbot dedicated to prayer, humility, and charity. Ryan or "Little King," was also considered a title of the infant Jesus.

Rychard *see Richard*

Rynald *see Ronald*

Ryszard *see Richard*

S

Sabas Saint; Hebrew; conversion

St. Sabas, St. Sabas of Serbia, St. Sabas Reyes Salazar

St. Sabas (439–532) was born in Cappadocia, near Caesarea. He was raised by an uncle, but he ran away as a child to a monastery. He later traveled to Jerusalem, where he entered a monastery. He then became a hermit in the desert near Jericho. He attracted many followers, was ordained a priest, and built monasteries and hospitals. He is known as one of the founders of Eastern monasticism.

Sabinian Saint; form of Sabine; Latin; member of a tribe in ancient Italy

St. Sabinian (d. 300) was the first bishop of Sens, France. He was martyred.

Sabinus Saint; form of Sabine; Latin; member of a tribe in ancient Italy

St. Sabinus (d. 303) was a bishop who was martyred at Spoleto, Italy, during the persecutions of Emperor Diocletian.

Sacer Saint; Latin; sacred

St. Sacer (seventh century) was an Irish abbot who founded the Monastery of Saggard, Dublin.

Sacerdos Saint; Latin; priest

Sardot, Serdon

St. Sacerdos (d. 551), also known as Sardot or Serdon,

was bishop of Lyons. He was a councilor of King Childebert I and presided over the Council of Orleáns.

Sadoth Saint

St. Sadoth (d. 345) attended the Council of Nicaea and was the head of the Church in Persia during the persecutions of Shapul II. He was tortured and then beheaded.

Sadwen Saint

St. Sadwen (sixth century) was from Wales and was a follower of St. Cadfan.

Sagar Saint; Indian; ocean

St. Sagar (d. 175) was a bishop of Laodicea in Phrygia (modern Turkey). He was martyred during the reign of Emperor Marcus Aurelius.

Saimon *see Simon*

Salaun Saint; Hebrew; peace

St. Salaun (d. 1358) was a poor man from Brittany who was considered a fool and was an object of derision. Later, he was recognized for his holiness.

Salbatore *see Salvatore*

Salo *see Solomon*

Saloman *see Solomon*

Salomon Saint; form of Solomon; Hebrew; peaceful

St. Salomon (d. 857) was martyred in Córdoba by being beheaded.

Salvador *see Salvatore*

Salvator *see Salvatore*

Salvatore Saint; Italian; savior

Salbatore, Salvador, Salvator, Salvattore, Salvidor, Sauveur

St. Salvatore of Horta (d. 1567) was born in Gerona, Spain. Orphaned as a child, he worked as a shoemaker before becoming a lay brother of the Franciscans in Barcelona. He worked as a cook but was known as a miracle worker and for living an austere life.

Salvattore *see Salvatore*

Salve *see Salvius*

Salvidor *see Salvatore*

Salvinus Saint; form of Salvatore; Spanish; savior

St. Salvinus (d. 420) was bishop of Verdun, France.

Salvius Saint; Latin; cured, healthy

Salve

St. Salvius, St. Salvius of Albi

St. Salvius (d. 768) was a missionary bishop who served in the area around Angoukme, France, and was sent to evangelize the Flemish. He was murdered by a local nobleman.

Samael *see Samuel*

Samaru *see Samuel*

Samauel *see Samuel*

Samaul *see Samuel*

Samel *see Samuel*

Sameul *see Samuel*

Samiel *see Samuel*

Samien *see Simon*

Sammail *see Samuel*

Sammel *see Samuel*

Sammuel *see Samuel*

Samouel *see Samuel*

Sampson *see Samson*

Samson Saint; Hebrew; like the
sun

*Sampson, Sansao, Sansim, San-
som, Sansome, Sanson, Sansone,
Sansum, Shymson*

Samson was one of twelve
heroes in ancient Israel whose
story is told in the book of
Judges (13–16). A fierce warrior, he is most remembered for
losing his strength when Deli-
lah tricked him and cut his hair
while he was asleep.

St. Samson (d. 530) was a physician and priest in Constantinople. He ministered to both the
physical and spiritual needs of
his patients. He founded a hospital and was known as "the
Father of the Poor."

Samuel Saint; Top 100 Name;
Hebrew; God has heard

*Samael, Samaru, Samauel, Sam-
aul, Samel, Sameul, Samiel, Sammail, Sammel, Sammuel, Samouel,
Samuele, Samuelis, Samuell,
Samuello, Samuil, Samuka, Samule, Samvel, Samwell, Sanko, Saumel, Shemuel, Simuel, Somhairle,
Zamuel*

St. Samuel, St. Samuel of Edessa

Samuel was a prophet in
ancient Israel. He anointed Saul
as the first king and selected
David to be his successor. His
story is told in 1 Samuel.

St. Samuel of Edessa (d. 496)
was an ecclesiastical writer who
wrote against the Nestorians
and other heretics.

Samuele *see Samuel*

Samuelis *see Samuel*

Samuell *see Samuel*

Samuello *see Samuel*

Samuil *see Samuel*

Samuka *see Samuel*

Samule *see Samuel*

Samvel *see Samuel*

Samwell *see Samuel*

Sancho *see Sanctan*

Sanctain *see Sanctan*

Sanctan Saint; Latin; holy, sacred

*Sancha, Sancho, Sancia, Sancta,
Sanctain, Sanctina*

St. Sanctan (sixth century) was
the son of a king in northern
Britain. He served as a missionary in Ireland and became
bishop of Kill-da-Les and Kill-
na-Sanctan (modern Dublin).

Sanctinus Saint; Latin; holy, sacred

St. Sanctinus (d. 300) was a follower of St. Denis of Paris. He
became the first bishop of Meux
and founded the diocese of Verdun, France.

Sandratus Saint

Shenudi

St. Sandratus (d. 986) was a
monk at St. Maximinus Monastery in Trier, Germany. King
Otto I sent him to St. Gall Monastery in Switzerland to help
reform that community. He
later served as abbot of Glad-
bach and Weissenburg.

Sanko *see Samuel*

Sansao *see Samson*

Sansim *see Samson*

Sansom *see Samson*

Sansome *see Samson*

Sanson *see Samson*

Sansone *see Samson*

Sansum *see Samson*

Saraf *see Seraphim*

Saraph *see Seraphim*

Sarbelius Saint; Latin

St. Sarbelius (d. 101) was a pagan high priest at Edessa, Mesopotamia, who converted to the faith. He was tortured and martyred during the reign of Emperor Trajan.

Sardot *see Sacerdos*

Sarmata Saint; Iranian; council

Sarmatas

St. Sarmata (d. 357) was a follower of the Desert Fathers in the Egyptian desert. He was murdered by a band of Bedouins.

Sarmatas *see Sarmata*

Saturninus Saint; Latin; related to Roman god Saturn

Saturnia

St. Saturninus (d. 450) was a leader of a group of 365 martyrs who were killed in Africa by Arian Vandals.

Saturus Saint; Latin; protector of the sown fields

St. Saturus (fifth century) was the master of the household of the Vandal King Genseric. He was tortured by the king and stripped of all he owned,

but he was allowed to live. He spent the rest of his days as a poor miner and cowherd. He is a patron of poor people.

Satyrus Saint; Latin; protector of the sown fields

St. Satyrus (d. 376) was the brother of Sts. Ambrose and Marcellina. Born in Germany, the family moved to Rome, where Satyrus became a lawyer. He served St. Ambrose as the manager of the secular affairs of the diocese of Milan.

Sauman *see Psalmodius*

Saumel *see Samuel*

Sauveur *see Salvatore*

Sawl Saint; Hebrew, English; asked for, prayed for

St. Sawl (sixth century) was a Welsh chieftain and father of St. Asaph.

Scannal Saint

St. Scannal (d. 563) was a follower of St. Columba and an Irish missionary in the area of Cell Coleraine.

Schotin Saint

St. Schotin (sixth century) was born in Ireland. He traveled to Wales to study under St. David. He returned home to live as a hermit. He also established a boy's school in Kilkenny.

Scubilion Saint

Bl. Scubilion Rousseau (1797–1867) was born in Burgundy, France. He entered the Christian Brothers and served as an elementary school teacher for ten years in France. He then was sent to Reunion Island in the Indian Ocean, where he taught the natives for thirty-four years. He was beatified by Pope John Paul II in 1989.

Seachnall Saint; Celtic; second

St. Seachnall (d. 457) was a follower of St. Patrick. He was named the first bishop of Dunsaugli, Meath. He later served as assistant bishop in Armagh. He wrote the hymn *Audites, Omnes Amantes Deum*.

Seameon *see Simeon*

Sean *see John*

Sebald Saint; German; bold victory

St. Sebald (d. 770) was from England. He traveled to Italy, where he lived as a hermit near Vicenza, before serving as a missionary with St. Willibald in the Reichswald. He was known as a miracle worker and is a patron saint of Nuremberg.

Sebashtian *see Sebastian*

Sebastain *see Sebastian*

Sebastao *see Sebastian*

Sebastian Saint; Top 100 Name; Greek, Latin; venerable, revered

Bastian, Bastien, Sebashtian, Sebastain, Sebastao, Sebastiane, Sebastiano, Sebastiao, Sebastin, Sebastine, Sebastyn, Sebo, Sepasetiano

St. Sebastian (d. 268) was born in Gaul and served as a soldier in the Roman army. Both Emperor Diocletian and Emperor Maximian had him serve as captain of the Praetorian Guards. Neither emperor knew that he was Christian. When Emperor Maximian discovered the truth, he ordered him to be executed. He was shot with arrows and was presumed dead. St. Castulus found that he was still alive and nursed him back to health. He then denounced the emperor, who this time ordered him beaten to death. He is a patron saint of archers, athletes, and soldiers.

Sebastiane *see Sebastian*

Sebastiano *see Sebastian*

Sebastiao *see Sebastian*

Sebastin *see Sebastian*

Sebastine *see Sebastian*

Sebastyn *see Sebastian*

Sebbe *see Sebbi*

Sebbi Saint; English

Sebbe

St. Sebbi (d. 694), also known as Sebbe, was king of Essex for thirty years. He was known for his devotion to prayer and almsgiving. He retired and became a monk in London.

Sebo *see Sebastian*

Secondo Saint; Latin; second

Bl. Secondo Pollo (1908–1941) was born in Caresanablot, Italy. He studied in Rome and was ordained a priest. He became the archdiocesan chaplain to the Italian Youth of Catholic Action and served as chaplain in a local prison. He then was drafted as a military chaplain and died on the battlefield while caring for the wounded. He was beatified in 1998 by Pope John Paul II.

Secundel Saint; Latin; second

St. Secundel (sixth century) was a hermit who lived with St. Friard on the island of Vindomitte, near Nantes.

Secundian Saint; Latin; second

St. Secundian (d. 250) was a government official who was martyred during the persecutions of Emperor Trajanus Decius.

Secundinus Saint; Latin; second

St. Secundinus (d. 306) was from Spain. He was martyred during the persecutions of Emperor Diocletian.

Secundus Saint; Latin; second

St. Secundus, St. Secundus of Ventimiglia

St. Secundus (d. 250) was an African who was martyred during the persecutions of Emperor Trajanus Decius.

Sedna Saint; Eskimo; well fed

St. Sedna (d. 570) was a bishop of Ossory, Ireland. He also served as abbot of Seir-Kiernan Abbey.

Seemeon *see Simeon*

Seimein *see Simon*

Seine *see Sequanus*

Seiriol Saint; Celtic; bright one

St. Seiriol (sixth century) was a son of King Owain Danwyn of Rhos. He became a monk and hermit in northern Wales.

Selestin *see Celestine*

Selestine *see Celestine*

Selestyn *see Celestine*

Seleucius Saint

St. Seleucius (d. 309) was martyred after he praised St. Porphyrius's behavior during his execution. He was beheaded.

Selim *see Solomon*

Selyf Saint; Hebrew, Welsh; peace

St. Selyf (sixth century) was a hermit in Cornwall, England.

Semein *see Simon*

Senach Saint; Gaelic

St. Senach (sixth century) was a follower of St. Finian. He became an Irish bishop and served as the head of the Clonard school.

Senan Saint; Spanish; living

Senen, Senin, Senón, Senyn

St. Senan (488–544) was born to a Christian farmer in County Clare, Ireland. He became a monk at Kilkenny and founded a monastery at Enniscorthy, Ireland, as well as several other churches and monasteries. He was a teacher of St. Aidan of Lindesfarne.

Senator Saint; Latin; old man

St. Senator (d. 480) was a priest who was sent by Pope St. Leo the Great to Constantinople as a papal legate. He was also present at the Council of Chalcedon. He later served as archbishop of Milan, Italy.

Sencio *see Inocencio*

Senen *see Senan*

Senin *see Senan*

Senoch Saint

St. Senoch (d. 576) was born to pagan parents in Gaul. He converted and became a hermit. He established a monastery in order to serve his large number of followers. He was known for his austere life. He was also a friend of St. Gregory of Tours.

Senón *see Senan*

Senyn *see Senan*

Sepasetiano *see Sebastian*

Seperatus Saint; Latin; separate

St. Seperatus (d. 180) was martyred in Africa during the persecutions of Vigellius.

Sequanus Saint; French

Seine

St. Sequanus (d. 580), also known as Seine, was born in Burgundy, France. He was a monk at Reomay and later founded the monastery at Segreste. He also lived as a hermit at Verreysous-Dree.

Serafin *see Seraphim*

Seraphim Saint, Angel; Hebrew; fiery, burning

Saraf, Saraph, Serafin, Seraphimus, Seraphin, Seraphinus

St. Seraphim of Montegranaro (d. 1604) was born into a poor family in Montegranaro, Italy. Uneducated, he worked as a shepherd in his youth. He entered the Capuchins at age sixteen and was known for his obedience, asceticism, and care for the poor. He was deeply devoted to the Eucharist and the Blessed Mother. He had the gifts of reading hearts and

prophecy. He was also known as a miracle worker.

Seraphimus *see Seraphim*

Seraphin *see Seraphim*

Seraphinus *see Seraphim*

Serapion Saint; Hebrew, Latin; ardent, fiery

St. Serapion, St. Serapion of Thmuis, St. Serapion the Scholastic, St. Serapion the Sindonite

St. Serapion the Scholastic (d. 370) was a monk in the Egyptian desert and companion of St. Anthony. He became the head of the Catechetical School of Alexandria and was known as a brilliant scholar and theologian who wrote about the divinity of the Holy Spirit.

Serdon *see Sacerdos*

Serenidus Saint; Latin; peaceful

St. Serenidus (d. 669) was a member of a noble family in Spoleto. He became a hermit in France. He attracted many followers and established a monastery near the Sarthe River.

Sereno *see Serenus*

Serenus Saint; Latin; calm, tranquil

Cerneuf, Sereno, Serino, Seryno

St. Serenus, St. Serenus the Gardener

St. Serenus the Gardener (fourth century), also known as Cerneuf, was born in Greece. He moved to Sirmium, where he was known for his garden. He was brought to court when falsely accused of insulting a wife of a member of the imperial guard. He was found innocent of that crime but was guilty of being a Christian. He was beheaded for refusing to sacrifice to pagan gods.

Serg *see Sergius*

Serge *see Sergius*

Sergei *see Sergius*

Sergios *see Sergius*

Sergius Saint; Latin; attendant

Serg, Serge, Sergei, Sergios, Sergus, Sirgio, Sirgios

St. Sergius, St. Sergius of Radonezh, Pope St. Sergius I

St. Sergius (d. 303) was an officer in the Roman army and was a friend of Emperor Maximian. When the emperor ordered him to sacrifice to pagan gods, he refused. Sergius was led through the streets of Arabissus in women's garb. He was then scourged and beheaded.

Sergus *see Sergius*

Serino *see Serenus*

Servais *see Servatus*

Servan Saint; Spanish; to serve

Servando, Servio

St. Servan (sixth century) was from Ireland and was consecrated a bishop by St. Palladius. He is called the Apostle of West Fife.

Servando *see Servan*

Servatus Saint; Latin; servant

Servais

St. Servatus (d. 384) was the bishop of Tongres and gave St. Athanasius refuge when that saint was exiled from Alexandria. Servatus attended the Council of Rimini in 359. Later in life, he served as bishop of Maastricht.

Servilian Saint; Latin; servant

St. Servilian (d. 117) was martyred during the persecutions of Emperor Trajan.

Servio *see Servan*

Servulus Saint; Latin; little servant

St. Servulus (d. 590) suffered from severe palsy from birth. He could not stand or sit unaided. He begged for alms at the door of St. Clement's Church but gave much of what he had to other beggars. He is a patron of handicapped people.

Servus Saint; Latin; servant

St. Servus (d. 484) was from Africa. He was martyred by Arian Vandals.

Seryno *see Serenus*

Severian Saint; Spanish; severe

St. Severian (d. 453) was a bishop of Scythopolis, Palestine. He opposed the Monophysite heretics at the Council of Chalcedon. He was martyred by followers of a Monophysite monk who sought to be bishop of Jerusalem.

Severinus Saint; Latin; severe

St. Severinus, St. Severinus Boethius

St. Severinus (sixth century) was born in Burgandy and became a monk at Agaunum. He was known as a miracle worker and cured King Clovis of a disease his doctors had been unable to help.

Severus Saint; Latin; severe

St. Severus, St. Severus of Alexandria

St. Severus (d. 483) was martyred by Monophysites in Alexandria, Egypt.

Seymeon *see Simon*

Seymon *see Simon*

Shawn *see John*

Shelomah *see Solomon*

Shemuel *see Samuel*

Shenudi *see Sandratus*

Shimon *see Simon*

Shymson *see Samson*

Sias *see Silas*

Sidnee *see Sidney*

Sidney Saint; French; from Saint-Denis, France

Cydney, Sidnee, Sidni, Sidnie, Sidny, Sydney

Bl. Sidney Hodgson (d. 1591) was an English layman who was martyred for helping priests during a time in which Catholicism was against the law in England. He was hung, drawn, and quartered in Tyburn, London, England.

Sidni *see Sidney*

Sidnie *see Sidney*

Sidny *see Sidney*

Sidonio *see Sidonius*

Sidonius Saint; form of Sidney; Latin; from Saint-Denis, France

Sidonio

St. Sidonius (d. 690) was a monk at Jumieges Abbey in France. St. Ouen of Rouen sent him to found Saint-Saens Monastery. He also founded several other monasteries.

Siegfred *see Sigfrid*

Siegfried *see Sigfrid*

Sigfrid Saint; German; victorious peace

Fredo, Siegfred, Siegfried, Sigfried, Sigfroi, Sigfryd, Sigifredo, Sigvard, Singefrid, Sygfred, Sygfreid, Sygfreyd, Sygfrid, Sygfried, Sygfryd, Zigfrid

St. Sigfrid (d. 690) was a deacon at Wearmouth Abbey. He served as coadjutor abbot for a time. He suffered from frail health and was known for his knowledge of scripture.

Sigfried *see Sigfrid*

Sigfroi *see Sigfrid*

Sigfryd *see Sigfrid*

Sigifredo *see Sigfrid*

Sigmund *see Zygmunt*

Sigvard *see Sigfrid*

Silas Saint; Latin; forest dweller

Sias

St. Silas (d. 50) was one of the early leaders of the church of Jerusalem. He accompanied St. Paul on his second missionary journey to Syria, Cilicia, and Macedonia. He was in prison with Paul in Philippi. He served as first bishop of Corinth.

Silvan *see Silvanus*

Silvanos *see Silvanus*

Silvanus Saint; Latin; forest dweller

Silvan, Silvanos

St. Silvanus (d. 165) was the son of St. Felicitas. He was martyred by being thrown off of a cliff during the persecutions of Emperor Antoninus.

Silverio *see Silverius*

Silverius Saint; Greek; Greek god of trees

Silverio, Sylvere

Pope St. Silverius (480–537) was the son of Pope Hormisdas. King Theodahad the Ostragoth pushed for his election as pope in 536, but Empress Theodora was attempting to put her own pick in place. Silverius was kidnapped, falsely accused of treason, and exiled to Ponza, Italy, where he died of starvation.

Silvestio *see Sylvester*

Sim *see Simon*

Simen *see Simon*

Simeon Saint; form of Simon; French; he heard

Seameon, Seemeon, Simion, Simione, Simmeon, Simmond, Simone, Symeon, Symyan

St. Simeon Barsabae, St. Simeon Metaphrastes, St. Simeon of Thou, St. Simeon the Stylite

St. Simeon the Stylite (390–459) was a shepherd in Turkey. He entered a monastery and lived as a hermit. He moved to the top of a pillar, where he devoted himself to prayer and preached twice a day to those who came to hear him. He converted many pagans and urged all to pray for the salvation of souls.

Simion *see Simeon*

Simione *see Simeon*

Simmeon *see Simeon*

Simmon *see Simon*

Simmond *see Simeon*

Simmonds *see Simon*

Simmons *see Simon*

Simon Saint, New Testament; Hebrew; he heard

Saimon, Samien, Seimein, Semein, Seymeon, Seymon, Shimon, Sim, Simen, Simmon, Simmonds, Simmons, Simonas, Simons, Simyon, Siomon, Siomonn, Symeon, Symon, Symonn, Symonns

St. Simon, St. Simon de Rojas, St. Simon of Cyrene, St. Simon the Zealot, St. Simon Stock, St. Simon Zelotes

St. Simon the Zealot (d. 107) was one of the less well-known apostles. He was known as a zealot for his rigid adherence to Jewish and Canaanite law. According to one tradition, he preached the faith in Egypt and Persia before suffering martyrdom. Another tradition has him dying peacefully in Edessa.

Simonas *see Simon*

Simone *see Simeon*

Simons *see Simon*

Simplicius Saint; Latin; simple

Pope St. Simplicius (d. 483) was born in Tivoli. He was elected pope in 468. He was an opponent of the heresy called Monothelitism and strove to maintain papal authority even as civil authority was collapsing.

Simuel *see Samuel*

Simyon *see Simon*

Singefrid *see Sigfrid*

Siomon *see Simon*

Siomonn *see Simon*

Sirgio *see Sergius*

Sirgios *see Sergius*

Siricius Saint; Latin

Pope St. Siricius (334–399) was born in Rome. He was elected pope in 384. He was the first pope to issue decretals that carried the force of law. He called for clerical celibacy. He also excommunicated Jovian for saying that Mary lost her virginity when she gave birth to Jesus. He also opposed Bonosus of Niassus when he said that Mary and Joseph had other children after Jesus.

Sisebut Saint; Teutonic; he who fulfills his leadership role wholeheartedly

St. Sisebut (d. 1082) was abbot of St. Peter Monastery in Cardena, Spain. He was known for his self-discipline and adherence to the monastic rule. He also gave the military hero Rodrigo Diaz (El Cid) refuge in the monastery when he had been exiled.

Sisinnius Saint

St. Sisinnius (d. 309) was a deacon in Rome who was arrested and sentenced to hard labor. He was martyred with the priest St. Saturninus.

Sissinius Saint; Latin

Pope St. Sissinius (d. 708) served as pope for only twenty days. He fortified the walls of Rome against attack.

Sixtus Saint; Latin; sixth

Pope St. Sixtus I (second century) was pope for ten years in the early part of the second century, although the exact dates are unknown. He was responsible for the following ordinances: that none but sacred ministers should touch the sacred vessels, that bishops summoned to Rome shall, upon their return, be received by their diocese only if they have an apostolic letter, and that the priest shall recite the Sanctus with the people.

Sly *see Sylvester*

Socrates Saint; Greek; wise, learned

Socratis, Sokrates, Sokratis

St. Socrates (d. 362) was martyred at Tiberiopolis.

Socratis *see Socrates*

Sokrates *see Socrates*

Sokratis *see Socrates*

Solaman *see Solomon*

Solamh *see Solomon*

Solange *see Solange (girl's name)*

Solmon *see Solomon*

Soloman *see Solomon*

Solomo *see Solomon*

Solomon Saint, Old Testament; Hebrew; peaceful

Salaun, Salo, Saloman, Selim, Shelomah, Solaman, Solamh, Solmon, Soloman, Solomo, Solomonas, Solomyn, Zelman, Zelmen

Solomon in scripture was the son of King David. He was the builder of the first Temple of Jerusalem and was known for his wisdom. Unfortunately, he turned to idolatry, which led to the kingdom being torn in two. Bl. Solomon le Clerq (1745–1792) was the son of a French wine merchant. He entered the Brothers of Christian Schools. He taught at several schools around France and then served as director of novices for his community. He later became secretary to the superior general of the order. He was imprisoned and martyred during the French Revolution.

Solomonas *see Solomon*

Solomyn *see Solomon*

Solutor Saint; Latin; payer

St. Solutor (d. 284) was martyred in Turin, Italy, and is regarded as a patron of that city.

Somhairle *see Samuel*

Sophronius Saint; Greek, Latin; self-controlled, sensible

St. Sophronius (d. 639) was born in Damascus, Syria, but traveled throughout both the East and West. He was known as an ecclesiastical writer and poet. He fought against Monothelitism. He served as patriarch of Jerusalem.

Soter Saint; Greek; savior

Pope St. Soter (d. 174) served as pope for about a decade. He declared that marriage was only a sacrament if blessed by a priest and also established Easter as an annual festival.

Soupire *see Exuperius*

Speciosus Saint; Latin; showy

St. Speciosus (d. 545) was a Roman noble who donated his wealth and joined St. Benedict's Monastery near Terracina, Italy.

Spiridon *see Spyridon*

Spyridon Saint; Greek, Latin; basket, spirit

Spiridon

St. Spyridon of Tremithius (270–348) was a native of Cyprus. He was a married sheep farmer who was tortured during the persecutions of Diocletian. After his wife's death, he entered a monastery. He went on to become bishop of Tremithius and attended the Council of Sardica.

Stanislao *see Stanislaus*

Stanislas *see Stanislaus*

Stanislau *see Stanislaus*

Stanislaus Saint; Latin, Slavik; stand of glory

Stanislao, Stanislas, Stanislau, Stanislus, Stanyslaus

St. Stanislaus (d. 1079) was born to a noble family near Krakow, Poland. He was ordained a priest and became known as a preacher and spiritual advisor. In 1072, he was named bishop of Krakow. He excommunicated King Boleslaus the Bold for his cruelty and kidnapping of the wife of a nobleman. Boleslaus killed Stanislaus while he was saying Mass. He is the patron saint of Krakow.

Stanislav *see Stanislaw*

Stanislaw Saint; form of Stanislaus; Slavik

Stanislav

St. Stanislaw Kostka (1550–1568) was the son of a Polish senator. He attended the Viennese Jesuit College when he was fourteen. While at the home of a Lutheran, he became gravely ill but was not allowed to call a priest. He called on St. Barbara who appeared to him in a vision. He was miraculously healed by Our Blessed Mother who then told him to become a Jesuit. He died of a high fever while attending the Jesuit college in Rome. He was a friend of St. Peter Canisius.

Stanislus *see Stanislaus*

Stanyslaus *see Stanislaus*

Stasio *see Anastasius*

Stefan Saint; form of Stephen; German, Polish, Swedish; crowned

Bl. Stefan Grelewski, Bl. Stefan Wincenty Frelichowski

Bl. Stefan Grelewski (1898–1941) was born in Dwikozy, Poland. He was ordained a priest and also worked as a journalist and translator. He died at the Dachau concentration camp. He is one of the 108 Polish Martyrs of World War II and was beatified by Pope John Paul II in 1999.

Stefanos *see Stephen*

Steffan *see Stephen*

Stefos *see Stephen*

Stepanos *see Stephen*

Stephan *see Stephen*

Stephanas *see Stephen*

Stephano *see Stephen*

Stephanos *see Stephen*

Stephanus *see Stephen*

Stephen Saint, New Testament; Greek; crowned

Estefan, Estevon, Stefanos, Steffan, Stefos, Stepanos, Stephan, Stephanas, Stephano, Stephanos, Stephanas, Stephens, Stephfan, Stephin, Stepven, Steven

St. Stephen, St. Stephen Harding, St. Stephen I, St. Stephen Min Kuk-Ka, St. Stephen of Grandmont, St. Stephen of Obazine, St. Stephen of Surosh, St. Stephen the Anchorite, St. Stephen the Great

St. Stephen (d. 33) was a deacon and preacher who became the first Christian martyr. He was stoned to death by angry Jews. Saul, who would later become St. Paul, was present at the execution.

Stephens *see Stephen*

Stephfan *see Stephen*

Stephin *see Stephen*

Stepven *see Stephen*

Steven *see Stephen*

Successus Saint; Latin; success

St. Successus (second century) was martyred in Numidia.

Suitbert *see Swithbert*

Sulpice Saint; Latin

Sulpicius

St. Sulpice II (d. 647) was a courtier of the Frankish King Thierry II of France. At night, he would visit churches to perform penance. St. Austregisilus, bishop of Bourges, convinced him to become a priest. Sulpice later served as bishop of Bourges himself. During his tenure, he convinced Bourges's Jews to embrace the Christian faith.

Sulpicius *see Sulpice*

Swidbert *see Swithbert*

Swithan *see Swithun*

Swithbert Saint; English; strong and bright

Swidbert, Suitbert

St. Swithbert (647–713) was from Northumbria. He traveled to Ireland and joined the Monastery of Rathmelsigi. He was sent to evangelize the Netherlands and became a regionary bishop for that area. He also served as a missionary in Germany but was deterred by a Saxon invasion. Late in life, he founded a monastery at Kaiserswerth where he lived out his days.

Swithen *see Swithun*

Swithon *see Swithun*

Swithun Saint; German; strong

Swithan, Swithen, Swithon, Swithun, Swithyn

St. Swithun (d. 862) was born in Wessex, England. He was ordained and became chaplain and counselor to King Egbert of the West Saxons. He became bishop of Winchester and was known for his care of the poor and needy.

Swithun *see Swithun*

Swithyn *see Swithun*

Sydney *see Sidney*

Sygfred *see Sigfrid*

Sygfreid *see Sigfrid*

Sygfreyd *see Sigfrid*

Sygfrid *see Sigfrid*

Sygfried *see Sigfrid*

Sygfryd *see Sigfrid*

Syl *see Sylvester*

Sylvanus Saint; Latin; forest dweller

St. Sylvanus (d. 950) was a hermit who was martyred by Moors in Spain.

Sylvere *see Silverius*

Sylverster *see Sylvester*

Sylvester Saint; Latin; forest dweller

Silvestio, Sly, Syl, Sylverster, Sylvestre, Sylvestro, Sylwester

Pope St. Sylvester, St. Sylvester II, Sylvester III

Pope St. Sylvester (d. 335) was born in Rome, survived the persecutions of Diocletian, and became pope in 314 when Constantine was emperor. During his pontificate, the Basilica of St. John Lateran, Santa Croce, and St. Peter's Basilica were built. He did not attend the First Council of Nicaea in 325 but sent representatives and approved the council's decision.

Sylvestre *see Sylvester*

Sylvestro *see Sylvester*

Sylwester *see Sylvester*

Symeon *see Simeon, Simon*

Symforian Saint

Bl. Symforian Ducki (1888–1942) was born in Warsaw, Poland. He was a Franciscan Capuchin friar who was arrested by the Nazis and sent to the Auschwitz concentration camp. He is one of the 108 Polish Martyrs of World War II and was beatified by Pope John Paul II in 1999.

Symmachus Saint; Greek, Latin

St. Symmachus (d. 514) was from Sardinia. He was an archdeacon in Rome when he was elected pope in 498. An antipope was elected by the opposition the same day, and the schism lasted several years. As pope, he sent aid to the bishops of North Africa and also ransomed captives, founded hospices, and helped victims of barbarian raids. He also expanded the use of the Gloria at Mass.

Symon *see Simon*

Symonn *see Simon*

Symonns *see Simon*

Symphorian Saint; Greek, Latin; carry, useful, good

St. Symphorian (d. 178) was the son of a Roman senator. He studied at Gaul where he was arrested for not worshipping the pagan goddess Cybele. He refused to deny the faith and was beheaded.

Symyan *see Simeon*

Syrell *see Cyril*

Syril *see Cyril*

Szymon Saint; Hebrew; to hear, to be heard

St. Szymon Lipnica (1437–1482) was born in the south of Poland and attended the Jagiellonian Academy in Krakow. He joined the Franciscans and was known as a powerful preacher. He died while taking care of plague victims. He was canonized by Pope Benedict XVI in 2007.

T

Tacla *see Thecla (girl's name)*

Tadeusz Saint; form of Thaddeus; Slavic; courageous

Bl. Tadeusz Dulny (1914–1942) was a Polish layman who was killed at the Dachau concentration camp. He is one of the Polish Martyrs of World War II and was beatified by Pope John Paul II in 1999.

Tadhg *see Timothy*

Taidgh *see Timothy*

Talacrian Saint

Tarkin

St. Talacrian (sixth century), also known as Tarkin, was a bishop of Caledonia.

Tamhas *see Thomas*

Tanco Saint

St. Tanco (d. 808) was abbot of Amalbarich Abbey in Saxony. He served as a missionary in Belgium and was later named bishop of Werden, Germany. He was martyred for destroying pagan statues.

Taracus *see Tharacus*

Tarasios *see Tarasius*

Tarasius Saint; Greek; prophet

Tarasios

St. Tarasius (750–806) served as consul and secretary of state to Emperor Constantine IV and Empress Irene. He was elected patriarch of Constantinople and worked to resolve the iconoclast controversy. He was also imprisoned for condemning the emperor for leaving his wife and marrying another woman. He was known for his asceticism.

Tarrance *see Terence*

Tarsicius Saint; Latin; born in Tarsus

St. Tarsicius (third or fourth century) was martyred while defending the Eucharist from a pagan mob. According to tradition, when the pagans searched him after he was killed, the Eucharist had miraculously disappeared. He is a patron saint of altar servers and first communicants.

Taso Saint; Greek; revival

St. Taso (eighth century) was from Benevento, Italy. He became a monk at Farfa Monastery in Sabina, Italy, where he later served as abbot.

Tassac *see Asicus*

Tassach *see Asicus*

Tathal Saint; Welsh

Athan, Tathan

St. Tathal (sixth century) was from Ireland and became a hermit in Glamorgen, Wales, where he ultimately started a school and monastery.

Tathan *see Tathal*

Tation Saint; Latin; he who is quiet

St. Tation (d. 304) was beheaded in Bithynia during the persecutions of Emperor Diocletian.

Tato Saint

St. Tato (eighth century) was from Benevento, Italy. He became a monk at Farfa Monastery in Sabina, Italy, where he later served as abbot. He was a brother of Sts. Paldo and Taso.

Tatwin *see Tatwine*

Tatwine Saint; English

Tatwin

St. Tatwine (670–734) was from Mercia, England. He became a monk at Bredon and was named archbishop of Canterbury in 731. He was a writer of riddles and also composed a Latin grammar.

Taurin *see Taurinus*

Taurinus Saint; Latin; bull

Taurin

St. Taurinus (d. 412) was a bishop of Evreux, Normandy, France.

Tavey *see Octavian*

Teadomiro *see Theodore*

Tebaldo *see Theobald*

Tecla *see Thecla (girl's name)*

Tedor *see Theodore*

Teilo Saint; Welsh

Teliaus, Theliau

St. Teilo (500–560) was from Penally, Pembrokshire, Wales. He traveled with St. David of Wales to Jerusalem. When he returned to Wales, he founded Llandaff Monastery in Dyfed.

Telemachus *see Almachius*

Telesphorus Saint; Greek; man from the countryside

Pope St. Telesphorus (d. 137) was born in Greece. He may have lived as a hermit. He served as pope from approximately 126 to 138. It is possible that he established the keeping of Lent for seven weeks prior to Easter. He was martyred for the faith.

Teliaus *see Teilo*

Tenenan Saint; French

St. Tenenan (seventh century) was from Britain. He lived as a hermit in Brittany, France, before serving as bishop of Leon, Spain.

Teobald *see Theobald*

Teobaldo *see Theobald*

Teobalt *see Theobald*

Teodor Saint; form of Theodore; Italian, Spanish; gift of God

Bl. Teodor Romza (1911–1947) was born at Velykyj Bychkiv, Transcarpathia, Ukraine. He was ordained a priest and received a licentiate in theology. He was drafted and served in the military. After his discharge he worked as a parish priest and taught at the seminary in Uzhorod. He was named bishop of the Mukachiv eparchy. He fought against the Soviet occupation. He was wounded in an assassination attempt and then poisoned while in the hospital. He was beatified by Pope John Paul II in 2001.

Teodorico *see Theodoric*

Teodus *see Theodore*

Teofil *see Theophilus*

Teos *see Theodore*

Terance *see Terence*

Terence Saint; Latin; smooth

Tarrance, Terance, Terince, Terrence, Terrance, Terron, Terronce, Terrynce, Terynce

St. Terence, St. Terence of Metz

St. Terence (first century) was bishop of Iconium.

Terentian Saint; Latin; soft, tender

St. Terentian (d. 118) was bishop of Todi, in Umbria, Italy. He was tortured and beheaded during the reign of Emperor Hadrian.

Terentianus Saint; Latin; soft, tender

St. Terentianus (first century) was the commander of an imperial Roman bodyguard. He witnessed the death sentencing of Sts. John and Paul. He converted and was martyred.

Terince *see Terence*

Ternan Saint; Celtic; high, noble

Torannan

St. Ternan (fifth century) served as a missionary bishop among the Picts in Scotland. He founded Culross Abbey in Fifeshire.

Ternatius Saint

St. Ternatius (d. 680) was bishop of Besancon, France. He was known for his holiness and charity.

Terrance *see Terence*

Terrence *see Terence*

Terron *see Terence*

Terronce *see Terrence*

Terrynce *see Terence*

Tertullian Saint; Latin

St. Tertullian (d. 490) was bishop of Bologna, Italy.

Tertullinus Saint; Latin

St. Tertullinus (d. 257) was martyred two days after being ordained a priest during the reign of Emperor Valerian.

Terynce *see Terence*

Tetricus Saint; Latin

St. Tetricus (d. 572) was the uncle of St. Gregory of Tours and the son of St. Gregory, bishop of Langres. When his father died, he took over leadership of the see.

Thais Saint; Greek; bond

St. Thais (fourth century) was a wealthy Christian woman raised in Alexandria. She lived as a courtesan, but she repented, gave up her money, and performed penance by being walled up for three years in a convent. She was released and lived with the other women at the convent for fifteen days before her death.

Thalassius Saint; Greek; to blossom

St. Thalassius (fifth century) was a hermit who lived in a cave near Cyrrhus.

Thalelaeus Saint

St. Thalelaeus (d. 284) was from Lebanon and was the son of a Roman general. He was a Christian doctor who treated his patients free of charge. He was captured and tortured during the reign of Emperor Numerian. He survived being cast into the sea but was then beheaded.

Thamel Saint; Aramaic; twin

St. Thamel (d. 125) was a pagan priest who converted to Christianity and was martyred during the reign of Emperor Hadrian.

Tharacus Saint

Taracus

St. Tharacus (d. 304), also known as Taracus, was an officer in the Roman army. During the reign of Emperor Diocletian, he was thrown to wild beasts but was unharmed. He was then beheaded.

Thasius *see Cyprian*

Theballd *see Theobald*

Thedric *see Theodoric*

Thedrick *see Theodoric*

Thedrik *see Theodoric*

Theliau *see Teilo*

Themistoeles Saint

St. Themistoeles (d. 253) was martyred by beheading during the persecutions of Emperor Valerian.

Theobald Saint; German; people's prince

Tebaldo, Teobald, Teobaldo, Teobalt, Theballd, Theobaldo, Theobalt, Theobanet, Thibault, Thyobald, Thyobaldo, Thyobalt, Tibald, Tibalt, Tibold, Tiebold, Tiebout, Tiobaid, Tioboid, Toiboid, Tybald, Tybalt, Tybault

St. Theobald, St. Theobald of Marly, St. Theobald of Vienne

St. Theobald of Marly (d. 1247) was born in Marly Castle, France. He was brought up at the court of King Philip II Augustus of France. He left court and became a Cistercian monk at the Abbey of Vaux-de-Cernay, where he later served as abbot.

Theobaldo *see Theobald*

Theobalt *see Theobald*

Theobanet *see Theobald*

Theodard Saint; Greek, Latin

Audard

St. Theodard (d. 893) was born at Montauban, France. He became a lawyer. He was named secretary to Archbishop Sigebold of Narbonne. He became a deacon and then succeeded Sigebold as archbishop. He helped rebuild the area after the Saracens had invaded.

Theodemar *see Thethmar*

Theodemir Saint; Greek, Latin

St. Theodemir (d. 851) was martyred in Córdoba, Spain, during the persecution of Emir Abd al-Rahman II.

Theodinaris *see Thiemo*

Theodon *see Theodore*

Theodor *see Theodore*

Theódor *see Theodore*

Theodore Saint; Greek; gift of God

Teadomiro, Tedor, Teodus, Teos, Theodon, Theodor, Theódor, Theodors, Theodorus, Theodosios, Theodrekr, Tivadar, Todor, Tolek

St. Theodore, St. Theodore of Bologna, St. Theodore of Chotep, St. Theodore of Egypt, St. Theodore of Emesa, St. Theodore of Pavia, St. Theodore of Pelusium, St. Theodore of Studites, St. Theodore of Sykeon, St. Theodore of Tabenna, St. Theodore of Tarsus

St. Theodore (d. 310) was a deacon at Pentapolis, Lybia. He and Sts. Irenaeus, Serapion, and Ammonius were tortured by having their tongues cut out. All survived the ordeal and died of natural causes, but they are considered martyrs due to their willingness to die.

Theodoret Saint; Greek; gift of God

St. Theodoret of Antioch (d. 362) was a Syrian Christian priest who was beheaded by Emperor Julian the Apostate.

Theodoric Saint; German; ruler of the people

Derek, Derrick, Teodorico, Thedric, Thedrick, Thedrik, Theodorick, Theodorik, Theodrick, Theodryc, Theodryck, Theodryk, Thierry

St. Theodoric, St. Theodoric of Emden, St. Theodoric of Orleans, St. Theodoric Balat

St. Theodoric of Orleans (d. 1022) was a monk at the Monastery of Saint Pierre-le-Vif before becoming a royal counselor and bishop of Orleans.

Theodorick *see Theodoric*

Theodorik *see Theodoric*

Theodors *see Theodore*

Theodorus *see Theodore*

Theodosios *see Theodore*

Theodosius Saint; form of Theodore; Greek; gift of God

St. Theodosius, St. Theodosius of Antioch, St. Theodosius Pechersky, St. Theodosius the Cenobiarch

St. Theodosius (d. 516) served as bishop of Auxerre, France.

Theodotus Saint; Greek, Latin; given to God

St. Theodotus (d. 325) was bishop of Cyrenia on Cyprus. He was imprisoned during the persecutions of Emperor Licinius Licinianus.

Theodrekr *see Theodore*

Theodrick *see Theodoric*

Theodryc *see Theodoric*

Theodryck *see Theodoric*

Theodryk *see Theodoric*

Theodulphus Saint; Greek, Latin

Thiou

St. Theodulphus (d. 776) was abbot at Lobbes Monastery near Liege, Belgium. He also served as a bishop.

Theodulus Saint; Greek, Latin; slave of God

St. Theodulus (d. 127) was the son of Sts. Exsuperius and Zoe. He was a slave owned by a pagan. When he and his family refused to sacrifice meat to an idol, they were all tortured and martyred.

Theofred *see Theofrid*

Theofrid Saint; Greek, Latin

Theofred, Chaffre

St. Theofrid, St. Theofird (Chaffre) of Orange

St. Theofrid (d. 732), also known as Chaffre, was abbot of Calmeliac near Le Puy. He defended the monastery against a Moorish invasion. The Moors found him praying and beat him. He was wounded, but a severe storm dispelled his attackers. He died a week later.

Theogenes Saint; Greek, Latin; Godly

St. Theogenes (d. 320) was a soldier in the Roman army who was martyred at Cyzicus on the Hellespont.

Theon *see Theonas*

Theonas Saint; Greek, Latin; Godly

Theon

St. Theonas, St. Theonas of Egypt, St. Theonas "Column of the Church"

St. Theonas (d. 284) was a pagan magician who converted to the faith and was martyred during the persecutions of Emperor Diocletian.

Theonestus Saint; Greek, Latin; Godly

St. Theonestus (d. 425) was a bishop of Philippi, Macedonia, who was exiled by Arians. The pope sent him as a missionary to Germany, but the Vandals invaded and he was also forced to leave there. He was martyred.

Theopemptus Saint; Greek, Latin

Theopompus

St. Theopemptus (d. 284) was a bishop of Nicomedia who was martyred during the persecutions of Emperor Diocletian.

Theophane Saint; Greek, Latin; manifestation of God

St. Theophane Venard (1829–1861) was from Poitiers, France. He joined the Foreign Missions of Paris and was sent to Vietnam where he taught in a seminary. He was tortured by being chained in a cage for months. He was martyred by being beheaded. One of the Martyrs of Vietnam, he was canonized in 1988 by Pope John Paul II.

Theophanes Saint; Greek, Latin; manifestation of God

St. Theophanes (d. 815) was an officer in the Byzantine court of Leo the Armenian. He was arrested and martyred for opposing Leo's iconoclasm.

Theophilus Saint; Greek; loved by God

Teofil, Theophlous, Theopolis

St. Theophilus, St. Theophilus of Corte, St. Theophilus the Lawyer, St. Theophilus the Penitent

St. Theophilus the Lawyer (d. 300) was beheaded in Caesarea in Cappadocia.

Theophlous *see Theophilus*

Theophylact Saint; Greek, Latin; God's guard

St. Theophylact (d. 845) was a bishop of Nicomedia who opposed Emperor Leo V's iconoclasm. He was exiled to Caria where he spent thirty years. He was known for his charity.

Theopistus Saint; Greek, Latin; God's beloved

St. Theopistus (d. 188) was the son of Sts. Eustachius and Theopistes. He was martyred during the persecutions of Emperor Hadrian by being cooked to death in a bronze bull.

Theopolis *see Theophilus*

Theopompus *see Theopemptus*

Theotimus Saint; Greek, Latin; honorable gift to God

St. Theotimus (d. 407) was bishop of Tomi on the Black Sea. He helped evangelize the Germanic tribes on the Danube Valley.

Theotonius Saint; Greek; godly

St. Theotonius (1088–1166) was born in Gonfeo, Spain. He studied in Portugal and became an archpriest of Viseu. After making a pilgrimage to the Holy Land, he entered the Augustinian Canons at Coimbra. He later served as an advisor to King Alfonso I Henriquez of Portugal.

Thespesius Saint; Greek; wondrous one

St. Thespesius (d. 230) was martyred in Cappadocia during the reign of Emperor Severus Alexander.

Thethmar Saint

Theodemar

St. Thethmar (d. 1152) was a canon who served as a missionary to the Wends, a tribe in Germany.

Thibault *see Theobald*

Thiemo Saint; German; people, race, great, famous

Theodinaris

St. Thiemo (d. 1102) was born into a noble family in Bavaria. He became a Benedictine monk at Niederltaich and was known for his skill as a painter, metalworker, and sculptor. He served as abbot of St. Peter's in Salzburg and was then named archbishop of that area. He was exiled by King Henry IV because of his position in the Investiture Controversy. He then traveled to Palestine to help in the crusades. He was captured and martyred by Muslims.

Thiento Saint; German

St. Thiento (d. 955) was an abbot in Bavaria, Germany. He and six of his monks were martyred by the Magyars of Hungary.

Thierry *see Theodoric*

Thillo *see Tillo*

Thiou *see Theodulphus*

Thomais *see Thomais (girl's name)*

Thomas Saint, New Testament; Top 100 Name; Aramaic; twin

Tamhas, Thomason, Thomaz, Thommas, Thumas, Tomcy, Tommasi, Tuomo

St. Thomas, St. Thomas Aquinas, St. Thomas Becket, St. Thomas Danki, St. Thomas Dien, St. Thomas Du, St. Thomas Garnet, St. Thomas Kozaki, St. Thomas More, St. Thomas of Antioch, St. Thomas of Dover, St. Thomas of Farfa

St. Thomas (d. 72) was one of the twelve apostles of Jesus. He is best known for his role after the Resurrection. He doubted the testimony of the other apostles that Jesus had risen from the dead. When Christ appeared to the group again, he was present, rebuked for his doubt, and able to see the nail holes and put his hand into Christ's side. He declared, "My Lord and God," thereby proclaiming the divinity of Jesus. According to tradition, he preached to the Parthians, Medes, and Persians, eventually reaching India. He was martyred by being pierced with a spear in Calamine, India. He is a patron saint of architects.

Thomason *see Thomas*

Thomaz *see Thomas*

Thomian Saint; form of Thomas; Greek, Aramaic; twin

Toiman, Toimen

St. Thomian (d. 660) served as archbishop of Armagh, Ireland. He was involved in the controversy over when Easter should be celebrated.

Thommas *see Thomas*

Thorfinn Saint; Gaelic; chief, thunder

Torfinn

St. Thorfinn (d. 1285) was born in Norway and became a Cistercian monk at Tautra Abbey. He served as canon of the Cathedral of Nidaros and was soon named as a bishop. He was exiled by King Eric for his opposition to state involvement in Church affairs. He then lived at TerDoest Abbey in Flanders. He died soon after returning from a pilgrimage to Rome.

Thorlac Saint; Latin

St. Thorlac Thorhallsson (1133–1193) was born to a poor family in Iceland. He became a priest and served his parish well. He then traveled to Europe where he studied at Paris, France, and Lincoln, England. He returned to Iceland and settled at Kirkjubaer and established the first nunnery in that area. He became abbot of the Augustinian Canonry at Thykkvibaer and was later elected bishop of Skálholt, a position he held for fifteen years.

Thraseas Saint

St. Thraseas (d. 170) was bishop of Eumenia, Phrygia, in Asia Minor, and was martyred at Smyrna during the reign of Emperor Marcus Aurelius.

Throstan *see Drostan*

Thumas *see Thomas*

Thyobald *see Theobald*

Thyobaldo *see Theobald*

Thyobalt *see Theobald*

Thyrsus Saint; Greek, Latin; staff carried in mythology

St. Thyrsus (d. 251) was martyred at Apollonia, Phrygia, in Asia Minor during the persecutions of Emperor Decius.

Tibald *see Theobald*

Tibalt *see Theobald*

Tiberias *see Tiberius*

Tiberio *see Tiberius*

Tiberious *see Tiberius*

Tiberiu *see Tiberius*

Tiberius Saint; Latin; from the Tiber River region

Tiberias, Tiberio, Tiberious, Tiberiu, Tibius, Tyberious, Tyberius

St. Tiberius (d. 303) was martyred at Agde, France, during the persecutions of Emperor Diocletian.

Tibius *see Tiberius*

Tibold *see Theobald*

Tiburtius Saint; Latin; from Tibur

St. Tiburtius (d. 288) was a Roman subdeacon who proved his faith by walking over hot coals barefoot without incurring any injury. He was beheaded at Via Labicana.

Tiebold *see Theobald*

Tiebout *see Theobald*

Tiege *see Timothy*

Tierney *see Tigernach*

Tierry *see Tigernach*

Tigernach Saint; Gaelic; lord

Tierney, Tierry

St. Tigernach (d. 549) was grandson of the Irish King Eochod. He was a godson of St. Brigid. He was kidnapped by pirates and given to the British king, who placed him at Rosnat Monastery where he later became a monk. He returned to Ireland and served as abbot of Cluanois Abbey and then bishop of Clogher.

Tigides Saint

St. Tigides (sixth century) served as a bishop in the French Alps.

Tigrius Saint; Latin; tigerlike

St. Tigrius (d. 405) was a priest in Constantinople who supported St. John Chrysostom during his exile. Because of his support, Tigrius was arrested on the false charge of attempting to burn down the Constantinople Cathedral. He was exiled.

Tilbert Saint; English

St. Tilbert (d. 789) served as bishop of Hexham, England.

Tillo Saint; Teutonic; skillful and praises God

Thillo, Tillon

St. Tillo (d. 702) was born in Saxony but was kidnapped and brought to the low countries as a slave. After being ransomed by St. Eligius of Noyon, he became a Benedictine monk at Solignac. He was ordained a priest and served as a missionary near Courtrai, France. He later lived as a hermit at Solignac.

Tillon *see Tillo*

Timan *see Timon*

Timathee *see Timothy*

Timathey *see Timothy*

Timathy *see Timothy*

Timen *see Timon*

Timethy *see Timothy*

Timin *see Timon*

Timithy *see Timothy*

Timito *see Timothy*

Timka *see Timothy*

Timkin *see Timothy*

Timmothy *see Timothy*

Timolaus Saint

St. Timolaus (d. 303) was beheaded in Caesarea, Palestine, during the persecutions of Emperor Diocletian.

Timon Saint, New Testament; Greek; honorable

Timan, Timen, Timin, Timyn

St. Timon (first century) was one of the seven deacons chosen by the apostles in Acts 6:5 to minister to the Nazarene community of Jerusalem.

Timontheo *see Timothy*

Timonthy *see Timothy*

Timót *see Timothy*

Timote *see Timothy*

Timoteus *see Timothy*

Timotheo *see Timothy*

Timotheos *see Timothy*

Timotheus *see Timothy*

Timothey *see Timothy*

Timothie *see Timothy*

Timothy Saint, New Testament; Greek; God's house

Tadhg, Taidgh, Tiege, Timathee, Timathey, Timathy, Timethy, Timithy, Timito, Timka, Timkin, Timmothy, Timok, Timontheo, Timonthy, Timót, Timote, Timoteus, Timotheo, Timotheos, Timotheus, Timothey, Timothie, Timthie, Tiomóid, Tomothy, Tymothy

St. Timothy, St. Timothy II, St. Timothy III, St. Timothy the Lector

St. Timothy (d. 97) was the son of a Greek father and a Jewish mother. He was converted to Christianity by St. Paul and became a close friend and worker with that saint. He served as the head of the church in Ephesus and was the recipient of two letters from St. Paul that are included in the Bible. He was martyred by being stoned to death.

Timthie *see Timothy*

Timyn *see Timon*

Tiobaid *see Theobald*

Tioboid *see Theobald*

Tiomóid *see Timothy*

Tipasio *see Tipasius*

Tipasius Saint; African

Tipasio, Typasius

St. Tipasius (d. 304) was a soldier who refused to worship pagan idols. He was beheaded during the persecutions of Emperor Diocletian.

Titan *see Titus*

Titas *see Titus*

Titek *see Titus*

Tites *see Titus*

Titian Saint; form of Titus; Latin, Greek; giant, hero

St. Titian (fifth century) was born in Germany and became bishop of Brescia, Italy.

Titus Saint, New Testament; Latin, Greek; giant, hero

Titan, Titas, Titek, Tites

St. Titus (d. 96) was a companion of St. Paul and is mentioned in several of Paul's letters. He accompanied Paul to Jerusalem and worked in Corinth, Greece. He later served in Crete as that community's first bishop.

Tivadar *see Theodore*

Todor *see Theodore*

Toiboid *see Theobald*

Toiman *see Thomian*

Toimen *see Thomian*

Tola Saint; form of Antonia (girl's name); Polish; flourishing, praiseworthy

St. Tola (d. 733) was a bishop in Meath, Ireland. He sent missionaries to Europe and helped expand scholastic efforts.

Tolek *see Theodore*

Tomas Saint; form of Thomas; German; twin

Tomaz, Tomcio, Tomek, Tomico, Tomislaw, Tommas, Tomo, Tonik

Bl. Tomas Cuartero Garcia (1915–1936) was one of the Passionist Martyrs of Daimiel who were killed during the Spanish Civil War. He was beatified by Pope John Paul II in 1989.

Tomaz *see Tomas*

Tomcio *see Tomas*

Tomcy *see Thomas*

Tomek *see Tomas*

Tomico *see Tomas*

Tomislaw *see Tomas*

Tommas *see Tomas*

Tommasi *see Thomas*

Tommaso Saint; form of Thomas; Italian; twin

Bl. Tommaso Maria Fusco, Bl. Tommaso Reggio

Bl. Tommaso Maria Fusco (1831–1891) was born in Pagani, Salerno. He was orphaned at the age of ten and was raised by his uncle who was a priest and teacher. He was ordained a priest and opened a school for boys in his home. He joined the Congregation of the Missionaries of Nocera and worked in southern Italy. He founded the Priestly Society of the Catholic Apostolate and the Daughters of Charity of the Most Precious Blood. He was beatified by Pope John Paul II in 2001.

Tomo *see Tomas*

Tomothy *see Timothy*

Tonik *see Tomas*

Topher *see Christopher*

Torannan *see Ternan*

Torfinn *see Thorfinn*

Toribio Saint; Greek; he who makes bows

St. Toribio Alfonso de Mogrovejo, St. Toribio Romo Gonzalez

St. Toribio Alfonso de Mogrovejo (1538–1606) was born in Mayorga, Spain. He became a lawyer and then a professor at Salamanca. He served as chief judge of the Court of Inquisition under King Philip II of Spain. He then became archbishop of Lima, Peru. He worked hard to reform the dioceses and helped the poor and the Indians who were in need. He founded schools, churches, hospitals, and the first seminary in the New World. He is a patron of Native rights and Latin American bishops.

Torpes Saint

Torpete, Tropez

St. Torpes (d. 65) was martyred during the reign of Emperor Nero. He is a patron of sailors.

Torpete *see Torpes*

Torquatus Saint; Latin; neck chain

St. Torquatus (first century) was sent by the apostles Peter and Paul to serve as a missionary to Spain. He worked near Granada and was martyred.

Tranquilino Saint; Latin; tranquil, serene

St. Tranquilino Ubiarco Robles (1899–1928) was born in Zapotlan, Mexico. He served as a dedicated parish priest. He was arrested one night while preparing to celebrate the Eucharist and bless a marriage. He was martyred by hanging. Pope John Paul II canonized him in 2000.

Tranquillinus Saint; Latin; tranquil, serene

St. Tranquillinus (d. 288) was a Roman martyr.

Trason Saint

St. Trason (d. 302) was martyred during the persecutions of Emperor Diocletian for giving aid to Christian prisoners.

Tremorus Saint

St. Tremorus (sixth century) was the son of St. Triphena. He was martyred by his stepfather, Count Conmore, while he was being educated at a monastery in Brittany.

Tresian *see Tressan*

Tressan Saint

Tresian

St. Tressan (d. 550) was from Ireland and served as a missionary in Gaul. He was ordained by St. Remigius.

Trien Saint

St. Trien (fifth century) was a follower of St. Patrick and served as a missionary. He later became abbot of Killelga Monastery in Ireland.

Trillo Saint; Welsh; assembly hill

St. Trillo (sixth century) was a Welsh saint who is patron of two sites in Gwynedd, Wales.

Trinity *see Trinity (girl's name)*

Triphyllius Saint

St. Triphyllius (d. 370) was a lawyer who converted to the faith and became bishop of Nicosia, Cyprus. He was an opponent of Arianism and was known for his eloquence.

Triverius Saint

St. Triverius (d. 550) was from Gaul. He became a hermit at a young age and lived out his days near the Monastery of Therouanne and Dombes.

Troadius Saint

St. Troadius (d. 250) was martyred in Pontus by being crucified during the reign of Emperor Trajanus Decius.

Trojan Saint; Greek; born in Troy

Troyen

St. Trojan (d. 533) was the son of a Jewish father and an Arabic mother. He converted to Christianity, became a priest, and later served as bishop of Saintes, France.

Tron *see Trudo*

Trond *see Trudo*

Tropez *see Torpes*

Trophimus Saint; Hebrew; well educated

St. Trophimus (d. 277) was martyred at Antioch during the persecutions of Emperor Probus.

Troyen *see Trojan*

Trudo Saint; German

Tron, Trond

St. Trudo (d. 695) was from France. He became a Benedictine monk and was ordained a priest. He founded an abbey near Louvain which was later named St. Trond in his honor.

Trudpert Saint; German

St. Trudpert (d. 644) was from Ireland and served as a missionary in Germany. He later lived as a hermit in Munstehal.

Trumwin Saint; English

St. Trumwin (d. 704) was born in England. He became bishop of the Picts in southern Caledonia (Scotland). He was forced to flee after the death of King Egfrith of Northumbria and spent the rest of his life as a monk at Whitby, England.

Tryphon Saint; Greek; softness, delicacy

St. Tryphon (d. 251) was a gooseherder near Apamea (modern Syria) who was martyred in Nicaea during the persecutions of Emperor Trajanus Decius.

Tuda Saint; Celtic

St. Tuda (d. 664) was an Irish bishop of Lindisfarne. He supported the use of the Roman Rite instead of the Celtic Rite. He died of the plague after serving as bishop for one year.

Tudno Saint; Welsh

St. Tudno (sixth century) was from Wales. Llandudno in Gwynedd, Wales, is named for him.

Tudwal Saint; Welsh; country ruler

St. Tudwal (d. 564) was a monk in Wales. He traveled to France with several members of his family and later became bishop of Treher (Treguier).

Tudy Saint

St. Tudy (fifth century) was a consecrated virgin in Wales.

Tuomo *see Thomas*

Turiaf Saint

Turiav

St. Turiaf (d. 750) was bishop of Dol, in Brittany, France.

Turiav *see Turiaf*

Turibius Saint; Latin

St. Turibius of Astorga (d. 460) was bishop of Astorga, Spain. He was an opponent of the Priscillianist heresy and was a supporter of Pope Leo the Great.

Turketil Saint; English

St. Turketil (d. 975) was the brother of King Edred of England. He served as chancellor but gave up that life to become a monk. He later served as abbot of Croyland and established a school.

Turninus Saint; Celtic

St. Turninus (ninth century) was an Irish priest who served as a missionary in the Netherlands.

Tutilo Saint

St. Tutilo (d. 915) was a Benedictine monk at St. Gall, Switzerland. He was known for his ability as a painter, sculptor, musician, and poet. He taught at the abbey school.

Tybald *see Theobald*

Tybalt *see Theobald*

Tybault *see Theobald*

Tyberious *see Tiberius*

Tyberius *see Tiberius*

Tychicus Saint, New Testament; Greek; casual, by chance

St. Tychicus (first century) is mentioned five times in scripture (Acts 20:4, Col 4:7, Eph 6:21, 2 Tm 4:12, Ti 3:12). He was from Asia and was a companion of St. Paul, who sent him to other Christians to offer encouragement. He later became bishop of Paphos, Cyprus.

Tychon Saint; Greek; accurate

St. Tychon (d. 450) was from Cyprus. He served as bishop of

Amathus and worked to root out pagan culture on the island. He is a patron of wine growers on Cyprus because he brought a dead vine leaf back to life.

Tydecho Saint; Welsh

St. Tydecho (sixth century) was from Wales and was the brother of St. Cadfan.

Tymothy *see Timothy*

Typasius *see Tipasius*

Tyran *see Tyrannus*

Tyrannus Saint

Tyran, Tyren, Tyrin, Tyron, Tyrone

St. Tyrannus (fourth century) was a priest in North Africa and an opponent of Arius, a heretic.

Tyren *see Tyrannus*

Tyrin *see Tyrannus*

Tyron *see Tyrannus*

Tyrone *see Tyrannus*

U

Ubald Saint; Teutonic; peace of mind

Ubaldas, Ubalde, Ubaldo, Uboldas, Uboldus

St. Ubald Baldassini (1084–1160) was born into a noble family in Gubbio, Italy. He was ordained a priest and became deacon of the cathedral before leaving a few years later to live as a hermit. He was later named bishop of Gubbio. In that position, he was able to convince Emperor Frederick II not to attack the area. He is a patron saint of people with autism and those suffering from obsessive-compulsive disorder.

Ubaldas *see Ubald*

Ubalde *see Ubald*

Ubaldo *see Ubald*

Uberto *see Hubert*

Uboldas *see Ubald*

Uboldus *see Ubald*

Ugine *see Eugene, Ugo*

Ugo Saint; Italian; thinker

Hugo, Ugine

St. Ugo (d. 1170) was born in France and was a follower of St. Bernard of Clairvaux. He served as the first abbot of Novara Abbey in Sicily.

Ulfred *see Ulfrid*

Ulfrid Saint; German; peaceful wolf

Ulfred, Ulfried, Ulfryd, Ulphrid, Ulphryd

St. Ulfrid (d. 1028) was from England. He served as a missionary in Germany and Sweden and was martyred after chopping down an idol of the god Thor.

Ulfried *see Ulfrid*

Ulfryd *see Ulfrid*

Uli *see Ulrich*

Ull *see Ulrich*

Ullric *see Ulric*

Ullrich *see Ulrich*

Ullrick *see Ulrich*

Ullrik *see Ulrich*

Ullryc *see Ulric*

Ullrych *see Ulrich*

Ullryck *see Ulrich*

Ullryk *see Ulrich*

Ulmar *see Wulmar*

Ulphrid *see Ulfrid*

Ulphryd *see Ulfrid*

Ulrech *see Ulrich*

Ulric Saint; form of Ulrich; German; wolf ruler

Ullric, Ullryc, Ulryc

St. Ulric (890–973) was born at Augsburg, Germany, and was educated in Switzerland. He became bishop of Augsburg. He led the efforts to rebuild the cathedral there after it had been attacked by the Magyars. He retired to St. Gall Abbey in Switzerland.

Ulrich Saint; German; wolf ruler

Uli, Ull, Ullrich, Ullrick, Ullrik, Ullrych, Ullryck, Ullryk, Ulrech, Ulrick, Ulrico, Ulrik, Ulrike, Ulrych, Ulryck, Ulryk

St. Ulrich (1029–1093) was born in Ratisbon, Germany. He worked as a page for Empress Agnes but left that life to become a religious. He served as archdeacon of the Cathedral at Freising. He later lived as a monk at Cluny and was ordained a priest. He founded a monastery at Zell in the Black Forest and a convent at Bollschweil. He lost his sight two years before he died.

Ulrick *see Ulrich*

Ulrico *see Ulrich*

Ulrik *see Ulrich*

Ulrike *see Ulrich*

Ulryc *see Ulric*

Ulrych *see Ulrich*

Ulryck *see Ulrich*

Ulryk *see Ulrich*

Ultan Saint; German; noble stone

Ulten, Ultin, Ultman, Ultmann, Ulton, Ultyn

St. Ultan (d. 657) was bishop of Ardbraccan, Ireland. He founded a school and cared for poor students. He also collected and illustrated the writings of St. Brigid.

Ulten *see Ultan*

Ultin *see Ultan*

Ultman *see Ultan*

Ultmann *see Ultan*

Ulton *see Ultan*

Ultyn *see Ultan*

Uni Saint; Norse

Huno

St. Uni (d. 936) was a Benedictine monk at New Corvey in Saxony. He became bishop of Bremen-Hamburga and worked to evangelize Denmark and Sweden.

Urbain *see Urban*

Urbaine *see Urban*

Urban Saint; Latin; city dweller, courteous

Urbain, Urbaine, Urbane, Urbano, Urbanus, Urvan, Urvane

Pope St. Urban, St. Urban of Langres

Pope St. Urban (d. 230) was born in Rome. He became pope in 222. He encouraged Christian martyrs and was responsible for the conversion of many.

Urbane *see Urban*

Urbano *see Urban*

Urbanus *see Urban*

Urbitius Saint; Latin

St. Urbitius (d. 420) was bishop of Metz, France. He helped evangelize that area and built a church in honor of St. Francis of Nola, which later became St. Clement Monastery.

Urciscenus Saint

St. Urciscenus (d. 216) was bishop of Pavia, Italy, during a time of increased persecutions.

Urfol *see Eval*

Urpasian Saint

St. Urpasian (d. 295) was a member of the household of Emperor Diocletian. He was burned alive for being a Christian.

Ursen *see Ursus*

Ursicinus Saint; Latin; bear

St. Ursicinus (d. 625) was from Ireland. He was a companion of St. Columbanus and went with him to Switzerland. He helped found the Monastery of St. Ursanne.

Ursicius Saint

St. Ursicius (d. 304) was a tribune from Illyria who served in the army of Emperor Diocletian. He was martyred by being beheaded in Nicomedia.

Ursin *see Ursus*

Ursinus Saint; Italian; bear

St. Ursinus (third century) was the first bishop of Bourges, France.

Ursmar Saint; German

St. Ursmar (d. 713) served as abbot-bishop of the Abbey of Lobbes in Flanders, Belgium. He helped organize missionary efforts in the region.

Urson *see Ursus*

Ursus Saint; Latin; bearlike

Ursen, Ursin, Urson, Ursyn

St. Ursus (d. 508) was a hermit for many years before becoming bishop of Auxerre, France, at the age of seventy-five.

Ursyn *see Ursus*

Urvan *see Urban*

Urvane *see Urban*

Usthazanes Saint

St. Usthazanes (d. 341) was an abbot in Persia who was martyred along with twelve of his monks at Ishtar.

Ustin *see Justin*

Uval *see Eval*

V

Vaast *see Vedast*

Vaclav *see Wenceslaus*

Vaise *see Vasius*

Valens Saint; Latin; healthy, strong

St. Valens (d. 531) was bishop of Verona, Italy. He fought against barbarian attacks and heretical groups.

Valentijn *see Valentin*

Valentin Saint; Latin; strong, healthy

Valentijn, Valentio, Valenton, Valenty, Valentyn, Valentyne, Velten

St. Valentin Faustine Berri Ochoa (1827–1861) was born in Elorrio, Spain. He became a Dominican and served as a missionary to the Phillipines and Vietnam. One of the Martyrs of Vietnam, he was beheaded. He was canonized in 1988 by Pope John Paul II.

Valentine Saint; Latin; strong, healthy

St. Valentine (d. 269) was a priest in Rome who assisted Christians who were imprisoned and tortured during the reign of Emperor Claudius II. He also performed Christian marriages. He was arrested, beaten with clubs, and beheaded. According to legend, he had healed his jailor's blind daughter. Before his death, he sent her a farewell note signed, "From your Valentine." He is a patron of love, young people, and happy marriages.

Valentinian Saint; Latin; strong, healthy

St. Valentinian (d. 500) was bishop of Salerno, Italy.

Valentio *see Valentin*

Valenton *see Valentin*

Valenty *see Valentin*

Valentyn *see Valentin*

Valentyne *see Valentin*

Valerian Saint; Latin; strong, healthy

Valeriano, Valerien, Valerio, Valerius, Valerya, Valeryan, Valeryn

St. Valerian (d. 178) was a companion of St. Pothinus of Lyons.

He was beheaded at Autun, France, during the persecutions of Emperor Commodus.

Valeriano *see Valerian*

Valerien *see Valerian*

Valerio *see Valerian*

Valerius Saint; form of Valerian; Latin; strong, healthy

St. Valerius (d. 315) was bishop of Saragossa, Spain. He assisted at the Council of Iliberis. He was imprisoned during the persecutions of Emperor Diocletian, but he survived and was exiled to Enet.

Valery *see Walericus*

Valerya *see Valerian*

Valeryn *see Valerian*

Vales Saint; Latin; from the valley

St. Vales (fourth century) was a priest in France.

Valter *see Walter*

Vandrille *see Wandrille*

Vanne *see Vitonus*

Vannie *see Giovanni*

Varus Saint; Latin; German

St. Varus (d. 307) was a soldier in Upper Egypt who guarded a group of monks awaiting execution. One of the monks died. Varus converted and asked to take that monk's place. He was martyred by hanging.

Vasil Saint; Greek; royal

Bl. Vasil Hopko (1904–1976) was born in Hrabske, eastern Slovakia. He was ordained and became a parish priest in Prague. He received a doctorate in theology and was named auxiliary bishop of Prjashev. He was arrested by the communist government. He was transferred from prison to prison and tortured. He was beatified by Pope John Paul II in 2003.

Vasius Saint

Vaise

St. Vasius (d. 500) was a wealthy Frenchman who gave his property to the poor. As a result, his family murdered him.

Vasos *see Vasyl*

Vassos *see Vasyl*

Vasyl Saint; form of William; German, Slavic; determined guardian

Vasos, Vassos

Bl. Vasyl Velchkovsky (1903–1973) was ordained a priest in Lviv and was a member of the Order of the Most Holy Redeemer. He became abbot of the Monastery of Ternopil. He was arrested by the Soviet government and sent to Kyiv. He was sentenced to ten years hard labor. In 1963, he was ordained a bishop. He was arrested again in 1969 and served three years. After his release, he was exiled. He was beatified in 2001 by Pope John Paul II.

Vaubert *see Walbert*

Vaune *see Vitonus*

Vedast Saint; German

Foster, Gaston, Vaast

St. Vedast (453–540) was from western France. He taught Clovis, king of the Franks. He served as bishop of Arras and Cambrai and worked to convert the people from paganism.

Veho *see Vouga*

Velleicus Saint

Willeic

St. Velleicus (eighth century) was an Anglo-Saxon abbot who served as a missionary in Germany. He served as abbot of Kaiserswerth, on the Rhine.

Velten *see Valentin*

Venantius Saint; Latin; a fan of hunting

St. Venantius (d. 250) was a fifteen-year-old who was beheaded at Camino during the persecutions of Emperor Decius.

Vencel *see Wenceslaus*

Vencent *see Vincent*

Venedict *see Benedict*

Venerandus Saint; Latin; worthy of veneration

St. Venerandus (d. 423) was bishop of Clermont, Auvergne, Gaul, and helped to evangelize the entire region.

Venerius Saint; Latin

St. Venerius (d. 408) was the second bishop of Milan, Italy. He sent representatives to the Council of Carthage in 401 and was a supporter of St. John Chrysostom. He is a patron saint of lighthouse keepers.

Venturino Saint; Italian

St. Venturino (1304–1346) was from Bergamo, Italy. He joined the Dominicans and was known for his ability as a preacher. Large crowds flocked to hear him. Because of a misunderstanding, he was imprisoned by Pope Benedict XII, but he was restored to favor by Pope Clement VI, who asked him to preach a crusade against the Turks.

Venustian Saint; form of Venus; Latin; love

St. Venustian (d. 303) was a convert to the faith who was martyred at Spoleto, Italy.

Veranus Saint; Latin

St. Veranus (513–590) was born at Vaucluse. He became a priest and soon attracted many followers. He then decided to live as a hermit in the mountains and later made a pilgrimage to Rome. On his return journey, he converted the people of Albenga in Sardinia. When he returned to France, he was made bishop of Cavaillon.

Verecundus Saint; Italian

St. Verecundus (d. 522) was bishop of Verona, Italy, during a time in which the Goths ruled the area.

Veremundus Saint; Latin

St. Veremundus (d. 1092) was born in Navarre, Spain. He became a Benedictine monk at the Abbey of Our Lady of Hirache, where he eventually served as abbot. He was known as a miracle worker and for his aid to the poor. During a famine, he fed up to three thousand people a day at the abbey.

Verge *see Vergil*

Vergel *see Vergil*

Vergil Saint; Latin; rod bearer, staff bearer

Verge, Vergel, Vergilio, Vergill, Vergille

St. Vergil of Salzburg (700–784) was born in Ireland. He traveled to mainland Europe where he spent two years at the court of Pepin the Short. He became abbot of St. Peter's and later was named bishop of Salzburg. He established many monasteries and is known as the Apostle to the Slovenes. He was one of the most learned men of his time.

Vergilio *see Vergil*

Vergill *see Vergil*

Vergille *see Vergil*

Verissimus Saint; Latin; very true

St. Verissimus (d. 302) was martyred in Lisbon, Portugal, during the persecutions of Emperor Diocletian.

Verulus Saint; Latin; truth

St. Verulus (d. 434) was martyred in North Africa by Arian Vandals.

Verus Saint; Latin; truth

St. Verus (fourth century) was a bishop of Salerno, Italy, who championed orthodoxy in that area.

Vetranio *see Bretannion*

Vetranion *see Bretannion*

Veturius Saint; Latin

St. Veturius (d. 180) was martyred in Carthage during the persecutions of Vigellius.

Viator Saint; Latin; voyager through life

St. Viator, St. Viator of Tremble-Vif-Sologne

St. Viator (d. 390) was a lector at the Cathedral of Lyons, where St. Justus presided. He accompanied St. Justus to Egypt where the two lived as hermits for several years. St. Viator outlived St. Justus by only a few weeks.

Vicelin Saint

Vicelinus, Vizelin, Wissel, Wizelin

St. Vicelin (1086–1154) was born in Lower Saxony in Germany. He studied at the cathedral school of Paderborn and at Laon, France. He served as a canon in Bremen, Germany, and then as a missionary among the Wends in Northern Germany. He founded several monasteries before being forced to flee the area to avoid an invasion of pirates. He was later named bishop of Staargard, but Emperor Frederick I Barbarossa would not allow him to take over the see. He spent the end of his life in Lorraine, France. He is known as the Apostle of Holstein.

Vicelinus *see Vicelin*

Vicenc *see Vincent*

Vicente Saint; form of Vincent; Latin, Spanish; victor, conqueror

Bl. Vicente Soler, Bl. Vicente Pinilla

Bl. Vicente Soler (d. 1936) was an Augustinian Recollect who was martyred during the Spanish Civil War. He led his fellow prisoners in prayer and heard their confessions. He was beatified in 1999 by Pope John Paul II.

Vicens *see Vincent*

Vicenzo *see Vincent*

Victer *see Victor*

Victor Saint; Spanish, Latin; victor, conqueror

Victer, Victorien, Victorin, Victorino, Vidor, Viktor, Vitin, Vyctor

St. Victor, St. Victor in Paris, St. Victor Maurus (St. Victor the Moor), St. Victor of Assyut, St. Victor of Piacenza, St. Victor of Vilae, St. Victor of Vita, St. Victor the Ninivite, Pope St. Victor I

St. Victor (d. 290) was a soldier in the Roman army in Marseilles. He was arrested for denouncing the worship of idols and for encouraging other Christians to be firm in their faith in the face of persecution. He converted three of his guards while he was imprisoned, who were also put to death for the faith. He was crushed in a millstone and beheaded.

Victorian Saint; form of Victor; Spanish; victor, conqueror

St. Victorian, St. Victorian of Asan

St. Victorian of Asan (d. 560) was from Italy. He traveled to France where he founded the Asan Monastery in the Pyrenees, which was later named for him.

Victoriano Saint; form of Victor; Spanish; victor, conqueror

St. Victoriano Pio (1905–1934) was born in San Millan de Lora, in Borgos, Spain. He became a member of the Brothers of the Christian Schools and was one of the Martyrs of Turón killed during the Spanish Civil War. He was canonized in 1999 by Pope John Paul II.

Victorianus Saint; form of Victor; Latin; victor, conqueror

St. Victorianus (d. 484) was the proconsul of Carthage and fought against Arianism. He was martyred by the Arian King Huneric.

Victoric *see Victoricus*

Victorice *see Victoricus*

Victoricus Saint; form of Victor; Latin; victor, conqueror

Victoric, Victorice

St. Victoricus (d. 287) was a missionary in Gaul who was martyred by being beheaded at Saint Aux-Bois.

Victorien *see Victor*

Victorin *see Victor*

Victorino *see Victor*

Victorinus Saint; Latin; victory

St. Victorinus of Pettau (third century) was from Greece. He wrote scholarly commentaries on the Old and New Testament. He served as bishop of Pettay and fought against several heresies. He was martyred during the persecutions of Emperor Diocletian.

Victorious Saint; Latin; victory

St. Victorious (d. 490) was a follower of St. Martin of Tours who became bishop of Le Mans, France.

Victorius Saint; Latin; victory

Victurus

St. Victorius (d. 259) was martyred in Carthage during the persecutions of Valerian.

Victricius Saint; Latin; victory

St. Victricius (330–407) resigned his position in the Roman Legion once he became a Christian. He was flogged and sentenced to death but managed to receive a discharge instead. He then served as a missionary in Belgium and became bishop of Rouen, France.

Victurus *see Victorius*

Vidor *see Victor*

Vigilius Saint; Latin; watchman

St. Vigilius of Trent (353–405) was born into a noble Roman family at Trent, Italy. He studied in Greece then returned home where he was named bishop of Trent. He worked to help the poor and convert pagans. He was stoned to death for commanding that a statue of Saturn be thrown into the river.

Vigor Saint; Latin; energy

St. Vigor (d. 537) was born in Artois, France. He was ordained a priest against his father's wishes and worked as a missionary until he was named bishop of Bayeux in 513. He also founded a monastery that was later named after him.

Vikent *see Vincent*

Vikenti *see Vincent*

Viktor *see Victor*

Vilhelm *see William*

Vili *see William*

Viliam *see William*

Viljo *see William*

Villanus Saint; Latin; worker in a large house

St. Villanus (d. 1237) became a monk at the Benedictine monastery at Fonte-Avellana. He was later named bishop of Gubbio, Italy.

Ville *see William*

Villiam *see William*

Villicus Saint; Latin; overseer of a large house

St. Villicus (d. 568) was bishop of Meta, France.

Vilmer *see Wulmar*

Vilmos Saint; Hungarian; desiring protector

Bl. Vilmos Apor (1892–1945) was born into a noble family in Hungary. He was ordained a priest and named bishop of Gyor. During World War II, he provided emergency supplies to Jews and sheltered the homeless. He also hid women to protect them from Russian soldiers. He was shot on Good Friday by a drunken Red Army officer. He was beatified by Pope John Paul II in 1997.

Vimin Saint

St. Vimin (sixth century) was a Scottish bishop who founded the monastery of Holywood.

Vincence *see Vincent*

Vincens *see Vincent*

Vincent Saint; Latin; victor, conqueror

Vencent, Vicenc, Vicens, Vicenzo, Vicenzo, Vikent, Vikenti, Vincence, Vincens, Vincentij, Vincentius, Vincenty, Vincenzio, Vincenzo, Vincien, Vincient, Vincint, Vinicent, Vinsent, Vinsint, Vinsynt, Vyncent, Vyncynt, Vyncynte, Vynsynt, Wicent

St. Vincent, St. Vincent de Paul, St. Vincent Diem, St. Vincent Ferrer, St. Vincent Kadlubek, St. Vincent Kaun, St. Vincent Liem, St. Vincent Madelgarus, St. Vincent of Agen, St. Vincent of Bevagna, St. Vincent of Collioure, St. Vincent of Digne

St. Vincent de Paul (1581–1660) was born to a peasant family in southwest France. He was educated by the Franciscan friars at Acq and then served as a tutor. He was ordained at age twenty. He was taken captive by Turkish pirates and sold into slavery. He was freed in 1607 when he converted one of his owners to Christianity. He then returned to France and served as a parish priest who was dedicated to helping the poor. He also helped found the Congregation of the Daughters of Charity and the Congregation of Priests of the Mission.

Vincente Saint; form of Vincent; Spanish; victor, conqueror

Bl. Vincente Soler (d. 1936) was an Augustinian monk who was killed in Grenada during the Spanish Civil War. He was beatified by Pope John Paul II in 1999.

Vincentij *see Vincent*

Vincentius Saint; form of Vincent; Latin; victor, conqueror

St. Vincentius (d. 380) was born in North Africa and served as a missionary in Digne, France, where he later served as bishop.

Vincenty *see Vincent*

Vincenzio *see Vincent*

Vincenzo *see Vincent*

Vincien *see Vincent*

Vincient *see Vincent*

Vincint *see Vincent*

Vindemialis Saint; Latin; vintage

St. Vindemialis, St. Vindemialis of Caspa

St. Vindemialis (d. 485) was an African bishop who was martyred by the Arian Vandal King Hunneric.

Vindician Saint

St. Vindician (632–712) was born at Bullecourt, France. He was named bishop of Cambrai and opposed the actions of the

Frankish King Thierry III who had executed Bishop St. Leodegarius of Autun.

Vinicent *see Vincent*

Vinsent *see Vincent*

Vinsint *see Vincent*

Vinsynt *see Vincent*

Vintila Saint

St. Vintila (d. 890) was a Benedictine monk who lived as a hermit in Pugino, Galicia, Spain. He attracted many followers.

Virge *see Virgil*

Virgial *see Virgil*

Virgil Saint; Latin; rod bearer, staff bearer

Virge, Virgial, Virgilio, Virgilius, Virgille, Virginlo, Vurgil, Vurgyl, Vyrge, Vyrgil, Vyrgyl

St. Virgil, St. Virgil of Arles

St. Virgil (530–610) was from Gascony, France. He became a monk at Lerins Abbey. He later served as archbishop of the city of Arles.

Virgilio *see Virgil*

Virgilius Saint; form of Virgil; Latin; rod bearer, staff bearer

St. Virgilius of Salzburg (700–784) was a native of Ireland. He served as abbot of Aghaboe. He traveled to the Holy Land on pilgrimage and then went to France and Bavaria. He became abbot of St. Peter Abbey at Salzburg and then bishop of Salzburg. He was denounced for believing that the world was round but was exonerated. He also arranged a missionary venture to Carinthia.

Virgille *see Virgil*

Virginlo *see Virgil*

Virila Saint; Latin, Spanish; strength, power

St. Virila (d. 1000) was a Benedictine abbot of St. Saviour Monastery in Navarre, France. He was known as a miracle worker.

Vital *see Vitalis*

Vitale *see Vitalis*

Vitali *see Vitalis*

Vitalian Saint; Latin; young and strong

Vitaliano, Vitalianus, Vitalicio

Pope St. Vitalian (d. 672) was born at Segni, Campania, Italy. He was elected pope in 657. During his time as pope, he fought with the eastern patriarchs over their support of Monithelite heresy and helped settle the dispute over the date of Easter between the English and Irish bishops. He also strengthened ties with England. He and Archbishop Maurus of Ravenna excommunicated each other, and the controversy wasn't settled for several years.

Vitaliano *see Vitalian*

Vitalianus *see Vitalian*

Vitalicio *see Vitalian*

Vitalicus *see Vitalis*

Vitalis Saint; Latin; life, alive

Vital, Vitale, Vitali, Vitalicus, Vitaliss, Vitaly, Vitalys, Vitalyss, Vytal, Vytalis, Vytalys

St. Vitalis, St. Vitalis of Gaza

St. Vitalis (d. 304) was either a slave or relative of St. Agricola. Vitalis's courage in facing his martyrdom convinced Agricola to convert and be martyred as well.

Vitaliss *see Vitalis*

Vitaly *see Vitalis*

Vitalys *see Vitalis*

Vitalyss *see Vitalis*

Vitas *see Vitus*

Vitin *see Victor*

Vitis *see Vitus*

Vitonus Saint; Latin; life

Vanne, Vaune

St. Vitonis (d. 525) was a monk who later became bishop of Verdun, France. He helped wipe out paganism in that area. He also founded a college for priests.

Vitus Saint; Latin; life, alive

Vitas, Vitis, Vytas, Vytus

St. Vitus (d. 1095) was a Benedictine monk at Bergamo, Italy. He was a follower of St. Albert.

Viventiolus Saint; Latin; life

St. Viventiolus (460–524) was archbishop of Lyons, France. He helped convene the Council of Epaone in 517.

Viventius Saint; Latin; life

St. Viventius (d. 400) was a Samaritan hermit who traveled to Europe. He helped St. Hilary of Poitiers in attacking Arian heretics.

Vizelin *see Vicelin*

Vladamar *see Vladimir*

Vladamir *see Vladimir*

Vladimar *see Vladimir*

Vladimeer *see Vladimir*

Vladimer *see Vladimir*

Vladimere *see Vladimir*

Vladimir Saint; Russian; famous prince

Vladamar, Vladamir, Vladimar, Vladimeer, Vladimer, Vladimere, Vladimire, Vladimyr, Vladmir, Vladymar, Vladymer, Vladymir, Vladymyr, Volodimir, Wladimir, Wladimyr

St. Vladimir (980–1015) was the grandson of St. Olga. He became ruler of Novgorod, but he was forced to flee to Scandinavia when war broke out among his brothers. He returned with an army and became sole ruler of Russia. He was known for his barbarism, but he became impressed by Christianity, converted, and reformed his life. He married Anne, the daughter of Eastern Emperor Basil II. He built many schools and churches. He is a patron of Russian Catholics.

Vladimire *see Vladimir*

Vladimyr *see Vladimir*

Vladmir *see Vladimir*

Vladymar *see Vladimir*

Vladymer *see Vladimir*

Vladymir *see Vladimir*

Vladymyr *see Vladimir*

Vodalus *see Vodoaldus*

Vodoaldus Saint; Latin; speaking

Vodalus, Voel

St. Vodoaldus (d. 725) was a native of Ireland or Scotland. He served as a missionary in France and later lived as a hermit near St. Mary's Convent at Soissons. He was known as a miracle worker.

Voel *see Vodoaldus*

Voloc Saint; Celtic; Welshman

St. Voloc (d. 724) was from Ireland and served as a missionary in Scotland.

Volodimir *see Vladimir*

Volodymyr Saint; form of Vladimir; Russian; famous prince

Bl. Volodymyr Pryjma (1906–1941) was born at Stradch, Yavoriv District, Ukraine. He was a Greek Catholic layman and father who served as a cantor and choir director at Stradch. He was martyred with Fr. Nicholas Konrad. He was beatified in 2001 by Pope John Paul II.

Volusian Saint; French

St. Volusian (d. 496) was a senator at Tours, France. He became bishop of Tours but was exiled to Spain by the Arian Visigoths. It is possible that he died as a martyr.

Vonny *see Giovanni*

Votus Saint; Latin; vowed, desired

St. Votus (d. 750) was from Saragossa, Spain. He and his brother, St. Felix, became hermits in the Pyrenees. They lived with another hermit, St. John, and their hermitage became the Benedictine Abbey of St. John de Ia Pena.

Vouga Saint

Veho, Vougar

St. Vouga (sixth century), also known as Vougar and Veho, was an Irish bishop who resigned his post to become a hermit near Lesneven.

Vougar *see Vouga*

Vulganius Saint; Latin

St. Vulganius (d. 704) was from Ireland or Wales and served as a missionary among the Atrebati in France. He then became a hermit at Arras.

Vulgis Saint; Latin; common

St. Vulgis (d. 760) was abbot of a monastery in Hainault, Belgium.

Vulmar *see Wulmar*

Vulphy Saint

St. Vulphy (d. 643) was from Rue, near Abbeville, France. His wife gave him permission to become a priest, and he later lived as a hermit.

Vulpian Saint; Latin; sly as a fox

Vulpiano

St. Vulpian (d. 304) was from Syria. He was martyred at Lebanon during the persecutions of Emperor Diocletian. According to tradition, he was killed by being sewn into a leather sack with a dog and a snake and thrown into the sea.

Vulpiano *see Vulpiano*

Vulsin *see Wulsin*

Vurgil *see Virgil*

Vurgyl *see Virgil*

Vyctor *see Victor*

Vyncent *see Vincent*

Vyncynt *see Vincent*

Vyncynte *see Vincent*

Vynsynt *see Vincent*

Vyrge *see Virgil*

Vyrgil *see Virgil*

Vyrgyl *see Virgil*

Vytal *see Vitalis*

Vytalis *see Vitalis*

Vytalys *see Vitalis*

Vytas *see Vitus*

Vytus *see Vitus*

W

Waccar Saint; Netherlands

St. Waccar (d. 755) was one of the Benedictine monks who were martyred with St. Boniface when they were attacked by pagans.

Walbert Saint; German; secure strengthening

Vaubert

St. Walbert (d. 678) was the duke of Lorraine, France, and count of Hainault, Belgium. He was the husband of St. Bertilia and father of Sts. Waldetrudis and Alegundis.

Walbert *see Waldebert*

Waldalenus Saint; German; ruler

St. Waldalenus (seventh century) was the founder of the Monastery of Beze. He was the brother of St. Adalsindis.

Waldebert Saint; French

Walbert, Gaubert

St. Waldebert (d. 668) was born into a noble French family. He entered Luxeuil Monastery where he lived as a hermit before serving as abbot. He held that position for forty years and instituted the Rule of St. Benedict. He also helped St. Salaberga found a convent at Laon.

Walder *see Walter*

Waleric *see Walericus*

Walericus Saint; Latin, French; strong, healthy

Valery, Waleric, Walric

St. Walericus (d. 622) was a monk at Luxeuil, France. He also founded the Monastery of Leuconay, on the Somme River.

Walfred *see Walfrid*

Walfredd *see Walfrid*

Walfredo *see Walfrid*

Walfrid Saint; German; peaceful ruler

Galfrido, Walfred, Walfredd, Walfredo, Walfridd, Walfried, Walfryd, Walfrydd, Wallfried

St. Walfrid (d. 765) was born in Pisa. He and his wife had five sons and a daughter, but both felt called to religious life. He and two friends founded the Abbey of Palazzuolo. They also started a convent for women, including his wife, eighteen miles away. He served as abbot for ten years.

Walfridd *see Walfrid*

Walfried *see Walfrid*

Walfryd *see Walfrid*

Walfrydd *see Walfrid*

Wallfried *see Walfrid*

Walric *see Walericus*

Walstan Saint; English

St. Walstan (d. 1016) was born near Norwich, England. He spent his life in prayer, gave away his wealth to the poor, and became a farmhand. He is a patron saint of farms, farmers, ranchers, and husbandrymen.

Waltar *see Walter*

Walter Saint; German; army ruler, general

Valter, Walder, Waltar, Waltir, Waltor, Waltur, Waltyr, Woulter, Wualter

St. Walter, St. Walter of Pontoise

St. Walter (d. 1070) was born into a noble family in Aquitaine. He entered a monastery at Dorat and was later named abbot of L'Esterp, a position he held for thirty-eight years.

Waltir *see Walter*

Waltor *see Walter*

Waltur *see Walter*

Waltyr *see Walter*

Wandrille Saint; French

Vandrille

St. Wandrille (d. 668), also known as Vandrille, was born to a noble family near Verdun, France. He was married, but the couple made a pilgrimage to Rome and decided to separate in order to enter religious life. He became a hermit, then entered the Benedictine Monastery of Montfaucon, in Champagne, France. He then returned to life as a hermit. He founded the monastery of Fontenelle in Normandy. He also established a school there.

Waningus Saint; French

St. Waningus (d. 683) was a native of Rouen, France. He was part of the court of King Clotaire III, but he gave up that life to become a monk. He assisted St. Wandrille in founding Fontenelle Abbey and established Holy Trinity Church and the Convent of Fecamp.

Ware *see Widradus*

Warinus Saint; German

St. Warinus (seventh century) was the son of St. Sigrada and brother of St. Leodegarius. Ebrion, the Frankish Mayor of the Palace, had a feud with Leodegarius and killed Warinus.

Wenceslao *see Wenceslaus*

Wenceslas *see Wenceslaus*

Wenceslaus Saint; Slavic; wreath of honor

Vaclav, Vencel, Wenceslao, Wenceslas, Wiencyslaw

St. Wenceslaus (907–935) was born near Prague and was the son of Duke Wratislaw. After his father was murdered, an anti-Christian ruler took over. But after a coup, Wenceslaus took over the throne. After his son was born, his brother and a group of his followers martyred Wenceslaus while he was on the way to Mass. He is the patron saint of Bohemia.

Wendolinus Saint

St. Wendolinus (d. 607) was an Irish hermit and shepherd. He may have also served as an abbot of a monastery near Trier.

Werenfrid Saint; Netherlands; warrior for peace

St. Werenfrid (d. 760) was from England and served as a Benedictine missionary to help convert the Frisians. He died in the Netherlands.

Wicent *see Vincent*

Wicho *see Wicterp*

Wicterp Saint; German

Wicho

St. Wicterp (d. 749) was abbot of Ellwangen Monastery. He founded several other monasteries in Germany. He later served as bishop of Augsburg, Austria.

Widradus Saint; German

Ware

St. Widradus (d. 747) was abbot of Flavigny, France. He also established the community of Saulieu, near Autun.

Wiencyslaw *see Wenceslaus*

Wigbert Saint; German; fighter, warrior, bright, famous

St. Wigbert (675–746) was born in England. He traveled to Germany where he became the abbot of Hersfeld Monastery in Hesse. He also worked as a missionary with St. Boniface. He later served as abbot of Ohrdruf in Thuringia.

Wilek *see William*

Wilferd *see Wilfrid*

Wilfred *see Wilfrid*

Wilfredo *see Wilfrid*

Wilfrid Saint; German; determined peacemaker

Wilferd, Wilfred, Wilfredo, Wilfride, Wilfried, Wilfryd, Willfred, Willfrid, Willfried, Willfryd

St. Wilfrid, St. Wilfrid the Younger

St. Wilfrid (633–710) was born in Northumberland. He was educated at Lindesfarne and spent time in Lyons and Rome before returning to England. He served as abbot of Ripon and supported Roman rites rather than the Celtic practices of northern England. He became bishop of York but faced considerable opposition and was exiled. During that time, he served as a missionary to the southern Saxons. He later retired to Ripon where he dedicated himself to prayer and penance.

Wilfride *see Wilfrid*

Wilfried *see Wilfrid*

Wilfryd *see Wilfrid*

Wilhelm *see William*

Wiliam *see William*

Wiliame *see William*

Willaim *see William*

Willam *see William*

Willeam *see William*

Willehad Saint; German

St. Willehad of Denmark (d. 1572) was born in Denmark. He

was exiled from that country at the onset of the Protestant Reformation. He entered the Franciscan friary at Gorkum, in the Netherlands. He was martyred by the Protestants at Biel. He was hanged at the age of ninety.

Willeic see *Velleicus*

Willem see *William*

Willfred see *Wilfrid*

Willfrid see *Wilfrid*

Willfried see *Wilfrid*

Willfryd see *Wilfrid*

William Saint; Top 100 Name; German; helmet, protection

Bill, Billy, Vasyl, Vilhelm, Vili, Viliam, Viljo, Ville, Villiam, Wilek, Wilhelm, Wiliam, Wiliame, Willaim, Willam, Willeam, Willem, Willil, Willium, Williw, Willyam, Wyliam, Wylliam, Wyllyam, Wylyam

St. William, St. William Arnaud, St. William Breteuil, St. William Firmatus, St. William Freeman, St. William of Bourges, St. William of Dijon, St. William of Eskilsoe, St. William of Gellone, St. William of Maleval, St. William of Norwich, St. William of Penacorada, St. William of Pontoise, St. William of Rochester, St. William of Roeskilde, St. William of Saint-Brieuc, St. William of Vercelli, St. William of York, St William the Abbot

St. William of York (d. 1154) was born in England, the son of Count Herbert. He became treasurer of the church of York, was ordained a priest, and served as chaplain to King Stephen. He was named archbishop of York, but his selection was opposed, and he was unjustly accused of several misdeeds. He was cleared by Pope Innocent but was removed by Pope Eugene III. He then became a monk at Winchester. Pope Anastasius IV once again named him archbishop of York a month before William's death.

Willibald Saint; German; will, desire, bold, brave

St. Willibald (700–786) was a native of Wessex, England, the brother of Sts. Winebald and Walburga. He was captured by Saracens while on a pilgrimage to the Holy Land. He was released and continued his journey. In Italy, he entered Monte Cassino, where he spent ten years. Pope St. Gregory III sent him to Germany to assist St. Boniface as a missionary. Boniface ordained him and appointed him as bishop of Eichstatt, in Franconia. He and his brother Winebald founded Heidenheim Monastery.

Willibrord Saint; English; will, spear, pike

St. Willibrord (658–739) was born in Northumbria, England. He spent twelve years studying in Ireland and then served as a missionary in Frisia. Pope Sergius I consecrated him archbishop of the Frisians, with his see at Utrecht. He founded the monastery of Echternach,

Luxembourg. He is known as the Apostle of the Frisians. He is a patron of epileptics.

Willigis Saint; German

St. Willigis (d. 1011) was born at Schoningen, Germany, the son of a wheelwright. He was ordained, named a canon at Hildesheim, and appointed as chaplain to Emperor Otto II. He then became chancellor of Germany, archbishop of Mainz, and vicar apostolic of Germany. He sent missionaries to Scandinavia, founded churches, and rebuilt the Cathedral of Mainz.

Willigod Saint

St. Willigod (seventh century) was a cofounder of the Monastery of Romont, France, where he later served as abbot.

Willil *see William*

Willium *see William*

Williw *see William*

Willyam *see William*

Winaman Saint

St. Winaman (d. 1040) was a missionary in Sweden who was martyred by pagan raiders.

Wincenty Saint; form of Vincent; Polish; victor, conqueror

Bl. Wincenty Matuszewski (1869–1940) was a Polish priest who was martyred in World War II. He is one of the 108 Polish Martyrs of World War II and was beatified by Pope John Paul II in 1999.

Winebald Saint; English

St. Winebald (d. 768) was born in Wessex, England, and was the brother of Sts. Willibald and Walburga. He traveled to Rome where he studied for seven years. St. Boniface invited him to serve as a missionary in Germany. He became a priest and worked in Thuringia and Bavaria. He helped found the Monastery of Heidenheim, Germany, where he served as abbot.

Winewald Saint; English

St. Winewald (d. 731) served as abbot of Beverley Monastery in England. He helped develop the monastery into a center for spirituality and culture.

Winnoc *see Winoc*

Winnow Saint; English; wind

St. Winnow (sixth century) was from Ireland and served as a missionary in Cornwall, England.

Winoc Saint; French; white, fair, blessed

Winnoc

St. Winoc (d. 717) was from Wales or Britain but was raised in Brittany, France, and entered St. Peter's Monastery at Sithiu. He later helped found a monastery near Dunkirk and served the Morini people at Wormhont.

Winwaloc Saint

Wonnow, Gwenno

St. Winwaloc (d. 532), also known as Wonnow and Gwenno, was born in Brittany, France. He became a monk at the monastery on Lauren Island. He later helped found

Landevenne Monastery near Brest.

Wiomad Saint

St. Wiomad (d. 791) served as abbot of Mettlach and bishop of Trier, Germany.

Wiro Saint; English

St. Wiro (eighth century) was from Northumbria, England. He traveled to Rome where he was consecrated as a bishop. He then served as a missionary in Germany under the leadership of St. Boniface. He became bishop of Utrecht, Netherlands. He later helped found a monastery at Odilienburg, in the lower Meuse River valley of Belgium and France.

Wissel *see Vicelin*

Wistan Saint; English; battle stone

St. Wistan (d. 850) was murdered by the king of Mercia for opposing the king's planned marriage to Wistan's mother.

Wizelin *see Vicelin*

Wladimir *see Vladimir*

Wladimyr *see Vladimir*

Wladyslaw Saint; form of Vladislav; Polish; glorious ruler

Bl. Wladyslaw Bladzinski, Bl. Wladyslaw Demski, Bl. Wladyslaw Goral, Bl. Wladyslaw Mackowiak, Bl. Wladyslaw Mackowski, Bl. Wladyslaw Miegon

Bl. Wladyslaw Bladzinski (1908–1944) was born in Ukraine. He was a priest of the

Congregation of St. Michael the Archangel and died at Gross-Rosen, Germany. He is one of the 108 Polish Martyrs of World War II and was beatified by Pope John Paul II in 1999.

Wlodzimierz Saint; Slavic; great, famous, ruler

Bl. Wlodzimierz Laskowski (1886–1940) was a priest of the Archdiocese of Poznan who was killed by the Nazis. He is one of the 108 Polish Martyrs of World War II and was beatified by Pope John Paul II in 1999.

Wojciech Saint; Polish; soldier of consolation

St. Wojciech (956–997) was born into a noble family in Bohemia. He was educated in Magdeburg. After he returned to Prague, he was named bishop. Because of conflict with the Duke of Bohemia, he left and went to Rome where he became a monk. He later returned to Prague and founded the Abbey of Brevnoc. He also served as a missionary to the Prussians of Pemerania. He was killed when he was suspected of being a Polish spy.

Wolfegang *see Wolfgang*

Wolfgang Saint; German; wolf quarrel

Wolfegang, Wolfgans

St. Wolfgang (d. 994) was born in Swabia, Germany. He taught at the cathedral school of Trier and entered the Benedictines at Einsiedeln. He was ordained a priest and served as a missionary in Hungary until Emperor Otto II named him bishop of Regensburg. He was known for his support of monasticism and education, as well as his aid to the poor.

Wolfgans *see Wolfgang*

Wolstan *see Wulfstan*

Wonnow *see Winwaloc*

Woulter *see Walter*

Wualter *see Walter*

Wulfhade Saint; English; wolf

St. Wulfhade (seventh century) was a prince of Mercia who was baptized by St. Chad and then executed by his pagan father.

Wulfram Saint; German; traveling wolf

St. Wulfram (d. 703) was born in Milly, France. He served in the court of King Thierry of Neustria. He served as bishop of Sens for two-and-a-half years before becoming a missionary among the Frisians.

Wulfric Saint; English; wolf ruler

St. Wulfric (1080–1154) was born near Bristol, England. He became a priest but was very attached to worldly goods. After meeting a beggar, he gave up his possessions and became a hermit at Heselbury, Somerset, England. He was known as a miracle worker.

Wulfstan Saint; English; old stone

Wolstan

St. Wulfstan (d. 1095) was born in Warwickshire, England. He became a priest and joined the Benedictines at Worcester. He was later named bishop of Worcester, a position he held for thirty years. He died while performing his daily ritual of washing the feet of a dozen poor men.

Wulmar Saint; English

Ulmar, Vilmer, Vulmar

St. Wulmar (d. 689) was born near Picardy, France. He was married but left his wife to enter the Benedictines at Haumont, in Hainault. He founded a monastery near Boulogne, where he served as abbot.

Wulsin Saint

Vulsin

St. Wulsin (d. 1002) was named by St. Dunstan to serve as abbot of Westminster, England. He was later named bishop of Sherborne.

Wyliam *see William*

Wylliam *see William*

Wyllyam *see William*

Wylyam *see William*

X

Xachary *see Zachary*

Xander *see Alexander*

Xarles *see Charles*

Xavier Top 100 Name; Arabic; bright

St. Francis Xavier (1506–1552) was born in the family castle near Pamplona in Spanish Navarre. He earned his licentiate from the University of Paris and was one of the seven who, with St. Ignatius Loyola, founded the Society of Jesus. He traveled with Fr. Simon Rodriguez to the Far East as one of the first Jesuit missionaries. He helped convert thousands of souls to Christianity. He is a patron of foreign missions.

Y

Yan *see Jan*

Yardcard *see Yrchard*

Yeremia *see Jeremiah*

Yeshak *see Isaac*

Yisrael *see Israel*

Ymar Saint

St. Ymar (d. 830) was a Benedictine monk at Reculver Abbey in Kent, England. He was martyred by Danish invaders.

Yoel *see Joel*

Yohan *see John*

Yon *see Jonas*

Yonah *see Jonah*

Yosef *see Joseph*

Yrchard Saint

Yardcard

St. Yrchard (fifth century) was a Scottish bishop who served as a missionary among the Picts.

Yrieix *see Aredius*

Ysarn *see Isarnus*

Yunus *see Jonah*

Yvan *see Ivan*

Yvann *see Ivan*

Yvo *see Ivo*

Ywi Saint; English

Iwi

St. Ywi (d. 690) was a Benedictine monk and hermit at Lindisfarne Abbey in England.

Z

Zabdas *see Zambdas*

Zacary *see Zachary*

Zacceus *see Zacchaeus*

Zacchaeus Saint; Hebrew; innocent, pure

Zacceus, Zacchious, Zachaios, Zacharcus, Zacharius, Zecharias

St. Zacchaeus (d. 116) was a bishop of Jerusalem.

Zacchary *see Zachary*

Zacchious *see Zacchaeus*

Zach *see Zachary*

Zacha *see Zachary*

Zachaery *see Zachary*

Zachaios *see Zacchaeus*

Zachar *see Zachary*

Zacharcus *see Zacchaeus*

Zacharay *see Zachary*

Zachari *see Zachary*

Zachariah Saint, New Testament; Hebrew; God remembered

Zacharias, Zacharius, Zacharyas, Zackarias, Zackoriah, Zaggery, Zakarias, Zakarius, Zakoryah, Zaquero, Zecharias, Zekarias, Zhachory

St. Zachariah (first century) was the father of St. John the Baptist. According to the first chapter of the Gospel of Luke, he received a vision from an angel informing him that his wife, St. Elizabeth, would have a baby. When he doubted, he was struck dumb until John was born and named.

Zacharias *see Zachariah*

Zacharius *see Zacchaeus*

Zacharry *see Zachary*

Zachary Saint; Top 100 Name; form of Zachariah; Hebrew; God remembered

Xachary, Zacary, Zacchary, Zach, Zacha, Zachaery, Zachar, Zacharay, Zachari, Zacharry, Zachaury, Zechary, Zeke

St. Zachary (d. 106) was a bishop of Vienne, Gaul, who was martyred during the persecutions of Emperor Trajan.

Zacharyah *see Zachariah*

Zachaury *see Zachary*

Zackarias *see Zachariah*

Zackoriah *see Zachariah*

Zaggery *see Zachariah*

Zakarias *see Zachariah*

Zakarius *see Zachariah*

Zakaryah *see Zachariah*

Zama Saint; Latin; one from Zama

St. Zama (d. 268) was ordained by Pope St. Dionysius and served as bishop of Bologna, Italy.

Zambdas Saint; Hebrew; meditation

Zabdas

St. Zambdas (d. 304) was a bishop of Jerusalem who was martyred during the persecutions of Emperor Diocletian.

Zamuel *see Samuel*

Zaquero *see Zachariah*

Zebedee New Testament; Hebrew; abundant, portion

Zebedee in the Bible was the father of the apostles James and John.

Zebinus Saint; Greek; hunter's dart

St. Zebinus (fifth century) was a hermit who lived in Syria.

Zecharias *see Zacchaeus*

Zechary *see Zachary*

Zef *see Joseph*

Zeferino Saint; Greek, Portuguese; west wind

Bl. Zeferino Agostini (1813–1896) was born in Verona, Italy, the son of a doctor. He was ordained a priest and served as a curate and teacher for eight years. He took over the parish in 1845 and dedicated himself to serving his parishioners. He founded the Pious Union of Sisters Devoted to St. Angela Merici and opened a school for poor girls. He was beatified in 1998 by Pope John Paul II.

Zekarias *see Zachariah*

Zeke *see Ezekiel, Zachary*

Zelman *see Solomon*

Zelmen *see Solomon*

Zenan *see Zeno*

Zenas *see Zeno*

Zeno Saint; Greek; cart, harness

Zenan, Zenas, Zenon, Zenos, Zenus, Zenys, Zino, Zinon

St. Zeno (300–371) was born in Africa. He served as a missionary and as bishop of Verona, Italy. He fought against Arianism. He was also known for his charity and writing on ecclesiastical subjects.

Zenobius Saint; Greek; sign, symbol

St. Zenobius (third century) was a physician in the town of Aegae, in Asia Minor. He and his sister Zenobia were martyred during the persecutions of Emperor Diocletian.

Zenon *see Zeno*

Zenos *see Zeno*

Zenus *see Zeno*

Zenys *see Zeno*

Zephyrinus Saint; Greek; west wind

Pope St. Zephyrinus (d. 217) was pope from 198–217. The antipope, Hippolytus, opposed him. Zephyrinus fought against the heresies of adoptionism, modalism, and monarchianism.

Zeticus Saint; Greek; investigator

St. Zeticus (d. 250) was a martyr from Crete who died during the persecutions of Emperor Decius.

Zhachory *see Zachariah*

Zigfrid *see Sigfrid*

Zigmund *see Zygmunt*

Zikmund *see Zygmunt*

Zino *see Zeno*

Zinon *see Zeno*

Zo *see Lorenzo*

Zoellus *see Zoe (girl's name)*

Zoilus Saint; Greek; life

St. Zoilus (d. 301) was martyred at Córdoba during the reign of Emperor Diocletian.

Zosimas Saint; Greek; he who fights

St. Zosimas (460–560) became a monk in Palestine. In his fifties, he chose to live as a hermit near the Jordan River. According to tradition, he was a friend of St. Mary of Egypt.

Zosimus Saint; Greek; he who fights

Pope St. Zosimus (d. 418) was a Greek of Jewish descent. He became pope in 417. He took part in a long dispute in Gaul over which see had primacy. He planned to excommunicate the people of Ravenna for plotting against him, but he died before he could follow through.

Zoticus Saint; Greek; of a long life

St. Zoticus (d. 204) was bishop of Comana, Italy. He opposed the Montanists and was martyred during the reign of Septimius Severus.

Zozimus Saint

St. Zozimus (d. 263) was martyred in Carthage during the persecutions of Valerian and Gallienus.

Zygismon *see Zygmunt*

Zygismond *see Zygmunt*

Zygismun *see Zygmunt*

Zygismund *see Zygmunt*

Zygismundo *see Zygmunt*

Zygmunt Saint; Polish; victorious protector

Sigmund, Zigmund, Zikmund, Zygismon, Zygismond, Zygis-mun, Zygismund, Zygismundo, Zygysmon, Zygysmond, Zygys-mondo, Zygysmun, Zygysmund, Zygysmundo

St. Zygmunt Gorazdowski, St. Zygmunt Szczesny Felinski

St. Zygmunt Gorazdowski (1845–1920) was born in Sanok, Podkarpackie, Poland. He studied law for two years before entering the seminary. He was ordained and served the parish of St. Nicholas in Lviv. He organized two shelters for the poor and hungry, as well as a shelter for abandoned children and single mothers. He also founded a convent for the Sisters of Mercy of St. Joseph. He was canonized by Pope Benedict XVI in 2005.

Zygysmon *see Zygmunt*

Zygysmond *see Zygmunt*

Zygysmondo *see Zygmunt*

Zygysmun *see Zygmunt*

Zygysmund *see Zygmunt*

Zygysmundo *see Zygmunt*

Girls'
Names

A

Aami *see Aimee*

Abagael *see Abigail*

Abaigael *see Abigail*

Abaigeal *see Abigail*

Abbee *see Abigail*

Abbegaele *see Abigail*

Abbegail *see Abigail*

Abbegale *see Abigail*

Abbegayle *see Abigail*

Abbeygayle *see Abigail*

Abbi *see Abigail*

Abbiegail, *see Abigail*

Abbiegayle *see Abigail*

Abby *see Abigail*

Abee *see Abigail*

Abelone *see Apollonia*

Abgail *see Abigail*

Abgale *see Abigail*

Abgayle *see Abigail*

Abi *see Abigail*

Abigail Old Testament; Top 100 Name; Hebrew; the father's joy

Abagael, Abaigael, Abaigeal, Abbee, Abbegaele, Abbegail, Abbegale, Abbegayle, Abbeygale, Abbi, Abbiegail, Abbiegayle, Abby, Abee, Abgail, Abgale, Abgayle, Abi, Abigaile, Abigaill, Abigal, Abigale, Abigayil, Abigayl, Abigel, Abigial, Abugail, Avigail, Avigayle

In the Bible, Abigail (1 Samuel 25) was the wife of a foolish man named Nabal. King David had stayed in the area of Nabal's flock and made sure that no harm came to his possessions.

In return, he asked Nabal for some food for his men. Nabal refused. In response, David decided to have Nabal and his whole household killed. Abigail rushed out to meet David and was able to persuade him to change his mind. When Nabal died of a heart attack soon after, David asked Abigail to marry him, which she did.

Abigaile *see Abigail*

Abigaill *see Abigail*

Abigal *see Abigail*

Abigale *see Abigail*

Abigayil *see Abigail*

Abigayl *see Abigail*

Abigel *see Abigail*

Abigial *see Abigail*

Abra Saint; Hebrew; mother of many nations

Abrah, Abrea, Abreana, Abre, Abree, Abri, Abria

St. Abra (ca. 342–ca. 360) was the daughter of St. Hilary of Poitiers, born before he converted to Christianity. At the urging of her father, she became a consecrated virgin and dedicated herself to good works before dying at the age of eighteen.

Abrah *see Abra*

Abrea *see Abra*

Abreana *see Abra*

Abree *see Abra*

Abre *see Abra*

Abria *see Abra*

Abugail *see Abigail*

Accidia Saint; Latin; sloth

St. Accidia was an African martyr.

Acquila *see Aquila (boy's name)*

Ada Saint; German, English, Hebrew; prosperous, happy

Adabelle, Adah, Adan, Adaya, Adda, Addiah, Aidah, Auda

St. Ada (seventh century) was a niece of St. Engelbert. A dedicated virgin, she was a nun at Soissons, France, and then an abbess at St. Julien de Prés Abbey in Le Mans, France. In France, she is considered a patroness of religious women and nuns.

Adabelle *see Ada*

Adalaid *see Adelaide*

Adalaide *see Adelaide*

Adalayd *see Adelaide*

Adalayde *see Adelaide*

Adaleana *see Adelina*

Adalena *see Adelina*

Adalina *see Adelina*

Adaline *see Adelina*

Adalsindis Saint

St. Adalsindis (d. 715) was the daughter of Sts. Adalbald and Rictrudis. She became a Benedictine nun, entering the convent at Hamayles-Marchiennes, France, where her sister, St. Eusebia, was abbess.

Adah *see Ada*

Adalyn *see Adelina*

Adan *see Ada*

Adarian *see Adrian (boy's name)*

Adaya *see Ada*

Adda *see Ada*

Addiah *see Ada*

Addison Top 100 Name; child of Adam

Ade *see Adrian (boy's name)*

Adela Saint; English; noble and serene

Adelae, Adelah, Adelista, Adella, Adelya, Adelyah

St. Adela (d. 1137) was the youngest daughter of William the Conqueror. Married to Stephen of Blois, she was very active in English politics and was known for endowing churches and monasteries.

Adelade *see Adelaide*

Adelae *see Adela*

Adelah *see Adela*

Adelaid *see Adelaide*

Adelaide Saint; German; noble and serene

Adalaid, Adalaide, Adalayd, Adalayde, Adelade, Adelaid, Adelais, Adelayd, Adelayde, Adelheid, Adeliade, Adelie, Adeliade, Adline, Aley, Delia, Edelaid, Edlaid, Edelaide, Edlaid, Laidey, Laidy

St. Adelaide, St. Adelaide of Bellich

St. Adelaide (ca . 932–999) was married as a teenager to Lothair of Italy. When he died three years later, his successor imprisoned her and tried to force her to marry his son. She escaped to Canossa where she begged Otto of Germany for help. Otto conquered Italy and married Adelaide in 951. The couple was crowned as rulers of the Holy Roman Empire the following year. She established many monasteries and churches and died at the convent at Seltz that she had founded.

Adelais *see Adelaide*

Adelayd *see Adelaide*

Adelayde *see Adelaide*

Adeleuna *see Adelina*

Adele Saint; English; noble and serene; short form of Adelaide

St. Adele (d. 730) was a daughter of King Dagobert II of Germany and was the grandmother of St. Gergory of Utrecht. After her husband died, she became a nun, founding a convent at Palatiolum where she served as abbess.

Adelei *see Adelaide*

Adelena *see Adelina*

Adelheid *see Adelaide*

Adeliade *see Adelaide*

Adeliana *see Adelina*

Adelice *see Alice*

Adelie *see Adelaide*

Adelina Saint; English; noble and serene

Adalina, Adaline, Adeleana, Adalena, Adalyn, Adeleuna, Adeliana, Adellena, Adellyna, Adileena, Adlena

St. Adelina (d. 1125) was a granddaughter of William the Conqueror and sister of St. Vitalis. She was abbess of the Benedictine Convent of La Blanche in Normandy, which

had been founded by her brother.

Adelista *see Adela*

Adella *see Adela*

Adellena *see Adelina*

Adellyna *see Adelina*

Adeloga Saint; German

Hadeloga

St. Adeloga (d. 745) or Hadeloga was a Frankish princess who founded the Benedictine Convent of Kitzingen in Franconia.

Adelya *see Adela*

Adelyah *see Adela*

Adeodata Saint; Latin; given by God

Bl. Adeodata Pisani (1806–1855) was born in Italy. She was raised by her grandmother after her mother left her father. She entered the Monastery of St. Peter in Malta when she was nineteen. She was known for her devotion to prayer, work, and love. She also suffered physical ailments, which she bore silently. She was beatified by Pope John Paul II in 2001.

Adileena *see Adelina*

Adilia *see Odilia*

Adlena *see Adelina*

Adline *see Adelaide*

Adrey *see Audrey*

Adrian *see Adrian (boy's name)*

Aeva *see Ava*

Affery *see Afra*

Affra *see Afra*

Affrah *see Afra*

Affrey *see Afra*

Affrie *see Afra*

Afra Saint; Hebrew, Arabic; young doe, earth color

Affery, Affra, Affrah, Affrey, Affrie, Afraa, Afrah, Afria, Afriah, Afrya, Afryah, Aphra

St. Afra (d. 304) was the daughter of the king of Cyprus. She lived a life of ill repute, either operating a brothel or serving as a prostitute, before being converted and baptized by Bishop Narcissus of Gerona, Spain, who sought lodging with her and her colleagues. She hid the bishop under a pile of flax when officials came searching for him. When Afra was arrested, she was burned to death. Her remains were buried in a church named after her.

Afraa *see Afra*

Afrah *see Afra*

Afria *see Afra*

Afriah *see Afra*

Afrya *see Afra*

Afryah *see Afra*

Agace *see Agatha*

Agacia *see Agatha*

Agafa *see Agatha*

Agafia *see Agatha*

Agafon *see Agatha*

Agaisha *see Agatha*

Agape Saint; Greek; love

St. Agape (d. 304) of Macedonia, and her sisters Chionia and Irene, were convicted of possessing scriptural texts, a crime punishable by death during the reign of Emperor Diocletian. When she refused to sacrifice to pagan gods, she was burned alive.

Agasha *see Agatha*

Agata *see Agatha*

Agatah *see Agatha*

Agatha Saint; Greek; good, kind

Agace, Agacia, Agafa, Agafia, Agafon, Agaisha, Agasha, Agata, Agatah, Agathe, Agathia, Agathiah, Agathya, Agathyah, Agatka, Agetha, Aggie, Agota, Agotha, Agueda, Agye, Agytha, Atka

St. Agatha, St. Agatha Kwon Chin-I, St. Agatha Lin

St. Agatha (d. 251) was born in Sicily. Determined to dedicate her life to God, she resisted the advances of lowborn Roman prefect Quintianus. He had her arrested and placed in a brothel, but she refused to submit to Quintianus or to renounce her faith. One of the tortures she underwent was to have her breasts cut off. An apparition of St. Peter healed her. She died in prison. She is considered the patron saint of bakers, bellfounders, and breast-cancer patients.

Agathe *see Agatha*

Agathia *see Agatha*

Agathiah *see Agatha*

Agathoclia Saint; Latin; good angel

St. Agathoclia (d. 230) was a virgin Christian slave owned by two pagans. They physically abused her in an effort to get her to renounce her faith.

When she refused, they brought her before the local magistrate. Her punishment was having her tongue cut out. She was later martyred.

Agathya *see Agatha*

Agathyah *see Agatha*

Agatka *see Agatha*

Agetha *see Agatha*

Aggie *see Agatha*

Agia Saint

St. Agia (d. 714) was the wife of St. Hiduiphus of Hainault. When he became a monk, she became a Benedictine nun.

Agilberta Saint; German; famous sword from combat

St. Agilberta (d. 680) was the second abbess of Joarre Monastery, which had been founded by St. Ado. She was a relative of Sts. Ebrigisil, Ado, and Agilbert.

Agna *see Agnes*

Agne *see Agnes*

Agneis *see Agnes*

Agnes Saint; Greek; pure

Agna, Agne, Agneis, Agnesa, Agnesca, Agnese, Agnesina, Agneska, Agness, Agnessa, Agnesse, Agneta, Agnete, Agnetha, Agneti, Agnetis, Agnetta, Agnette, Agnies, Agniya, Agnola, Agnus, Aignéis, Aneska, Anezka, Anka

St. Agnes, St. Agnes De, St. Agnes of Assisi, St. Agnes of Bohemia, St. Agnes of Montepulciano, St. Agnes of Poitiers, St. Agnes of Rome

St. Agnes (d. 304) had vowed to remain a virgin at a very young age. Many young men wanted to marry her, but she refused them all, saying, "Jesus Christ is my only spouse." Procop, the governor's son, wouldn't take no for an answer. To retaliate, he reported her as a Christian to his father. The governor tried to offer her gifts in exchange for her renunciation of the faith, but she refused. Ultimately, she was sentenced to death. She was only thirteen years old when she was martyred for the faith. She is a patron saint of chastity, gardeners, engaged couples, rape victims, and virgins.

Agnesa *see Agnes*

Agnesca *see Agnes*

Agnese *see Agnes*

Agnesina *see Agnes*

Agneska *see Agnes*

Agness *see Agnes*

Agnessa *see Agnes*

Agnesse *see Agnes*

Agneta *see Agnes*

Agnete *see Agnes*

Agnetha *see Agnes*

Agneti *see Agnes*

Agnetis *see Agnes*

Agnetta *see Agnes*

Agnette *see Agnes*

Agnies *see Agnes*

Agniya *see Agnes*

Agnofleda Saint

St. Agnofleda (d. 638) was a virgin recluse in the care of St. Longis, who founded a monastery in Maine, France. When false rumors were circulated about the two, their innocence was proved miraculously.

Agnola *see Agnes*

Agostina *see Agnes*

Agnus *see Agnes*

Agostina Saint; female form of Augustine; Italian; majestic

St. Agostina Livia Pietrantoni (1864–1894) was born in the village of Pozzaglia Sabina, the daughter of faith-filled farmers. She helped her mother care for her nine younger siblings and also helped in the fields. She began work as a seasonal worker at the age of seven. She joined the Sisters of Charity when she was twenty-two. She was sent to work at the Hospital of Santo Spirito, a place very hostile to religious faith. She was forbidden to even speak of God. Yet, she prayed for her patients' physical and spiritual health. One such patient, Joseph Romanelli, threatened her life several times and followed through on that threat, killing her on November 13, 1894. She was canonized by Pope John Paul II on April 18, 1999.

Agota *see Agatha*

Agotha *see Agatha*

Agripa *see Agrippina*

Agripah *see Agrippina*

Agripina *see Agrippina*

Agripinah *see Agrippina*

Agripine *see Agrippina*

Agrippah *see Agrippina*

Agrippina Saint; Latin; born feet first

Agripa, Agripah, Agripina, Agripinah, Agripine, Agrippah, Agrippinah, Agrippine, Agrypina, Agrypinah, Agrypine, Agryppina, Agryppine

St. Agrippina (d. 262) was from a noble Roman family and was either beheaded or scourged for the faith. Her body was taken to Mineo, Sicily, where her tomb became a popular pilgrimage destination. She is a patron saint against evil spirits, leprosy, thunderstorms, and bacterial diseases.

Agrippinah *see Agrippina*

Agrippine *see Agrippina*

Agrypina *see Agrippina*

Agrypinah *see Agrippina*

Agrypine *see Agrippina*

Agryppina *see Agrippina*

Agryppinah *see Agrippina*

Agryppine *see Agrippina*

Agueda *see Agatha*

Agusta *see Augusta*

Agye *see Agatha*

Agytha *see Agatha*

Ahnna *see Anna*

Ahriel *see Ariel (boy's name)*

Aidah *see Ada*

Aidan *see Adain (boy's name)*

Aignéis *see Agnes*

Aime *see Aimee*

Aimee Saint; Latin, French; loved

Aami, Aime, Aimey, Ame, Amee, Amei, Ammy, Amy, Amylyn, Aymee

Bl. Louise-Aimee Dean de Luigne (1759–1794) was a laywoman who was martyred during the French Revolution. She was beatified by Pope John Paul II in 1984.

Aimey *see Aimee*

Aindrea *see Andrea (boy's name)*

Airick *see Airick (boy's name)*

Albina Saint; Latin; white

St. Albina (d. 250) was a young martyr for the faith. Born in Caesarea, she was persecuted under Emperor Trajanus Decius.

Alaxandra *see Alexandra*

Alburga Saint; English

St. Alburga (d. 810) was the sister of King Egbert of Wessex. While married to Wulfstan of Wiltshire, she founded Wilton Abbey. After his death, she lived there and became the abbess.

Aldegunais Saint; German; noble warrior

St. Aldegunais (ca. 639–684) was the daughter of St. Walbert and St. Bertila. She grew up in Flanders and refused several offers of marriage in order to become a nun. She then founded a convent at a desert site called Malbode. She died of breast cancer and is a patron saint of those suffering from cancer or wounds.

Aldo Saint; Latin, German; old, elder

St. Aldo (seventh century?) was a native of Siena. After her husband died, she gave away all her possessions and spent her life serving the poor and sick. She was a mystic who experienced visions and ecstasies during her lifetime.

Aleana *see Alena*

Aleanah *see Alena*

Aled *see Almedha*

Aleece *see Alice*

Aleese *see Alice*

Aleina *see Alena*

Alena Saint; a form of Helen; Russian; light

Aleana, Aleanah, Aleina, Alenah, Alene, Alenea, Aleni, Alenia, Alenka, Alenna, Alennah, Alenya, Aleyna, Aliena, Ilena

St. Alena (d. 640) was born into a pagan family near Brussels, Belgium. She became a Christian in secret and was arrested and martyred during a secret Mass.

Alenah *see Alena*

Alene *see Alena*

Alenea *see Alena*

Aleni *see Alena*

Alenia *see Alena*

Alenka *see Alena*

Alenna *see Alena*

Alennah *see Alena*

Alenya *see Alena*

Alesia *see Alice*

Alexa Top 100 Name; a short form of Alexandra; Greek; defender of mankind

Alexande *see Alexandra*

Alexandera *see Alexandra*

Alexandra Saint; Top 100 Name; Greek; defender of mankind

Alaxandra, Alexande, Alexandera, Alexandrine, Alexina, Alexine, Alexis, Alexius, Alexxandra, Alexxandrah, Alixsandra, Aljexi, Alla, Lexandra

St. Alexandra (d. 300) was burned to death during the persecution of Emperor Diocletian.

Alexandera *see Alexandra*

Alexandrina Saint; a form of Alexandra; Greek; defender of mankind

Bl. Alexandrina Maria da Costa (1904–1955) was born in Balasar, Oporto, Portugal. At age fourteen, a man tried to rape her. She jumped from a window to escape and was paralyzed as a result of the fall. She spent the rest of her life bedridden. She became a member of the Salesian Cooperators and was known as a mystic. For the last thirteen years of her life, she existed only on daily Communion. She was beatified by Pope John Paul II in 2004.

Alexandrine *see Alexandra*

Alexina *see Alexandra*

Alexine *see Alexandra*

Alexis *see Alexandra*

Alexius *see Alexandra*

Alexxandra *see Alexandra*

Alexxandrah *see Alexandra*

Aley *see Adelaide*

Aleydis *see Alice*

Aleyna *see Alena*

Alfreda Saint; English; elf counselor, wise counselor

Alfredah, Alfredda, Alfredia, Alfreida, Alfrida, Alfridah, Alfrieda, Alfryda, Alfrydah, Alfrydda, Elfreda

St. Alfreda (d. 795) was the daughter of King Offa of Mercia, England. When St. Ethelbert, king of the East Angles, went to King Offa to ask for Alfreda's hand in marriage, he was killed by Offa's queen, Cynethritha. Alfreda then became a hermit, living in the marshes of Crowland until her death.

Alfredah *see Alfreda*

Alfredda *see Alfreda*

Alfredia *see Alfreda*

Alfreida *see Alfreda*

Alfrida *see Alfreda*

Alfridah *see Alfreda*

Alfrieda *see Alfreda*

Alfryda *see Alfreda*

Alfrydah *see Alfreda*

Alfrydda *see Alfreda*

Alice Saint; Greek, German; truthful, noble

Adelice, Aleece, Aleese, Alesia, Aleydis, Alicea, Alicie, Alics, Aliece, Aliese, Alise, Alisse, Alla, Alleece, Alles, Allesse, Allice, Alysa, Elissa, Leece, Lissa

St. Alice, or St. Aleydis, (1204–1250) was born near Brussels. She entered a Cistercian convent called Camera Sanctae Mariae at the age of seven and remained there the rest of her life. She contracted leprosy, which led to her becoming paralyzed and blind. She suffered greatly but took great comfort in receiving the Holy Eucharist. She is a patron saint of the blind and paralyzed.

Alicea *see Alice*

Alicie *see Alice*

Alicja Saint; English; truthful, noble

Alicya

Bl. Alicja Jadwiga Kotowska (1899–1939) was a Polish nun, head of the Resurrectionist convent in Wejherowo. She was martyred by the German Nazis in 1939 and is one of the 108 Martyrs of World War II. She was beatified in 1999 by Pope John Paul II.

Alics *see Alice*

Alicya *see Alicja*

Aliece *see Alice*

Aliena *see Alena*

Aliese *see Alice*

Alise *see Alice*

Alisse *see Alice*

Alix Saint; a short form of Alexander; Greek; defender of mankind

Bl. Alix Le Clercq (1576–1622) was born in Remiremont in the area of Lorraine, France. She became a nun and, together with Fr. Peter Fourier, founded a new convent dedicated to the education of children. They received papal approval for the

Augustinian Canonesses of the Congregation of Our Lady.

Alixsandra *see Alexandra*

Alizabeth *see Elizabeth*

Aljexi *see Alexandra*

Alkeld Saint; English

Athilda

According to legend, St. Alkeld (tenth century), or Athilda, was an Anglo-Saxon princess and possibly a nun who was strangled by Danish invaders.

Alla *see Alexandra, Alice*

Alleece *see Alice*

Alles *see Alice*

Allesse *see Alice*

Allice *see Alice*

Allison Top 100 Name; a form of Alice; truthful, noble

Almedha Saint; Welsh; shapely

Aled, Elined, Eluned, Eliwedd, Filuned

St. Almedha (sixth century), also known as Aled or Filuned, was the daughter of King Brychan. Having taken a vow of virginity, she fled from home to avoid marrying a neighboring prince. She took refuge in Brecon, but the prince arrived and demanded her return. When she refused, he beheaded her.

Alodia Saint; Basque; free land

St. Alodia (d. 851) was the daughter of a Muslim father and a Christian mother in Spain. She and her sister were dedicated to the Christian faith. When they were arrested, they refused to renounce the faith. They were placed in a brothel and later beheaded.

Aloisa *see Louisa*

Aloise *see Louise*

Alphonsa Saint; form of Alphonse; German; noble and eager

St Alphonsa Muttathupadathu (1910–1946) was born as Annakkutty (little Anna) in Travancore, part of present-day India. Because her mother died when she was very young, she was raised by her aunt. In 1923, she fell into a pit of burning chaff and badly burned her feet. She was left permanently disabled. In 1927, she joined the Poor Clares convent at Bharananganam where she took the name Alphonsa. She worked as a teacher for some time, but her health was weak. She suffered from various medical problems before dying of a stomach problem at the age of thirty-five. Her tomb has become a pilgrimage site where several miracles have been reported.

Alysa *see Alice*

Alyssa Top 100 Name; a form of Alice; Greek; rational

Amabilis Saint; Latin; lovable

St. Amabilis (d. 634) was the daughter of an Anglo-Saxon king. She became a nun at Saint-Amand in Rouen, France.

Amalberga Saint; German; work, protection

Amelia

St. Amalberga (d. 690), or Amelia, was married to Witgar and was the mother of Sts. Emembertus, Gudila, and Reinalda. She and her husband, through mutual agreement, separated and became religious.

Amalia *see Emily*

Amalie *see Emily*

Amata Saint; Latin; beloved

St. Amata (d. 1250) was a niece of St. Clare of Assisi. After she was miraculously cured of an illness, she entered the Poor Clares.

Ame *see Aimee*

Amee *see Aimee*

Amei *see Aimee*

Amelberga Saint; German; protected work

St. Amelberga (d. 900) was the abbess of a Benedictine monastery in Susteren, Netherlands. Her abbey educated two daughters of the king of Lorraine, France.

Amelia Top 100 Name; a form of Emily; German, Latin; hard-working

Ammia Saint; Latin; dearly loved

According to legend, St. Ammia (d. 270) was the foster mother of St. Mamas. She was martyred in Cappadocia during the reign of Emperor Aurelian.

Ammonaria Saint

St. Ammonaria (d. 250) was martyred along with another young woman by the same name and two other women named Mercuria and Dionysia. They were killed during the persecution of Emperor Decius.

Ammy *see Aimee*

Amor *see Amor (boy's name)*

Amunia Saint

St. Amunia (d. 1069) was the mother of St. Aurea. After her husband died, she joined her daughter in living as a hermitess.

Amy *see Aimee*

Amylyn *see Aimee*

Ana *see Anna*

Anabel *see Anna*

Anabella *see Anna*

Anah *see Anna*

Anastacia *see Anastasia*

Anastascia *see Anastasia*

Anastase *see Anastasia*

Anastasee *see Anastasia*

Anastasha *see Anastasia*

Anastashia *see Anastasia*

Anastasia Saint; Greek; resurrection

Anastacia, Anastascia, Anastase, Anastasee, Anastasha, Anastashia, Anastasie, Anastasija, Anastassia, Anastassya, Anastasya, Anastatia, Anastaysia, Anastazia, Anastice, Anestasia, Annastacia, Annastaciah, Annastasia, Annastasija, Annastaysia, Annastazia, Annestasia, Annestassia, Annstás, Anstace, Anstice, Asia, Ayzia, Stacy, Stasa, Staska, Tasia, Tasya

St. Anastasia, St. Anastasia Patricia

St. Anastasia (fourth century) was the daughter of Roman nobles. Her father was a pagan, but her mother was a Christian who had her child baptized and taught her the faith. Anastasia in turn was married to another pagan, who upon discovering her Christianity began to treat her like a slave. After he met an untimely death while traveling, she was free to live her Christian life fully. She spent her time consoling and helping Christian prisoners. In time, she was arrested and brought before Emperor Diocletian. She was miraculously preserved during several attempts to take her life, but she was ultimately burned to death.

Anastasie *see Anastasia*

Anastasija *see Anastasia*

Anastassia *see Anastasia*

Anastassya *see Anastasia*

Anastasya *see Anastasia*

Anastatia *see Anastasia*

Anastaysia *see Anastasia*

Anastazia *see Anastasia*

Anastice *see Anastasia*

Anatolia Saint; Greek; from the east

St. Anatolia (d. 250) lived with her sister, Victoria. When Anatolia refused the advances of a young man named Aurelius, he had the sisters arrested as Christians. She was banished to Thora where she was locked in a room with a poisonous snake. The snake, however, did not attack her. This fact converted her guard, Audax, to Christianity. Both Audax and Anatolia were martyred.

Andee *see Andrea (boy's name)*

Andera *see Andrea (boy's name)*

Anderea *see Andrea (boy's name)*

Andra *see Andrea (boy's name)*

Andraia *see Andrea (boy's name)*

Andraya *see Andrea (boy's name)*

Andrea *see Andrea (boy's name)*

Andreah *see Andrea (boy's name)*

Andreaka *see Andrea (boy's name)*

Andreea *see Andrea (boy's name)*

Andreja *see Andrea (boy's name)*

Andreka *see Andrea (boy's name)*

Andrel *see Andrea (boy's name)*

Andrell *see Andrea (boy's name)*

Andrelle *see Andrea (boy's name)*

Andreo *see Andrea (boy's name)*

Andressa *see Andrea (boy's name)*

Andrette *see Andrea (boy's name)*

Andriea *see Andrea (boy's name)*

Andrieka *see Andrea (boy's name)*

Andrietta *see Andrea (boy's name)*

Andris *see Andrea (boy's name)*

Andrya *see Andrea (boy's name)*

Andryah *see Andrea (boy's name)*

Ane *see Anne*

Aneska *see Agnes*

Anestasia *see Anastasia*

Aneta *see Anne*

Anezka *see Agnes*

Angadresma Saint

St. Angadresma (615–695) was educated by St. Omer and St. Iaambert. She was betrothed to be married but prayed that she might live as a religious instead. She contracted leprosy, and her betrothed released her from the commitment. The leprosy disappeared after she entered a monastery. She became abbess of the Benedictine monastery Arver, near Beauvais, France, and is remembered as a miracle worker.

Angala *see Angela*

Anganita *see Angela*

Angel Top 100 Name; Greek; angel, messenger

Angela Saint; Greek; angel, messenger

Angala, Anganita, Angelanell, Angelanette, Angele, Angelina, Angelo, Angil, Angiola, Anglea, Anjel, Anjella, Anjellah, Anjelle

St. Angela de la Cruz, St. Angela Merici

St. Angela de la Cruz (1846–1932) was born in Seville, Spain, to pious parents who taught her the faith from the earliest age. As a young girl, she went to work in shoe repair. Her boss was a holy woman who had her employees pray the rosary and read the lives of the saints. Fr. José Torres Padilla became Angela's spiritual director when she was sixteen. She attempted to enter religious life twice, but her health was too frail. In 1873 she received a vision from God in which she saw an empty cross directly in front of one on which Christ was hanging. She understood that she was to be "poor with the poor to bring them to Christ." Three women joined her in her efforts, and they served the poor day and night. They became known as the Sisters of the Company of the Cross. During Mother Angela's lifetime, twenty-three other convents were established. She was canonized on May 4, 2003, by Pope John Paul II.

Angelanell *see Angela*

Angelanette *see Angela*

Angele *see Angela*

Angelina Top 100 Name; a form of Angela; Greek, Latin; angel, messenger

Angelo *see Angela*

Angil *see Angela*

Angiola *see Angela*

Anglea *see Angela*

Anice *see Anna, Anne*

Aniela *see Anna*

Anita *see Anna*

Anjel *see Angela*

Anjella *see Angela*

Anjellah *see Angela*

Anjelle *see Angela*

Anka *see Agnes*

Anmaree *see Anne-Marie*

Anmari *see Anne-Marie*

Anmarie *see Anne-Marie*

Anmary *see Anne-Marie*

Anmarya *see Anne-Marie*

Anmaryah *see Anne-Marie*

Ann *see Anne*

Anna Saint, New Testament; Top 100 Name; German, Italian, Czech, Swedish; gracious, one who gives

Ahnna, Ana, Anabel, Anabella, Anah, Anice, Aniela, Anita, Annaka, Annice, Annina, Annora, Anona, Anyu, Aska

St. Anna the Prophetess (first century) was a daughter of Phanuel, from the tribe of Aser. She was married for seven years as a young woman and spent the remainder of her life as a widow, living in the Temple. She was present at the Temple when Jesus was brought for his presentation. Her story is told in Luke 2:26–38.

Annaka *see Anna*

Annastaciah *see Anastasia*

Annastasia *see Anastasia*

Annastasija *see Anastasia*

Annastaysia *see Anastasia*

Annastazia *see Anastasia*

Annchen *see Anne*

Anne Saint; English; gracious, one who gives

Ane, Aneta, Anice, Anita, Ann, Annchen, Anneka, Annella, Annelle, Annze, Anouche

Through tradition, St. Anne is held to be the mother of Mary and grandmother of Jesus. An angel appeared to St. Anne and her husband, St. Joachim, telling them that they would have a child. Anne, in turn, promised to dedicate this child to God. She is the patron saint of Christian mothers and women in labor.

Anneka *see Anne*

Annella *see Anne*

Annelle *see Anne*

Annemarie *see Anne-Marie*

Anne-Marie Saint; combination of Anne and Mary; English

> *Anmaree, Anmari, Anmarie, Anmary, Anmarya, Anmaryah, Annemarie, Ann-Marie, Annmaree, Annmari, Annmarie, Annmary*

> Bl. Anne-Marie Jahouvey (1779–1851) was born in Jallanges, France, the daughter of a wealthy farmer. She entered several convents but none felt like a good fit. She wanted to minister to poor black children, so she and eight other women founded the Sisters of St. Joseph of Cluny. She founded convents in Europe, South America, and Africa.

Annestasia *see Anastasia*

Annestassia *see Anastasia*

Annice *see Anna*

Annina *see Anna*

Annmaree *see Anne-Marie*

Annmari *see Anne-Marie*

Annmarie *see Anne-Marie*

Ann-Marie *see Anne-Marie*

Annmary *see Anne-Marie*

Annora *see Anna*

Annstás *see Anastasia*

Annunciata Saint; Spanish; annunciation

> *Anunciación, Anunciada, Nunciata, Nunzia*

> Bl. Annunciata Cocchetti (1800–1882) was born in Italy and raised by her grandmother after her parents died. She started a home for needy girls based in her grandmother's home in Rovato but was forced to move to Milan. She later became a teacher at a Catholic girls' school in Cemmo. She then founded the Sisters of Saint Dorothy of Cemmo devoted to the service of teaching girls. She was beatified by Pope John Paul II in 1991.

Annze *see Anne*

Anona *see Anna*

Anouche *see Anne*

Ansonia *see Antonia*

Ansonya *see Antonia*

Anstace *see Anastasia*

Anstice *see Anastasia*

Anstrude *see Anstrudis*

Anstrudis Saint

> *Anstrude*

> St. Anstrudis (d. 688), or Anstrude, was the daughter of Sts. Salaberga and Blandinus, who had founded St. John the Baptist Convent at Laon. Her brother was St. Baldwin. When St. Salaberga became abbess at the convent, Anstrudis accompanied her. Upon her mother's death, she reluctantly took up the post of abbess herself. Ebroin, the mayor of the locality, made her life very difficult until Bl. Pepin of Landen involved himself in the dispute

and put an end to the harassment. She is remembered for her kindness and her austere life.

Antania *see Antonia*

Anthia Saint; Greek; flower

Antia

St. Anthia (d. 121) was the widow of a consul named Eugenius and was the mother of St. Eleutherius. She took her son to Anicetus, the bishop of Rome, who educated him. He was ordained and ultimately became a bishop. Both he and his mother were arrested as Christians and martyred. St. Anthia was beheaded.

Anthusa Saint; perfect bloom

St. Anthusa, St. Anthusa the Younger

St. Anthusa (eighth century) was a hermitess who became abbess of a convent near Constantinople. She was arrested by the emperor because she venerated sacred images. She was tortured until the empress intervened and arranged for her release.

Antia *see Anthia*

Antinia *see Antonia*

Antona *see Antonia*

Antonee *see Antonia*

Antoney *see Antonia*

Antoni *see Antonia*

Antonia Saint; Latin, Greek; flourishing, praiseworthy

Ansonia, Ansonya, Antania, Antinia, Antona, Antonee, Antoney, Antoni, Antoñia, Antoniah, Antonice, Antonie, Antoniya, Antonnea, Antonnia, Antonniah, Antonya, Antonyah, Toinetta, Tonya

Bl. Antonia Mesina (1919–1935) was born to a peasant family in Sardinia, Italy. She went to school for four years before needing to take over care of her large family when her mother was bedridden. She joined Catholic Action when she was ten years old. She was murdered when she resisted being raped by another teenager. She is considered a martyr to purity. She was beatified by Pope John Paul II in 1987.

Antoñia *see Antonia*

Antoniah *see Antonia*

Antonice *see Antonia*

Antonie *see Antonia*

Antoniya *see Antonia*

Antonnea *see Antonia*

Antonnia *see Antonia*

Antonniah *see Antonia*

Antonya *see Antonia*

Antonyah *see Antonia*

Anuarite Saint; African; one who laughs at war

Bl. Anuarite Nengapeta (1939–1964) was a member of the Holy Family Sisters in Bafwabaka, Belgian Congo. She was killed during Congo's civil war when she resisted being raped by a soldier. She was beatified by Pope John Paul II in 1985.

Anunciación *see Annunciata*

Anunciada *see Annunciata*

Anysia Saint; Greek; satisfaction

St. Anysia (284–304) was born into a wealthy Christian family in Salonika. She took a vow of chastity and dedicated her life to helping the poor. A Roman soldier discovered she was a Christian and attempted to drag her to a pagan sacrifice. She spit in his face, and he murdered her with his sword.

Anyu *see Anna*

Aphra *see Afra*

Apoline *see Apollonia*

Apollonia Saint; form of Apollo; Greek

Abelone, Apoline, Apolloniah, Apollonya, Apollonyah, Apollyne, Apolonia, Apoloniah, Apolonie, Apolonya, Apolonyah, Appollonia, Appolloniah, Appollonya, Appollonyah

St. Apollonia (d. 249) was arrested and tortured during the reign of Emperor Philip. After having all her teeth knocked out, she was threatened with death by fire unless she gave up her faith. She jumped into the flames voluntarily. She is a patron of those with toothaches.

Apolloniah *see Apollonia*

Apollonya *see Apollonia*

Apollonyah *see Apollonia*

Apollyne *see Apollonia*

Apolonia *see Apollonia*

Apoloniah *see Apollonia*

Apolonie *see Apollonia*

Apolonya *see Apollonia*

Apolonyah *see Apollonia*

Appollonia *see Apollonia*

Appolloniah *see Apollonia*

Appollonya *see Apollonia*

Appollonyah *see Apollonia*

Apronia Saint; Latin;

St. Apronia (sixth century) was born near Trier, Germany. Her brother was Bishop St. Aprus of Toul who received her into a convent in Troyes, France, where she lived out her days.

Aquila *see Aquila (boy's name)*

Aquilla *see Aquila (boy's name)*

Aquille *see Aquila (boy's name)*

Aquilina Saint; a form of Aquila; Latin; eagle

St. Aquilina (281–293) was born to Christian parents in Biblus, Phoenicia. At the age of twelve, she set out to preach the faith and converted many young people. She attracted the attention of the authorities and was arrested. She was flogged but still refused to renounce her faith. She was then lacerated with a sharp rake, and her eardrums were punctured with flaming iron rods, and she was left for dead. When she miraculously survived, the magistrate ordered her to be beheaded, but she died in prison before the sentence could be carried out.

Araght *see Attracta*

Archelais Saint

St. Archelais (d. 293) was a companion of Thecla and Susanna. The three women were from the Romagna region of Italy. They traveled to Nola, in Campania, where they were arrested, tortured, and martyred for the faith.

Arela *see Aurelia*

Arella *see Aurelia*

Aretius Saint; Greek; virtuous

St. Aretius was an early Roman martyr whose relics were found in the catacombs along the Appian Way.

Ariadne Saint; Greek; holy

St. Ariadne (d. 130) was a slave in the home of a Phrygian prince. She refused to take part in pagan rites at the prince's birthday celebration and was hunted by the authorities. She escaped into a chasm in a ridge which miraculously closed behind her.

Arian *see Arian (boy's name)*

Ariana *see Arian (boy's name)*

Ariane *see Arian (boy's name)*

Ariann *see Arian (boy's name)*

Arianna *see Arian (boy's name)*

Arianne *see Arian (boy's name)*

Ariel Hebrew; lioness of God

Arilda Saint; German; hearth maiden

St. Arilda (fifth century?) was a consecrated virgin who was martyred resisting sexual advances. She is the patron saint of Oldbury on the Hill, Gloucestershire.

Arrian *see Arian*

Arrieal *see Ariel*

Arsema *see Rhipsime*

Arthelais Saint

St. Arthelais (544–560) was the daughter of Proconsul Lucius and his wife, Anthusa. Because she had taken vows of chastity, she fled Constantinople in order to avoid the advances of Emperor Justinian. She went to her uncle's home in Benevento where she died of a fever at age sixteen.

Ascelina Saint; Latin, French; noble, high birth

St. Ascelina (1121–1195) was a nun at the Cistercian convent at Boulancourt, Haute-Marne, France, where she was known for her mystical gifts.

Asella Saint; Latin, Spanish; ascension

St. Asella (d. 406) consecrated herself to the Lord at the age of ten. She lived in a small cell in Rome and was referred to as a "flower of the Lord" by St. Jerome.

Asheley *see Ashley (boy's name)*

Ashelie *see Ashley (boy's name)*

Ashely *see Ashley (boy's name)*

Ashlan *see Ashley (boy's name)*

Ashlea *see Ashley (boy's name)*

Ashlee *see Ashley (boy's name)*

Ashleigh *see Ashley (boy's name)*

Ashlen *see Ashley (boy's name)*

Asheley *see Ashley*

Ashley *see Ashley (boy's name)*

Ashli *see Ashley (boy's name)*

Ashlie *see Ashley (boy's name)*

Ashlin *see Ashley (boy's name)*

Ashling *see Ashley (boy's name)*

Ashlinn *see Ashley (boy's name)*

Ashlone *see Ashley (boy's name)*

Ashly *see Ashley (boy's name)*

Ashlyn *see Ashley (boy's name)*

Ashlynn *see Ashley (boy's name)*

Asia short form of Anastasia

> *Ayziz, Esia, Esiah, Esya, Esyah*

Aska *see Anna*

Asteria Saint; Greek; star

> St. Asteria (d. 307) was the sister of St. Grata. The two virgins were martyred at Bergamo, in Sicily.

Athanasia Saint; Greek; immortal

> St. Athanasia (790–860) lived on an Aegean Island. She lost her first husband after only two weeks of marriage when he was killed fighting Saracens. Her second husband decided to become a monk, and she agreed to become a nun as well. She converted her home into a convent where she served as abbess. Later, she moved the convent to Timia. She also served as an advisor to the Byzantine empress.

Athilda *see Alkeld*

Athracht *see Attracta*

Atka *see Agatha*

Attala *see Attala (boy's name)*

Attalia Saint; Hebrew; the Lord is exalted

> St. Attalia (d. 741) was the niece of St. Odilia. She served as abbess of St. Stephen's Convent in Salzburg, Austria.

Attracta Saint; Latin, Celtic

> *Araght, Athracht, Taraghta*

> St. Attracta (sixth century) was born into a noble Irish family. Against her father's wishes, she went to St. Patrick at Coolavin and became a nun. She founded a hospice on Lough Gara and was known as a miracle worker. She is the patron of Tourlestrane, County Silgo, Ireland.

Aubrey *see Aubrey (boy's name)*

Auda *see Ada*

Audey *see Audrey*

Audra *see Audrey*

Audrah *see Audrey*

Audray *see Audrey*

Audre *see Audrey*

Audrey Saint; Top 100 Name; English; noble strength

> *Adrey, Audey, Audra, Audrah, Audray, Audre, Audrienna, Audrienne, Audrin, Audriya, Audrye, Ethelreda, Etheidreda, Etdelreda*

> St. Audrey (d. 679), also known as Ethelreda or Etheidreda, was an English princess. She had taken a vow of virginity but was married anyway. Her first marriage ended after three years when her husband died. The marriage had never been consummated. Her second husband did not wish to live a celibate life and asked St. Wilfrid

to release Audrey from her vow of virginity, but he refused. He instead helped her to escape. Her husband followed her, but he eventually gave up and married someone else, and Audrey became a nun. She founded the Abbey of Ely and lived an austere life. She died of a large tumor on her neck.

Audrienna *see Audrey*

Audrienne *see Audrey*

Audrin *see Audrey*

Audriya *see Audrey*

Audrye *see Audrey*

Augusta Saint; form of Augustine; Latin; majestic

Agusta, Augustah, Augustia, Augustina, Austina, Austine, Austyne

St. Augusta (fifth century) was the daughter of the duke of Fruili, Italy. His father was so angered by her conversion to Christianity that he killed her.

Augustah *see Augusta*

Augustia *see Augusta*

Augustina *see Augusta*

Aundrea *see Andrea (boy's name)*

Auralea *see Aurelia*

Auraleah *see Aurelia*

Auralia *see Aurelia*

Aurea Saint; Latin; she who has blond hair

St. Aurea (1042–1069) was born in Villavelayo, Spain, an area controlled by the Moors. She joined the Convent of San Millán de la Cogolla. She was known as a visionary and miracle worker. She died of a painful disease at the age of twenty-seven.

Aureah *see Aurelia*

Aureal *see Aurelia*

Aurel *see Aurelia*

Aurela *see Aurelia*

Aurelah *see Aurelia*

Aurele *see Aurelia*

Aurelea *see Aurelia*

Aurelia Saint; Latin; golden

Arela, Arella, Auralea, Auraleah, Auralia, Aurea, Aureah, Aureal, Aurel, Aurela, Aurelah, Aurele, Aurelea, Aureliana, Aurella, Aurellah, Auria, Auriah, Aurie, Auriel, Aurilia, Auriola, Auriolah, Auriolla, Auriollah, Aurita, Oralia, Oralie

St. Aurelia (d. 1027) was a member of the royal family of Hugh Capet. She became a hermitess in a Benedictine abbey in Salzburg, Austria, in order to avoid marriage. She was a friend of St. Wolfgang.

Aureliana *see Aurelia*

Aurella *see Aurelia*

Aurellah *see Aurelia*

Auria *see Aurelia*

Auriah *see Aurelia*

Aurie *see Aurelia*

Auriel *see Aurelia*

Aurilia *see Aurelia*

Auriola *see Aurelia*

Auriolah *see Aurelia*

Auriolla *see Aurelia*

Auriollah *see Aurelia*

Aurita *see Aurelia*

Austell Saint; German; August
Hoystill

St. Austell (sixth century), or Hoystill, was a daughter of Brychan of Wales. She was a disciple of St. Newman of Cornwall, England.

Austina *see Augusta*

Austine *see Augusta*

Austreberta Saint
Eustreberta

St. Austreberta (630–704), or Eustreberta, was born to Count Palatine Badefrid and St. Framechildis near Therouanne, Artois, France. She became a nun to escape an unwanted marriage. She entered the Convent of Abbeville, Port-sur-Somme, where she was elected abbess and helped to reform the convent. She was known for her visions and miracles.

Austyne *see Augusta*

Ava Saint; Top 100 Name; Hebrew; life
Aeva, Avada, Avae, Avah, Ave, Aveen, Avis

St. Ava (ninth century) was the daughter of King Pepin. She was cured of blindness by St. Rainfredis. She became a Benedictine nun at Dinart, Hainault, where she was later elected abbess.

Avada *see Ava*

Avae *see Ava*

Avah *see Ava*

Ave *see Ava*

Aveen *see Ava*

Averil *see Everild*

Avery Top 100 Name; form of Aubrey; English; noble, bear-like, blond ruler

Avigail *see Abigail*

Avigayle *see Abigail*

Avis *see Ava*

Aydan *see Aidan (boy's name)*

Aydin *see Aidan (boy's name)*

Aymee *see Aimee*

Ayzia *see Asia*

B

Babara *see Barbara*

Babb *see Barbara*

Babbette *see Barbara*

Babbie *see Barbara*

Babel *see Barbara*

Babette *see Barbara*

Babina *see Barbara*

Babs *see Barbara*

Balbina Saint; Latin; little stutterer

St. Balbina (d. 130) was the daughter of Quirinus the martyr. She was baptized by Pope St. Alexander and died for the faith. She was buried on the Appian Way.

Balda Saint; Phoenician; God protect the king

St. Balda (seventh century) was a Benedictine abbess in Jouarre, Meaux.

Baldegundis Saint

St. Baldegundis (d. 580) was an abbess of Saint-Croix in Poitiers, France.

Barbara Saint; Latin; stranger, foreigner

Babara, Babb, Babbette, Babbie, Babel, Babette, Babina, Babs, Barbarina, Barbarit, Barbarita, Barbary, Barbeeleen, Barbel, Barbera, Barbette, Barbey, Barbica, Barbora, Barborah, Barborka, Barbraann, Barbro, Baruska, Basha, Berbera

St. Barbara (fourth century) was brought up as a pagan. Her father, Dioscorus, kept her secluded in a tower, where she dedicated herself to prayer and study and received Baptism in secret from a priest. Angered by her conversion, her father turned her over to the civil tribunal. She was tortured and beheaded by her father's own hand. She is a patron of the US Army Field Artillery.

Barbarina *see Barbara*

Barbarit *see Barbara*

Barbarita *see Barbara*

Barbary *see Barbara*

Barbe Saint; Latin; foreign woman

Bl. Barbe Aurillot (1566–1618) was the daughter of a French government official. She thought about becoming a nun but married Pierre Acarie, an aristocrat, when she was sixteen. She had six children, three of whom became Carmelites, and one a priest. When Henry VI became king, he seized the Acarie estates and exiled the family. Barbe went to court over the matter and won. After she was widowed, she became a Carmelite sister, taking the name Mary of the Incarnation. She founded five Carmelite houses in France.

Barbeeleen *see Barbara*

Barbel *see Barbara*

Barbera *see Barbara*

Barbette *see Barbara*

Barbey *see Barbara*

Barbica *see Barbara*

Barbora *see Barbara*

Barborah *see Barbara*

Barborka *see Barbara*

Barbraann *see Barbara*

Barbro *see Barbara*

Barta *see Bertha*

Bartha *see Bertha*

Bartholomea Saint; Hebrew; child of Talmai

St. Bartholomea Capitanjo (1807–1833) was born in Lovere, Italy, and founded the Sisters of Charity of Lovere with St. Vincenzia Gerosa. The order was dedicated to education and nursing. She was canonized in 1950 by Pope Pius XII.

Baruska *see Barbara*

Basha *see Barbara*

Basila *see Basilla*

Basilia *see Basilla*

Basiliah *see Basilla*

Basilie *see Basilla*

Basilissa *see Basilla*

Basilla Saint; Greek, Latin; royal, queenly

Basila, Basilia, Basiliah, Basilie, Basilissa, Basillah, Basillie, Basyla, Basylah, Basyle, Basyll, Basylla,

Basyllah, Basylle, Bazila, Bazilah, Bazile, Bazilie, Bazill, Bazilla, Bazillah, Bazille, Bazillia, Bazilliah, Bazillie, Bazyla, Bazylah, Bazyle, Bazyll, Bazylla, Bazyllah, Bazylle

St. Basilla (d. 304), or Basilissa, was born into a Roman noble family. She converted to Christianity and refused to marry Pompeius, a Roman patrician. He turned her over to Emperor Galienus who had her beheaded for her faith.

Basillah *see Basilla*

Basillie *see Basilla*

Bassa Saint; Spanish; wood, forest

St. Bassa (d. 304) was the wife of a pagan priest. When her three sons were condemned during the persecution of Emperor Diocletiall, she joined them.

Bastienne *see Sebastiana*

Basyla *see Basilla*

Basylah *see Basilla*

Basyle *see Basilla*

Basyll *see Basilla*

Basylla *see Basilla*

Basyllah *see Basilla*

Basylle *see Basilla*

Bathilda *see Bathildis*

Bathildah *see Bathildis*

Bathilde *see Bathildis*

Bathildis Saint; Latin; to fight a battle

Bathilda, Bathildah, Bathilde, Bathylda, Bathyldah, Bathylde, Batilda, Batilde

St. Bathildis (626–680) was born in England, but she was taken as a slave to Neustria, which was part of the Frankish kingdom. She became part of King Clovis II's court and married him in 649, giving birth to three future kings. When Clovis II died, she became regent for Clotaire III. After he assumed the throne, she retired to Chelles Convent, one of several abbeys and convents she had founded.

Bathylda *see Bathildis*

Bathyldah *see Bathildis*

Bathylde *see Bathildis*

Batilda *see Bathildis*

Batilde *see Bathildis*

Bazila *see Basilla*

Bazilah *see Basilla*

Bazile *see Basilla*

Bazilie *see Basilla*

Bazill *see Basilla*

Bazilla *see Basilla*

Bazillah *see Basilla*

Bazille *see Basilla*

Bazillia *see Basilla*

Bazilliah *see Basilla*

Bazillie *see Basilla*

Bazyla *see Basilla*

Bazylah *see Basilla*

Bazyle *see Basilla*

Bazyll *see Basilla*

Bazylla *see Basilla*

Bazyllah *see Basilla*

Bazylle *see Basilla*

Bea *see Beatrice*

Beata *see Beatrice*

Beate *see Beatrice*

Beatrica *see Beatrice*

Beatrice Saint; Latin; blessed, happy, bringer of joy

Bea, Beata, Beate, Beatrica, Beatricia, Beatriks, Beatris, Beatrisa, Beatrise, Beatriss, Beatrissa, Beatrix, Beatriz, Beatryx, Beatryz, Beattie, Beatty, Bebe, Bee, Beitris, Betrys, Brites, Trice

St. Beatrice da Silva Meneses (1424–1490), also known as Beatrix or Brites, was born in Ceuta, Portugal, the daughter of the count of Viana. Raised in the household of Princess Isable, she accompanied her when she married John II of Castile. Beatrice resigned from court life and entered the Cistercian convent in Toledo. She founded the Congregation of the Immaculate Conception of the Blessed Virgin Mary. She was canonized by Pope Paul VI in 1976.

Beatricia *see Beatrice*

Beatriks *see Beatrice*

Beatris *see Beatrice*

Beatrisa *see Beatrice*

Beatrise *see Beatrice*

Beatriss *see Beatrice*

Beatrissa *see Beatrice*

Beatrix *see Beatrice*

Beatriz *see Beatrice*

Beatryx *see Beatrice*

Beatryz *see Beatrice*

Beattie *see Beatrice*

Beatty *see Beatrice*

Bebe *see Beatrice*

Bedelia *see Bridget*

Bee *see Beatrice*

Bega Saint; German; illustrious, brilliant

Bee

St. Bega (seventh century), or Bee, was an Irish princess. She had taken a vow of virginity and refused to marry a prince from Norway. She fled her homeland, going to Cumberland in England where St. Aidan received her vows as a nun. She founded St. Bee's Monastery where she served as abbess until her death.

Begga Saint; Celtic, Danish; might, strength, valor

St. Begga (615–693) was the daughter of Pepin of Landen and St. Itta. She married Ansegilius and gave birth to Pepin of Herstal, who was the founder of the Carolingian dynasty of rulers in France. After her husband died, she built a church and convent at Andenne where she lived out the rest of her days.

Beitris *see Beatrice*

Belina Saint; French, Italian; goddess, beautiful

St. Belina (d. 1135) was from Troyes, France. She died defending her virginity from a feudal lord.

Belita *see Isabel*

Bella *see Isabel*

Bellaude *see Berlinda*

Belle *see Isabel*

Benadette *see Bernadette*

Bendite *see Benedicta*

Benedetta Saint; form of Benedicta; Latin; blessed

St. Benedetta Cambiagio Frassinello (1791–1858) wanted to become a religious, but her parents wanted her to marry, and she honored their wishes. After two years of marriage, she and her husband decided to live together as brother and sister and devote their lives to God. They later both entered religious life. Benedetta joined the Ursuline Sisters but only stayed one year due to poor health. After receiving a miraculous cure, her bishop asked her to devote herself to the education of young girls. She eventually began the Congregation of the Benedictine Sisters of Providence. She was canonized by Pope John Paul II in 2002.

Benedattah *see Benedicta*

Benedicta Saint; Latin; blessed

Bendite, Benedetta, Benedettah, Benedicte, Benedictina, Benedikta, Benedycta, Benedykta, Benedyta, Bengta, Benita, Benna, Bennicia, Benoite, Binney

St. Benedicta (sixth century) was a mystic who lived in a convent founded by St. Galla in Rome.

Benedicte *see Benedicta*

Benedictina *see Benedicta*

Benedikta *see Benedicta*

Benedycta *see Benedicta*

Benedykta *see Benedicta*

Benedyta *see Benedicta*

Bengta *see Benedicta*

Benita *see Benedicta*

Benna *see Benedicta*

Bennicia *see Benedicta*

Benoite *see Benedicta*

Bera *see Bernadette*

Beradette *see Bernadette*

Berbera *see Barbara*

Berget *see Bridget*

Berlinda Saint; German; bear

Berlindis, Bellaude

St. Berlinda (d. 702) was a niece of St. Amandus. Her father disowned her after he contracted leprosy, believing that she would not take care of him. She fled to a convent at Moorsel where she became a nun. After her father's death, she became a hermit at Meerbeke. She was known for helping the poor and suffering.

Berlindis *see Berlinda*

Berna *see Bernadette*

Bernadeen *see Bernardine*

Bernadeena *see Bernardine*

Bernadeenah *see Bernardine*

Bernadeene *see Bernardine*

Bernaden *see Bernardine*

Bernadena *see Bernardine*

Bernadet *see Bernadette*

Bernadeta *see Bernadette*

Bernadetah *see Bernadette*

Bernadete *see Bernadette*

Bernadett *see Bernadette*

Bernadetta *see Bernadette*

Bernadettah *see Bernadette*

Bernadette Saint; form of Bernadine; French; brave as a bear

Benadette, Bera, Beradette, Berna, Bernadet, Bernadeta, Bernadetah, Bernadete, Bernadett, Bernadetta, Bernadettah, Bernadit, Bernadita, Bernaditah, Bernadite, Bernadyta, Bernadytah, Bernadyte, Bernarda, Bernardette, Bernedet, Bernedette, Bernessa, Berneta, Bernina, Bernita

St. Bernadette Soubirous (1844–1879) was born in Lourdes, France, into very poor circumstances. On February 11, 1858, she received a vision of the Blessed Virgin Mary in a cave on the banks of the Gave River near Lourdes. Crowds began to gather at the area as she experienced further visions. Despite repeated questioning from the authorities, she never changed her story. Mary gave her name as the "Immaculate Conception." Bernadette, at Mary's direction, dug a spring at the location, which had miraculous properties. Bernadette became a Sister of Notre Dame in Nevers, where she died of tuberculosis of the knee.

Bernadit *see Bernadette*

Bernadita *see Bernadette*

Bernaditah *see Bernadette*

Bernadite *see Bernadette*

Bernadyta *see Bernadette*

Bernadytah *see Bernadette*

Bernadyte *see Bernadette*

Bernarda *see Bernadette*

Bernardette *see Bernadette*

Bernardina Saint; a form of Bernard; Spanish; brave as a bear

Bernardine, Berni

Bl. Bernardina Maria Jablonska (1878–1940) was born in Pyzuny Lukawica, Poland. She became a cofoundress of the Sisters of the Third Order of Saint Francis Servants of the Poor (Albertine Sisters), whom she served as superior. She founded hospices for the sick and poor and was known as a mystic. She was beatified by Pope John Paul II in 1997.

Bernardine *see Bernardine (boy's name)*

Bernedet *see Bernadette*

Bernedette *see Bernadette*

Bernessa *see Bernadette*

Berneta *see Bernadette*

Berni *see Bernardina, Bernardine*

Bernina *see Bernadette*

Bernita *see Bernadette*

Berta *see Bertha*

Berth *see Bertha*

Bertha Saint; a form of Alberta; German; bright, illustrious

Barta, Bartha, Berta, Berth, Berthe, Bertille, Bertita, Bertrona, Bertus, Berty, Birdy, Birtha, Birthe, Byrth, Byrtha, Byrthah

St. Bertha of Kent (539–612) was a Frankish princess who became the first Christian queen of England. She married Ethelbert of Kent, a pagan king. She restored a Christian church in Canterbury, dedicating it to

St. Martin of Tours. With Bertha's encouragement, King Ethelbert welcomed St. Augustine of Canterbury to England.

Berthe *see Bertha*

Bertilda *see Bertilia, Bertilla*

Bertilia Saint; German; she who fights, the distinguished one
Bertilda

St. Bertilia (d. 687) was married, but she and her husband took vows of celibacy and remained virgins. After his death, she became a hermitess near a church she had founded at Maroeuil, France.

Bertilla Saint; German; she who fights, the distinguished one
Bertilda

St. Bertilla Boscardin (1888–1922) was born Anna Francesca Boscardin into an Italian peasant family. She was thought to be intellectually slow and did not receive much schooling. She was accepted as a member of the Teachers of St. Dorothy, Daughters of the Sacred Heart, in 1904, where she took the name Maria Bertilla. She served as a laundress and kitchen maid. She was then sent to Treviso where she learned nursing. She was known for her care of sick children and victims of air raids during World War I. She died of a painful tumor and was canonized in 1961.

Bertille *see Bertha*

Bertita *see Bertha*

Bertoara Saint

St. Bertoara (d. 614) was abbess of Notre-Dame-de-Sales in Bourges, France.

Bertrona *see Bertha*

Bertus *see Bertha*

Berty *see Bertha*

Bethany New Testament; Aramaic; the house of figs

Bethany is a village near the foot of the Mount of Olives. It was the home of Jesus' friends, Lazarus, Martha, and Mary.

Betrys *see Beatrice*

Bibiana Saint; Latin; lively
Bibianah, Bibiane, Bibiann, Bibianna, Bibiannah, Bibianne, Bibyan, Bibyana, Bibyanah, Bibyann, Bibyanna, Bibyannah, Bibyanne, Bybian, Bybiana, Bybianah, Bybiane, Bybiann, Bybianna, Bybiannah, Bybianne

St. Bibiana (fourth century) was the daughter of Flavian, a Roman knight, and Dafrosa, his wife, both of whom died for the faith. Bibiana and her sister Demetria lost all their possessions but stayed in their house, fasting and praying. When they were arrested, Demetria fell dead at the feet of the governor of Rome. Bibiana was placed with a wicked woman who attempted to corrupt her, but Bibiana remained faithful. She was then tied to a pillar and beaten to death.

Bibianah *see Bibiana*

Bibiane *see Bibiana*

Bibiann *see Bibiana*

Bibianna *see Bibiana*

Bibiannah *see Bibiana*

Bibianne *see Bibiana*

Bibyan *see Bibiana*

Bibyana *see Bibiana*

Bibyanah *see Bibiana*

Bibyann *see Bibiana*

Bibyanna *see Bibiana*

Bibyannah *see Bibiana*

Bibyanne *see Bibiana*

Bichier Saint

St. Bichier (1773–1838) was born near LeBlanc, France, and was sent to a convent at Poitiers when she was ten. Under the direction of St. Andrew Fournet, she devoted herself to caring for the sick and needy. She lived as a Carmelite and a member of the Society of Providence before helping to found the Daughters of Charity, also known as the Sisters of St. Andrew. She encouraged Fr. Michael Garicoits to start the Priests of the Sacred Heart of Betharram. She was canonized in 1947.

Bilhild Saint

St. Bilhild (d. 710) was the widow of the duke of Thuringia. She founded the Convent of Altenmunster in Mainz, Germany, where she served as abbess.

Binney *see Benedicta*

Birdy *see Bertha*

Birgitta *see Bridget*

Birgitte *see Bridget*

Birtha *see Bertha*

Birthe *see Bertha*

Blaesilla Saint

St. Blaesilla (d. 384) was the daughter of St. Paula. She was married for seven months, when her husband died. She then dedicated herself to a very ascetical lifestyle under the direction of St. Jerome. Her body was so weakened by this life that she died four months later.

Blandina Saint; Latin; flattering

St. Blandina (162–177) was a Christian slave who was tortured and martyred for the faith after watching her younger brother die a painful death. She is a patroness of young girls.

Blath Saint; Celtic; fair haired, white

Flora

St. Blath (d. 523), also known as Flora, was the cook in St. Brigid's convent in Kildare, Ireland. She was known for her holiness and her loyalty to St. Brigid.

Boleslawa Saint; Slavic; the most glorious of the glorious

Bl. Boleslawa Maria Lament (1862–1946) was born in Lowicz, Poland. She studied in Warsaw and then opened a tailoring business with her sister. She joined the Congregation of the Family of Mary, which was organized in secrecy because of persecution. Nine years later, she left and returned home with the intent of later entering an enclosure. Instead, she became director of a home for the homeless. She entered the Franciscan Third Order. She later joined with two other sisters and founded the Sisters of the Sacred Family, which she served as superior. She was beatified by Pope John Paul II in 1991.

Bonifacia Saint; Latin; do-gooder

Saint Bonifacia Rodriguez Castro (1837–1905) was from Salamanca, Spain. She worked as a cord maker and opened a shop in her mother's home. On Sundays, a group of like-minded women would meet there. They founded the Association of the Immaculate and Saint Joseph, which later became the Servants of Saint Joseph. Bonifacia served as superior for eight years before being unjustly removed from that office. She later began another house in Zamora, but it wasn't until after her death that the two houses were reconciled. She was canonized by Pope Benedict XVI in 2011.

Branca *see Breaca*

Branka *see Breaca*

Breaca Saint; Celtic

Branca, Branka, Breque

St. Breaca (fifth or sixth century), also known as Breque, Branca, and Branka, was a disciple of St. Brigid. She traveled from Ireland to England, and she and her companions settled on the bank of the Hoyle River.

Breda *see Bridget*

Breque *see Breaca*

Brianna Top 100 Name; female form of Brian; Gaelic; strong, virtuous, honorable

Bride *see Bridget*

Bridey *see Bridget*

Bridger *see Bridget*

Bridget Saint; Gaelic; strong

Bedelia, Berget, Birgitta, Birgitte, Breda, Bride, Bridey, Bridger, Bridgeta, Bridgetah, Bridgete, Bridgid, Bridgit, Bridgita, Bridgitah, Bridgite, Bridgot, Brietta, Brigada, Briget, Brigida, Brydget, Brydgeta, Brydgetah, Brydgete

St. Bridget, St. Bridget of Sweden

St. Bridget of Sweden (1303–1373), also known as Birgitta, was born into a pious noble family. She was married at the age of thirteen to Ulf Gudmarsson and gave birth to eight children. She served as lady-in-waiting to the Queen of Sweden. Her husband died when she was forty-one. She then founded a religious order. She was a mystic. Through her visions, she received messages that she passed on to kings and popes. She is a patron saint of Sweden.

Bridgeta *see Bridget*

Bridgetah *see Bridget*

Bridgete *see Bridget*

Bridgid *see Bridget*

Bridgit *see Bridget*

Bridgita *see Bridget*

Bridgitah *see Bridget*

Bridgite *see Bridget*

Bridgot *see Bridget*

Brietta *see Bridget*

Brigada *see Bridget*

Briget *see Bridget*

Brigid Saint; a form of Bridget; Gaelic; strong

St. Brigid of Ireland (453–523) was born at Faughart, Ireland, to parents who had been baptized by St. Patrick. She became a nun at a young age. She settled with seven other virgins at the foot of Croghan Hill. She later founded a monastery at Kildare, the first convent in Ireland, where she served as abbess. She founded a school of art, best known for the Book of Kildare, an illuminated manuscript. While there are many legends that surround her life, she was truly a remarkable woman who had great charity and compassion. She is a patron saint of Ireland.

Brigida Saint; a form of Bridget; Gaelic; strong

Bl. Brigida of Jesus Morello (1610–1679) was born in Genoa, Italy. She became the foundress of the Institute of the Ursuline Sisters of Mary Immaculate. She was beatified by Pope John Paul II in 1998.

Brites *see Beatrice*

Britta Saint; Swedish; strong

St. Britta (fourth century) was a virgin who was martyred with St. Maura. Their relics were discovered by St. Euphronius.

Bronach Saint; Gaelic; sorrowful

St. Bronach (fourth century?) was an Irish mystic known for her beauty and spiritual gifts. She is reputed to have founded Cell Brónche in County Down.

Brydget *see Bridget*

Brydgeta *see Bridget*

Brydgetah *see Bridget*

Brydgete *see Bridget*

Buriana Saint; Ukranian; lives near weeds

St. Buriana (sixth century) was the daughter of an Irish king who served as a missionary to Dumnonia. She also lived as a hermit and was known for her holiness.

Bybian *see Bibiana*

Bybiana *see Bibiana*

Bybianah *see Bibiana*

Bybiane *see Bibiana*

Bybiann *see Bibiana*

Bybianna *see Bibiana*

Bybiannah *see Bibiana*

Bybianne *see Bibiana*

Byrth *see Bertha*

Byrtha *see Bertha*

Byrthah *see Bertha*

C

Caaran *see Caron*

Caaren *see Caron*

Caarin *see Caron*

Caaron *see Caron*

Cachi *see Casimir (boy's name)*

Cacilia *see Cecilia*

Caciliah *see Cecilia*

Caecilia Saint; Latin; blind

St. Caecilia (d. 304) was one of a large group of Christians arrested and martyred for the faith in northwestern Africa.

Caeciliah *see Cecilia*

Caellainn Saint; Gaelic

Caoilfionn

St. Caellainn (sixth century), also known as Caoilfionn, was an Irish martyr.

Caesarea Saint; Latin; longhaired

Caesarn

St. Caesarea (date unknown), also known as Caesarn, was a virgin who became a hermit in Otranto in southern Italy in order to maintain her virtue.

Caesaria Saint; Latin; longhaired

St. Caesaria (sixth century) was the sister of Bishop St. Caesarius of Arles, Gaul. She became an abbess of a convent that he had founded and was known for her care of the poor, sick, and children.

Caesarn *see Caesarea*

Cain *see Keyne*

Cainder *see Cannera*

Cairena *see Catherine*

Cairene *see Catherine*

Cairina *see Catherine*

Cait *see Catherine*

Caitlin *see Catherine*

Caitrin *see Catherine*

Cajetana *see Gaetana*

Caline *see Celine*

Callie *see Caroline*

Callinica Saint; Latin; she who secures a beautiful victory

St. Callinica (d. 250) was a wealthy matron who, together with Basilissa, cared for imprisoned Christians in her area. She was martyred.

Calliope Saint; Greek; beautiful voice

Kalliopi

St. Calliope (third century), also known as Kalliopi, refused the hand of a pagan man. He arranged for her to be arrested. When she was sentenced, the suitor vowed to withdraw the charges if she should accept him, but she refused. She was flogged, and her face was scarred with branding irons. Still alive after all that torture and still steadfast in her faith, she was beheaded.

Camella *see Camila*

Camila Saint; Top 100 Name; Latin; child born to freedom

Camella, Camilah, Camile, Camilia, Camilla, Camillah, Camille, Camillia, Camilya, Cammila, Cammilah, Cammilla, Cammyla, Cammylah, Cammylla, Cammyllah, Chamika, Chamila, Chamilla, Chamylla, Chamyllah, Kamila, Kamilah

St. Camilla, St. Camilla Battista da Varano

St. Camilla Battista da Varano (1458–1524) was an Italian princess who received a noble education. Even as a child, she meditated on Christ's passion. As a teen, she began to fast and keep night vigils, even as she maintained other youthful pursuits such as dancing and singing at court. At the age of twenty-one, she took a vow of chastity. Against her father's wishes, she became a Poor Clare two years later. She was a mystic who had visions of Our Lord and St. Clare of Assisi. She became abbess of the monastery and was later sent by Pope Julius II to establish a monastery in Fermo. She was canonized by Pope Benedict XVI on October 17, 2010.

Camilah see *Camila*

Camile see *Camila*

Camilia see *Camila*

Camilla see *Camila*

Camillah see *Camila*

Camille see *Camila*

Camillia see *Camila*

Camilya see *Camila*

Cammila see *Camila*

Cammilah see *Camila*

Cammilla see *Camila*

Cammyla see *Camila*

Cammylah see *Camila*

Cammylla see *Camila*

Cammyllah see *Camila*

Candida Saint; a form of Candace; Greek; glittering white, glowing
St. Candida, St. Candida the Elder, St. Candida the Younger, St. Candida Maria de Jesus

St. Candida (d. 798) was the mother of St. Memerius. She lived as a hermit near the Abbey of St. Stephen of Banoles in Spain.

Cannera Saint
Cainder, Kinnera
St. Cannera (d. 530), also known as Cainder or Kinnera, was an Irish hermitess who lived near Bantry. She was a friend of St. Senan.

Cantianilla Saint; Latin
St. Cantianilla (d. 304), with her siblings St. Cantius and St. Cantianus, was a member of the Roman Anicii family, orphaned as a child and raised by a Christian named Protus. After freeing their slaves and giving their money to the poor, she and her siblings fled to Aquileia, Italy, to escape Diocletian's persecution. They were captured at Aquae Gradatae and were beheaded.

Caoilfionn see *Caellainn*

Capitolina Saint; Latin; she who lives with the gods
St. Capitolina (d. 304) was martyred with her handmaid, Erotheis, in the persecutions of Diocletian.

Caralyn see *Caroline*

Caran see *Caron*

Carane see *Caron*

Carciliah see *Cecilia*

Carelyn see *Caroline*

Carene see *Caron*

Carilyn see *Caroline*

Carilynn see *Caroline*

Carilynne *see Caroline*

Carin *see Caron*

Carinn *see Caron*

Carissima Saint; Latin; loved, appreciated

St. Carissima (fifth century) was born at Albi. She lived as a hermit and then became a nun at Viants, France.

Carita *see Charity*

Carman *see Carmel*

Carmel Hebrew; vineyard, garden

Carman, Carmen, Carmon, Carmyn

Carmel is one of the titles of Our Blessed Mother. Mount Carmel was the first place dedicated to our Blessed Virgin—a chapel was established in her honor there while she was still living. On July 16, 1251, Our Lady of Mount Carmel appeared to St. Simon Stock, general of the Carmelites at Cambridge, England, and gave him the scapular, promising special protection to all who would wear it and live Christian lives.

Carmen *see Carmel*

Carmon *see Carmel*

Carmyn *see Carmel*

Caro *see Caroline*

Carol *see Caroline, Karol (boy's name)*

Carolean *see Caroline*

Caroleane *see Caroline*

Caroleen *see Caroline*

Carolin *see Caroline*

Carolina *see Caroline*

Caroline Saint; Top 100 Name; French; little and strong

Callie, Caralyn, Carelyn, Carilyn, Carilynn, Carilynne, Caro, Carol, Carolean, Caroleane, Caroleen, Carolin, Carolina, Carolyn, Carrie, Carroleen, Carroleene, Carrolene, Carrolin, Carroline, Karolina, Karolyn

Bl. Caroline Kozka (1898–1914) was born into a farm family in Wal-Ruda, Poland. She resisted being raped by a Russian soldier and was martyred. She was beatified by Pope John Paul II in 1987.

Carolyn *see Caroline*

Caron Saint; Welsh; loving, kind-hearted, charitable

Caaran, Caaren, Caarin, Caaron, Caran, Carane, Carene, Carin, Carinn, Caronne, Carran, Carron, Carrone, Carrun, Carun

St. Caron (date unknown) is a saint associated with Tregaron, Wales.

Caronne *see Caron*

Carran *see Caron*

Carrie *see Caroline*

Caroleen *see Caroline*

Carroleene *see Caroline*

Carrolene *see Caroline*

Carrolin *see Caroline*

Carroline *see Caroline*

Carron *see Caron*

Carrone *see Caron*

Carrun *see Caron*

Carun *see Caron*

Cas *see Casimir (boy's name)*

Cashemere *see Casimir (boy's name)*
Cashi *see Casimir (boy's name)*
Cashmeire *see Casimir (boy's name)*
Cashmere *see Casimir (boy's name)*
Casilda Saint; Arabic; virgin carrier of the lance

St. Casilda (d. 1050) was the daughter of a Muslim king of Toledo. She, however, cared for Christian prisoners, hiding bread in her clothes in order to feed them. When Muslim soldiers stopped her and asked her what she was carrying, she opened up her skirts and the bread turned into roses. She was later baptized and lived as a hermitess near Briviesca, Burgos.

Casimere *see Casimir (boy's name)*
Casimir *see Casimir (boy's name)*
Casimire *see Casimir (boy's name)*
Castimer *see Casimir (boy's name)*
Cat *see Catherine*
Cate *see Catherine*
Catereana *see Caterina*
Catereanah *see Caterina*
Catereane *see Caterina*
Catereena *see Caterina*
Catereenah *see Caterina*
Catereene *see Caterina*
Caterin *see Caterina*
Caterina Saint; a form of Catherine; German; pure

Catereana, Catereanah, Catereane, Catereena, Catereenah, Catereene, Caterin, Caterinah, Caterine, Cateryna, Caterynah, Cateryne, Catrina, Katerina, Katrina

St. Caterina Volpicelli (1839–1894) was born into an upper middle-class family in Naples, Italy. She was educated at the Royal Educational Institute of San Marcellino. She became a Franciscan Tertiary and later joined the Perpetual Adorers of the Blessed Sacrament but had to leave because of ill health. She founded the Institute of Handmaidens of the Sacred Heart and opened an orphanage. She also set up the Association of the Daughters of Mary. She was canonized by Pope Benedict XVI in 2009.

Caterinah *see Caterina*
Caterine *see Caterina*
Cateryna *see Caterina*
Caterynah *see Caterina*
Cateryne *see Caterina*
Cathann *see Catherine*
Cathanne *see Catherine*
Cathenne *see Catherine*
Catheren *see Catherine*
Catherene *see Catherine*
Catheria *see Catherine*
Catherin *see Catherine*
Catherina *see Catherine*
Catherinah *see Catherine*
Catherine Saint; Greek; pure

Cairena, Cairene, Cairina, Cait, Caitlin, Caitrin, Cat, Cate, Cathann, Cathanne, Cathenne, Catheren, Catherene, Catheria, Catherin, Catherina, Catherinah, Cathleen, Cathrine, Cathy, Catlaina, Catreeka, Catrelle, Catrice, Catricia, Catrika, Kaitlyn

St. Catherine de Ricci, St. Catherine Laboure, St. Catherine of Alexandria, St. Catherine of Bologna, St. Catherine of Siena, St. Catherine of Sweden

St. Catherine of Siena (1347–1380) was the twenty-third of twenty-five children born to a wool dyer and his wife. She had her first vision of Christ when she was six and took a vow of chastity at the age of seven. Her parents wished her to marry her older sister's widower, but she refused. At the age of sixteen, she became a Dominican tertiary. In the 1370s, she began dictating letters, writing to people in power. She had a long correspondence with Pope Gregory XI, trying to convince him to return to Rome. She also wrote "The Dialogue of Divine Providence." She is a Doctor of the Church.

Catheria *see Catherine*

Catherin *see Catherine*

Cathleen *see Catherine*

Cathrine *see Catherine*

Cathy *see Catherine*

Catlaina *see Catherine*

Catreeka *see Catherine*

Catrelle *see Catherine*

Catrice *see Catherine*

Catricia *see Catherine*

Catrika *see Catherine*

Catrina *see Caterina*

Cazimier *see Casimir (boy's name)*

Cazimir *see Casimir (boy's name)*

Ceara *see Cera*

Ceceley *see Cecilia*

Cecil *see Cecilia*

Cecila *see Cecilia*

Cecile *see Cecilia*

Cecilea *see Cecilia*

Cecilia Saint; Latin; blind

Cacilia, Caciliah, Caecilia, Caeciliah, Carciliah, Ceceley, Cecil, Cecila, Cecile, Cecilea, Ceciliah, Cecilija, Cecillia, Cecilya, Ceclia, Cecylia, Cecyliah, Cecylja, Cecylyah, Cee, Ceil, Ceila, Ceilagh, Ceileh, Ceileigh, Ceilena, Sheila, Sisiliya

St. Cecilia (third century) was a Roman virgin who married Valerian. She was determined to preserve her virginity and told her husband that there was an angel that guarded her. He was able to see this angel once he was baptized. Valerian was martyred for burying Christians. St. Cecilia preached the faith and converted over four hundred. She was arrested and condemned to die by being suffocated in the baths. When that didn't kill her, she was sentenced to be beheaded. Three strikes couldn't remove her head. She lived for three more days. She is the patroness of music.

Ceciliah *see Cecilia*

Cecilija *see Cecilia*

Cecillia *see Cecilia*

Cecilya *see Cecilia*

Ceclia *see Cecilia*

Cecylia *see Cecilia*

Cecyliah *see Cecilia*

Cecylja *see Cecilia*

Cecylya *see Cecilia*

Cecylyah *see Cecilia*

Cee *see Cecilia*

Ceil *see Cecilia*

Ceila *see Cecilia*

Ceilagh *see Cecilia*

Ceileh *see Cecilia*

Ceileigh *see Cecilia*

Ceilena *see Cecilia*

Céin *see Cian (boy's name)*

Celeane *see Celine*

Celeene *see Celine*

Celestine *see Celestine (boy's name)*

Celestyn *see Celestine (boy's name)*

Celin *see Celine*

Celina *see Celine*

Celine Saint; Greek; moon

> *Caline, Celeane, Celeene, Celin, Celina, Cellinn, Celyn, Celyne, Ciline, Cilline, Selena*

> St. Celine (fifth century) was the mother of St. Remigius, bishop of Rheims. His birth is considered a miracle because of her advanced age.

Cellinn *see Celine*

Celyn *see Celine*

Celyne *see Celine*

Cenobie *see Zenobia*

Centolla Saint; Arabic; light of knowledge

> St. Centolla (d. 304) was martyred in Burgos, Spain, with another woman named Helen during the persecutions of Diocletian.

Cera Saint; French; cherry red

> *Ceara, Cerea, Ceri, Ceria, Cerise, Cerra, Ciar, Ciara, Cior, Cyra*

> St. Cera (seventh century), also known as Ciar, Cior, Cyra, and Ceara, and five other Irish virgins asked St. Fintan Munnu for land. He gave them their abbey in Heli, which may have been in County Westmeath. The monastery was named after St. Telle. She also founded another monastery in Killchree.

Cerea *see Cera*

Cerelia *see Cyrilla*

Cerella *see Cyrilla*

Cerena *see Serena*

Ceri *see Cera*

Ceria *see Cera*

Cerise *see Cera*

Cerra *see Cera*

Chamika *see Camila*

Chamila *see Camila*

Chamilla *see Camila*

Chamylla *see Camila*

Chamyllah *see Camila*

Chana *see Hannah*

Chanah *see Hannah*

Chanton *see Chanton (boy's name)*

Chareese *see Charity*

Chariety *see Charity*

Charista *see Charity*

Charita *see Charity*

Charitah *see Charity*

Charitas *see Charity*

Charitea *see Charity*

Charitee *see Charity*

Charitey *see Charity*

Chariti *see Charity*

Charitia *see Charity*

Charitiah *see Charity*

Charitie *see Charity*

Charitina Saint; form of Charity; Latin; charity, kindness, love

St. Charitina (d. 304) was a virgin from Asia Minor. She was orphaned as a young girl and was raised by Claudius, who taught her the faith. She led a life of fasting and prayer and brought others to the Christian faith. She was arrested during the reign of Emperor Diocletian. He had her hair cut off and burning coals put on her head, but she lived. She also survived being drowned and being tied to a wheel. When he decided to have her raped, she begged God to take her before her virginity was lost. She died while praying.

Charitine *see Charity*

Charity Saint; Latin; charity, kindness, love

Carita, Chareese, Chariety, Charista, Charita, Charitah, Charitas, Charitea, Charitee, Charitey, Chariti, Charitia, Charitiah, Charitie, Charitine, Charitye, Charityna, Charityne, Chariza, Charyt, Charytey, Charytia, Charytiah, Charyty, Charytya, Charytyah

St. Charity (first or second century) was the daughter of St. Sophia, also known as St. Wisdom, and the sister of St. Faith and St. Hope. The mother and daughters were martyred for

the faith. St. Charity, who was nine years old, was beheaded after being unhurt in a furnace.

Charitye *see Charity*

Charityna *see Charity*

Charityne *see Charity*

Chariza *see Charity*

Charlotte Saint; Top 100 Name; French; little and strong

Bl. Charlotte Lucas (1752–1794) was a laywoman from the diocese of Angers, France, who was martyred during the French Revolution. She is one of the martyrs of Anjou. She was beatified by Pope John Paul II in 1984.

Charyt *see Charity*

Charytey *see Charity*

Charytia *see Charity*

Charytiah *see Charity*

Charyty *see Charity*

Charytya *see Charity*

Charytyah *see Charity*

Cheara *see Chiara*

Chelidonia Saint; Phoenician; new town

St. Chelidonia (d. 1152) was born in Ciculum, Italy. She became a hermitess in the mountains near Subiaco.

Chelle *see Michael (boy's name)*

Chi *see Chi (boy's name)*

Chiara Saint; a form of Clara; Latin; clear, bright

Chearan, Chiarra, Chyara

Bl. Chiara Badano (1971–1990) was born in Savona, Italy, the daughter of a truck driver and his wife. She was a very active girl and wanted to be a flight attendant. She joined the Focolare movement at age nine and at age sixteen became drawn to life as a religious missionary. She was diagnosed with cancer of the shoulder, which spread quickly. She lost the use of her legs and spent her remaining days devoted to prayer. She was beatified by Pope Benedict XVI in 2010.

Chiarra *see Chiara*

Chloe New Testament; Top 100 Name; Greek; blooming, verdant

Chloea, Chloee, Chloey, Chloie, Cloe, Cloey

Chloe (first century) was a prominent member of the Christian church of Corinth. She is mentioned in 1 Corinthians 1:11.

Chloea *see Chloe*

Chloee *see Chloe*

Chloey *see Chloe*

Chloie *see Chloe*

Chlotilda *see Clotilde*

Chrisopherson *see Christopher (boy's name)*

Christa *see Christian (boy's name)*

Christé *see Christian (boy's name)*

Christeana *see Christina*

Christeanah *see Christina*

Christeena *see Christina*

Christeenah *see Christina*

Christeina *see Christina*

Christeinah *see Christina*

Christella *see Christina*

Christiaan *see Christian (boy's name)*

Christian *see Christian (boy's name)*

Christiana *see Christian (boy's name)*

Christiane *see Christian (boy's name)*

Christiann *see Christian (boy's name)*

Christianna *see Christian (boy's name)*

Christina Saint; Greek; Christian, anointed

Christeana, Christeanah, Christeena, Christeenah, Christeina, Christeinah, Christella, Christinaa, Christinah, Christine, Christinea, Christinia, Christinna, Christinnah, Christna, Christyna, Christynah, Christynna, Chryst, Chrystena, Chrystina, Chrystyna, Chrystynah, Kristian, Kristine

St. Christina (third century) was the daughter of a wealthy pagan magistrate named Urbanus. He had her tortured because of her faith. She survived many of these tortures, but she was ultimately martyred at Bolsena in Turkey.

Christinaa *see Christina*

Christinah *see Christina*

Christine *see Christina*

Christinea *see Christina*

Christinia *see Christina*

Christinna *see Christina*

Christinnah *see Christina*

Christipher *see Christopher (boy's name)*

Christna *see Christina*

Christoher *see Christopher (boy's name)*

Christyan *see Christian (boy's name)*

Christyna *see Christina*

Christynah *see Christina*

Christynna *see Christina*

Christyon *see Christian (boy's name)*

Chritian *see Christian (boy's name)*

Chryst *see Christina*

Chrystain *see Christian (boy's name)*

Chrystena *see Christina*

Chrystina *see Christina*

Chrystyna *see Christina*

Chrystynah *see Christina*

Chyara *see Chiara*

Ciar *see Cera*

Ciara *see Cera*

Ciline *see Celine*

Cilinia Saint; Latin; heaven
St. Cilinia (d. 458) was the mother of St. Principius and St. Remigius.

Cilla *see Priscilla*

Cillene *see Cillene (boy's name)*

Cilline *see Celine*

Cinia *see Cinia*

Ciniah *see Cinnia*

Cinnia Saint; Latin; curly haired
Cinia, Ciniah, Cinniah, Cinnie, Sinia, Siniah, Sinnia, Sinniah
St. Cinnia (fifth century) was a princess of Ulster, Ireland. St. Patrick converted her and welcomed her into religious life.

Cinniah *see Cinnia*

Cinnie *see Cinnia*

Cior *see Cera*

Cira *see Cyrilla*

Cirah *see Cyrilla*

Ciri *see Cyrilla*

Cirila *see Cyrilla*

Cirilah *see Cyrilla*

Cirilla *see Cyrilla*

Cirylla *see Cyrilla*

Cissa *see Cissa (boy's name)*

Claire *see Clare*

Clar *see Clare*

Clare Saint; Latin, English; clear, bright
Claire, Clar
St. Clare, St. Clare of Montefalco
St. Clare (1194–1253) was born Chiara Offreduccio to an Italian count and his wife. She was always devoted to prayer. Her parents wanted her to marry, but she heard St. Francis preach and decided to give her life to God. She ran away. St. Francis cut her hair and gave her a veil and placed her in a Benedictine monastery. Her sister soon joined her, and they moved to the Church of San Damiano. Other women joined them, and they became the Poor Clares, known at the time as the Order of San Damiano. St. Clare served as abbess and remained great friends with St. Francis for as long as he lived, taking care of him in his final illness. She is the patron saint of television.

Clauda *see Claudia*

Claudah *see Claudia*

Claudea *see Claudia*

Claudeen *see Claudia*

Claudia Saint; form of Claude; Latin; lame

Clauda, Claudah, Claudea, Claudeen, Claudiah, Claudie, Claudy, Claudine, Claudya, Clodia

St. Claudia (first century) was the daughter of the British King Caractacus. When he was defeated by Aulus Plautius, he and his family were brought to Rome in chains. After Emperor Claudius released them, one of his daughters took the name Claudia and stayed in Rome. She was baptized and is mentioned in St. Paul's Second Letter to Timothy (4:21).

Claudiah *see Claudia*

Claudie *see Claudia*

Claudine Saint; form of Claude; Latin; lame

St. Claudine Thevenet (1774–1837) was from Lyons, France. Her two brothers were executed during the French Revolution. As they died, they begged her to "forgive, as we also forgive." She did forgive but was forever scarred by the sight of watching them murdered. She founded the Congregation of Jesus and Mary, dedicated to the needy and formation of girls. She took the name Mary of St. Ignatius. She also founded a home for Catholic women authors. She was canonized by Pope John Paul II in 1993.

Claudy *see Claudia*

Claudya *see Claudia*

Clelia Saint; form of Cecilia; Latin; blind

St. Clelia Barbierc (1847–1870) was born in Italy to very religious, poor hemp workers. Her father died when she was only eight years old, and she worked with her mother to help support the family. She joined the Workers of Christian Catechism as an assistant teacher when she was fourteen. She founded the Sisters Minims of Our Lady of Sorrows when she was only twenty-one. She died two years later of tuberculosis. She was canonized by Pope John Paul II in 1989.

Clodia *see Claudia*

Cloe *see Chloe*

Cloette *see Colette*

Cloey *see Chloe*

Clotilda *see Clotilde*

Clotilde Saint; Greek; heroine

Chlotilda, Clotilda, Klothilda, Klothilde

St. Clotilde (474–545) was the wife of King Clovis, whom she converted to Christianity a few years after they married. They were the founders of the Merovingian dynasty, although the infighting among her children caused her great pain. After her husband's death, she retired to Tours where she was known for her charity and works of mercy.

Clotsend *see Clotsindis*

Clotsindis Saint

Clotsend, Glodesind

St. Clotsindis (635–714), also known as Clotsend and Glodesind, was the daughter of Sts. Adalbald and Rictrudis. She became the abbess of Machiennes Abbey in Flanders.

Cocha Saint

St. Cocha (sixth century) was the nurse of St. Kieran of Saighir when he was an infant. She later became an abbess.

Coe *see Colette*

Coetta *see Colette*

Cointha Saint; Latin; fifth

Quinta, Quintah

St. Cointha (d. 249), also called Quinta, was martyred by being dragged through the streets of Alexandria with her feet tied to a horse. She died during the reign of Emperor Trajunus Decius.

Colet *see Colette*

Coleta *see Colette*

Colete *see Colette*

Colett *see Colette*

Coletta *see Colette*

Colettah *see Colette*

Colette Saint; a form of Nicole; Latin; victorious people

Cloette, Coe, Coetta, Colet, Coleta, Colete, Colett, Coletta, Colettah, Collet, Collete, Collett, Colletta, Kolette

St. Colette (1381–1447) was christened Nicolette but was always called Colette. The daughter of a French carpenter, she was orphaned at seventeen. She gave away her inheritance and became a Franciscan tertiary. She lived in a cell at Corby Abbey. She had a vision in 1406 that directed her to reform the Poor Clares. She joined that community and reformed several convents and started seventeen more. She was known for her holiness and her mysticism.

Collet *see Collette*

Collete *see Collette*

Collett *see Collette*

Colletta *see Collette*

Colombe *see Columba (boy's name)*

Columba *see Columba (boy's name)*

Columbia *see Columba (boy's name)*

Columbina *see Columba (boy's name)*

Columbinah *see Columba (boy's name)*

Comnika *see Dominica*

Concessa Saint; Latin; award

St. Concessa (date unknown) was a martyr from Carthage.

Connat Saint

St. Connat (d. 590) was an abbess of St. Brigid's Convent at Kildare, Ireland.

Consortia Saint; Latin; association

St. Consortia (d. 570) started a convent endowed by King Clotaire I of the Franks. She cured Clotaire's daughter of a serious illness.

Constance *see Constantia*

Constancia *see Constantia*

Constancy *see Constantia*

Constanta *see Constantia*

Constantia Saint; Latin; firm, constant

> *Constance, Constancia, Constancy, Constanta, Constantina, Constanza*
>
> St. Constantia (d. 68) was martyred with St. Felix in Nocera, Italy, during a persecution ordered by Emperor Nero.

Constantina *see Constantia*

Constanza *see Constantia*

Crescentia Saint; Latin; growth

> St. Crescentia (d. 303) was martyred with Sts. Vitus and Modestus in the Roman province of Lucania. Crescentia was an attendant of Vitus.

Crescentiana Saint; Latin; growth

> St. Crescentiana (fifth century) was a martyr honored by a church in Rome.

Crispina Saint; Latin; curly haired

> St. Crispina (d. 304) was born at Thagora, Africa. She married a wealthy Roman and had several children. She was brought before Proconsul Anulinus and was ordered to deny Christ. She refused. After having her head shaved and being mocked by the crowds, she was beheaded.

Cristeena *see Christina*

Cristena *see Christina*

Cristine *see Christina*

Cunegunda Saint; German; brave, famous

> *Kinga, Kunigunde*
>
> St. Cunegunda (1224–1292), also known as Kunigunde

or Kinga, was born into a royal Hungarian family. Her aunts included St. Elizabeth of Hungary, St. Hedwig, and St. Agnes of Prague. She married the future king of Poland, Boleslaus V, when she was fifteen. Both took vows of chastity and lived as brother and sister for forty years. The queen took care of her younger sister and dedicated her life to visiting the sick. After the king died, she became a Poor Clare and served as abbess of her community. She is the patron saint of Poles and Lithuanians. Pope John Paul II canonized her in 1999.

Cuthburg *see Cuthburga*

Cuthburga Saint; English

> *Cuthburg, Cuthburh*
>
> St. Cuthburga (d. 725), also known as Cuthburh or Cuthburg, was the sister of Ine, king of Wessex, and was married to Aldfrith, king of Northumbria. After several years of marriage and the birth of sons, she and her husband decided to become celibate. She entered Barking Abbey, which was under the direction of St. Hildelitha. Cuthberga and her sister later founded a double monastery at Wimborne.

Cuthburh *see Cuthburga*

Cyan *see Cian (boy's name)*

Cyra *see Cera*

Cyrah *see Cyrilla*

Cyrella *see Cyrilla*

Cyrelle *see Cyrilla*

Cyrenia Saint; Greek; enchanter

St. Cyrenia (d. 306) was martyred by being burned to death at Tarsus, Turkey, during the reign of Coemperor Galerius.

Cyriaca Saint; Greek; of the Lord

St. Cyriaca (d. 249) was a Roman widow. She opened her home to St. Laurence, deacon and martyr, so that he could distribute alms and food to the poor. She was martyred by scourging.

Cyrila *see Cyrilla*

Cyrilla Saint; Greek; noble

Cerelia, Cerella, Cira, Cirah, Ciri, Cirila, Cirilah, Cirilla, Cirylla, Cyrah, Cyrella, Cyrelle, Cyrila, Cyrille, Cyryll, Cyrylla, Cyrylle, Siri, Sirilla

St. Cyrilla (d. 300) was an elderly widow who was arrested, tortured, and martyred for her faith in Cyrene in Libya.

Cyrille *see Cyrilla*

Cyryll *see Cyrilla*

Cyrylla *see Cyrilla*

Cyrylle *see Cyrilla*

D

Dafrosa Saint

St. Dafrosa (fourth century) was the mother of St. Bibiana. She was martyred during the persecution of Julian the Apostate.

Daiana *see Diana*

Daianna *see Diana*

Dalasina Saint

St. Dalasina (third century) was martyred at Luxor during the persecution of Emperor Diocletian.

Damhnade Saint; Celtic

St. Damhnade (date unknown) was an Irish virgin.

Daniele *see Danielle*

Danielle form of Daniel; Hebrew; God is my judge

Daniele

Dardulacha *see Darulagdach*

Darerca Saint; Celtic

St. Darerca (fifth century) was the sister of St. Patrick. She was married twice, to Conan Meriadoc and to Chonas the Briton. She had many children—some say as many as seventeen sons, many of whom became bishops. Many of her sons and daughters became saints.

Dari *see Daria*

Daria Saint; Greek; wealthy

Dari, Darian, Dariane, Darice, Dariya, Darria, Darriah

St. Daria (d. 283) was a Greek priestess of Minerva. She married Chrysanthus who converted her to Christianity. They lived in chastity. The couple was arrested for having converted. They brought many to the faith. She was stoned and then buried alive.

Darian *see Dari*

Dariane *see Daria*

Darice *see Daria*

Dariya *see Daria*

Darria *see Daria*

Darriah *see Daria*

Darulagdach Saint; Celtic
Dardulacha
St. Darulagdach (d. 524), also known as Dardulacha, was an abbess of Kildare, Ireland.

Dasha *see Dorothy*

Dasya *see Dorothy*

Dayana *see Diana*

Deana *see Diana*

Deb *see Deborah*

Debbee *see Deborah*

Debbera *see Deborah*

Debberah *see Deborah*

Debborah *see Deborah*

Debera *see Deborah*

Deberah *see Deborah*

Debor *see Deborah*

Deborah Old Testament; Hebrew; word, thing, a bee
Deb, Debbee, Debbera, Debberah, Debborah, Debera, Deberah, Debor, Deboran, Deborha, Deborrah, Debra, Debrah, Debrena, Debrina, Debroah, Dobra
Deborah is the only female judge mentioned in the Bible. She was the wife of Lapidoth and gave her judgments beneath a palm tree. She was the fourth judge of Israel. Her story is told in the book of Judges.

Deboran *see Deborah*

Deborha *see Deborah*

Deborrah *see Deborah*

Debra *see Deborah*

Debrah *see Deborah*

Debrena *see Deborah*

Debrina *see Deborah*

Debroah *see Deborah*

Deitra *see Demetria*

Delia *see Adelaide*

Demeetra *see Demetria*

Demeetrah *see Demetria*

Demeta *see Demetria*

Demeteria *see Demetria*

Demetria Saint; Greek; cover of the earth
Deitra, Demeetra, Demeetrah, Demeta, Demeteria, Demetriana, Demetrianna, Demetrias, Demetrice, Demetriona, Demetris, Demetrish, Demetrius, Demi, Dimetria, Dimitra, Dymeetra, Dymeetrah, Dymetra, Dymetrah, Dymitra, Dymitrah, Dymitria, Dymitriah, Dymytria, Dymytriah, Dymtrya, Dymytrah
St. Demetria (d. 363) was the daughter of Sts. Flavian and Dafrosa and the sister of St. Bibiana. When she was arrested with her sister, she dropped dead before she could be martyred.

Demetriana *see Demetria*

Demetrianna *see Demetria*

Demetrias *see Demetria*

Demetrice *see Demetria*

Demetriona *see Demetria*

Demetris *see Demetria*

Demetrish *see Demetria*

Demetrius *see Demetria*

Demi *see Demetria*

Devota Saint; Latin; devoted to God

St. Devota (d. 303) was born in Corsica. She had devoted herself fully to devotion to God and was imprisoned and tortured for her faith. Her body was dragged through rocks and brambles before she was martyred on the rack. She is a patron saint of Corsica and Monaco.

Diaana *see Diana*

Diaanah *see Diana*

Diana Saint; Latin; divine

Daiana, Daianna, Dayana, Deana, Dianna, Diaanah, Dianah, Dianalyn, Dianarose, Dianatris, Dianca, Diane, Dianelis, Diania, Dianiah, Dianiella, Dianielle, Dianita, Dianna, Dianya, Dianyah, Dianys, Didi, Dihana, Dihanah, Dihanna, Dihannah, Dyana

Bl. Diana d'Andalo (d. 1236) was born into a noble family in Bologna, Italy. She became a Dominican nun and helped found the Monastery of St. Agnes. She was one of the first three Dominican nuns in Bologna.

Dianah *see Diana*

Dianalyn *see Diana*

Dianarose *see Diana*

Dianatris *see Diana*

Dianca *see Diana*

Diane *see Diana*

Dianelis *see Diana*

Diania *see Diana*

Dianiah *see Diana*

Dianiella *see Diana*

Dianielle *see Diana*

Dianita *see Diana*

Dianna *see Diana*

Dianya *see Diana*

Dianyah *see Diana*

Dianys *see Diana*

Didi *see Diana*

Digna Saint; Latin; worthy

St. Digna (fourth century) was a virgin who lived as a hermitess in the mountains of Todi, Italy.

Dihana *see Diana*

Dihanah *see Diana*

Dihanna *see Diana*

Dihannah *see Diana*

Dimetria *see Demetria*

Dimitra *see Demetria*

Dimpna *see Dymphna*

Dina Saint; Hebrew; vindicated

Dinah, Dinna, Dinnah, Dyna, Dynah, Dynna, Dynnah

Bl. Dina Belanger (1897–1929) was born in St-Roch, Quebec, Canada. She studied music in New York and planned to become a concert pianist. When she returned home, she entered the Congregation of Jesus-Marie at Sillery, where she taught music. She was beatified by Pope John Paul II in 1993.

Dinah *see Dina*

Dinna *see Dina*

Dinnah *see Dina*

Dionysia Saint; Greek; celebration

St. Dionysia (first century) rebuked a fellow Christian

when he was being tortured and recanted Christ. Because of this, she was taken prisoner and turned over to three men to abuse her. She was protected by an angel and escaped. She demanded to be martyred and was beheaded.

Do *see Dorothy*

Doa *see Dorothy*

Dobra *see Deborah*

Doe *see Dorothy*

Domenica *see Dominica*

Domineca *see Dominica*

Domineka *see Dominica*

Dominga *see Dominica*

Domini *see Dominica*

Dominia *see Dominica*

Dominiah *see Dominica*

Dominica Saint; Latin; belonging to the Lord

Comnika, Domenica, Domineca, Domineka, Dominga, Domini, Dominia, Dominiah, Dominicah, Dominicka, Dominikah, Dominique, Dominyika, Domka, Domnica, Domnicah, Domnicka, Domnika, Domonica, Domonice, Domonika, Domynica

St. Dominica (fourth century) was martyred in Campania, Italy, during the reign of Emperor Diocletian. She was sentenced to be attacked by wild beasts, but they didn't harm her and she was beheaded instead.

Dominicah *see Dominica*

Dominicka *see Dominica*

Dominikah *see Dominica*

Dominique *see Dominica*

Dominyika *see Dominica*

Domka *see Dominica*

Domnica *see Dominica*

Domnicah *see Dominica*

Domnicka *see Dominica*

Domnika *see Dominica*

Domnina Saint; Latin; lord, master

St. Domnina (d. 310) was martyred in Syria with her daughters Berenice and Prosdoce.

Domonica *see Dominica*

Domonice *see Dominica*

Domonika *see Dominica*

Domynica *see Dominica*

Donata Saint; Latin; gift

St. Donata (d. 180) was one of twelve Martyrs of Scillium, martyred during the reign of Emperor Marcus Aurelius.

Donwen *see Dwynwen*

Donwenna *see Dwynwen*

Doortje *see Dorothy*

Dora *see Theodora*

Dorathea *see Dorothy*

Dorathee *see Dorothy*

Dorathey *see Dorothy*

Dorathi *see Dorothy*

Dorathie *see Dorothy*

Dorathy *see Dorothy*

Dordei *see Dorothy*

Dordi *see Dorothy*

Dorefee *see Dorothy*

Dorethie *see Dorothy*

Doretta *see Dorothy*

Dorifey *see Dorothy*

Dorika *see Dorothy*

Dorita *see Dorothy*

Doritha *see Dorothy*

Dorka *see Dorothy*

Dorle *see Dorothy*

Dorlisa *see Dorothy*

Doro *see Dorothy*

Dorofey *see Dorothy*

Dorolice *see Dorothy*

Dorosia *see Dorothy*

Dorota *see Dorothy*

Dorothea *see Dorothy*

Dorothey *see Dorothy*

Dorothi *see Dorothy*

Dorothie *see Dorothy*

Dorothy Saint; Greek; gift of God

Dasha, Dasya, Do, Doa, Doe, Doortje, Dorathea, Dorathee, Dorathey, Dorathi, Dorathie, Dorathy, Dordei, Dordi, Dorefee, Dorethie, Doretta, Dorifey, Dorika, Dorita, Doritha, Dorka, Dorle, Dorlisa, Doro, Dorofey, Dorolice, Dorosia, Dorota, Dorothea, Dorothey, Dorothi, Dorothie, Dorothya, Dortha, Dorthy, Doryfey, Dosha, Dosi, Dossie, Dosya, Dote

St. Dorothy of Montau (1347–1394) was born a peasant in Montau, Prussia. She married an ill-tempered, wealthy swordsmith from Poland and bore nine children. Eight of them died—four in infancy and four of the plague. The sole remaining daughter became a Benedictine. In time, Dorothy was able to convert her husband. After his death, she became a hermitess at Marienswerder. She was known for her visions and spiritual gifts and was canonized in 1976.

Dorottya *see Dorothy*

Dortha *see Dorothy*

Dorthy *see Dorothy*

Doryfey *see Dorothy*

Dosha *see Dorothy*

Dosi *see Dorothy*

Dosia *see Theodosia*

Dossie *see Dorothy*

Dosya *see Dorothy*

Dote *see Dorothy*

Dula Saint; Greek; slave

Theodula

St. Dula (date unknown), also known as Theodula, was the slave of a pagan soldier who was martyred defending her chastity.

Dulcissima Saint; Latin; sweet

St. Dulcissima (date unknown) was a virgin martyr who is a patron saint of Sutri, Italy.

Dwyn *see Dwynwen*

Dwynwen Saint; Welsh; white wave

Dwyn, Donwen, Donwenna

St. Dwynwen (d. 460), also known as Dwyn, Donwen, and Donwenna, was the daughter of King Brychan of Brecknock. Despite her love for a man named Maelon, who shared her feelings, she wanted to become a nun. She prayed for him and that all lovers should find happiness. She became a nun and lived on Llanddwyn Island. She is a patron saint of lovers and sick animals.

Dyana *see Diana*

Dymeetra *see Demetria*

Dymeetrah *see Demetria*

Dymetra *see Demetria*

Dymetrah *see Demetria*

Dymitra *see Demetria*

Dymitrah *see Demetria*

Dymitria *see Demetria*

Dymitriah *see Demetria*

Dymphna Saint; Gaelic; convenient

Dimpna, Dympna

St. Dymphna (seventh century), also known as Dympna and Dimpna, was the daughter of a pagan Irish king and his Christian wife. Her mother died when she was fourteen years old, and her father became mentally ill. He wanted to find someone who reminded him of his wife to marry, but finding none, he turned to his daughter. To escape his advances, she fled to Belgium with her confessor. Her father followed them, and when she continued to refuse him, he drew his sword and cut off her head. She is the patron saint of those suffering from nervous and mental afflictions.

Dympna *see Dymphna*

Dymytria *see Demetria*

Dymytriah *see Demetria*

Dymytrya *see Demetria*

Dymytryah *see Demetria*

Dyna *see Dina*

Dynah *see Dina*

Dynna *see Dina*

Dynnah *see Dina*

E

Eaden *see Eden (boy's name)*

Eadin *see Eden (boy's name)*

Eadith *see Edith*

Eadyn *see Eden (boy's name)*

Ealsitha *see Etheidwitha*

Eanfleda Saint; English; very fertile

St. Eanfleda (d. 700) was the daughter of King St. Edwin and St. Ethelberga of Kent. After she was widowed, she became a Benedictine nun at Whitby, where her daughter, St. Elfieda, was abbess.

Eanswida Saint; English; strong lamb

St. Eanswida (d. 640) was the daughter of a king of Kent. She refused to marry a pagan Northumbrian prince, instead starting a convent at Folkestone in Kent, England.

Eav *see Eve*

Eave *see Eve*

Ebba Saint; German; wild boar

St. Ebba (d. 874) governed the monastery of Coldingham, Scotland. When the monastery was attacked by Danish pirates, she feared for her own and her fellow sisters' chastity. She took a razor and cut off her nose and upper lip. The other sisters followed her example.

The invaders did not touch the sisters but set fire to the monastery, and all were martyred.

Eda see Edith

Edan see Edana

Edana Saint; Gaelic; ardent, flame

Edan, Edanah, Edanna

St. Edana (date unknown) was an Irish saint who lived near the Boyle and Shannon Rivers.

Edanah see Edana

Edanna see Edana

Ede see Edith

Edelaid see Adelaide

Edelaide see Adelaide

Eden see Eden (boy's name)

Edenson see Eden (boy's name)

Edetta see Edith

Edette see Edith

Edie see Edith

Edifelda see Elfleda

Edit see Edith

Edita see Edith

Edite see Edith

Edith Saint; English; rich gift

Eadith, Eda, Ede, Edetta, Edette, Edie, Edit, Edita, Edite, Editha, Edithe, Editta, Ediva, Edyta, Edyth, Edytha, Edythe

St. Edith of Polesworth, St. Edith of Wilton, St. Edith Stein

St. Edith Stein (1891–1942) was born in Breslau, Poland, the youngest child of a large Jewish family. She became an atheist in her teen years and devoted herself to the study of philosophy, in which she earned a doctorate degree. In 1921, she read an autobiography of St. Teresa of Avila which caused her to convert to Catholicism. She entered the Discalced Carmelite Monastery of Our Lady of Peace at Cologne in 1933 and became Sr. Teresa Benedicta of the Cross. She was transferred to the Netherlands in order to avoid the growing Nazi threat. In 1942, all Jewish converts were ordered to be arrested. She was sent to Auschwitz where she died in the gas chamber on August 9, 1942. She was canonized by Pope John Paul II in 1998.

Editha see Edith

Edithe see Edith

Editta see Edith

Ediva see Edith

Edlaid see Adelaide

Edwen Saint; form of Edwin; English; prosperous friend

St. Edwen (seventh century) was the daughter of King Edwin of Northumbria. She is the patroness of Llanedwen, Anglesey, Wales.

Edyn see Eden (boy's name)

Edyta see Edith

Edyth see Edith

Edytha see Edith

Edythe see Edith

Eeva see Eva

Eiden see Eden (boy's name)

Eileen see Helen

Eimile see Emily

Einhildis Saint; German

St. Einhildis (eighth century) was abbess of Niedermunster,

near Hohenburg, Alsace, France.

Ekaterina *see Katherine*

Ekatrinna *see Katherine*

Elana *see Helen*

Elda *see Hilda*

Eleanor *see Eleanora*

Eleanora Saint; Greek; sun ray, shining light

Eleanor, Eleanore, Elianora, Elleanora

Bl. Eleanora (d. 1226) was the daughter of Count Raymond IV of Provence, France. She was married to King Henry III of England for thirty-seven years. After his death, she became a Benedictine nun.

Eleanore *see Eleanora*

Elena *see Helen*

Elfeda *see Elfleda*

Elfleda Saint

Edifelda, Elfeda, Elgiva, Ethelfieda

St. Elfleda (d. 714) was the sister of King Oswy of Northumbria, England. She was raised in the Convent of Hartlepool under the direction of St. Hilda. Hilda took Elfleda to Whitby where Elfleda was named abbess. She was responsible for mediating a dispute between Sts. Wilfrid and Theodore.

Elfreda *see Alfreda*

Elgiva Saint

St. Elgiva (d. 944) was the wife of King Edmund the First. She bore two future kings, King Eadwig of the Saxons and King Edgar of England. She was a patron of the convent of Shaftesbury.

Eliabeth *see Elizabeth*

Elianora *see Eleanora*

Elide *see Hilda*

Elined *see Almedha*

Elisa *see Elisabeth*

Elisabet *see Elisabeth*

Elisabeth form of Elizabeth; Hebrew; consecrated to God

Elisa, Elisabet, Elisabethe, Elisabith, Elisebeth, Elisheba, Elishebah, Ellisabeth, Elsabeth, Elsbeth, Elysabeth, Liese, Liesel, Lise

Elisabethe *see Elisabeth*

Elisabith *see Elisabeth*

Elisebeth *see Elisabeth*

Elisheba *see Elisabeth*

Elishebah *see Elisabeth*

Elissa *see Alice*

Eliwedd *see Almedha*

Eliza *see Elizabeth*

Elizabea *see Elizabeth*

Elizabee *see Elizabeth*

Elizabeth Saint, New Testament; Top 100 Name; Hebrew; consecrated to God

Alizabeth, Eliabeth, Eliza, Elizabea, Elizabee, Ellizabeth, Elshen, Elysabeth, Elzbieta, Elzsébet, Helsa, Ilizzabet, Lizette, Lusa

St. Elizabeth, St. Elizabeth Ann Seton, St. Elizabeth Rose, St. Elizabeth of Hungary, St. Elizabeth of Portugal, St. Elizabeth of Schonau

St. Elizabeth (first century) was a cousin of Mary, the Mother of God. Her husband, Zachary, was a priest in Jerusalem. He was told by an angel that his wife, who was beyond child-bearing age, would have a son. When he doubted this, he lost the ability to speak until after their child, John the Baptist, was born. While Mary was pregnant with Jesus, she went to visit the pregnant Elizabeth. Elizabeth's story is told in the first chapter of the Gospel of Luke.

Ella Top 100 Name; form of Eleanora; English; elfin, beautiful fairy woman

Elleanora *see Eleanora*

Ellisabeth *see Elisabeth*

Ellizabeth *see Elizabeth*

Eloisa *see Louisa*

Eloise *see Louise*

Elsabeth *see Elisabeth*

Elsbeth *see Elisabeth*

Elshen *see Elizabeth*

Eluned *see Almedha*

Elysabeth *see Elisabeth, Elizabeth*

Elzbieta *see Elizabeth*

Elzsébet *see Elizabeth*

Emerentiana Saint; Latin; she who will be rewarded

St. Emerentiana (third century) was a catechumen when she was stoned to death after she was found praying at St. Agnes's grave.

Emilia *see Emily*

Emiliana Saint; Latin; friendly, industrious

St. Emiliana (sixth century) was an aunt of St. Gregory the Great. She and her sister Tarsilla lived in their father's house as if in a monastery.

Emilie Saint; Latin; friendly, industrious

Bl. Emilie Tavernier Gamelin, Bl. Emilie van der Linden d'Hooghvorst

Bl. Emilie Tavernier Gamelin (1800–1851) was born in Montreal. Her parents died when she was young, and she was raised by her aunt. She became a debutante and married an older man. They had three children before he died, but all died while very young. As a widow, she devoted herself to charitable works. She joined the Confraternity of the Holy Family. She opened a shelter for sick and elderly women. She later helped found the Daughters of Charity, Servants of the Poor (now known as the Sisters of Providence). She died of cholera and was beatified by Pope John Paul II in 2001.

Emilis *see Emily*

Emily Saint; Top 100 Name; Latin, German; flatterer, industrious

Amalia, Amalie, Amelia, Eimile, Emilia, Emilie, Emilis, Emilye, Emmaley, Emmaline, Emmaly, Emmélie, Emmye, Emyle

St. Emily de Rodat, St. Emily de Vialar

St. Emily de Vialar (1797–1856) was born to Baron James

Augustine de Vialar and his wife, Antoinette, in Gaillac in Languedoc. She was educated in Paris but left school at the age of fifteen to be a companion to her widowed father. She spent the next fifteen years serving the poor and needy children in her hometown. When her maternal grandfather died, she inherited quite a bit of money and was able to buy a large house where she began a religious order, the Congregation of the Sisters of St. Joseph of the Apparition. They dedicated themselves to the care of the needy and the education of children. She was canonized in 1951.

Emilye *see Emily*

Emma Saint; Top 100 Name; form of Emily; German; flatterer, industrious

Hemma

St. Emma (980–1045), also known as Hemma, was raised at the court of Emperor Henry II. She married Landgrave William of Friesach. After their two children were murdered and her husband died while on pilgrimage, Emma devoted her life to God. She gave to the poor and founded several convents and monasteries. She may have become a nun.

Emmaley *see Emily*

Emmaline *see Emily*

Emmaly *see Emily*

Emmélie *see Emily*

Emmye *see Emily*

Emyle *see Emily*

Ena *see Helen*

Encratia Saint; Greek, Latin; in control, temperate

Encratide, Engracia

St. Encratia (d. 304), also known as Encratide or Engracia, was from Saragossa, Spain. She was tortured for the faith but survived.

Encratide *see Encratia*

Endelienta *see Endellion*

Endellion Saint; Gaelic; fire soul

Endelienta

St. Endellion (sixth century), also known as Endelienta, was a daughter of King Brychan of Brecknock. She and her siblings helped convert the citizens of North Cornwall to Christianity. She later lived as a hermit at Trentinney. According to legend, she was the goddaughter of King Arthur.

Engracia *see Encratia*

Epifania *see Epiphania*

Epiphania Saint; manifestation; Greek, Spanish

Epifania

St. Epiphania (d. 800) was the daughter of King Ratchis of the Lombards. She was a Benedictine nun of Pavia, Italy.

Ercnacta *see Ergnad*

Eremberta Saint; German; mighty bright

St. Eremberta (seventh century) served as abbess of Wierre Monastery, which her uncle, St. Wulmur, had founded for her.

Erena *see Irene*

Erene *see Irene*

Erentrude Saint; German; strong spear

Erentrudis

St. Erentrude (d. 710) served as abbess of the newly formed Benedictine convent in Salzburg, known as Nonnberg. She was very close to St. Rupert, a missionary bishop who served as her spiritual father. She died only a few days after him.

Erentrudis *see Erentrude*

Erfyl Saint; Welsh; wept over

St. Erfyl (date unknown) founded the parish of Llanerfyl, in Powys, Wales.

Ergnad Saint

Ercnacta

St. Ergnad (fifth century) was an Irish nun, also known as Ercnacta. She lived a life of prayer and penance in seclusion.

Erica *see Eric (boy's name)*

Ermelinda Saint; Teutonic; offers sacrifices to God

St. Ermelinda (d. 595) lived as a hermitess in Meldaert, Belgium.

Ermenberga Saint; German; strong city

St. Ermenberga (d. 700) was the wife of Merewald, a king of Mercia, England, and the mother of Sts. Mildred, Milburga, Ermengytha, and Mildgytha. She founded the convent of Minster, on Thanet Isle. Her uncle, King Egbert of Kent, donated the land for the convent to atone for his sins.

Ermengild Saint; German; soldier

Ermenilda

St. Ermengild (d. 700), also known as Ermenilda, was the daughter of a king of Kent, England, and St. Sexburga. After marrying the king of Mercia, she helped to spread the faith in that area. After his death, she became a nun at Milton at Minster, Sheppey, where her mother was abbess. After her mother retired, she became abbess herself. She later also served as abbess at Ely.

Ermengytha Saint; German; soldier

St. Ermengytha (d. 680) was either a daughter or sister of St. Ermenberga. She was a Benedictine nun at a monastery in Minster, on Thanet Isle, England.

Ermenilda *see Ermengild*

Esia *see Asia*

Esiah *see Asia*

Estar *see Esther*

Esther Old Testament; Persian; star

Estar, Esthur, Eszter, Eszti

Esther in the Bible was a Queen of Persia. She was Jewish by birth and had been raised by her cousin Mordecai. When Mordecai refused to bow down to Haman, one of the princes of the realm, Haman then planned to kill all Jews in the empire. Esther took a great risk in approaching the king and asking him to host a banquet with the king and Haman. During the banquet, she revealed Haman's plan to kill all the Jews, including her. She thus stopped the slaughter. The feast of Purim is held in honor of this event. Esther's story is told in the book of Esther.

Esthur *see Esther*

Esya *see Asia*

Esyah *see Asia*

Eszter *see Esther*

Eszti *see Esther*

Etdelreda *see Audrey*

Etheidreda *see Audrey*

Etheidwitha Saint; English

> *Ealsitha*
>
> St. Etheidwitha (ninth century), also known as Ealsitha, was an Anglo–Saxon princess who became the wife of King Alfred the Great of England. She founded a convent at Winchester and became abbess there after the king's death.

Ethelburga Saint; English; noble fortress

> St. Ethelburga (d. 647) was the daughter of St. Ethelbert of Kent. She married and brought King St. Edwin of Northumbria, England, into the faith. After his death, she founded a convent at Lyminge where she served as abbess.

Ethelfieda *see Elfleda*

Ethelgiva Saint; English; noble gift

> St. Ethelgiva (d. 896) was a daughter of King Alfred the

Great of England. She became a Benedictine abbess at Shaftesbury.

Ethelreda *see Audrey*

Ethenea Saint

> St. Ethenea (d. 433) was a daughter of King Leoghaire of Ireland. She and her sister, St. Fidelmia, were baptized by St. Patrick and died in ecstasy shortly after receiving their First Communion.

Eudocia Saint; Greek; famous, knowledgeable

> St. Eudocia (d. 100) was from Coele, Syria. She spent much of her life doing penance for her sins. She lived in Heliopolis, Egypt, and was beheaded during the reign of Emperor Trajan.

Eugeena *see Eugenia*

Eugeenah *see Eugenia*

Eugeenia *see Eugenia*

Eugeeniah *see Eugenia*

Eugenia Saint; Greek; born to nobility

> *Eugeena, Eugeenah, Eugeenia, Eugeeniah, Eugeniah, Eugenina, Eugina, Eujania, Eujaniah, Eujanya, Eujanyah, Evgenia, Evgeniah, Evgenya, Evgenyah, Geena, Gena*
>
> St. Eugenia (d. 258) was the daughter of Philip, governor of Egypt. She left her father's house disguised as a man in order to be baptized. Still in men's clothing, she later became an abbot. She was accused by a woman of adultery and was taken to court

where she appeared before her father who was the judge. At the trial, she revealed her true identity and was exonerated. She converted her father, who became bishop of Alexandria and was martyred. St. Eugenia was also martyred.

Eugeniah *see Eugenia*

Eugenie Saint; Greek; born to nobility

St. Eugenie Milleret de Brou (1817–1898) was born in France. She entered the Sisters of the Visitation for a time but did not take vows with that order. She made a pilgrimage to the shrine of Sainte-Anne d'Auray in 1825, when she felt a call to begin a new teaching order that would work in the world but keep monastic observances. She founded the Congregation of the Assumption.

Eugenina *see Eugenia*

Eugina *see Eugenia*

Eujania *see Eugenia*

Eujaniah *see Eugenia*

Eujanya *see Eugenia*

Eujanyah *see Eugenia*

Eulalia Saint; Greek; well-spoken

St. Eulalia of Merida (d. 304) was born in Spain. When she was twelve years old, she appeared before Judge Dacian of Merida and refused to deny the faith. Her body was torn by iron hooks and set on fire. She is a patron saint of runaways, torture victims, and widows.

Eulampia Saint; Greek; brilliant

St. Eulampia (d. 310) was martyred with her brother St. Eulampius in Nicomedia during the reign of the Eastern Roman Emperor Maximinus Daia.

Euna *see Eunice*

Eunice New Testament; Greek; happy, victorius

Euna, Eunie, Eunique, Eunise, Euniss, Eunisse, Eunys, Eunysa, Eunysah, Eunyse, Eunyss, Unice

Eunice (first century) was the mother of Timothy and is mentioned in the letters to Timothy and in the Acts of the Apostles. She was a Jewish convert to the faith.

Eunie *see Eunice*

Eunique *see Eunice*

Eunise *see Eunice*

Euniss *see Eunice*

Eunisse *see Eunice*

Eunys *see Eunice*

Eunysa *see Eunice*

Eunysah *see Eunice*

Eunyse *see Eunice*

Eunyss *see Eunice*

Euphemia Saint; Greek; well-spoken

St. Euphemia (d. 307) was born in Chalcedon to a senator named Philophronos and his wife, Theodosia. She consecrated herself to virginity at a young age. The governor of Chalcedon demanded that all the citizens take part in a ceremony worshiping Ares.

Euphemia and several other Christians refused and were tortured. She was slain by a wild lion.

Euphrasia Saint; Greek; mirth

St. Euphrasia, St. Euphrasia Pelletier

St. Euphrasia Pelletier (1796–1868) was born on the island of Noirmoutier off the coast of Brittany. She was sent to school in Tours and came to know the Institute of Our Lady of Charity of the Refuge. She joined the convent and was later elected superior. She started other houses and created a centralized organization. They became known as the "Good Shepherd Nuns." She was canonized in 1940.

Euphrosyne Saint; Greek; mirth, merriment

St. Euphrosyne, St. Euphrosyne of Alexandria, St. Euphrosyne of Polotsk

According to legend, St. Euphrosyne (fifth century) was the much-longed-for daughter of a wealthy citizen of Alexandria and his wife. After her mother died, when she was eleven, her father promised her in marriage to an older man. After speaking with an old monk, she decided to forget about the things of this world. While her father was away, she changed into men's clothes, took on an assumed name, and slipped out of the house to a local monastery. There she lived as a man for many years, growing in holiness. Her father eventually sought out this wise monk's advice. She did not reveal who she was, however, until she was on her deathbed. He then retreated from the world and took her place in the monastery.

Eurosia Saint; Greek; eloquent

Orosia

St. Eurosia (d. 714) was born into a noble family at Bayonne, France. She was promised to a Moor in an arranged marriage, but she escaped and hid in a cave. She was found, dragged by her hair, and martyred.

Eusebia Saint; Greek; with good feelings

St. Eusebia, Bl. Eusebia Palomino Yenes

St. Eusebia (d. 680) was the daughter of Sts. Adalbald and Rictrudis. She was raised by her aunt, St. Gertrude, at Hamage Abbey in France. Eusebia was elected abbess at the age of twelve.

Eustadiola Saint; Greek

St. Eustadiola (594–684) was a widow from Bourges, France, who used her wealth to build a convent where she served as abbess.

Eustochium Saint; Greek; produces many ears of corn

St. Eustochium, St. Eustochium Calafato

St. Eustochium (370–419) was the third daughter of St.

Paula. She took the veil from St. Jerome. She traveled with her mother and St. Jerome to Bethlehem, where she assisted the scholar in the translation of the Bible. She became abbess of three convents founded by St. Jerome.

Eustolia Saint; Greek; agile

St. Eustolia (seventh century) was one of the daughters of Emperor Maurice of Constantinople. Little is known of her life, but she has long been revered as a saint.

Eustreberta *see Austreberta*

Euthalia Saint; Greek; gets along well

St. Euthalia (third century) became a Christian after her mother, St. Eutropia, experienced a miraculous healing. Her brother wanted them to recant their faith. They both refused. Her mother fled, but Euthalia stayed and was beheaded by her brother.

Euthymia Saint; Greek; in good spirits

Bl. Euthymia Uffing (1914–1955) was born in Halverde, Germany. At eighteen months, she came down with rickets and suffered with poor health the rest of her life. She entered the Sisters of the Congregation of Compassion. She went to work at St. Vincent's Hospital in Dinslaken, Germany. She studied to become a nurse and served in that capacity during World

War II. She died of cancer. She was beatified in 2001 by Pope John Paul II.

Eutropia Saint; Greek; good character

St. Eutropia (fifth century) was a widow of Auvergne, France, known for her holiness.

Eva Saint; Top 100 Name; Greek; life

Eeva, Evah, Evalea, Evaleah, Evalee, Evalei, Evaleigh, Evaley, Evali, Evalia, Evalie, Evaline, Evaly, Evani, Evike, Evva, Ewa, Ewah

Bl. Eva of Liege (thirteenth century) was a recluse who was a close friend of St. Juliana of Liege. She gave Juliana shelter when she was driven from Cornillon, and Eva continued Juliana's work to have the feast of Corpus Christi established after she died. Her efforts were successful, and Pope Urban IV instituted the feast and had St. Thomas Aquinas compile a special office for the day.

Evah *see Eva*

Evalea *see Eva*

Evaleah *see Eva*

Evalee *see Eva*

Evalei *see Eva*

Evaleigh *see Eva*

Evaley *see Eva*

Evali *see Eva*

Evalia *see Eva*

Evalie *see Eva*

Evaline *see Eva*

Evaly *see Eva*

Evani *see Eva*

Eve Saint, Old Testament; Hebrew; living, enlivening

Eav, Eave, Evelyn, Evita, Evuska, Evyn

Eve was the first woman created by God. Her story is told in the book of Genesis. She was the wife of Adam and is the mother of all the living. She gave into temptation and ate the fruit that God had forbidden them to eat. She then shared the fruit with Adam who also ate it. For this action, Adam and Eve were expelled from the Garden of Eden.

St. Eve of Dreux (date unknown) was a martyr.

Evelyn Top 100 Name; form of Eve; English; hazelnut

Everild Saint; English

Averil

St. Everild (seventh century), also known as Averil, was a noblewoman of Wessex, England. St. Wilfrid gave her a place called "the bishop's Farm" where she became a Benedictine abbess.

Evgenia *see Eugenia*

Evgeniah *see Eugenia*

Evgenya *see Eugenia*

Evgenyah *see Eugenia*

Evike *see Eva*

Evita *see Eve*

Evuska *see Eve*

Evva *see Eva*

Evyn *see Eve*

Ewa Saint; Hebrew, Persian; mother

Bl. Ewa Noiszewska (1885–1942) was a member of the Congregation of Sisters of the Immaculate Conception of the Blessed Virgin Mary. She was shot for her faith during World War II. She was beatified as one of the 108 Polish Martyrs of World War II in 1999 by Pope John Paul II.

Ewah *see Eva*

F

Fabiola Saint; Latin; bean grower

Fabiolah, Fabiole, Fabyola

St. Fabiola (fourth century) was from a wealthy Roman family. She was married twice and had left the Church, but after the death of her second husband, she returned to the faith and dedicated herself to helping the poor, building churches, and starting the first Christian public hospital in the West. She also opened a hospice for poor pilgrims.

Fabiolah *see Fabiola*

Fabiole *see Fabiola*

Fabyola *see Fabiola*

Faeth *see Faith*

Faethe *see Faith*

Faith Saint; Top 100 Name; English; belief

Faeth, Faethe, Faithe

St. Faith (third century) was martyred by being tortured to

death with a red-hot brazier during the persecutions of Emperor Diocletian.

Faithe *see Faith*

Fanchea Saint; Gaelic; free

St. Fanchea (d. 585) started Rossara Convent in Fermanagh, Ireland, where she served as abbess.

Fandila *see Fandila (boy's name)*

Fara Saint; English; beautiful, pleasant

Farah, Fare, Faria, Fariah, Farra, Farrah, Farria, Fayre

St. Fara (seventh century), also known as Fare, was the daughter of Count Agneric who served King Theodoric II. She refused to marry, instead convincing her father to build a convent, where she served as abbess for thirty-seven years.

Farah *see Fara*

Fare *see Fara*

Faria *see Fara*

Fariah *see Fara*

Farra *see Fara*

Farrah *see Fara*

Farria *see Fara*

Fausta Saint; Latin; lucky, fortunate

Faustah

St. Fausta (third century) was the virtuous mother of St. Anastasia of Sirmium, Serbia, Yugoslavia.

Faustah *see Fausta*

Fausteana *see Faustina*

Fausteanah *see Faustina*

Fausteane *see Faustina*

Fausteen *see Faustina*

Fausteena *see Faustina*

Fausteenah *see Faustina*

Fausteene *see Faustina*

Faustin *see Faustina*

Faustina Saint; Latin; lucky, fortunate

Fausteana, Fausteanah, Fausteane, Fausteen, Fausteena, Fausteenah, Fausteene, Faustin, Faustinah, Faustine, Faustyn, Faustyna, Faustynah, Faustyne, Fawstine

St. Faustina Kowalska (1905–1938) was born Helen Kowalska in a small village in Poland. When she made her vows to become a member of the Sisters of Our Lady of Mercy, she took the name Sr. Maria Faustina of the Most Blessed Sacrament. In the 1930s, she began to receive from the Lord a message of mercy that she was told to spread throughout the world. She united her sufferings with Christ in order to help atone for the sins of others; she devoted herself to bringing joy and peace to others, and she wrote about God's mercy. Jesus also asked her to commission a painting of him with rays of light coming from his heart and the words "Jesus, I Trust in You." Her diary, *Divine Mercy in My Soul,* has shared this message of mercy with the world. She was canonized by Pope John Paul II in 2000.

Faustinah *see Faustina*

Faustine *see Faustina*

Faustyn *see Faustina*

Faustyna *see Faustina*

Faustynah *see Faustina*

Faustyne *see Faustina*

Fawstine *see Faustina*

Fayre *see Fara*

Febronia Saint; Latin; sacrifice of atonement

St. Febronia (284–304) was a nun at Nisbis, Mesopotamia. She was arrested but offered her freedom by Emperor Diocletian if she would marry his nephew, Lysimachus. She refused and was tortured and martyred. Lysimachus was so impressed by her faith that he converted to Christianity.

Felice *see Felice (boy's name)*

Felicita *see Felicitas*

Felicitah *see Felicitas*

Felicitas Saint; Latin, Italian, Spanish; fortunate, happy

Felicita, Felicitah, Felicitee, Felicity, Felicyta, Felicytah, Felicytas, Felise, Felisita, Felycita, Felycitah, Felycyta, Felycytah, Felycytas

St. Felicitas (101–165) was martyred and buried in the Cemetery of Maximus. She may have been the mother of seven other martyrs and for that reason is the patron of parents who have had a child die.

Felicitee *see Felicitas*

Felicity *see Felicitas*

Felicula Saint; Latin; kitty

St. Felicula (d. 90) was the foster sister of St. Petronilla. Flaccus, an important Roman, proposed to Petronilla and she refused. After she was martyred, Felicula, who was imprisoned, refused to eat or drink. She was then thrown into a sewer to die.

Felicyta *see Felicitas*

Felicytah *see Felicitas*

Felicytas *see Felicitas*

Felise *see Felicitas*

Felisita *see Felicitas*

Felycita *see Felicitas*

Felycitah *see Felicitas*

Felycyta *see Felicitás*

Felycytah *see Felicitas*

Felycytas *see Felicitas*

Fermina *see Firmina*

Fidelmia Saint; Latin; my faithful one

St. Fidelmia (d. 433) was a daughter of King Laoghaire. She and her sister, St. Ethenea, were baptized by St. Patrick and died shortly after making their First Communion.

Filimena *see Philomena*

Filomena *see Philomena*

Filumena *see Philomena*

Filuned *see Almedha*

Fina Saint; Hebrew, Spanish; God increases, angelic

Seraphina

St. Fina (d. 1253), also known as Seraphina, was born in San Geminiano, Tuscany, to a very poor family. Even in her youth, she lived a holy life, giving generously to others and spending much of her time in prayer. While still young, she suffered from a disease that attacked many of her organs. She was in great pain but never complained. After her parents died, she only had one friend that would care for her, but she was largely left unattended. She prayed to St. Gregory the Great to help her. In a vision, he appeared to her and told her she would die soon on his feast day. When she died and her body was lifted from the board, the rotten wood was found to be covered in while violets.

Fiora *see Flora*

Fiore *see Flora*

Fiorella *see Flora*

Fiorenza *see Florentina*

Fiorenze *see Florentina*

Fiori *see Flora*

Fiorincia *see Florentina*

Firmina Saint; Latin; firm, sure

Fermina

St. Firmina (d. 303) was the daughter of a Roman prefect. Olympiadis attempted to seduce her, but she instead converted him to Christianity. After he was martyred, she lived as a recluse near the city of Amelia in Umbria, Italy. She was martyred during the persecution of Emperor Diocletian.

Flannery *see Flannan (boy's name)*

Flarance *see Florentina*

Flaura *see Flora*

Flaurah *see Flora*

Flauria *see Flora*

Flauriah *see Flora*

Flaury *see Flora*

Flaurya *see Flora*

Flauryah *see Flora*

Flavere *see Flavia*

Flavia Saint; Latin; blond, golden haired

Flavere, Flaviah, Flavianna, Flavianne, Flavien, Flavienne, Flaviere, Flavya, Flavyah, Flawia, Flawya, Flawyah, Fulvia

St. Flavia, St. Flavia Domitilla

St. Flavia Domitilla (second century) was related to Emperors Diocletian and Titus. She was martyred with her two foster sisters, Euphrosyna and Theodora.

Flaviah *see Flavia*

Flaviana Saint; Latin; blond, golden haired

St. Flaviana (date unknown) was a virgin who was martyred in Auxerre, France, along with St. Firmatus.

Flavianna *see Flavia*

Flavianne *see Flavia*

Flavien *see Flavia*

Flavienne *see Flavia*

Flaviere *see Flavia*

Flavya *see Flavia*

Flavyah *see Flavia*

Flawia *see Flavia*

Flawya *see Flavia*

Flawyah *see Flavia*

Fliora *see Flora*

Flo *see Flora*

Flora Saint; Latin; flower

Fiora, Fiore, Fiorella, Fiori, Flaura, Flaurah, Flauria, Flauriah, Flaury,

Flaurya, Flauryah, Fliora, Flo, Florah, Flore, Florelle, Florey, Floria, Florica

St. Flora (1309–1347) was born in France. She refused her parents' efforts to find her a husband and instead entered the Priory of Beauliew of the Hospitaller Nuns of St. John of Jerusalem. She was known as a mystic and a prophet. Many sought out her wise counsel. She is the patron saint of those who have been abandoned, converts, single laywomen, and victims of betrayal.

Florah *see Flora*

Florance *see Florentina*

Florancia *see Florentina*

Floranciah *see Florentina*

Florancie *see Florentina*

Flore *see Flora*

Florean *see Florian*

Florelle *see Flora*

Floren *see Florentina*

Florena *see Florentina*

Florenca *see Florentina*

Florence *see Florentina*

Florencia *see Florentina*

Florenciah *see Florentina*

Florencija *see Florentina*

Florency *see Florentina*

Florencya *see Florentina*

Florendra *see Florentina*

Florene *see Florentina*

Florentia *see Florentina*

Florentina Saint; Latin; blooming

Fiorenza, Fiorenze, Fiorincia, Flarance, Florance, Florancia,

Floranciah, Florancie, Floren, Florena, Florenca, Florence, Florencia, Florenciah, Florencija, Florency, Florencya, Florendra, Florene, Florentia, Florentyna, Florenza, Florina, Florine

St. Florentina (d. 612) was born in Cartagena, Spain, the sister of Sts. Leander, Isidore, and Fulgentius. She became an ascetic, and together with a group of like-minded women formed a religious community at St. Maria de Valle near Ecija.

Florentyna *see Florentina*

Florenza *see Florentina*

Florey *see Flora*

Floria *see Flora*

Floria *see Flora*

Florian *see Florian (boy's name)*

Florida Saint; Latin, Spanish; blooming, flowery

Floridah, Floridia, Floridiah, Florind, Florinda, Florinde, Florita, Floryda, Florydah, Florynd, Florynde

Bl. Florida Cevoli (1685–1767) was born Elena Lucrezia Cevoli in Pisa, the daughter of a count. She entered the convent of the Capuchin Poor Clares in Citta di Castello where she took the name Florida. She was beatified in 1993 by Pope John Paul II.

Floridah *see Florida*

Floridia *see Florida*

Floridiah *see Florida*

Florien *see Florian (boy's name)*

Florina *see Florentina*

Florind *see Florida*

Florinda *see Florida*

Florinde *see Florida*

Florine *see Florentina*

Florion *see Florian (boy's name)*

Florita *see Florida*

Florrian *see Florian*

Flortyna *see Florentina*

Flory *see Florian (boy's name)*

Floryan *see Florian (boy's name)*

Floryante *see Florian (boy's name)*

Floryda *see Florida*

Florydah *see Florida*

Florynd *see Florida*

Florynde *see Florida*

Foila Saint; Latin, French, English; leaf

> St. Foila (sixth century) was from Ireland and was the sister of St. Colgan. She is a copatroness of Kil-Faile and Kil-Golgan parishes.

Fortuna *see Fortunata*

Fortunah *see Fortunata*

Fortunata Saint; Latin; fortune, fortunate

> *Fortuna, Fortunah, Fortunate, Fortune, Fortunia, Fortuniah, Fortunya*
>
> St. Fortunata (d. 303) was a virgin martyred with her brothers, Sts. Carphonius, Evaristus, and Priscian, in Caesarea, Israel.

Fortunate *see Fortunata*

Fortune *see Fortunata*

Fortunia *see Fortunata*

Fortuniah *see Fortunata*

Fortunya *see Fortunata*

Fotina *see Photina*

Franca Saint; short form of Frances; Latin; free, from France

> St. Franca Visalta (1170–1218) was born in Piacenza, Italy. At the age of seven, she entered the St. Syrus Benedictine Convent. She later served as abbess but was removed because of her strictness. She then became abbess of a convent at Montelana, which adopted the Cistercian rule. She lived a most austere life and dedicated herself to many hours of prayer.

France *see Frances*

Francena *see Frances*

Frances Saint; Latin; free, from France

> *France, Francena, Francesca, Francess, Francesta, Francille, Francina*
>
> St. Frances Bizzocca, St. Frances de Croissy, St. Frances of Rome, St. Frances Xavier Cabrini
>
> St. Frances Xavier Cabrini (1850–1917) was born in Lombardi, Italy. She wanted to be a nun but suffered from poor health, so she stayed home and helped her parents. A local priest asked her to teach in a girls' school, which she did for six years. Her bishop then asked her to begin a religious order dedicated to caring for poor children in schools and hospitals. She founded the Missionary Sisters of the Sacred Heart. In 1889, Pope Leo XIII asked her to serve as a missionary to America to help the Italian immigrants. In 1946, she

became the first American citizen to be canonized. She is the patroness of immigrants.

Francesca *see Frances*

Francess *see Frances*

Francesta *see Frances*

Francille *see Frances*

Francina *see Frances*

Francisca Saint; form of Frances; Italian; free, from France

Franciska, Franciszka, Frantiska, Franziska

Bl. Francisca Ana Cirer Carbonell (1781–1855) wanted to become a nun, but her father was opposed. After he died, she founded the Community of the Sisters of Charity in the diocese of Majorca. She was a mystic who frequently had visions of angels. She was beatified by Pope John Paul II in 1992.

Franciska *see Francisca*

Franciszka *see Francisca*

Francoise *see Francois (boy's name)*

Frantiska *see Francisca*

Franziska *see Francisca*

Freda *see Winifred*

Frideswide Saint; English; strong peace

Frideswinda

St. Frideswide (d. 735) was the daughter of Prince Didan of the Upper Thames region of England. She fled to Thomry Wood in Birnsey in order to avoid marrying Prince Algar. She became a hermitess and started the convent of St. Mary's in Oxford.

Frideswinda *see Frideswide*

Fulvia *see Flavia*

Fusca Saint; Latin; dark

St. Fusca (d. 250) was a young girl martyred in Ravenna, Italy.

Fyncana Saint

St. Fyncana (date unknown) was martyred with St. Fyndoca.

G

Gabbrielle *see Gabrielle*

Gabby *see Gabrielle (boy's name)*

Gabielle *see Gabrielle*

Gabis *see Gabriel (boy's name)*

Gabrael *see Gabriel (boy's name)*

Gabraiel *see Gabriel (boy's name)*

Gabreil *see Gabriel (boy's name)*

Gabrell *see Gabriel (boy's name)*

Gabrealle *see Gabrielle*

Gabriana *see Gabrielle*

Gabriel *see Gabriel (boy's name)*

Gabriël *see Gabriel (boy's name)*

Gabriella *see Gabrielle*

Gabrielle Saint; Top 100 Name; Hebrew, French; devoted to God

Gabbrielle, Gabielle, Gabrealle, Gabriana, Gabriella, Gabrille, Gabrina, Gabryell, Gabryelle

Bl. Gabrielle Androuin (1755–1794) was a laywoman from the diocese of Angers, France, who was martyred during the French Revolution. One of the Martyrs of Anjou, she was beatified by Pope John Paul II in 1984.

Gabrielus *see Gabriel (boy's name)*

Gabrile *see Gabriel (boy's name)*

Gabrille *see Gabrielle*

Gabrina *see Gabrielle*

Gabris *see Gabriel (boy's name)*

Gabryel *see Gabriel (boy's name)*

Gabryell *see Gabrielle*

Gabryelle *see Gabrielle*

Gaetana Saint; Italian; from Gaeta, a city in southern Italy

Cajetana, Gaetanna, Gaetanne, Gaitana, Gaitanah, Gaitann, Gaitanna, Gaitanne, Gaytana, Gaytane, Gaytanna, Gaytanne

Bl. Gaetana Sterni (1827–1889) was born at Cassola, Vicenza, Italy. She married Liberale Conte, a widower with three children. She was soon pregnant, but she received a vision that her husband would die. She was a widow before her child was born. Her baby died soon after birth, and her in-laws wanted the other three children returned to their family. At age nineteen, she returned home. After her mother's death, she cared for her siblings. She later began work at a hospice for beggars in Bassano and helped found the Daughters of the Divine Will. She was beatified by Pope John Paul II in 2001.

Gaetanna *see Gaetana*

Gaetanne *see Gaetana*

Gaitana *see Gaetana*

Gaitanah *see Gaetana*

Gaitann *see Gaetana*

Gaitanna *see Gaetana*

Gaitanne *see Gaetana*

Galla Saint; Norwegian; singer

St. Galla (d. 550) was a Roman noblewoman, the daughter of Quintus Aurelius Symmachus. Her husband died within a year of their marriage, and she joined a community of women living on Vatican Hill, Italy. She cared for the poor and sick before dying of breast cancer.

Garvais *see Gervase (boy's name)*

Garvaise *see Gervase (boy's name)*

Garvas *see Gervase (boy's name)*

Garvase *see Gervase (boy's name)*

Gaudentia Saint; Latin, Spanish; happy, content

St. Gaudentia (date unknown) was a virgin who was martyred in Rome with three companions.

Gaytana *see Gaetana*

Gaytane *see Gaetana*

Gaytanna *see Gaetana*

Gaytanne *see Gaetana*

Gebereal *see Gabriel (boy's name)*

Gebetrude Saint; German; strength of the spear

Gertrude

St. Gebetrude (d. 675), also known as Gertrude, was an abbess of the Benedictine Abbey of Remiremont, France.

Gebreil *see Gabriel (boy's name)*

Gebrell *see Gabriel (boy's name)*

Geena *see Eugenia*

Geertrud *see Gertrude*

Geertruda *see Gertrude*

Geertrude *see Gertrude*

Geertrudi *see Gertrude*

Geertrudie *see Gertrude*

Geertrudy *see Gertrude*

Geitruda *see Gertrude*

Geltrude Saint; German, Italian; spear, strength, power

St. Geltrude Comensoli (1847–1903) was born in Val Camonica, Brescia. Unable to resist the attraction, at the age of seven she went to Mass alone and secretly made her First Communion. She was deeply devoted to the Eucharist. She joined the Sisters of Charity, but she became very ill and was asked to leave the community. When she recovered, she worked as a servant for the future bishop of Lodi. She took a private vow of chastity and began educating the children of San Gervasio. In 1880, Pope Leo XIII gave her permission to begin the Congregation of the Sacramentine Sisters of Bergamo. She was canonized by Pope Benedict XVI in 2009.

Gem *see Gemma*

Gema *see Gemma*

Gemah *see Gemma*

Gemee *see Gemma*

Gemey *see Gemma*

Gemia *see Gemma*

Gemiah *see Gemma*

Gemie *see Gemma*

Gemma Saint; Latin, Italian; jewel, precious stone

Gem, Gema, Gemah, Gemee, Gemey, Gemia, Gemiah, Gemie, Gemmah, Gemmi, Gemmia, Gemmiah, Gemmie, Gemmy, Gemy, Jemma, Jemsa

St. Gemma Galgani (1878–1903) was born in a small Italian town near Lucca. She was a quiet, sickly child who experienced many mystical experiences, for which she was ridiculed. Her father died when she was nineteen, and she took care of her seven younger siblings. She wanted to become a nun but was prevented because of her ill health. In 1899, she received the stigmata. The wounds would appear every Thursday and last until Friday night or Saturday. She often saw her guardian angel, whom she sent on errands to help her. She died at the age of twenty-five and was canonized in 1940.

Gemmah *see Gemma*

Gemmi *see Gemma*

Gemmia *see Gemma*

Gemmiah *see Gemma*

Gemmie *see Gemma*

Gemmy *see Gemma*

Gemy *see Gemma*

Gena *see Eugenia*

Genaveeve *see Genevieve*

Genaveve *see Genevieve*

Genavie *see Genevieve*

Genavieve *see Genevieve*

Genavive *see Genevieve*

Generosa Saint; Latin, Spanish; generous

St. Generosa (d. 180) was martyred in northwestern Africa.

Genes *see Genesis*

Genese *see Genesis*

Genesha *see Genesis*

Genesia *see Genesis*

Genesis Old Testament; Top 100 Name; Greek, Latin; beginning, origin, birth

Genes, Genese, Genesha, Genesia, Genesiss, Genessa, Genesse, Genessie, Genicis, Genises, Genysis, Jennasis, Yenesis

Genesis is the first book of the Bible.

Genesiss *see Genesis*

Genessa *see Genesis*

Genesse *see Genesis*

Genessie *see Genesis*

Geneva *see Genevieve*

Geneveve *see Genevieve*

Genevie *see Genevieve*

Genevieve Saint; form of Guinevere; German, French; white wave, white phantom

Genaveeve, Genaveve, Genavie, Genavieve, Genavive, Geneva, Geneveve, Genevie, Genevievre, Genevive, Genivive, Genvieve, Ginetta, Ginette, Gineveve, Ginevieve, Ginevive, Guinevieve, Guinivive, Guynieve, Guyniviv, Guynivive, Gwenevieve, Gwenivive, Gwiniviev, Gwinivieve, Gwynivive, Gynevieve, Janavieve, Jenerieve, Jennavieve

St. Genevieve (422–512) was born near Paris. She consecrated herself as a virgin at the age of seven. When Attila was marching on Paris, she convinced the people to turn to fasting and prayer rather than abandon the city. With God's protection, Attila did not attack. She was known for her austerity and prayer.

Genevievre *see Genevieve*

Genevive *see Genevieve*

Genicis *see Genesis*

Genises *see Genesis*

Genivive *see Genevieve*

Genoveva Saint; form of Genevieve; German, French; white wave, white phantom

St. Genoveva Torres Morales (1870–1956) was born in Castille, Spain. By the time she was eight, both of her parents and four siblings had died. Genoveva had to care for her home and her younger brother. At age thirteen, she lost her left leg to gangrene. From 1885 to 1894, she lived at the Mercy Home with the Carmelites of Charity. She wanted to join that order but was rejected because of her physical deformity. In 1911 she started a small community in Valencia dedicated to helping poor women. Soon, many other houses of the order were started. In 1953, the Congregation of the Sacred Heart of Jesus and the Holy Angels received pontifical approval. She was canonized by Pope John Paul II in 2003.

Genvieve *see Genevieve*

Genysis *see Genesis*

Georgia Saint; Greek; farmer

Giorgia

St. Georgia (sixth century) was a native of Clermont, France. She lived as an anchoress, spending her life almost continually praying in church. During her funeral procession, a large flock of birds hovered overhead. They remained on the church for the duration of the funeral. The people took this as a sign of God's favor.

Gerda *see Gertrude*

Gerivas *see Gervase (boy's name)*

Germain *see Germaine*

Germaine Saint; French, English; from Germany, sprout, bud

Germain, Germane, Germayn, Germayne, Germin, Germon, Germyn, Jermaine

St. Germaine Cousin (1579–1601) was born with a right hand that was deformed and paralyzed. After her mother died, her stepmother, Hortense, treated her very badly. She fed her so little that she would eat out of the dog's dish. She left her in a drain for three days. She also poured boiling water on the little girl's legs. Her father did nothing to stop this abuse. Germaine developed scrofula and was soon plagued by sores. Afraid her own children would catch the disease, Hortense had Germaine sleep in the barn. Germaine developed a deep faith in God. She attended Mass every day. She shared the little she had with beggars. Hortense finally softened toward her and invited her back into the house, but Germaine refused and was found dead in the barn when she was twenty-two.

Germane *see Germaine*

Germayn *see Germaine*

Germayne *see Germaine*

Germin *see Germaine*

Germon *see Germaine*

Germyn *see Germaine*

Gerruda *see Gertrude*

Gerrudah *see Gertrude*

Gerta *see Gertrude*

Gertina *see Gertrude*

Gertraud *see Gertrude*

Gertraude *see Gertrude*

Gertrud *see Gertrude*

Gertruda *see Gertrude*

Gertrudah *see Gertrude*

Gertrude Saint; German; beloved warrior

Geertrud, Geertruda, Geertrude, Geertrudi, Geertrudie, Geertrudy, Geitruda, Gerda, Gerruda, Gerrudah, Gerta, Gertina, Gertraud, Gertraude, Gertrud, Gertruda, Gertrudah, Gertrudia, Gertrudis, Gertruide, Gertruyd, Gertruyde, Girtrud, Girtruda, Girtrude, Trudi, Trudy

St. Gertrude, St. Gertrude of Hamage, St. Gertrude of Nivelles, St. Gertrude the Great

St. Gertrude the Great (1256–1302) was born in Eisleben, Thuringia. She went to live with the Benedictines at the Monastery of St. Mary at Helfta as a young girl. She was a scholar who studied scripture and theology. She produced many writings and was known as a mystic. She is invoked for the souls in purgatory.

Gertrudia *see Gertrude*

Gertrudis *see Gertrude*

Gertruide *see Gertrude*

Gertruyd *see Gertrude*

Gertruyde *see Gertrude*

Gervais *see Gervase (boy's name)*

Gervas *see Gervase (boy's name)*

Gervase *see Gervase (boy's name)*

Gervasio *see Gervase (boy's name)*

Gervaso *see Gervase (boy's name)*

Gervasy *see Gervase (boy's name)*

Gervayse *see Gervase (boy's name)*

Gervis *see Gervase (boy's name)*

Gerwazy *see Gervase (boy's name)*

Gessica *see Jessica*

Ghabriel *see Gabriel (boy's name)*

Giacinda *see Jacinta*

Giacinthia *see Jacinta*

Gian *see Gianna*

Gianah *see Gianna*

Gianel *see Gianna*

Gianela *see Gianna*

Gianele *see Gianna*

Gianell *see Gianna*

Gianella *see Gianna*

Gianelle *see Gianna*

Gianet *see Gianna*

Gianeta *see Gianna*

Gianete *see Gianna*

Gianett *see Gianna*

Gianetta *see Gianna*

Gianette *see Gianna*

Gianina *see Gianna*

Gianinna *see Gianna*

Gianna Saint; Hebrew; God is gracious

Gian, Gianah, Gianel, Gianela, Gianele, Gianell, Gianella, Gianelle, Gianet, Gianeta, Gianete, Gianett, Gianetta, Gianette, Gianina, Gianinna, Giannah, Gianne, Giannee, Giannetta, Gianni, Giannie, Giannina, Gianny, Gianouia, Gyan, Gyana, Gyanah, Gyann, Gyanna, Gyannh

St. Gianna Beretta Molla (1922–1962) was an Italian pediatrician. She and her husband Pietro were the parents of four children. When pregnant with her fourth child she refused both an abortion and a hysterectomy in order to save her baby's life. She later died of complications from this pregnancy. With her husband and daughter in attendance, she was canonized by Pope John Paul II in 2004.

Giannah *see Gianna*

Gianne *see Gianna*

Giannee *see Gianna*

Giannetta *see Gianna*

Gianni *see Gianna*

Giannie *see Gianna*

Giannina *see Gianna*

Gianny *see Gianna*

Gianoula *see Gianna*

Gibitrudis Saint; German; strong gift

St. Gibitrudis (d. 665) was a Benedictine nun at Faremoutieren Brie, in France.

Ginata *see Virginia*

Ginetta *see Genevieve*

Ginette *see Genevieve*

Gineveve *see Genevieve*

Ginevieve *see Genevieve*

Ginevive *see Genevieve*

Ginger *see Virginia*

Gingia *see Virginia*

Ginia *see Virginia*

Giorgia *see Georgia*

Giosafata *see Josaphata*

Girtrud *see Gertrude*

Girtruda *see Gertrude*

Girtrude *see Gertrude*

Giuditta *see Judith*

Giulia Saint; form of Julia; Italian; youthful

> *Guila, Guiliana, Guilietta, Guiliette*

St. Giulia Salzano (1846–1929) was educated by the Sisters of Charity in the Royal Orphanage of St. Nicola La Strada until she was fifteen. She worked as a teacher and catechist in Casoria, Naples. She was deeply devoted to the Virgin Mary and the Sacred Heart of Jesus. She founded the Congregation of the Catechetical Sisters of the Sacred Heart of Jesus in 1905. Pope Benedict XVI canonized her in 2010.

Giuseppina Saint; form of Joseph, Josephine; Italian; God will add, God will increase

Bl. Giuseppina Gabriella Bonino (1843–1906) was born in Savigliano, Italy. After going through back surgery in her twenties, she traveled to Lourdes to give thanks for her health. There, she felt called to devote her life to caring for the poor. She began caring for orphans and founded the Sisters of the Holy Family. She was beatified in 1995 by Pope John Paul II.

Giustina *see Justina*

Givonni *see Giovanni (boy's name)*

Glad *see Gladys*

Gladdis *see Gladys*

Gladdys *see Gladys*

Gladis *see Gladys*

Gladiz *see Gladys*

Gladness *see Gladys*

Gladuse *see Gladys*

Gladwys *see Gladys*

Glady *see Gladys*

Gladys Saint; Latin, Gaelic; small sword, princess

> *Glad, Gladdis, Gladdys, Gladis, Gladiz, Gladness, Gladuse, Gladwys, Glady, Gladyss, Gleddis, Gleddys*

St. Gladys (sixth century) was a daughter of Brychan of Brecknock, Wales. She was the wife of St. Gundleus and the mother of St. Cadoc. The romance between Gundleus and Gladys became part of the Arthurian legend.

Gladyss *see Gladys*

Glaphyra Saint; Greek; fine, elegant

St. Glaphyra (d. 324) was a slave owned by Empress Constantia, wife of Coemperor Licinius Licinianus. She fled court in order to protect her chastity but was captured and condemned to death. She died en route to her execution.

Gleddis *see Gladys*

Gleddys *see Gladys*

Glodesind Saint

St. Glodesind (d. 608) was getting married, but on her wedding day her intended was arrested and executed. She became a nun and later became abbess in Metz, Germany.

Glyceria Saint; Latin; sweetness

St. Glyceria (d. 177) was a daughter of a Roman senator. She was arrested for being a Christian and destroying a statue of Jupiter. She was thrown to wild animals at the Heraclea in the Propontis, in Greece, but she died before the animals could attack her.

Gobnait *see Gobnata*

Gobnata Saint; Celtic; mouth, beak

Gobnait

St. Gobnata (sixth century), also known as Gobnait, was the abbess of a convent in Ballyvourney, County Cork, Ireland, that had been founded by St. Abban.

Godebertha Saint; German; God bright

St. Godebertha (640–700) was born at Boves, near Amiens, to a noble family. Her parents wanted her to marry, but St. Eligius helped her fulfill her desire to become a nun. Clovis II gave her a small palace at Noyon where she started a convent and served as abbess. She was known as a miracle worker.

Gorgonia Saint; Greek; the violent one

St. Gorgonia (d. 375) was the daughter of St. Gregory Nazianzus and St. Nonna. She was married and had several children. She converted her husband, and the whole family was baptized. At her death, she was held up as a model for Christian married women. She is a patron saint of people afflicted by bodily ills or sickness.

Graca *see Grace*

Grace Saint; Top 100 Name; Latin; graceful, gift of God

Graca, Gracea, Gracelia, Gracella, Gracia, Graciane, Grasia, Gratia, Gratiana, Grayce, Graziella

St. Grace (d. 304) was a virgin martyred during the persecutions of Emperor Diocletian. Her breasts were cut off, and then she was returned to her prison cell to die of the wounds.

Gracea *see Grace*

Gracelia *see Grace*

Gracella *see Grace*

Gracia *see Grace*

Graciane *see Grace*

Grasia *see Grace*

Grata Saint; Latin; favor, blessing

St. Grata (fourth or eighth century) was a holy widow from Bergamo, Italy, who secured Christian burial for martyrs.

Gratia *see Gratia (boy's name)*

Gratiana *see Grace*

Grayce *see Grace*

Graziella *see Grace*

Grimonia Saint

St. Grimonia (fourth century) was the daughter of a pagan Irish chief. She converted to Christianity when she was twelve and took a vow of virginity. She refused to marry, and her father locked her up. When she escaped, she fled to France where she lived as a hermit in the forest of Thierache in Picardy. Her father's messengers eventually found her. When she still refused to marry, they beheaded her.

Gudelia Saint; Latin; God

St. Gudelia (d. 340) was a Persian maiden who was martyred during the persecution of King Shakur II.

Gudula Saint; Latin; God

St. Gudula (d. 712) was the daughter of Count Witger and St. Amalberga. She was taught by St. Gertrude of Nivelles and lived with her until St. Gertrude died. She was known for her great charity. She is a patron saint of Brussels and single laywomen.

Guibar *see Wioborada*

Guila *see Giulia*

Guiliana *see Giulia*

Guilietta *see Giulia*

Guiliette *see Giulia*

Guinevieve *see Genevieve*

Guinivive *see Genevieve*

Gundelindis Saint; German; gentle fight

Gwendoline

St. Gundelindis (d. 750), also known as Gwendoline, was the daughter of the duke of Alsace, France, and a niece of St. Ottilia. She served as abbess of Niedermunster.

Guynieve *see Genevieve*

Guyniviv *see Genevieve*

Guynivive *see Genevieve*

Gwen Saint; Welsh; white wave, white browed

Gwenesha, Gweness, Gwenessa, Gweneta, Gwenetta, Gwenette, Gweni, Gwenisha, Gwenishia, Gwenita, Gwenite, Gwenitta, Gwenitte, Gwenn, Gwenna, Gwenneta, Gwennete, Gwennetta, Gwennette, Gwennie, Gwenny, Gwyn

St. Gwen (fifth century) was a daughter of Brychan of Brecknock. She married St. Fragan and was martyred by pagans. According to legend she had three breasts. For this reason, she is invoked for women's fertility.

Gwendoline *see Gundelindis*

Gwenesha *see Gwen*

Gweness *see Gwen*

Gwenessa *see Gwen*

Gweneta *see Gwen*

Gwenetta *see Gwen*

Gwenette *see Gwen*

Gwenevieve *see Genevieve*

Gweni *see Gwen*

Gwenisha *see Gwen*

Gwenishia *see Gwen*

Gwenita *see Gwen*

Gwenite *see Gwen*

Gwenitta *see Gwen*

Gwenitte *see Gwen*

Gwenivive *see Genevieve*

Gwenn *see Gwen*

Gwenna *see Gwen*

Gwenneta *see Gwen*

Gwennete *see Gwen*

Gwennetta *see Gwen*

Gwennette *see Gwen*

Gwennie *see Gwen*

Gwenny *see Gwen*

Gwiniviev *see Genevieve*

Gwinivieve *see Genevieve*

Gwyn *see Gwen*

Gwynivive *see Genevieve*

Gyan *see Gianna*

Gyana *see Gianna*

Gyanah *see Gianna*

Gyann *see Gianna*

Gyanna *see Gianna*

Gyannah *see Gianna*

Gynevieve *see Genevieve*

H

Hadas *see Hadassah*

Hadasah *see Hadassah*

Hadassa *see Hadassah*

Hadassah Old Testament; Hebrew; a myrtle tree; joy

Hadas, Hadasah, Hadassa, Haddasa, Haddassah

Hadassah was the original name of Esther, who became queen of Persia and helped save the Jewish people from a mass killing.

Haddasa *see Hadassah*

Haddasah *see Hadassah*

Hagar Old Testament; Hebrew; a stranger, one that fears

Hagara, Hagarah, Hagaria, Hagariah, Hagarya, Hagaryah, Hager, Haggar, Hagir, Hagor, Hagyr

Hagar was the handmaiden of Sarai (Sarah), the wife of Abraham. When Sarah was unable to conceive a child, she gave Hagar to Abraham as a concubine. She conceived and gave birth to Ishmael. Later, after Sarah had given birth to Isaac, she saw Ishmael mocking Isaac. With Abraham's permission, she sent Hagar and Ishmael away. Yahweh assured both Abraham and Hagar that Ishmael would be the head of a great nation. Her story is told in the book of Genesis.

Hagara *see Hagar*

Hagarah *see Hagar*

Hagaria *see Hagar*

Hagariah *see Hagar*

Hagarya *see Hagar*

Hagaryah *see Hagar*

Haggar *see Hagar*

Halayna *see Helena*

Halaynah *see Helena*

Halena *see Helena*

Halina *see Helen, Helena*

Hanna *see Hannah*

Hannaa *see Hannah*

Hannah Old Testament; Top 100 Name; Hebrew; gracious, merciful, he that gives

Chana, Chanah, Hanna, Hannaa, Hanneke, Hannele, Hannon, Honnah

Hannah was the wife of Elkanah. Her story is told in the 1 Samuel. Hannah was childless and went up to the temple and prayed for a child, vowing to give the son back to God. She conceived and gave birth to Samuel.

Hanneke *see Hannah*

Hannele *see Hannah*

Hannon *see Hannah*

Harlindis Saint; German; Lord, army, shield

St. Harlindis (eighth century) and her sister Relindis became nuns at the Valenciennes Convent in France. They then established a convent in Maaseyk, Belgium, that their father had built for them. Soon, many other women joined them, and Harlindis served as abbess. The sisters made ecclesiastical furnishings and copied liturgical manuscripts for the Divine Office.

Heda *see Hedda*

Hedah *see Hedda*

Hedaya *see Hedda*

Hedda Saint; German; battler

Heda, Hedah, Hedaya, Heddah, Hedia, Hedie, Hedu

St. Hedda (d. 870) was the Benedictine abbot of Peterborough, England. When the Danes invaded, he and eighty-four other monks were killed.

Heddah *see Hedda*

Hedia *see Hedda*

Hedie *see Hedda*

Hedu *see Hedda*

Hedvig *see Hedwig*

Hedvige *see Hedwig*

Hedvika *see Hedwig*

Hedwig Saint; German; warrior

Hedvig, Hedvige, Hedvika, Hedwiga, Hedwyg, Hedwyga, Jadviga

St. Hedwig, St. Hedwig, Queen of Poland

St. Hedwig, Queen of Poland (1373–1399), was the daughter of King Louis I of Hungary and Elizabeth of Bosnia. She ascended to the Polish throne when she was thirteen. Her official title was "king" rather than "queen," indicating that she was the sovereign by her own right and not as consort. She spoke six languages and was very well educated. She was also known for her piety. She married Jagielloe of Lithuania, and the couple actively promoted Christianity in that area. She died because of complications from childbirth. She is a patron saint of queens and a united Europe. She was canonized by Pope John Paul II in 1997.

Hedwiga *see Hedwig*

Hedwyg *see Hedwig*

Hedwyga *see Hedwig*

Hela *see Helen*

Helan *see Helen*

Helayna *see Helena*

Helaynah *see Helena*

Hele *see Helen*

Helean *see Helen*

Heleana *see Helena*

Heleanah *see Helena*

Heleen *see Helen*

Heleena *see Helena*

Heleenah *see Helena*

Helen Saint; Greek; light

> *Eileen, Elana, Elena, Ena, Halina, Hela, Helan, Hele, Helean, Heleen, Helene, Helin, Helon, Helyn, Holain, Ileana, Ilene, Ilyne, Yolanda*
>
> St. Helen, St. Helen of Skovde, Sts. Centolla and Helen
>
> St. Helen of Skovde (d. 1160) was born to a noble family in Sweden. After her husband died, she gave all her possessions to the poor and made a pilgrimage to Rome. When she returned, she was falsely accused of being involved in her son-in-law's death. By the time her innocence was proven, she had already been executed. Many miracles were reported at her tomb.

Helena Saint; Greek; light

> *Halayna, Halaynah, Halena, Halina, Helayna, Helaynah, Heleana, Heleanah, Heleena, Heleenah, Helenah, Helenka, Helenna, Hellaina, Hellana, Hellanah, Hellanna, Hellena, Hellenna, Helona, Helonna*

St. Helena (248–328) was the mother of Emperor Constantine the Great. She was married to Constantius Chlorus, coregent of the Western Roman empire. He ultimately left her for a second marriage with better political connections. After his death, Constantine assumed the throne and brought his mother home. She used her position to help build churches throughout the empire. Late in life, she traveled to the Holy Land to search for the true Cross of Jesus. She is a patron saint of archeologists, converts, difficult marriages, and divorced people.

Helenah *see Helena*

Helene *see Helen*

Helenka *see Helena*

Helenna *see Helena*

Heliconis Saint; Greek

> St. Heliconis (d. 250) was martyred by being beheaded at Thessalonica, Greece.

Helin *see Helen*

Hellaina *see Helena*

Hellana *see Helena*

Hellanah *see Helena*

Hellanna *see Helena*

Hellena *see Helena*

Hellenna *see Helena*

Heloisa *see Louisa*

Heloise *see Louise*

Helon *see Helen*

Helona *see Helena*

Helonna *see Helena*

Helsa *see Elizabeth*

Helyn *see Helen*

Hemma *see Emma*

Hendvyg *see Hedwig*

Hereswitha Saint

St. Hereswitha (d. 690) was a sister of St. Hilda. She married Aethelhere, king of East Anglia, and became the mother of Sts. Sexburga, Withburga, and Ethelburga. After her husband died, she became a Benedictine nun in Chelles, France.

Herma *see Hermina*

Hermalina *see Hermina*

Hermia *see Hermina*

Hermina Saint; Latin, German; noble, soldier

Herma, Hermalina, Hermia, Herminah, Hermine, Herminia, Herminna

St. Hermina Grivot (1866–1900) was born in Beaune, France. Despite being a sickly child, she entered the Franciscan Missionaries of Mary, but had to make a longer than usual novitiate in order to prove she could survive missionary life. She cared for the sick in Marseilles before being sent to China as a missionary, where she was beheaded. She is one of the Martyrs of China canonized by Pope John Paul II in 2000.

Herminah *see Hermina*

Hermine *see Hermina*

Herminia *see Hermina*

Herminna *see Hermina*

Hermion *see Hermione*

Hermiona *see Hermione*

Hermione Saint; Greek; earthy

Hermion, Hermiona, Hermoine, Hermyone

St. Hermione (d. 117) was the daughter of Philip the Deacon. She was referred to as a prophetess in the Acts of the Apostles and was martyred at Ephesus.

Hermoine *see Hermione*

Hermyone *see Hermione*

Hi *see Hilary (boy's name)*

Hideltha *see Hildelitba*

Hieu Saint; Vietnamese; respectful

St. Hieu (d. 657) was an abbess of Tadcaster Abbey, in Yorkshire, England.

Hil *see Hilary (boy's name)*

Hilair *see Hilary (boy's name)*

Hilaire *see Hilary (boy's name)*

Hilare *see Hilary (boy's name)*

Hilaria Saint; Latin; happy, content

St. Hilaria (d. 304) was the mother of St. Afra of Augsburg, Austria. She and her three maids were burned alive at the tomb of St. Afra.

Hilarie *see Hilary (boy's name)*

Hilary *see Hilary (boy's name)*

Hilda Saint; form of Hildegarde, Brunhilda; German; fortress

Elda, Elide, Hildah, Hilde, Hildee, Hildey, Hildi, Hildia, Hildie, Hildur, Hildy, Hillda, Hilldah, Hilldee, Hilldey, Hilldi, Hilldia, Hilldie, Hilldy, Hulda, Hylda, Hyldah, Hyldea, Hyldee, Hyldey, Hyldi, Hyldie, Hyldy

St. Hilda, St. Hilda of Whitby

St. Hilda (614–680) was a daughter of the king of

Northumbria, England. She entered Chelles Monastery in France when she was thirty-three. St. Aidan asked her to return to Northumbria and become abbess of Hartlepool. She then became the head of the double monastery of Streaneschalch, at Whitby.

Hildaagard *see Hildegard*

Hildaagarde *see Hildegard*

Hildagard *see Hildegard*

Hildagarde *see Hildegard*

Hildah *see Hilda*

Hilde *see Hilda*

Hildee *see Hilda*

Hildegard Saint; German; fortress

> *Hildaagard, Hildaagarde, Hildagard, Hildagarde, Hildegard, Hildegaurd, Hyldaagard, Hyldaagarde, Hyldaaguard, Hyldaaguarde, Hyldagard, Hyldagarde, Hyldegard, Hyldegarde*

> St. Hildegard of Bingen (1098–1179) was born in Bockelheim, Germany. A sickly child, she was given to the Church at the age of eight. She grew up under the care of Jutta at an enclosure at Disisbodenberg in the Palatinate Forest. She founded Rupertsberg Convent near Bingen. She was known as a mystic, poetess, musician, and prophetess. Her best-known work is the *Scivias*, which tells of twenty-six of her visions. She was made a Doctor of the Church in 2012.

Hildegund German *see Hildegard*

> St. Hildegund (1130–1183) was the daughter of Count Herman of Lidtberg and Countess Hedwig. She married Count Lothair of Meer and had three children. After her husband died, she went on a pilgrimage to Rome. When she returned, she became a Praemonstratensian nun and converted her castle into a convent where she served as abbess.

Hildegaurd *see Hildegard*

Hildelitba Saint; German

> *Hideltha*

> St. Hildelitba (d. 712), also known as Hideltha, was an Anglo-Saxon princess, who became a nun at Chelles in France but then was asked to serve as abbess at Barking, England.

Hildemarca Saint; German; noble warrior

> St. Hildemarca (d. 670) was a nun at St. Eulalia in Bordeaux before being invited by St. Wandrille to serve as abbess of a monastery in Fecamp, France.

Hildey *see Hilda*

Hildi *see Hilda*

Hildia *see Hilda*

Hildie *see Hilda*

Hildur *see Hilda*

Hildy *see Hilda*

Hilery *see Hilary (boy's name)*

Hill *see Hilary (boy's name)*

Hillary *see Hilary (boy's name)*

Hillda *see Hilda*

Hilldah *see Hilda*

Hilldee *see Hilda*

Hilldey *see Hilda*

Hilldi *see Hilda*

Hilldia *see Hilda*

Hilldie *see Hilda*

Hilldy *see Hilda*

Hillery *see Hilary (boy's name)*

Hilliary *see Hilary (boy's name)*

Hillie *see Hilary (boy's name)*

Hilly *see Hilary (boy's name)*

Hiltrude Saint; German; strength in battle

St. Hiltrude (d. 790) was a hermitess at Liessies Abbey in France.

Holain *see Helen*

Honnah *see Hannah*

Honorata Saint; Spanish; honorable

St. Honorata (d. 500) was a nun at Pavia, Italy. When she was kidnapped by the Germanic chieftain Odoacer, her brother, St. Epiphanus, who was bishop of Pavia, ransomed her.

Honorina Saint; Latin; honorable

St. Honorina (d. 303) was a virgin martyr in Normandy, France. She is a patron of boatmen.

Hope Saint; English; hope

St. Hope (second century) was one of the daughters of St. Wisdom (Sophia) who were martyred during Hadrian's persecution of Christians. After emerging unharmed from a furnace, she was beheaded. She was ten years old.

Hoystill *see Austell*

Hulda *see Hilda*

Humbeline Saint; French

St. Humbeline (d. 1135) was the younger sister of St. Bernard of Clairvaux. She was married, but her husband allowed her to enter the Benedictine convent at Jully les Nonnais. She later served that community as abbess.

Humilitas Saint; Latin; humble

Humility

St. Humilitas (1226–1310), also known as Humility, was born in Faenza, Italy, and was married at the age of fifteen. She bore two children who both died in infancy. After nine years of marriage, the couple decided to separate to enter religious life. She was a hermit until she was asked to start two Vallumbrosan convents.

Humility *see Humilitas*

Hunna Saint

St. Hunna (d. 679) was a noblewoman of Strasbourg, France, who devoted herself to the poor. Because she would wash them, she became known as "the Holy Washerwoman." She is a patron saint of laundresses, laundry workers, and washerwomen.

Hyacintha *see Hyacinth (boy's name)*

Hyacinthia *see Hyacinth (boy's name)*

Hyacinthie *see Hyacinth (boy's name)*

Hycinth *see Hyacinth (boy's name)*

Hycynth *see Hyacinth (boy's name)*

Hylarie *see Hilary (boy's name)*

Hylary *see Hilary*

Hylda *see Hilda*

Hyldaagard *see Hildegard*

Hyldaagarde *see Hildegard*

Hyldaaguard *see Hildegard*

Hyldaaguarde *see Hildegard*

Hyldagard *see Hildegard*

Hyldagarde *see Hildegard*

Hyldah *see Hilda*

Hyldea *see Hilda*

Hyldee *see Hilda*

Hyldegard *see Hildegard*

Hyldegarde *see Hildegard*

Hyldey *see Hilda*

Hyldi *see Hilda*

Hyldie *see Hilda*

Hyldy *see Hilda*

I

Ia Saint; Greek; voice, shout

Ives

St. Ia (d. 450), also known as Ives, was the sister of St. Ercus, educated under St. Baricus. She was a missionary to Cornwall, and St. Ives, Cornwall, is named for her.

Ileana *see Helen*

Ilena *see Alena*

Ilene *see Helen*

Ilizzabet *see Elizabeth*

Illuminata Saint; Latin; shining

St. Illuminata (d. 320) was a virgin who is venerated in Todi, Italy.

Ilyne *see Helen*

Imma Saint; German; water pourer

Immina

St. Imma (eighth century), also known as Immina, was an abbess of Karlburg, in Francona.

Immina *see Imma*

Inger *see Ingrid*

Ingrede *see Ingrid*

Ingrid Saint; Scandinavian; hero's daughter, beautiful daughter

Inger, Ingrede

St. Ingrid of Sweden (d. 1282) was the first Dominican nun in Sweden. She founded St. Martin's in Skänninge, the first Dominican cloister in Sweden.

Ioudith *see Judith*

Iphgena *see Iphigenia*

Iphigenia Saint; Greek; sacrifice

Iphgena, Iphigeniah, Iphigenya, Iphigenyah

St. Iphigenia (first century) was a virgin from Ethiopia converted by St. Matthew.

Iphigeniah *see Iphigenia*

Iphigenya *see Iphigenia*

Iphigenyah *see Iphigenia*

Irais Saint; Greek; descendent of Hera (Greek goddess)

Rhais

St. Irais (d. 303), also known as Rhais, was martyred in Egypt during the persecutions of Emperor Diocletian.

Irean *see Irene*

Ireane *see Irene*

Ireen *see Irene*

Irén *see Irene*

Irena *see Irene*

Irene Saint; Greek; peaceful

> *Erena, Erene, Irean, Ireane, Ireen, Irén, Irena, Irien, Irine, Iryn, Iryne, Jereni*
>
> St. Irene (d. 379) was the sister of Pope St. Damasus. At age twenty, she made a vow to remain a virgin. She spent much of her time praying at the tombs of martyrs. Her brother wrote her a book on consecrated virginity. She was known for her holiness and purity.

Irien *see Irene*

Irine *see Irene*

Irmina Saint; Latin; noble

> St. Irmina (d. 716) was the daughter of King Dagobert II. She was engaged to be married, but her intended died prior to the marriage. Her father then built Oehren Convent for her near Trier. She served as abbess there. She also founded Echternacht for St. Willibrord.

Irsaline *see Ursula*

Irsula *see Ursula*

Iryn *see Irene*

Iryne *see Irene*

Isabal *see Isabel*

Isabeal *see Isabel*

Isabel Saint; Spanish; consecrated to God

> *Belita, Bella, Belle, Isabal, Isabeal, Isabele, Isabeli, Isabelia, Isabelita, Isabella, Isabelle, Isabello, Isbel, Iseabal, Ishbel, Issabel, Issie, Izabel, Izabele, Sabella, Ysabella*
>
> St. Isabel of France (d. 1270) was a daughter of King Louis VIII of France and Blanche of Castile. She received several offers of marriage but refused them all because she had consecrated herself to God. She devoted herself to serving the sick and poor. She also founded the Franciscan Monastery of the Humility of the Blessed Virgin Mary at Longchamps in Paris. She lived there but never became a nun.

Isabele *see Isabel*

Isabeli *see Isabel*

Isabelia *see Isabel*

Isabelita *see Isabel*

Isabella *see Isabel*

Isabelle *see Isabel*

Isabello *see Isabel*

Isadoria *see Isidora*

Isadoriah *see Isidora*

Isadorya *see Isidora*

Isadoryah *see Isidora*

Isbel *see Isabel*

Isberga Saint; German; she who battles with sword

> St. Isberga (d. 800) was a sister of Charlemagne. She was a Benedictine nun at a convent at Aire in Artois, France.

Iseabal *see Isabel*

Ishbel *see Isabel*

Isidora Saint; Latin; gift of Isis

Isadoria, Isadoriah, Isadorya, Isadoryah, Izadora, Izadorah, Izadore, Ysadora

St. Isidora, St. Isadora the Simple

St. Isidora (fourth century) was a nun in Egypt. She then became a hermit in the desert where she lived out the rest of her days.

Isidora *see Isidora*

Issabel *see Isabel*

Issie *see Isabel*

Ita Saint; Gaelic; thirsty

Itah

St. Ita (475–570) was born at Decies, Waterford, Ireland. She founded a community of women dedicated to God in Killeedy, Limerick. She also started a school for boys where she taught St. Brendan. She was known as a miracle worker and is a patron of Limerick, Ireland.

Itah *see Ita*

Iulia *see Julia*

Iuliana *see Julia*

Ives *see Ia*

Izabel *see Isabel*

Izabele *see Isabel*

Izadora *see Isidora*

Izadorah *see Isidora*

Izadore *see Isidora*

J

Jacanta *see Jacinta*

Jacent *see Jacinta*

Jacenta *see Jacinta*

Jacentah *see Jacinta*

Jacente *see Jacinta*

Jacinta Saint; form of Hyacinth; Greek; plant with colorful, fragrant flowers

Giacinda, Giacinthia, Jacanta, Jacent, Jacenta, Jacentah, Jacente, Jacintah, Jacinthe, Jacintia, Jacynta, Jacyntah, Jasinta, Jasintah, Jasinte, Jaxinta, Jaxintah, Jaxinte, Jazinta, Jazintah, Jazynte, Jecinda

Bl. Jacinta Marto (1910–1920) was the youngest visionary of Our Lady of Fatima. She was born to a poor family in Fatima, Portugal. She, her brother Francisco, and their cousin Lucia received visions of Our Lady in 1917. After seeing a vision of hell, she devoted herself to penance and sacrifice in order to save sinners. She died as a result of the influenza epidemic. She was beatified in 2000 by Pope John Paul II.

Jacintah *see Jacinta*

Jacinthe *see Jacinta*

Jacintia *see Jacinta*

Jacynta *see Jacinta*

Jacyntah *see Jacinta*

Jadviga *see Hedwig*

Jaeen *see Jane*

Jaeene *see Jane*

Jaen *see Jane*

Jaene *see Jane*

Jahn *see Jan (boy's name)*

Jahne *see Jane*

Jain *see Jane*

Jaine *see Jane*

Jan *see Jan (boy's name)*

Jana *see Jan (boy's name)*

Janae *see Jan (boy's name)*

Janavieve *see Genevieve*

Jane Saint; Hebrew; God is gracious

Jaeen, Jaeene, Jaen, Jaene, Jahne, Jain, Jaine, Janet, Janetta, Janette, Janka, Jasia, Johanna, Joane, Juanetta

St. Jane Antide Thouret, St. Jane Elizabeth Bichier des Ages, St. Jane Frances de Chantal

St. Jane Frances de Chantal (1572–1641) was the daughter of the president of the Parliament of Burgandy. Her mother died when she was only eighteen months old. She married the Baron de Chantal when she was twenty years old and became a mother of four. Her husband died in a hunting accident eight years later. She took a personal vow of chastity and went to live with her father-in-law. In Lent of 1604, she met St. Francis de Sales, who became her spiritual director and good friend. In 1610, she founded the Order of the Visitation of Our Lady at Annecy, France. The order was designed for widows and lay women. In time, Jane oversaw sixty-nine convents.

Janet *see Jane*

Janetta *see Janette*

Janette *see Jane*

Janka *see Jane*

Jann *see Jan (boy's name)*

Janne *see Jan (boy's name)*

Jano *see Jan (boy's name)*

Januaria *see Januarius (boy's name)*

Jardan *see Jordan (boy's name)*

Jasia *see Jane*

Jasinta *see Jacinta*

Jasintah *see Jacinta*

Jasinte *see Jacinta*

Jaxinta *see Jacinta*

Jaxintah *see Jacinta*

Jaxinte *see Jacinta*

Jazinta *see Jacinta*

Jazintah *see Jacinta*

Jazynte *see Jacinta*

Jean *see Jean (boy's name)*

Jéan *see Jean (boy's name)*

Jeane *see Jean (boy's name)*

Jeanette *see Jeanne*

Jeannah *see Jean (boy's name)*

Jeanne Saint; French; God is gracious

Jeanette, Jeannett, Jeannetta, Jeannette

St. Jeanne Delanoue, St. Jeanne de Lestonnac, St. Jeanne Jugan

St. Jeanne Jugan (1792–1879) was born to a poor fisherman who died when Jeanne was four years old. Her mother raised the family, supporting them by farming. She taught them the faith even during the French Revolution when the faith was suppressed. Jeanne worked as a maid for a time, before deciding to dedicate herself to God and serving the poor. After six years, she was exhausted and returned to life as a maid. At age forty-five, she began to work as a spinner and gave much of her money to the poor. Others joined her, and the Little Sisters of the Poor were founded. She was canonized by Pope Benedict XVI in 2009.

Jeannett *see Jeanne*

Jeannetta *see Jeanne*

Jeannette *see Jeanne*

Jeannie *see Jean (boy's name)*

Jeannot *see Jean (boy's name)*

Jeano *see Jean (boy's name)*

Jeanot *see Jean (boy's name)*

Jeanty *see Jean (boy's name)*

Jecinda *see Jacinta*

Jeen *see Jean (boy's name)*

Jemma *see Gemma*

Jemsa *see Gemma*

Jenda *see Jan (boy's name)*

Jene *see Jean (boy's name)*

Jenevieve *see Genevieve*

Jennasis *see Genesis*

Jennavieve *see Genevieve*

Jeremaya *see Jeremiah (boy's name)*

Jeremia *see Jeremiah (boy's name)*

Jeremya *see Jeremiah (boy's name)*

Jeremyah *see Jeremiah (boy's name)*

Jereni *see Irene*

Jescee *see Jesse (boy's name)*

Jese *see Jesse (boy's name)*

Jesee *see Jesse (boy's name)*

Jesi *see Jesse (boy's name)*

Jesicka *see Jessica*

Jesika *see Jessica*

Jessaca *see Jessica*

Jessalin *see Jessica*

Jessca *see Jessica*

Jesscia *see Jessica*

Jesse *see Jesse (boy's name)*

Jessé *see Jesse (boy's name)*

Jessia *see Jessica*

Jessica Saint; Top 100 Name; Hebrew; wealthy

Gessica, Jesicka, Jesika, Jessaca, Jessalin, Jessca, Jesscia, Jessia, Jessicah, Jessicia, Jessicka, Jessieka, Jessiqua, Jessiquah, Jessique, Jezeca, Jezecah, Jezecka, Jezeka, Jezekah, Jezica, Jezicah, Jezicka, Jezika, Jezikah, Jeziqua, Jeziquah, Jezyca, Jezycah, Jezycka, Jezyka

St. Jessica (first century) is another name for Joanna, the wife of Chuza. She was one of the women who helped serve Jesus and was one of the three women who discovered the empty tomb on Easter morning.

Jessicah *see Jessica*

Jessicia *see Jessica*

Jessicka *see Jessica*

Jessieka *see Jessica*

Jessiqua *see Jessica*

Jessiquah *see Jessica*

Jessique *see Jessica*

Jestena *see Justina*

Jestine *see Justina*

Jewelea *see Julia*

Jeweleah *see Julia*

Jewelia *see Julia*

Jeweliah *see Julia*

Jewelie *see Julie*

Jewelya *see Julia*

Jewlie *see Julie*

Jewlya *see Julia*

Jewlyah *see Julia*

Jezeca *see Jessica*

Jezecah *see Jessica*

Jezecka *see Jessica*

Jezeka *see Jessica*

Jezekah *see Jessica*

Jezica *see Jessica*

Jezicah *see Jessica*

Jezicka *see Jessica*

Jezika *see Jessica*

Jezikah *see Jessica*

Jeziqua *see Jessica*

Jeziquah *see Jessica*

Jezyca *see Jessica*

Jezycah *see Jessica*

Jezycka *see Jessica*

Jezyka *see Jessica*

Jezze *see Jesse (boy's name)*

Jezzee *see Jesse (boy's name)*

Jhan *see Jan (boy's name)*

Jhoana *see Joanna*

Jisica *see Jessica*

Jisicah *see Jessica*

Jisicka *see Jessica*

Jisikah *see Jessica*

Jisiqua *see Jessica*

Jisiquah *see Jessica*

Joahna *see Joanna*

Joan Saint; Hebrew; God is gracious

> *Joananette, Joaneil, Joanmarie, Joayn, Joen, Joenn, Jonette, Jonni*

St. Joan de Lestonnac, St. Joan of Arc, St. Joan of Valois

St. Joan of Arc (1412–1431) was born in Lorraine, France. At age thirteen, she began receiving visions from St. Margaret of Antioch, St. Catherine of Alexandria, and St. Michael the Archangel. These visions told her to find the true king of France and help him regain the throne. Three years later, she went to Charles VII in Chinon and told him of her visions. She led the troops in battle and helped bring him to the throne. She was captured by the Burgundians and sold to the English, who put her on trial. She was executed as a heretic by being burned at the stake. In 1456, the verdict was reversed and she was acquitted. She was canonized in 1920. She is a patron saint of France, imprisoned people, soldiers, and the Women's Army Corps.

Jo-Ana *see Joanna*

Joanah *see Joanna*

Joananette *see Joan*

Joananna *see Joanna*

Joandra *see Joanna*

Joane *see Jane*

Joaneil *see Joan*

Joanka *see Joanna*

Joanmarie *see Joan*

Joanna Saint, New Testament; form of Joan; English; grace or gift of the Lord

> *Jhoana, Johna, Jo-Ana, Joanah, Joananna, Joandra, Joanka, Jo-Anna, Joannah, Joanne, Joayna, Joeana, Joeanah, Joeanna, Joeannah, Joena, Joenah, Joenna, Joennah, Ohanna*

St. Joanna (first century) was the wife of Chuza. She was one of the women who helped serve Jesus and was one of the three women who discovered the empty tomb on Easter morning.

Jo-Anna *see Joanna*

Joannah *see Joanna*

Joanne *see Joanna*

Joayn *see Joan*

Joayna *see Joanna*

Joeana *see Joanna*

Joeanah *see Joanna*

Joeanna *see Joanna*

Joeannah *see Joanna*

Joelle *see Joel (boy's name)*

Joen *see Joan*

Joena *see Joanna*

Joenah *see Joanna*

Joenn *see Joan*

Joenna *see Joanna*

Joennah *see Joanna*

Johanna *see Jane*

Johsua *see Joshua (boy's name)*

Johusa *see Joshua (boy's name)*

Joleta *see Julitta*

Joletah *see Julitta*

Jolyon *see Julian (boy's name)*

Jonette *see Joan*

Jonni *see Joan*

Jordaan *see Jordan (boy's name)*

Jordae *see Jordan (boy's name)*

Jordain *see Jordan (boy's name)*

Jordaine *see Jordan (boy's name)*

Jordan *see Jordan (boy's name)*

Jordane *see Jordan (boy's name)*

Jordani *see Jordan (boy's name)*

Jordann *see Jordan (boy's name)*

Jordano *see Jordan (boy's name)*

Jordany *see Jordan (boy's name)*

Jordayne *see Jordan (boy's name)*

Jorden *see Jordan (boy's name)*

Jordian *see Jordan (boy's name)*

Jordun *see Jordan (boy's name)*

Jorrdan *see Jordan (boy's name)*

Josaphata Saint; Hebrew; God's judgment

Giosafata

Bl. Josaphata Hordashevska (1869–1919) was born in Lviv, Ukraine. She entered the Basilian Sisters and was chosen to lead a new active congregation known as the Sisters Servants of Mary Immaculate. This congregation was devoted to teaching and caring for the sick. She was beatified by Pope John Paul II in 2001.

Josaphine *see Josephine*

Josefa Saint; form of Joseph; Hebrew; God will add

Josepha

Bl. Josefa Naval Girbes (1820–1893) was born in Algemesi, Valencia, Spain. She took a personal vow of chastity as a young woman and opened a school for girls in her home. She was a member of the Third Order Secular of Our Lady of Mount Carmel and St. Teresa of Jesus. She was beatified by Pope John Paul II in 1988.

Josefine *see Josephine*

Josepha *see Josefa*

Josephin *see Josephine*

Josephina *see Josephine*

Josephine Saint; form of Joseph; French; God will add

Josaphine, Josefine, Josephin, Josephina, Josephiney, Josephyn, Josephyne, Jozephine, Sefa, Yosephina

St. Josephine Bakhita (1868–1947) was born to a wealthy Sudanese family. She was kidnapped and sold into slavery when she was nine years old. She was sold to Callisto Legnani, who planned to free her. She went with him to Italy where she worked as a nanny. She joined the Catholic Church in 1890. Three years later, she joined the Institute of Canossian Daughters of Charity. She served the poor and worked as a public speaker to help support the missions. She was canonized in 2000 by Pope John Paul II.

Josephiney *see Josephine*

Josephyn *see Josephine*

Josephyne *see Josephine*

Joveda *see Jovita*

Jovet *see Jovita*

Joveta *see Jovita*

Joveta *see Jovita*

Jovete *see Jovita*

Jovett *see Jovita*

Jovetta *see Jovita*

Jovette *see Jovita*

Jovi *see Jovita*

Jovida *see Jovita*

Jovidah *see Jovita*

Jovit *see Jovita*

Jovita Saint; Latin; jovial

Joveda, Jovet, Joveta, Jovete, Jovett, Jovetta, Jovette, Jovi, Jovida, Jovidah, Jovit, Jovitah, Jovite, Jovitt, Jovitta, Jovitte, Jowita

St. Jovita (d. 120) and his brother, St. Faustinus, were natives of Brescia who preached the faith fearlessly. They were arrested and tortured. The Emperor Hadrian, who happened to be traveling through Brescia, commanded them to be beheaded.

Jovitah *see Jovita*

Jovite *see Jovita*

Jovitt *see Jovita*

Jovitta *see Jovita*

Jovitte *see Jovita*

Jowita *see Jovita*

Jozephine *see Josephine*

Juana Saint; form of Jane, Joan; Spanish; God is gracious

Juanah, Juanell, Juaney, Juanika, Juanit, Juanita, Juanna, Juannah, Juannia

Bl. Juana Maria Condesa Lluch (1862–1916) was born into a wealthy family in Valencia, Spain. She opened a shelter to help factory workers and their families. She then opened a school for their children. Other women joined her, and she founded the Congregation of the Handmaids of the Immaculate Coneption, Protectress of Workers. She was beatified by Pope John Paul II in 2003.

Juanah *see Juana*

Juanell *see Juana*

Juanetta *see Jane*

Juaney *see Juana*

Juanika *see Juana*

Juanit *see Juana*

Juanita *see Juana*

Juanna *see Juana*

Juannah *see Juana*

Juannia *see Juana*

Jucunda Saint; Latin; pleasant

> St. Jucunda (d. 466) was a virgin of Reggio, Italy. St. Prosper taught her how to live an eremitical life.

Judett *see Judith*

Judetta *see Judith*

Judette *see Judith*

Judine *see Judith*

Judit *see Judith*

Judita *see Judith*

Judite *see Judith*

Judith Old Testament; Hebrew; praised

> *Giuditta, Ioudith, Judett, Judetta, Judette, Judine, Judit, Judita, Judite, Juditha, Judithe, Juditt, Juditta, Juditte, Judyta, Judythe, Judytt, Judytta, Judytte, Jutka, Yudita*

> Judith in the Bible was a widow who traveled to the camp of the enemy general Holofernes. She gained his trust and then cut off his head, thereby saving the Israelites. Her story is told in the book of Judith.

Juditha *see Judith*

Judithe *see Judith*

Juditt *see Judith*

Juditta *see Judith*

Juditte *see Judith*

Judyta *see Judith*

Judythe *see Judith*

Judytt *see Judith*

Judytta *see Judith*

Judytte *see Judith*

Juel *see Julie*

Juelea *see Julia*

Jueleah *see Julia*

Juelee *see Julie*

Juelei *see Julie*

Jueleigh *see Julie*

Jueli *see Julie*

Juelie *see Julie*

Juely *see Julie*

Jula *see Julia*

Jule *see Julie*

Julea *see Julia*

Juleah *see Julia*

Julean *see Julian (boy's name)*

Juleet *see Julitta*

Juleeta *see Julitta*

Juleetah *see Julitta*

Juleete *see Julitta*

Julei *see Julie*

Juleigh *see Julie*

Julene *see Julie*

Julet *see Julitta*

Juleta *see Julitta*

Juletah *see Julitta*

Julett *see Julitta*

Juletta *see Julitta*

Julette *see Julitta*

Juli *see Julie*

Julia Saint; Top 100 Name; Latin; youthful

Iulia, Iuliana, Jewelea, Jeweleah, Jewelia, Jeweliah, Jewelya, Jewlya, Jewlyah, Juelea, Jueleah, Jula, Julea, Juleah, Juliah, Julica, Juliea, Julienne, Julija, Julita, Julity, Juliya, Julka, Julya

St. Julia Maria Ledochowska, St. Julia of Billiart, St. Julia of Carthage, St. Julia of Corsica, St. Julia of Merida, St. Julia of Troyes

St. Julia of Corsica (seventh century) was born in Carthage to a noble Christian family. She was captured by Vandals and sold into slavery to a pagan named Eusebius. When the ship landed at Corsica, she was commanded to take part in a pagan festival. She refused. Her hair was torn out of her head, and she was martyred.

Juliaan *see Julian (boy's name)*

Juliah *see Julia*

Julian *see Julian (boy's name)*

Juliana Saint; form of Julia; Czech, Spanish; youthful

Julianah, Juliannah, Julieana, Julieanah, Juliena, Julienna, Juliennah, Julijana, Julijanah, Julijanna, Julijannah, Julina, Julinah, Julliana, Jullianna, Julyana, Julyanah, Julyanna, Julyannah, Yuliana

St. Juliana, St. Juliana Falconieri, St. Juliana of Cumae, St. Juliana of Nicomedia, St. Juliana of Norwich, St. Juliana of Pavilly

St. Juliana Falconieri (1270–1341) was born to a wealthy Florentine family in 1270. After her father died, she was raised by her mother and her uncle, who was one of the founders of the Servites. Her family wanted her to marry, but she instead became a Servite tertiary. She lived at home until her mother died, at which time she became the foundress of a community of women dedicated to prayer and good works. The rule was approved 120 years later. She is considered the foundress of the Servite nuns.

Julianah *see Juliana*

Juliannah *see Juliana*

Julianne *see Julian (boy's names)*

Julica *see Julia*

Julie Saint; form of Julia; English; youthful

Jewelie, Jewlie, Juel, Juelee, Juelei, Jueleigh, Jueli, Juelie, Juely, Jule, Julei, Juleigh, Julene, Juli, Julle, Jullee, Julli, Jullie, Jully, July

St. Julie Billiart (1751–1816) was born in Cuvilly, France. She took a vow of virginity while still young. She was afflicted with an illness and became crippled until 1804, when she was miraculously healed. That same year, she started the Institute of Notre Dame. By the time of her death, there were fifteen convents of the Sisters of Notre Dame. She is a patron saint against poverty, bodily ills, and disease.

Juliea *see Julia*

Julieana *see Juliana*

Julieanah *see Juliana*
Juliena *see Juliana*
Julienna *see Juliana*
Juliennah *see Juliana*
Julienne *see Julia*
Julija *see Julia*
Julijana *see Juliana*
Julijanah *see Juliana*
Julijanna *see Juliana*
Julijannah *see Juliana*
Julina *see Juliana*
Julinah *see Juliana*
Julion *see Julian (boy's name)*
Julit *see Julitta*
Julita *see Julia*
Julitah *see Julitta*
Julite *see Julitta*
Julitt *see Julitta*
Julitta Saint; form of Julia; Spanish; youthful

> *Joleta, Joletah, Juleet, Juleeta, Juleetah, Juleete, Julet, Juleta, Juletah, Julett, Juletta, Julette, Julit, Julitah, Julite, Julitt, Julittah, Julitte, Julyta*
> St. Julitta (d. 303) was martyred by being burned at the stake in Cappadocia, in modern Turkey.

Julittah *see Julitta*
Julitte *see Julitta*
Julity *see Julia*
Juliya *see Julia*
Julka *see Julia*
Julle *see Julie*
Jullee *see Julie*
Julli *see Julie*
Julliana *see Juliana*
Jullianna *see Juliana*

Jullie *see Julie*
Jully *see Julie*
July *see Julie*
Julya *see Julia*
Julyan *see Julian (boy's name)*
Julyana *see Juliana*
Julyanah *see Juliana*
Julyanna *see Juliana*
Julyannah *see Juliana*
Julyin *see Julian (boy's name)*
Julyon *see Julian (boy's name)*
Julyta *see Julitta*
Jushua *see Joshua (boy's name)*
Justa Saint; Latin; just

> St. Justa (d. 287) was a Christian woman of Seville, Spain, who together with St. Rufina sold earthenware. Pagan worshippers destroyed their products when the two women refused to sell them vessels that would be used in heathen ceremonies. In response, the women destroyed an image of a pagan goddess. They were arrested and then stretched on the rack and torn with hooks. St. Justa died on the rack, and then her body was burned.

Justeana *see Justina*
Justeanah *see Justina*
Justeena *see Justina*
Justeenah *see Justina*
Justeina *see Justina*
Justeinah *see Justina*
Justeyna *see Justina*
Justeynah *see Justina*
Justice *see Justice (boy's name)*

Justicia *see Justina*

Justina Saint; form of Justin; Latin; just, righteous

Giustina, Jestena, Jestine, Justeana, Justeanah, Justeena, Justeenah, Justeina, Justeinah, Justeyna, Justeynah, Justicia, Justinah, Justine, Justinna, Justyna

St. Justina of Antioch, St. Justina of Padua

St. Justina of Padua (d. 304) was a young woman who had taken a private vow of chastity. She was martyred during the persecutions of Emperor Diocletian.

Justinah *see Justina*

Justine *see Justina*

Justinna *see Justina*

Justyna *see Justina*

Juthware Saint; English

St. Juthware (seventh century) was from England, the sister of St. Sidwell. She was martyred, possibly by beheading.

Jutka *see Judith*

Jutta Saint; Hebrew; from Judea

St. Jutta (1200–1260) was a noblewoman of Thuringia. She married and bore several children, all of whom entered monasteries or convents. After her husband's death, she sold her property, moved to Prussia, and devoted her life to caring for the poor and sick. Her reputation for holiness was well-known, and many visitors sought her counsel.

Jysica *see Jessica*

Jysicah *see Jessica*

Jysicka *see Jessica*

Jysika *see Jessica*

Jyssicah *see Jessica*

Jyssicka *see Jessica*

Jyssika *see Jessica*

Jyssikah *see Jessica*

Jyssiqua *see Jessica*

Jyssiquah *see Jessica*

Jyssyca *see Jessica*

Jyssycka *see Jessica*

Jyssyka *see Jessica*

Jyssykah *see Jessica*

Jysyka *see Jessica*

Jysykah *see Jessica*

Jysyqua *see Jessica*

Jysyquah *see Jessica*

K

Kaitlyn *see Catherine*

Kalliopi *see Calliope*

Kamila *see Camila*

Kamilah *see Camila*

Karal *see Karol (boy's name)*

Karalos *see Karol (boy's name)*

Karen *see Katherine*

Karol *see Karol (boy's name)*

Karolek *see Karol (boy's name)*

Karolina *see Caroline*

Karolis *see Karol (boy's name)*

Károly *see Karol (boy's name)*

Karolyn *see Caroline*

Karrel *see Karol (boy's name)*

Karrol *see Karol (boy's name)*

Karroll *see Karol (boy's name)*

Kasen *see Katherine*

Kasimir *see Casmir (boy's name)*

Kat *see Katherine*

Katarzyna Saint; form of Katherine; Czech; pure

Bl. Katarzyna Celestyna Faron (1913–1944) was a sister who had offered her life for the conversion of a priest. She was arrested and placed in the Auschwitz concentration camp. She died on Easter Sunday in 1944. She is one of the 108 Polish Martyrs of World War II. She was beatified by Pope John Paul II.

Katchen *see Katherine*

Kateri Saint; form of Katherine; Greek; pure

St. Kateri Tekakwitha (1656–1680) was the daughter of a Christian Algonquin woman who was married to a non-Christian Mohawk chief. She contracted smallpox as a child and was badly scarred and lost much of her eyesight. She converted to the Christian faith and was shunned by her relatives. She took a vow of chastity and was known for her prayer life and austerities. She was canonized by Pope Benedict XVI in 2012.

Katerina *see Caterina*

Kathann *see Katherine*

Kathanne *see Katherine*

Kathereen *see Katherine*

Katheren *see Katherine*

Katherene *see Katherine*

Katherenne *see Katherine*

Katherine Saint; Top 100 Name; Greek; pure

Ekaterina, Ekatrinna, Karen, Kasen, Kat, Katchen, Kathann, Kathanne, Kathereen, Katheren, Katherene, Katherenne, Kathleen, Kathrina, Kathyrine, Katlaina, Katoka, Katreeka, Katreen, Katrin, Katrine, Katya

St. Katherine Drexel (1858–1955) was born to a wealthy railroad entrepreneur and his wife in Philadelphia, Pennsylvania. Her parents opened their home to the poor several days a week, and she learned from their example. When she asked Pope Leo XIII to send missionaries to Wyoming to work with the Native American population, he asked her to do it. She spent millions of dollars of her fortune helping them. She entered the Sisters of Mercy and then founded the Sisters of the Blessed Sacrament. She started forty-two Catholic schools for black children, fifty Indian missions, and Xavier University, the first United States university for blacks.

Kathleen *see Katherine*

Kathrina *see Katherine*

Kathyrine *see Katherine*

Katlaina *see Katherine*

Katoka *see Katherine*

Katreeka *see Katherine*

Katreen *see Katherine*

Katrin *see Katherine*

Katrina *see Caterina*

Katrine *see Katherine*

Katya *see Katherine*

Kea see Kea (boy's name)

Keane see Keyne

Keene see Keyne

Keeran see Kieran (boy's name)

Keeren see Kieran (boy's name)

Keerin see Kieran (boy's name)

Keeron see Kieran (boy's name)

Kennera Saint; Scottish; land to the west

St. Kennera (fourth century) was a hermitess who lived in Kirk Kenner, Galloway, Scotland.

Kennocha Saint; Celtic; lovely

Kyle, Kylie

St. Kennocha (d. 1007), also known as Kyle, lived in a convent in Fife, Scotland.

Kentigerna Saint; Gaelic; kind ruler

St. Kentigerna (d. 734) was the daughter of Kelly, a prince of Leinster, Ireland. She married and became the mother of St. Coellan. After her husband's death, she became a hermitess at Inchebroida Island in Loch Lomond, Scotland.

Kevoca Saint; Scottish

St. Kevoca (seventh century) is a saint honored in Kyle, Scotland.

Keyna see Keyne

Keyne Saint; Celtic; fighter, sharp eye

Keane, Keene, Keyna, Cain

St. Keyne (fifth century), also known as Keyna or Cain, was a child of King Brychan of Brecknock, Wales. She refused to marry, instead becoming a hermitess on the banks of the Severn River in Somersetshire, England. Later in life, she returned to Wales. During her travels she founded several churches.

Khloe Top 100 Name; form of Chloe; Greek; blooming, verdant

Kian see Cian (boy's name)

Kiara Saint; Gaelic; little and dark

St. Kiara (d. 680) was an Irish abbess who lived near Nenagh, in Tipperary, Ireland.

Kiaron see Kieran (boy's name)

Kiarron see Kieran (boy's name)

Kieran see Kieran (boy's name)

Kierien see Kieran (boy's name)

Kierin see Kieran (boy's name)

Kiernan see Kieran (boy's name)

Kierrian see Kieran (boy's name)

Kinga see Cunegunda

Kinnera see Cannera

Kinnia Saint; Celtic

St. Kinnia (fifth century) was a nun baptized by St. Patrick.

Klemensa Saint; Latin; merciful

Bl. Klemensa Staszewska (1890–1943) was born in Zloczew, Wielkopolskie. She joined the Ursuline Convent and later became superior of the convent. She was arrested by the Nazis for helping sick Polish and Jewish children escape from Poland. She died in Auschwitz and was beatified in 1999 by Pope John Paul II.

Klothilda see Clotilde

Klothilde *see Clotilde*

Kolette *see Collette*

Kristin *see Krystyn (boy's name)*

Kristina *see Christina*

Kristine *see Christina*

Krys *see Krystyn (boy's name)*

Krystein *see Krystyn (boy's name)*

Krystek *see Krystyn (boy's name)*

Krystin *see Krystyn (boy's name)*

Krystyn *see Krystyn (boy's name)*

Kunigunde *see Cunegunda*

Kylie *see Kennocha*

Kyneburga Saint; English

St. Kyneburga (d. 680) and her sister, St. Kyneswide, were daughters of King Penda of Mercia. Kyneburga founded an abbey at Castor, Northamptonshire.

Kyneswide Saint; English

St. Kyneswide (d. 680) was a daughter of King Penda of Mercia. She joined the abbey at Castor, Northamptonshire, which had been founded by her sister, St. Kyneburga.

L

Lacrecia *see Lucretia*

Laidey *see Adelaide*

Laidy *see Adelaide*

Landrada Saint; Teutonic, Spanish; counselor

St. Landrada (d. 690) founded Munsterbilzen Abbey in Belgium, where she served as abbess.

Larance *see Laurence (boy's name)*

Larrance *see Laurence (boy's name)*

Lasar Saint

Lassera

St. Lasar (sixth century), also known as Lassera, was a niece of St. Forchera. She became a nun at Clonard, Ireland.

Lassera *see Lasar*

Laura Saint; Latin; crowned with laurel

Laurah, Laure, Laurea, Laureen, Laurella, Lauren, Laurka, Lavra, Lawra, Lawrah, Lawrea, Loura

St. Laura (d. 864) was born in Córdoba, Spain. After her husband died, she became a nun at Cuteclara, where she later served as abbess. She was taken captive by Muslims who martyred her by placing her in a vat of boiling lead. She is one of the Martyrs of Córdoba.

Laurah *see Laura*

Laure *see Laura*

Laurea *see Laura*

Laureen *see Laura*

Laurella *see Laura*

Lauren Top 100 Name; form of Laura; English; crowned with laurel

Laurentia Saint; form of Laura; Latin; crowned with laurel

St. Laurentia (d. 302) was a Christian slave of St. Palatias. She converted Palatias, and the two women were arrested and martyred at Fermo, Italy.

Laurka *see Laura*

Lavra *see Laura*

Lawis *see Louise*

Lawisa *see Louisa*

Lawisah *see Louisa*

Lawise *see Louise*

Lawra *see Laura*

Lawrah *see Laura*

Lawrea *see Laura*

Lea Saint; form of Leah; Hebrew; weary

St. Lea (fourth century) was a Roman widow who entered a monastery after her husband's death, where she later served as abbess.

Leah Old Testament; Top 100 Name; Hebrew; weary

Leah in the Bible was the first wife of Jacob. She was the daughter of Laban. Jacob wanted to marry Leah's younger sister, Rachel, but Laban tricked him and had him marry Leah instead. She gave birth to several children who would become the first six of the twelve tribes of Israel, but she was never able to gain the love of her husband. Her story is told in the book of Genesis.

Leece *see Alice*

Lelia Saint; Greek, Hebrew, Aramaic; fair speech, dark beauty, night

Leliah, Lelika, Lelita, Lellia, Lelliah

St. Lelia (date unknown) was a daughter of Prince Cairthenn. She lived in Limerick and Kerry, Ireland, and became abbess of a convent in Munster.

Leliah *see Lelia*

Lelika *see Lelia*

Lelita *see Lelia*

Lellia *see Lelia*

Lelliah *see Lelia*

Lena *see Madeleine*

Leocadia Saint; Greek; shining, white

St. Leocadia (d. 303) was martyred in Toledo, Spain.

Leocrita Saint; Latin; to succeed

Lucretia

St. Leocrita (d. 859), also known as Lucretia, lived in Córdoba, Spain, the daughter of Muslim parents. After her conversion, she found shelter with St. Eulogius. They were both scourged and beheaded.

Leona *see Leonie*

Leonee *see Leonie*

Leoney *see Leonie*

Leoni *see Leonie*

Leonie Saint; German; brave as a lioness

Leona, Leonee, Leoney, Leoni, Leonni, Leonnie, Leony

St. Leonie Francoise de Sales Aviat (1844–1914) was born in Sezanne, France, the daughter of a shopkeeper. Together with Fr. Louis Brisson and Mother Marie Therese de Sales Chappuis, she founded the Sister Oblates of St. Francis de Sales in Troyes, which helped young women who were coming to the city to work in factories. They also opened homes and schools for working-class girls. Because of religious persecution in France, she was forced to go to Italy, where she rebuilt the congregation with Perugia as its base. She was canonized in 2001 by Pope John Paul II.

Leonni *see Leonie*

Leonnie *see Leonie*

Leony *see Leonie*

Leweese *see Louise*

Leweez *see Louise*

Lewina Saint; English; friend

St. Lewina (fifth century) was an English virgin who was martyred by invading Saxons.

Lexandra *see Alexandra*

Liberata Saint; Latin; the liberated one

St. Liberata (fifth century) was the sister of Sts. Honorata and Epiphanius of Pavia, Italy.

Lida *see Lydia*

Lidia *see Lydia*

Lidmila *see Ludmilla*

Liduina Saint; German; friend of the village

Bl. Liduina Meneguzie (1901–1941) was born into a poor farm family in Albano Terme, Padua, Italy. She joined the Sisters of the Congregation of St. Francis de Sales. She worked at the Santa Croce boarding school in various capacities, including as a housekeeper, sacristan, and nurse. She then became a missionary, serving in Ethiopia. She worked as a nurse in the Parini Civil Hospital and took care of wounded soldiers during World War II. She spoke of God to all who would listen.

She was beatified by Pope John Paul II in 2002.

Liese *see Elisabeth*

Liesel *see Elisabeth*

Lil *see Lillian*

Lila *see Lillian*

Lileane *see Lillian*

Lilla *see Lillian*

Lilli *see Lillian*

Lillia *see Lillian*

Lillian Saint; Top 100 Name; Latin; lily flower

Lil, Lila, Lileane, Lilla, Lilli, Lillia, Lilliane, Lilliann, Lillianne, Lily, Lilyann

St. Lillian (d. 852) was a married laywoman in an area of Spain controlled by the Moors. At first, she kept her faith a secret, but once she heard of Christians being persecuted, she began to openly live her faith. She was martyred.

Lilliane *see Lillian*

Lilliann *see Lillian*

Lillianne *see Lillian*

Lily *see Lillian*

Lilyann *see Lillian*

Limbania Saint

St. Limbania (d. 1294) was born in Cyprus and became a hermitess in Genoa.

Lioba Saint; German; beloved, valued

St. Lioba (d. 781) was born in Wessex, England, and became a nun at Wimbourne Monastery in Dorsetshire. She later became abbess of Bischofheim

Monastery in Mainz, Germany, a position she held for twenty-eight years.

Lise *see Elisabeth*

Lissa *see Alice*

Lizette *see Elizabeth*

Loeasa *see Louisa*

Loeasah *see Louisa*

Loeaza *see Louisa*

Loeazah *see Louisa*

Loeaze *see Louise*

Loisa *see Louisa*

Loisah *see Louisa*

Loise *see Louise*

Looesa *see Louisa*

Looesah *see Louisa*

Looise *see Louise*

Loucea *see Lucia*

Loucey *see Lucy*

Loucia *see Lucia*

Louciah *see Lucia*

Loucilah *see Lucilla*

Loucilla *see Lucilla*

Loucillah *see Lucilla*

Loucrecia *see Lucretia*

Loucrezia *see Lucretia*

Loucy *see Lucy*

Louisa Saint; form of Louise; English; famous warrior

Aloisa, Eloisa, Heloisa, Lawisa, Lawisah, Loeasa, Loeasah, Loeaza, Loeazah, Loisa, Loisah, Looesa, Looesah, Louisah, Louisetta, Louisan, Louisina, Louiza, Louizah, Louyza, Louyzah, Lovisa, Loyisa, Luisina, Luyiza

Bl. Louisa Therese de Montaignac de Chauvance (1821–1885)

was a member of a noble French family. She founded the Congregation of the Oblates of the Sacred Heart of Jesus and was devoted to helping churches and orphans and supporting priestly vocations. She spent many years of her life bedridden because of a disease that affected her legs. She was beatified in 1990 by Pope John Paul II.

Louisah *see Louisa*

Louisane *see Louise*

Louise Saint; German; famous warrior

Aloise, Eloise, Heloise, Lawis, Lawise, Leweese, Leweez, Loeaze, Loise, Looise, Louisane, Louisette, Louisiane, Louisine, Louiz, Louize, Louyz, Louyze, Lowise, Loyce, Loyise, Luis, Luise, Luiz, Luize, Lujzika, Luys, Luyse, Luyz, Luyze

St. Louise de Marillac (1591–1660) was born near Meux, France. She was educated by Dominican nuns and married Antony LeGras. After her husband died, she met St. Vincent de Paul, who would become her friend and spiritual advisor. She directed his Ladies of Charity, which later became the Daughters of Charity. She traveled throughout France, establishing several houses for the order. She is a patroness of social workers.

Louisetta *see Louisa*

Louisette *see Louise*

Louisian *see Louisa*

Louisiane *see Louise*

Louisina *see Louisa*

Louisine *see Louise*

Louiz *see Louise*

Louiza *see Louisa*

Louizah *see Louisa*

Louize *see Louise*

Loura *see Laura*

Louyz *see Louise*

Louyza *see Louisa*

Louyzah *see Louisa*

Louyze *see Louise*

Lovisa *see Louisa*

Lowise *see Louise*

Loyce *see Louise*

Loyisa *see Louisa*

Loyise *see Louise*

Lua *see Lua (boy's name)*

Luca *see Lucy*

Luce *see Lucy*

Lucea *see Lucia*

Lucetta *see Lucy*

Lucette *see Lucy*

Lucia Saint; form of Lucy; Latin; light, bringer of light

Loucea, Loucia, Louciah, Lucea, Luciana, Lucija, Lucinenne, Luciya, Lucya, Lucyah, Luzia, Luziah, Luzya, Luzyah

St. Lucia Park Huisun (d. 1839) was one of the Korean martyrs canonized by Pope John Paul II in 1984. She was hung on a cross and then beheaded.

Luciana *see Lucia*

Lucie *see Lucy*

Lucija *see Lucia*

Lucika *see Lucy*

Lucila *see Lucilla*

Lucilah *see Lucilla*

Lucilla Saint; form of Lucy; English; light, bringer of light

Loucilah, Loucilla, Loucillah, Lucila, Lucilah, Lucillah, Lucilynne, Lucyla, Lucylah, Lucylla, Lucyllah, Luisella, Lusila, Lusilah, Lusilla, Lusillah, Lusyla, Lusylah, Lusylla, Lusyllah, Luzela, Luzelah, Luzella, Luzellah, Luzilla

St. Lucilla (d. 260) was the daughter of St. Nemesius, who was a deacon. Both father and daughter were martyred for the faith during the persecutions of Emperor Valerian. She was beheaded.

Lucillah *see Lucilla*

Lucilynne *see Lucilla*

Lucina Saint; form of Lucy; Latin; light, bringer of light

St. Lucina (d. 250) ministered to other martyrs before being martyred herself.

Lucine *see Lucy*

Lucinenne *see Lucia*

Lucita *see Lucy*

Luciya *see Lucia*

Lucrece *see Lucretia*

Lucrecia *see Lucretia*

Lucreciah *see Lucretia*

Lucreecia *see Lucretia*

Lucreeciah *see Lucretia*

Lucresha *see Lucretia*

Lucreshia *see Lucretia*

Lucreshiah *see Lucretia*

Lucreshya *see Lucretia*

Lucreshyah *see Lucretia*

Lucretia Saint; Latin; rich, rewarded

Lacrecia, Loucrecia, Loucrezia, Lucrece, Lucrecia, Lucreciah, Lucreecia, Lucreeciah, Lucresha, Lucreshia, Lucreshiah, Lucreshya, Lucreshyah, Lucrezia, Lucrisha, Lucrishah, Lucrishia, Lucrishiah

St. Lucretia (d. 306) was a virgin from western Spain who was martyred in Merida.

Lucrezia see *Lucretia*

Lucrisha see *Lucretia*

Lucrishah see *Lucretia*

Lucrishia see *Lucretia*

Lucrishiah see *Lucretia*

Lucy Saint; Top 100 Name; Latin; light, bringer of light

Lleulu, Loucey, Loucy, Luca, Luce, Lucetta, Lucette, Lucie, Lucika, Lucine, Lucita, Lucye, Lucyee, Luiseach, Luzca, Luzi, Luzie, Luzy

St. Lucy, St. Lucy Filippini

St. Lucy (fourth century) was from Syracuse and was martyred. According to legend, she had vowed herself to Christ, but her mother wanted to arrange a marriage for her. To convince her mother of the wisdom of her choice, she brought her to the tomb of St. Agatha, where her mother was cured of a long-standing illness. Her mother then supported Lucy's wishes, but her rejected bridegroom turned her over to the authorities. She is a patron saint of the blind because, according to some, her eyes were put out by Emperor Diocletian as part of her torture.

Lucya see *Lucia*

Lucyah see *Lucia*

Lucye see *Lucy*

Lucyee see *Lucy*

Lucyla see *Lucilla*

Lucylah see *Lucilla*

Lucylla see *Lucilla*

Lucyllah see *Lucilla*

Ludie see *Ludmilla*

Ludka see *Ludmilla*

Ludmila see *Ludmilla*

Ludmilah see *Ludmilla*

Ludmile see *Ludmilla*

Ludmilla Saint; Slavic; loved by the people

Lidmila, Ludie, Ludka, Ludmila, Ludmilah, Ludmile, Ludmyla, Ludmylah, Ludmylla, Ludmyllah, Ludmylle, Lyuda, Lyudmila, Lyuka

St. Ludmilla (860–921) was a Slavic princess who married Duke Borivoy of Bohemia. The couple converted to Christianity, but when they attempted to convert the people of Bohemia, they were exiled for a time. When they stepped down, their son Spytihinev ruled for two years. At his death, their other son, Ratislav, took the throne. Ludmilla helped raise his son, who would become known as Good King Wenceslaus. When Wenceslaus became king, Ludmilla served as regent, but the young king's mother was jealous and had her killed. She is a patroness of Bohemia, converts, the Czech Republic, and problems with in-laws.

Ludmyla *see Ludmilla*

Ludmylah *see Ludmilla*

Ludmylla *see Ludmilla*

Ludmyllah *see Ludmilla*

Ludmylle *see Ludmilla*

Lugud *see Lua (boy's name)*

Luis *see Louise*

Luise *see Louise*

Luiseach *see Lucy*

Luisella *see Lucilla*

Luisina *see Louisa*

Luiz *see Louise*

Luize *see Louise*

Lujzika *see Louise*

Lusa *see Elizabeth*

Lusila *see Lucilla*

Lusilah *see Lucilla*

Lusilla *see Lucilla*

Lusillah *see Lucilla*

Lusyla *see Lucilla*

Lusylah *see Lucilla*

Lusylla *see Lucilla*

Lusyllah *see Lucilla*

Lutgardis Saint; German; people of the enclosure

> *Luthgard*
>
> St. Lutgardis (1182–1246) was born at Tangares in the Netherlands. She went to live at the Benedictine Convent of St. Catherine near St. Trond when she was twelve. She had no desire to enter religious life until she had a vision of Christ. She officially became a Benedictine at age twenty. She was a mystic who frequently had visions of Jesus and Mary. She spent the last thirty years of her life at a Cistercian convent at Aywieres. She suffered from blindness for eleven years before her death.

Luthfild Saint; German

> St. Luthfild (d. 850) was a hermitess in Cologne, Germany.

Luthgard *see Lutgardis*

Luyiza *see Louisa*

Luys *see Louise*

Luyse *see Louise*

Luyz *see Louise*

Luyze *see Louise*

Luzca *see Lucy*

Luzela *see Lucilla*

Luzelah *see Lucilla*

Luzella *see Lucilla*

Luzella *see Lucilla*

Luzellah *see Lucilla*

Luzi *see Lucy*

Luzia *see Lucia*

Luziah *see Lucia*

Luzie *see Lucy*

Luzilla *see Lucilla*

Luzy *see Lucy*

Luzya *see Lucia*

Luzyah *see Lucia*

Lybe Saint

> St. Lybe (d. 303) was a virgin who was martyred by being beheaded in Syria.

Lydia Saint; Arabic; strife

> *Lida, Lidia, Lydie, Lydya, Lydyah*

St. Lydia Purpuraria (first century) was born at Thyatira in Asia Minor. She was St. Paul's first convert in Philippi, and Paul stayed at her home.

Lydie *see Lydia*

Lydwina *see Lydwine*

Lydwine Saint; Netherlands; friend of the people

Liduina, Lydwina

St. Lydwine (1380–1433) was born in Schiedam, Holland. When she was sixteen, she was injured ice-skating. An abscess formed inside her body which later burst, causing her extreme suffering. She also suffered from a series of mysterious illnesses which plagued her the rest of her life. She was a mystic who experienced visions. She also received the stigmata. She offered up her sufferings for the sins of humanity. She is a patron of ice-skaters, the chronically ill, and the town of Schiedam.

Lydya *see Lydia*

Lydyah *see Lydia*

Lyuda *see Ludmilla*

Lyudmila *see Ludmilla*

Lyuka *see Ludmilla*

M

Maarya *see Martha*

Mabyn Saint; Welsh; youth

St. Mabyn (sixth century) was a daughter of King Brychan of Brecknock, Wales. The village and church of St. Mabyn are named for her.

Machael *see Michael (boy's name)*

Machas *see Michael (boy's name)*

Macia *see Matilda*

Macra Saint; Greek; she who grows

St. Macra (d. 287) was a virgin from Rheims, France, who was martyred during the persecutions of Emperor Diocletian.

Macrina Saint; form of Macra; Greek; she who grows

St. Macrina the Elder, St. Macrina the Younger

St. Macrina the Elder (d. 340) lived at Neocaesarea in Pontus. Because of Christian persecution, she fled to the shores of the Black Sea. She was the mother of St. Basil the Elder and grandmother of St. Basil the Great, St. Gregory of Nyssa, St. Peter of Sebaste, and St. Macrina the Younger. She is a patroness of widows and against poverty.

Mada *see Madeleine*

Máda *see Matilda*

Madalberta Saint; German; bright place

St. Madalberta (seventh century) was the sister of St. Aldetrudis and the daughter of Sts. Vincent Madelgarus and Waldetrudis. She became abbess of Maubeuge Abbey.

Madalyn *see Madeleine*

Maddalena *see Magdalena*

Madelain *see Madeleine*

Madelaine *see Madeleine*

Madelane *see Madeleine*

Madelayne *see Madeleine*

Madelein *see Madeleine*

Madeleine Saint; French; high tower

Lena, Mada, Madalyn, Madelain, Madelaine, Madelane, Madelayne, Madelein, Madeleyn, Madeleyne, Madelina, Madeline, Madelyn

St. Madeleine Brideau, St. Madeleine Lidoine, St. Madeleine Sophie Barat

St. Madeleine Sophie Barat (1779–1865) was born in Joigny, Burgundy, France. She joined a new order, the Society of the Sacred Heart of Jesus, and was appointed superior, a position she held for sixty-three years. During her life, she opened more than a hundred convents and schools in twelve countries.

Madeleyn *see Madeleine*

Madeleyne *see Madeleine*

Madelina *see Madeleine*

Madeline *see Madeleine*

Madelyn *see Madeleine*

Madzia *see Magdalen*

Maeree *see Mary*

Maerey *see Mary*

Maeri *see Mary*

Maerie *see Mary*

Maery *see Mary*

Mafalda *see Matilda*

Magdala *see Magdalen*

Magdalane *see Magdalen*

Magdaleen *see Magdalen*

Magdalen Saint; Hebrew, Greek; from Magdala

Madzia, Magdala, Magdalane, Magdaleen, Magdaline, Magdalyn, Magdalyne, Magdalynn, Magdelan, Magdelane, Magdelen, Magdelene, Magdelin, Magdeline, Magdelon, Magdelone, Magdelyn, Magdelyne, Magdlen, Magola, Maighdlin, Mala, Malaine, Malene

St. Maria Magdalen of Canossa (1774–1835) was the daughter of the Marquis of Canossa, who died when she was three; She managed her father's estates until she was thirty-three; then she founded the Daughters of Charity at Verona, Italy. She was canonized in 1988 by Pope John Paul II.

Magdalena Saint; Greek; woman from Magdala

Maddalena

Bl. Magdalena Catarina Morano (1847–1908) was born in Chieri, Italy. She began working at age eight after her father and older sister died. She also managed to continue her education and earned a teaching certificate. At age thirty-one, she entered the Daughters of Mary Help of Christians. She went to Sicily to help establish new schools and houses for the order. She died of cancer. She was beatified by Pope John Paul II in 1994.

Magdalene Saint, New Testament; form of Magdalen; Greek, Hebrew; from Magdala

St. Mary Magdalene (first century) was called "the Penitent." According to St. Luke, she had had seven devils removed from her. She visited Jesus when he was at dinner and wept at his feet and wiped them with her hair. She was also present at our Lord's crucifixion and at Jesus' empty tomb. She was one of the first people that Jesus appeared to after his resurrection. She later traveled to France where she lived as a hermitess.

Magdaline *see Magdalen*

Magdalyn *see Magdalen*

Magdalyne *see Magdalen*

Magdalynn *see Magdalen*

Magdelan *see Magdalen*

Magdelane *see Magdalen*

Magdelen *see Magdalen*

Magdelene *see Magdalen*

Magdelin *see Magdalen*

Magdeline *see Magdalen*

Magdelon *see Magdalen*

Magdelone *see Magdalen*

Magdelyn *see Magdalen*

Magdelyne *see Magdalen*

Magdlen *see Magdalen*

Magola *see Magdalen*

Mahaut *see Matilda*

Maie *see Maria*

Maighdlin *see Magdalen*

Maikal *see Michael (boy's name)*

Mair *see Mary*

Makael *see Michael (boy's name)*

Makal *see Michael (boy's name)*

Makayla Top 100 Name, form of Michael; Hebrew; who is like God?

Makel *see Michael (boy's name)*

Makell *see Michael (boy's name)*

Makilde *see Matilda*

Makis *see Michael (boy's name)*

Mala *see Magdalen*

Malaine *see Magdalen*

Malaney *see Melanie*

Malanie *see Melanie*

Malene *see Magdalen*

Malgerita *see Margarita*

Malgherita *see Margarita*

Malkin *see Matilda*

Mara *see Maria*

Marana Saint; Spanish; jungle

St. Marana (d. 450) grew up in Berea, Syria, the daughter of wealthy parents. She and her sister Kyra became hermitesses and lived in a small hut for forty years, living an extremely ascetic life.

Marcella Saint; Latin; martial, warlike

St. Marcella (325–410) was a Roman. She married, only to be widowed after nine months of marriage. She gave her wealth to the poor and formed a group of women devoted to living an ascetical life.

Marcella *see Marcia*

Marcellina Saint; Latin; warlike

St. Marcellina (d. 398) was born at Trier, Gaul, the sister of St. Ambrose. Her family moved to Rome when she was young. Pope Liberius consecrated her to religious life, and she dedicated herself to a life of great austerity.

Marcena *see Marcia*

Marcene *see Marcia*

Marci *see Marcia*

Marcia Saint; Latin; dedicated to Mars, the Roman god of war

Marcella, Marcena, Marcene, Marci, Marciana, Marcile, Marcsa, Marcy, Marsha, Marsia

St. Marcia (d. 284) was martyred during the persecutions of Emperor Diocletian.

Marciana Saint; Italian, Spanish; martial, warlike

St. Marciana (d. 303) was a virgin from Mauretania. She was arrested for vandalizing a statue of the goddess Diana. She was martyred by being torn apart by a bull and leopard in the amphitheater of Caesarea. She is invoked to help heal wounds.

Marcile *see Marcia*

Marcsa *see Marcia*

Marcy *see Marcia*

Marea *see Maria*

Mareah *see Maria*

Mareana *see Marina*

Mareanah *see Marina*

Mareas *see Maria*

Maree *see Marie, Mary*

Marella *see Mary*

Marelle *see Mary*

Marena *see Marina*

Marenka *see Marina*

Marga *see Margaret*

Margala *see Margaret*

Marganit *see Margaret*

Margara *see Margaret*

Margaret Saint; Greek; pearl

Marga, Margala, Marganit, Margara, Margarett, Margarette, Margaro, Margarta, Margat, Margeret, Margeretta, Margerette, Margetha, Margetta, Margiad, Margisia

St. Margaret Bourgeoys, St. Margaret Clitherow, St. Margaret Mary Alacoque, St. Margaret of Antioch, St. Margaret of Cortona, St. Margaret of England, St. Margaret of Hungary, St. Margaret of Scotland, St. Margaret the Barefooted

St. Margaret of Scotland (d. 1093) was an English princess. She and her mother traveled to Scotland to escape from a new king who had conquered their land. King Malcolm of Scotland fell in love with her, and they were soon married. She helped soften her husband's rough manners, and she served as an example of piety and devotion. She and the king were generous to the poor. They also founded many churches. She had eight children, the youngest of whom was St. David. When she was near death, she learned that her husband and her son Edward had been killed in battle.

Margareta *see Margarita*

Margarete *see Marguerite*

Margaretha *see Marguerite*

Margarett *see Margaret*

Margaretta *see Margarita*

Margarette *see Margaret*

Margarida *see Margarita*

Margarita Saint; form of Margaret; Italian, Spanish; pearl

Malgerita, Malgherita, Margareta, Margaretta, Margarida, Margaritis, Margaritta, Margeretta, Margharita, Margherita, Margo, Margrieta, Margrita, Marguita, Margurita, Marguryta, Marjarita

St. Margarita of Amelia (d. 1666) was a Benedictine abbess at St. Catherine of Amelia Abbey. She was known as a mystic.

Margarite *see Marguerite*

Margaritis *see Margarita*

Margaritta *see Margarita*

Margaro *see Margaret*

Margarta *see Margaret*

Margat *see Margaret*

Margeret *see Margaret*

Margeretta *see Margaret*

Margeretta *see Margarita*

Margerette *see Margaret*

Margerite *see Marguerite*

Margetha *see Margaret*

Margetta *see Margaret*

Marghanita *see Marguerite*

Margharita *see Margarita*

Margherita *see Margarita*

Margiad *see Margaret*

Margisia *see Margaret*

Margo *see Margarita*

Margrieta *see Margarita*

Margrita *see Margarita*

Marguareta *see Marguerite*

Marguarete *see Marguerite*

Marguaretta *see Marguerite*

Marguarette *see Marguerite*

Marguarita *see Marguerite*

Marguaritta *see Marguerite*

Marguerita *see Marguerite*

Marguerite Saint; French; pearl

Margarete, Margaretha, Margarite, Margerite, Marghanita, Marguareta, Marguarete, Marguaretta, Marguarette, Marguarita, Marguaritta, Marguerette, Marguerita, Margueritta, Margueritte, Margurite, Marguritte, Marguryt, Marguryte

St. Marguerite Bourgeoys, St. Marguerite d'Youville

St. Marguerite d'Youville (1701–1771) was born in Quebec, Canada. She married Francis d'Youville in 1722 and was widowed eight years later. She supported her three children and volunteered with the Confraternity of the Holy Family. In 1737, she and three companions founded the Sisters of Charity, also known as the Grey Nuns. She was canonized by Pope John Paul II in 1990.

Margueritta *see Marguerite*

Margueritte *see Marguerite*

Marguita *see Margarita*

Margurita *see Margarita*

Margurite *see Marguerite*

Marguritte *see Marguerite*

Marguryt *see Marguerite*

Marguryta *see Margarita*

Marguryte *see Marguerite*

Maria Saint; Top 100 Name; form of Mary; Hebrew, Italian, Spanish; bitter, sea of bitterness

Maie, Mara, Marea, Mareah, Mareas, Mariabella, Mariae, Mariesa,

Mariessa, Maritza, Marrea, Marria, Mayria, Moriah

St. Maria Crocifissa Di Rosa, St. Maria de Cerevellon, St. Maria Dominic Mazzarello, St. Maria Francesca Gallo, St. Maria Giuseppe Rossello, St. Maria Goretti, St. Maria Magdalen Dei Pazzi, St. Maria Magdalen of Canossa, St. Maria Michaela Desmaisieres

St. Maria Goretti (1890–1902) was born in Carinaldo, Ancona, Italy. In 1902, an eighteen-year-old neighbor, Alexander, attempted to rape her. When she refused to submit, he stabbed her. When she was dying in the hospital, she forgave her attacker. She later visited her attacker via a dream when he was in prison. When he awoke, he repented of his crime and reformed his life. He was present at Maria's canonization in 1950. She is a patron saint of youth, young women, purity, and victims of rape.

Mariabella *see Maria*

Mariae *see Maria*

Mariah Top 100 Name; form of Mary; Hebrew; bitter, sea of bitterness

Mariam Saint; form of Miriam and Mary; Hebrew; bitter, sea of bitterness

Mariame, Mariem, Meriame, Meryam

Bl. Mariam Thresia Chiramel Mankidiyan (1876–1926) was born in Trichur, Kerala, India.

She made a private vow of chastity at age ten. Her mother died two years later, and she devoted herself to caring for the poor and sick. She founded the Congregation of the Holy Family. She was beatified by Pope John Paul II in 2000.

Mariame *see Mariam*

Marian Saint; form of Mary Ann; Latin; combination of Mary and Ann

Marien, Mariene, Marienn, Marienne, Marrian, Marriane, Marriann, Marrianne

St. Marian (fifth century) was a monk at the monastery at Auxerre under the direction of St. Mamertinus. He served as a cowman and shepherd and was known to have a strange power over animals.

Mariana Saint; form of Marian; Spanish

Marianah, Mariena, Marienah, Marienna, Mariennah, Marriana, Marrianna, Maryana, Maryanna, Maryannah

St. Mariana, St. Mariana de Paredes

St. Mariana (1618–1645) was born at Quito, Ecuador, to noble Spanish parents. Her parents died when she was young, and she was raised by her older sister and her husband. She lived a solitary life in her sister's home and was under the direction of a Jesuit confessor. She had the gift of prophesy and was a miracle worker. She lived a most austere life, sleeping and eating little. She is known as "the Lily of Quito" because she offered herself up as a victim when the area was stricken by an earthquake and epidemic. After she did so, the epidemic subsided.

Marianah *see Mariana*

Marianna Saint; form of Marian; Spanish

Bl. Marianna Biernacka (1888–1943) gave her life in place of her pregnant daughter-in-law and was shot in Naumowicze near Grodno. She is one of the 108 Polish Martyrs of World War II. She was beatified in 1999 by Pope John Paul II.

Maricara *see Mary*

Marie Saint; form of Mary; French; bitter, sea of bitterness

Maree, Mariette, Marrie

St. Marie Claude Brard, St. Marie Croissy, St. Marie Dufour, St. Marie Hanisset, St. Marie Magdalen Desjardin, St. Marie Magdalen Fontaine, St. Marie Magdalen Postel, St. Marie Meunier, St. Marie St. Henry, St. Marie Teresa Couders

St. Marie Claude Brard (d. 1794) was a member of the Carmelite Nuns of Compiegne. The community was martyred by officials of the French revolutionary government.

Mariem *see Mariam*

Marien *see Marian*

Mariena *see Mariana*

Marienah *see Mariana*

Mariene *see Marian*

Marienn *see Marian*

Marienna *see Mariana*

Mariennah *see Mariana*

Marienne *see Marian*

Mariesa *see Maria*

Mariessa *see Maria*

Mariette *see Marie*

Marila *see Mary*

Marina Saint; Latin; sea

Mareana, Mareanah, Marena, Marenka, Marinae, Marinah, Marinka, Marni, Marrina, Marrinah, Marrinia, Maryna, Marynah, Marynna, Marynnah, Marynne, Mayne, Merina, Mirena, Myrena, Myrenah

St. Marina (eighth century) was a virgin who lived as a monk in Bithynia. She was known for her humility, meekness, and patience.

Marinae *see Marina*

Marinah *see Marina*

Marinka *see Marina*

Mariquilla *see Mary*

Mariquita *see Mary*

Maritza *see Maria*

Marjarita *see Margarita*

Marla *see Mary*

Marni *see Marina*

Marrea *see Maria*

Marrey *see Mary*

Marria *see Maria*

Marrian *see Marian*

Marriana *see Mariana*

Marriane *see Marian*

Marriann *see Marian*

Marrianna *see Mariana*

Marrianne *see Marian*

Marrie *see Marie*

Marrina *see Marina*

Marrinah *see Marina*

Marrinia *see Marina*

Marry *see Mary*

Marsha *see Marcia*

Marsia *see Marcia*

Marta Saint; form of Martha and Martina; Aramaic; lady, sorrowful

Martah, Marte, Marttaha, Merta, Merte

Bl. Marta Wolowska (1879–1942) was a member of the Sisters of the Immaculate Conception. She is one of the 108 Polish Martyrs of World War II. She was beatified in 1999 by Pope John Paul II.

Martah *see Marta*

Martaha *see Martha*

Martaina *see Martina*

Martainah *see Martina*

Martana *see Martina*

Martanah *see Martina*

Martanna *see Martina*

Martannah *see Martina*

Martayna *see Martina*

Martaynah *see Martina*

Marte *see Marta*

Marteana *see Martina*

Marteanah *see Martina*

Marteena *see Martina*

Marteina *see Martina*

Martella *see Martina*

Martelle *see Martha*

Marth *see Martha*

Martha Saint, New Testament; Aramaic; lady, sorrowful

Maarya, Martaha, Martelle, Marth, Marthan, Marthy, Marticka, Martila, Martita, Martus, Martuska, Masia

St. Martha, St. Martha Wang

St. Martha (first century) was a close friend of Jesus. He often visited the home in Bethany that she shared with her sister Mary and her brother Lazarus. According to Luke 10:38–42, she was the one who kept house and was eager to serve Jesus while Mary sat at his feet and listened. Jesus told her that she was worried about many things and that Mary had chosen the better part. When Jesus came to see them after Lazarus died, she rushed out to meet him and declared her faith in him. He then raised Lazarus from the dead (Jn 11:20–32). Nothing is known of her life after Jesus' resurrection.

Marthan *see Martha*

Marthe Saint; form of Martha; Aramaic; lady, sorrowful

Bl. Marthe Le Bouteiller (1816–1883) was born into a poor French family. She joined the Sisters of the Christian Schools of Mercy and worked in the farm, garden, and kitchen. She was beatified by Pope John Paul II in 1990.

Marthena *see Martina*

Marthina *see Martina*

Marthy *see Martha*

Martia Saint; Latin; martial, warlike

Marcia

St. Martia (first century) was martyred in Syracuse, Sicily.

Marticka *see Martha*

Martie *see Martina*

Martila *see Martha*

Martina Saint; Latin; martial, warlike

Martaina, Martainah, Martana, Martanah, Martanna, Martannah, Martayna, Martaynah, Marteana, Marteanah, Marteena, Marteina, Martella, Marthena, Marthina, Martie, Martinah, Martine, Martinia, Martine, Martino, Martosia, Martoya, Martricia, Martrina, Martyna, Martynah

St. Martina (d. 228) was the daughter of a wealthy Christian Roman consul. When her parents died, she gave away her money and devoted herself to a life of prayer. She refused to sacrifice to pagan gods and was martyred. She is a patron of nursing mothers.

Martinah *see Martina*

Martine *see Martina*

Martinia *see Martina*

Martino *see Martina*

Martita *see Martha*

Martosia *see Martina*

Martoya *see Martina*

Martricia *see Martina*

Martrina *see Martina*

Marttaha *see Marta*

Martus *see Martha*

Martuska *see Martha*

Martyna *see Martina*

Martynah *see Martina*

Marura Saint; Hebrew; bitter

St. Marura (d. 250) was martyred in Ravenna, Italy.

Mary Saint, New Testament; Hebrew; bitter, sea of bitterness

Maeree, Maerey, Maeri, Maerie, Maery, Mair, Maree, Marella, Marelle, Maricara, Marila, Mariquilla, Mariquita, Marla, Marrey, Marry, Marye, Maryla, Marynia, Mavra, Mayra, Meridel, Mirja, Morag, Moya

St. Mary, St. Mary Cleophas, St. Mary Di Rosa, St. Mary MacKillop, St. Mary Magdalen Postel, St. Mary Magdalene de Pazzi, St. Mary Magdalene, St. Mary of Egypt, St. Mary Salome, St. Mary the Consoler, St. Mary the Slave

St. Mary (first century) is the Mother of God. According to tradition, she was the daughter of Sts. Joachim and Anne and was presented at the Temple at a young age. When she was betrothed to St. Joseph, the angel Gabriel appeared to her and told her she was to be the mother of Jesus. Scripture tells of his birth in Bethlehem, the Holy Family's flight into Egypt, and the search for the child Jesus when he was twelve years old. Mary was present at the crucifixion, when she was entrusted to the care of St. John. She was present with the disciples in the days before Pentecost. According to tradition, she spent her last years on earth in Ephesus. She was then assumed into heaven, body and soul.

Maryana *see Mariana*

Maryanna *see Mariana*

Maryannah *see Mariana*

Marye *see Mary*

Maryla *see Mary*

Maryna *see Marina*

Marynah *see Marina*

Marynia *see Mary*

Marynna *see Marina*

Marynnah *see Marina*

Marynne *see Marina*

Masia *see Martha*

Mat *see Matilda*

Matelda *see Matilda*

Mathild *see Matilda*

Mathilda *see Matilda*

Mathilde *see Matilda*

Mathildis *see Matilda*

Matilda Saint; German, English; powerful battler

Macia, Máda, Mafalda, Mahaut, Makilde, Malkin, Mat, Matelda, Matilly, Mathild, Mathilda, Mathilde, Mathidis, Matilde, Mattilda, Mattylda, Matusha, Matyld, Matylda, Matyldah, Matylde, Metild, Metilda, Metildah, Metilde, Metyld, Metylda, Metyldah, Metylde, Tilda, Tilde, Tylda

St. Matilda (895–968) was the daughter of Theodoric, a Saxon count. She grew up at the Monastery of Erfurt, where her grandmother served as abbess. She was married in 913 to Henry "the Fowler" who later became King of Germany. Queen Matilda worked for the sick, poor, and prisoners. Her children included Otto, who became emperor, Henry, who served as duke of Bavaria, and St. Bruno, archbishop of Cologne.

Matilde Saint; form of Matilda; German; powerful battler

Bl. Matilde del Sagrado Corazon Tellez Robles (1841–1902) was born in Robledillo de la Vera, Cáceres, Spain. She founded the Congregation of the Daughters of Mary, Mother of the Church. She was beatified by Pope John Paul II in 2004.

Matilly *see Matilda*

Matrona Saint; Latin; mother

St. Matrona (d. 300) was burned to death at Paphlagonia during the persecutions of Emperor Diocletian.

Mattilda *see Matilda*

Mattylda *see Matilda*

Matusha *see Matilda*

Matyld *see Matilda*

Matylda *see Matilda*

Matyldah *see Matilda*

Matylde *see Matilda*

Maura Saint; Gaelic; dark

Maurah, Maure, Mauree, Maurette, Mauri, Mauricette,

Maurie, Maurita, Mauritia, Maury, Maurya, Mora

St. Maura, St. Maura Troyes

St. Maura (fourth century) was a Scottish princess who was murdered while on pilgrimage to Rome.

Maurah *see Maura*

Maure *see Maura*

Mauree *see Maura*

Maurette *see Maura*

Mauri *see Maura*

Mauricette *see Maura*

Maurie *see Maura*

Maurita *see Maura*

Mauritia *see Maura*

Maury *see Maura*

Maurya *see Maura*

Mavra *see Mary*

Maxellendis Saint; Latin

St. Maxellendis (d. 670) was from Caudry, near Cambrai, France. She fled an intended marriage to Harduin of Solesmes because she wanted to become a nun. He chased her down and killed her with his sword. He was immediately struck blind, and his sight was only returned when he begged for forgiveness at her coffin three years later.

Maxentia Saint; Latin; greatest

St. Maxentia of Beauvais (date unknown) was from either Ireland or Scotland. She went to France in order to escape marriage to a pagan. She became a hermitess, but her intended husband followed her and beheaded her at Pont-Sainte-Maxence.

Maxima Saint; Latin; greatest

St. Maxima (d. 302) was martyred in Lisbon, Portugal, during the persecutions of Emperor Diocletian.

Mayne *see Marina*

Mayra *see Mary*

Mayria *see Maria*

Me *see Melanie*

Mechtildis Saint; German; mighty in battle

St. Mechtildis, St. Mechtildis of Helfta

St. Mechtildis (d. 1160) was the daughter of Count Berthold of Andechs and his wife, Sophia. They had founded a monastery, and Mechtildis went to live there when she was five years old. She later served as abbess. In 1153, she was asked by the bishop of Augsburg to become abbess of Edelstetten. She was known as a mystic and miracle worker.

Medana Saint; Celtic; St. Medana

St. Medana (eighth century) was an Irish virgin who traveled to Galloway, Scotland.

Meikil *see Michael (boy's name)*

Meikyl *see Michael (boy's name)*

Meila *see Melanie (boy's name)*

Meilani *see Melanie (boy's name)*

Meilin *see Melanie (boy's name)*

Mekil *see Michael (boy's name)*

Mekyl *see Michael (boy's name)*

Melaine *see Melanie (boy's name)*

Melainie *see Melanie (boy's name)*

Melane *see Melanie (boy's name)*

Melanee *see Melanie (boy's name)*

Melangell Saint; Welsh; sweet angel

Monacella

St. Melangell (d. 590), also known as Monacella, was an Irish or Scottish princess who went to Wales to live as a hermitess. She founded a community of women, whom she served as abbess for thirty-seven years.

Melania Saint; form of Melanie; Greek; having black skin

St. Melania, St. Melania the Elder

St. Melania (383–439) was born to a wealthy Christian Roman family. She was married to Valerius Pinianus, but after two of their children died in infancy, they agreed to live a celibate life and devote themselves to God. After her father died, she inherited his wealth and used it to found monasteries in Egypt, Syria, and Palestine. Melania, her husband, and her mother made a pilgrimage to the Holy Land and settled in Jerusalem. After her husband and mother died, she became a hermitess, attracted followers, and started a convent where she served as abbess.

Melanie *see Melanie (boy's name)*

Melanka *see Melanie (boy's name)*

Melayne *see Melanie (boy's name)*

Melaysa *see Melanie (boy's name)*

Melenee *see Melanie (boy's name)*

Meleney *see Melanie (boy's name)*

Meleni *see Melanie (boy's name)*

Melenia *see Melanie (boy's name)*

Melenie *see Melanie (boy's name)*

Meleny *see Melanie (boy's name)*

Melinda *see Melitina (boy's name)*

Melitina Saint; Latin; honey

Melinda

St. Melitina (second century) was a virgin who was martyred in Thrace during the reign of Emperor Antoninus Pius.

Mella Saint; Greek; black, dark

St. Mella (d. 780) was the mother of Sts. Cannech and Tigernach. She lived in Connaught, Ireland. After her husband's death, she became the abbess of Doire Melle, Leitrim.

Mellanee *see Melanie (boy's name)*

Mellaney *see Melanie (boy's name)*

Mellani *see Melanie (boy's name)*

Mellanie *see Melanie (boy's name)*

Mellany *see Melanie (boy's name)*

Mellenee *see Melanie (boy's name)*

Melleney *see Melanie (boy's name)*

Melleni *see Melanie (boy's name)*

Mellenie *see Melanie (boy's name)*

Melleny *see Melanie (boy's name)*

Mellony *see Melanie (boy's name)*

Melya *see Melanie (boy's name)*

Menefrida Saint; Welsh

St. Menefrida (fifth century) was a member of the family of King Brychan of Brecknock. She is the patron saint of Tredresick, in Cornwall, England.

Menna Saint; Greek; month

St. Menna (d. 395) was a virgin from Lorraine, France, who was related to Sts. Eucherius and Elaptius.

Menodora Saint; Greek; gift of Mene, the moon goddess

St. Menodora (d. 306) and her sisters, Metrodora and Nymphodora, were from Bithynia, in Asia Minor. The three were martyred for refusing to worship pagan gods. Menodora was beaten to death.

Mercedes Saint; Latin, Spanish; reward, payment, merciful

Bl. Mercedes of Jesus Molina (1828–1886) was born in Baba, Ecuador. She became a nun and founded the Institute of the Sisters of Saint Mary Ann of Jesus. She was beatified by Pope John Paul II in 1985.

Merewenna Saint; English

Merwenna, Merwinna

St. Merewenna (d. 970) served as abbess of Romsey, in Hampshire, England.

Meriame *see Mariam*

Meridel *see Mary*

Merina *see Marina*

Merta *see Marta*

Merte *see Marta*

Merwenna *see Merewenna*

Merwinna *see Merewenna*

Meryam *see Mariam*

Messalina Saint; Latin; she who has an insatiable appetite

St. Messalina (d. 251) received the veil from St. Felician, the bishop of Foligno. She refused to sacrifice to pagan gods and was beaten to death.

Metild *see Matilda*

Metilda *see Matilda*

Metildah *see Matilda*

Metilde *see Matilda*

Metyld *see Matilda*

Metylda *see Matilda*

Metyldah *see Matilda*

Metylde *see Matilda*

Mhichael *see Michael (boy's name)*

Micaela *see Michael (boy's name)*

Micah *see Michael (boy's name)*

Micahel *see Michael (boy's name)*

Mical *see Michael (boy's name)*

Micha *see Michael (boy's name)*

Michael *see Michael (boy's name)*

Michaela *see Michael (boy's name)*

Michaele *see Michael (boy's name)*

Michaell *see Michael (boy's name)*

Michak *see Michal (boy's name)*

Michal *see Michal (boy's name)*

Michalek *see Michal (boy's name)*

Michalel *see Michael (boy's name)*

Michall *see Michal (boy's name)*

Michau *see Michael (boy's name)*

Michelet *see Michael (boy's name)*

Michella *see Michael (boy's name)*

Michelle *see Michael (boy's name)*

Michiel *see Michael (boy's name)*

Micho *see Michael (boy's name)*

Michoel *see Michael (boy's name)*

Mieczyslawa Saint; Polish

Bl. Mieczyslawa Kowalska (1902–1941) was a Polish sister who was killed at Dzialdowo.

She is one of the 108 Polish Martyrs of World War II and was beatified by Pope John Paul II in 1999.

Miekil *see Michael (boy's name)*

Miekyl *see Michael (boy's name)*

Mihail *see Michael (boy's name)*

Mihalje *see Michael (boy's name)*

Mihkel *see Michael (boy's name)*

Mil *see Mildred*

Milburga Saint; German; pleasant city

St. Milburga (d. 715) was the daughter of a king of Mercia and sister of Sts. Mildred of Thanet and Mildgytha. She served as abbess of Wenlock Abbey in Salop, Shropshire, England. She was known to have the power of levitation.

Milda *see Mildred*

Mildgytha Saint; English; St. Mildgytha

St. Mildgytha (d. 676) was the daughter of Merewald and St. Ermenburga. Her sisters were Sts. Milburga and Mildred. She became abbess of a Northumbrian convent.

Mildred Saint; English; gentle counselor

Mil, Milda, Mildrene, Mildrid, Milly, Mylda, Myldred, Myldreda

St. Mildred (d. 700) was the daughter of Merewald and St. Ermenburga. A young man wanted to marry her, but she entered Minster Monastery, where she later served as abbess. She was known for her compassion for the poor.

Mildrene *see Mildred*

Mildrid *see Mildred*

Milly *see Mildred*

Milya *see Melanie*

Mirena *see Marina*

Mirja *see Mary*

Misha *see Michael (boy's name)*

Modesta Saint; Latin; modest

Modestah, Modestia

St. Modesta (d. 680) was a niece of St. Modoald, who appointed her abbess of Oehren Convent at Trier.

Modestah *see Modesta*

Modestia *see Modesta*

Modesty Virtue; Latin; modest

Modwenna Saint; Celtic

Monenna

St. Modwenna (seventh century), also known as Monenna, founded Burton-on-Trent Abbey in Staffordshire, England. She was known as a miracle worker.

Molly Top 100 Name; form of Mary; bitter, sea of bitterness

Mona *see Monica*

Monacella *see Melangell*

Monca *see Monica*

Moneeca *see Monica*

Monegundis Saint; German; good woman

St. Monegundis (d. 570) was born in Chartres, France. She was married, but after her daughters died in childhood, her husband gave her permission to leave and become a hermitess. She attracted followers, which led to the establishment of St. Pierre-le-Puellier convent in Tours.

Monenna *see Modwenna*

Monennaa Saint; Celtic

St. Monennaa (d. 518) was a nun at Sliabh Cuillin in Ireland, where she served as abbess. She was known for her austere life.

Monessa Saint; German; protection

St. Monessa (d. 456) was the daughter of an Irish chieftain. She was converted by St. Patrick and died immediately after being baptized.

Monia *see Monica*

Monic *see Monica*

Monica Saint; Greek, Latin; solitary, advisor

Mona, Monca, Moneeca, Monia, Monic, Monicah, Monice, Monicia, Monicka, Monika, Monique, Monise, Monn, Monnica, Monnicah, Monnicka, Monnie, Monnyca, Monya, Monyca, Monycah. Monycka

St. Monica (d. 387) was married to a violent pagan official in North Africa. Her mother-in-law also lived with them and made Monica's life difficult. Yet, through her patient example, she was able to convert both her husband and his mother to the faith. Her two daughters entered religious life, but her son Augustine was lazy

and lived a dissolute life. She prayed for him for seventeen years before he converted. He went on to become one of the greatest saints of the Church. She is a patron saint of wives and abuse victims.

Monicah *see Monica*

Monice *see Monica*

Monicia *see Monica*

Monicka *see Monica*

Monika *see Monica*

Monique *see Monica*

Monise *see Monica*

Monn *see Monica*

Monnica *see Monica*

Monnicah *see Monica*

Monnicka *see Monica*

Monnie *see Monica*

Monnyca *see Monica*

Monya *see Monica*

Monyca *see Monica*

Monycah *see Monica*

Monycka *see Monica*

Mora *see Maura*

Morag *see Mary*

Morgan *see Maughold (boy's name)*

Moriah *see Maria*

Morwenna Saint; Latin, Welsh; maiden, white seas

St. Morwenna (fifth century) was a Cornish virgin. Several places in that region were named for her.

Moya *see Mary*

Mura Saint; village

Muran

St. Mura McFeredach (d. 645), also known as Muran, was abbot of Fahan in County Derry, Ireland. He was a follower of St. Columba.

Muran *see Mura*

Musa Saint; Greek; inspiration

St. Musa (sixth century) was a virgin child from Rome who had visions and ecstasies.

Mylda *see Mildred*

Myldred *see Mildred*

Myldreda *see Mildred*

Myrena *see Marina*

Myrenah *see Marina*

Myrope Saint

St. Myrope (d. 251) and a Roman soldier, St. Ammianus, were arrested in Chios, Greece, for recovering the remains of St. Isidore after he was martyred. She was scourged and died in prison.

Myshell *see Michael (boy's name)*

N

Nacia *see Natalia*

Namadia Saint

St. Namadia (sixth or seventh century) was the widow of St. Calminius. After his death, she entered a convent and lived at Marsat.

Naoma *see Naomi*

Naome *see Naomi*

Naomee *see Naomi*

Naomey *see Naomi*

Naomi Old Testament; Top 100 Name; Hebrew; pleasant, beautiful

Naoma, Naome, Naomee, Naomey, Naomia, Naomiah, Neoma, Neomah, Neomee, Neomi, Neomie, Neomy, Nioma, Noami, Noemi

Naomi in the Bible was the mother-in-law of Ruth. Naomi encouraged Ruth to marry Boaz, and they give birth to Obed, who became the grandfather of King David. Her story is told in the book of Ruth.

Naomia *see Naomi*

Naomiah *see Naomi*

Narcessa *see Narcisa*

Narcisa Saint; Greek; daffodil

Narcessa, Narcissa, Narcissah, Narcisse, Narcyssa, Narkissa

St. Narcisa de Jesus Martillo Moran (1832–1869) was from Nobol, Ecuador. An orphan, she worked as a seamstress to help support her family. She didn't enter a religious order but consecrated her virginity and spent her life in prayer and penance, practicing various mortifications. She was a mystic who experienced ecstasies. She was canonized by Pope Benedict XVI in 2008.

Narcissa *see Narcisa*

Narcissah *see Narcisa*

Narcisse *see Narcisa*

Narcyssa *see Narcisa*

Narkissa *see Narcisa*

Natala *see Natalia*

Natalah *see Natalia*

Natalea *see Natalia*

Nataleah *see Natalia*

Natalka *see Natalia*

Natali *see Natalia*

Natalia Saint; Top 100 Name; form of Natalie; Russian; born on Christmas day

Nacia, Natala, Natalah, Natalea, Nataleah, Natalka, Natali, Nataliah, Natalie, Nataliia, Natalija, Nataliya, Nataliyah, Natalja, Natalka, Natalla, Natallah, Natallea, Natallia, Natalya, Natelea, Nateleah, Natelia, Nateliah, Nathalia, Natila, Natilea, Natileah, Natilia, Natileah, Natlea, Natleah, Natlia, Natliah, Nattalea, Nattaleah, Nattaleya, Nattaleyah, Nattalia, Nattaliah, Nattlea, Nattleah, Nattlia, Nattliah, Natylea, Natyleah, Natylia, Natyliah

St. Natalia (d. 311) was a Christian woman married to Adrian, a non-Christian Nicomedian imperial officer. Adrian was so impressed by Christians who were being persecuted by Emperor Diocletian that he converted himself and was arrested. Natalia visited him in prison and cared for other prisoners as well. When her husband was sentenced to death and was no longer allowed visitors, she dressed as a boy and bribed her way in to see him. After he was martyred, she moved to Argyropolis where she lived out her days alone.

Nataliah *see Natalia*

Natalie *see Natalia*

Nataliia *see Natalia*

Natalija *see Natalia*

Nataliya *see Natalia*

Nataliyah *see Natalia*

Natalja *see Natalia*

Natalka *see Natalia*

Natalla *see Natalia*

Natallah *see Natalia*

Natallea *see Natalia*

Natallia *see Natalia*

Natalya *see Natalia*

Natelea *see Natalia*

Nateleah *see Natalia*

Natelia *see Natalia*

Nateliah *see Natalia*

Nathalia *see Natalia*

Natila *see Natalia*

Natilea *see Natalia*

Natileah *see Natalia*

Natilia *see Natalia*

Natiliah *see Natalia*

Natlea *see Natalia*

Natleah *see Natalia*

Natlia *see Natalia*

Natliah *see Natalia*

Nattalea *see Natalia*

Nattaleah *see Natalia*

Nattaleya *see Natalia*

Nattaleyah *see Natalia*

Nattalia *see Natalia*

Nattaliah *see Natalia*

Nattlea *see Natalia*

Nattleah *see Natalia*

Nattlia *see Natalia*

Nattliah *see Natalia*

Natylea *see Natalia*

Natyleah *see Natalia*

Natylia *see Natalia*

Natyliah *see Natalia*

Nazaria Saint; Spanish; dedicated to God

> Bl. Nazaria Ignacia of St. Teresa of Jesus March Mesa (1889–1943) was born in Madrid, Spain. Her family moved to Mexico, and she joined the Little Sisters of the Abandoned Elderly. She worked in Bolivia. Later, she helped found the Congregation of the Missionary Sisters of the Papal Crusade. She was beatified by Pope John Paul II in 1992.

Neoma *see Naomi*

Neomah *see Naomi*

Neomee *see Naomi*

Neomi *see Naomi*

Neomie *see Naomi*

Neomy *see Naomi*

Nicarete Saint; Greek; gift of virtue

> St. Nicarete (fifth century) was from Nicomedia. She moved to Constantinople where she devoted herself to caring for the poor. She cared for St. John Chrysostom when he was ill.

Nichele *see Nicholas (boy's name)*

Nichola *see Nicholas (boy's name)*

Nichole *see Nicholas (boy's name)*

Nicholl *see Nicholas (boy's name)*

Nina Saint; Spanish; girl

> *Ninacska, Ninah, Ninetta, Ninita, Ninja, Ninna, Nino, Ninosca, Ninoshka, Nyna*

St. Nina (300–332) was born in Cappadocia. It is possible that she was a slave who traveled to Georgia. She was known for her piety and evangelization. She healed Queen Nana of a disease and, in doing so, converted the queen. King Mirian also became a Christian and declared it to be the official religion of the area. She spent the rest of her life preaching in Georgia.

Ninacska *see Nina*

Ninah *see Nina*

Ninetta *see Nina*

Ninita *see Nina*

Ninja *see Nina*

Ninna *see Nina*

Ninosca *see Nina*

Ninoshka *see Nina*

Nioma *see Naomi*

Noami *see Naomi*

Noemi *see Naomi*

Non Saint; Welsh; ninth

> *Nonna, Nonnita*

> St. Non (sixth century), also known as Nonnita or Nonna, was the mother of St. David of Wales. She was a noble born in Dyfed, Wales, who married a local chieftain. She later traveled to Cornwall and died in Brittany.

Nonna *see Non*

Nonnita *see Non*

Notburga Saint; German; protected beauty

> St. Notburga (1265–1313) was born to a peasant family in Rattenburg. She served as a

servant of Count Henry of that area but was dismissed by his wife for giving food to the poor. She then became a servant of a farmer. After the count's wife died, he rehired Notburga, and she was his housekeeper. She was known for her care of the poor and as a miracle worker.

Nouna Saint

St. Nouna (fourth century) was the wife of St. Gregory of Nazianzus. She brought that saint to the faith. She was also the mother of Sts. Gregory Nazianzus the Younger, Caesarius of Nazianzus, and Gorgonius.

Noyala Saint

St. Noyala (date unknown) was a virgin who was from Britain and beheaded at Beignan.

Nunciata see *Annunciata*

Nunzia see *Annunciata*

Nyna see *Nina*

O

Obdulia Saint; Latin; she who takes away sadness and pain

St. Obdulia (date unknown) was a nun who is associated with Toledo, Spain. Details of her life have been lost.

Octavia see *Octavian (boy's name)*

Oda Saint; Scandinavian; rich

St. Oda (680–726) was born blind in Scotland. She was cured at the tomb of St. Lambert in Leige. She then returned

home to Scotland, vowing to dedicate her life to God. Her father wanted her to marry, so she fled, eventually making her home in the Netherlands.

Odeelia see *Odilia*

Odeleya see *Odilia*

Odelia see *Odilia*

Odeliah see *Odilia*

Odelina see *Odilia*

Odelinah see *Odilia*

Odelinda see *Odilia*

Odeline see *Odilia*

Odellah see *Odilia*

Odelyn see *Odilia*

Odetta see *Odilia*

Odette see *Odilia*

Odiel see *Odilia*

Odila see *Odilia*

Odilah see *Odilia*

Odile see *Odilia*

Odilia Saint; Greek, Hebrew; ode, melodic, I will praise God

Adilia, Odeelia, Odeleya, Odelia, Odeliah, Odelina, Odelinah, Odelinda, Odeline, Odellah, Odelyn, Odetta, Odette, Odiel, Odila, Odilah, Odile, Odille, Odyla, Odylah, Odyle, Odyll, Odylla, Odyllah, Odylle

St. Odilia (660–720) was born blind and disabled to the duke of Alsace. Because of her disability, they sent her to live with a peasant family, and then she was put into a convent at age twelve. When she was baptized, her sight was returned to her. Her brother then wanted her back in order to have her be married, but she fled the convent. She later founded Hohenburg Abbey in Alsace. After she died, she reportedly returned briefly to tell her fellow sisters about heaven and to take Communion one last time. She is invoked against eye diseases and is a patron saint of Alsace, France.

Odille *see Odilia*

Odyla *see Odilia*

Odylah *see Odilia*

Odyle *see Odilia*

Odyll *see Odilia*

Odylla *see Odilia*

Odyllah *see Odilia*

Odylle *see Odilia*

Offa Saint; English

St. Offa (d. 1070) was abbess of the Benedictine Convent of St. Peter's near Benevento, Italy.

Ohanna *see Joanna*

Olga Saint; Scandinavian; holy

Olgah, Olgy, Olia, Olivia, Ollya, Olva

St. Olga (890–969) was married to Prince Igor I of Russia. She was a cruel woman who scalded her husband's murderers to death and killed thousands of their followers by burying some alive and burning others. She reformed after she was baptized and asked for missionaries to be sent to Kiev. The efforts did not succeed, but her grandson, St. Vladimir,

would bring Christianity to the region.

Olgah *see Olga*

Olgy *see Olga*

Olia *see Olga*

Oliva Saint; form of Olivia, Olga; Latin, English; olive tree, holy

Olivia

St. Oliva (d. 138) was martyred in the last year of the reign of Emperor Hadrian.

Olivia *see Oliva, Olga*

Ollya *see Olga*

Olva *see Olga*

Olympia Saint; Greek; heavenly

Bl. Olympia Bida (1903–1952) was born at Tsebliv, Lviv District, Ukraine. She joined the Congregation of the Sisters of Saint Joseph. She worked as a teacher and with the sick and aged. She was a convent superior in Kheriv. She was arrested and exiled to a labor camp where she organized other sisters into prayer groups. She was beatified by Pope John Paul II in 2001.

Olympias Saint; Greek; heavenly

Olympia

St. Olympias (368–408) was born into a wealthy family in Constantinople but was orphaned when she was young. She married Nebridius, who was prefect of Constantinople. After his death, she dedicated herself to a life of good works. She was a consecrated deaconess. She built a hospital and orphanage and looked after some monks that had been exiled. Her support of St. John Chrysostom led to her being exiled herself, and she spent the rest of her life at Nicomedia.

Ondria *see Andrea (boy's name)*

Opportuna Saint; Latin; opportune

St. Opportuna (d. 770) was born near Hyesmes, Normandy. She became a nun at Monasteriolum Convent, where she later served as abbess. She was the sister of St. Chrodegang, bishop of Seez.

Oralia *see Aurelia*

Oralie *see Aurelia*

Orosia *see Eurosia*

Orsala *see Ursula*

Osanna *see Osmanna*

Osburga Saint; English

St. Osburga (d. 1018) was abbess of a convent at Coventry, England.

Osith *see Osyth*

Osmanna Saint; Latin; we pray

Osanna

St. Osmanna (d. 700), also known as Osanna, was a Benedictine nun in Jouarre, France.

Osyth Saint; Spanish; divinely strong

Osith, Sytha

St. Osyth (d. 700) was born in England, the daughter of a chieftain of the Mercians and Wilburga. She wanted to become a nun but was forced to marry King Sighere of Essex. After giving birth to a son, he gave her permission to enter

a convent. He donated land, where she established a monastery and served as abbess. She was martyred by Danish raiders.

P

Palatias Saint; Latin

St. Palatias (d. 302) was a noblewoman from Ancona, Italy, who was brought to the faith by her slave, Laurentia. The two were arrested and martyred at Fermo during the persecutions of Emperor Diocletian.

Paliki *see Paula*

Panacea Saint; Greek, Latin; remedy for all diseases

Panassia, Panexia

St. Panacea (1378–1383) was from Quarona, near Novara, Italy. She was martyred by her stepmother while she was praying.

Panassia *see Panacea*

Pandwyna Saint; Celtic; all gifts

Pandonio

St. Pandwyna (tenth century) was from Scotland or Ireland. A church in Cambridgeshire, England, is named for her.

Panexia *see Panacea*

Paola Saint; form of Paula; Italian; small

Paoli, Paolina, Paoline, Paula

St. Paola Elisabetta Cerioli, St. Paola Frassinetti

St. Paola Frassinetti (1809–1882), also known as Paula, was

born in Genoa, Italy. She helped her brother, who was a parish priest, by teaching and caring for poor children. Other women soon joined her in her efforts, which led to the founding of the Sisters of St. Dorothy. She was canonized by Pope John Paul II in 1984.

Paoli *see Paola*

Paolina *see Paola*

Paoline *see Paola*

Paras *see Paris (boy's name)*

Paree *see Paris (boy's name)*

Pares *see Paris (boy's name)*

Parese *see Paris (boy's name)*

Parie *see Paris (boy's name)*

Paris *see Paris (boy's name)*

Parys *see Paris (boy's name)*

Paschasia Saint; Hebrew, Latin; relating to Easter

St. Paschasia (second century) was martyred in Dijon, France.

Pasha *see Pelagia*

Patience Virtue; English; patient

Patientia Saint; Latin; patient

St. Patientia (d. 240) and her husband, St. Orentius, were martyred. They are traditionally considered the parents of St. Lawrence of Rome.

Patresa *see Patricia*

Patrica *see Patricia*

Patricah *see Patricia*

Patrice *see Patricia*

Patriceia *see Patricia*

Patrichea *see Patricia*

Patricia Saint; Latin; noblewoman

Patresa, Patrica, Patricah, Patrice, Patriceia, Patrichea, Patriciah, Patriciana, Patricianna, Patricja, Patricka, Patrickia, Patrika, Patrisha, Patrisia, Patrissa, Patryka

St. Patricia (d. 665) was from a noble family in Constantinople. She left her family in order to escape an arranged marriage. She traveled to Rome and became a nun. After her father's death, she returned home and gave away all her property to the poor. She was shipwrecked on her way to Jerusalem and died on the island of Megarides.

Patriciah *see Patricia*

Patriciana *see Patricia*

Patricianna *see Patricia*

Patricja *see Patricia*

Patricka *see Patricia*

Patrickia *see Patricia*

Patrika *see Patricia*

Patrisha *see Patricia*

Patrisia *see Patricia*

Patrissa *see Patricia*

Patryka *see Patricia*

Paula Saint; Latin; small

Paliki, Paulane, Paulann, Pauletta, Paulette, Pauli, Paulla, Pavia

St. Paula, St. Paula Frasinetti, St. Paula Montal Fornes de San Jose de Calasanz

St. Paula (347–404) was born to a noble Roman family. She married Toxotius and had five children. After her husband's death, she devoted herself to helping the poor. She became friends with St. Jerome and helped him in his work while he was in Rome. She traveled with him to the Holy Land and settled in Bethlehem where she helped build a hospice, monastery, and convent. She is a patron saint of widows.

Paulane *see Paula*

Paulann *see Paula*

Paule *see Pauline*

Pauleen *see Pauline*

Paulene *see Pauline*

Pauletta *see Paula*

Paulette *see Paula*

Pauli *see Paula*

Paulien *see Pauline*

Paulin *see Pauline*

Pauline Saint; form of Paula; French; small

Paule, Pauleen, Paulene, Paulien, Paulin, Paulyn, Paulyne, Paulynn, Polline, Pouline

St. Pauline of the Agonizing Heart of Jesus (1865–1942) was born Amabile Lucia Visintainer to a poor family in Trent, Italy. When she was ten, her family moved to Brazil in search of a better life. In her teens, she taught children the faith and visited the sick. In 1890, she and her friend Virginia Rosa Nicolodi began the Congregation of the Little Sisters of the Immaculate Conception, which she served as superior. She served the sick and aged and worked to spread the religious community. She spent the last twenty years of her life at the congregation's motherhouse, serving her fellow sisters and praying. She died of complications of diabetes. She was canonized by Pope John Paul II in 2002.

Paulla *see Paula*

Paulyn *see Pauline*

Paulyne *see Pauline*

Paulynn *see Pauline*

Pavia *see Paula*

Pedrine *see Petronilla*

Pega Saint; English

St. Pega (673–719) was the sister of St. Guthlac. She lived as a hermitess on the western edge of Peterborough Fen, not far from where he lived as a hermit. When she attended her brother's funeral, she cured a blind man from Wisbech. She died while on pilgrimage to Rome.

Pelage *see Pelagia*

Pelageia *see Pelagia*

Pelagia Saint; Greek; sea

Pasha, Pelage, Pelageia, Pelagiah, Pelagie, Pelagya, Pelagyah, Pelasha, Pelga, Pelgia, Pellagia

St. Pelagia, St. Pelagia of Antioch, St. Pelagia of Tarsus, St. Pelagia the Penitent

St. Pelagia of Antioch (d. 311) was a virgin from Rome. She was fifteen when soldiers came to arrest her. Rather than submit to imprisonment and possible rape, she jumped from the roof and died.

Pelagiah *see Pelagia*

Pelagie *see Pelagia*

Pelagya *see Pelagia*

Pelagyah *see Pelagia*

Pelasha *see Pelagia*

Pelga *see Pelagia*

Pelgia *see Pelagia*

Pellagia *see Pelagia*

Peronel *see Petronilla*

Peronella *see Petronilla*

Peronelle *see Petronilla*

Perpetua Saint; Spanish, Latin; perpetual

St. Perpetua (d. 203) was a noblewoman martyred with her maid and friend, St. Felicity, in Carthage, North Africa. They were killed by beheading.

Perseveranda Saint; Latin; she who perserveres

Pezaine

St. Perseveranda (d. 726), also known as Pezaine, was from Spain. She traveled with her sisters to Poitiers, France, where she founded a convent. A group of pirates attacked the community, and she died while attempting to escape.

Peternella *see Petronilla*

Petrenela *see Petronilla*

Petrina *see Petronilla*

Petrine *see Petronilla*

Petrisse *see Petronilla*

Petrona *see Petronilla*

Petronela *see Petronilla*

Petronella *see Petronilla*

Petronelle *see Petronilla*

Petronilla Saint; Greek, Latin; small rock

Pedrine, Peronel, Peronella, Peronelle, Peternella, Petrenela, Petrina, Petrine, Petrisse, Petrona, Petronela, Petronella, Petronelle, Petronille, Pierretta

St. Petronilla (first century) was long thought to be the biological daughter of St. Peter the Apostle. Now, it is thought that she may have been related or served in his household. St. Peter cured her of palsy. She is listed as a martyr, and her remains are in St. Peter's Cathedral in Rome, Italy.

Petronille *see Petronilla*

Pezaine *see Perseveranda*

Phaebe *see Pheobe*

Pharaildis Saint

Vareide, Varelde, Veerle, Verylde

St. Pharaildis (650–740) was a Flemish virgin who was married against her will and beaten by her husband for not consummating the marriage. She was known for her nighttime visits to churches and as a miracle worker. She is a patron saint of childhood diseases, difficult marriages, victims of abuse, and widows.

Pheabe *see Pheobe*

Phebea *see Pheobe*

Pheebea *see Pheobe*

Pheebee *see Pheobe*

Pheeby *see Pheobe*

Pheibee *see Pheobe*

Pheibey *see Pheobe*

Pheobi *see Phoebe*

Pheoby *see Phoebe*

Pheybee *see Pheobe*

Pheybey *see Pheobe*

Phiala Saint; Celtic

St. Phiala (fifth century) was the sister of St. Fingar. She was martyred in Cornwall, England, by pagans.

Philipine *see Philip (boy's name)*

Philippa *see Philip (boy's name)*

Philippina *see Philip (boy's name)*

Philippine *see Philip (boy's name)*

Philomena Saint; Greek; loved one

Filimena, Filomena, Filumena, Philoméne, Philomina, Philomine, Phylomina, Phylomine, Phylomyna, Phylomyne

St. Philomena (date unknown) was a martyr in the early Church. Her relics were found in 1802 in the catacomb of St. Priscilla on the Via Saleria in Rome, Italy, and were enshrined in a chapel in Mugnano. Many miracles began to be reported at that site. She is a patron saint of many things, including children, desperate causes, infants, poor people, test takers, and against infertility, mental illness, and sickness.

Philoméne *see Philomena*

Philomina *see Philomena*

Philomine *see Philomena*

Phoebe Saint, New Testament; Greek; shining

Phaebe, Pheabe, Phebea, Pheebea, Pheebee, Pheeby, Pheibee, Pheibey, Pheobi, Pheoby, Pheybee, Pheybey, Phoebey

St. Pheobe (first century) is mentioned in St. Paul's Letter to the Romans (Rom 16:1). She may have been the person who brought it to the Romans. It is possible that she was a benefactor of Paul. She is listed as a "diakonos," which can be translated as either a deaconess or a servant. The debate continues as to which one she was.

Phoebey *see Pheobe*

Photina Saint, New Testament; Greek; light

Fotina, Photine, Photyna, Photyne

St. Photina (first century) has traditionally been considered the Samaritan woman at the well that Jesus spoke to in John 4. Various traditions exist as to the remainder of her life, but they agree that she was ultimately martyred for the faith.

Photine *see Photina*

Photyna *see Photina*

Photyne *see Photina*

Phylomina *see Philomena*

Phylomine *see Philomena*

Phylomyna *see Philomena*

Phylomyne *see Philomena*

Pia Saint; Italian; devout

Piah, Pya, Pyah

St. Pia (second century) was martyred in Nicomedia.

Piah *see Pia*

Piedad Saint; Spanish; piety, devotion

Bl. Piedad de la Cruz Ortiz Real (1842–1916) was born in Bocairente, Valencia, Spain. She founded the Congregation of Salesian Sisters of the Sacred Heart of Jesus. She was beatified by Pope John Paul II in 2004.

Pierina Saint; form of Petra; French; rock

Bl. Pierina Morosini (1931–1957) was born into a poor family in Fiobbio di Albani, Italy. She began work in a fabric factory when she was fifteen. She had made a private vow of chastity and wanted to become a nun, but she instead stayed at home and helped her mother take care of her younger siblings. She died while resisting a rape attempt. She was beatified by Pope John Paul II in 1987.

Pierretta *see Petronilla*

Pina Saint; Hebrew, Italian; God will add

Bl. Pina Suriano (1915–1950) was born in Sicily. In 1922, she made her First Holy Communion and Confirmation. She also joined the Catholic Action group. She would eventually become the president of her parish chapter of Catholic Action. In 1948, she began the Association of the "Daughters of Mary," which she served as president until her death. She wanted to enter religious life, but her family opposed her. She took a private vow of chastity. In 1940, her parents finally granted their permission, but she was only able to stay for eight days before failing a medical exam. She died of a heart attack at the age of thirty-five. She was beatified by Pope John Paul II in 2004.

Piri *see Priscilla*

Placida *see Placide*

Placide Saint; Latin; serene

Placida

Bl. Placide Viel (1815–1877) was born in Normandy, France, as Eulalie Victorie Jacqueline Viel. She joined the Sisters of the Christians Schools and ultimately became Mother General of that order. She held that position for thirty years. She also helped provide relief during the Franco-Prussian War.

Placidia Saint; Latin; serene

St. Placidia (d. 460) was a virgin from Verona, Italy, known for her holiness.

Platonides Saint; Greek; broad shouldered

St. Platonides (d. 308) was the founder of a convent in Nisibis, Mesopotamia. She was martyred in Ascalon.

Plautilla Saint; Latin

St. Plautilla (d. 67) was a Roman widow who, tradition holds, was baptized by St. Peter and witnessed the martyrdom of St. Paul.

Polline *see Pauline*

Polyxena Saint; Greek; hospitable

St. Polyxena (first century) was a virgin who was a disciple of the apostles. She died in Spain.

Pomponia *see Pomponius (boy's name)*

Pomposa Saint; Latin; lavish, magnificent

St. Pomposa (d. 835) was a nun from Córdoba who was beheaded by Muslims.

Potamioena Saint

Potamon

St. Potamioena the Elder, St. Potamioena the Younger

St. Potamioena the Elder (d. 202) was a young virgin who was martyred by being boiled to death in pitch. Her example led to the conversion of St. Basilides of Alexandria.

Pouline *see Pauline*

Praxedes Saint; Greek; active

Praxides

St. Praxedes (d. 164) was the daughter of a Roman senator and St. Pudens. Her sister was St. Prudentiana. She was a virgin who cared for Christians who were being persecuted by Emperor Marcus Antoninus.

Praxides *see Praxedes*

Precila *see Priscilla*

Precilla *see Priscilla*

Prema *see Prima*

Prescilla *see Priscilla*

Presilla *see Priscilla*

Pressilia *see Priscilla*

Prima Saint; Latin; first

Prema, Primah, Primalia, Primara, Primaria, Primariah, Primetta, Primina, Priminia, Pryma, Prymarya, Prymaryah

St. Prima (d. 304) was martyred in Carthage.

Primah *see Prima*

Primalia *see Prima*

Primara *see Prima*

Primaria *see Prima*

Primariah *see Prima*

Primetta *see Prima*

Primina *see Prima*

Priminia *see Prima*

Primitiva Saint; form of Prima; Latin; first

St. Primitiva (first century) was martyred in Rome during the early days of the Church.

Principia Saint; Latin; head, manager

St. Principia (d. 420) was a Roman virgin who was a follower of St. Marcella.

Prisca Saint; form of Priscilla; Latin; ancient

St. Prisca (third century) was a virgin who was martyred in Rome.

Priscela *see Priscilla*

Priscella *see Priscilla*

Priscill *see Priscilla*

Priscilla Saint, New Testament; Latin; ancient

Cilla, Piri, Precila, Precilla, Prescilla, Presilla, Pressilia, Prisca, Priscela, Priscella, Priscill, Priscille, Priscilla, Priscillie, Prisella, Prisila, Prisilla, Prissila, Prissilla

St. Priscilla (first century) and her husband Acquila are mentioned by St. Paul in Romans 16:3–4. St. Paul stayed with the couple in Corinth and may have converted them. They followed him to Ephesus. When they returned to Rome, their home was used as a church. They were martyred.

Priscille *see Priscilla*

Priscillia *see Priscilla*

Priscillian Saint; Latin; ancient
St. Priscillian (d. 362) was martyred during the persecutions of Emperor Julian the Apostate.

Priscillie *see Priscilla*

Prisella *see Priscilla*

Prisila *see Priscilla*

Prisilla *see Priscilla*

Prissila *see Priscilla*

Prissilla *see Priscilla*

Prudence Virtue; Latin; cautious, discreet

Pryma *see Prima*

Prymarya *see Prima*

Prymaryah *see Prima*

Publia Saint; Latin; from the village
St. Publia (d. 362) was a widow from Antioch. She was arrested by Emperor Julian the Apostate after he heard her singing Psalm 115 in public. She was sentenced to die, but the emperor died in battle and the sentence was not carried out.

Puicheria Saint; Latin; pretty
St. Puicheria Augusta (399–453) was born in Constantinople, the daughter of Emperor Arcadius and Empress Aelia Eudoxia. She served as regent for her younger brother, Theodosius II. After his death, she became empress. She married General Marcian after he agreed to respect her vow of virginity. She fought against the heresies of Eutychianism and Nestorianism. She also built many hospitals and churches and the School of Constantinople.

Pusinna Saint; Latin; child
St. Pusinna (sixth century) was a virgin who formed a religious community with six other sisters in Champagne, France.

Pya *see Pia*

Pyah *see Pia*

Q

Quinta *see Cointha*

Quintah *see Cointha*

Quintana *see Quentin (boy's name)*

Quiteria Saint; Latin, French; tranquil
St. Quiteria (fifth century) was the daughter of a Galacian prince. When her father wanted her to abandon the Christian faith and marry, she fled. Her father's men hunted her down and beheaded her.

R

Rachail *see Rachel*

Racheal *see Rachel*

Rachel Old Testament; Top 100 Name; Hebrew; female sheep

Rachail, Racheal, Rachela, Rachelann, Racquel, Rahel, Raiche, Raichel, Raichele, Raichell, Raichelle, Raishel, Raishele, Raquel, Raquelle, Ruchel, Ruchelle

Rachel in the Bible was the much-loved second wife of Jacob. She was the mother of Joseph and Benjamin. Her story is told in the book of Genesis.

Rachela *see Rachel*

Rachelann *see Rachel*

Rachilidis Saint

St. Rachilidis (d. 946) was a Benedictine hermitess who lived near the Monastery of St. Gall, Switzerland.

Racquel *see Rachel*

Rada *see Rose*

Radegund Saint; German

St. Radegund (d. 1300) was a serving girl in Wellenburg Castle, near Augsburg, Germany. She was known for her charity and goodness. She was killed by a pack of wolves.

Radegunde Saint; German

St. Radegunde (d. 586) was the daughter of a king of Thuringia. She was taken captive by King Clotaire I of Neustria, who later married her. She spent her time serving the poor and sick and accepting the cruel behavior of her husband until he murdered her brother. At that time, she left and became a nun at Saix. She founded the double Monastery of the Holy Cross at Poitiers.

Raegina *see Regina*

Rafaela Saint; form of Raphael *(boy's name)*; Spanish; God has healed

Rafaelah, Rafaelia, Rafaeliah, Rafaella, Rafaellah, Raffaela, Raffaelah, Raffaella, Raffaellah, Rafia, Rafiah

Bl. Rafaela Ybarra de Villalongo (1843–1900) was from Bilbao, Spain. She was a widow who founded the Institute of the Sisters of Guardian Angels. She was beatified in 1984 by Pope John Paul II.

Rafaelah *see Rafaela*

Rafaelia *see Rafaela*

Rafaeliah *see Rafaela*

Rafaella *see Rafaela*

Rafaellah *see Rafaela*

Raffaela *see Rafaela*

Raffaelah *see Rafaela*

Raffaella *see Rafaela*

Raffaellah *see Rafaela*

Rafia *see Rafaela*

Rafiah *see Rafaela*

Rafka *see Rafqa*

Rafqa Saint; Lebanese; wide

Rafka

St. Rafqa Pietra Choboq Ar-Rayes (1832–1914) was born in Lebanon. Her mother died when she was young, and she never got along well with her stepmother. She worked as a maid until she entered the Marian Order of the Immaculate Conception at the age of twenty-one. In 1871, that order merged with another one. She left and joined the Order of

St. Anthony of the Maronites. In 1885, her health began to weaken, and she was left blind and crippled. She spent thirty years in pain but continued to pray and work. She was canonized by Pope John Paul II in 2001.

Rahel *see Rachel*

Raiche *see Rachel*

Raichel *see Rachel*

Raichele *see Rachel*

Raichell *see Rachel*

Raichelle *see Rachel*

Raina *see Regina*

Raishel *see Rachel*

Raishele *see Rachel*

Raquel *see Rachel*

Raquelle *see Rachel*

Rasia *see Rose*

Rasine *see Rose*

Raven *see Ravennus (boy's name)*

Ravenne *see Ravennus (boy's name)*

Raziela *see Rosalia*

Reda *see Rita*

Reeta *see Rita*

Reetah *see Rita*

Reetta *see Rita*

Reettah *see Rita*

Rega *see Regina*

Regeana *see Regina*

Regeanah *see Regina*

Regeena *see Regina*

Regeenah *see Regina*

Regena *see Regina*

Regennia *see Regina*

Regiena *see Regina*

Regina Saint; Latin; queen

Raegina, Raina, Rega, Regeana, Regeanah, Regeena, Regeenah, Regena, Regennia, Regiena, Reginah, Reginia, Regyna, Regynah

St. Regina (third century) was born, in Autun, France. Her mother died when Regina was born, and her father sent her to a Christian nurse. She was engaged to a proconsul named Olybrius, but when she refused to give up her faith, she was beheaded.

Reginah *see Regina*

Reginia *see Regina*

Regula Saint; Latin; small king

St. Regula (d. 286) and her brother St. Felix fled to Switzerland in an attempt to avoid the persecutions of Coemperor Maximian. They were captured and beheaded near Zürich. They are patron saints of Zürich.

Regyna *see Regina*

Regynah *see Regina*

Reida *see Rita*

Reinelde *see Reineldis*

Reineldis Saint; German

Reinelde

St. Reineldis (630–700) was the daughter of Count Witgar and St. Arnalberga. She made a pilgrimage to the Holy Land and then devoted herself to a life of caring for others. She was martyred by barbarian invaders in Belgium.

Relindis Saint; German

Renule

St. Relindis (d. 750), also known as Renule, was a daughter of Count Adelard. The count built an abbey at Maaseik for his daughters. St. Herlindis served as abbess until her death, at which point her sister, St. Relindis, took over that role.

Renee *see Rene (boy's name)*

Renule *see Relindis*

Reparata Saint; Latin; renewed

St. Reparata (third century) was a twenty-year-old virgin from Caesarea who was martyred during the persecutions of Emperor Trajanus Decius. She survived being thrown in a furnace and was beheaded.

Restituta Saint; Latin; she who returns to God

St. Restituta (d. 304) was martyred in Carthage during the persecution of Emperor Diocletian.

Rhais *see Irais*

Rheeta *see Rita*

Rheta *see Rita*

Rhian *see Rhian (boy's name)*

Rhipsime Saint

Ripsima, Arsema

St. Rhipsime (d. 290) was a member of a community of virgins in Rome. Emperor Diocletian was enamored with her because of her beauty, and she was forced to flee. She settled in Valarshapat where she attracted the notice of King Tiridates. When she refused his offer, she was burned to death. All the other virgins who had fled with her, except one, were also martyred. They are known as the first martyrs of Armenia.

Rhita *see Rita*

Rhyan *see Rhian (boy's name)*

Richardis Saint; form of Richard; German, English; rich and powerful ruler

St. Richardis (840–895) was the daughter of the count of Alsace. She wed Emperor Charles the Fat. They lived together for nineteen years until she was falsely accused of infidelity with a bishop. She endured an ordeal of fire to prove her innocence, but she still went to go live as a nun, first at Hohenburg in Germany and later at Andlau Abbey where she died.

Richrudis Saint

Rictrude

St. Richtrudis (614–688) was born into a noble family in Gascony, France. She married St. Adalbald and gave birth to four children, all of whom went on to become saints. After her husband was murdered, she rejected the pressure to remarry and instead became a nun at Marchiennes, Flanders, Belgium, a monastery which she had founded. She served as abbess there for forty years.

Rictrude *see Richtrudis*

Rida *see Rita*

Riel *see Gabriel (boy's name)*

Riet *see Rita*

Ripsima *see Rhipsime*

Rita Saint; short form of Margarita; Spanish; pearl

Reda, Reeta, Reetah, Reetta, Reettah, Reida, Rheeta, Rheta, Rhita, Rida, Riet, Ritah, Ritamae, Ritamarie, Ritta, Rittah, Ryta, Rytah, Rytta, Ryttah

St. Rita, St. Rita Amada de Jesus

St. Rita (1381–1457) was born in Spoleto, Italy. She wanted to enter a convent, but her parents arranged a marriage for her to an ill-tempered man who treated her poorly. They were married for nearly twenty years. He was stabbed by an enemy and repented of his cruelty before he died. After her two sons also died, St. Rita devoted her life to prayer, fasting, penance, and good works. She joined the Augustinian nuns at Cascia. She was deeply devoted to the Passion of Christ, and one day she was pierced by a thorn on a crucifix. The wound never healed. She is the patroness of impossible cases.

Ritah *see Rita*

Ritamae *see Rita*

Ritamarie *see Rita*

Ritta *see Rita*

Rittah *see Rita*

Rois *see Rose*

Roma *see Romana*

Romana Saint; Latin; from Rome, Italy

Roma

St. Romana (d. 324) was a virgin hermitess who lived near the Tiber River in Rome, Italy.

Romlua Saint

St. Romlua (sixth century) was a companion of St. Redempta. The two lived as hermitesses near the Church of Mary Major in Rome. Romlua was paralyzed for the last years of her life.

Ronica *see Veronica*

Ronika *see Veronica*

Rooth *see Ruth*

Rosa Saint; form of Rose; Spanish, Italian; rose

Rosae, Rosah, Rosula

St. Rosa Venerini (1656–1728) was born in Viterbo, Italy. After her fiancé died, she entered a convent, but she left to care for her widowed mother. With the help of a Jesuit priest, she discerned that she would better serve God as a teacher than as a contemplative nun. She opened a free school for girls. She was asked to take over the training of teachers for the diocese of Montefiascone and organized many schools in Italy. She also founded a sodality of women who became known as the Venerini Sisters. She was canonized by Pope Benedict XVI in 2006.

Rosae *see Rosa*

Rosah *see Rosa*

Rosalea *see Rosalia*

Rosaleah *see Rosalia*

Rosalee *see Rosalie*

Rosaleen *see Rosalie*

Rosalia Saint; English; fair rose

Raziela, Rosalea, Rosaleah, Rosaliah, Rosalla, Rosallah, Roseleah, Roselia, Roseliah, Rosezella, Rozalea, Rozaleah, Rozalia, Rozaliah, Rozlea, Rozleah, Rozlia, Rozliah

St. Rosalia (d. 1160) was born in Palermo, Sicily, and was a descendant of Charlemagne. She lived as a hermitess in a cave and later moved to Mount Pellagrino where she also lived secluded from the world. She is a patron saint of Palermo.

Rosaliah *see Rosalia*

Rosalie Saint; English; fair rose

Rosalee, Rosaleen

Bl. Rosalie Rendu (1786–1856) was born in Confort, Gex, France. The French Revolution broke out when she was only three years old. Her family hid priests who were ministering to Catholics. She began to work with the Daughters of Charity at a local hospital. She then joined the order and worked in the slums for fifty-four years, serving and teaching the sick and poor. She suffered from blindness the last two years of her life. She was beatified by Pope John Paul II in 2003.

Rosalla *see Rosalia*

Rosallah *see Rosalia*

Rose Saint; Latin; rose

Rada, Rasia, Rasine, Rois, Rosea, Rosetta, Rosina, Rosita, Roza, Roze, Rozelle

St. Rose of Lima, St. Rose Philippine Duchesne

St. Rose of Lima (1586–1617) was born in Lima, Peru. She was born with the name Isabel but was so beautiful that everyone soon started calling her Rose. She took that name as her Confirmation name. She worked to hide her beauty and refused when her parents wanted her to marry. Her father allowed her to live by herself in their home. She became a Dominican tertiary and took a vow of perpetual virginity. She dedicated herself to fasting, prayer, and good works. She was the first Catholic from the Americas to be declared a saint.

Rosea *see Rose*

Roseleah *see Rosalia*

Roselia *see Rosalia*

Roseliah *see Rosalia*

Rosetta *see Rose*

Rosezella *see Rosalia*

Rosina *see Rose*

Rosinda *see Roswinda*

Rosita *see Rose*

Rosula *see Rosa*

Roswinda Saint; German; famous warrior

Rosinda

St. Roswinda (eighth century) was the sister of St. Ottilia. She lived as a nun at the Benedictine Monastery of Hohenburg in Alsace, France.

Roza *see Rose*

Rozalea *see Rosalia*

Rozaleah *see Rosalia*

Rozalia *see Rosalia*

Rozaliah *see Rosalia*

Roze *see Rose*

Rozelle *see Rose*

Rozlea *see Rosalia*

Rozleah *see Rosalia*

Rozlia *see Rosalia*

Rozliah *see Rosalia*

Ruchel *see Rachel*

Ruchelle *see Rachel*

Rufa *see Rufina*

Rufeana *see Rufina*

Rufeanah *see Rufina*

Rufeane *see Rufina*

Rufeena *see Rufina*

Rufeenah *see Rufina*

Rufeene *see Rufina*

Rufeine *see Rufina*

Ruffina *see Rufina*

Ruffine *see Rufina*

Rufina Saint; Latin; redhead

> *Rufa, Rufeana, Rufeanah, Rufeane, Rufeena, Rufeenah, Rufeene, Rufeine, Ruffina, Ruffine, Rufinah, Rufine, Rufinia, Rufiniah, Rufynia, Rufyniah, Rufynya, Rufynyah, Ruphina, Ruphinah, Ruphinia, Ruphiniah*

St. Rufina (d. 287) and St. Justa were two virgins from Seville, Spain, who sold earthenware. They refused to sell their goods for use in pagan ceremonies. When pagans attacked their business, they responded by destroying an image of a goddess. They were arrested and sentenced to be stretched on the rack and to have their sides torn with hooks. Rufina was also strangled.

Rufinah *see Rufina*

Rufine *see Rufina*

Rufinia *see Rufina*

Rufiniah *see Rufina*

Rufynia *see Rufina*

Rufyniah *see Rufina*

Rufynya *see Rufina*

Rufynyah *see Rufina*

Ruphina *see Rufina*

Ruphinah *see Rufina*

Ruphinia *see Rufina*

Ruphiniah *see Rufina*

Rusticula Saint; Latin; country dweller

St. Rusticula (d. 632) was raised by nuns in a convent at Arles, France. She chose to remain there and became a nun. She was named the abbess at the age of eighteen and was known for her meekness, obedience, and prudence. She often spent all night in prayer and once experienced a vision of St. Lucy.

Ruth Old Testament; Hebrew; friendship

> *Rooth, Rutha, Ruthe, Ruthia, Ruthina, Ruthine*

Ruth in the Bible was a widow who followed her mother-in-law, Naomi, to Bethlehem. With Naomi's encouragement, she married Boaz and gave birth to Obed. Obed became the father of Jesse, who was the father of King David. Ruth is an ancestor of Jesus and is mentioned in the genealogy of the Gospel of Matthew.

Rutha *see Ruth*

Ruthe *see Ruth*

Ruthia *see Ruth*

Ruthina *see Ruth*

Ruthine *see Ruth*

Ryan *see Ryan (boy's name)*

Ryta *see Rita*

Rytah *see Rita*

Rytta *see Rita*

Ryttah *see Rita*

S

Sabella *see Isabel*

Sabina Saint; form of Sabine; Latin; member of a tribe in ancient Italy

St. Sabina (second century) was a wealthy Roman who was converted to Christianity by her Syrian servant Serapia. Sabina was martyred during the persecutions of Emperor Hadrian.

Sabine *see Savina*

Sadie *see Sarah*

Saethryth Saint; English

Sethrida

St. Saethryth (d. 660), also known as Sethrida, was the stepdaughter of King Anna of East Anglia. She became abbess of a convent in Gaul.

Sahra *see Sarah*

Salaberga Saint; German; she who defends the sacrifice

St. Salaberga (d. 665) was cured of blindness by St. Eustace of Lisieux when she was young. Her first husband died after only two months of marriage. She and her second husband, St. Blandinus, had five children, including Sts. Baldwin and Anstrude, before agreeing to separate and enter religious life. She entered a convent at Poulangey and later founded the convent of St. John the Baptist at Laon.

Sallustia Saint; Latin

St. Sallustia (d. 251) was a convert to Christianity and the wife of St. Caerealis. She was martyred during the persecutions of Emperor Decius.

Salome Saint, New Testament; Hebrew; peaceful

St. Salome (first century), also known as Mary Salome, was a follower of Jesus. She was the wife of Zebedee and the mother of the apostles James and John. She was present at the crucifixion and was one of the women who went to anoint the body on Sunday morning and were greeted by an angel.

Salve *see Salvius (boy's name)*

Samthan *see Samthann*

Samthann Saint; Celtic; dove of the Church

Samthan

St. Samthann (d. 739) was a maiden from Ulster, Ireland, who was a ward of the Irish King Cridan. The king arranged a marriage for her against her wishes. Her future husband saw her bathed in a heavenly light as she slept the night before their wedding and again after their wedding. Both the king and her husband agreed to allow her to keep her vow of virginity. She became abbess of Clonbroney in County Longford.

Sancha *see Sanctan (boy's name)*

Sancia *see Sanctan (boy's name)*

Sancja Saint; Polish; sacred

Santia

Bl. Sancja Szymkowiak (1910–1942) was born into a well-to-do family in Mozdzanów, Poland. She was well educated and studied literature and languages at the University of Poznan. She was a member of the Sodality of Mary and was known for her generosity. She spent a year with the Congregation of the Oblate Sisters of the Sacred Heart and then entered the Congregation of the Daughters of Our Lady of Sorrows. She always strove to do God's will. She was put under house arrest during World War II and served the German soldiers. She died of tuberculosis. She was beatified by Pope John Paul II in 2002.

Sancta *see Sanctan (boy's name)*

Sanctina *see Sanctan (boy's name)*

Sandila Saint

St. Sandila (d. 855) was martyred by the Moors in Cordoba, Spain.

Santia *see Sancja*

Sara *see Sarah*

Sarae *see Sarah*

Sarah Old Testament; Top 100 Name; Hebrew; princess

Sadie, Sahra, Sara, Sarae, Saraha, Sarai, Sari, Sorcha, Zara, Zarah, Zareh, Zarra, Zarrah

Sarah in scripture was the wife of Abraham and the mother of Isaac. Her name was originally Sarai, but God changed it to Sarah in Genesis 17:15. She suffered from infertility, but God kept his promise to give Abraham an heir, and at an advanced age she gave birth to Isaac.

Saraha *see Sarah*

Sarai *see Sarah*

Sareana *see Serena*

Sareanah *see Serena*

Sareena *see Serena*

Sareenah *see Serena*

Sari *see Sarah*

Sarmata *see Sarmata (boy's name)*

Sarmatas *see Sarmata*

Saryna *see Serena*

Saturnina *see Saturninus (boy's name)*

Sava *see Savina*

Savean *see Savina*

Saveana *see Savina*

Saveanah *see Savina*

Saveane *see Savina*

Saveen *see Savina*

Saveena *see Savina*

Saveenah *see Savina*

Saveene *see Savina*

Savina Saint; Latin; member of a tribe in ancient Italy

Sabina, Sabine, Sava, Savean, Saveana, Saveanah, Saveane, Saveen, Saveena, Saveenah, Saveene, Savinah, Savine

St. Savina (d. 311) was from Milan. She gave aid to Christians who were being held prisoner and also helped bury them after they were martyred. She died while praying at the tomb of Sts. Nabor and Felix.

Savinah *see Savina*

Savine *see Savina*

Scholastica Saint; Latin; orator

St. Scholastica (d. 543) was the twin sister of St. Benedict of Nursia. She founded a monastery at Plombariola. St. Benedict served as their spiritual director. The two remained close all of their lives and frequently conversed about spiritual matters. She is a patron saint of nuns and convulsive children and is invoked against rainstorms.

Seana *see Sina*

Sebastia *see Sebastiana*

Sebastiana form of Sebastian (boy's name); Greek, Latin; venerable, revered

Bastienne, Sebastia, Sebastianah, Sebastianna, Sebastiannah, Sebastyanna, Sebastyna

Sebastianah *see Sebastiana*

Sebastianna *see Sebastiana*

Sebastiannah *see Sebastiana*

Sebastyanna *see Sebastiana*

Sebastyna *see Sebastiana*

Secunda Saint; Latin; second

St. Secunda (d. 304) was martyred in North Africa during the persecutions of Emperor Diocletian.

Secundilla Saint; Latin; second

St. Secundilla (d. 305) was martyred at Porto Romano during the persecutions of Emperor Diocletian.

Secundina Saint; Latin; second

St. Secundina (d. 250) was flogged to death in Rome during the persecutions of Emperor Trajanus Decius.

Sedna *see Sedna (boy's name)*

Sefa *see Josephine*

Selena *see Celine*

Selestin *see Celestine (boy's name)*

Selestine *see Celestine (boy's name)*

Selestyn *see Celestine (boy's name)*

Senobe *see Zenobia*

Senobia *see Zenobia*

Senorina Saint; Latin; aged

St. Senorina (d. 982) was placed into the care of her aunt who was an abbess at a convent in Venaria. She stayed at the convent, where she later served as abbess. She moved the convent to Basta in Portugal.

Senovia *see Zenobia*

Serafeena *see Seraphina*

Serafina *see Seraphina*

Seraina *see Serena*

Serana *see Serena*

Seraphe *see Seraphina*

Serapheena *see Seraphina*

Seraphia *see Serapia*

Seraphina Saint; Hebrew, Latin; fiery, burning

Fina, Serafeena, Serafina, Seraphe, Serapheena, Seraphita, Seraphyna, Seraphynah, Serapia

St. Seraphina (d. 1253) was born into a poor family at San Geminiano, Tuscany, Italy. Despite her poverty, she was always generous with others. She lived as a hermit in her home, living under the Benedictine Rule even though she never joined an order. She was stricken with a painful illness that made movement difficult, and she lived in a state of constant suffering.

Seraphita *see Seraphina*

Seraphyna *see Seraphina*

Seraphynah *see Seraphina*

Serapia Saint; Hebrew, Latin; ardent, fiery

Seraphia

St. Serapia (d. 119) was a servant of St. Sabina and led her to conversion to Christianity. Both she and Sabina were beheaded during the persecutions of Emperor Hadrian.

Sereana *see Serena*

Sereanah *see Serena*

Sereina *see Serena*

Serena Saint; form of Serenus (boy's name); Latin; peaceful

Cerena, Sareana, Sareanah, Sareena, Sareenah, Saryna, Seraina, Serana, Sereana, Sereanah, Sereina, Serenah, Serene, Serenea, Serenia, Serenity, Serenna, Serreana, Serrena, Serrenna, Seryna

Serenah *see Serena*

Serene *see Serena*

Serenea *see Serena*

Serenia *see Serena*

Serenity *see Serena*

Serenna *see Serena*

Serreana *see Serena*

Serrena *see Serena*

Serrenna *see Serena*

Seryna *see Serena*

Sethrida *see Saethryth*

Severa Saint; Spanish; severe

St. Severa (d. 680) was abbess of St. Gemma Convent at Villeneuve.

Sexburga Saint; German; shelter of the victorious one

St. Sexburga (d. 699) was a daughter of the king of East Anglia. Married to King Erconbert of Kent, she had four children, two of whom became saints. She was known for her piety and humility. After her husband's death, she entered a convent at Minster-in-Sheppey, later transferring to a convent at Ely founded by her sister, St. Etheldreda.

Shauna *see John (boy's name)*

Shawna *see John (boy's name)*

Sheila *see Cecilia*

Silvia *see Sylvia*

Simone *see Simeon (boy's name)*

Sina Saint; form of Jane; Gaelic; God is gracious

Seana

St. Sina (fourth century) was martyred in Egypt during the persecutions of Emperor Diocletian.

Sinia *see Cinia*

Siniah *see Cinia*

Sinnia *see Cinia*

Sinniah *see Cinia*

Siri *see Cyrilla*

Sirilla *see Cyrilla*

Sisiliya *see Cecilia*

Sofeea *see Sofia*

Sofeeia *see Sofia*

Sofia Saint; Top 100 Name; form of Sophia; Greek; wise

Sofeea, Sofeeia, Soficita, Sofija, Sofiya, Sofka, Sofya, Sophia, Sophie, Sophy, Wisdom, Zofya

St. Sofia (second century) was the mother of Faith, Hope, and Charity, three virgins who were martyred for the faith during the reign of Emperor Hadrian. She died three days later while praying at their tomb.

Soficita *see Sofia*

Sofija *see Sofia*

Sofiya *see Sofia*

Sofka *see Sofia*

Sofya *see Sofia*

Solange Saint; French; dignified

St. Solange (d. 880) was born into a poor family near Bourges, France. She made a vow of virginity at the age of seven, but her beauty attracted the son of the count of Poitiers. He kidnapped her, but she jumped from the horse she was being carried away on. He then followed her and beheaded her.

Sophia *see Sofia*

Sophie *see Sofia*

Sophy *see Sofia*

Soprata Saint; Latin; high

St. Soprata (seventh century) was a daughter of Emperor Maurice of Constantinople.

Sorcha *see Sarah*

Sosana *see Susanna*

Soteris Saint; Greek; savior

St. Soteris (d. 304) was a beautiful young virgin from Rome. She was arrested for the faith and struck repeatedly in the face. She was martyred by being beheaded.

Stacy *see Anastasia*

Stasa *see Anastasia*

Staska *see Anastasia*

Stefanie form of Stephen (boy's name); crowned

Stephanie form of Stephen (boy's name); crowned

Sueann *see Susanna*

Suesanna *see Susanna*

Susan *see Susanna*

Susana *see Susanna*

Susane *see Susanna*

Susanka *see Susanna*

Susanna Saint; Hebrew; lily

Sosana, Sueann, Suesanna, Susan, Susana, Susane, Susanka, Susannah, Suzanne

St. Susanna (fourth century) was the daughter of Gabinius, a priest, and niece of Pope Caius.

She refused to marry Emperor Diocletian's son-in-law. In addition, she converted two of the court officers that Diocletian sent to her. She was ultimately beheaded.

Susannah *see Susanna*

Suzanne *see Susanna*

Sylvette *see Sylvia*

Sylvia Saint; Latin; forest

Silvia, Sylvette, Sylvie

St. Sylvia (515–592) was from Sicily and married St. Gordian. She was the mother of St. Gregory the Great. After her husband died, she lived a quasi-monastic life near the Church of St. Sava.

Sylvie *see Sylvia*

Symphorosa Saint; Greek, Latin; carry, useful, good

St. Symphorosa (d. 284) was martyred in Italy during the persecutions of Emperor Diocletian.

Syncletica Saint

St. Syncletica of Alexandra (fourth century) was the daughter of an emperor of Rome. She disguised herself as a man and went to the desert where she lived as a hermit. Her sex was discovered upon her death.

Sytha *see Osyth*

T

Tabatha *see Tabitha*

Tabetha *see Tabitha*

Tabiatha *see Tabitha*

Tabita *see Tabitha*

Tabitha Saint, New Testament; Greek, Aramaic; gazelle

Tabatha, Tabetha, Tabiatha, Tabita, Tabithia, Tabotha, Tabtha

St. Tabitha (first century), also known as Dorcas, was a widow from Joppa mentioned in Acts 9:36–42 as one "completely occupied with good deeds and almsgiving." She was raised from the dead by St. Peter.

Tabithia *see Tabitha*

Tabotha *see Tabitha*

Tabtha *see Tabitha*

Tacjana *see Tatiana*

Tacla *see Thecla*

Taedra *see Theodora*

Taitiann *see Tatiana*

Taitianna *see Tatiana*

Talida Saint; German; noble

St. Talida (fourth century) was abbess of a group of convents in Egypt.

Tanca Saint

St. Tanca (d. 637) was born in Troyes, France, and was murdered while defending her virginity.

Taraghta *see Attracta*

Tarba *see Tarbula*

Tarbo *see Tarbula*

Tarbula Saint; Arabic; square, block

Tarba, Tarbo

St. Tarbula (d. 345), also known as Tarba or Tarbo, was a consecrated virgin who was accused of causing the anti-Christian

Persian King Shapur to become ill. She was martyred by being sawed in half.

Taresa *see Teresa*

Taressa *see Teresa*

Tarissa *see Teresa*

Tarsicia Saint; Latin; born in Tarsus

St. Tarsicia (d. 600) was a granddaughter of King Clotaire I of France. She lived as a hermit near Rodez, France.

Tarsilla Saint; Latin

Tharsilla

St. Tarsilla (d. 581) was an aunt of Pope St. Gregory the Great. She and her sister Emiliana lived together in Rome and were known for their austerity and prayers.

Tarsykia Saint; Ukranian

Bl. Tarsykia Matskiv (1919–1944) was born in Khodoriv, Lviv District, Ukraine. She entered the Sister Servants of Mary Immaculate and gave her life for the conversion of Russia and the good of her church. She answered the door when Bolsheviks came to the convent and was shot without warning. She was beatified in 2001 by Pope John Paul II.

Tasia *see Anastasia*

Tasya *see Anastasia*

Tatania *see Tatiana*

Tataniah *see Tatiana*

Tatanya *see Tatiana*

Tatanyah *see Tatiana*

Tateana *see Tatiana*

Tateanna *see Tatiana*

Tateonna *see Tatiana*

Tateyana *see Tatiana*

Tati *see Tatiana*

Tatia *see Tatiana*

Tatiana Saint; Slavic; fairy queen

Tacjana, Taitiann, Taitianna, Tatania, Tataniah, Tatanya, Tatanyah, Tateana, Tateanna, Tateonna, Tateyana, Tati, Tatia, Tatianah, Tatiania, Tatianiah, Tatiayana, Tatie, Tatihana, Tationna, Tatiyona, Tatiyonna, Tatjana, Tiatiana

St. Tatiana (third century) was raised Christian. She was arrested and asked to make a sacrifice to Apollo. She refused, was blinded and beaten, and then given to a hungry lion, but the lion would not touch her. As a result, she was beheaded.

Tatianah *see Tatiana*

Tatiania *see Tatiana*

Tatianiah *see Tatiana*

Tatiayana *see Tatiana*

Tatie *see Tatiana*

Tatihana *see Tatiana*

Tationna *see Tatiana*

Tatiyona *see Tatiana*

Tatiyonna *see Tatiana*

Tatjana *see Tatiana*

Tecla *see Thecla*

Tedra *see Thodora*

Telchildis *see Theodichildis*

Teodora *see Theodora*

Teodosia *see Theodosia*

Teodosiah *see Theodosia*

Teodosya *see Theodosia*

Teodosyah *see Theodosia*

Teofila *see Theophila*

Terasa *see Teresa*

Tercza *see Teresa*

Tereasa *see Teresa*

Tereasah *see Teresa*

Tereatha *see Teresa*

Tereesa *see Teresa*

Tereesah *see Teresa*

Teresa Saint; form of Theresa; Greek, Spanish; late summer

Taresa, Taressa, Tarissa, Terasa, Tercza, Tereasa, Tereasah, Tereatha, Tereesa, Tereesah, Teresah, Terese, Teresea, Teresha, Teresia, Teresina, Tereson, Teretha, Tereza, Terezia, Terezie, Terezijya, Terezon, Terezsa, Terisa, Terisah, Terisha, Teriza, Terrasa, Terreasa, Terreasah, Terresa, Terresha, Terresia, Terrisa, Terrisah, Terrysa, Terrysah, Tersita, Teruska, Tess, Tessa, Treza, Tyresa, Tyresia

St. Teresa de los Andes, St. Teresa Kim Im-I, St. Teresa Margaret Redi, St. Teresa of Avila, St. Teresa of Jesus Jornet Ibars, St. Teresa of Portugal, Bl. Teresa of Calcutta, St. Teresa de Jesus Solar, St. Teresa Eustochio Verzeri

St. Teresa of Avila (1515–1582) was born to Spanish nobility. She was crippled when young but was cured after prayer to St. Joseph. Her mother died when she was twelve, and her father refused to allow Teresa to enter religious life. She left home anyway. She became a Carmelite at seventeen. She began to experience visions and was a mystic for the rest of her life. She founded a reformed Carmelite Convent of St. John of Avila. She is known for her writings, especially *The Interior Castle.* She was proclaimed a Doctor of the Church in 1970.

Teresah *see Teresa*

Terese *see Teresa*

Teresea *see Teresa*

Teresha *see Teresa*

Teresia *see Teresa*

Teresina *see Teresa*

Tereson *see Teresa*

Teresse *see Therese*

Teretha *see Teresa*

Tereza *see Teresa*

Terezia *see Teresa*

Terezie *see Teresa*

Terezijya *see Teresa*

Terezon *see Teresa*

Terezsa *see Teresa*

Terisa *see Teresa*

Terisah *see Teresa*

Terisha *see Teresa*

Teriza *see Teresa*

Terrasa *see Teresa*

Terreasa *see Teresa*

Terreasah *see Teresa*

Terresa *see Teresa*

Terresha *see Teresa*

Terresia *see Teresa*

Terrisa *see Teresa*

Terrisah *see Teresa*

Terrysa *see Teresa*

Terrysah *see Teresa*

Tersita *see Teresa*

Teruska see Teresa

Tess see Teresa

Tessa see Teresa

Tetta Saint; Teutonic; ruler of the house

St. Tetta (d. 772) was a Benedictine abbess of Wimborne Convent in Dorsetshire, England. She sent some of her nuns to help St. Boniface evangelize in Germany.

Thaney see Theneva

Tharsilla see Tarsilla

Thea Saint; form of Althea; Greek; goddess

Theah, Theia, Theiah, Theta, Theya, Theyah, Thia

St. Thea (d. 307) was a virgin from Palestine who was martyred in Alexandria, Egypt.

Theah see Thea

Thecla Saint; Greek; God's fame

Tacla, Tecla

According to legend, St. Thecla (first century) was a native of Iconomium. After hearing St. Paul preach on virginity, she broke off her engagement. She was arrested and ordered to be burned to death, but a storm put out the flame, and she escaped with St. Paul and traveled with him to Antioch. She eventually became a hermit, living in a cave near Meriamlik for seventy-two years.

Theda see Theodora

Thedorsha see Theodora

Thedosia see Theodosia

Thedosiah see Theodosia

Thedosya see Theodosia

Thedosyah see Theodosia

Thedrica see Theodora

Theia see Thea

Theiah see Thea

Thenaw see Theneva

Theneva Saint

Thaney, Thenaw, Thenova

St. Theneva (seventh century) was a British princess. When her family discovered that she was pregnant out of wedlock, they threw her off a cliff. She survived the fall and sought refuge on an unmanned boat. She sailed to Culross, where she was cared for by St. Serf. Her son became St. Kentigern.

Thenova see Theneva

Theoctiste Saint; Greek, Latin

St. Theoctiste (tenth century) was from the island of Lesbos where she was raised in a monastery. At the age of eighteen, she was kidnapped by Arab raiders. She managed to escape and subsequently lived for thirty years as a hermitess on the island of Paros.

Theodichildis Saint; Greek, Latin

Telchildis

St. Theodichildis (d. 660) was abbess of Jouarre in Meaux, France.

Theodora Saint; Greek; gift of God

Dora, Taedra, Tedra, Teodora, Theda, Thedorsha, Thedrica, Theodoria, Theodorian, Theodosia, Theodra, Tossia

St. Theodora (d. 120) was the sister of St. Hermes. She cared for her brother while in prison. Both she and Hermes were martyred in Rome.

Theodoria *see Theodora*

Theodorian *see Theodora*

Theodosia Saint; form of Theodora; Greek; gift of God

Dosia, Teodosia, Teodosiah, Teodosya, Teodosyah, Thedosia, Thedosiah, Thedosya, Thedosyah, Theodosiah, Theodosya, Theodosyah, Tossia

St. Theodosia, St. Theodosia of Constantinople

St. Theodosia of Constantinople (d. 745) was orphaned when young. She later became a nun at St. Anastasia Monastery. She and her fellow nuns defended an icon of Christ against soldiers representing the iconoclast Emperors Leo III and Constantine V. The sisters were arrested and tortured. Theodosia died in prison.

Theodosiah *see Theodosia*

Theodosya *see Theodosia*

Theodosyah *see Theodosia*

Theodota Saint; Greek, Latin; given to God

Theodra

St. Theodata (d. 304) was a noblewoman from Nicaea who was martyred with her three sons by being burned to death in a furnace.

Theodra *see Theodora*

Theodula *see Dula*

Theofilia *see Theophila*

Theofilie *see Theophila*

Theophila Saint; Greek; loved by God

Teofila, Theofilia, Theofilie, Theophyla, Theophylah

St. Theophila (d. 303) was martyred in Nicomedia during the persecutions of Emperor Diocletian.

Theophyla *see Theophila*

Theophylah *see Theophila*

Theopistes Saint; Greek, Latin; God's beloved

St. Theopistes (d. 188) was married to St. Eustachius and was the mother of Sts. Agapitus and Theopistus. She was martyred during the persecutions of Emperor Hadrian.

Theoregitha *see Thordgith*

Theorigitha Saint; Greek, English

St. Theorigitha (seventh century) was mistress of novices at Barking Convent in England, where St. Ethelburga was abbess. Theorigitha was sick for many years and had a vision foretelling St. Ethelburga's death.

Thereasa *see Theresa*

Theresa Saint; Greek; late summer

Thereasa, Theresah, Theresia, Theresie, Theresina, Theresita, Theressa, Thereza, Therisa, Therisah, Therise, Therissie, Therrisa, Therrisah, Therrysa, Therrysah, Thersea, Therysa, Therysah

St. Theresa Coudere (1805–1885) was born in Le Mans,

France. She entered the Sisters of St. Regis in Lalouvesc in 1825, but she helped found the Sisters of the Cenacle with Fr. John-Pierre Etienne Terme the following year. For many years, she served as superior of the order.

Theresah *see Theresa*

Therese Saint; form of Theresa; Greek, French; late summer

Teresse, Theresse, Therise, Therra, Therressa, Therris, Therrise, Therrys, Therryse, Theryse

St. Thérèse of Lisieux (1873–1897) was born in Alcon, Normandy, to Bl. Louis Martin and Bl. Marie-Azelie Guerin. Her mother died when she was only four. The family moved to Lisieux, and her older sister Pauline took over the care of her. A statue of the Virgin Mary smiled at her when she was eight and cured her of an illness. At age fourteen, she tried to join the Carmelites but was refused because of her age. Her father brought her to Rome to ask Pope Leo XIII for permission. The pope did not grant it, but she was allowed to enter the monastery at the age of fifteen. Under the direction of her superiors, she wrote her autobiography, *Story of a Soul*, which was published after her death from tuberculosis. Known for her "Little Way," she was declared a Doctor of the Church in 1997.

Theresia *see Theresa*

Theresie *see Theresa*

Theresina *see Theresa*

Theresita *see Theresa*

Theressa *see Theresa*

Theresse *see Therese*

Thereza *see Theresa*

Therisa *see Theresa*

Therisah *see Theresa*

Therise *see Therese*

Therissie *see Theresa*

Therra *see Therese*

Therressa *see Therese*

Therris *see Therese*

Therrisa *see Theresa*

Therrisah *see Theresa*

Therrise *see Therese*

Therrys *see Therese*

Therrysa *see Theresa*

Therrysah *see Theresa*

Therryse *see Therese*

Thersea *see Theresa*

Therysa *see Theresa*

Therysah *see Theresa*

Theryse *see Therese*

Theta *see Thea*

Theya *see Thea*

Theyah *see Thea*

Thia *see Thea*

Thomais Saint; form of Thomas (boy's name); Greek, Aramaic; twin

St. Thomais (d. 476) was the Christian wife of a fisherman in Alexandria, Egypt. She was killed by her father-in-law for refusing his advances.

Thordgith Saint

Theoregitha

St. Thordgith (d. 700) was a novice mistress at Barking Convent in England, where St. Ethelburga served as abbess.

Tiatiana *see Tatiana*

Tibba Saint; form of Tiberia; Latin; the Tiber River in Italy

St. Tibba (d. 680) was a nun at an abbey at Castor, Northamptonshire. She was a member of the Mercian royal family in England and was related to Sts. Kyneburga and Kyneswide who were abbesses of the same convent.

Tigridia Saint; Latin; tiger like

St. Tigridia (d. 925) was the daughter of Count Sancho Garcia of Castile. She entered a Benedictine convent at Burgos, Spain, which her father had founded. She later served as its abbess.

Tilda *see Matilda*

Tilde *see Matilda*

Toinetta *see Antonia*

Tola *see Tola (boy's name)*

Tonya *see Antonia*

Tossia *see Theodora, Theodosia*

Trallen *see Triduna*

Trea Saint; Gaelic; strength, intensity

St. Trea (fifth century) was converted by St. Patrick and became a hermit at Ardtree, Derry, Ireland.

Trenedy *see Trinity*

Treza *see Teresa*

Trice *see Beatrice*

Triduna Saint; Scottish

Trallen

St. Triduna (eighth century) was a consecrated virgin who worked with St. Regulus in Scotland.

Trifina *see Triphina*

Trinidad *see Trinity*

Trinidade *see Trinity*

Trinidy *see Trinity*

Trinitee *see Trinity*

Trinitey *see Trinity*

Triniti *see Trinity*

Trinitie *see Trinity*

Trinity Top 100 Name; Holy Trinity;

Trenedy, Trinidad, Trinidade, Trinidy, Trinitee, Trinitey, Triniti, Trinitie, Trynyty

Triphina Saint; Greek; fun

Trifina

St. Triphina (sixth century) was the mother of St. Tremorus, who was murdered by her husband, Count Conmore of Brittany. After her son died, she spent the rest of her days in a convent in Brittany.

Trudi *see Gertrude*

Trudy *see Gertrude*

Trynyty *see Trinity*

Trypbaena Saint, New Testament

St. Trypbaena (first century) was a convert to Christianity mentioned as a "worker in the Lord" in St. Paul's Letter to the Romans.

Tryphonia Saint; Greek; softness, delicacy

St. Tryphonia (third century) was a Roman widow who was martyred.

Tydfil Saint; Welsh

St. Tydfil (d. 480) was a daughter of King Brychan of Brycheiniog in Wales. She was martyred by a group of pagans.

Tylda *see Matilda*

Tyresa *see Teresa*

Tyresia *see Teresa*

U

Ulphia Saint; English; a lovely woman

Wulfe, Wulfia

St. Ulphia (d. 750) was a hermitess who lived near Amiens, France, under the spiritual direction of St. Domitius.

Ulrica *see Ulricha*

Ulricha Saint; German; wolf ruler

Ulrica

Bl. Ulricha Nisch (1882–1913) was born in Oberdorf, Germany. She worked for several years to help support her family. She became ill and was hospitalized. She met the Sisters of the Holy Cross while she was there and decided to enter their order. She was known for her piety and humility. She died of tuberculosis. She was beatified by Pope John Paul II in 1987.

Unice *see Eunice*

Ursala *see Ursula*

Ursel *see Ursula*

Ursela *see Ursula*

Ursella *see Ursula*

Ursely *see Ursula*

Ursilla *see Ursula*

Ursillane *see Ursula*

Ursley *see Ursula*

Ursola *see Ursula*

Ursula Saint; Greek; little bear

Irsaline, Irsula, Orsala, Ursala, Ursel, Ursela, Ursella, Ursely, Ursilla, Ursillane, Ursley, Ursola, Ursule, Ursulina, Ursuline, Ursulyn, Ursulyna, Ursylyn, Urszula, Urszuli, Urzsulah, Urzula, Urzulah

St. Ursula (fifth century) was the daughter of a Christian British king. She and eleven companions were tortured to death for the faith. She is the namesake of the Ursuline order, which was founded to educate young Catholic girls.

Ursule *see Ursula*

Ursulina *see Ursula*

Ursuline *see Ursula*

Ursulyn *see Ursula*

Ursulyna *see Ursula*

Ursylyn *see Ursula*

Urszula Saint; form of Ursula; Latin; little bear

St. Urszula Ledochowska (1865–1939) was born in Austria, the daughter of a Polish noble and Austrian mother and the sister of St. Theresa Ledochowska. Her family moved to Poland in 1873. She became an Ursuline nun and founded the

Ursulines of the Sacred Heart (Gray Ursulines) in Pniewy, Poland. Pope Pius X sent her to Russia as a missionary, but she was expelled during the Communist Revolution. Pope Benedict XV asked her to move to Rome. She became known as an orator and worked for Polish independence. She was canonized by Pope John Paul II in 2003.

Urszuli *see Ursula*

Urzsulah *see Ursula*

Urzula *see Ursula*

Urzulah *see Ursula*

V

Valantina *see Valentina*

Valaree *see Valeria*

Valarey *see Valeria*

Valencia *see Valentina*

Valensia *see Valentina*

Valenteana *see Valentina*

Valenteane *see Valentina*

Valenteen *see Valentina*

Valenteena *see Valentina*

Valenteene *see Valentina*

Valentena *see Valentina*

Valentia *see Valentina*

Valentina Saint; Latin; strong, healthy

Valantina, Valencia, Valensia, Valenteana, Valenteane, Valenteen, Valenteena, Valenteene, Valentena, Valentia, Vallatina

St. Valentina (d. 308) was a virgin who was martyred in Palestine during the reign of Emperor Galerius.

Valeree *see Valeria*

Valeri *see Valeria*

Valeria Saint; Top 100 Name; Latin; strong, healthy

Valaree, Valarey, Valeree, Valeri, Valerie, Vallory, Valory, Valry

St. Valeria (first or second century) was the wife of St. Vitalis of Milan and the mother of Sts. Gervase and Protase. She was martyred for providing burial to Christian martyrs.

Valerie *see Valeria*

Vallatina *see Valentina*

Vallory *see Valeria*

Valory *see Valeria*

Valry *see Valeria*

Vareide *see Pharaildis*

Varelde *see Pharaildis*

Varonica *see Veronica*

Varonicca *see Veronica*

Varoniccah *see Veronica*

Varyn *see Verena*

Varyna *see Verena*

Varyne *see Verena*

Veep Saint

Wennapa

St. Veep (sixth century) is a Cornish saint who was possibly a member of the celebrated clan of King Brychan.

Veerle *see Pharaildis*

Venaranda Saint; Latin; worthy of veneration

St. Venaranda (second century) was a virgin who was martyred in Gaul.

Venusta see *Venustian (boy's name)*

Vera see *Verena*

Verah see *Verena*

Verean see *Verena*

Vereana see *Verena*

Vereane see *Verena*

Vereen see *Verena*

Vereene see *Verena*

Vereena see *Verena*

Verena Saint; Latin; truthful

> *Varyn, Varyna, Varyne, Vera, Verah, Verean, Vereana, Vereane, Vereen, Vereena, Vereene, Verenah, Verene, Verenia, Verin, Verina, Verine, Verinka, Verna, Vernah, Veroshka, Verunka, Verusya, Veryn, Veryna, Veryne, Virna*

St. Verena (fourth century) was from Egypt. She went to Rhaetia (modern Switzerland) as a companion and nurse of her relative St. Victor, who served in the Theban Legion. When the members of the Legion were martyred, she became a hermitess, living in a cave near present-day Zurich. She cared for young girls, using her expertise as a nurse to help care for them both physically and spiritually.

Verenah see *Verena*

Verene see *Verena*

Verenia see *Verena*

Vergie see *Virginia*

Verginia see *Virginia*

Verginya see *Virginia*

Verhonica see *Veronica*

Veridiana Saint; Latin; truthful

St. Veridiana (1182–1242) was born into a noble family in Castelfiorentino, Tuscany, Italy. Even as a child, she was known for her generosity. She made a pilgrimage to Santiago de Compstela. When she returned, she took up residence as a hermitess in a cell near the oratory of San Antonio, where she lived for thirty-four years. She may have been visited by St. Francis of Assisi.

Verin see *Verena*

Verina see *Verena*

Verine see *Verena*

Verinica see *Veronica*

Verinka see *Verena*

Verna see *Verena*

Vernah see *Verena*

Vernice see *Veronica*

Verohnica see *Veronica*

Veron see *Veronica*

Verona see *Veronica*

Verone see *Veronica*

Veronee see *Veronica*

Veronica Saint; Latin; true image

> *Ronica, Ronika, Varonica, Varonicca, Varoniccah, Verhonica, Veronika, Veronique, Verinica, Vernice, Verohnica, Veron, Verona, Verone, Veronee, Veronice, Veronika, Veronique, Veronne, Veronnica, Veruszhka, Vironica, Vironicah, Vironicca, Vironiccah, Vironiqua, Vron, Vronica, Vronicah, Vyronica, Vyronicah, Vyronicca, Vyroniccah*

St. Veronica, St. Veronica Giuliani

St. Veronica (first century) was a woman from Jerusalem who wiped the face of Jesus as he carried the Cross on his way to be crucified. The cloth was imprinted with the image of Jesus' face. According to legend, Veronica later used the cloth to cure Emperor Tiberius of an illness. Her act of kindness toward Jesus is remembered in the Stations of the Cross.

Veronice *see Veronica*

Veronika *see Veronica*

Veronique *see Veronica*

Veronne *see Veronica*

Veronnica *see Veronica*

Veroshka *see Verena*

Verunka *see Verena*

Verusya *see Verena*

Veruszhka *see Veronica*

Verylde *See Pharaildis*

Veryn *see Verena*

Veryna *see Verena*

Veryne *see Verena*

Vesta *see Vestina*

Vestina Saint; Latin; keeper of the house

Vesta

St. Vestina (d. 180) was martyred in Carthage during the persecutions of Emperor Vigellius.

Vevay *see Vivian*

Vevey *see Vivian*

Vicenta *see Vincentia*

Vicentia *see Vincentia*

Victoire *see Victoria*

Victoria Saint; Top 100 Name; Latin; victorious

Victoire, Victorice, Victorie, Victorine, Victoriya, Victorria, Victorriah, Victory, Victorya, Victrice, Viktoria, Vitoria, Vitorie, Vittoria, Vyctoria, Vyctoriah

St. Victoria (d. 253) was from Tivoli, Italy. She was engaged to marry a pagan nobleman when she met St. Anatolia, who convinced her of the virtue of consecrated virginity. She then broke her engagement. Her fiancé imprisoned her in his home and attempted to starve her, but she would not relent. He then turned her over to the Roman authorities, who beheaded her.

Victorice *see Victoria*

Victorie *see Victoria*

Victorine *see Victoria*

Victoriya *see Victoria*

Victorria *see Victoria*

Victorriah *see Victoria*

Victory *see Victoria*

Victorya *see Victoria*

Victrice *see Victoria*

Viktoria *see Victoria*

Vincensa *see Vincentia*

Vincensah *see Vincentia*

Vincensia *see Vincentia*

Vincensiah *see Vincentia*

Vincenta *see Vincentia*

Vincentah *see Vincentia*

Vincentena *see Vincentia*

Vincentia Saint; Latin; victor, conqueror

Vicenta, Vicentia, Vincensa, Vincensah, Vincensia, Vincensiah, Vincenta, Vincentah, Vincentena, Vincentina, Vincentine, Vincenza, Vincenzah, Vincenzia, Vincenziah, Vincy, Vinnie

St. Vincentia Maria Lopez y Vicuna (1847–1896) was born at Cascante, Spain. She took a vow of chastity and organized a group of women to minister to working girls. This group eventually became the Daughters of Mary Immaculate for Domestic Service.

Vincentina *see Vincentia*

Vincentine *see Vincentia*

Vincenza Saint; form of Vincentia; Latin, Spanish; victor, conqueror

St. Vincenza Gerosa, St. Vincenza Mary Lopez y Vicuna

St. Vincenza Gerosa (1784–1847) was from Lovere, Italy. She and St. Bartolomea Capitanio founded the Sisters of Charity of Lovere, which were dedicated to helping the poor and sick and educating children. Vincenza later served as director of the order.

Vincenza *see Vincentia*

Vincenzah *see Vincentia*

Vincenzia *see Vincentia*

Vincenziah *see Vincentia*

Vincy *see Vincentia*

Vinnie *see Vincentia*

Virge *see Virginia*

Virgeen *see Virginia*

Virgeena *see Virginia*

Virgeenah *see Virginia*

Virgeenia *see Virginia*

Virgeeniah *see Virginia*

Virgen *see Virginia*

Virgenae *see Virginia*

Virgene *see Virginia*

Virgenia *see Virginia*

Virgenya *see Virginia*

Virgie *see Virginia*

Virginae *see Virginia*

Virgine *see Virginia*

Virginia Saint; Latin; pure, virginal

Ginata, Ginger, Gingia, Ginia, Vergie, Verginia, Verginya, Virge, Virgeen, Virgeena, Virgeenah, Virgeenia, Virgeeniah, Virgen, Virgenae, Virgene, Virgenia, Virgenya, Virgie,Virginae, Virgine, Virginio, Virginnia, Virgins, Virgy, Virjeana, Virjinea, Virjineah, Virjinia, Vyrginia, Vyrginiah, Vyrgynia, Vyrgyniah, Vyrgynya, Vyrgynyah

St. Virginia Centurione Bracelli (1587–1651) was the daughter of the doge of Genoa. She entered into an arranged marriage to Gasparo Grimaldi Bracelli, who was a drinker and gambler. He died after five years, and she was left a widow with two small children. She raised her children and spent her free time in prayer and charity. After her children were grown, she devoted herself entirely to charitable efforts, opening her home to the needy. She built extra housing and started a hospital. She started the Sisters of Refuge in Mount Calvary and the Daughters of Our Lady on Mount Calvary. She was canonized by Pope John Paul II in 2003.

Virginio *see Virginia*

Virginnia *see Virginia*

Virgins *see Virginia*

Virgy *see Virginia*

Virjeana *see Virginia*

Virjinea *see Virginia*

Virjineah *see Virginia*

Virjinia *see Virginia*

Virjiniah *see Virginia*

Virna *see Verena*

Vironica *see Veronica*

Vironicah *see Veronica*

Vironicca *see Veronica*

Vironiccah *see Veronica*

Vironiqua *see Veronica*

Visa *see Vissia*

Vissia Saint; Latin; strength, vigor
Visa

St. Vissia (d. 250) was a virgin who was martyred at Fermo, Italy, during the persecutions of Emperor Trajanus Decius.

Vitalia *see Vitalina*

Vitalina Saint; Latin; life, alive
Vitalia

St. Vitalina (d. 390) was a hermitess at Artonne, France. She is a patroness of Artonne.

Vitoria *see Victoria*

Vitorie *see Victoria*

Vittoria *see Victoria*

Viv *see Vivian*

Viva *see Vivian*

Viveca *see Vivian*

Vivi *see Vivian*

Vivia *see Vivian*

Vivian Saint; Latin; full of life
Vevay, Vevey, Viv, Viva, Viveca, Vivi, Vivia, Viviani, Viviann, Viviano, Vivina, Vivion, Vivyan, Vivyann, Vivyanne, Vyvian, Vyvyan, Vyvyann, Vyvyanne

St. Vivian (d. 460) was bishop of Saintes, France. He worked to relieve the suffering of those who had been invaded by the Visigoths.

Viviani *see Vivian*

Viviann *see Vivian*

Viviano *see Vivian*

Vivina *see Vivian, Wivina*

Vivion *see Vivian*

Vivyan *see Vivian*

Vivyann *see Vivian*

Vivyanne *see Vivian*

Vron *see Veronica*

Vronica *see Veronica*

Vronicah *see Veronica*

Vyctoria *see Victoria*

Vyctoriah *see Victoria*

Vyrginia *see Virginia*

Vyrginiah *see Virginia*

Vyrgynia *see Virginia*

Vyrgyniah *see Virginia*

Vyrgynya *see Virginia*

Vyrgynyah *see Virginia*

Vyronica *see Veronica*

Vyronicah *see Veronica*

Vyronicca *see Veronica*

Vyroniccah *see Veronica*

Vyvian *see Vivian*

Vyvyan *see Vivian*

Vyvyann *see Vivian*

Vyvyanne *see Vivian*

W

Walburga Saint; German; ruler of the fortress

St. Walburga (710–779) was born in Devonshire, England, the sister of Sts. Willibald and Winebald. She became a nun at Wimborne Monastery in Dorset and traveled to Germany to help St. Boniface with his missionary work. She later served as abbess of the double monastery at Heidenheim.

Waldetrudis Saint; German; battlefield, loved, powerful

Waltrude

St. Waldetrudis (d. 668) was the daughter of Sts. Walbert and Bertilia. She married St. Vincent Madelgarius and became the mother of Sts. Landericus, Madalberta, Adeltrudis, and Dentelin. She and St. Vincent both entered religious life. He founded the Monastery of Hautrnont, France. She established a convent at Chateaulieu.

Waltrude *see Waldetrudis*

Wastrada Saint

St. Wastrada (d. 760) was the mother of St. Gregory of Utrecht. Late in life, she joined a religious community.

Welbrath *see Wiborada*

Wenfreda *see Winifred*

Wennafred *see Winifred*

Wennapa *see Veep*

Werburg Saint; English

St. Werburg (d. 785) was from Mercia, England. After her husband died, she entered a convent where she later served as abbess.

Werburga Saint; German; protector of the army

St. Werburga (d. 699) was born in Staffordshire, the daughter of King Wulfhere of Mercia and St. Ermenilda. She refused marriage, instead entering the convent of Ely. She later founded communities at Hanbury, Trentham, and Wedon. She was known as a miracle worker and is a patroness of Chester, England.

Wiborada Saint; German; female counselor

Guibor, Welbrath

St. Wiborada (d. 926) was a member of the Swabian nobility in Switzerland. She became a hermitess and wanted to be walled up as an anchoress near the monastery of St. Gall. Before they would allow her to do so, they forced her to endure a trial by fire. She was known for her holiness and gifts of prophecy. She foretold her own martyrdom at the hands of the Magyars of Hungary.

Wilfretrude *see Wilfretrudis*

Wilfretrudis Saint

Wilfretrude

St. Wilfretrudis (sixth century) was the niece of St. Gertrude.

She served as abbess of Nivelles Convent at Brabant, Belgium.

Wilfrida Saint; German; determined peacemaker

St. Wilfrida (d. 988) was the mother of St. Edith of Wilton, who was also the daughter of King Edgar (to whom Wilfrida was not married). After her daughter's birth, she entered the convent of Wilton, England, where she later became abbess. She spent her life in penance.

Wiltrude *see Wiltrudis*

Wiltrudis Saint; German; will, desire, strength, power

Wiltrude

St. Wiltrudis (d. 986) was the wife of a duke of Bavaria. After he died, she became a nun. She later founded the Convent of Bergen, near Neuburg, where she later served as abbess.

Winafred *see Winifred*

Winefred *see Winifred*

Winefrid *see Winifred*

Winefride *see Winifred*

Winfreda *see Winifred*

Winfrieda *see Winifred*

Winiefrida *see Winifred*

Winifred Saint; German; peaceful friend

Freda, Wenfreda, Wennafred, Winafred, Winefred, Winefrid, Winefride, Winfreda, Winfrieda, Winiefrida, Winifrid, Winifryd, Winifryda, Winnafred, Winnafreda, Winnefred, Winniefred, Winnifred, Winnifreda, Winnifrid, Winnifrida, Wynafred, Wynafreda,

Wynafrid, Wynafrida, Wynefred, Wynefreda, Wynfryd, Wynette, Wynifred, Wynne, Wynnifred

St. Winifred (d. 660) was born in Wales. She was martyred for refusing the advances of Caradog of Hawarden.

Winifrid *see Winifred*

Winifryd *see Winifred*

Winifryda *see Winifred*

Winnafred *see Winifred*

Winnafreda *see Winifred*

Winnefred *see Winifred*

Winniefred *see Winifred*

Winnifred *see Winifred*

Winnifreda *see Winifred*

Winnifrid *see Winifred*

Winnifrida *see Winifred*

Winnow *see Winnow (boy's name)*

Wisdom *see Sofia*

Withburga Saint; English

St. Withburga (d. 743) was the daughter of King Anna of East Anglia, England. After her father died, she established a convent and church at Dereham.

Wivina Saint; Netherlands

Vivina

St. Wivina (1103–1170) was from Flanders, Belgium. She refused all offers of marriage and became a hermitess at the age of twenty-three. Several followers joined her. Count Godfrey of Brabant gave her the land to build a convent, where she served as abbess.

Wulfe *see Ulphia*

Wulfhilda Saint; German; one who fights with the wolves

St. Wulfhilda (d. 1000), an Anglo-Saxon noble, refused the hand of King Edgar in marriage and became a nun at Wilton Abbey. She later became abbess of the convents of Barking and Ilorton.

Wulfia *see Ulphia*
Wynafred *see Winifred*
Wynafreda *see Winifred*
Wynafrid *see Winifred*
Wynafrida *see Winifred*
Wynefred *see Winifred*
Wynefreda *see Winifred*
Wynefryd *see Winifred*
Wynette *see Winifred*
Wynifred *see Winifred*
Wynne *see Winifred*
Wynnifred *see Winifred*

Y

Yan *see Jan (boy's name)*
Yenesis *see Genesis*
Yolanda *see Helen*
Yosephina *see Josephine*
Ysabella *see Isabel*
Ysadora *see Isidora*
Yudita *see Judith*
Yuliana *see Juliana*

Z

Zara *see Sarah*
Zarah *see Sarah*
Zareh *see Sarah*

Zarra *see Sarah*
Zarrah *see Sarah*
Zdenka Saint; Latin, Czech; woman from Sidon

Bl. Zdenka Schelingova (1916–1955) was born in Slovakia. She studied nursing and radiology. She entered the Congregation of the Sisters of Charity of the Holy Cross. She worked as a nurse in Bratislava and took care of many who had been tortured by the communists. She helped save a condemned priest from death and tried to help three other priests and seminarians escape, but she failed and was arrested and tortured. She was released after three years, but died from the abuse she had received. She was beatified by Pope John Paul II in 2003.

Zdislava Saint; German; glory, honor

St. Zdislava of Lemberk (1220–1252) was the daughter of an aristocratic Czech family. She wanted to become a hermitess but was brought home by her family. She married the count of Lemberk and had four children. She was very devout and attended Mass frequently. She cared for the poor and brought refugees into her castle. She was also a mystic. Her husband helped fulfill her desire to found a Dominican convent. She died from an illness while still young.

Zeata *see Zita*

Zeba *see Zenobia*

Zeeba *see Zenobia*

Zeeta *see Zita*

Zeita *see Zita*

Zenna *see Zenobia*

Zenobia Saint; Greek; sign, symbol

Cenobie, Senobe, Senobia, Senovia, Zeba, Zeeba, Zenna, Zenobiah, Zenobie, Zenobyah, Zenovia, Zinovia

St. Zenobia (third century) was the sister of St. Zenobius. The two were from Asia Minor and were martyred during the persecutions of Emperor Diocletian.

Zenobiah *see Zenobia*

Zenobie *see Zenobia*

Zenobyah *see Zenobia*

Zenovia *see Zenobia*

Zinovia *see Zenobia*

Zita Saint; Spanish; rose

Zeata, Zeeta, Zeita, Zitah, Zyta, Zytah, Zytka

St. Zita (1212–1272) was born in Tuscany into a holy Christian family. At age twelve, she became a housekeeper in the home of a rich weaver and spent forty-eight years in their service. She attended daily Mass and carried out all her duties perfectly. She considered her work to be part of her faith life. She was also generous with the poor and visited the sick and those in prison. She is a patron saint of domestic servants.

Zitah *see Zita*

Zoa *see Zoe*

Zoe Saint; Top 100 Name; Greek; life

Zoa, Zoee, Zoelie, Zoeline, Zoelle, Zoellus, Zowe, Zowey, Zowie, Zoya

St. Zoe (d. 286) was a noblewoman in Rome who was martyred during the persecutions of Emperor Diocletian.

Zoee *see Zoe*

Zoelie *see Zoe*

Zoeline *see Zoe*

Zoelle *see Zoe*

Zoey Top 100 Name; form of Zoe; Greek; life

Zofya *see Sofia*

Zowe *see Zoe*

Zowey *see Zoe*

Zowie *see Zoe*

Zoya *see Zoe*

Zyta *see Zita*

Zytah *see Zita*

Zytka *see Zita*

Appendices

I. Recently Canonized Saints

Rodrigo Aguilar Aleman
Julio Álvarez Mendoza
Luis Bátiz Sáinz
Agustín Caloca Cortés
Augustine Chao and 119 companions
Katharine Drexel
Josephine Bakhita

2001

Luigi Scrosoppi
Agostino Roscelli
Bernard of Corleone
Joseph Marello
Paula Montal Fornés de San José de
   Calasanz
Maria Crescentia Höss

2002

Alphonsus de Orozco
Ignatius of Santhià
Humilis de Bisignano
Benedetta Cambiagio Frassinello
Pio of Pietrelcina
Juan Diego Cuauhtlatoatzin
Josemaría Escrivá
Pedro Poveda Castroverde
José María Rubio y Peralta

2004

Gianna Beretta Molla
Luigi Orione
Hannibal Mary Di Francia
Josep Manyanet i Vives
Nimatullah Kassab Al-Hardini
Paola Elisabetta Cerioli

SAINTS CANONIZED BY
POPE BENEDICT XVI

2005

Josef Bilczewski
Gaetano Catanoso
Zygmunt Gorazdowski
Felice da Nicosia

2006

Bishop Rafael Guizar Valencia
Mother Theodore Guerin
Filippo Smaldone
Rosa Venerini

2007

Antônio de Sant'Anna Galvão
George Preca
Charles of Mount Argus
Marie-Eugénie de Jésus

2008

Alphonsa Muttathupadathu
Gaetano Errico
Narcisa de Jesus Martillo Moran
Maria Bernarda Bütler

2009

Arcangelo Tadini
Bernardo Tolomei
Nuno Álvares Pereira
Geltrude Comensoli
Caterina Volpicelli
Zygmunt Szczęsny Feliński
Francisco Coll Guitart
Damien de Veuster
Rafael Arnáiz Barón
Jeanne Jugan

2010

Stanisław Sołtys
André Bessette
Candida Maria de Jesus
Mary MacKillop
Giulia Salzano
Camilla Battista da Varano

2011

Guido Maria Conforti
Luigi Guanella
Bonifacia Rodríguez De Castro

2012

Jacques Berthieu
Pedro Calungsod
Giovanni Battista Piamarta
Maria del Monte Carmelo Sallés y
   Barangueras
Marianne Cope
Kateri Tekakwitha
Anna Schäffer
Caius of Korea

II. Top 100 Names

According to the US Social Security Administration (http://www.socialsecurity.gov/OACT/babynames/index.html) these are the top names for 2011 in the United States.

Rank	Male Names	Female Names
1.	Jacob	Sophia
2.	Mason	Isabella
3.	William	Emma
4.	Jayden	Olivia
5.	Noah	Ava
6.	Michael	Emily
7.	Ethan	Abigail
8.	Alexander	Madison
9.	Aiden	Mia
10.	Daniel	Chloe
11.	Anthony	Elizabeth
12.	Matthew	Ella
13.	Elijah	Addison
14.	Joshua	Natalie
15.	Liam	Lily
16.	Andrew	Grace
17.	James	Samantha
18.	David	Avery
19.	Benjamin	Sofia
20.	Logan	Aubrey
21.	Christopher	Brooklyn
22.	Joseph	Lillian
23.	Jackson	Victoria
24.	Gabriel	Evelyn
25.	Ryan	Hannah
26.	Samuel	Alexis
27.	John	Charlotte
28.	Nathan	Zoey
29.	Lucas	Leah
30.	Christian	Amelia
31.	Jonathan	Zoe
32.	Caleb	Hailey
33.	Dylan	Layla
34.	Landon	Gabriella
35.	Isaac	Nevaeh
36.	Gavin	Kaylee
37.	Brayden	Alyssa
38.	Tyler	Anna
39.	Luke	Sarah
40.	Evan	Allison
41.	Carter	Savannah
42.	Nicholas	Ashley
43.	Isaiah	Audrey

Rank	Male Names	Female Names
44.	Owen	Taylor
45.	Jack	Brianna
46.	Jordan	Aaliyah
47.	Brandon	Riley
48.	Wyatt	Camila
49.	Julian	Khloe
50.	Aaron	Claire
51.	Jeremiah	Sophie
52.	Angel	Arianna
53.	Cameron	Peyton
54.	Connor	Harper
55.	Hunter	Alexa
56.	Adrian	Makayla
57.	Henry	Julia
58.	Eli	Kylie
59.	Justin	Kayla
60.	Austin	Bella
61.	Robert	Katherine
62.	Charles	Lauren
63.	Thomas	Gianna
64.	Zachary	Maya
65.	Jose	Sydney
66.	Levi	Serenity
67.	Kevin	Kimberly
68.	Sebastian	Mackenzie
69.	Chase	Autumn
70.	Ayden	Jocelyn
71.	Jason	Faith
72.	Ian	Lucy
73.	Blake	Stella
74.	Colton	Jasmine
75.	Bentley	Morgan
76.	Dominic	Alexandra
77.	Xavier	Trinity
78.	Oliver	Molly
79.	Parker	Madelyn
80.	Josiah	Scarlett
81.	Adam	Andrea
82.	Cooper	Genesis
83.	Brody	Eva
84.	Nathaniel	Ariana
85.	Carson	Madeline
86.	Jaxon	Brooke
87.	Tristan	Caroline
88.	Luis	Bailey
89.	Juan	Melanie
90.	Hayden	Kennedy

Rank	Male Names	Female Names
91.	Carlos	Destiny
92.	Jesus	Maria
93.	Nolan	Naomi
94.	Cole	London
95.	Alex	Payton
96.	Max	Lydia
97.	Grayson	Ellie
98.	Bryson	Mariah
99.	Diego	Aubree
100.	Jaden	Kaitlyn

III. Most Popular
Catholic Names by Decade

According to the US Social Security Administration (http://www.socialsecurity.gov/OACT/babynames/index.html) these are lists of the most popular baby names over the last five decades.

Popular names of the 2000s

Rank	Male Names	Female Names
1.	Jacob	Emily
2.	Michael	Madison
3.	Joshua	Emma
4.	Matthew	Olivia
5.	Daniel	Hannah
6.	Christopher	Abigail
7.	Andrew	Isabella
8.	Ethan	Samantha
9.	Joseph	Elizabeth
10.	William	Ashley
11.	Anthony	Alexis
12.	David	Sarah
13.	Alexander	Sophia
14.	Nicholas	Alyssa
15.	Ryan	Grace
16.	Tyler	Ava
17.	James	Taylor
18.	John	Brianna
19.	Jonathan	Lauren
20.	Noah	Chloe
21.	Brandon	Natalie
22.	Christian	Kayla
23.	Dylan	Jessica
24.	Samuel	Anna
25.	Benjamin	Victoria

Popular names of the 1990s

Rank	Male Names	Female Names
1.	Michael	Jessica
2.	Christopher	Ashley
3.	Matthew	Emily
4.	Joshua	Sarah
5.	Jacob	Samantha
6.	Nicholas	Amanda
7.	Andrew	Brittany
8.	Daniel	Elizabeth
9.	Tyler	Taylor

Rank	Male Names	Female Names
10.	Joseph	Megan
11.	Brandon	Hannah
12.	David	Kayla
13.	James	Lauren
14.	Ryan	Stephanie
15.	John	Rachel
16.	Zachary	Jennifer
17.	Justin	Nicole
18.	William	Alexis
19.	Anthony	Victoria
20.	Robert	Amber
21.	Jonathan	Alyssa
22.	Austin	Courtney
23.	Alexander	Rebecca
24.	Kyle	Danielle
25.	Kevin	Jasmine

Popular names of the 1980s

Rank	Male Names	Female Names
1.	Michael	Jessica
2.	Christopher	Jennifer
3.	Matthew	Amanda
4.	Joshua	Ashley
5.	David	Sarah
6.	James	Stephanie
7.	Daniel	Melissa
8.	Robert	Nicole
9.	John	Elizabeth
10.	Joseph	Heather
11.	Jason	Tiffany
12.	Justin	Michelle
13.	Andrew	Amber
14.	Ryan	Megan
15.	William	Amy
16.	Brian	Rachel
17.	Brandon	Kimberly
18.	Jonathan	Christina
19.	Nicholas	Lauren
20.	Anthony	Crystal
21.	Eric	Brittany
22.	Adam	Rebecca
23.	Kevin	Laura
24.	Thomas	Danielle
25.	Steven	Emily

Popular names of the 1970s

Rank	Male Names	Female Names
1.	Michael	Jennifer
2.	Christopher	Amy
3.	Jason	Melissa
4.	David	Michelle
5.	James	Kimberly
6.	John	Lisa
7.	Robert	Angela
8.	Brian	Heather
9.	William	Stephanie
10.	Matthew	Nicole
11.	Joseph	Jessica
12.	Daniel	Elizabeth
13.	Kevin	Rebecca
14.	Eric	Kelly
15.	Jeffrey	Mary
16.	Richard	Christina
17.	Scott	Amanda
18.	Mark	Julie
19.	Steven	Sarah
20.	Thomas	Laura
21.	Timothy	Shannon
22.	Anthony	Christine
23.	Charles	Tammy
24.	Joshua	Tracy
25.	Ryan	Karen

Rank	Male Names	Female Names
23.	Gregory	Sharon
24.	Ronald	Debra
25.	Donald	Teresa Patrice

Popular names of the 1960s

Rank	Male Names	Female Names
1.	Michael	Lisa
2.	David	Mary
3.	John	Susan
4.	James	Karen
5.	Robert	Kimberly
6.	Mark	Patricia
7.	William	Linda
8.	Richard	Donna
9.	Thomas	Michelle
10.	Jeffrey	Cynthia
11.	Steven	Sandra
12.	Joseph	Deborah
13.	Timothy	Tammy
14.	Kevin	Pamela
15.	Scott	Lori
16.	Brian	Laura
17.	Charles	Elizabeth
18.	Paul	Julie
19.	Daniel	Brenda
20.	Christopher	Jennifer
21.	Kenneth	Barbara
22.	Anthony	Angela

Patrice Fagnant-MacArthur is a lifelong Roman Catholic, homeschooling mom, and freelance writer on topics of women's spirituality. She is a senior editor at *Catholic Lane* and the author of *Letters to Mary from a Young Mother*. She holds a bachelor of arts in history and fine art and a master of arts in applied theology. Fagnant-MacArthur lives in western Massachusetts with her husband and two children.

Founded in 1865, Ave Maria Press,
a ministry of the Congregation of
Holy Cross, is a Catholic publishing
company that serves the spiritual and
formative needs of the Church and its
schools, institutions, and ministers;
Christian individuals and families; and
others seeking spiritual nourishment.

———◆———

For a complete listing of titles from

Ave Maria Press

Sorin Books

Forest of Peace

Christian Classics

visit www.avemariapress.com

 **ave maria press®** / Notre Dame, IN 46556
A Ministry of the United States Province of Holy Cross